BRICS and International Tax Law

Series on International Taxation

VOLUME 61

Series Editors

Prof. Ruth Mason, University of Virginia School of Law
Prof. Dr Ekkehart Reimer, University of Heidelberg

Introduction & Contents

The Series on International Taxation deals with a wide variety of topics in the global tax arena. The authors include many of the field's leading experts as well as talented newcomers. Their expert views and incisive commentary has proven highly useful to practitioners and academics alike.

Objective

The volumes published in this series are aimed at offering high-quality analytical information and practical solutions for international tax practitioners.

Readership

Practitioners, academics and policy makers in international tax law.

Frequency of Publication

2-3 new volumes published each year.

The titles published in this series are listed at the end of this volume.

BRICS and International Tax Law

Peter Antony Wilson

Published by:
Kluwer Law International B.V.
PO Box 316
2400 AH Alphen aan den Rijn
The Netherlands
Website: lrus.wolterskluwer.com

Sold and distributed in North, Central and South America by:
Wolters Kluwer Legal & Regulatory U.S.
7201 McKinney Circle
Frederick, MD 21704
United States of America
Email: customer.service@wolterskluwer.com

Sold and distributed in all other countries by:
Air Business Subscriptions
Rockwood House
Haywards Heath
West Sussex
RH16 3DH
United Kingdom
Email: international-customerservice@wolterskluwer.com

Printed on acid-free paper.

ISBN 978-90-411-9435-0

e-Book: ISBN 978-90-411-9436-7
web-PDF: ISBN 978-90-411-9437-4

© 2018 Peter Antony Wilson

All rights reserved. No part of this publication may be reproduced, stored in a retrieval system, or transmitted in any form or by any means, electronic, mechanical, photocopying, recording, or otherwise, without written permission from the publisher.

Permission to use this content must be obtained from the copyright owner. More information can be found at: lrus.wolterskluwer.com/policies/permissions-reprints-and-licensing

Printed in the United Kingdom.

Table of Contents

Preface	xiii
List of Abbreviations	xv
Acknowledgements	xxi

CHAPTER 1
Introduction 1
1.1 Background 1
1.2 Birth of the BRICS 2
1.3 FDI 3
1.4 Political Cooperation 5
1.5 BRICS Tax Cooperation 6
1.6 Illicit Trade Flows 7
1.7 Tax Authority Capacity 9
1.8 Hypotheses, Assumptions and Questions 14
1.9 Research Methods 16

CHAPTER 2
Core International Tax Policy and Law 19
2.1 Introduction 19
    2.1.1 BRICS and Policy 19
        2.1.1.1 Aid Agencies 19
        2.1.1.2 Investment Treaties 21
        2.1.1.3 WTO 23
    2.1.2 OECD Model DTC: Core BRICS Policy and Law 25
        2.1.2.1 OECD Model DTC 25
        2.1.2.2 OECD Policy and the Prisoners' Dilemma 37
    2.1.3 MNEs and Core Policy Influence 46
        2.1.3.1 Industry and Trade Groups 46
        2.1.3.2 Government Lobbying 48

Table of Contents

	2.1.4	Significance of the Policy Influencers	48
	2.1.5	Next Chapter	49

CHAPTER 3
Evasion and Avoidance According to the BRICS — 51

3.1	Introduction			51
3.2	Special Focus			52
3.3	BRICS: Evasion			53
	3.3.1	Introduction		53
	3.3.2	Concealing Income		53
		3.3.2.1	Purposely Not Paying Existing Liability	59
		3.3.2.2	Wilful or Intentional Fraudulent Conduct	61
		3.3.2.3	Significance: Criminal Conduct	64
3.4	BRICS: Avoidance			64
	3.4.1	Introduction		64
	3.4.2	Reducing Tax Liability		66
	3.4.3	Loopholes and Intent		69
	3.4.4	Substance Over Form		71
3.5	Meanings: Significance			76
3.6	BRICS Coordination: Avoidance			77
3.7	Divergences: Consequences			77
3.8	Mispriced Transactions and Tax Havens: Evasion or Avoidance			77
3.9	Next Chapter			77

CHAPTER 4
Countering Avoidance: SAARs — 79

4.1	Introduction		79
4.2	Thin Capitalization		79
	4.2.1	Exchange Controls	80
	4.2.2	India and Thin Capitalization	81
	4.2.3	Ratio or Arm's Length	82
	4.2.4	Associates	85
	4.2.5	Hybrids and Thin Capitalization	88
	4.2.6	Lender's Residence	89
	4.2.7	Safe Harbours	90
	4.2.8	Exemptions	91
	4.2.9	Excess Interest: Deemed Dividend	92
	4.2.10	Treaty Override	93
	4.2.11	Thin Capitalization: Anti-avoidance Rule?	95
	4.2.12	Thin Capitalization and GAAR	95
	4.2.13	BRICS DTCs: Affirmative Savings	96
	4.2.14	BRICS and Coordination	96
	4.2.15	Thin Capitalization: Significance of Widening the Rules	96
4.3	Transfer Pricing		97
	4.3.1	Background	97

	4.3.2	Associates	99
	4.3.3	Transactions	100
	4.3.4	CCAs	102
	4.3.5	Excessive Leverage	103
	4.3.6	Methods	103
	4.3.7	Safe Harbours	108
	4.3.8	Documentation	111
	4.3.9	APA	113
	4.3.10	Audit Selection	116
	4.3.11	Burden of Proof	119
	4.3.12	UN Transfer Pricing Manual	119
	4.3.13	Compensatory Adjustments and Double Taxation	120
	4.3.14	Transfer Pricing: BRICS Cooperation	123
	4.3.15	BRICS: Significance of Widening of TP	123
4.4	CFC Rules		124
	4.4.1	Background	124
	4.4.2	Exchange Controls and OFDI	124
	4.4.3	Evolution of the Rules	126
	4.4.4	Control	128
	4.4.5	Potentially Attributed Income	129
	4.4.6	Substance	131
	4.4.7	Exemptions	133
	4.4.8	Notification	138
	4.4.9	Tax Credits	140
	4.4.10	BPA Override	141
		4.4.10.1 What Is the Argument?	141
		4.4.10.2 Treaties and Interpretation	142
		4.4.10.3 BRICS and BPA Override	142
	4.4.11	CFCs: Anti-avoidance Rule?	145
	4.4.12	CFCs and GAAR	146
	4.4.13	CFCs: DTCs and BPA Override	146
	4.4.14	BRICS: Cooperation and CFC Rules	147
	4.4.15	Significance: Divergences from the Developed World	147
4.5	Next Chapter		148

CHAPTER 5
Information Exchange 149
5.1	Introduction	149
5.2	Exchanging Architecture	150
5.3	Exchanging Information	151
5.4	DTCs-Article 26	153
5.5	TIEAs	155
5.6	Multilateral Agreements	155
	5.6.1 Exchanging Prior Information	157
5.7	Financial Account Information	157

Table of Contents

		5.7.1	BRICS and Peer Reviews	158
			5.7.1.1 Global Forum: Roles of Influence	158
			5.7.1.2 AEOI: Legal Basis for Exchange	159
			5.7.1.3 AEOI: Procedures Facilitating Exchange	159
5.8	BRICS and Coordination			161
5.9	BRICS: Consequences of Exchanging			161
5.10	Next Chapter			162

CHAPTER 6
Countering Treaty Benefits   163

6.1	Introduction			163
6.2	Resident			163
	6.2.1	Introduction		163
	6.2.2	POEM		165
		6.2.2.1	Highest Decision Making	166
		6.2.2.2	Economic Activities	167
	6.2.3	Residence and DTCs		167
	6.2.4	BRICS: DTC Residence and POEM		169
	6.2.5	Residence: Effectiveness in Denying DTC Benefits		171
6.3	Beneficial Ownership, Limitation of Benefits, Principal Purpose			171
	6.3.1	Introduction		171
	6.3.2	Beneficial Ownership		172
		6.3.2.1	Contractual Obligations	173
		6.3.2.2	Possession, Use, Risk and Control	176
	6.3.3	BRICS: DTCs and Beneficial Ownership		179
	6.3.4	Limitation of Benefits (LOB)		180
		6.3.4.1	BRICS and LOBs	181
	6.3.5	MPT		185
	6.3.6	DTCs: LOB and MPTs		185
		6.3.6.1	LOBs	186
		6.3.6.2	MPT	187
		6.3.6.3	Significance of LOB and MPT Approach	189
		6.3.6.4	Coordination: LOB and MPT	189
	6.3.7	Non-cooperative Countries and Indirect Transfers		189
		6.3.7.1	Introduction	189
		6.3.7.2	Non-cooperative Countries	190
		6.3.7.3	Indirect Asset Transfers	190
		6.3.7.4	Domestic Rule	191
		6.3.7.5	Indirect Transfers and DTCs	194
	6.3.8	BRICS and Coordination		195
	6.3.9	Significance: Non-cooperative and Indirect Asset Transfers		196
6.4	Next Chapter			196

Table of Contents

CHAPTER 7
BEPS Final 2015 Reports 197
7.1 Introduction 197
7.2 Strengthening Anti-abuse Rules 199
    7.2.1 Introduction 199
    7.2.2 Domestic Actions 200
        7.2.2.1 Hybrid Mismatches 200
        7.2.2.2 CFC Rules 201
        7.2.2.3 Interest Deductibility 202
        7.2.2.4 Harmful Tax Practices 203
    7.2.3 International Actions 205
        7.2.3.1 Digital Economy 205
        7.2.3.2 DTC Abuse 206
            7.2.3.2.1 LOB 207
            7.2.3.2.2 MPT 207
        7.2.3.3 PEs 208
            7.2.3.3.1 Commissionaire Agreements: Business Presence 208
            7.2.3.3.2 Dependent Agency PEs 209
            7.2.3.3.3 Excluded Activities 210
    7.2.4 Value Creation Actions 210
        7.2.4.1 Location Savings and Other Local Market Features 211
        7.2.4.2 Assembled Workforces 212
        7.2.4.3 MNE Group Synergies 212
        7.2.4.4 Intangibles 212
            7.2.4.4.1 Identification 212
            7.2.4.4.2 DEMPE 213
            7.2.4.4.3 Cost Contribution Agreements (CCA) 215
            7.2.4.4.4 Intra-group Services 216
                7.2.4.4.4.1 Benefits Test 217
                7.2.4.4.4.2 Shareholder Activities and Duplication 217
                7.2.4.4.4.3 Centralized Services 217
    7.2.5 Information Gathering Actions 219
        7.2.5.1 Disclosure of Aggressive Tax Planning 219
        7.2.5.2 Country-by-Country (CbyC) Reporting 220
    7.2.6 MAP and Mandatory and Binding Dispute Resolution 221
7.3 Multilateral Instrument ('MI') and the BRICS 223
    7.3.1 Introduction 223
    7.3.2 DTC Abuse 223
    7.3.3 Binding MAP 223
    7.3.4 Opt Out 224
7.4 Recommendations: BRICS Coordination 224
7.5 Next Chapter 225

Table of Contents

CHAPTER 8
Dispute Resolution 227
8.1 Introduction 227
8.2 Arbitration 227
8.3 Investment Treaties 230
8.4 WTO 234
8.5 Human Rights 236
8.6 Human Rights Defence 238
8.7 Conclusion 239

CHAPTER 9
BRICS and FDI: DTC Anti-abuse and Dispute Resolution 241
9.1 Introduction 241
9.2 DTC Anti-abuse 243
    9.2.1 Application 243
    9.2.2 Domestic Rules 245
        9.2.2.1 Transfer Pricing 245
            9.2.2.1.1 APA Programme 246
            9.2.2.1.2 Safe Harbours 248
            9.2.2.1.3 Country-by-Country Reporting 249
        9.2.2.2 Thin Capitalization 250
            9.2.2.2.1 ND Article Override 250
            9.2.2.2.2 Arm's Length Lenders Resident in Tax Privileged Countries 251
        9.2.2.3 Hybrid Debt 251
        9.2.2.4 Residence 252
            9.2.2.4.1 Place of Incorporation and POEM 252
            9.2.2.4.2 POEM Tie-Breaker: Decision Makers' Location v. Economic Activities Location 253
        9.2.2.5 Beneficial Ownership 254
            9.2.2.5.1 DTCs: *Contractual Control v. Economic Control* 254
    9.2.3 International Rules 255
        9.2.3.1 Limitation of Benefits 255
            9.2.3.1.1 BRICS and Treaty Shopping 256
            9.2.3.1.2 BEPS Recommendation 257
        9.2.3.2 Main Purpose Tests 257
            9.2.3.2.1 BRICS and MPTs 257
            9.2.3.2.2 BEPS Recommendation 258
        9.2.3.3 Indirect Asset Transfers 259
            9.2.3.3.1 Domestic Rules 259
            9.2.3.3.2 BRICS and DTCs 260
            9.2.3.3.3 BEPS Recommendation 260
        9.2.3.4 Third Country PEs 261

		9.2.3.4.1	Domestic Rules	261
		9.2.3.4.2	BEPS Recommendation	261
	9.2.3.5	DTCs and Business Purpose		262
	9.2.3.6	DTC and Savings Provisions		263
		9.2.3.6.1	BEPS Recommendation	263
		9.2.3.6.2	BRICS and DTCs Savings Clauses	264
	9.2.3.7	Contract Splitting		264
		9.2.3.7.1	BRICS and Contract Splitting	265
		9.2.3.7.2	BEPS Recommendation	265
	9.2.3.8	Multilateral Instrument		266
		9.2.3.8.1	Changes and Sovereignty	266
		9.2.3.8.2	The Instrument	267
		9.2.3.8.3	BRICS and the Instrument	267
9.3	Supplementary Dispute Resolution			269
	9.3.1	MAP		269
		9.3.1.1	MAP and BRICS Dispute Resolution	269
		9.3.1.2	The MI and Sovereignty	270
		9.3.1.3	BRICS, MAP and Sovereignty	271
	9.3.2	Binding and Mandatory Arbitration		271
		9.3.2.1	BEPS Recommendation	271
		9.3.2.2	Arbitration Rules	273
	9.3.3	Human Rights		274
9.4	Conclusion			275

CHAPTER 10
Summary of Conclusions 277
10.1 Research Problems and Hypotheses 277
10.2 Tax Authority Capacity 277
10.3 Tax Coordination and Cooperation 278
10.4 International Tax Law 278

ANNEX
Communiqué of BRICS, Heads of Revenue Meeting 283

Bibliography 287

Table of Cases 335

Index 345

Preface

This book, which is a Thesis, studies a new and evolving area of international tax law, namely, the international tax law of Brazil, Russia, India, China and South Africa, the 'BRICS', and concludes that the thrust of their divergences from the developed world's international tax law evolves from the necessity to counter the significant illicit outflow of funds while not disturbing inbound FDI or, in recent times, their outbound FDI while ensuring profits are taxed where created. The design of the divergences reflects more on the initial limited manpower capacity of their emerging tax authorities to deal with the complex international tax law issues and politically encouraged policy cooperation amongst the BRICS than it does of actual tax authority cooperation although not wishing to underestimate the importance of that cooperation.

Relevant to my conclusions are the published positions of international governance organizations and financing institutions, BRICS tax administrations, scholars and precedent, and I have used that information, both for and against, to arrive at the most rational conclusions. While economic theories may be relevant, they are not relevant to this study.

My research questions include what is the basis of the BRICS approach to core international tax law, in what way has their approach to defining evasion and avoidance been driven by the magnitude of profits shifted offshore, and particularly to tax havens, and whether their divergences from the developed world's approach to countering thin capitalization, transfer pricing and controlled foreign companies have been fashioned by the necessity for countering the elevated level of abuse. My conclusions also reflect my research on whether the divergences have been designed to counter treaty abuse affiliated with the transactions implemented by MNEs intending to shift profits offshore or accumulating passive income in tax havens and, on whether were the BRICS to localize the BEPS recommendations, would their capacity to counter this abuse be improved. My research also considers whether resolving the disputation arising from the increasing level of tax authority cross border audits and investigations can be facilitated through the adoption of alternative dispute resolution procedures. I also study whether the BRICS' response to the world's growing information exchanging architecture reflects their elevated necessity for gathering information to be used in

Preface

stemming illicit flows, countering international evasion and avoidance and ensuring profits are taxed where created.

I conclude the study with recommendations for the BRICS *Heads of Revenue* to include in a Communique for updating their tax law and procedures which would counter the abuse and assist in dispute resolution.

List of Abbreviations

Academy	(OECD) International Academy for Tax Crime Investigation
Ad hoc Group	Ad hoc Group of Experts on Tax Treaties Between Developed and Developing Countries
ADB	African Development Bank
ALP	Arm's Length Price
ALS	Arm's Length Standard
ANC	African National Congress Party
ASIAN DB	Asian Development Bank
ATC	Law of the People's Republic of China on the Administration of Tax Collection (2001)
Automatic Exchange	Standard for Automatic Exchange of Financial Account Information in Tax Matters, 2014
BEE	Black Economic Empowerment
BEPS	Base Erosion and Profit Shifting
BIAC	Business Investment Advisory Council
BIT	Bi-lateral Investment Treaty
BNTC	Brazil National Tax Code
CA	Competent Authority
Cahiers	Cahiers de droit fiscal international
CbC MCAA	Multilateral Competent Authority Agreement on the Exchange of CbC Reports
CBDT	Central Board of Direct Taxes
CBR	Central Board of Revenue
CCA	Cost Contribution Agreement
CCC	Chinese Criminal Code

List of Abbreviations

CCPR	Covenant on Civil and Political Rights
CFE	Confederation Fiscale Europeenne
CIAT	Inter-American Center of Tax Administration
CIETAC	China International Economic and Trade Arbitration Commission
CIFA	Cooperation and Investment Facilitation Agreement
CIGI	Centre for International Governance Innovation
CEEC	Committee of European Economic Co-operation
CEE	Central Eastern Europe
CEPCIL	Committee of Experts on Progressive Codification of International Law
CFA	Committee on Fiscal Affairs
CFC	Controlled Foreign Corporation
CIAT	Inter-America Centre of Tax Administration
CJEU	Court of Justice of the European Union
CLT	Comprehensive Liability Test
Committee	Committee of Experts on International Cooperation in Tax Matters
Common Reporting Standard	Common Standard on Reporting and Due Diligence For Financial Account Information
Competent Authority Agreement	Model Agreement Between the Competent Authorities of Jurisdiction A and B on the Automatic Exchange of Financial Account Information To Improve International Compliance
COR	Certificate of Residence
COT	Commission on Taxation
CPHRFF	Convention for the Protection of Human Rights and Fundamental Freedoms
CTPA	Centre for Tax Policy and Administration
Customary IL	Customary International Law
Davis Tax Committee	Davis Tax Committee
DEMPE	Development, Enhancement, Maintenance, Protection and Exploitation
DRP	Dispute Resolution Panel
DSB	Dispute Settlement Body
DSU	Dispute Settlement Understanding
DTC	Double Taxation Convention
ECB	European Central Bank

List of Abbreviations

ECHR	European Convention on Human Rights
ECOSOC	UN Department of Economic and Social Council
ECJ	European Court of Justice
EEU	Eurasian Economic Union
EIB	European Investment Bank
EITL	Enterprise Income Tax Law of the People's Republic of China
EURODAD	European Network on Debt and Development
FAD	Fiscal Affairs Department
FATCA	Foreign Account Tax Compliance Act
FATF	Financial Action Task Force
FBE	Foreign Business Establishment
FDI	Foreign Direct Investment
FEITL	Income Tax Law of the People's Republic of China Concerning Chinese-Foreign Equity Joint Ventures and Income Tax Law of the People's Republic of China for Foreign Enterprises
FIE	Foreign Invested Enterprise
FfD Office	Financing for Development Office
FTA	Forum on Tax Administration
FTC	Foreign Tax Credit
FTP	(Russia) Federal Tax Police Service of the Russian Federation
FTS	(Russian) Federal Tax Service
GAAR	General Anti-Avoidance (Abuse) Rule
GATT	General Agreement on Tariff and Trade
Global Forum	Global Forum on Transparency and Exchange of Information for Tax Purposes
HNTEs	High and New Technology Enterprises
HRC	Human Rights Council
Human Rights Council	UN Human Rights Council Advisory Committee
IATJ	International Association of Tax Justices
IBAHRI	International Bar Association Human Rights Institute
ICC	International Chamber of Commerce
ICJ	International Court of Justice
ICSID	International Centre for Settlement of Investment Disputes
IDB	Inter-American Development Bank

List of Abbreviations

IFA	International Fiscal Association
IFC	International Finance Corporation
IGA	Inter-Governmental Agreements
IIA	International Investment Agreements
ILC	International Law Commission
ILCA	International Labour and International Civil-Aviation Organisations Agreements
IMF	International Monetary Fund
IRC	US Internal Revenue Code
International Academy	OECD International Academy for Tax Crime Investigation
IRS	Internal Revenue Service
ITLEFIFE	Income Tax Law on Enterprises with Foreign Investment and Foreign Enterprises
International Covenant	International Covenant on Civil and Political Rights
ITD	International Tax Dialogue
ITLCFEJV	Income Tax Law of the People's Republic of China on Chinese-Foreign Equity Joint Ventures
JITSIC	Joint International Tax Shelter Information Centre on Shared Intelligence and Collaboration
Katz Commission	Katz Commission Report into Taxation
League	Assembly of League of Nations
League Evasion Report	League of Nations Double Taxation and Evasion Report
Lima Declaration	Lima Declaration on Tax and Human Rights
LTB	Local Taxation Bureau
LOB	Limitation of Benefits
MAC	Multilateral Convention on Mutual Administrative Assistance in Tax Matters, Amended by 2010 Protocol
Margo Commission	Margo Commission's Report into the Tax Structure of South Africa
MFN	Most Favoured Nation
MIGA	Multilateral Investment Guarantee Agency
MNE	Multi-National Enterprise
MPT	Main Purpose Test
MS	Member State/s
NPC	National People's Congress

List of Abbreviations

OECD Convention	Convention on the Organisation for Economic Co-operation and Development
OECD Model Convention	Model Convention with Respect to Taxes on Income and on Capital
OECD Commentary	Commentaries on the Articles of the Model Tax Convention
OEEC	Organisation for European Economic Co-operation
Paris Conference	Paris Conference on International Economic Co-operation
PE	Permanent Establishment
Peer Review Reports	Global Forum Peer Review Reports
POEM	Place of Effective Management
RCC	Criminal Code of The Russian Federation No. 63-FZ of June 13, 1996
RDTA	Research and Development Technical Assistance
RDP White Paper	Reconstruction and Development Programme White Paper
REIS	Regional Economic Integration Support Programme
RFB	Secretaria da Receita Federal do Brasil
RTC	Tax Code of the Russian Federation
RIITL	Rules for the Implementation of the Income Tax Law of the People's Republic of China on Enterprises with Foreign Investment and Foreign Enterprises.
RET	Regulations of the People's Republic of China on the Implementation of the Enterprise Income Tax Law
Russian Model	Russian Federation Model Double Tax Treaty
SAAR	Specific Anti-Avoidance Rule
SAARC	South Asian Association for Regional Cooperation
SADC	South African Development Community
SAFE	State Administration of Foreign Exchange
SAT	State Administration of Taxation
SACU	Southern African Customs Union
Settlement Convention	Convention on Settlement of Investments Disputes Between States and Nationals of Other States

List of Abbreviations

SCM	Subsidy and Countervailing Measures Agreement
SEA	Special Economic Area
SEZ	Special Economic Zone
SIT	Special Investigation Team Report
SOE	State Owned Enterprise
SPEPHR	Special Rapporteur on Extreme Poverty and Human Rights
Standard	Standard for Automatic Exchange of Financial Account Information in Tax Matters, 2014
TAL	Tax Administration Law (China)
TCCC	Transnational Corporations Code of Conduct
TCL	Tax Collection Law (China)
TFOND	Task Force on Tax and Development
TIEA	OECD Model Tax Information Exchange Agreement
TIPs	Treaties with Investment Provisions
TIWB	Tax Inspectors Without Borders
Transfer Pricing Guidelines	OECD Transfer Pricing Guidelines for MNEs and Tax Administrations, 2010
TPRM	Trade Policies Review Mechanism
UN	United Nations
UN Model DTC	United Nations Model Double Taxation Convention between Developed and Developing countries
UN Negotiating Manual	Manual For Negotiating of Bilateral DTC Between Developed and Developing Countries
UN TP Manual	United Nations Practical Manual on Transfer Pricing for Developing Countries
UN Overview	Overview of Cooperation on Capacity Building in Taxation
UNCTAD	United Nations Council on Trade and Development
Vienna Convention	Vienna Convention on the Law of The Treaties
WGBHR	Working Group on Business and Human Rights
WHT	Withholding Tax
WTO	World Trade Organisation

Acknowledgements

A decision to venture into a topic with the breadth as mine comes with an expectation that many people have both deep technical knowledge and extensive practical experience on aspects of my focus, and this is what I found. That knowledge, together with the continual change established the background for my study and the basis for much learning. Many changes have taken place, and my writing represents only a snapshot in time!

Without the support, advice and encouragement of my supervisors Dr Tom O'Shea, Dr Christiana HJI Panayi, Professor Rafael Leal-Arcas and Professor Spyros Maniatis, all from Queen Mary, University of London not simply in the academic challenge but in the mechanisms for processing the volume of information, my task would have been immensely more complicated. A special thanks to Dr O'Shea for reviewing the draft chapters and to Julie Bacon, for assisting on process and procedures.

While much can be learned from the literature, a consequence of my topic being new and so broad was the need for first hand research, even though that by necessity was limited. Therefore, I am extremely grateful for contributions from Professors Bianco, Dias, Rolim, Schoueri and Valadao (Brazil), Mr Victor Matechkin and Professor Balco (Russia), T.P. Ostwal, Judge Kumar and Nishith Desai (India), Professors Wei Xiong, Ying Feng Long, Zhengwen Shi and Sharkey (China) and Professors Roeleveld and West (South Africa). I also thank Ms Teixeira for her comments on Peer Reviews, Professor Owens for commenting on Arbitration and Professor Vann for commenting on residence and source. In the end, I am responsible for any errors or omissions.

Finally, I would not have been able to complete this study without the understanding, dedication and support of my wife, Mary and our daughter, Elizabeth each of whom lived the journey with me and without their love, understanding and support, I would have found the completion of this mammoth task, considerably more difficult.

CHAPTER 1
Introduction

1.1 BACKGROUND

The problem researched in this study is whether the shape of the BRICS international tax law has diverged from the core of the developed world's international tax law and, if so, whether that divergence reflects the necessity to counter an elevated level of evasion and avoidance in the BRICS, achieved by MNEs international transactions or the adoption of tax haven structures to facilitate illicit outflows. This study also researches whether the form taken by the BRICS international tax laws has been influenced by their, in the main, limited tax authorities work force to identify and counter those transactions or structures and whether the formulation of those procedures has been influenced by any coordination between their tax authorities or international governance institutions. The answer to this research is then used as the basis for formulating recommendations for the BRICS Revenue Ministers to adopt to strengthen their international tax laws countering the evasion and avoidance that has facilitated the illicit outflows.

One outcome of the research therefore will be an extension to the body of knowledge on BRICS international tax law beyond that of factual presentations in order to assist in the development of a coherent response by the BRICS to countering evasion and avoidance: an approach which should limit interference in both outbound and inbound FDI while simplifying tax authority administration and establishing a basis for resolving international tax disputes, which the BRICS can adopt into their tax laws and practice. This is a new area of study and therefore with little to be seen research on the group as a whole, except for projects conducted in the *Master of Laws Program at the Catholic University of Brasilia, 2009*[1] and in the David R.Tillinghast *Research Conference on International Tax Principles in the BRICS and OECD Countries: Divergences and*

---
1. BRIC, tax system structures and effects on development and foreign trade performance-lessons and solutions, ABDI, 2011.

Convergences[2] and in the IBFD research publication which discusses the potential implications of the BRICS coordinating international tax edited, by *Pistone* and *Brauner*.[3] The economic justification for the BRICS grouping has been examined in many reports including those authored by *Prabhakar*,[4] *Xinhua*[5] *and Cassiolata*[6] but this study will not consider them because taxation is the central core of this study.

The specific plan adopted in this study is to introduce the key background factors which include the emergence of the BRICS and the relevance to the world of the BRICS inbound and outbound FDI. Also a key factor is the political co-ordination between their Governments as is the extent to which that coordination is influencing their tax authorities' coordination of their approaches to countering the transactions and behaviour facilitating the substantial illicit flows. Additionally relevant is the manpower numbers within their tax authorities capable of identifying, auditing and closing investigations on the transactions and behaviour and whether that manpower is a hindrance to stemming the illicit outflows. In subsequent chapters, the research focuses on selected aspects of their international tax law and forms a conclusion on a rational analysis, on whether the formulation of their approach to international tax law has been influenced by any of the key background factors. A discussion of the key background factors now follows.

1.2 BIRTH OF THE BRICS

The liberalizing of the individual BRICS began in the late 1970s for China and the early 1990s for the other members, but it was not before *Dr Jim O'Neill's* 2001 Research Paper[7] examining the relationship between the world's leading economies and the larger emerging market economies, that interest in the countries as a grouping began to arise. Dr O'Neill's theory was that while the BRICS then controlled 8% of the world GDP their anticipated significant GDP growth in the subsequent decade would see their combined GDP reaching 30% of the global GDP by 2014.[8] He was proven to be correct! In absolute terms, the BRICS combined GDP, which was $10trn in 2001 reached $32.5trn by 2014 with trade between the BRICS increasing by 70% in 2014 to $US291bn. SA joined the grouping in December 2010 in order, as *Pinto*[9] observes, to provide a base for the other BRIC(S) investment in Africa. Having regard to this

---

2. David R. Tillinghast Research Conference, University of Sao Paulo, Law School, 30 Sep. and 1 Oct. 2013, on *International Tax Principles in BRICS and OECD Countries: Divergences and Convergences*.
3. BRICS and the Emergence of International Tax Coordination, IBFD, 2015.
4. BRICS Economy, The New Emerging Markets of Asia, Eastern Europe, Africa and Latin America, Lambert Academic Publishing, 2011.
5. A Guide to Doing Business in BRICS, Intercultural Publishing, 2012.
6. BRICS and Development Alternatives, Innovative Systems and Policies, 2011 European Communities.
7. Building Better Global Economies BRICs, Goldman Sachs Global Economic Paper No. 66, November 2001.
8. Ulyukayev, Russian Minister of Economic Development published at BRICS Trade Ministers meeting in Moscow, http://en.brics2015.ru/news/20150707/277026.html.
9. Fair Observer, makes sense of the world, 29 Mar. 2012, http://www.fairobserver.com/region/africa/why-south-africa-brics/.

Chapter 1: Introduction

information, it is rationale to conclude that first, the BRICS are seen to be a quasi-economic grouping attractive for investment by developed countries and second, that intra-BRICS trade is growing.

1.3 FDI

Since liberalization, substantial FDI[10] has been introduced into the BRICS and in recent years the members have themselves become providers of FDI (OFDI). According to *Andref*,[11] Indian and Brazilian firms began outbound FDI earlier than the Chinese and Russian MNEs. In relation to intra-BRICS investment, it remains relatively small as *UNCTAD*[12] confirms, with just 3.2% of Indian outward stock, 2.2% of Chinese stock and 0.3% for Russian and Brazilian outward stock respectively even though it amounted to $291bn in absolute terms by 2014. With intra-BRICS investment representing around 2.5% of global FDI, this must be viewed as being relatively insignificant.

The statistics also confirm a lack of consistency in members receiving FDI, because around 2005, Russia and China were the largest recipients while by 2015 this changed to Brazil and China, with India's FDI increasing at a relatively modest rate during that period (Table 1.1). In relation to OFDI, that same period evidences relatively modest outbound flows except for China and Russia and in Russia's case, OFDI since 2013 accelerated and now substantially exceeds its inbound FDI, a phenomenon perhaps explained by geopolitical issues. Since 2014 China's OFDI has almost equalled its inbound FDI, which reflects the growing success of the *'Going Out'*[13] and the *'One Belt- One Road'*[14] policies (Table 1.1). In relation to the countries providing FDI to the BRICS, except for SA, the leading providers were based in tax havens or privileged tax jurisdictions ('tax preferred jurisdictions'): Brazil, 38% Russia, 75%, India, 64% and 77% for China (Table 1.2). With the top OFDI locations for each of the BRICS (except SA) being respectively 36%, 68%, 58% and 69% tax preferred jurisdictions, the BRICS' MNEs use of tax preferred jurisdictions is substantially similar for OFDI as inbound even though the per country contribution differs (Table 1.3).

---

10. Investment made to acquire lasting interest in enterprises operating outside of the economy of the investor where the investor´s purpose is to gain an effective voice in the management of the enterprise, UNCTAD definitions, http://unctad.org/en/Pages/DIAE/Foreign-Direct-Investment-(FDI),aspx.
11. Outward FDI from BRIC countries: Comparing strategies of Brazilian, Russian, Indian and Chinese multinational companies, EJCE Volume 12, No. 2, p. 80.
12. Rise of BRICS FDI and Africa, Special Edition, 25 Mar. 2013, http://unctad.org/en/publicationslibrary/webdiaeia2013d6_en.pdf.
13. Wang, A Deeper Look at China's 'Going Out' Policy, CIGI Commentary, March 2016, https://www.cigionline.org/sites/default/files/hongying_wang_mar2016_web.pdf.
14. At https://www.clsa.com/special/onebeltoneroad/.

Table 1.1 BRICS Inbound and Outbound FDI

	2005/2007	2012	2013	2014	2015
Inbound FDI					
Brazil	22,824	65,271	64,045	73,086	64,648
Russia	35,579	50,587	79,262	29,152	9,825
India	17,766	24,196	28,199	34,582	44,208
China	76,214	121,080	123,911	128,500	135,610
SA	4,499	4,559	8,187	5,771	1,772
Outbound FDI					
Brazil	12,595	- 5,301	- 1,180	2,230	3,072
Russia	30,145	28,423	70,685	64,203	26,558
India	11,501	8,486	1,679	11,783	7,501
China	18,800	87,804	107,844	123,120	127,560
SA	3,320	2,988	6,649	7,669	5,349

Source: World IR 2016, Investor Nationality: Policy Challenges. For the purposes of this study, FDI is an investment made which provides a lasting interest in an enterprise operating outside the investor's home jurisdiction, http://unctad.org/en/Pages/DIAE/World%20Investment%20Report/Country-Fact-Sheets.aspx; Global Investment Trends, Figure 1.5, http://unctad.org/en/PublicationChapters/wir2016ch1_en.pdf; Nistor,FDI Implications on BRICS Economic Growth, Procedia Economics and Finance 32 (2015) p. 984.

Table 1.2 BRICS

Main Inbound FDI(Non Stock) Investor Countries % of Total Inbound FDI 2012

Brazil		Russia		India		China		SA[1]	
Country	%	Country	%	Country	%	Country	%	Country	Amount ($m)
US	21	Luxembourg	21	Mauritius	44	HK	59	UK	8,036
Netherlands	18	Netherlands	21	Netherlands	9	BVI	7	Luxembourg	844
Luxembourg	12	Ireland	20	Singapore	9	Japan	7	Japan	370
Switzerland	8	BVI	5	Japan	7	Singapore	6	Germany	316
France	4	Germany	5	UK	6	Korea, Republic of	3	US	250
Mexico	4	Bahamas	4	France	3	Taiwan	3	France	217
Chile	3	Cyprus	4	Poland	3	US	2	Italy	195
UK	3	Sweden	3	US	3	Cayman Islands	2	Denmark	190

Chapter 1: Introduction

Main Inbound FDI(Non Stock) Investor Countries % of Total Inbound FDI 2012									
Brazil		Russia		India		China		SA[1]	
Country	%	Country	%	Country	%	Country	%	Country	Amount ($m)
Spain	3	France	2	Germany	2	Samoa	2	Switzerland	129
Canada	2	Austria	2	Cyprus	2	Germany	1	Finland	41

Source: UNCTAD Bilateral FDI Statistics http://unctad.org/en/Pages/DIAE/FDI%20Statistics/FDI-Statistics-Bilateral.aspx, last visited 1 Sep. 2016.
1. SA FDI inflow for 2012 was less than total of amount of absolute inbound FDI from leading ten providers due to repatriations.

Table 1.3 BRICS

Main Outbound FDI (Non Stock) Investor Countries (% of Total Outbound FDI 2012)									
Brazil		Russia		India		China		South Africa	
Country	%	Country	%	Country	%	Country	%	Country	%
Spain	25	Cyprus	43	Singapore	17	HK	58	Nigeria	33
Dominican Republic	20	BVI	15	Mauritius	16	US	5	Panama	22
Chile	16	Turkey	9	US	13	Kazakhstan	4	US	19
Belgium	9	Netherlands	5	Netherlands	9	UK	3	Zambia	15
Mexico	8	France	3	Azerbaijan	7	BVI	3	Mauritius	3
Colombia	5	Singapore	3	UAE	7	Australia	2	France	3
Argentina	4	Bermuda	2	UK	5	Venezuela	2	Italy	2
BVI	3	Germany	2	Switzerland	5	Singapore	2	Uganda	1
Bahamas	2	Canada	2	BVI	4	Indonesia	2	Mexico	1
Panama	2	Austria	2	Australia	2	Luxembourg	1	Germany	1

Source: https://en.portal.santandertrade.com/establish-overseas/russia/foreign-investment, last visited February 2017.

1.4 POLITICAL COOPERATION

While the BRICS individually are members of many international governance institutions and economic groupings,[15] the countries only meet as a bloc at the BRICS Meetings. The *Delhi Declaration (2012)*[16] of the BRICS Leaders explained that because they represented 43% of the world's population they should be accepted as a platform facilitating dialogue and cooperation for achieving peace, security and development in

---

15. EG: Mercosur for Brazil, EEU for Russia, SAARC for India, APEC for China and SADC for SA.
16. Fourth BRICS Summit: Delhi Declaration, New Delhi, 29 Mar. 2012, p. 3.

an interdependent and globalizing world. The later *Fortaleza Declaration (2014)*[17] supported this objective but this time because the countries were the main engines for sustaining the world's economic growth away from the 2008/2010 economic and financial global crisis. They argued that this economic role provided them with moral authority for expecting their strategies to be respected by other countries and governance institutions. While the adoption of these policy positions represented a shift from the BRICS solely being an economic engine, as Dr O'Neill predicted, they were formulated off the back of discussions and cooperation between the BRICS[18] first formalized in 2009[19] which then grew from ministerial meetings and establishing institutions,[20] protocols and financial arrangements facilitating their intra BRICS trade. The *Fortaleza* achievement of formalizing an agreement for the establishment of an economic partnership[21] and the subsequent political decision to press ahead with it as part of the 2020 plans[22] is indicative that the BRICS plan to move from a political to an economic agenda. The economic partnership plan continues to commit the BRICS to the WTO and the opportunities it presents for furthering free trade but also confirms that the G20 should be the premier forum for international economic cooperation[23] rather than the OECD or the UN, even though they highly respect the UN. The BRICS Leaders' communiques rarely mention the OECD.

1.5 BRICS TAX COOPERATION

While not an integral feature of the early BRICS Leaders' communiques, tax cooperation has featured more prominently recently, particularly their objective of countering evasion and avoidance through enhanced cooperation and coordination, both amongst themselves and more widely. They have agreed on the importance of exchanging information and mandated their Revenue Ministers to widely cooperate, first, through a seven-point plan but more recently in individual task areas. A central focus of the BRICS Leaders is the taxing of revenue in the jurisdiction where the economic activity occurred and value created (*Fortaleza Declaration*)[24] together with countering evasion, transnational fraud and aggressive tax planning. Countering aggressive tax avoidance and non-compliance practices has also become a focus and the *Ufa Declaration*[25] directed their tax authorities to explore enhanced cooperation towards countering base erosion and promoting information exchange including localizing the *BEPS Action*

---

17. Sixth BRICS Summit: Fortaleza Declaration, 15 Jul. 2014, p. 6.
18. At http://www.brics.utoronto.ca/docs/.
19. Joint Statement of the BRIC Countries' Leaders, Yekaterinburg, Russia, 16 Jun. 2009.
20. New Development Bank and the Contingent Reserve Arrangement.
21. BRICS Economic Cooperation Strategy and a Framework of BRICS Closer Economic Partnership, to promote intra-BRICS economic, trade and investment cooperation, p. 20 published as Strategy for BRICS Economic Partnership Released at Ufa 9 Jul. 2015.
22. Media Note on Informal Meeting of the BRICS Leaders on the Margins of the G20 Summit in Antalya, Turkey, 15 Nov. 2015.
23. Strategy for BRICS Economic Partnership, Sections III.2 and IV, *supra* n. 10.
24. 6th BRICS Summit, *supra* n. 17, p. 17.
25. 2015 Ufa Declaration, Ufa, Russia, 9 Jul. 2015, p. 18.

Plans[26] and the *Common Reporting Standard*. In private meetings held away from the annual leaders meetings, the *Heads of Revenue* (first in *Delhi*)[27] have focussed on tax administration cooperation intended to counter base erosion through tax treaty abuse, incomplete disclosure of information and fraudulent claims, capacity building and multilateral cooperation including establishing a central contact point in each country. The research confirms that none of the BRICS has published the details of the central contact points even though at the *Moscow*[28] meeting they stipulated that the central points would be established. The *Moscow* meeting additionally discussed practical issues designed to help members and other developing countries counter evasion and also the localizing of the *BEPS* recommendations, including the *Common Reporting Standard*. It also provided for continuing the exchanging of experiences between the members including how best to cooperate in combating base erosion and profit shifting, while continuing to improve the compliance of international tax law. In agreeing to assist other developing countries in their localizing of the BEPS recommendations, the BRICS saw this as being instrumental in their influencing other developing countries' development of their own international tax law.

They also agreed on the necessity for increasing in their tax administrations' capacity when implementing the *Common Reporting Standard* providing each member had fulfilled the legal requirements to do so. Furthering the objective of helping developing countries, they agreed to document the BRICS Tax Administrations' experience in assisting developing countries build tax administration capacity, focussing on BEPS and the *Common Reporting Standard*.

1.6 ILLICIT TRADE FLOWS

As the *GFI Report*[29] confirms, the need to counter illicit flows is of supreme importance to the BRICS because those countries occupy five of the top seven positions in the listing of countries' illicit outflows. The aggregate accumulated outflow for all countries was estimated to be \$3.3trn[30] over the ten-year period to 2013 and according to the *GFI Report*, 83.4% arose through 'deliberate trade mispricing and leakages in the balance of payments'. This means that approx. \$2trn of the illicit flows amounted to export under-pricing (Table 1.4). Supporting *UNCTAD*[31] explains that more than \$100bn of annual tax revenues are lost by developing countries each year from 'mispriced intangible and financing transactions' written through 'offshore hubs' of MNE groups. It also explains that other devices adopted by MNEs to relocate moneys include tax rate differentials (TP manipulations such as trade mispricing, intangibles and commissionaire arrangements), loopholes (hybrids, derivatives, disguised domestic investments and deferred repatriation) or DTC abuse (treaty shopping, triangular structures and

---

26. BEPS 2015 Final Reports, http://www.oecd.org/ctp/beps-2015-final-reports.htm.
27. Communiqué of BRICS Heads of Revenue Meeting, New Delhi, 18 Jan. 2013.
28. BRICS Heads of Tax Administrations Meeting, 19 Nov. 2015, Moscow.
29. Kar and Spanjer, Illicit Financial Flows from Developing Countries, 2004/2013, Appendix 2, p. 28, http://www.gfintegrity.org/wp-content/uploads/2015/12/IFF-Update_2015-Final-1.pdf.
30. *Ibid.*, at p. 8.
31. World Investment Report, 2015, p. 190.

circumvention of DTC thresholds).[32] In further support, the *Tax Justice Network*[33] asserts that evasion is the primary reason for the illicit funds flows which they argue is accomplished through mispriced trade transactions, mispriced related party transactions and 'round tripping'.[34] Supporting a contrary theory to how funds flow illicitly, is the effective increase in BRICS corporation taxes arising from the dismantling of incentives[35] introduced to attract FDI, but with China being the only BRICS' member having genuinely substantially restructured a very wide range of corporation tax incentives since 2000 and only from 2008, this does little to support this theory.

These Reports therefore support the theory that the BRICS are losing substantial amounts of tax through illicit offshore flows structured primarily through mispriced related party trades (Table 1.5) and mispriced intangible and financing transactions, although other structures, including 'round tripping' and DTC avoidance are used. With inbound FDI to the BRICS, except for SA, predominantly emanating from tax preferred jurisdictions (Russia 75%, India 64% and 77% for China) and with the top OFDI locations for each of the BRICS except SA, (Russia 68%, India 58% and China 69%) also being tax preferred jurisdictions, the importance of establishing procedures to stem the flow to them cannot be overestimated while not drying up the inbound FDI.

Table 1.4 BRICS

	Illicit Financial Outbound Flows-($USm)							
	2003	2005	2007	2009	2011	2012	Cumulative (1)	Export Underpricing (2)
Brazil	12.06	16.7	17.2	22.3	34.1	33.9	217	145
Russia	41.3	57.5	82.1	129.4	187.7	122.8	973	824
India	10.1	20.1	34.6	29.0	86.0	94.7	439	125
China	64.4	82.3	107.0	140.0	162.7	249.5	1,252	828
SA	0	3.3	18.6	19.6	15.2	29.1	122	95
Total							**3,003**	**2,017**

Source: Data extracted from Table 3 p. 30/33, pages Kar and Spanjer, Global Financial Integrity: Illicit Financial Flows from Developing Countries: 2003-2012, December 2014, Table C, p. 8, updated 2015.
1. Total of all years commencing 2003 and concluding 2012.
2. Excludes tax havens and offshore centres due to unreliability of data.

---

32. *Ibid.*, at p. 192.
33. Closing the Floodgates, p. 17, http://www.taxjustice.net/cms/upload/pdf/Closing_the_Floodgates_-_1-FEB-2007.pdf, p. 16/17/18.
34. Domestic sourced investment disguised as FDI.
35. Introduction of EITL replacing Income Tax Law of PRC Concerning Foreign-funded Enterprises and Foreign Enterprises (9 Apr. 1991) and Interim Regulation of PRC Concerning Enterprise Income Tax (promulgated on 13 Dec. 1993).

Chapter 1: Introduction

Table 1.5 BRICS

	Analysis of BRICS Trade Mispricings			
	Import Mis-invoicing		Export Mis-invoicing	
	Over Pricing	Under Pricing	Over Pricing	Under Pricing
Brazil	59,742	184,742	92,645	145,750
Russia	78,635	558,130	798,941	824,938
India	309,938	348,797	142,185	125,012
China	228,908	3,141,045	832,126	828,352
SA	23,335	6,744	2,908	95,041

Source: Gosling, What comfort does SA's Protection of Investment Act provide to foreign investors?, Norton Rose Fullbright, April 2016, http://www.insideafricalaw.com/blog/what-comfort-does-south-africa-s-protection-of-investment-act-provide-to-foreign-investors, last visited January 2017.

1.7 TAX AUTHORITY CAPACITY

The tax authorities of Brazil, India and SA,[36] were formed prior to the growth in inbound FDI, and when formed had little need to establish teams of officials to investigate international transactions because before liberalization, there was little cross-border activity to administer. Also relevant for tax authority capacity at that time was the countries adoption of the territorial basis for taxing companies. With China's[37] tax authority prior to liberalization being confined to supervising indirect taxes, it too had little need to develop an international tax capacity while Russia's tax authority[38], which had been formed in the dying days of the Soviet Union, had little reason to establish teams investigating international transactions because domestic tax planning was positively encouraged.

While it is rational to expect that BRICS' tax authority manpower has increased since liberalization, statistics on the BRICS manpower in the tax authorities[39] before 2009 does not support the theory. Similar statistics (*see* Table 1.6) available for the 2009–2013[40] period disclose that only Brazil substantially increased its manpower while Russia suffered a 33% reduction.

---

36. RFB, formed in 1968; CBDT formed in 1963 following breakup of the CBR, formed in 1924; SARS formed in 1997 from Directorate of Internal Revenue.
37. SAT, formed in 1958 to administer indirect taxes and then direct taxation from 1993.
38. FTS, formed in 2004 after dissolution of FTP formed in 1992.
39. 2016 *FTA* (Communiqué 10th Meeting of the OECD Forum on Tax Administration Beijing, 13 May 2016, http://www.oecd.org/tax/forum-on-tax-administration/meetings/fta-communique-2016.pdf)agreed that by OECD, CIAT, IOTA and IMF collecting comparative data on tax administrations publishing them in the Tax Administration Series, transparency of staffing levels would improve.
40. In 2013, 24,500 (Brazil); 133,000 (Russia); 41,500 (India); 756,000 (China);15,000 (SA), Table 4.6: Staff metrics – arrivals, departures, age profile and academic qualifications, http://www.oecd.org/tax/forum-on-tax-administration/database/; 2009, 8000 (Brazil); 180,000 (Russia); 42,000 (India); 750,000 (China);15,000 (SA).

Table 1.6 Tax Authority Aggregate Manpower

	Brazil	Russia	India	China	SA
2009	8,000	180,000	42,000	750,000	15,000
2013	24,500	133,000	41,500	756,000	15,000

These raw numbers depict relatively large tax authority forces in Russia and China but more relevant to this study are the officer numbers dealing with international audit and investigation which are found in Tables 1.7/1.8 and 1.9. During the period 2009–2013,[41] the audit and investigation manpower in Brazil and SA were both below the sample average, while Russia's manpower was above. Without specific information available for India and China in 2013 drawing a conclusion is not possible. However, the numbers show relatively large number of audit and investigation officers in Russia and China but whether these are accurate or misleading requires further investigation.

Table 1.7 Tax Authority Audit and Investigation Manpower-Absolute

	Brazil	Russia	India	China	SA
2009[42]	2,560	57,600	13,400	240,000	4,800
2013	4,900	62,500	NA	NA	2,550

Table 1.8 Tax Authority Audit and Investigation Manpower-Percentages

	Brazil	Russia	India	China	SA	OECD
2013	19.7%	47.1%	NA	NA	16.6%	36.2%

These statistics do not breakdown into manpower focussing on international audit and investigation but, rationally, the relatively absolute small number of officers in Brazil, India and SA focussing on audit and investigation supports a deduction that in those countries only a small number were focussing on international audit and investigation, even in 2013. A conclusion on the international manpower in China and Russia cannot be drawn from these statistics.

Looking at other sources, can more accurate conclusions be drawn? With the FTS employing approx. only forty TP officers in 2011, this indicates a small Russian TP team as did the SAT and STB specialist TP manpower of around 1,000 officers[43] in 2014

---

41. 2013: 20% (Brazil); 47% (Russia); NA (India); NA (China);16.7% (SA), Table 5.7: Staff usage (2013) by major tax functional groupings (% of total usage); in 2009 an average of 32% of officers were involved in audit in non OECD countries, Tax Administration in OECD and Selected Non OECD Countries: Comparative Information Series (2010) 3 Mar. 2011, p. 139.
42. In 2009 an average of 32% of officers were involved in audit in Non-OECD countries, Tax Administration in OECD and Selected Non OECD Countries: Comparative Information Series (2010) 3 Mar. 2011, p. 139.
43. Around 1996 China tax officials began discussing international tax matters with the OECD and the necessity for training has become evident from the training colleges established in China in conjunction with the OECD and from SAT's decision to train 1,000 officials on taxation matters

Chapter 1: Introduction

with approx. 200 being SAT based from around the 100 which *Jinyan Li*[44] suggested were employed in 2012. The manpower in China focussing on international investigations was relatively small when compared with the numbers of officers centred on audit and investigation generally. While small in percentage terms, the rapid China increase arose, as *Yuan*[45] explained, can be misleading because before 2008[46], China had little need for officers to investigate cross border transactions when compared to China's later diverse approach to audit. In relation to Brazil, Orsini's[47] explanation that the availability of few administration resources had contributed to Brazil's adoption of the fixed margin TP approach and the RFB's employment in 2011 of (only) twelve officers dealing with TP matters supports his position. In India, the CBDT employed approx. seventy TP officers in 2012, which according to TP Ostwal has grown to 252 in 2016. No information is publicly available on SARS TP manpower.

Table 1.9   Tax Authority TP Manpower

	Brazil	Russia	India	China	SA
2011/2012	12	40	70		NA
2014				1,000	

However, were the individual BRICS members to implement the *Dehli* and *Moscow* communiques and the *Fortaleza* and *Ufa* Declarations of working together in building tax administration capacity, systems and sharing resources, knowledge and best practices then achieving these objectives would require a substantial increase in tax authority manpower. That training should focus on international tax law and how to apply that law to transactions and structures used by MNEs for international evasion and avoidance. There is some evidence of this education process having begun, including the BRICS officials (except for Russia) attending training courses conducted by the *Academy* under the *Oslo Dialogue*[48] on countering tax crime, establishing of the Yangzhou Tax Centre in China in conjunction with the OECD,[49] the OECD's

---

under the National Talent Training programme and pursuant to the 'Belt and Road', Tax Administrations and Capacity Building, A collective Challenge, 2016, http://www.keepeek.com/Digital-Asset-Management/oecd/taxation/tax-administrations-and-capacity-building_978926 4256637-en#.V7yqt_krLIU#page15, (Box 3.10); With FTS having 140 tax officers on non-routine work with approx. 100 dealing with EOI, Russian Peer Review Report, p. 135.

44. Around 150 TP officers in 1997, 500 by 1998 with 1,000 by 2000 with reinforcements from proposed review panel for substantial cases and National database (*Eighth Session, UN Committee of Experts on International Cooperation in Tax Matters, 15/19 October 2012 Geneva*).
45. MNEs conducted business for many years without audit: Yuan, China Changing TP Landscape: Like It or Not, ITPJ, 2013 (Volume 20), No. 4, p. 259/260/261.
46. Fewer than 233 TP audits conducted until recent years partially explained by limited resources, SAT 2013 APA Report: 6 officials in APA programme and 2006/2011 audits increased from 177 to 207.
47. Mitchell, Daily Tax Report, 10 Jun. 2011 Lead Report http://www.rickmitchell.com/developing .pdf; TP Ostwal email exchange with author.
48. Closing Statement by Norway as host of Oslo Dialogue, 23 Mar. 2011.
49. At http://www.oecd.org/ctp/50250817.pdf.

involvement[50] in training Indian tax officers at the Nagpur National Tax Academy and training Russian and SA officials[51] on TP and exchange of information. The IMF has also been training China tax officials on a range of tax matters (Table 1.10).

Table 1.10   China

Summary of Technical Assistance, 2001–13		
Department	Purpose	Date
Tax System Reform		
FAD	Mission on VAT and inheritance tax	April 2001
FAD	Mission on tax preference	September 2001
FAD	Mission on financial sector taxation	August/September 2002
FAD	Mission on personal income tax reform	November 2003
LEG	Seminar on basic tax law	December 2005
FAD	Mission on VAT treatment of financial services	April 2006
FAD	Mission on estimation of VAT gap and capacity	June 2009
FAD	Mission on VAT treatment of financial services	June 2010
FAD	Mission on tax gap analysis	September 2011
FAD	Mission on VAT and inheritance tax	April 2001
Tax Administration Reform		
FAD	Five missions on computerizations	June 2000–October 2002
FAD	Two missions on strategic planning	November 2001–August 2002
FAD	Seminar on Strategic Planning in Washington	October 2002
FAD	Mission on revenue administration	November 2003
FAD	Review of computerization project	September 2004
FAD	Mission on business process reengineering pilot	November 2005
FAD	Mission on IT modernization	June 2006

---

50. At http://www.oecd.org/tax/tax-global/India_Impact_of_OECD_tax_co-operation.pdf.
51. At http://www.oecd.org/ctp/50250817.pdf.

Chapter 1: Introduction

Summary of Technical Assistance, 2001–13

Department	Purpose	Date
FAD	Mission on strategic planning, risk management, and taxpayer services	September 2006
FAD	Mission on VAT invoice cross-checking and other administration issues	March 2007
FAD	Mission on business process re-engineering and Golden Tax Project 3	August 2007
FAD	Seminar on Strategic Planning and Management	January 2008
FAD	Mission on VAT on services, resource tax policy	October 2009
FAD	Mission on project management Golden Tax Project 3	June 2010
FAD	Expert Visit on Strategic Planning	October 2010
FAD	Mission on Tax Administration: Large Taxpayers	October 2010
FAD	Peripatetic Expert Visit on Tax Administration	October 2010
FAD	Tax Policy and Administration	September 2011
FAD	Tax Administration (Peripatetic Expert Visit 4 of 5)	October 2011
FAD	Tax Administration (Peripatetic Expert Visit 5 of 5)	October 2011
FAD	Tax System Reform	October 2011
FAD	Tax Administration Reform	December 2012
FAD	Large Taxpayer Compliance	January 2013
FAD	Workshop on practical tax analysis for tax officials	June 2000–Oct. 2002
FAD	Large taxpayer admin mission	November 2001–August 2002

Source: China Staff Report for the 2013 Article IV Consultation, Informational Annex, IMF, page 18, 27 June 2013.

1.8 HYPOTHESES, ASSUMPTIONS AND QUESTIONS

Based on the key background factors discussed above, one hypothesis is that the BRICS tax authorities have responded to the substantial increase in MNE cross-border transactions facilitating illicit trade flows causing evasion or avoidance by increasing the deterrent inherent in their international tax law by widening the laws' coverage and increasing notifications, because the manpower numbers and their experience levels were then both incompatible with the task. A second hypothesis is that outside of TP, there is little evidence of practical coordination between the BRICS in formulating their international tax law even though there is political agreement at the *BRICS Leaders'* level for this to happen.

This study is about international tax law, which makes fundamental to an understanding of the results, an appreciation of what constitutes international tax law. As *Avi Yonah* and *Ring*[52] confirm, international tax law is difficult to define but many have tried. Some define it as an amalgam of customary international law[53] and international agreements[54] including States rights to tax, tax treaties and dispute settlement. Others suggest it constitutes the international aspects of tax systems arising in national environments[55] and the distribution of revenue between countries requiring substantial coordination if that allocation is to be fair.[56] It may also be the global rules applicable to business and investment transactions between two or more States or territories encompassing all tax issues arising under one country's income tax laws which contain a foreign element[57]. It may be all international and domestic tax provisions relating specifically to situations involving the territory of more than one State, or so-called cross-border situations.[58] In this study, the author defines international tax law as constituting the amalgam of public, private and customary international law (but excluding indirect tax laws) applicable to cross-border business and investment transactions of corporations including the body of 'soft'[59] and 'black letter'[60] law designed domestically and bilaterally for that purpose, including the rules for resolving cross-border taxation disputes. He also assumes in this study that the

---

52. International Tax as International Law, Law & Economics Working Papers Archive: 2003–2009, Art. 7 [2004]; Ring, The Promise of International Tax Scholarship, published by Saint Louis University Law Journal (2010) Volume 55, p. 319.
53. At http://www.judicialmonitor.org/archive_1206/generalprinciples.html.
54. Quereshi, The Public International Law of Taxation, Text, Cases and Materials, Kluwer Law International; 1994.
55. Isenbergh, International Taxation, published by Thomson/Reuters 2010, p. 3.
56. Rixen, The Political Economics of International Tax Governance, Transformation of the State Series, Palgrave Macmillan, 2008.
57. Rohatgi, Basic International Taxation, Richmond Law, 2005.
58. Vogel, Double Tax Treaties and Their Interpretation, Berkeley J. Int'l Law, Volume 4, Issue 1 (Article 1) Spring 1986.
59. Rules in treaties, nonbinding or voluntary resolutions, recommendations, codes of conduct, and standards, Oxford Bibliographies, http://www.oxfordbibliographies.com/view/document/obo-9780199796953/obo-9780199796953-0040.xml, January 2014.
60. Basic standard rules generally known and free from doubt. The black letter law on any subject consists of rules for application in a very mechanical way without moral qualms or other considerations, Cornell University Law School, https://www.law.cornell.edu/wex/black_letter_law.

Chapter 1: Introduction

'developed world' international tax law which the BRICS law is compared with is that recommended by the OECD rather than by the UN or the EU, as doing so enables the research questions to be manageable. Also, tax authority capacity refers to work force numbers and the nature of the expertise, which that manpower has to deal with evasion or avoidance transactions or behaviour.

Having set out two hypotheses and assumptions, the main questions which are intended to breakdown the main research question into manageable sub-questions, the outcomes of which will enable the hypotheses to be test are considered. Chapter 2 shows how it came about that the BRICS core international tax policy and law reflects the basic formulation of the developed world's core international tax policy and law and the significance of the influence of the inbound MNEs on the development of that policy and law. Chapter 3 focuses on whether countering evasion and avoidance has become a special BRICS focus and if so why, and whether the BRICS approach to evasion and avoidance diverges from the developed world's approach and whether that special focus has influenced the divergences. Chapter 3 also further researches whether the BRICS treatment of mispriced transactions and tax haven use as evasion can be explained by the necessity to increase the deterrent effect. Chapter 4 discusses whether the BRICS widened approach to countering thin capitalization, TP and controlled foreign corporations from the developed world's approach was formulated to counter those abuses. Studied in Chapter 5, is whether the BRICS approach to exchanging information is compatible with the developed world's exchanging architecture and whether the BRICS have sought to influence the design of that architecture so that the new methods provide them with information to counter transactions or behaviour facilitating illicit outflows or investment of funds in lowly taxed jurisdictions, but without additional demands on their tax authorities. Chapter 6 researches whether the BRICS approach to residence both domestically and in their DTCs is intended to widen the laws countering DTC abuse and whether their widening of the beneficial ownership, limitation of benefit and main purpose tests results in the countering of abuse by persons who satisfy the residence test. Chapter 6 also analyses whether declaring countries to be non-cooperative or applying indirect asset disposal rules widens the options available to counter DTC abuse. Chapter 7 researches whether were the BRICS to localize the *BEPS Final Action Reports*[61] recommendations, that their procedures for countering abuse would be strengthened and whether the formulation of localization proposals published by the BRICS has been influenced by coordination amongst their tax authorities and whether their signing of the *Multi-lateral Instrument*[62] would improve their ability to counter DTC abuse. Chapter 8 questions whether the BRICS failure to embrace the other approaches for resolving international tax disputes can be explained by their reluctance to compromise their right to sovereignty over tax dispute resolution. Chapter 9 researches any link between FDI and dispute resolution.

The significance of the influence on the design of the BRICS international tax law of their political and tax authority coordination and cooperation is researched.

---

61. At http://www.oecd.org/ctp/beps-2015-final-reports.htm.
62. Developing a Multi-lateral Instrument to Modify Bi-lateral DTCs, Action 15.

1.9 RESEARCH METHODS

The research in this study requires conclusions be drawn on questions directed at the five BRICS members, both with respect to themselves as countries and also with respect to their relationships with the developed world. In conducting this research, the comparative, doctrinal and participatory methods of legal research have been followed. First, the comparison was set up and then in researching the comparisons, the doctrinal approach has been adopted and, in order to sensitize the research for the practicalities of the real world, the participatory approach has been followed.

In relation to the comparative method, the sensitivity of the method is acknowledged but as *Paris*[63] confirms, there is no exclusively correct method. This led to a careful selection of the 'approach' and the 'accomplishment', and the approach adopted involved carefully selecting the material while the comparators are the BRICS and the developed world. In managing the research process, the most important only of the materials available have been considered together with the analysis of them because the significant volume of material would otherwise overwhelm the analysis resulting in a failure to draw realistic conclusions. The doctrinal method has been adopted because of the logic of the law and the importance which it allocates to the valid legal sources including 'black letter' law. Research results based on the doctrinal method may suffer from a failure to deal with justness embedded in 'black letter' law as Kilcommins[64] observes, and this potential failing was dealt with by adopting the participatory approach. As *Londras*[65] observes, the participatory research method involves the participation of other persons in the research study. By incorporating the participatory research into the study, this limits the failings of the doctrinal method and it also reflects in the conclusions on the hypotheses, the views of persons who may deal with some of the issues on a day-to-day basis. Mindful of the importance of selecting the right persons to participate in the research and in order to avoid the conclusions being contaminated by persons promoting their bias or personal agendas, leading academics were carefully selected and, where possible, justices and professional advisers who would understand the necessity for their responses to be objective. The participation of Brazil and India took the form of responses to questionnaires together with limited interviews while for Russia, China and SA questionnaires and in SA's case, a limited questionnaire.

Having regard then to these research methods, features of both the 'black letter' and 'soft law' of the developed world and of the BRICS and the relevant literature were considered, as were the decisions of the BRICS domestic dispute resolving bodies and the decisions of the international dispute resolving institutions, where relevant. Relevant materials published by international governance institutions was considered and 'first hand' research conducted through interviews with leading BRICS academics and practitioners, each review or investigation being designed to shed light on the

---

63. Doctrinal Legal Method, Assumptions, Commitments and Shortcoming, Legal Research Methods, Principles and Practicalities, Clarus Press, May 2016, p. 48/49.
64. *Ibid.*, 63, at p. 14.
65. *Ibid.*, 63, at p. 150.

Chapter 1: Introduction

research questions and the hypotheses. Also of relevance were discussions at a meeting of the Committee of Experts on International Cooperation in Tax Matters of the UN with senior international tax representatives of the BRICS tax authorities. An appreciation of the methods adopted by the BRICS in dealing with international tax law conflict was also relevant as were publications of the author including those presented at conferences[66]. Since some of the materials examined for this study were not written in English, working version English language translations have been used instead of official transactions. These should be obtained through were a closer examination of the subject matter be required in further research.

The results of the literature review have been directly incorporated into the Chapters where relevant because separating the results into a stand-alone Chapter would neither have facilitated testing the hypotheses nor arriving at conclusions to the individual research questions nor would it have facilitated a reader's understanding of the research and the relevance of it to the conclusions, including how tax authorities and governance institutions may benefit from the research.

The book has the following chapter structure: Chapter 1: Introduction; Chapter 2: BRICS: Core international tax policy and law; Chapter 3: Evasion and avoidance: BRICS and widening the developed world's meaning of the concepts; Chapter 4: Countering avoidance: specific anti-avoidance rules; Chapter 5: Information Exchange; Chapter 6: BRICS and DTCs: Countering treaty benefits; Chapter 7: BRICS and BEPS: Final Reports; Chapter 8: Dispute Resolution and Chapter 9: Summary of Conclusions. There is also an Annex containing draft recommendations for the BRICS Revenue Ministers which if implemented would strengthen their international tax law countering evasion and avoidance arising from transactions or behaviour facilitating illicit outflows.

Finally, the author reaffirms his goal of extending the existing body of knowledge beyond that of factual presentations of the BRICS international tax laws in order to assist in developing an understanding of the BRICS approach to dealing with evasion and avoidance: an approach which facilitates both outbound and inbound FDI, simplifies tax authority administration and establishes a basis for resolving international disputes which is compatible with sovereignty.

The law is at 31 July 2016, and 1 January 2017 for Chapter 9.

---

66. Including Russia and Model International Tax Treaties –Parts 1/2, July/August 2012, International Tax Report; UK CFC Rules and the BRICS, International Tax Report, September/November 2013; WTO and Direct Taxation; David R. Tillinghast Research Conference, University of Sao Paulo, Law School, 30 Sep. and 1 Oct. 2013, on International Tax Principles in BRICS and OECD Countries: Divergences and Convergences; QMUL Summer Tax Programme 2013 and 2014 BRICS' Conferences.

CHAPTER 2
Core International Tax Policy and Law

2.1 INTRODUCTION

This Chapter studies how it came about that the BRICS core international tax policy and law has reflected the basic formulation of the developed world's core international tax policy and international tax law. It also examines what was the significance of the MNEs influence in the development of that policy and law.

2.1.1 BRICS and Policy

This subsection researches the influence, if any, that the international aid agencies, bilateral and multilateral investments treaties and the WTO have had on the development of the BRICS core international tax law and concludes that neither the aid agencies nor international investment treaties have significantly influenced the core, while the WTO has had an influence.

2.1.1.1 Aid Agencies

The years leading up to 2015 has produced little evidence of the IMF, World Bank or other international aid agencies having had much success in exerting real influence on the BRICS to adopt the developed world's policy. One reason for this is the general push back by the BRICS[67] against the influence of the World Bank and the IMF reflecting the BRICS belief that their representation on those institutions governing councils is not

---

67. Gang, Alternate Governor of IMF for China, October 2014; Mayaram, Alternate Governor of IMF at the Joint Annual Discussion, October 2014; Kudrin, Governor of the Bank and the Fund for Russia at Joint Annual Discussion, October 2009; Manuel, Chairman of Joint Ministerial Committee of Boards of Governors on the Transfer of Real Resources to Developing Countries at the Joint Annual Discussion, September 2006.

reflective of the BRICS growing role in world trade.[68] Another reason is the failure of the *World Bank*[69] to link the adoption of the developed world's tax policy to the granting of loans and other financial accommodation, a policy which is contrary to the Bank's established policy of linking developed world finance to the adoption by developing countries of the developed world's rules and regulations.[70] One illustration is the *CEE Report*[71] which required the post-World War Two European economies to increase both international trade and the free flow of goods and labour as a pre-condition for *Marshall Plan*[72] financing[73] with the linkage in practice involving the '*Working Group on Double Taxation*'[74] (established in 1956) which by 1971 had morphed into the OECD's *CFA*. Examples exist of the financial institutions seeking to exert influence, but none of the instances is of such significance that it resulted in the BRICS core policy being shaped in the image of the developed world's. So far as the *World Bank*[75] is concerned, one example is its *Report No. 8147-R*[76] which recommended Brazil replicate the corporate tax law policy of inbound investors, including USA, Japan, Germany and UK but this recommendation had little success while another is the *World Bank*[77] influencing of the BRICS' adoption of the developed world's VAT[78] system which has been successful but, VAT, is not core international tax policy, as defined in this study. A similar story is evident for the *IMF*,[79] where other than encouraging the adoption of VAT, seeking involvement in shaping China's tax administration reform (*see* Chapter 1 Table 1.10) and shaping[80] Russia's policy on 'offshore financial centres' and taxing natural resources[81] profits, there is little evidence. However, *Zhu's*[82] recommendation that the IMF should improve its tax policy relationship with the OECD evidences China attempting to influence the tax policy adopted by the IMF.

In relation to the regional funding institutions, such as the African Development Bank, EBRD, European Investment Bank and the Inter-American Development Bank,

---

68. Joint Statement of the BRIC Leaders, Yekaterinburg, Russia, 16 Jun. 2009, p. 3.
69. Guidelines on the Treatment of FDI, Legal Framework for the Treatment of FDI: Volume II: Guidelines, 1992.
70. Development of policy integral to the growth of trade because of how it facilities FDI and portfolio investment.
71. General Report-Volume 1, Paris, 21 Sep. 1947.
72. Marshall convinced Truman that without US financial assistance Europe would become Communist, http://marshallfoundation.org/marshall/the-marshall-plan/marshall-plan-speech, last visited 20 Jun. 2016.
73. Progress monitored by the OEEC (General Report, *supra* n. 71, p. 2, point viii) which became *OECD in 1960*.
74. First term of reference was: avoidance of double taxation with respect to taxes on income, capital and estates of deceased persons, http://archives.eui.eu/en/fonds/173529?item=OEEC.FC, last visited August 2015.
75. Financing For Development, Post 2015, p. 10.
76. Agenda for Tax Reform, Volume III: Assessment of Brazilian Direct Taxes, February 1990 Country Operations Division Brazil Department LA and the Caribbean Region, para. 15, p. 111.
77. *Supra* n. 75, at p. 10; IMF, FAD at a Glance, 2015, p. 4.
78. Reports on Technical Assistance provided by FAD are private unless countries publish them and the only published Report by a BRICS member is the August 2015 Report on VAT.
79. Spillovers in International Taxation, May 2014.
80. Press Release 23 Sep. 2000.
81. Energy Tax Reform in Russia, September 1998.
82. Statement by Vice Minister, October 2013.

there is also little evidence of them requiring any linkage between the provision of finance to borrowers and the borrowers adopting the developed world's core policy. The *Asian DB's*[83] exerting influence on tax authority capacity building is evident, from the Bank's concern that tax authority manpower levels were insufficient.

2.1.1.2 Investment Treaties

There is little evidence directly linking the *BITs*[84] with a purposive shaping of the BRICS core international tax policy in the image of the developed world even though a country's adoption of a BIT generally precedes large scale inbound FDI and liberalization. This follows from FDI providers wishing to limit their expropriation risk and occurs by the BITs taxation provisions. With increased taxation potentially a form of expropriation,[85] as *Gregoire*[86] discusses, economically prudent foreign investors are more likely to invest in a country having an effective BIT than one which does not. As *Guzman*[87] observes, since the mid-1990s, BITs have become the main form of international treaty regulating cross-border investment and because MNEs can limit their exposure to expropriation through an MIGA[88] (which presupposes a BIT having been implemented), then as *Schachter*[89] writes, any tax provisions incorporated into a BIT becomes part of the parties international tax law as a consequence of the provisions mere presence in the BIT. This practice has grown in importance since the *Hull Rule's*[90] redundancy.

As FDI globalization spread to the BRICS, the investors requirement for investment protection increased and by deduction, this must be one explanation for the increase in the number of BITs and multilateral investment treaties[91] entered into by the BRICS.[92] Since those treaties contain some international tax provisions and with those provisions modelled on the developed world's policy, this must be one

---

83. Tax Policy and Administration Research and Capacity Development, Project Number: 47231-001, RDTA, September 2013.
84. Agreement between two countries for promotion and protection of investments made by an investor from one of them to the other, UNCTAD, Investment Policy HUB.
85. UNCTAD Series on Issues in International Investment Agreement, 'Taxation', Geneva, 2000.
86. Taxation and Expropriation under BITs: Setting the Standard, 30 Butterworths, JIBFL, 629, November 2015.
87. Why LDCs Sign Treaties That Hurt Them: Explaining the Popularity of BITs, Berkeley Law Scholarship Repository, 1997, p. 640, http://scholarship.law.berkeley.edu/facpubs/904.
88. MIGA coverage is conditional on BITs being entered into because MIGA can cover expropriation which is a feature of most BITs.
89. Compensation for Expropriation, 78 AM. J. INT'L L 121 (1984).
90. American Secretary of State, Cordell Hull, published the full compensation standard, which required 'prompt, adequate and effective' compensation against Mexico for expropriation claims.
91. Investment Agreements and Investment Related Instruments with EEC; World Bank Investment Guidelines; Transnational Corporation Code of Conduct (TNCC) and Agreements Protecting Reciprocal Investments.
92. BITS signed with OECD Members: none of Brazil's BITs are effective, so difficult to conclude they formally shaped Brazil's policy. This is contrasted with BITs signed/enforced by other members with OECD members such as Canada (Russia, 1989; China, 2012; SA, 1995, NIF; France (India, 1997, China, 1994, replaced 2007, SA 1995); Germany (Russia, 1989, India, 1995, China, 1983, replaced 2003, SA, 1995, terminated); Netherlands (Russia, 1989, India, 1995,

explanation for some of the BRICS core policy reflecting the developed world's core. However, their influence on a BRICS member's international tax law is extremely limited, because, broadly, it relates only to the expropriation clause since the MFN and double tax provisions are usually excluded from these treaties[93] but just how effective the influence is must be tested against the BRICS' BITs which have become effective. A discussion on which BRICS BITs are effective is as follows.

With none of Brazil's[94] BITs and approx. one-third of SA's BITs being effective, the tax provisions in these BITs are potentially of persuasive[95] influence only, except for the BITs enforced by SA. With most of SAs enforced BITs entered into with the developed world members, it indicates an influence on SAs international tax law by the developed world. In relation to Russia, India and China with many or most of their BITs enforced (Russia more than 60% and most of India's and China's) this gives rise to a potential influence on their core international tax policy; but since a study of the tax provisions in the enforced BITs is beyond this research, little conclusions can be drawn except for the Russia/US BIT which preserves the parties' rights to use DTC procedures to ensure fair and equitable treatment in tax matters[96] and to deduct taxes from dividends[97] payable to non-residents. However, with this BIT continuing to be unenforced, it is difficult to judge the impact, if any, it has had on Russian international tax law and policy (*see* Chapter 8 Yukos discussion). In relation to the BRICS *TIPs,* most are enforced but conducting wide ranging research into whether *TIPs* contain tax provisions is also beyond this study. However, the limited research undertaken for this study has identified the 1983 (Draft) *Transnational Corporations Code of Conduct*[98] which, according to *Sauvant*,[99] was designed to prevent MNEs practising TP[100] or base erosion[101] strategies in their dealings with developing countries, which can be argued as an attempt to influence. With the *TCCC* not having been enforced, this leaves as open whether the draft had any real impact on shaping the BRICS international tax law and policy. Other limited research for this study has identified that the EC Co-operation

---

China, 1985, replaced 2001), SA, 1995, terminated); UK (Russia, 1989, India, 1994, China, 1986, SA, 1994), with US (Russia (1992-NIF)) yet to have effective BITs with any member.
93. Discussion on these provisions is furthered in Chapter 8 of this study.
94. Lemos argued that evidence of whether BITs encourage FDI is inconclusive, *see*, The Non-Ratification of BITs in Brazil: A Story of Conflict in a Land of Cooperation, Government of Brazil, April 2013.
95. Effective 2002, BITs enforcement removed from legislative agenda. Government has applied most of the policies required by foreign investors, *see* 'Blue Book', 1992 between fourteen MNCs to the Finance Minister requiring, *inter alia*, lower taxation of capital transfers; *see* '*Multinacionais querem divulgar novo tratamento ao capital estrangeiro*'. Gazeta Mercantil, March 1992.
96. Russia/US BIT, June 1992, Article 11(1).
97. *Ibid.*, Article IV(3)(a), .
98. Draft UN Code of Conduct on Transnational Corporations, 1983 version, http://investmentpolicyhub.unctad.org/Download/TreatyFile/2891, last viewed 2 Jan. 2016.
99. Negotiations of UN Code of Conduct on TC, The Journal of World Investment & Trade, 16 (2015) 11–87, p. 20.
100. *Supra* n. 98, Article 33.
101. *Ibid.*, Article 34.

Agreements with Russia[102] and with SA[103] influence their international tax policy and law, but those with Brazil,[104] India[105] and China[106] do not, in the latter case because they only apply to indirect taxes. In Russia's case, the agreement recognizes DTCs while rejecting the MFN policy, and in SA's case, they confirm that States have rights to counter avoidance or evasion while accepting that tax laws can differentiate between taxpayers not in identical situations, particularly in relation to places of residence.

2.1.1.3 WTO

There is evidence that the WTO influences the shape of the BRICS international tax law in the developed world's image. Brazil, India and SA became WTO members through their prior GAAT membership but each of Russia[107] and China[108] became WTO members in 2012 and 2001 respectively. The WTO package of Agreements allows members to influence corporate tax law because, according to *Japan-Alcohol Beverages II*,[109] *'members of the WTO are free to pursue their own domestic goals* through internal taxation .... *so long as they do not do so in a way that violates Article III or any other commitments they have made in the WTO Agreement'*. The Reports of the WTO Working Parties and the *TPRM*[110] periodic reporting, provides further evidence that the BRICS corporate tax laws have been, and continue to be influenced by the WTO Package as *Wilson*[111] observes, with examples of influence including the removal or

---

102. Agreement on Partnership and Cooperation between EC/Member States and Russia, 1994, Article 58(2).
103. Trade, Development and Cooperation between the European Community and Member States and SA, Article 98.
104. Interregional Framework Cooperation Agreement between EC and MERCUSOR and respective Members, December 1995.
105. Cooperation Agreement between EC and India on Partnership and Development, December 1993.
106. Agreement on Trade and Economic Cooperation between EEC and China, 1985.
107. WT/ACC/RUS/70 WT/MIN(11)/2 17 Nov. 2011, p. 281/290, file:///C:/Users/Peter%20 Wilson/Downloads/2.pdf.
108. WT/L/432 23 Nov. 2001, p. 72 and following pages.
109. WT/DS8/AB/R.
110. Brazil Secretariat Report, 17 May 2013 published at http://www.wto.org/english/tratop_e/tpr _e/s283_e.pdf; No Report on Russia; India Secretariat Report, 28 Apr. 2015 published at https://docs.wto.org/dol2fe/Pages/FE_Search/FE_S_S009-DP.aspx?language=E&Catalogue IdList=134359,131826,92476,107561,81496,25701,42365,75303&CurrentCatalogueIdIndex= 1&FullTextHash=; China notification, 15 Jun. 2016 published at https://docs.wto.org/dol2fe /Pages/FE_Search/FE_S_S009-DP.aspx?language=E&CatalogueIdList=229416,130052,12754 4,127372,124880,117621,115743,64045,103878,83884&CurrentCatalogueIdIndex=0&FullText Hash= including notification of tax incentives at https://docs.wto.org/dol2fe/Pages/FE_ Search/FE_S_S009-Html.aspx?Id=229416&BoxNumber=3&DocumentPartNumber=1&Lang uage=E&Window=L&PreviewContext=DP&FullTextHash=371857150#KV_GENERATED_ FILE_000132.htm; SACU Report, 5 Feb. 2015, published at https://docs.wto.org/dol2fe/Pages /FE_Search/FE_S_S009-DP.aspx?language=E&CatalogueIdList=226744,134794,97313,817 45,14288,106990&CurrentCatalogueIdIndex=1&FullTextHash=.
111. *Supra* n. 66.

reduction of Russian[112] subsidies[113] or incentives and for China[114] the very introduction of the EITL[115] within the permitted seven years from Accession.[116] The recognition by Russia that its SEZs must be compatible with the SCM is evidence of the influence as is India's retention of otherwise prohibited subsidies because of its Annex VII (b) SCM Member status. Also indicative of the WTO influence is the procedure for information on members' tax incentives to be made available to the WTO and its members through the periodic *TPRM* process, an arrangement which affords other members the opportunity to comment and question other members' tax incentives. When the *UN Overview*[117] failed to recognize the WTO as having had any influence on international tax policy, let alone BRICS tax policy, it was in the author's opinion, incorrect.

---

112. Accession Agreement, para. 698; export subsidies and those contingent on using domestic over imported goods (local content subsidies) are prohibited because they directly affect trade. Under SCM, prohibited subsidies are extended for developing country member subject to transition rules. Local content subsidy involves inducing customers to purchase domestically manufactured goods.
113. Subsidy, defined by Article 1, SCM includes financial contributions by a government, any public body within the territory e.g. grants, loans and equity, potential direct transfers of funds or liabilities (e.g., loan guarantees) and foregone or not collected government revenue (e.g., tax credits) within the meaning of Article 3, SCM.
114. Jinyan Li, Relationship Between International Trade Law and National Tax Policy: case Study of China, in 2005 IBFD Bulletin, para. 5.1, p. 83; Annex 6 listed duty rates and products subject to export duty. The changes WTO Accession brought to China's taxation included requirement to notify the *WTO* (Accession Protocol, Article 2B(1)) of its *SEAs* laws (Notification within sixty days of zone details including additions, modifications together with the laws, regulations and other measures benefitting from regulations and other measures). Also impact on SOE's corporation taxation due to the requirement to make tax incentives granted to them 'specific subsidies' (i.e., prohibited and removed) where the *SOE* was the predominant recipient of the subsidy or where the *SOE* received a disproportionately large subsidy. Accession also required the benefits (Including grants and the forgiving of tax liabilities) granted to the SOEs, listed in Annex 5B (Accession Protocol, p. 90/92) be phased out. With tax notifications covering more than twenty pages (Accession Protocol, p. 68/90) they clearly influenced China's taxation. Corporation tax benefits to be removed listed on Annex 5A including preferential corporation tax rates, exemptions from corporation tax for businesses conducted in SEAs, concessions for businesses conducted within those SEAs, foreign invested enterprises high-tech companies, companies utilizing waste and businesses in poverty stricken areas and businesses transferring technology.
115. EITL from 1 Jan. 2008 (5th Session of the 10th National People's Congress, 16 Mar. 2007) has been subject of many theories with some asserting it was 'positive signalling, that compensation and hospitality effects' of *FEITL* were no longer required to make China a country to invest in. Others China's domestic lobby fearing the competition to businesses from increased inbound FDI resulting from Accession while others suggested decision to replace the *FEITL* was national treatment principle (Li, The Rise and Fall of Chinese Tax Incentives and Implications for the International Tax Debates, CLPE Research Paper 05/2008, Volume 04 No. 01 (2008) at p. 10/33; Interview with SAT officials on Issue of Tax Policy Adjustment and Accession to the WTO, Peoples Daily, 6 Apr. 2000 at 2 (overseas edition)).
116. Accession Protocol and repeal fit neatly within the permitted seven years allowed under the *SCM* for a transforming country (as China then was) to repeal prohibited subsidies.
117. UN's Role in International Tax Policy, A Research and Policy Brief for the Use of the NGO Committee on Financing for Development, 7 Mar. 2012, http://www.ngosonffd.org/wp-content/uploads/2010/11/UN-Role-in-International-Tax-Policy-2012.pdf.

2.1.2 OECD Model DTC: Core BRICS Policy and Law

2.1.2.1 *OECD Model DTC*

This subsection investigates the reasons that the *OECD* has been able to exert influence on the BRICS' core international tax policy and law and deduces that because the major FDI providers were resident in OECD Member countries and because those resident countries were required to use the OECD Model[118] in their negotiations for DTCs[119] with the BRICS and because the BRICS did not want to dissuade the providers from investing, this led the BRICS to adopt the core OECD Model as their international tax policy. This is likely to have resulted in the BRICS being 'locked in' to the OECD Model as their core international tax policy.

The inbound BRICS FDI having grown from around $20bn in 1990 to approx. $957bn in 2013 (*Nistor*) evidences an immense increase. China and Brazil have been the two most impacted members in percentage terms, since approx. 63% and 17% of the total amount was invested in them, respectively. With much of the BRICS inbound FDI channelled through conduits and other intermediaries (*see* Chapter 1 Table 1.2), it is difficult to identify the ultimate sources of the investment, but with *UNCTAD*[120] confirming that developed economies' FDI outflows represented approx. 50% of the world's outflows during the 2005/2015 period (approx. 60% in 2007/2008) and with Asia constituting the main recipient of Chinese ODI,[121] the rational conclusion is that most inbound BRICS FDI ultimately emanates from the developed world. This conclusion supports the hypothesis that investor nations require recipient States to shape their core international tax and law policy in a fashion compatible with the OECD, as *Baistrocchi*[122] observed (meaning the *OECD Model* version published before 1990).[123] This conclusion is further supported by the BRICS taking few reservations or positions on the Articles in the OECD Model or in the Commentary thereto (Tables 2.1 and 2.2). Aligning with the OECD Model and Commentary has, according to the *UN Ad Hoc*

---

118. Model Convention with Respect to Taxes on Income and on Capital, https://www.oecd.org/ctp/treaties/2014-model-tax-convention-articles.pdf, last visited 1 Dec. 2015.
119. OECD recommended members use OECD Model DTC for bilateral DTCs with both members and non-members. Associated Commentary (Article 5 OECD Convention provides OECD with the right 'in order to achieve its aims of taking decisions which ..., shall be binding on all the Members and make recommendations to Non Members) was also recommended as a guide for DTC interpretation.
120. Global Investment Trends, Figure 1.5, http://unctad.org/en/PublicationChapters/wir2016ch1_en.pdf; Nistor, FDI Implications on BRICS Economic Growth, Procedia Economics and Finance 32 (2015) p. 984.
121. *García-herrero*, China's outward FDI, 28 Jun. 2015, http://bruegel.org/2015/06/chinas-outward-foreign-direct-investment/.
122. OECD Document C(97) 195/Final, Recommendations 1 (1-3); OECD[C(71),41]; Use and Interpretation of DTCs in the Emerging World: Theory and Implications, (2008) BTR, No. 4, p. 353.
123. 1963 and 1977 OECD Model DTC, Andean Community Income and Capital DTC 1971, 1979 UN Manual for Negotiation of bilateral DTCs between Developed and Developing Countries; 1980 UN Income and Capital Model Convention, 1981 US Model Income Tax Convention.

Group of Experts,[124] resulted in the BRICS being 'locked-in' to the OECD core Model DTC provisions in their bilateral DTCs (Table 2.3).

Table 2.1 BRICS Reservations and Positions on OECD Model DTC and Commentary by Article

Article	Brazil	Russia	India	China	South Africa
1	Y				
2	Y				Y
3			Y		
4	Y	Y	Y	Y	
5	Y	Y	Y	Y	Y
6			Y		
7	Y	Y	Y	Y	
8	Y	Y	Y		Y
9	Y	Y			Y
10	Y	Y	Y		Y
11	Y	Y	Y	Y	
12	Y	Y	Y	Y	Y
13	Y		Y	Y	
14			Deleted		
15			Y		
16		Neither reservations nor provisions by BRICS			
17		Y	Y		
18	Y				Y
19			Y		
20	Y		Y	Y	
21	Y				Y
22	Y		Y	Y	
23A & 23 B	Y			Y	
24	Y	Y	Y		Y
25	Y		Y	Y	
26	Y		Y		
29				Y	
Total	19	10	18	11	9

---

124. OECD Model DTC as main reference takes advantage of technical expertize in Convention and Commentary and for practical convenience because OECD Model had been used by Member States when negotiating DTCs not only with each other but with developing countries. UN, Introduction to Model Treaty, available at www.un.org/esa/ffd/tax/secondsession/Taxation-EC18-2006-7-part2-R.doc.

Table 2.2   BRICS Positions/Reservations from OECD Model DTC and Commentary

Article	Brazil	Russia	India	China	South Africa
1				China is not bound by its stated position or its reservations or positions	
2					Reserves on including local authority taxes in 'taxes'
3					
4		Definition of residence to include place of incorporation, partnerships to be treated as residents, inserts practical day-to-day management into POEM irrespective of location of overriding management	Partnerships are treated as residents, deems POEM to be the place where main and substantial activity of the company is carried on rather than the place of key commercial and management decisions	Reserves on POEM because it prefers 'head office'	
5	Believes building and construction with more than six-months duration should be a PE; disagrees	Excludes 'delivery' from paragraph 4, deems a PE where person acting on its behalf habitually maintains stock	Extends PE definition to sales outlet and farm, plantation, etc. inserts 'assembly' after construction,	To negotiate time from which a building or construction, assembly becomes a PE, creates a PE where	To negotiate time from which a building or construction, installation becomes a PE, creates a PE where

Article	Brazil	Russia	India	China	South Africa
	with OECD on electronic commerce and Commentary on source at 42.11 to 42.88	of goods or merchandise in other state from which deliveries are made	Excludes 'delivery' from paragraph 4 and extends definition of PE by a place where orders are habitually secured, removes from agent of independent status a person whose activities are wholly or almost wholly on behalf of a single enterprise, reserves on twelve-months test applying to individual sites because it believes short-term sales give rise to a PE, preserves India's national system for personal services after withdrawal of Article 14, aggregates separate projects, scientific work is not preparatory, participating in contract negotiation	supervisory activities in relationship to building, construction, assembly site, creates a PE where consulting services provided by employees including connected for more than 183 days in any twelve-month period, deems a person to be a PE if providing independent services in China for more than 183 days in any twelve-month period	supervisory activities in relationship to building, construction, installation site, treats a PE arising where exploitation of natural resources extends beyond sixmonths

Chapter 2: Core International Tax Policy and Law

Article	Brazil	Russia	India	China	South Africa
			can amount to a PE, local presence in a multinational supply chain can be a PE, a website can be a PE as can a hosted website, gross fees from technical services can be taxed, disagrees that two or more contracts for services to same clients cannot amount to a PE		
6	Neither reservations nor provisions by Brazil and Russia		*India* to address 'including income from agriculture or forestry' through bilateral negotiations	Neither reservations nor provisions by China and SA	
7	Business profits to include independent personal services but *exclude deductibility of expenses incurred outside PE's presence* and	Business profits to include independent personal services but *exclude deductibility of expenses incurred outside PE's presence*	Any income gain attributable to a PE which is not received until after PE ceases is taxable, insert into Articles 11, 12, 13 and 21 the	Includes independent services and excludes a deduction for foreign expenses	

Article	Brazil	Russia	India	China	South Africa
	reject apportionment of costs on Convention principles and not be bound to same method in year 2 as in year 1		taxing right after PE cessation, disagrees with transactions between different sections of an enterprise not having legal consequences		
8			Applies Article 12 and not 8 to profits from ships or aircraft leasing, not to include inland waterways in DTCs and taxes income from ancillary services		Reserves on treating container leasing sourced in SA, profits from leasing ships, aircraft on a bareboat charter to be taxed in same manner as transportation when incidental, not extended to inland waterways
9	*Does not allow compensatory adjustments*	*Does not allow automatically compensatory adjustments*			
10	Imposes WHT on PE's profits at same date as in paragraph 2	Reserves on limited rate in paragraph 2, minimum percentages in sub-paragraph (a), not allowing CS to negotiate paragraph 2 limited rate, right to apply	*Does not settle disputes by MAP*, CA not to agree rate in bilateral DTCs, define dividends differently to OECD Model definition		Reserves position on tax rates and minimum percentage shareholding

Chapter 2: Core International Tax Policy and Law

Article	Brazil	Russia	India	China	South Africa
		thin cap rules regardless of any provision in Convention			
11		Not allowing CS to negotiate paragraph 2 limited rate	Reserves on the rate in paragraph 2 and not to use MAP to settle disputes		
12	Taxes royalties at source and includes as royalties payments for leasing of industrial, commercial or scientific equipment and containers, payments for use of or right to use industrial, commercial or scientific equipment, fees for technical services and technical assistance, payments for transmission by cable satellite, fibre optic or similar technology, and to define source on the same basis as used in interest	Taxes royalties at source and includes as royalties payments for leasing of industrial, commercial or scientific equipment and containers, payments for use of or right to use industrial, commercial or scientific equipment	Taxes royalties and technical fees at source, define terms under Indian definition which extends beyond sub-paragraph (5), *deems payments at paragraphs 8.2, 10.1, 10.2, 14, 14.1, 14.2, 14.4, 15, 16 and 17.3 to be royalties*, disagree that industrial, commercial or scientific experience are interpreted by reference to previous experience	Taxes royalties at source, treats payments for the use of or the right to use as royalties and also payment for exclusive distribution rights for a product or services and defines source in the same way as for interest	Taxes royalties at source and defines source in the same way as for interest

31

Article	Brazil	Russia	India	China	South Africa
13	Right to tax in source country, a gain on sale of property not covered by paragraphs 1,2 and 3 of Article		Right to tax in source country, a gain on sale of property not covered by paragraphs 1,2 and 3 of Article when more than *50% by value is Indian immoveable property*	Right to tax in source country, a gain on sale of shares where a substantial portion (i.e. 25%) is sold	
14	With Article 14 deleted from the OECD Model DTC, reservations and positions of the BRICS are no longer relevant.				
15			Adjusts period of stays in DTCs, reconsider period of stay when partner is a non-resident, Indian does not accept a partner as an employee in a fiscally transparent entity		
16	Neither reservations nor provisions by BRICS				
17	Neither reservations nor provisions by Brazil	Russia reserves the right to exclude from the benefits, artistes and sportsmen employed in publicly funded organisations	India reserves the right to exclude from the benefits, income from activities performed in a Contracting State by	Neither reservations nor provisions by China or SA	

Chapter 2: Core International Tax Policy and Law

Article	Brazil	Russia	India	China	South Africa
			entertainers or sportspersons when the activities were substantially public funded.		
18	Brazil reserves the right to specifically refer to annuities	Neither reservations nor provisions by Russia, India or China			SA reserves the right to specifically refer to annuities
19	Neither reservations nor provisions by Brazil or Russia		India reserves on whether public bodies, including State Railways and Post Offices are undertaking business activities.	Neither reservations nor provisions by China or SA	
20	Brazil reserves the right to grant to visiting students the same tax exemptions, reliefs or reductions which are granted to residents for subsidies, grants and payments for dependent personal services. It also reserves the right to	Neither reservations nor provisions by Russia	India reserves the right to address the situation of teachers, professors and researchers, subject to various conditions. It also reserves the right to exclude 'business apprentice' from this Article and reserves the right to provide that	China reserves the right to address the situation of teachers, professors and researchers, subject to various conditions.	Neither reservations nor provisions by SA

33

Article	Brazil	Russia	India	China	South Africa
	address the situation of teachers, professors and researchers, subject to various conditions.		remuneration for services rendered by a student in a Contracting State shall not be taxed in that State provided that such services are directly related to his studies. It also reserves on the right to limit the exemption to a six-year period.		
21	Other income to be taxed in source country	Other income to be taxed in source country	Other income to be taxed in source country		Other income to be taxed in source country
22			Reserves a right to tax capital in the same manner as applies under Indian domestic law		
23A and 23B	Tax sparing to be included, tax deemed to have been paid by a matching credit on interest and royalties as a form of eliminating double		Reserves on requiring tax sparing be included to protect tax incentives provided under national law	Reserves on requiring tax sparing be included to protect tax incentives provided under national law	

Chapter 2: Core International Tax Policy and Law

Article	Brazil	Russia	India	China	South Africa
	taxation and reserves rights for dividends to be exempted through matching credit				
24	Apply rules to stateless persons, calculate a PE's taxable income on royalties payable by PE to head office since such payments not deductible in Brazil, profits not more burdensomely taxed in company owned by one or several residents of third state and confines taxes to those covered by Convention	Apply rules to stateless persons	Not to apply rules to stateless persons, extends protection to PEs from third countries, not to tax a PE at a rate higher than applicable to a resident of the PE state		Reserves on right to confirm that SA can impose tax on PE profits at a rate not more than the normal company rate, by 5%
25			Permit CA to agree a dispute while domestic claim is being heard but then requires claimant to withdraw the domestic claim,	Reserves right to resolve disputes through a joint commission	

35

Article	Brazil	Russia	India	China	South Africa
			prevents a taxpayer deferring a decision pending resolution of domestic law decision and disagrees that economic taxation arises from TP under Articles 11 and 12 which can be resolved by MAP		
26	Neither reservations nor provisions by Brazil or Russia		India reserves the right to include documents or certified copies of the documents within the scope of this Article.	China will only exchange information relating to taxable periods after the agreement came into operation.	Neither reservations nor provisions by SA
29				Reserves right to extend territorial application	

Table 2.3 BRICS DTC Network – Pre and Post Liberalization (Including TIEA but Excluding Transport, Social Security, Regional) – March 2013

	Brazil	Russia	India	China	SA
Pre 1995	20(1)				
Pre 1995 – terminated	2				
Post 1994	18				
Pre 1993 – ongoing		5			
Pre 1993 – terminated		15(2)(3)			

Chapter 2: Core International Tax Policy and Law

	Brazil	Russia	India	China	SA
Post 1992		89			
Pre 1992 – ongoing			16(4)		
Pre 1992 – terminated			25(5)		
Post 1991			91		
Pre 1981				0	
Post 1980 – ongoing				107 (6)	
Post 1980 terminated				7	
Pre 1990					18(7)
Post 1990 – ongoing					67(8)
Post 1990 – terminated					0

Notes:
1. Of the pre-1995 treaties one became effective in the 1960s, three became effective in the 1970s and four became effective in the 1980s. *This confirms Brazil's participation in treaties is long standing.*
2. Of the treaties terminated, one, Spain Treaty was entered into after 1992. *Russia's DTCs are essentially post liberalization.*
3. Of the treaties entered into before 1993, fifteen were terminated with the most recent termination being 2003.
4. India's oldest but still effective treaty was entered into in 1956 with Sierra Leone. *This confirms India's participation in treaties is long standing.*
5. India's oldest but terminated treaty was entered into with Germany in 1957 and three additional treaties were entered into before 1963 for Sweden (1958), Japan (1961) and Austria (1962).
6. Of the treaties entered into since 1980, fifteen were entered into in the 1980s and sixteen were entered into before 1997. *This confirms China's participation in treaties is long standing.*
7. Of the treaties entered into since 1990, 6 were entered into in the 1950s and seven were entered into 1960s and 1970s. *This confirms SA's participation in treaties is long standing.*
8. Of the ongoing treaties nineteen are with African countries.

2.1.2.2 OECD Policy and the Prisoners' Dilemma

Another explanation for the BRICS following the core of the OECD Model is the 'prisoner's dilemma'. According to *Baistrocchi*,[125] two or more developing countries are locked by the dilemma when competing for the same FDI[126] because each offers incentives (Table 2.4) to win the FDI, with the successful party likely to benefit from

---

125. *Supra* n. 122.
126. Following Dagan, National Interests in the International Tax Game, 18 Virginia Tax Review, 363, who wrote that countries are self-interested in international tax policy.

the ensuing market distribution benefits[127] including positive externalities[128] offered by the *OECD Model*.[129] While the prisoner's dilemma is one explanation for the OECD policy being influential, other explanations include *McLure's*[130] *'political clout'* theory which argues that the BRICS adoption of the OECD Model as the core because they 'lack the *political clout* to prevail in bilateral DTC negotiations with developed countries'. An example of this *'political clout'* is the Brazilian DTC network with asymmetric countries (countries having unequal trade flows) being closer to the *UN Model* than it is to the *OECD Model* because Brazil had *political clout* with those countries. *Brauner's*[131] 'benefit *theory*' is another possible explanation: it argues that developing countries adopt the OECD Model when doing so benefits them.

Table 2.4 BRICS

	\multicolumn{5}{c}{TAX Incentives Intended to Attract FDI}				
	Brazil	Russia	India	China	SA
Tax Holiday/tax exemption	Y	Y	Y	Y	Y
Reduced tax rate	Y	Y	Y	Y	N
R & D Allowances	Y		Y	Y	N
Duty/VAT reduction	Y	Y	N	Y	N
Investment allowances/tax credits	N	N	N	Y	Y
Deductibility of qualified expenses	N	Y	Y	N	N
Double tax treaties	Y	Y	Y	Y	Y

Source: UNCTAD, Geneva, ASIT Advisory Studies, No. 16, Tax Incentives and Foreign Direct Investment, A Global Survey, 2000.

What evidence then is there of the *'prisoner's dilemma'* driving the BRICS core tax policy?[132] Having researched a wide number of the BRICS DTCs (Tables 2.5 and 2.6), the author concludes that the DTCs entered into by Russia, China and SA more generally resemble the OECD core principles (discussion on trade flows at page 16) than the UN core while the DTCs entered into by Brazil and India more closely resemble the UN core principles than the OECD. The author further concludes that the

---

127. *Supra* n. 122, at p. 380.
128. Including minimizing communication and enforcement costs, minimizing international double taxation, e.g. APA, secondary adjustment procedure, predictability and legal stability.
129. *Supra* n. 122, at p. 375/380.
130. TP and Tax Havens: Mending the LDC Revenue Net, at 5, unpublished manuscript on file held by Baistrocchi.
131. An International Tax Regime in Crystallization – Realities, Experiences and Opportunities, (2003) 56 Tax Law Review 259.
132. BRICS have incorporated the OECD Model DTC and Commentary into their core DTC policy since 1997 because they have few reservations from and positions on the DTC and Commentary except for India and Brazil with substantial divergences: Vega, Explaining Reservations to the OECD Model DTC: An Empirical Approach, www.indret.com, Barcelona 2011, p. 3.

Chapter 2: Core International Tax Policy and Law

'prisoner's dilemma' explains the DTCs entered into by Russia, China and SA, because that dilemma is reflective of their trading patterns but the *'prisoner's dilemma'* does not explain the position for both Brazil and India because their trading patterns and FDI are asymmetric. In relation to symmetric trading patterns (countries where trade flows are roughly equal), the author's analysis of the BRICS DTCs entered into in the immediate post liberalization period by Russia and China (Table 2.5) evidences that the *'prisoner's dilemma'* is the likely reason for their adoption of the OECD core policy but the analysis does not permit a conclusion be drawn for SA because its DTCs with the developed countries are reflective of both the OECD and the UN Models. Brazil and India's DTCs reflect a closer resemblance to the UN Model. The reasons that the BRICS might wish to break away from the OECD 'lock in' are studied in Chapter 3, while the international tax policies the BRICS have adopted in order to implement this break are analysed in subsequent Chapters of this study.

Table 2.5 BRICS

BRICS DTC with Developed and Developing Countries, Pre and Post Liberalization-Compared to UN Model and OECD Model	
Developed Countries (1)	Developing Countries (2)
Brazil	
Pre-liberalization-11A	
8 DTCs in force contain a TP Article but *none permit compensatory adjustments* (OECD and UN require compensatory adjustments) each of the 8 DTCs includes in a PE a mine, quarry but not oil well (OECD and UN deems an oil well); *None has a Services PE* and none contain a connected projects provision (UN deems a Services PE and a connected projects provision while OECD deems a Services PE but does deem connected projects); *all 8 DTCs contain a technical fees Article* based on the independent personal services provision (neither UN nor OECD contains a technical services fee Article but UN has independent services Article); taxing of profits on disposal of shares may be taxed in both source and residence country in 6 DTCs and only in the residence country for Japan with no special rule for companies owning immovable property (OECD 50%)	Brazil entered into a DTC only with Argentina pre-liberalization. That DTC provided for a TP Article *with no compensatory adjustments*; extended the definition of PE to include a mine, and quarry but not oil well; included *neither a Services PE* nor a connected projects provision; contained a technical fees article based on the independent personal services provision; taxing of profits on disposal of shares is allocated to both source and residence country with no rule for companies owning immoveable property.

39

BRICS DTC with Developed and Developing Countries, Pre and Post Liberalization-Compared to UN Model and OECD Model	
Post-liberalization-11B	
7 DTCs in force contain a TP Article but *none permit compensatory adjustments*; each of the 7 DTCs includes in a PE a mine, quarry but not oil well (OECD and UN deems an oil well); *none has a Services PE* and none contain a connected projects provision, (UN deems a Services PE and a connected projects provision while OECD does deem a Services PE but does deem connected projects); 7 DTCs contain a technical fees Article (neither UN nor OECD contains a technical services fee Article); taxing of profits on disposal of shares may be taxed in both source and residence country in 6 DTCs and only in the residence country for Japan with no special rule for companies owning immoveable property (OECD 50%). German treaty was terminated and not replaced	3 DTCs (Argentina, Philippines and Venezuela) in force and each provides for a TP Article with *no compensatory adjustments;* extends the definition of PE to include a mine, quarry (in Philippines) and oil well in Venezuela; includes *neither a Services PE* nor a connected projects provision; each contain a technical fees Article based on the independent personal services provision; taxing of profits on disposal of shares is allocated to source and residence country with no rule for companies owning immovable property (OECD 50%)
Russia	
Pre-liberalization-11C	
6 DTCs in force *but none contain TP coverage* nor applicability to extractive industries taxation (OECD and UN deems extractive industries to be a PE); *none contain a services PE* nor reference to 'connected projects (UN includes a Services PE and connected projects and OECD does not contain a Services PE but contains connected projects); none contain separate technical fees article but three contain a fees article based on the independent personal services Article (neither UN nor OECD include a technical fees Article but UN includes an independent Services Article) while 3 DTCs permit the source country to tax profits on disposal of shares and where the company owns immovable property the value must be mainly (OECD 50%)	Russia entered into no DTCs with the researched countries pre-liberalization

Chapter 2: Core International Tax Policy and Law

BRICS DTC with Developed and Developing Countries, Pre and Post Liberalization-Compared to UN Model and OECD Model

Post-liberalization-11D	
11 DTCs in force each containing TP Article with *9 providing compensatory adjustments*; extending PE to mine, quarry oil well (UN and OECD provide for the same rule); *no DTC contains a services PE* nor a reference to 'connected projects' (UN contains a Services PE and connected projects while OECD only contained connected projects); none contain separate technical fees Article but 11 contain a fees Article based on the independent personal services Article (OECD does not contain the independent services Article while the UN does); in relation to profits on disposal of shares 4 DTCs exempt the resident in the source country while 7 DTCs provide for both the resident and source to tax and where immovable property is involved the underlying ownership needs to be the greater part of the value/mainly/50%/principally (OECD 50%)	7 DTCs in force each containing a TP Article with *5 providing compensatory adjustments and 2 not*; 7 DTCs extend the definition of PE to mine, quarry, oil well; 5 DTCs contain services PE with 'connected projects' provision in 1; 7 DTCs contain a technical fees Article based on independent personal services; profits on disposal of shares where the value is substantially attributable to immoveable property is exempt in source country in 2 DTCs and taxable in source and resident country in 5 DTCs where value of company from immovable property is principally/+50%/75% (OECD 50%)

India	
Pre-liberalization-11E	
5 DTCs in force each containing TP but *none containing compensatory adjustments*; 1 DTC treats a mine, oil well, quarry as a PE (UN and OECD deem all three to be a PE); no DTC includes a services PE nor a reference to 'connected projects (UN deems a Services PE and connected projects while OECD only deems connected projects); *all 5 DTCs referred to technical fees with 4 containing a separate Article and 1 based on independent services provisions* (UN does not contain a technical fees Article but does contain and independent services Article while OECD contains neither); 4 DTCS refer to the taxing right on profits on disposal of shares being extended to the country of source defined to be the place of the	2 DTCs (Singapore and Sri Lanka) in force each contained TP but *neither contained compensatory adjustments*; extended definition of PE to a mine, quarry, oil well; neither Services PE nor 'connected project' in either DTC; reference to technical fees in 1 DTC based on independent services provisions and not included in the other DTC; profits on disposal of shares not covered in 1 DTC with both residence and source country in other and no reference to immovable property (OECD 50%)

41

BRICS DTC with Developed and Developing Countries, Pre and Post Liberalization-Compared to UN Model and OECD Model	
company's incorporation or where the shares were located at the sale, and where immovable property is involved the value mainly/principally (OECD 50%)	
Post-liberalization-11F	
12 DTCs in force containing coverage of TP with *8 DTCs providing compensatory adjustments*; all 12 DTCS extend PE definition to a mine, quarry, oil well (in both UN and OECD); 5 DTCs include services PEs and 5 DTCs provide for connection but not services PEs (UN deems a services PE and connected projects while OECD only contains connected projects); all 12 DTCs have separate technical fees Articles (neither UN nor OECD contain a separate technical service fees article); all 12 DTCS extend taxing right on share profits to source country and where immovable property is mentioned the tests is by reference to mainly/principally/50% (OECD 50%)	6 DTCs in force with coverage of TP in all 6 DTCs with *2 not providing for compensatory adjustments and with 4 permitting;* 6 DTCs extend the definition of PE to a mine, quarry, oil field; 3 DTCs contain Services PE and 2 'connected project' provisions; 6 DTCs with 4 having separate technical fees Articles and 2 DTCs based on independent services article; profits on disposal of shares contained in 6 DTCs, with 3 DTCs taxable in both source and resident countries and 2 DTCs in resident only, and 1 DTC (Singapore) and where the company's assets are immovable property there is a principally tests (OECD 50%)
China	
Contiguous with Liberalization-11G	
6 DTCs in force and each contain a TP provision with *4 without compensatory adjustment and 2 with such adjustments*; all 6 DTCs extend PE definition to a mine, quarry, oil well (Both UN and OECD); 4 DTCs contained a services PE while 4 contain a 'connected projects' provision (UN contain a Services PE and a connected projects and OECD only contains a connected projects); *5 DTCs cover a technical service fees Article based on the independent services Article with the UK DTC containing a full technical services Article* (deleted from the 2014 UK-China DTC) (Neither UN nor OECD contain a technical services fee Article but UN contains an independent services Article); for profits on disposal of shares where the value is attributable	China entered into DTCs with none of the researched countries pre-liberalization

Chapter 2: Core International Tax Policy and Law

BRICS DTC with Developed and Developing Countries, Pre and Post Liberalization-Compared to UN Model and OECD Model

China	
Contiguous with Liberalization-11G	
to immovable property, 6 DTCs extend the taxing right to the source country with mainly/25%/50% of value in immovable property in 3 (OECD 50%)	
Post-Liberalization-11H	
12 DTCs in force all containing a TP provision with *6 of the 12 containing a compensatory adjustment clause*; all 12 DTC extend the PE definition to include a mine, quarry, oil well (Both UN and OECD contain this); 10 of the 12 DTCs contain a services PE with 10 of the 12 DTCs containing a 'connected projects' Article (UN contains a Services PE and connected projects and OECD only connected projects); 12 DTCs cover technical service fees based on the independent services Article (neither UN nor OECD contains a technical fees Article but UN contains an independent services Article); for profits on disposal of shares where the value is attributable to immovable property, all 12 DTCs do not interfere in the source country's right to tax but with different values in immovable property including wholly/principally/25%/50% (OECD 50%)	8 DTCs in force all containing a TP provision with *7 DTCs having a compensatory adjustment clause and the other not*; 8 DTCS extending the PE definition include a mine, oil well, etc. 5 DTCs contain a services PE and a 'connected projects' provision while 3 DTCs have not; all 8 DTCs contain technical service fees with 7 DTCs based on independent services Article and other separate Article; profits on disposal of shares, 7 DTCs provide for the source country to retain its taxing right as well as resident while one grants resident sole taxing right and where immovable property is an asset it must be worth principally/more than 50% of the company (OECD 50%)
South Africa	
Pre-Liberalization-11I	
2 DTCs in force and both contain a TP provision with *one having a compensatory adjustment clause while the other not*; both DTCs extend the PE definition to include a mine, oil well (UN and OECD contain this); neither DTC contains a services PE nor a connected projects provision (UN contains a Services PE and a connected projects provision while OECD contains connected projects); both DTCs cover technical service fees based on the independent services Article (neither UN nor OECD contain a technical	South Africa entered into DTCs with none of the researched countries pre-liberalization

BRICS DTC with Developed and Developing Countries, Pre and Post Liberalization-Compared to UN Model and OECD Model	
services fee article but UN contains an independent services fees Article); for profits on disposal of shares where the value is substantially attributable to immovable property, both DTCs prevent the source country from taxing	
Post-Liberalization-11J	
11 DTCs in force and *all contain a TP provision with a compensatory adjustment clause*; 9 DTCs extend the definition of a PE to include a mine, oil well (both UN and OECD contain this); 3 DTCs deem the provisions of services to be included in PE with 1 DTC including a 'connected projects' provision (UN contains a Services Fees and connected provision while OECD only contains a connected projects provision); 8 DTCs contain technical service fees provisions based on the independent services Article (Neither UN nor OECD contain a technical service fees Article but UN contains an independent services Article), with one covering through the PE Article; for profits on disposal of shares where the value is substantially attributable to immovable property, 4 DTCs prevent the source country from taxing the gain while permit the source and residence country to tax	6 DTCs in force with each containing a TP *provision with a compensatory adjustment clause*; 6 DTCs extend the definition of PE to include a mine, oil well, etc. 3 DTCs contain a services PE and a 'connected projects' provision with 3 DTCs not; 6 DTCs contain technical service fees with five based on the independent services Article and one dedicated Article; for profits on disposal of shares, 2 DTCs provide for the source and the residence country to have taxing rights, 3 DTCs provide the residence country with the exclusive taxing right and 1 DTC (Singapore) does not contain a capital gains article and where immovable property is owned by the company it must be principally the value (OECD 50%)

1. Developed countries: Australia, Austria, Belgium, Canada, Denmark, Estonia, France, Germany, Japan, Spain, US, UK.
2. Developing countries (G77 Members): Argentina, Ghana, Indonesia, Nigeria, Pakistan, Paraguay, Philippines, Singapore, Sri Lanka, South Korea, Uruguay, Venezuela.
3. Where Table refers to fewer than 12 DTCs this is because the BRICS have not entered into a DTC with the balance.

Chapter 2: Core International Tax Policy and Law

Table 2.6 BRICS DTC with Quasi Developed Countries, Pre and Post Liberalization-Compared to UN and OECD Model

Brazil
Pre-Liberalization- 12A
Brazil did not enter into any DTCs with the countries pre liberalization
Post-Liberalization- 12B
The DTCs contain a TP Article but *none permit compensatory adjustments* (not compliant with either UN or OECD policy); each of the DTCs includes in a PE a mine, quarry, oil well in PE (compliant with both UN and OECD); none has a Services PE nor a connected projects provision (not compliant either with UN nor OECD); the DTCs contain a technical fees Article based on the independent personal services article (compliant with UN but not OECD); profits on disposal of shares are taxable in source and resident country with no reference to immovable property (not compliant with UN or OECD).
Russia
Pre-Liberalization -12C
Russia did not enter into any DTCs with these countries pre-liberalization
Post-Liberalization-12D
The DTCs each contain TP Article with all *providing compensatory adjustments* (Compliant with both UN and OECD); each DTC extends PE to mine, quarry oil well (Compliant with both UN and OECD); 1 DTC contains a services PE but none contain a reference to 'connected projects' (neither compliant with UN nor OECD); Contain technical fees Article based on the independent personal services Article (Compliant with UN but not with OECD); profits on disposal of shares are taxed in source and residence countries and there is no reference to profits on sale of shares where immovable property is owned (not compliant with UN or OECD).
India
Pre-Liberalization-12E
India did not enter into any DTCs with these countries pre-liberalization
Post-Liberalization-12F
China
Pre-Liberalization-12F
China did not enter into any DTCs with these countries pre-liberalization
Post-Liberalization-12H
2 DTCs in force containing a TP provision *with compensatory adjustments* (Compliant with UN and OECD); both DTC extend the PE definition to include a mine, oil well (Compliant with UN and OECD); 1 DTC contains both a services PE and a connection while the other does not (one is UN compliant and the other partially OECD compliant); 2 DTCs cover technical service fees based on the independent services Article (both are UN compliant but neither OECD compliant); profits on disposal of shares are taxed in residence and source where the immovable property value is company's principal value (neither UN nor OECD compliant).

	South Africa
	Pre-Liberalization-12I
	SA did not enter into any DTCs with these countries pre-liberalization
	Post-Liberalization 12J
	3 DTCs in force containing a TP provision with *all having a compensatory adjustments* (UN and OECD compliant); DTCs extend the PE definition to include a mine, oil well (UN and OECD compliant); 1 DTC contains a services PE and connection while the other does not (one is UN compliant while the other is partially OECD compliant); 1 DTC covers technical service fees based on the independent services Article the other 2 do not (one is UN Compliant and the others are OECD Compliant); profits on disposal of shares are taxed in source and residence country and where company owns immovable property it is principal/50% asset value (UN and OECD compliant)

1. **Quasi developed countries** (members of both OECD and G77, or OECD members but considered developing): Chile, Mexico and Turkey.
2. Where Table refers to fewer than 3 DTCs this is because the BRICS member has not entered into a DTC with the others.

2.1.3 MNEs and Core Policy Influence

This subsection investigates whether within the BRICS, there exists a formal system by which inbound MNEs may exert influence over the shaping of the BRICS core international tax policy and law in the developed world's image. The conclusion is that even though formal procedures for exchanging views exist, the evidence of direct influence is inconclusive.

2.1.3.1 Industry and Trade Groups

The author investigated[133] whether MNEs can through industry and trade groups directly influence the BRICS policy and law and concluded that *AMCHAM* and the *British Trade Councils*[134] provide such an opportunity for US and British MNEs. *AMCHAM*[135] provides a formal mechanism to lobby for tax changes while the *British Trade Councils* provide an informal basis for UK MNEs[136] to do the same. The *AMCHAM* formal route arises from the BRICS branches having integrated into the local business communities through their long-term existence, many of which were established before liberalization. The *AMCHAM* tax study group[137] is the specific method

---

133. Email exchange between author and Prof Rolim, Brazil, 22 Aug. 2015, Victor Matchekhin, Russia and Dmitry Zapol, IFS, London 21 Aug. 2015; Associate Professor West, Dept of Finance and Tax, UCT, 19 Aug. 2015; Caldas, Departmento Tributario, Raizen, Brazil, 19 Aug. 2015.
134. AMCHAM branch formation years: Brazil, 1919; Russia 1991; India 1992; China, 2000; SA, 1978; British Trade Council formation years: Brazil, approx. 1915; Russia, 1916; India, uncertain; China, 1953 and SA, uncertain.
135. Each AMCHAM chapter has a tax working group.
136. British Councils focus on general regulatory issues except for Russia where there is a tax focus.
137. AMCHAM Brazil's Tax Task Force (lawyers and executives) since 2002 has recommended improvements to Brazil's tax policy (http://www.amcham.com.br/en/what-we-do) to make

Chapter 2: Core International Tax Policy and Law

adopted by it to present tax policy options to the respective member's tax authorities. Since the *British Trade Councils*[138] constitute a broader network with a much greater agenda, its lobbying capability is inferior[139] to *AMCHAM*. *Mvovo*[140] explained that the SA Treasury established a formal route for representations on international tax and DTC issues but it was discontinued in 2012 because of insufficient MNE interest. In relation to the format[141] the informal representations to the BRICS' tax authorities largely take the same but a less sophisticated format to that offered by the HMRC[142] to MNEs lobbying for changes to British tax policy.

MNEs more competitive, such as a proposed Brazil/US DTC (including TP designed by the Brazilian Treasury and EOI on taxes between Brazil and US). Russia AMCHAM (http://www.amcham.ru/eng/article/roots, last visited 21 Aug. 2015) confirms it is a resource for designing business legislation including taxation and cooperation (AMCHAM Russia Annual Report 2004, p. 11) which includes senior FTS officers discussing tax issues covering foreign legal entities. AMCHAM India (http://amchamindia.com/tax-tariff-and-regulatory-affairs/, last visited 21 Aug. 2015) influenced (Committee (AMCHAM India Annual Report 2009-2010, p. 3, 2009-2010 Annual Report, p. 4) Central Government to discuss the DTC and pre-Budget and post-Budget Sessions with the Revenue Secretary and MOF. Established programme with CBEC and tax officials discussing 'Obama Administration's Tax Proposals on US MNCs in India' and through Tax, Tariff and Regulatory Affairs Committee discussing tax issues including India/US DTC and TP. AMCHAM China (http://www.amchamchina.org/policy-advocacy/policy-spotlight/tax#sthash.00WSLqWF.dpuf, last visited 21 Aug. 2015) focussed on developing China's policy and particularly its Policy Spotlight Series covering TP, Large Cross-Border Payments, DTC qualification, anti-DTC shopping. AMCHAM's SA Tax Policy Forum (2013 Annual Report AMCHAM Forums, p. 3) from 2013 discusses TP, VAT and indirect tax and provides SA based American business community with opportunity for dialogue on tax issues with the National Treasury, SARS and DTI.

138. Indian Society and Establishment of British Supremacy, 1765/1818, Oxford History of the British Empire, ed. by P. J. Marshall, (1998), p. 508/29.
139. Russian/British Chamber of Commerce (http://www.rbcc.com/index.php?option=com_content&view=category&layout=blog&id=41&Itemid=191&lang=en, last visited 21 Aug. 2015). The UKIBC applied to secure favourable regulatory environment for UK trade and investment in India, http://www.ukibc.com/business-services/policy_and_research/, last visited 21 Aug. 2015, updates Indian politicians on UK/India trade issues while Government to Government negotiations on market liberalization and market access are conducted through JETCO with UKIBC promoting views of UK business community. CBBC's focus on opening China to FDI in the 1980s helped British businesses capitalize on opportunities. http://www.cbbc.org/about-us/history/#sthash.uLg2JYiX.dpuf.
140. Director, SA International Tax and Treaties, Legal Tax Design, Tax & Financial Policy Sector, in email exchange with author on 25 Aug. 2015.
141. Brazil: FRS accepts recommendations from persons dealing with more important tax policy issues and more likely to receive representations where the organization is important, email exchange with Prof Dr JD Rolim, Brazil, 22 Aug. 2015; SA MNEs have sought to influence the Government's policy through representations to National Treasury, email exchange with Dr C West, 21 Aug. 2012.
142. At https://www.gov.uk/government/publications/announcements-in-2014-of-changes-to-uk-double-taxation-treaties/announcement-by-hmrc-of-the-uks-tax-treaty-negotiating-priorities-for-the-year-to-31-march-2014; https://www.gov.uk/government/publications/announcements-in-2014-of-changes-to-uk-double-taxation-treaties/4hm-revenue-customs-hmrc-announces-details-of-the-uks-treaty-negotiating-priorities-for-the-year-to-31-march-2015; HMRC acknowledges feedback on desirable tax policy changes from British Embassies, British Chambers of Commerce based in those countries having relationship with Embassy's Commercial Officers, UK trade bodies such as the CBI, BBA and others – Ingreji, HMRC, CTIS Tax Treaty Team, email with author on 20 Aug. 2015 and in Brazil, FRS takes into account views of the Confederation of Brazilian Industry, Financial Institutions Associations, Association of

2.1.3.2 Government Lobbying

Investor Government Ministers may lobby on behalf of their MNEs for the host country to adopt features of the developed world's core international tax policy, a conclusion confirmed by *James*[143] in a 2010 UN Paper surveying the literature. One practical example is that of (former) the UK Chancellor Osborne's[144] lobbying the Indian Government on behalf of *Vodafone* on the proposed retro-active application of India's indirect asset transfer laws.

2.1.4 Significance of the Policy Influencers

The author concludes that the BRICS adoption of the developed world's core international tax policy and law is due neither to their tax capacity issues nor to the substantial illicit outflows.

He has however concluded that their adopting of the developed world's core approach arises from the investor countries requiring the investee countries to adopt laws compatible with the investor's own international taxation laws, with the investee countries doing so because the majority of FDI is provided by enterprises based in developed countries (*see* discussion on page 41) which axiomatically adopt developed world policies in their bilateral DTCs. This approach is the reason for the Russia, China and SA DTCs more generally resembling the OECD core principles than the UN principles and the ongoing applicability of this approach is explained by the '*lock-in*' and '*prisoner's dilemma*'. The DTCs entered into by Brazil and India more closely reflect the UN principles than they do the OECD core, even though the core is based on the developed world but the difference is, explained by Brazil and India having used '*political clout*' to push back on the FDI provider demands. This is further developed in subsequent chapters of this study.

In arriving at this conclusion, the force of the tax recommendations contained in the *TCCC* and the BITs/TIPs should not be ignored even though the effect (if any) is difficult to measure for where the treaties are ineffective. The WTO's influence is clear. However, it is significant that the focus in the *TCCC* was to discourage MNEs from entering into mispriced related party transactions (such as those covered by TP rules or transactions designed to reduce the investee's tax base), either when structuring the FDI or when operating the businesses acquired or established from that FDI and the

---

Foreign Financial Institutions and other associations/organizations including private/public organizations dedicated to taxation, explained in email exchange with Prof Dr JD Rolim, *supra* n. 141.

143. Committee of Experts on International Cooperation in Tax Matters, Sixth Session Geneva, 18–22 Oct. 2010, Item 3 (o) of provisional agenda: Tax competition in corporate tax: use of tax incentives in attracting FDI, E/C.18/2010/CRP.13.

144. At http://articles.economictimes.indiatimes.com/2012-04-03/news/31281435_1_indian-tax-authorities-vodafone-group-capital-gains-tax, 3 Apr. 2012; UK Chancellor Osborne when Vodafone was disputing Finance Act 2012, retroactive application of tax liability on indirect asset transfer, noted to Indian reporters at Third Annual Bilateral Economic and Financial Dialogue April 2012, 'we are concerned that (Indian) Budget will not just impact one company like Vodafone but will damage the overall climate for investment in India'.

author concludes this approach is one explanation for the BRICS tax laws countering such abuse being relatively unsophisticated in the early days

2.1.5 Next Chapter

This Chapter concludes that the BRICS core international tax policy and international tax law reflects the basic formulation of the developed world's core international tax policy and international tax law because of the influence of the FDI providers when funding the substantial inbound FDI and the international trade taking place, directly and indirectly with developed world counterparties and because of the WTO and to a lesser extent the BITs and TIPs. It also concludes that the encouragement given to the developed world's MNEs providing that FDI or participating in the trades, to avoid transactions which artificially reduced the host country's tax base is a reason for the BRICS being slow to adopt tax laws which countered abuses. The significance of the influence of the inbound MNEs in the development of the core policy and law for Russia, China and SA is that they were 'locked in' through the 'prisoner's dilemma' while in Brazil and India the core is not wholly the developed world's because they were able to exercise some 'political clout'.

In the next Chapter, the research centres on how the BRICS determine which transactions or structures constitute evasion or avoidance and also whether in adopting their approach to evasion or avoidance, they deviate from similar concepts adopted by the developed world, and if so, whether the divergences can be explained by the need to ensure the BRICS international tax laws are a deterrent for a wider group of transactions or behaviour.

CHAPTER 3
Evasion and Avoidance According to the BRICS

> The problem is that the definition of the tax crime is often quite vague not only in China but also in Western countries.
>
> – Prof. Frans Vanistendael

3.1 INTRODUCTION

Chapter 2 concluded that the core BRICS international tax policy and law reflected the developed world's core, primarily because doing so was in the BRICS best interests for attracting inbound FDI from the developed countries. Once their law was conformed, the BRICS became 'locked in'. Further, the developed world's MNEs which provided that FDI were discouraged from entering into artificial TP or base erosion strategies which avoided or evaded the host country taxation taxes. In this Chapter, the author investigates whether countering evasion and avoidance has become a special focus of the BRICS and if so, whether their reason for making it a focus was because the MNEs had failed to abide by the direction to avoid transactions or behavior which resulted in evasion or avoidance. This Chapter also studies whether the BRICS approach to evasion and avoidance diverges from the developed world's and, if so, whether that special focus has influenced the shape of the divergences. It also investigates whether the BRICS' deeming of mispriced transactions to constitute evasion arose from the necessity to increase the deterrent against evasion or avoidance in order to compensate for the lacking of manpower in the tax authority.

3.2 SPECIAL FOCUS

Chapter 1 described the magnitude of the illicit outflows from the BRICS. With an average of 83.4% of the BRICS illicit flows arising from deliberate trade mispricing and leakages in the balance of payments', (discussion at page 20), it is unsurprising that such transactions and behaviour resulted in the BRICS developing that special focus. One of the uses of mispriced transactions is to facilitate local businesses 'round tripping' of domestically generated profits and cash to foreign entities which are thereby positioned to enjoy tax incentives when reinvested which are specifically intended to attract foreign persons to provide that FDI. Round-tripping establishes a link between mispricing and FDI and the relative importance of mispriced transactions to inbound BRICS FDI is evident from materials published by the *Tax Justice Network*[145] and more generally in the Russian literature[146] (probably 70/80% if inbound Russian FDI flows from Cyprus), India[147] (around $600m annually) and China[148] (around 40%). Information on Brazil and SA round-tripping is not readily available.

In working out whether the mispriced transactions used to facilitate round-tripping are primarily tax induced (and therefore to be included in the special focus), it requires determining whether there is reasonable evidence of non-tax reasons being the primary explanation. The other major reasons asserted for round tripping transactions are investment protection (*UNCTAD*)[149] and avoiding bureaucratic regulations (*Peng*)[150] but an analysis of the favourite round trip destinations of the BRICS and whether those countries have entered into a BIT with the BRICS member presents a clear position. According to *Peng*, round-tripping avoids Brazilian and Indian bureaucratic regulations while Mauritius has an effective BIT with India.[151] *Quartz*[152] argues that establishing an intermediary in The Netherlands for a Brazil investment is justified by the investment protection available to the investor under Netherlands/Brazil BIT. The author believes *Quartz*'s conclusion is suspect since that particular BIT is yet to be enforced. The same conclusion follows for FDI into Russia from Cyprus because the

---

145. Reported Trade Figuring discrepancy, regulatory arbitrage and round-tripping: Evidence from the China-HK Trade Data, Journal of International Business Studies (2011), p. 42; p. 18/19, *supra* n. 33.
146. Ledyaeva, Offshore FDI Round tripping and Corruption: Empirical Analysis of Russian Regions, Economic Geography, Volume 91 No. 3 2015.
147. Rovnick, Most foreign investment in BRICs isn't foreign at all—it's tycoons using tax havens, March 2013, http://qz.com/66944/the-brics-biggest-investment-sources-are-tax-havens-which-mostly-shows-the-rich-stealing-from-the-poor/.
148. Round-Tripping Foreign Direct Investment and the People's Republic of China, ADB Institute Research Paper Series No. 58 July 2004, p. 7; Reported Trade Figuring discrepancy, regulatory arbitrage and round-tripping: Evidence from the China-HK Trade Data, Journal of International Business Studies, (2011), p. 42.
149. ASIT Advisory Studies No. 16, Tax Incentives and FDI, A Global Survey, 2000 p. 3; Reuter, Draining Development: Flight of Illicit Moneys from Developing Countries, World Bank p. 45/53.
150. Global Strategy, 3rd Edition, Emphasizing Institutions, Cultures and Ethics, Emerging Markets, 4.3, South-Western, Cengage-Learning, p. 103/104.
151. Quartz, Most foreign investment, *supra* n. 75.
152. Most foreign investment in BRICS is not foreign at all – it is tycoons using tax havens; Netherlands/Brazil November 1998 BIT.

Russia/Cyprus BIT is also yet to be effective. Hong Kong, British Virgin Islands, Japan and Singapore are the principal sources of inbound China FDI, but with the Japan and Singapore/China BITs of the four enforced, only Japan and Singapore FDI investors can rely on that defence. For these reasons, the better view is that round-tripping is a reason for the special focus.

3.3 BRICS: EVASION

3.3.1 Introduction

This subsection investigates how the BRICS define evasion and whether their definition/s diverges from the developed world's and concludes that because they treat mispriced transactions as evasion as they also do for entities established in havens without having appropriate business purpose, they diverge. It is arguable that the BRICS also deem both mispriced transactions and entities without business purpose to be criminal evasion. The author concludes that this treatment is designed to encourage compliance because treating these breaches as criminal increases the adverse consequences for senior company executives who sanction the behavior which results in, or assists with the illicit outflows.

3.3.2 Concealing Income

In this subsection the study examines how the BRICS define evasion and compare their approaches with those of the developed world where transactions or behaviour are deemed to be evasion when they conceal income, purposely not pay an already existing tax liability or participate in conduct which is inherently illegal.[153] Behaviour

---

153. Committee of Experts on Double Taxation and Tax Evasion (League of Nations, 1927) noted 'necessity of dealing with ... evasion and double taxation in coordination with each other'. Constituents of evasion in various OECD countries include *Germany (Section 370 Tax Code)*- incomplete/incorrect return, failing to inform the tax authority of significant tax matter leading to income understatement, obtaining an unwarranted tax advantage. *Canada* (http://www.cra-arc.gc.ca/gncy/lrt/vvw-eng.html) deliberately under reporting taxable profits by inflating deductions, wilfully refusing to comply with reporting requirements; *Australia* (ATO https://www.ato.gov.au/forms/tax-evasion-reporting-form/) failing to report all income; *USA* (IRAS, http://www.iras.gov.sg/irashome/page.aspx?id=6510#What_is_tax_evasion?) deliberately providing inaccurate or incomplete information, not declaring all income, claiming deductions for inflated or not legally deductible expenses. Baker, Short Paper on Tax Avoidance, Tax Evasion and Tax Mitigation, p. 8, May 2000, www.taxbar.com; Baker, Improper Use of Tax Treaties, Tax Avoidance and Tax Evasion, p. 1.5, Paper No. 9-A, Papers on Selected Topics in Administration of Tax Treaties for Developing Countries for the UN, May 2013; Blesgen, German Act to Combat Tax Evasion: Scope and Practical Implications, Eur. Taxn, February/March 2010, p. 106; Grinberg, Taxing Capital Income in Emerging Countries: Will FATCA Open the Door? World Tax J, October 2013 p. 327; Prebble, Comparing the GAAR of Income Tax Law with the Civil Law Doctrine of Abuse of Law, Eur. Taxn, April 2008, p. 151; Dunbar, Statutory GAAR: Lessons for the UK from the British Commonwealth, Bull. Intl. Taxn, December 2008, p. 533; Van den Hurk, Starbucks versus the People, Bull. Intl. Taxn, January 2014, p. 32; O'Connell, Combating Large-Scale Tax Evasion-Australia's Experience, Bull. Intl. Taxn, April 2008, p. 145; HMRC Report on Tax Evasion, https://www.gov.uk/report-an-unregistered-

constituting evasion includes the keeping of (at least) two sets of financial records for the purpose of concealing income, claiming deductions for amounts shown on invoices which overstate the actually incurred expenses, altering existing accounting entries in order for the net profits to be hidden, concealing the sources of income in order to confuse the tax authority, destroying business records and structuring transactions as shams. Legislatively, mispriced related party transactions are not treated by the developed world as evasion even where the counterpart resides in a tax haven, because, as *Essers*[154] observes, conducting business 'with a legal person in a tax haven, does not necessarily imply tax fraud unless (doing so) relies on the non-transparency by the haven, such as banking secrecy or the failure to exchange information'. Examples of concealing income amounting to criminal evasion[155] include where a US tax agent[156] deducts fake business losses in client returns so that refunds can be obtained or complex offshore secrecy arrangements designed to evade tax[157] but, as the HMRC[158] recently recognized, there is considerable difficulty in attributing evasion to a company when the transaction or behaviour was carried out by its representatives in a business transaction.

The Brazil *Crimes Against the Tax, Economic and Consumer Relations Systems Act*[159] establishes that evasion in Brazil amounts to the deceiving, neglecting to provide information, providing false information or neglecting to provide the truth in a document requested by the RFB. This definition is little different from that of the

---

trader-or-business, last visited 15 Sep. 2015; Spies v. United States, 1943; United States v. First Security, 1972; Brittingham v. IRS, 1979; Case IR 16/78, 1982; Case AZ IIR 39/89, 1992; RMM Canadian Enterprises, 1997; Snook v. London & West Riding, 1967; Behaviour and transaction examples include Essers: reducing tax by concealing and/twisting crucial facts, Krever: deliberately cheating by knowingly and willingly breaking the law, O'Connell: wilful non-compliance with tax law to reduce or avoid tax e.g. fraudulently misstating taxable income by not declaring income, overstating expenses, Baker: information deliberately omitted from details supplied to the Tax Authority; Blesgen: taxpayer's conducting business relationships with a person resident of a non-cooperative country increases the suspicion that the association has given rise to evasion, Prebble: lying about one's income e.g. a cash business understating its takings, Van den Hurk: company establishing a business structure which then is not used to conduct business through it or where the business structure is not supported by facts or a trustee manages a business which no reasonable shareholder would permit a trustee to manage; Global Tax Justice, Tax avoidance, evasion and havens', http://www.globaltaxjustice.org/wp-content/uploads/2015/02/Studie_tax_avoidance.pdf, May 2015.

154. International Tax Justice between Machiavelli and Habermas, Bull. Intl. Taxn, February 2014, p. 59.
155. Office of Chief Tax Counsel, IRS Tax Crimes Handbook Criminal Tax Division 2009 p. 4; falsely/delayed declaration of taxes, failure to declare taxes is evasion under German Criminal Tax Fraud Law as a felony, misdemeanour or infraction, depending on the gravity of charge while intentional fraud is a felony or a misdemeanour with grossly negligent criminal evasion an infraction, Barandt.
156. United States v. Morrison, F.3d, 2016 U.S. App. LEXIS 14888 (5th Cir. 2016).
157. At https://www.ato.gov.au/General/the-fight-against-tax-crime/tax-crime-explained/.
158. Tackling offshore evasion: a new corporate criminal offence of failure to prevent facilitation of tax evasion, Summary of Responses, December 2015, para. 1.9.
159. Law No. 8, 137/1990; the company's legal representative or administrator held criminally liable for evasion and imprisoned for between two and four years: Article 29, Criminal Code, prescribes a company as not being criminally liable.

Chapter 3: Evasion and Avoidance According to the BRICS

developed world. However, the 1997[160] Law extended the definition of what constitutes concealing income, as *Torres*[161] observed, by including mispriced transactions, simulations[162] and dis-simulations and transactions entered into with tax haven residents whether or not related. Brazil's extension constitutes a divergence from that of the developed world, subject to the RFB's application of the simulation concept being constitutional.[163] If simulations are constitutional, then the secondary question is whether the applicability of the concept is overridden by the 'legality principle', which preserves a taxpayer's right to tax plan as *Schoueri*[164] observes. Were simulations to be constitutional but overruled by the 'legality principle', the concept would be inapplicable because the Brazil Government is yet to incorporate the simulation concept into Brazil's municipal law.[165] For this study, the author researched the Brazilian constitutionality of simulations with Profs *Bianco, Schoueri, Rolim, Dias* and *Dr Rosenblatt* each of whom confirmed that simulations were unconstitutional because the 'legality principle' override, while *Prof Valadao*[166] took a different approach when confirming they were constitutional when used to counter abusive transactions such as those devoid of business purpose, as discussed in *No. 1402-001.404*[167] or for SPVs resident in preferred tax jurisdictions such as in *Marcopolo SA*.[168] The 2009 amendment to the Criminal Code which extended evasion to include any transaction with a resident of a country which kept the entity ownership confidential, creates a strict liability which requires little effort by the tax authority to apply. This extension to the evasion definition is relevant to the research in Chapter 5 of this study of Brazil's role in the evolving information exchanging architecture.

---

160. Law 9,430: A tax preferred jurisdiction charges tax at less than 20% (Treasury Ruling N°. 188/02) since reduced to 17%.
161. Brazil: Tax Treaties and Tax Avoidance: Application of Anti-avoidance Provisions, Cahiers, International Volume 95A, section 1, Relative simulation: dissimulation (Law 104/2011, Article 116 BTC) providing the RFB with authority to disregard legal acts or transactions implemented for purposes of dissimulating the occurrence of taxable events or dissimulating the nature of elements triggering tax obligations.
162. According to RFB, when transaction form is different from the substance e.g. sale not occurring because money did not change hands or occurred differently from that indicated by the taxpayer. Simulations: structuring sales as loans to hide consideration from the RFB (Complementary Law 104, Article 167) e.g. gifts; Doria: Simulation is fraudulent action undertaken by taxpayer to evade, reduce or delay tax payment; Filho: deliberate and direct ignorance of a tax provision in order to reduce a person's liability, whether by omission or by fraud.
163. Complementary Law 104, Article 116; Martins: FRB cannot rely on 'simulation' because it is unconstitutional since it limits a taxpayer's right to plan taxes making it contrary to the 'legality' principle i.e. a law cannot injure vested rights, perfect juridical acts and res judicata', Brazil Constitution, Article 5, XXXVI.
164. GAARs – a key element of tax systems in Post BEPS World-Brazil, WU Institute for Austrian and International Tax Law, IBFD Volume 3, p. 110.
165. FRB has not enacted ordinary law (*Article 116, BTC*) even though President Cardozo sought to do so (*Provisional Measure 66*).
166. Valadao and Dias were CARF members when interviewed.
167. CARF, Judgment No. 1402-001.404, 9 Jul. 2013.
168. Marcopolo SA, Case 105-17083, 25 Jun. 2008.

Russia deems evasion to be both a civil[169] and a criminal offence[170] with the concealing of income constituting criminal[171] evasion when it arises from using false accounting records. In the developed world, this offence would be civil. Russia extends evasion to transactions or structures which conceal income where the transaction or structure has insufficient commercial purpose or substance. It also includes in evasion, circular transactions (such as round tripping facilitated through mispriced transactions) or those involving entities existing for short time periods[172] or business entities registered in low tax jurisdictions (*Dvortsovy Ryad-MS and Syktyvkarsky Dairy Factory*)[173] or deductions claimed for payments to Marshall Island entities *(Tulazheldormash)*.[174] Examples of civil and criminal evasion are evident from the *State Arbitration Court of Moscow*[175] decision that the use by a Russian resident individual of a company to derive his personal consulting income which should have been derived by him personally was civil evasion because doing so was a breach of public order.[176] If a company is created without an intention to trade but with an intention to be used to embezzle assets[177] then this constitutes criminal evasion.

India historically has treated the concealing of income to be a criminal offence.[178] This has been the case when the party knowingly fails to provide accurate information to civil servants or where it breaches the tax law[179] offence of knowingly providing false information.[180] The misreporting or non-reporting of income earned in a legally enforceable transaction or in an illegal or fraudulent transaction also constitutes evasion under the *Black Money and Anti-avoidance White Paper*[181] and later Act. The constituents of evasion in India were also considered in *Provident Investment*[182] where the deliberate modification of commercial agreements was held to constitute evasion while in *Sree Meenakshi*[183] the use of dummy intermediaries to conceal information also amounted to evasion. Other examples include *Cartier Shipping*[184] which considered the failure to disclose in a tax return or in a later audit, all relevant information and *Durga Prasad*[185] which concerned a company funding its shareholder by loans instead

---

169. Article 166/181 Russian Civil Code, 1996.
170. Russian Criminal Code, Federal Law No. 64-FZ of 13 Jun. 1996, Article 198/199/159/173.
171. Imprisonment for up to four years and for large scale offences imprisonment for two to seven years: Articles 199, *supra* n. 170.
172. Case 160-0, Constitutional Court, 1 Apr. 2004.
173. Dvortsovy Ryad-MS, Russian Federation Supreme Court, 25 Feb. 2009, Decision No. 12418/08.
174. Tulazheldormash, Supreme Commercial Court No. 12093/11, dated 14 Feb. 2012.
175. 29 Nov. 2004.
176. Section 169, *supra* n. 170 i.e. contracts and transactions contrary to public order.
177. Plenum of the Supreme Court 51, 2007.
178. Indian Penal Code, 1860, section 177; Concealing income and transaction particulars breached Penal Code: T. S. Baliah, 1968.
179. Chapter XXI/II of the Income Tax Act, 1961, amended 2013.
180. Treated as evasion under the ITA, allows evader to concede offence and pay tax to avoid gaol, together with a substantial penalty. Should the tax and penalty not be paid then IRD can seize taxpayer's assets.
181. Black Money: White Paper, 2012, para. 1.3.1; Report on GAAR in Income Tax Act, 1961, Expert Committee (2012).
182. Commissioner Of Income-Tax v. The Provident Investment Co., Ltd, 15 May, 1957.
183. Sree Meenakshi Mills Ltd v. CIT (1957) 31 ITR 28.
184. Cartier Shipping Co. Ltd. v. DDIT, 7 Jun. 2010, ITA No. 3036/Mum/07.
185. CIT v. Durga Prasad More, AIR 1971 SC 2439.

of by dividend in order to avoid the dividend taxes. Except for the immediately preceding examples, India's approach conforms with the developed world but a widening of the meaning is evident in cases involving the use of tax haven entities as repositories of diverted income, such as *Keshavji Ravji; Aztec Software; Coco Cola; Iljin Automotive; Motif India Infotech and Nortel Networks*[186] or in cases covering legal transactions not having a business purpose, such as those involving the mispricing of intra group sales of immoveable property in *CB Gautum*[187] or transactions having an evasion motive as in *Maersk Global*.[188] Examples of transactions not constituting evasion in India include treaty shopping in *Azadi Bachao Andolan*[189] and in the later *Dynamic India Fund* and *Armstrong World*[190] cases.

Different views exist on whether evasion can be found from the structure employed or the behaviour adopted, including how the parties behave towards the tax authority. *Gupta* and *Diaz*[191] argue that structure is the more relevant factor, while *Lampreave* and *Ostwal*[192] argue that the behaviour is the focus. *Jain and Bhutani*[193] focus on the nature of the relationship between the taxpayer and the tax authority and, as an example, suggest taxpayers using the authority's inability to identify and counter excessive use of tax incentives, loopholes or mispriced transactions constitutes evasion. The author believes *Jain and Bhutani's* analysis is supportable since the mispricing of transactions arises from behaviour while using tax havens is structural.

Indicative of the seriousness with which evasion is treated in China is the post 2008[194] approach that it constitutes a crime only, when before 2008 it was both a crime and a tax law offence. The tax law definition of evasion before 2008 included the concealing[195] or misrepresenting[196] of information or the understating of taxable

---

186. Keshavji Ravji & Co. v. CIT, 1990 SCR (1) 243, 1990 SCC (2) 231; Aztec Software And Technology v. ACIT, 2007, 294 ITR 32 Bang, 12 Jul. 2007; Coca Cola India Inc. v. ACIT, Gurgaon, (2008) 116 TTJ Pune 880, 17 Dec. 2008; Iljin Automotive (P.) Ltd. v. ACIT, 30 Nov. 2011; Motif India Infotech Pvt. Ltd. v. ACIT, 25 Mar. 2014; M/S Nortel Networks India International Inc. DDIT, 13 Jun. 2014.
187. C.B. Gautam v. Union Of India & Ors, 17 Nov. 1992.
188. Maersk Global Service Centres (India) Pvt. Ltd. v. ACIT, 29 Feb. 2012.
189. (Civil) 8163-8164 of 2003.
190. Dynamic India Fund, 18 Jul. 2012 AAR No. 1016, 2010; Armstrong World Industries Mauritius Multi Consult Ltd, AAR No. 1044 of 2011, 22 Aug. 2012.
191. GAAR, and Indian and International Perspective, Asia-Pac. Tax Bull, 2013 p. 97/107; Punishment Under Criminal Tax Laws in Argentina, IBFD Bulletin 2006, p. 339/406.
192. Anti-avoidance measures in China and India, an evaluation of Specific Court Decisions, Bull. Intl. Taxn, Volume 67, No. 1, p. 49/60; Anti-avoidance Measures in India, National Law School of India Review, 2010, p. 59/103.
193. Tax Evasion and Corruption: Indian Perspective, Asia-Pac. Tax Bull, p. 124/127; Tax Treaty Interpretation, Asia-Pac. Tax Bull, 2004, p. 54/69.
194. Neither EITL (http://www.fdi.gov.cn/1800000121_39_3339_0_7.html) nor RET (http://www.fdi.gov.cn/1800000121_39_1563_0_7.html) discuss evasion but evasion is discussed in Article 63, Law of the PRC People's on the Administration of Tax Collection, http://www.china.org.cn/business/laws_regulations/2007-06/22/content_1214782.htm.
195. Deliberate violations of tax law including forging, altering or destroying ledgers, receipts or vouchers for entry account entries.
196. Overstating costs and expenditures.

income or earnings (based on the 1982 tax regulations)[197] making the definition broadly similar to that of the developed world, a position confirmed by *Na Li*.[198] However, when *Lampreave* and *Zhang*[199] explained that using tax havens and arrangements without reasonable business purpose (such as mispriced related party transactions) constituted evasion, they widened the China approach from that of the developed world. If this explanation is correct then how can it follow that *Circular 2* and *Special Measures*,[200] both of which are designed to counter tax havens and mispriced related party transactions, sit squarely in the EITL Chapter countering 'avoidance' rather than a section covering evasion? In order to resolve this conflict, the author interviewed leading China academics but those interviews failed to find a common belief that using tax havens constituted evasion[201] in China. The interviews did find a common belief though that mispriced offshore related party transactions[202] constituted evasion, a position supported by *SAT*[203] and the *LTBs*[204] decisions.

Evasion in SA is a breach of both the criminal and tax laws.[205] SA includes in evasion the provision of false information,[206] preparing false accounting books, contrivances or false statements which were made for the purpose of obtaining an exemption. In *SARS'*[207] including in evasion the falsification of expenses,[208] failing to submit returns and providing fraudulent employment records[209] and with *Honibell*[210] explaining that the failure to provide SARS with income information, failing to keep

---

197. RIITL (1982), Article 44, http://www.asianlii.org/cn/legis/cen/laws/rftiotitlffe705/; Criminal Law of the PRC, section 201, http://www.fmprc.gov.cn/ce/cgvienna/eng/dbtyw/jdwt/crimelaw/t209043.htm.
198. *Supra* n. 164, p. 186.
199. *Supra* n. 192; SATs Efforts towards Anti-Avoidance, Asia-Pac. Tax Bull, Volume 18, p. 439/441.
200. Article 41/48, *supra* n. 35; Article 92(iv)/(v), *Circular No. 2*, SAT Implementation of Special Tax Adjustments Measures, January 2009.
201. Dr Wei XIONG and Dr Zhengwen SHI confirming while Dr Ying Feng LONG deciding on avoidance, doctoral research.
202. Confirmed by Drs Wei XIONG, Ying Feng LONG and Zhengwen SHI, doctoral research.
203. M case where company conceded that shifting profits from China was evasion 2014 http://knowledge.ckgsb.edu.cn/2015/03/17/policy-and-law/the-crackdown-on-tax-evasion-in-china/.
204. Guangzhou's Municipal Government Report on evasion by foreign funded companies; Guangdong Province confirmed 9,465 foreign funded firms investigated for TP evasion (Chen Yao, China Business weekly), November 2004.
205. Section 104(1a/d), Income Tax Act 58, 1962; section 235(a/e)Tax Administration Act, 2011 guilty on conviction, subject to fine or imprisonment, not exceeding five years.
206. Without reasonable grounds for believing it to be true or providing false response to oral or written questions.
207. How to report suspected non-compliance to SARS, 2013, p. 3; http://www.sars.gov.za/TargTaxCrime/WhatTaxCrime/Pages/default.aspx.
208. Including business mileage and medical contributions.
209. SARS Discussion Paper, November 2005, p. 22; http://www.sars.gov.za/Media/MediaReleases/Pages/10-January-2014---SARS-Enforcement-and-Customs-Operations-for-December-2013-.aspx, last visited 12 Sep. 2015.
210. International Tax, SA Perspective, 2011, non-resident failing to notify SARS of taxable income and resident failing to disclose foreign income, p. 509.

proper records[211] or failing to correctly deal with deducted taxes[212] constitutes evasion, they describe examples common with the developed world. However, in *Ramaphosa*[213] (SA's then Deputy President), widening the evasion definition by including strategies relying on 'mismatches and gaps between tax rules (loopholes) and different jurisdictions (i.e. tax havens)...designed to minimise ... corporation tax, ... either by making tax profits disappear (shifting profits)', he confirmed that mispriced transactions and using tax havens constituted evasion. *Richardson's*[214] explanation that SARS does not normally treat transactions as shams when the parties follow through on the terms of the legal agreements, represents a narrowing of the developed world's position. This explanation conflicts with *Accolla Pillay*,[215] but conforms with the later *NWK*[216] decision where the implementation of unrealistic transaction steps[217] even though they were deliberately disguised to conceal their true nature[218] did not amount to evasion. *Richardson* has been confirmed in *Bosch*[219] providing there is commercial sense to the transactions.

The author concludes in this subsection that each of the BRICS deem mispriced related party transactions to be evasion and that each of the BRICS, except China, (but potentially China), confirm that using tax havens constitutes evasion. Since each of the BRICS treats evasion as a criminal offence, it follows that TP and misusing tax havens constitute BRICS criminal offences.

3.3.2.1 Purposely Not Paying Existing Liability

Baker[220] describes that in the developed world, evasion is to be found when a person having a degree of knowledge and an absence of honest belief concludes that he is not liable to pay an 'already arisen tax liability'. Baker's definition is supported by the *Internal Revenue Code's*[221] granting to the IRS of the right to sue any person who

---

211. Falsification of tax returns or accounting records resulting in tax payments being deliberately avoided (Oguttu, Curbing offshore avoidance: Case of SA Companies and Trusts, Doctor of Laws Thesis, 2007), failing to maintain adequate accounting records for business transactions (Richardson, Tax treatment of corporate losses – SA, 1998).
212. Input credits for goods not subject to VAT, failing to (Honibell, 'International Tax', p. 510) pay over to SARS deducted PAYE instalments (Kumarasingam, Tax Avoidance and Tax Evasion Explained and Exemplified, SA Tax Guide, http://www.sataxguide.co.za/tax-avoidance-and-tax-evasion-explained-and-exemplified,2015).
213. IOL, April 2014, http://www.iol.co.za/news/politics/tax-evasion-a-crime-against-sa---ramaphosa-1742247.
214. *Supra* n. 211.
215. Accolla Pillay v. Newlands Sport Bar Liquor Store 2010 (3) SA 116.
216. SARS v. NWK (27/10) [2010] ZASCA 168 (1 Dec. 2010), ENSafrica tax team, simulated transactions: welcome clarification from the Supreme Court of Appeal, https://www.ensafrica.com/news/simulated-transactions-welcome-clarification-from-the-Supreme-Court-of-Appeal?Id=1389&STitle=tax%20ENSight, last visited 15 Sep. 2015.
217. *Supra* n. 216, at para. 52.
218. Lewis JA *supra* n. 216, at para. 37.
219. Unreported Case No. A94/2012, 20, Davis J and Waglay, J.
220. Short Paper on Tax Avoidance, *supra* n. 153.
221. Section 6672(a).

'wilfully fails to pay over collected taxes' and *Bursey v. Bursey*[222] which held that purposely not paying taxes known to be due and payable constitutes evasion.

How the BRICS deal with 'purposely not paying an existing liability' is broadly consistent with that of the developed world but with some widening to encourage compliance. Brazil and Russia align with the developed world by, in Brazil's case, the treating the failure to pay taxes[223] or the (mis)appropriation of taxes deducted at source[224] to be evasion while Russia treats as evasion, the failure to pay taxes when due.[225] Russia narrows the definition by exempting any failure to pay tax by taxpayers who were acting in 'good faith'.[226] This approach is a throwback to the early 1990s Russian financial crisis where, when a Bank was requested by a taxpayer to remit the tax money it was in funds, but was out of funds when acting on the instruction, did not result in the taxpayer having evaded taxes. The meaning of evasion is widened in India when it includes the obtaining of tax refunds through group amalgamations *(Star Television)*[227] as evasion even when commercial reasons existed to support the reorganization. China and SA align with the developed world when treating as evasion, the refusal to pay taxes[228] or the paying of less tax than the taxpayer is legally obliged to do so,[229] while both China and SA widen the meaning when including as evasion late payments (China) or the failure to pay taxes due after having registered *(SARS)*.[230]

This subsection concludes that each of the BRICS has aligned with the developed world on whether purposely not paying tax is evasion with Russia narrowing the concept for good faith behaviour, India has widened the definition to catch tax refunds claimed through transactions or structures entered into which have a commercial purpose while both China and SA widen for administrative matters.

---

222. Bursey v. Bursey (1999, Newfoundland Court of Appeal) 47 RFL 4th 1.
223. Law 8137/90, Fraud involves using malicious and intentional acts or omissions resulting in delay in, or obstruction of taxable events, removing or varying any of the transaction's essential features leaving payment postponed or avoided (Lei No. 4.502, de 30 de novembro de 1964, D.O.U. de 30.11.1964, Article 72), e.g. recording untrue facts solely for purpose of not paying taxes.
224. Law 4357/64, Article 11.
225. Presidium No. 9408/00, 2001; Constitutional Court No. 4-O, 2002; Presidium No. 7374/01, 2002; Presidium No. 11259/02, 2002.
226. Constitutional Court No. 138-O, 2001; Presidium 6294/01, 2002; and letter No. C5-5/уП-342 of the Deputy President of the Supreme Commercial Court dated 17 Apr. 2002, except for tax benefits exceeding the investment then is evasion.
227. Re: Star Television Entertainment Ltd., (2010) 321 ITR 1 (AAR).
228. ITLEFIFE, http://www.npc.gov.cn/englishnpc/Law/2007-12/12/content_1383884.htm, Article 25, includes timeliness of payments as evasion with the refusal to pay taxes included first in the 1982 Regulations, then in the 1991 Regulations (Article 107, RET, 1991). 1992 Tax Collection Rules (Article 63, Law of PRC on the Administration of Tax Collection (Order of the President No. 49), 1992 provides that taxpayers which evades tax can have the tax reclaimed by the authority tax and subject to a fine not less than 50% but not more than five times evaded tax and where 'serious', criminally investigate, and 2007 Law on Tax Administration (Article 63 Law on Tax Administration, 2007 promulgated by Order of the Chairman of the NPC, 2001 No. 60, 28 Apr. 2001 extended to filing fraudulent returns).
229. Tax Avoidance and Tax Evasion, *supra* n. 212.
230. *Supra* n. 207, at p. 3.

3.3.2.2 Wilful or Intentional Fraudulent Conduct

Wilful or intentional fraudulent conduct is generally treated by the developed world as criminal evasion. The *HMRC*[231] treats *wilful or intentional fraudulent* conduct as a criminal offence, while *Judges Pizzitelli* and *Panuthos*[232] confirmed that *wilful cheating, criminal intent and illegal means* constitute fraudulent evasion. *LexisNexis*[233] also explains that the payment of too little tax or situations of companies wrongly claiming tax repayments through *dishonest acts* constitutes criminal behavior. The *ATO*[234] argues that abusing the tax system through '*intentional and dishonest behaviour*' gives rise to criminal sanctions with criminal behaviour being something as simple as failing to report cash wages or as complex as foreign secrecy arrangements.

While the BRICS, bar Brazil, adopt the same core approach to evasion, they widen the behaviour constituting criminal evasion. *Baker and McKenzie*[235] observes that the absence of a reason for Brazil widening evasion is because evasion already results in the company's legal officers being held criminally liable.[236] Law No. 8.317/90 criminalizes tax evasion and sets a standard prison sentence of between two to five years, plus a fine. Russia widens evasion by including the making of false declarations in accounting documents[237] concerning income or expenses as being criminal but the treating of such matters as criminal evasion had little consequence before the 1998 Tax Code[238] because at that time companies resident in high tax zones were encouraged to reduce taxes by shifting profits to related parties in domestic tax free zones, as *Samoylenko*[239] observed. TP[240] arranged in this way was, by 2004 in decline, because of the FTS' decision to treat that behaviour as criminal evasion, as explained in

---

231. UK *Taxes Management Act 1970*:person 'knowingly concerned' in fraudulent evasion of income tax by him or another person (http://www.gov.uk/government/news/new-criminal-offences-in-clampdown-on-tax-evasion, last visited September 2015); 26 U.S. Code § 7201: affirmative act to evade/attempt to evade tax, possession of the specific intent to evade a known legal duty to pay.
232. Judge Pizzitelli (*Canada*): fraud against Treasury with a criminal intent to avoid payment on an agreed liability, Judge Panuthos (*US*): wilful evading or defeating a legally due liability in any manner, act of fraud, where 'wilfully' involves voluntarily or intentionally breaching legal duty.
233. Lexis PSL Corporate Crime, https://www.lexisnexis.com/uk/lexispsl/corporatecrime/document/391421/55KB-9471-F188-N1BB-00000-00/Tax+evasion+offences%E2%80%94overview, last visited 15 Feb. 2016.
234. At https://www.ato.gov.au/General/the-fight-against-tax-crime/tax-crime-explained/, last visited 10 Feb. 2016.
235. Dispute Resolution Around the World, Brazil, 2010, p. 13.
236. Law No. 8,137/1990, *supra* n. 159.
237. Imprisonment up to four years, where offence was large scale- imprisonment for two to seven years: Articles 199, Russian Criminal Code, *supra* n. 170.
238. Part One No. 146-FZ, July 1998; 1995: President Yeltsin proposed a Unified Tax Code encouraging investment in manufacturing sector, fully collecting taxes repealing arbitrary preferences and evasion, not enacted until 1998.
239. Government approved zones, e.g. *FEZs* and *ZATOs* used widely by oil companies; Government Policies for Internal Tax Havens in Russia, Tax Notes Int'l, 5 Apr. 2004, p. 78.
240. Mispriced transactions were countered by treating them as criminal evasion rather the applying TP rules.

Yukos[241] unless the transactions were in 'good faith'. Compliance with this treatment was made difficult because 'good faith' remained undefined in the Russian tax context, even though the *Moscow Arbitration Court*[242] had argued it was a moral concept. The *Constitutional Court in N9-P* [243] held that 'good faith' meant not dishonest behaviour *('male fide')*.[244] Both these approaches failed to categorically define 'good faith', and it was not until the Supreme Arbitration Court issued *Resolution 53*[245] (2006) that what 'good faith' meant began to be understood. The Resolution gave rise to the doctrine of '*unjustified tax benefit*' (a GAAR equivalent) which broadly counters transactions having insufficient business substance. According to *Bruck*,[246] this applied to countering 'optimization' strategies (including those involving mispriced related party transactions) which lacked substance or business purpose. Therefore, because the 'unjustified tax benefit' concept grew out of criminal evasion (i.e. *Yukos*), structures and behaviour to which it is applied are treated by Russia as criminal evasion, a view supported by the proposed inclusion of 'unjustified tax benefit' as an offence in the *Criminal Code*.[247] It is also supported by *Oriflame Cosmetics*[248] which held that Russian

---

241. Charged with evading over US$27bn taxes through shifting profits between zones which FTS argued was ineffective because behaviour failed to respect the license conditions. Yukos was later liquidated for unpaid taxes and declared *bankrupt* in August 2006. *Yukos* and its Directors were held to have criminally evaded tax (*Arbitration, Veteran Petroleum Limited (Cyprus) and Russia, PCA Case No. AA 228 p. 14*). No similar claims were filed against similar strategies used by Lukoil, TNK-BP, Sibneft, https://en.wikipedia.org/wiki/Yukos, last visited October 2015.
242. No. A41-K1-11473/02.
243. 27 May 2003.
244. Behaviour which failed to be 'good faith' included one-off transactions, transactions with related parties or with companies having previous tax offences, transactions using newly formed companies, transactions with real business purpose even though there was a tax purpose, company's increased share capital to obtain cash to pay a non-Russian shareholder dividends rather than interest because of the lesser withholding tax, *see* EY Tax Insights, July 2014.
245. Reversed 'good faith' presumption for transactions documented/booked in a manner contrary to the economic substance ('sham'), or lacking business purpose to support taxpayer's activities where the taxpayer could not function as contemplated by agreements due to absence of staff, production capacity and the taxpayer dealt with counterparties (customers/suppliers including legal entities commonly owned with, associates) knowingly involved in evasion. Supplementary indications of 'unjustified tax benefit' included one-time unusual transactions, wide use of intermediaries, tax offences committed in past, conducting business mainly with contractors committing tax offences; conducting transactions outside of taxpayer's 'seat'. Transactions not in 'good faith' including VAT deducted from 'fake' transactions where parties did not have resources to conduct business, *Supreme Arbitration Court, 9 October 2007*. Examples of 'bad faith': obtaining tax reduction through using a deduction or exemption, a lower tax rate and obtaining right to tax credit or refund from the Budget (*53, section 2*), recording transactions not in compliance with business conducted, absence of business purpose or connection with any business transactions (*53, Sections 3–4*) or tax benefit being sole (or main) purpose (*53, section 9*).
246. Tax Treaties and tax avoidance: application of anti-avoidance provisions-Russia, IFA Cahiers 2010, p. 687.
247. May 2015, Duma attempted to consolidate into Tax Code and Criminal Code (Draft law 529775-6) the importance of economic activity when determining whether payments were deductible, main purpose of the payment being the non-payment or incomplete payment and/or a refund of Russian tax. Also proposed incorporating 'unjustified tax benefit' into the Criminal Code (Article 198/199).
248. Oriflame Cosmetics, 9th Arbitration Court, dated 4 Jun. 2015, No. A40-138879/14-75-404.

Chapter 3: Evasion and Avoidance According to the BRICS

deductions for payments to a non-resident should be denied on evasion grounds with the amount of foreign taxes paid by the direct and indirect recipients being relevant factors for this purpose. Integral to the Court's reasoning here was its decision to lift the corporate veil because there was insufficient commercial substance in the direct foreign intermediary to leave it unchallenged. The decision in *Oriflame* is seen as being contrary to *Element Trade (Monteka)*[249] which covered a similar fact pattern but is consistent with *Tulazheldormash*[250] and represents current Russian law on whether using intermediaries amounts to evasion. This conclusion supports the hypothesis that Russia treats mispriced transactions as evasion and potentially criminal evasion.

India treats '*wilful* and *intentional*' conduct as evasion, with examples including the deliberate modification of commercial agreements as in *Provident Investment*[251] or the using of dummy intermediate companies as in *Sree Meenaskshi*[252] but neither case was seen as constituting criminal evasion. This approach changed in March 2015, when the *Indian Finance Minister (Jaitley)*[253] explained that the mere holding of foreign assets giving rise to the concealment of foreign income was a 'predicate offence'[254] under anti-money laundering laws and thereby, a criminal offence for Indian purposes. This policy change grew out of the 2014 *Special Investigating Task Force's*[255] decision to hold the mere ownership of a Liechtenstein bank account as being evasion,[256] regardless of any failure to disclose.[257] This approach evolved into the *2015 Black Money Act*[258] which made an offence out of the misreporting or failure to disclose in a return or to provide information[259] concerning a resident's foreign income or foreign assets[260] or, in the case of a non-resident, assets financed from non-disclosed Indian sources, when justification for having the foreign asset or income was considered unsatisfactory by the tax authority (section 10). With the tax authority retaining

---

249. Element Trade (Monetka) No. A60-32327/2010.
250. Supreme Commercial Court No. 12093/11, dated 14 Feb. 2012.
251. 15 May 1957.
252. *Supra* n. 183.
253. Indian Economic Times, 2 Mar. 2015, http://articles.economictimes.indiatimes.com/2015-03-02/news/59684142_1_criminal-offence-tax-evasion-predicate-offence.
254. International Compliance Association, http://www.int-comp.org/careers/a-career-in-aml/what-is-money-laundering/. A crime that is a component of a more serious criminal offence.
255. International Tax Review, December 2014.
256. Public Interest Litigation, filed by Ram Jethmalani, https://www.quora.com/What-was-the-case-by-Ram-Jethmalani-on-which-the-Supreme-Court-of-India-asked-the-Central-Government-to-form-an-SIT-What-specifically-is-the-SIT-set-up-by-the-Narendra-Modi-government-investigating, last visited 15 May 2016.
257. At http://timesofindia.indiatimes.com/india/Centre-gives-names-of-all-account-holders-in-Liechtenstein-Bank-to-Supreme-Court/articleshow/34387090.cms, April 2014.
258. Black Money (Undisclosed Foreign Income and Assets) and Imposition of Tax Act, 2015, where person wilfully avoids disclosure can be imprisoned for up to seven years, section 49/50.
259. Wilful failure where information was controlled by, or in books of account or other documents containing a false entry or statement, furnish a return or any information covering income and asset located outside India. A mental state is presumed, section 49/58 Black Money Act, *supra* n. 258.
260. 'Undisclosed asset located outside India' means an asset (including financial interest in an entity) located outside India, held by the taxpayer in his name or as a beneficial owner, and where he has no explanation about funding of investment or the explanation is in AO's opinion unsatisfactory', section 2(11).

the right to make the final decision on whether a taxpayer's behaviour was criminal, it has left open whether doing so is a breach of human rights. This question is considered in Chapter 8 of this study.

China's Criminal Law[261] (Article 201) criminalizes evasion but by widening[262] it to situations involving the fraudulently reclaiming of taxes already paid through using deceptive means, such as fraudulently declaring the commodities a person produces to be exports (when they are sold domestically), increases its potential application. With sanctions for breaches (*Article 211*) being imposed on senior company officers and with those sanctions extending to preventing the executives from leaving[263] China, preventing the company issuing bonds, restricting access to State funds and being named and shamed in the media, the commercial consequences of the failure to comply are becoming more obvious.

In SARS[264] focussing on the use of contrivances or the making of false statements for the purpose of obtaining tax exemptions or the claiming of VAT input credits for VAT not actually paid,[265] its approach is essentially aligned with the developed world.

3.3.2.3 Significance: Criminal Conduct

This subsection concludes that evasion in each of the BRICS is a criminal offence and that because mispriced transactions and using tax havens lacking commercial substance amount to evasion, they will also constitute criminal evasion in the BRICS. One reason for treating such behaviour as criminal evasion is that where evasion exists there are increased sanctions on the senior company executives. This is intended to encourage compliance, especially in Brazil, Russia and China. Treating such offences as being criminal is understandable having regard to the magnitude of the illicit outflows to be countered and the insufficiency of manpower in the tax authority to identify and investigate. Further, the evidence suggests that there is no cooperation or coordination at the practical level amongst the BRICS on what constitutes evasion.

3.4 BRICS: AVOIDANCE

3.4.1 Introduction

This subsection studies the methodology used by the BRICS for defining avoidance and considers whether the BRICS methods diverge from those used by the developed world's. The author also researches the significance of those divergences. The

---

261. At http://www.fmprc.gov.cn/ce/cgvienna/eng/dbtyw/jdwt/crimelaw/t209043.htm, last visited 21 Jun. 2016.
262. Interpretation of the Supreme People's Court on Some Issues concerning the Specific Application of Laws in the Trial of Criminal Cases for Tax Evasion and Refusal to Pay Tax.
263. The declaration (China's crackdown on evasion to impact cross-border transactions, SCMP, 5 Jan. 2015, last visited 21 Jun. 2016) entered into by twenty-one ministries and departments.
264. *Supra* n. 207, at p. 3.
265. Honibell, *supra* n. 212, p. 509.

Chapter 3: Evasion and Avoidance According to the BRICS

conclusion drawn is that their methods are different from those of the developed world with those used by Brazil and India being less effective than those adopted by China, SA and Russia.

The developed world's approach to determining what constitutes avoidance has been well documented and rehearsed over many years, but relevant to this study is that the developed world's approach continues to evolve. While the early twentieth century approach[266] generally allowed taxpayers the freedom of organizing their affairs in a manner resulting in the saving of tax providing the transaction, behaviour or structure used to save the tax was legal, the right to behave in that way or to use transactions or structures for that purpose, has weakened in recent years. Different Governments[267] have formulated their approach for narrowing the confines of what is legitimate avoidance having regard to different fact patterns, pronouncements of governance institutions,[268] scholars[269] and the Courts.[270] If a principle could be drawn from all these materials, it would be that avoidance arises from transactions, structures or behaviour entered into by one or more persons which was arranged in a manner having

---

266. Fisher's Executors v. CIR [1926] AC395; Ayrshire Pullman v. CIR (1929) 14TC75; IRC v. Duke of Westminster [1935] All ER 259, (1935); Partington v. Attorney-General (1869) L.R. 4 E. & I. App. 100.
267. UK Parliament investigation of *Google* UK was unable to conclude on whether Google's main purpose was arranging sales to UK clients for Google Ireland or a device to avoid including 'so-called' UK income in UK tax returns, House of Commons, Committee of Public Accounts, Tax Avoidance- Google, Ninth Report of Session 2013/2014, 13 Jun. 2013; US Congress Investigation into *Apple US* was unable to conclude on whether combining a cost sharing agreement with a 'check the box' election was business or tax driven, Permanent Sub-committee on Investigations, Hearings Offshore Profit Shifting and the U.S. Tax Code - Part 2 (Apple Inc.), 21 May 2013.
268. UN Handbook on Selected issues in Administration of DTCs for Developing Countries, UN, 2013, p. 385; Malaysia IFA and IBFD 75th Jubilee Asia-Pacific Tax Conference-Panel 1B: Developments in Model Tax Treaties – Impact on Asia, November 2013.
269. Baker, A Short Paper on Tax Avoidance, Tax Mitigation and Tax Evasion, 2000, www.taxbar.com, p. 1; Prebble, Comparing the GAAR of Income Tax Law with the Civil Law Doctrine of Abuse of Law, Bull. Intl. Taxn, April 2008, p. 151/155; transactions directly/indirectly altering the incidence of income tax, relieving/reducing income tax liability or a pre-ordained series of transactions with steps inserted which have no commercial purpose other than avoiding tax absent a practical likelihood of events not taking place in the order ordained, Freedman, Designing a GAAR: Striking a Balance, Asia-Pac. Tax Bull, 2014 (Volume 20), No. 3, p. 168; engineered business transaction, Krever, Managers and Their Lawyers: Minimizing Tax, Maximizing Ethics and The Business Decision Making Process, Journal of Macau, Business of Science and Technology, Volume 1, No. 1, 30 Jun. 2007, p. 95/98; mispricing related party transactions, Vann, Taxing International Business Income: Hard-Boiled Wonderland and the End of the World; arranging income to be derived by persons tax resident in a more favourable jurisdiction, Wheeler, Attribution of Income in the Netherlands and the UK, World Tax J, Volume 3, Issue 1, February 2011, p. 40; abusive use of DTCs, Jung, Trends and Developments in Swiss Anti-Treaty Shopping Legislation and Treaty Shopping Case Law, Derivs. & Fin. Instrums, 2011 (Volume 51), No. 6, April 2011, p. 230; Vogel, DTCs and Their Interpretation, *supra* n. 58, p. 78/83; Pistone, From tax avoidance to aggressive tax planning: Outlining the path towards international tax fairness, http://ibdt.org.br/material/arquivos/Palestras/Pasquale%20Pistone.pdf.
270. Betty M. Ellis v. Commissioner of Internal Revenue, 30 Sep. 1985; CIR v. Challenge Corporation Ltd [1986] STC 548 (PC); Patrick McGrath and Ors v. Inspector of taxes JE McDermott, 7 Jul. 1988 3 ITR 683 (1988); Bayfine UK v. HMRC, [2011] EWCA Civ 304; transactions finding gaps, exploiting reliefs, using unnatural assets or transactions resulting in pre-ordained transaction and descriptively, 'dodgy' offshore schemes, Lord Walker of Gestingthorpe.

a motive of reducing a person's tax liability (when legal), providing the transaction, structure or behaviour conflicts with the intent of the law it purports to follow[271] or the economic substance of the transaction, structure or behaviour, differs from the legal form.[272] This means therefore that legally misusing loopholes or incentives[273] constitutes avoidance where the predominant purpose of that misuse is the saving of tax.[274]

3.4.2 Reducing Tax Liability

In this subsection, the research is on whether it is necessary to conclude that taxes have been reduced for the transaction, structure or behaviour to constitute avoidance. This subsection concludes that it is the position in the developed world and is now the position in China, SA and Russia (it was not the position in Russia or China in the immediate post liberalization period) but is not yet the position in Brazil or in India. In relation to Brazil, because the 'legality principle'[275] overrides avoidance, even when the transaction relies on a loophole or had insufficient business purpose,[276] this made reducing a liability irrelevant while in Russia during the 1990s and early 2000s with avoidance confined to breaching administrative provisions,[277] this left reducing a liability irrelevant[278] to a determination of whether the transaction, structure or

---

271. OECD, Centre For Tax Policy and Administration, Glossary of Tax Terms, http://www.oecd.org/document/29/0,3343,en_2649_34897_33933853_1_1_1_1,00.html last visited 31 Jul. 2015; Tax Law Reform Committee, published Countering Tax Avoidance in the UK: Which way forward, Bowler, Institute for Fiscal Studies, TLRC Discussion Paper No. 7, Feb. 2009, p. 10/14; Ramsay twenty-five years on: some reflections on tax avoidance, address to the Chancery Bar Association, 23 Mar. 2004; Final Report of the Review of Business Taxation, A Tax System Redesigned, Australian Government Printing Service, July 1999.
272. Gregory v. Helvering, 293 U.S. 465, 1935; Higgins v. Smith, 308 U.S. 473, 477 (1940); Commissioner v. Court Holding Co, 324 U.S. 331, 334 (1945); WT Ramsay Ltd v. IRC [1982] AC 300; Associated Wholesale Grocers, Inc. v. United States, 927 F.2d 1517, 1521 [67 AFTR 2d 91-837] (10th Cir. 1991); Del Commercial Properties, Inc. v. Commissioner of Internal Revenue, 8 Jun. 2001.
273. Financing equipment through double deduction loopholes, UK Tax Law Reform Committee; Exploiting loopholes to achieve outcomes not intended by Parliament, Ralph Report; obtaining tax advantages from unintended consequences of loopholes, Murray, Tax Avoidance, Sweet and Maxwell, 2012; Fussi, A legal and economic analysis of the effects of the Savings Tax Directive-Combating International Tax Avoidance, published by Aarhus School of Business, Aarhus, Fall of 2009, in p. 2.2/2.3.
274. Cecil B. Furstenberg v. Commissioner of Internal Revenue, 26 Nov. 1984; Del Commercial Properties, Inc. v. Commissioner of Internal Revenue, 8 Jun. 2001; raising finance through share issues instead of debt issuance because ongoing losses prevent using tax benefits from interest expense; year-end share sales generating losses to avoid taxes arising from net gains on sale of other assets in same year, UK Tax Law Reform Committee; artificial transactions used to obtain tax advantages not intended by the Government; transaction's business purpose being insubstantial when compared to tax advantage, http://www.hmrc.gov.uk/avoidance/overview.htm, last visited 3 Jul. 2015.
275. Deffenti, Introduction to Brazilian law, Kluwer International, p. 201; Ferreira, Form v. Substance a Comparison of Brazil's Tax System, University of Miami Inter-Am Law Review, p. 329; Torres, *supra* n. 161, p. 153; Schoueri, the post-BEPS world, *supra* n. 164, p. 2.
276. Profs Bianco; Dias and Schoueri in research for this Thesis.
277. Incorrect bookkeeping, failing to register with the FTS to make tax payments, untimely reporting of the opening of bank account, avoiding registration with FTS.
278. Part One No. 146-FZ, 31 Jul. 1998, Articles 120/116/119/121/117/124/126.

behavior was avoidance Reducing tax liabilities became relevant in Russia under *Resolution 53*,[279] but absent an avoidance definition in the *RTC*, it was generally seen to be a reference to actions taken by a taxpayer in reducing its liability which were not formally prohibited by the law ('optimization'), as *Pustovalov*[280] observed. *Pustovalov*[281] also argues that the 'unjustified tax benefit' doctrine established a basis for countering 'optimization', but his claim is difficult to accept when relying on the Court's 'unjustified tax benefit' definition. One fact which can be relied on though is that where arrangements which reduce tax have a 'business purpose' such as in *Vinco*,[282] the Court is unlikely to hold them to be avoidance.

The relationship in India, China and SA between the reduction of taxes and avoidance is different because those countries establish certain kinds of transactions, structures or behaviour as constituting avoidance, an approach which substantially simplifies tax authority administration. In India, the *Minister of Finance*[283] has confirmed that avoidance is the 'legal exploitation of tax laws to one's advantage' but the determination of whether, and if so when Indian tax laws have been 'exploited', was left to the *McDowell*[284] 'colourable device' doctrine which has since been reaffirmed in *Mathuram Agrawal*,[285] amongst others. Whether a 'colourable device' needed to be qualified by its use leading to a reduction in taxes for it to constitute avoidance was settled in *Azadi*[286] when the Court held that it was unnecessary for the State to suffer an economic detriment (i.e. a reduction in taxation) for a transaction to be avoidance:

> an act ... otherwise valid in law could be treated as non-est (not enforceable) merely because of *some underlying motive supposedly resulting in an economic detriment or prejudice to the national interests*, as perceived by the respondents.

In China, before 2008, avoidance was not associated with a reduction in tax because, as *Hann*[287] observed, the then laws[288] usually incorporated tax saving provisions, such as lower rates, accelerated capital allowances and SEZs, leaving it unnecessary for enterprises to enter into transactions, structures or behavior designed to reduce tax. In any event, before 1982 with a foreign enterprises' China tax liability typically being paid by the China partner, there was no China tax to be mitigated and therefore no need

---

279. *Supra* n. 245.
280. 2016: Tax Avoidance Revisited: The Russian Federation, http://www.eatlp.org/uploads/public/Russia%20(11%20Dec%202015).pdf, last visited 1 Jul. 2016.
281. *Ibid.*, at p. 1.
282. Vinco, Moscow Federal District Commercial Court No. KA-A40/8959-07, 10 Sep. 2007.
283. Statement of the Finance Minister on GAAR, January 2013.
284. McDowell and Co. Ltd. v. Commercial Tax Officer, 1986 AIR 649, 1985 SCR (3) 79117 April 1985.
285. Mathuram Agrawal v. State of M.P., Civil Appeal No. 1990 of 1995, AIR 2000 SC 109.
286. *Supra* n. 189.
287. PRC's FEITL and Regulations, Santa Clara Law Digital Comms, p. 704/5.
288. Section 3, Rules for the Implementation of the Income Tax Law of PRC Concerning Chinese-foreign Equity Joint Venture; Interim Provisions of the State Council concerning the Reduction of and Exemption from EIT and Consolidated Industrial and Commercial Tax in SEZs and the Fourteen Coastal Port Cities, 1984; Income Tax Law of PRC for Enterprises with Foreign Investment and Foreign Enterprises (1991), section 7 for SEZ.

for a transaction, structure or behaviour. This meant, according to *Hann*,[289] there was little reason for a foreign enterprise to enter into a strategy which reduced tax. Additionally, as *Jinya Li*[290] observed, there was no reason for residents to enter into a strategy reducing China tax because doing so was seen to be culturally incompatible. The need for both foreign enterprises and their China subsidiaries to rethink whether tax planning was needed changed from 2008 with the newly enacted EITL containing provisions which wound back tax incentives. Consequently, many inbound MNEs entered into transactions, establish new business entities, changed their behaviour or varied operational structures for the purpose of reducing their tax liabilities under the EITL to amounts which were compatible with amounts prevailing before 2008.

Paying less tax is integral to SA's approach to what constitutes avoidance, but transaction forms exist which do not constitute avoidance even if a reduction of tax results. According to *Oguttu*,[291] a transaction or behaviour does not give rise to avoidance even if tax has been reduced when what was done was a 'perfectly legal method of arranging one's affairs, ... through loopholes in tax laws ... with exploitation being within legal parameters'. This reflects the *Margo Commission's*[292] position and that of the judiciary in *Sunnyside and Conhage*[293] where transactions were held not to be avoidance even when taxes were reduced because the transaction form was legal, or in *Randles*,[294] when the transaction form was transparent. In order to counter the principles from these cases, SARS,[295] according to *Honibell*,[296] established the unacceptable transactions 'hallmarks'[297] as a GAAR. Where this approach gave rise to a consideration of substance and form, as in *Vasco Drycleaners; Ladysmith; Zandberg*

---

289. *Supra* n. 287, at p. 706.
290. Ideological basis of a person's right to avoid tax is based on right to be free from overreaching governments, freedom of property and freedom to contract, Barker, The Ideology of Tax Avoidance, 40 LOY. U. CHI. L.J. 229 (2009), but China lacks an equivalent. In China the duty to pay taxes is based on traditional values of collective rights, social harmony and relationship between Governments and taxpayers being more of a 'duty' to support the State than 'deprivation' of private property, Jinyan Li, Tax Transplants and Local Culture: A Comparative Study of the Chinese and Canadian GAAR, Theoretical Inquiries in Law, Research Paper No. 04 Volume 11/ Issue; 01/ (2015), p. 100. Taxpayers and Government are not seen as equals because paying taxes was seen as supporting a parent with the Emperor 'head' of the nation-family;Tax transplants, *ibid.*, p. 100. The taxpayer/child's duty was 'unconditional' and a moral obligation with the official position being that paying taxes was honourable to better serve the people (*que zhi yu min, yong zhi yu min*) with noncompliance shameful.
291. Curbing offshore tax avoidance, the case of SA companies and Trusts, Doctor of Laws Thesis, University of SA, p. 2.
292. Margo Commission's Report into the Tax Structure of South Africa, Old Mutual, 1987.
293. Commissioner of IR v. Sunnyside Centre (86/95) [1996] ZASCA 102; Commissioner for IR v. Conhage (Pty) Ltd (606/97) [1999] ZASCA 64.
294. Commissioner of Customs and Excise v. Randles, Bros and Hudson Ltd 1941 AD 369 at 395-6.
295. 2005 Discussion Paper, *supra* n. 51; section 103 of the Income Tax Act, 1962, November 2005 p. 10.1 referencing International benchmarking with Australia, Canada and New Zealand, p. 9.
296. *Supra* n. 212, at p. 511.
297. SARS Discussion Paper, *supra* n. 209, p. 19, complexity, insubstantial business substance, participation of irrelevant parties or embedded techniques devoid of business purpose, paying high fees to promoters and the non-commercial use of tax havens (Musviba, SA Tax Guide, http://www.sataxguide.co.za/tax-avoidance-and-tax-evasion-the-differences/) later became avoidance hallmarks.

and ABC Limited,[298] it led to difficulties in countering the transactions, especially when they had the effect which they purported to have, an approach discussed in *Bank Windhoek and Relier*.[299] The position became further complicated when the transaction or behaviour constituted a 'trick', as discussed in *Matrix Securities*.[300]

This subsection concludes, that the transaction, structure or behaviour must result in the reduction of taxes in China, SA and Russia (it was neither necessary in Russia before *Resolution 53* nor in China before the introduction of the EITL) to constitute avoidance but does not need to do so in Brazil (where the legality principle overrides) or in India (where the colourable device concept prevails).

3.4.3 Loopholes and Intent

The developed world generally treats the misusing of loopholes as being avoidance but the BRICS do not treat that misuse in the same way.

Brazil generally does not strike down the use of loopholes to generate tax savings because the 'legality principle' overrides, and as *Schoueri*[301] observes, the 'sham' doctrine is 'left aside' in favour of business purpose. Some examples of loophole misuse which have not been struck down in Brazil are reverse merger reorganizations which facilitate deducting prior year losses *(107-07.596)*[302] or reorganizations which create internally generated goodwill for amortization *(1101-00.708)*.[303]

Russia does not treat the misusing of loopholes as avoidance because transactions and structures giving rise to 'unjustified tax benefits', as defined by *Resolution 53*, are treated as evasion. This means therefore that were a loophole to be abused it would likely be seen as evasion (rather than avoidance), and this is clear from *Dvortsovy Ryad-MS*[304] where using a structure to provide the ultimate beneficial owner with tax benefits was held to be an unjustified tax benefit. The author concludes that on the basis of this information, in Russia avoidance and evasion have merged, a position supported by *Worstall's*[305] observation that neither form, content nor purpose of a transaction determines whether it constitutes avoidance. This conclusion contradicts the views of *Hansam, Bruk and Franklin*[306] who argued that both paying salaries in

---

298. Vasco Drycleaners v. Twycross 1979 (1) SA 603 (A) at 615H in fin to 616A; Erf 3183/1 Ladysmith (Pty) Ltd and Another v. Commissioner for Inland Revenue 1996 (3) SA 942 (A) at (953D-E); Zandberg v. Van Zyl 1910 AD 302 *Innes JA, p. 309;* ABC Limited v. SARS (VAT 189) [2010] ZATC 2, 6 May 2010.
299. Bank Windhoek Bpk v. Rajie en 'n Ander 1994(1) SA 115 (A); Relier (Pty) Ltd. v. Commissioner for Inland Revenue (256/96) [1997] ZASCA 105.
300. R v. IRC ex parte Matrix Securities Ltd [1994] 1 WLR (HL) at p. 345C.
301. *Supra* n. 164, at p. 129.
302. 4 Apr. 2004.
303. 4 Nov. 2012.
304. Decision No. 12418/08, *supra* n. 173.
305. Worstall, Forbes/Tech, March 2013, http://www.forbes.com/sites/timworstall/2013/03/27/russians-in-cyprus-its-not-about-tax-its-about-the-rule-of-law-and-property-rights/.
306. Hansam, Sunshine Isle Lures Moscow Billions, Evening Standard, July 1991, p. 35; Franklin, Tax avoidance by Citizens of the Russian Federation, DJCIL, Volume 8, No. 1 (1997); Bruk, Russia Supreme Arbitration Court Adopts 'Disregard of Legal Entity' approach to Combat Tax Fraud, Eur. Taxn, 2010.

kind and the provision of interest free loans to shareholders amounted to avoidance, but based on *Dvortsovy*,[307] in the author's opinion, these examples give rise to 'unjustified tax benefits' which makes them evasion.

Raman[308] established that Indian taxpayers had the right to plan their business affairs in a manner resulting in a tax reduction. That principle was, however, watered down by the *McDowell*[309] 'colourable device' doctrine, which confirmed that using loopholes in a manner unintended by the legislature[310] constituted avoidance providing the device used was something dubious and different from something normally see in business planning.[311] In *McDowall*, Misra J[312] wrote that:

> Tax avoidance postulates the assessee (being) in receipt of an amount which is really and in truth his income liable to tax but on which he avoids payment of tax by some *artifice or device* ... showing the income as accruing to another person, at the same time making it available for use and enjoyment to the assesse ... or mask(ing) the true character of the income by disguising it as a capital receipt ... or other diverse forms ... . Tax planning may be legitimate provided it is within the framework of law. Colourable devices cannot be part of tax planning and it is wrong to encourage or entertain the belief that it is honourable to avoid paying tax by resorting to dubious methods.

Shah J[313] also in *McDowell* defined:

> a 'colourable device' as being a transaction or a device designed to avoid tax, ... ' or (one) 'using dubious methods'.

Therefore relying on *Shah J*, the misusing of a loophole is not necessarily a 'colourable device' because its misuse may or may not be avoidance because its use may not have been intended to reduce tax. Focussing on the device used to obtain the benefit therefore, rather than whether a loophole was exploited sets India apart from the developed world and a consequence of India adopting this approach is the introduction of some simplicity for the Indian tax administration and compensation for the smaller manpower numbers available to identify, audit and counter the transactions.

The necessity for enterprises before 2008 to plan to avoid China tax was limited because the available tax incentives resulted in little tax being due. Consequently, focussing on loopholes to achieve tax savings had not been relevant. However, as *Jinyan Li*[314] notes, this did not stop foreign taxpayers from entering into transactions or

---

307. *Supra* n. 173.
308. Raman & Co, 1968, 67 ITR 11.
309. *Supra* n. 284.
310. Expert Committee, Final Report on GAAR in India Income Tax Act, 1961, 2012 p. 19/21; Deferred payment of tax liability, re-characterization of receipt or payments to lower rate or nil, permanent elimination of liabilities, income shifting from high taxed to lower taxed persons, Ostwal, 'Anti-avoidance Measures in India', http://www.manupatra.co.in/newsline/articles/Upload/C8034670-1E8E-4E9D-A68B-35D1E7AF7B29.pdf, p. 62.
311. Device used to obtain tax benefits within the law is not colourable (Kumar, India's taxation regime: perspectives on the proposed changes. Fourth NLSIR Symposium Rapporteur Report, 23 National Schedule India Rev 2011/2012, p. 28; Ostwal, *ibid.*; Kapadia, *supra* n. 164, p. 323).
312. *Supra* n. 284.
313. *Supra* n. 284.
314. Tax Transplants, *supra* n. 290.

establishing structures which misused China's tax incentives, unfairly accessed DTC benefits, abused the company legal form, used offshore haven entities to accumulate profits or misused other loopholes, all in order to save tax. This meant that while misusing loopholes reduced tax liabilities, their misuse did not constitute avoidance. It is also evident that despite the SAT being aware of some of these strategies (through the periodic discussions with the OECD on tax avoidance from around 1996,[315]) the SAT was unable to effectively counter the behaviour because before 2008 its tax legislation did not contain a broad based anti-avoidance rule which treated loophole misuse as avoidance, as *Jinyan Li*[316] writes. However, China sought to counter avoidance through applying the substance over form doctrine which is discussed in the next subsection of this study.

Identifying misused loopholes in SA's transactions[317] has become an important feature of SA's approach to determining what constitutes avoidance, as *Oguttu*[318] confirms. However, the assertion that to be avoidance a transaction, structure or behaviour must both misuse a loophole and be devoid of substance is incorrect because transactions having some business substance but which involve a trick[319] have been held to be avoidance.

This subsection concludes that misusing loopholes does not constitute avoidance in Brazil, Russia, or China but does in SA. It also concludes that it constitutes avoidance in India but only when the loophole had been exploited by the use of a 'colourable device' which was dubious and also different from a structure normally found in planning.

3.4.4 Substance Over Form

The developed world and the BRICS are alike in that while the substance of a transaction is important when determining whether there has been avoidance, the form cannot always be discarded. However, the BRICS substance and form concept diverges from that generally adopted by the developed world, leaving it of little relevance in Brazil and in India but very widely and liberally applied in China. SA and Russia have broadly aligned with the developed world's approach, but in Russia's case 'substance and form' is embedded in evasion.

As *Defferenti, Ferreira and Torres*[320] observe, Brazil's 'legality principle' ensures that even transactions with insignificant substance will not likely be treated as avoidance, while structures with little or no business purpose will also not likely be

---

315. At http://www.oecd.org/ctp/countryprogrammeontaxationwiththepeoplesrepublicofchina.htm, last visited 10 May 2016.
316. Other than for TP SAT did not aggressively pursue avoidance because challenging based on general principle was difficult, Tax Transplants, *supra* n. 290, p. 99.
317. SARS 2005 Discussion Paper and section 103 of the Income Tax Act, 1962 (Act No. 58 of 1962), p. 4.
318. *Supra* n. 291, at p. 2.
319. R v. IRC ex parte Matrix Securities Ltd [1994] 1 WLR (HL) at p. 345C.
320. Introduction to Brazilian law, *supra* n. 275; Form v. Substance, *supra* n. 275 p. 329; Tax Treaties and Tax Avoidance, *supra* n. 161, p. 153; A key element of post BEPS World, *supra* n. 164, p. 2.

treated as avoidance, as *Bianco, Dias* and *Schoueri* [321] observe. The contrary view advanced by *Valdes and Greco*[322] *(*which has been confirmed by *Rolim, Valadao and Rosenblatt*[323]) is that the 'legality principle' can be overridden when the arrangement's substance differs from its form, or where the tax saving arose from 'trickery' or abuse of rights or of the form. The RFB followed the *Valdes and Greco* approach in *Gerdau Açominas*,[324] a case involving a scheme to amortize internally generated goodwill. The he Court however rejected the RFB's argument on the grounds that the reorganization had been legally entered into ('legality principle') even though the amortized principal had been 'conjured by a scheme'. The decision was reversed by the CARF in No 1402-001.404[325] on the grounds of the scheme not being economically sound although it had been legally entered into. *Schoueri*[326] has recently argued in relation to 'substance over form' that if substance can prevail over form (Complementary Law 104/01), then it is only to the extent necessary to disregard 'sham' transactions thereby allowing the real transaction to be revealed. This must make the Law ineffective because it establishes a procedure only to strike down shams rather than establishing 'substance over form' as a doctrine. Whether *Schoueri's* explanation is the preferred view remains to be seen, but because arbitrariness is forbidden in Brazil[327] and the substance and form doctrine can be arbitrary, there is merit in *Schoueri's* opinion.

Disagreement between eminent scholars and judges on something as fundamental as 'substance over form' indicates a need for statutory resolution which the RFB sought to do in 2015, in a practical way, by requiring taxpayers to include in an annual return[328] all details of their planning transactions which eliminate, reduce or defer taxes or transactions not having business or economic purposes or those which were implemented through unusual structures. Such a notification process would have simplified identification of potentially abusive transactions, and as a consequence allowed the RFB to concentrate manpower on the investigations requiring intensive labour use and allowing its limited manpower to be used most effectively. However, since this notification process was excluded from the enacted version of Law 13,202/2015, the RFB has been left with the need to make a decision on whether to apply 'substance over form' to a transaction, structure or behaviour with the knowledge of questionable support in the Courts.

Russia adopted 'substance over form' in *Resolution 53*,[329] but unlike the other BRICS, it uses the concept to counter evasion instead of avoidance given that avoidance is limited to administrative breaches

---

321. Profs Bianco, Dias and Schoueri in original research for this study.
322. Regional Seminar on International Tax Law, IFA Chile, Day 2, July 2009; Greco, Formalism Crisis in Brazilian Tax law, 1 Revista da PGFN, 2011 p. 9/18.
323. Profs Rolim, Valadao and Rosenblatt in original research for this study.
324. Gerdau Açominas S/A v. National Treasury, Administrative Proceedings n. 10680.724392/2010-28.
325. CARF Judgment No. 1402-001.404, 9 Jul. 2013.
326. *Supra* n. 164, at p. 113.
327. Prof Dias, original research for this study.
328. Provisional Measure 685/2015, July 2015.
329. *Supra* n. 245.

India generally does not apply the 'substance over form' doctrine to reveal avoidance unless the colourable device had little substance or business purpose. Having decided in *McDowell* that in India it was unnecessary for an 'economic detriment' to arise from a transaction, structure or behaviour to establish avoidance, the *Azadi* decision to not see treaty shopping as being avoidance, seems correct. Were treaty shopping to result in India suffering an 'economic detriment' then it would still not be avoidance unless the treaty shopping was a colourable device and then only if the conduit transaction of structure adopted had insufficient substance as discussed in *Star Television* or *KSPG Netherlands*.[330] Where India suffers an 'economic detriment' as it did in *Aztec Software*[331] from mispriced related party transactions, the decision to treat it as avoidance is correct because the device, in this instance, mispriced transactions, has little substance. This conclusion is also evident in *Ardex Investments*[332] where the fact that a taxpayer had owned shares for many years on which dividends had not been paid was found to be relevant when holding that the transaction was not a colourable device and in *Vodafone International*[333] where the ownership structure was accepted as a normal commercial instance. When applying the same logic in *IDBI Trusteeship*,[334] a case concerning the use of intermediate companies to circumvent India's FDI policy, the Court held that the particular conduit form chosen was a 'colourable device' because the form lacked business purpose or substance.

This means that the extent of business purpose or substance is relevant to determining whether the transaction or structure was a 'colourable device' but there is little guidance on what that level should be. One extreme however is found in *Aricent Technologies* and in *Tata Sons*[335] where the Courts held that the derivation of trading profits through foreign branches of Indian companies, not to be a colourable device because the taxpayers merely relied on the relevant DTCs for the exemption. Another example is *Star Television*[336] where the restructuring of a company's ownership for the purpose of allowing gains on any later sale (if any) to be free from Indian tax was also not seen as a colourable device, because at completion of the reorganization there was no certainty of any later sale. The *Star Television* decision supports *Vodafone International* but contradicts *Mehta's*[337] observation that companies inserted into structures as part of sale planning remain vulnerable to be treated as colourable.

Non-colourable conduct is evident in *Ansaldo Energia*[338] where a single contract was broken into discrete components (onshore and offshore) with each being subject

---

330. In Re: Star Television Entertainment Ltd., (2010) 321 ITR 1 (AAR); KSPG Netherlands Holding v. Director of Income Tax International, Mumbai, 25 Feb. 2010.
331. Aztec Software, *supra* n. 186.
332. Ardex Investments Mauritius Ltd, A.A.R. No. 886 of 2010, 14 Nov. 2011.
333. Vodafone International Holdings BV v. India, 2014.
334. IDBI Trusteeship Services Limited v. Hubtown Limited, LSI-511-HC-Mumbai-2015.
335. Aricent Technologies (Holding) Limited v. DCIT, 21 Jan. 2011; Tata Sons Limited v. DCIT, 24 Nov. 2010.
336. Star Television, *supra* n. 161.
337. Vodafone's Supreme Court Victory in India, Slaughter and May, February 2012, p. 2, https://www.slaughterandmay.com/media/1750169/vodafones-supreme-court-victory-in-india.pdf.
338. M/S. Ansaldo Energia Spa v. The Income Tax Appellate Tribunal on 12 Jan. 2009.

to separate contracts, reflecting the different sources. Contract splitting such as this, has come under scrutiny in BEPS Action Plan Seven[339] discussed in Chapter 7 of this study.

Running parallel to the debate on colourable devices is the relevance of the foreign person's COR, especially where that person is an intermediary for third country investors and, even more so after *Azadi*, where the intermediary was a Mauritius resident, as many of India's inbound FDI providers evidently are. While India proposed legislation[340] to reduce the effectiveness of a COR, as *Kumar*[341] observes, this gave rise to 'tedious issues', but the proposed changes would not likely result in conduiting being deemed avoidance because the legislation did not seek to override *Azadi*.

Substance and form began as a China focus after the 2008 introduction of the EITL which, as *Sharkey*[342] observed, led to an increase in transactions, structures and behaviour entered into for the purpose of preserving the previously applicable low effective tax rates. While the *EITL*[343] authorized SAT to counter avoidance, it was not before the 2009 issue of *Circular 2*[344] that SAT was armed with a 'reasonable business purpose' test to apply to potentially avoidance transactions. At the 'reasonable business purpose' core was 'substance over form'[345] which in turn required the transaction, structure or behaviour to have sufficient 'economic substance'[346] for it to withstand challenge.

Circular 2 is a complicated instruction requiring the tax authorities to make many subjective judgements and absent manpower capacity for dealing objectively with the issues, has resulted in practical, rather than legally analysed decisions being made on disputed items. When examining *Circular 2* in more depth it is apparent that some bright line tests were established in order to minimize areas of dispute, such as the mere use of haven enterprises being deemed to constitute avoidance, as were foreign enterprise structures devoid of economic substance. A review of the published decisions on *Circular 2* concludes how these principles have been applied. In *Xingjiang*[347] the person's foreign tax residence was held to be artificial, in *Chongqing*,

---

339. Preventing the Artificial Avoidance of PE Status, Action 7 – 2015 Final Report.
340. Finance Act, 2012 proposed enactment but in 2013 removed because of investor anxiety arising from MOF confirming that possessing a COR is necessary but not sufficient (non-resident is required to provide prescribed information to IRD) to access DTC benefits (except for Mauritius, Circular 789).
341. India: Tax Residency Certificate Requirement in India – Bumpy Road Ahead? 3 Jun. 2013, http://www.mondaq.com/india/x/238218/Income+Tax/Tax+Residency+Certificate+Requirement+in+India+Bumpy.
342. Forum: China's New EITL: Continuity and Change, UNSW Law Journal, Volume 30(3), p. 836.
343. Chapter VI, Special Tax Adjustments gave tax authority the right to counter specific avoidance transactions but failed to define avoidance.
344. *Supra* n. 200, Circular 2, Article 92/97, Implementation Measures of Special Tax Adjustments requires understanding of transaction's substance, implementing method and connectivity of steps. Substance was identified having regard to assets, liabilities of the intermediary and published materials of the parent including Annual Reports, Financial Statements and share sale agreement.
345. *Ibid.*, Article 93(i/vi).
346. *Ibid.*, Article 94.
347. 2006.

Chapter 3: Evasion and Avoidance According to the BRICS

Jiangdu, Nantong and *Zhuizheng*[348] the immediate foreign intermediaries were held to have insufficient substance, in *Mudan* and *Xinjiang*[349] the immediate foreign intermediaries were held not to be the beneficial owners, in *Xiangshan*[350] the company was held to be a tax haven company, in *Suzhou*[351] the substance of a Mauritius structure was held to be different from the form, in *Taizhou*[352] it was held necessary to protect China's sovereign right to tax and in *Beijing, Xiamen, Guangzhou*[353] the shifting offshore of China profits was held to be relevant. While not all of these decisions focus on substance and form, their adoption of a substance test is clear, as is identifying whether the foreign structure has economic substance and if so, to what extent.

The meaning of avoidance in China was further considered in the July 2014 draft[354] focussing on GAAR and the relevance of economic substance became clearer from that draft. This draft extended avoidance countered by GAAR to cover transactions where the obtaining of a tax benefit was the 'sole or main purpose' but in a 'nod' to substance and form, where the legally compliant arrangements were not commensurate with economic substance. *Liao Tizhong*[355] further cemented the importance of economic substance in September 2014[356] when stating that holding structures or transactional arrangements not having economic substance or those designed to achieve double non-taxation[357] constituted avoidance. In concluding that an insufficiency of economic substance or a lack of transparency amounts to avoidance, this conflicts with the decision to treat the same items as evasion or suggests that evasion and avoidance overlap in China.

SA treats 'substance over form' as being integral to the meaning of avoidance and has widened its application as evident in *Bank Windhoek*[358] where the Court adopted substance instead of form even though the transactions had been honestly entered into and had the intention the parties intended and were without fraud or disguise. In following this approach, the Court relied on the common law principle of *plus valet quod agitur quam quod simulate concipitur* (what is actually done is more important than that which seems to have been done), as *Barry Ger*,[359] observes. However, while *Honibell*[360] has argued that it is not always clear when that rule applies, the decisions

---

348. June 2010, 2009 and 2012, March 2013.
349. July 2010 and 2008.
350. 2011.
351. 2011.
352. 2013.
353. At http://finance.china news. Com/cj/2013/05-17/4827643.shtml, last visited 28 Aug. 2015.
354. SAT discussion draft on Administrative Measures for GAAR, 3 Jul. 2014; Administrative Measures for General Anti-avoidance Rules (SAT Order [2014] No. 32. http://www.chinatax.gov.cn/n810341/n810755/c1395341/content.html).
355. Director General, SAT International Tax Department.
356. SAT Conference on BEPS Deliverables and Tax Avoidance, 25 Sep. 2014.
357. Double non-taxation, hybrid mismatches.
358. Bank Windhoek Bpk v. Rajie en 'n Ander 1994(1) SA 115 (A).
359. High Court challenges SCA's interpretation of simulated transactions, http://www.saflii.org/za/journals/DEREBUS/2013/25.pdf.
360. *Supra* n. 212, p. 514.

in *Zandberg; Vasco Drycleaners; Ladysmith* and *ABC Limited*[361] to treat transactions as avoidance where the substance differs from the form, suggest that *Honibell* may have been too conservative in his thinking.

This subsection concludes, that substance and form is of little relevance in Brazil and also of little relevance in India unless the 'colourable device' has little substance or insufficient business purpose, while it has been widely and arguably, liberally applied in China. SA and Russia have broadly aligned with the developed world, but in Russia's case substance and form is embedded in evasion and in SA, the meaning has widened to apply to transactions honestly entered into even absent fraud or disguise.

3.5 MEANINGS: SIGNIFICANCE

In relation to defining what constitutes avoidance, the author concludes that the transactions, structures or behaviour is required to result in the reduction of taxes in China, SA and Russia but not in Brazil (where the legality principle overrides) or in India (where the colourable device concept prevails) and also did not in Russia before *Resolution 53* or in China before the introduction of the EITL. A taxpayer's misusing of loopholes is not indicative of avoidance in Brazil, Russia, or China but it is in SA and in India, when the loophole was misused by dubious devices. With respect to substance over form as an indicator of avoidance, the concept has little relevance in Brazil (because of the legality principle) and of little relevance in India (unless the 'colourable device' has little substance or business purpose), while it is widely applied in China through its 'reasonable business purpose' and 'economic substance' tests. SA and Russia have broadly aligned with the developed world on the meaning of substance over form but in Russia's case it has embedded the concept into evasion while in SA, the meaning has widened to apply to transactions honestly entered into by parties without fraud or disguise.

The significance of the inability of Brazil and to a significant extent India to establish avoidance as an effective concept is the necessity to adopt broad based SAARs to counter certain forms of abuse, especially in the absence of GAARs. With China and SA having developed sophisticated approaches to identifying avoidance (including GAARs), the necessity for them to establish the broad based SAARs is not as pressing. Russia has struggled to establish the meaning of avoidance but has a broad based approach to evasion.

With India and China treating mispriced transactions as avoidance as well as evasion, it evidences a merger of avoidance and evasion for mispriced transactions used to shift profits offshore in those countries. Russia also merges avoidance into evasion for transactions giving rise to unjustified tax benefits which includes all transactions and structures where the substance differs from the form. This convergence however does not apply where the avoidance arises from transactions which misuse loopholes which delineates the difference between avoidance and evasion in China.

---

361. *Supra* n. 298.

3.6 BRICS COORDINATION: AVOIDANCE

Having regard to the constituents of avoidance in the BRICS, there is no evidence of any cooperation or coordination between the BRICS in their legislative or administrative development or in their judicial interpretation.

3.7 DIVERGENCES: CONSEQUENCES

The consequence of the difficulty in identifying what constitutes avoidance in Brazil is the relatively few cases where transactions, structures or behaviour have been overturned and the failure to enact the proposed 2015 notification obligation means that the RFB is left with few tools to counter avoidance. In Russia, the consequence of the breadth of the unjustified tax benefits doctrine (evasion) is that it counters structures or transactions which the developed world would treat as avoidance leaving avoidance to represent sundry administrative breaches. With India considerably narrowing the constituents of avoidance by its reliance on 'colourable devices', the number of structures or transactions countered by it is limited and suggests the urgent need for a GAAR. China's widened meaning of avoidance results in many structures or transactions being countered, as has become clear with the wide range of cases. SA's adoption of the developed world's approach together with a GAAR provides it with the tools it needs to counter avoidance. All this means that it is more important for Brazil and India (than the other BRICS) to implement SAARs to counter transactions which, in the developed, world would be avoidance and for the BRICS to implement GAARs to deny benefits for transactions, structures or behaviour not covered by the SAARs.

3.8 MISPRICED TRANSACTIONS AND TAX HAVENS: EVASION OR AVOIDANCE

This Chapter thus concluded that mispriced transactions and tax haven structures which do not have sufficient business purpose constitute evasion in the BRICS and the author deduces the BRICS have adopted this approach because the volume of illicit outflows requires strong action to counter and to increase the compliance deterrent as well as to compensate for the relatively limited tax authority manpower. The author has also deduced that by treating mispriced transactions and tax haven structures as criminal evasion, the compliance deterrent is further enhanced through the prospect for criminal sanctions being levied on senior company officers who fail to comply being a reason alone for them to comply.

3.9 NEXT CHAPTER

As discussed, this Chapter concludes that countering evasion and avoidance has become a special BRICS focus because of the need to counter transactions, structures or behaviour used to facilitate the substantial illicit outflows and that the BRICS have widened their approach to evasion from the developed world's approach principally by including mispriced transactions and tax haven usage in evasion, because by doing so they increase the incentive for companies and senior company officers to comply and compensate for their lack of tax authority manpower. In Chapter 4, the research focuses on whether the BRICS approach to countering thin capitalization, TP and controlled foreign corporations (SAARs) diverges from the developed world's and investigate the reasons for those divergences.

CHAPTER 4
Countering Avoidance: SAARs

4.1 INTRODUCTION

Chapter 3 concluded that the BRICS diverged from the development world's meaning of evasion and avoidance when countering transactions, structures and behavior used to facilitate illicit outflows.[362] In Chapter 4, the focus is on whether the BRICS have widened their approach to countering the thin capitalization, TP and controlled foreign corporation practices from that of the developed world and whether the formulation of those divergences by the BRICS can be explained by the BRICS necessity to increase the deterrent in order to compensate for their comparatively small tax authority manpower capacity dealing with the audit, investigation and prosecution of those arrangements. The study also researches whether there is evidence that the divergences have been influenced by intra-BRICS coordination.

4.2 THIN CAPITALIZATION

Thin capitalization is the term describing financial arrangements between related parties where either the principal borrowing amount[363] or the interest rate is not supportable by reference to arm's length lending arrangements. Either excess debt or excess interest leads to lower borrower taxable profits and the developed world's thin capitalization rules are intended to counter the resulting tax leakages by applying fixed debt[364] to asset or equity ratios[365] to limit the deductions available in respect of the

---

362. WIR, Reforming International Investment Governance, p. 190/192, particularly financing and intangibles based TP schemes.
363. Blouin, IMF Working Paper, Thin Capitalization Rules and Multinational Firm Capital Structure, WP/14/12.
364. Aggregate internal from related parties, total internal, total internal foreign, or total foreign debt.
365. OECD, Thin Capitalization Legislation: Background Paper for Country Tax Administrations, Initial draft, August 2012, p. 8, Ratio might represent arm's length.

interest expense The excess interest amount is treated as equity or dividends and is usually subject to dividend WHT rather than interest WHT. Some countries apply the arm's length standard (ALS)[366] to calculate the deductible amount in respect of the interest expense while some developed countries limit that deductible amount to a fixed percentage of trading profits.

Where the lender and borrower reside in different countries and providing the two countries have entered into a bilateral DTC containing an Article 9 based on the *OECD Model Convention*,[367] the DTC may preserve the denial of the interest deductions made domestically or override it, preserve or reject the domestic interest limitation[368] or preserve or reject the reclassification of the actual interest into a loan or a dividend[369] subject to WHT.

The developed world has argued that applying a fixed ratio provides more certainty than the ALS and is also simpler to administer for both taxpayers and the tax authority,[370] especially a tax authority with limited manpower capacity.

Leverage is important because the amount of approved debt or interest provided to a related party as a loan can influence the taxes paid by the related party borrower on its profits[371] and the lender on the amount it receives.[372] The difficulties tax authorities have in countering leverage either by applying the fixed ratio, ALS or the interest rate limitation have been well documented in the *OECD/G20 BEPS 2015 Final Reports*,[373] and are discussed in Chapter 7 of this study.

As concluded in this subsection, tax based thin capitalisation rules are of less importance to the BRICS than the developed world because the BRICS continue to rely on exchange controls for regulating the terms and conditions of inbound related party debt. In India's case in the absence of a tax based thin capitalization rule, the reliance on exchange controls is even more important. However, notwithstanding the BRICS de-emphasizing(other than India) of the tax based thin capitalisation rules, they have still widened important features of those rules in order to ensure that additional forms of financial accommodation or financial assistance provided by parties which seem at be at arm's length, come within the fixed ratio's ambit.

4.2.1 Exchange Controls

Some countries control inbound lending through exchange control regulations and where that procedure exists, lending is permitted only to the extent it is compatible with the banking regulations and those regulations become, de facto, the tax based thin

---

366. Article 9, OECD Model Convention.
367. OECD, Thin Capitalization; Taxation of Entertainers, Artistes and Sportsmen, Issues in International Taxation, No. 2, 1987; Thin Capitalization Legislation: A Background Paper, *supra* n. 365, p. 7/8.
368. Articles 9(1) and 11(6), *supra* n. 366.
369. Article 11(6), *supra* n. 366.
370. *Supra* n. 365, at p. 12.
371. The greater the deductible interest the lower the corporate profits.
372. Extracting profits as interest may reduce source country taxes on lender.
373. At http://www.oecd.org/ctp/beps-2015-final-reports.htm.

capitalization rules. While the BRICS have not entirely abrogated the responsibility of controlling interest tax deductibility to the exchange control authorities, the exchange rules provide an important tool for controlling excessive interest and a tool which in part deals with the consequences of limited tax authority capacity.

The Brazil Central Bank[374] still controls the terms and conditions of all inbound loans, and as observed by *NortonRoseFullbright*,[375] ensures that the terms are compatible with 'international standards'. A similar policy existed in Russia[376] until 1992 when the controls were substantially relaxed. They continue to be relevant in both India[377] and China,[378] with India having established fixed rates for capital inflows together with thresholds for related party loans[379] including loans provided by sister companies, while China prevents related party debt exceeding the difference between the enterprise's total investment and its registered capital. SA's[380] exchange control rules limit foreign loans to R10,000 without prior Treasury approval.

4.2.2 India and Thin Capitalization

With India not incorporating thin capitalization rules (fixed ratio[381] or ALS) into its tax legislation, interest deductibility depends upon the loan satisfying both the exchange control limitation together and the general interest[382] deduction rules. Whether an interest expense meets the general interest deductibility test is established by reference to the 'commercial' considerations of the borrower drawing down the loan, as was confirmed in *Hindustan Conductors*.[383] This is not to say that the IRD has not sought to deny deductions for interest expenses by relying on the ALS, but its approach was rejected in *Mittal Metal*.[384] In that case, the Court held an 18% interest payment on a

---

374. Central Bank of Brazil, Resolution 3,844, Article 9, Law 4,595, December 1964, 23 Mar. 2010, based on Article 4 http://www.bcb.gov.br/rex/LegCE/Ingl/Ftp/Resolution3844.pdf; CMN's Resolution 4,373 (2014), BCB's Circular 3,689.
375. NortonRoseFullbright, Registration of Foreign Loans in Brazil, November 2013.
376. 173-FZ, Currency Regulation and Currency Control, 1992, departure for exchange control, IFLR/September 2004.
377. Foreign Exchange Management (borrowing or lending in foreign exchange) Regulations, 2000 Notification No FEMA 3 /2000-RB 3 May 2000 RBI (Exchange Control Department) Central Office Mumbai 400 001.
378. Debt not exceeding difference between total investment and registered capital; Renminbi conditionally convertible for current accounts under Administrative Rules, January 1996, amended 14 Jan. 1997, 5 Aug. 2008.Circulars of SAFE; Yang, China: Tax Treaties and Tax avoidance: application of anti-avoidance provisions, IFA Cahiers 2010 – Volume 95A, p. 214/215/209.
379. 4:1 ratio for +$5m related party loans (providing equity holder owning at least 25% of the borrower's paid up capital) with an all-in cost of funds of six month LIBOR plus margin.
380. Notices R1111, December 1961, clause 16(1)(a) and 2.
381. Thincap rules drafted in 2011 but Finance Minister failed to approve: Jain, Director General of International Tax and TP, Internationaltaxreview.com, June 2010, p. 22; Anti-avoidance provision in Chapter X, ITA do not extend to thincap.
382. Section 36(1)(iii), ITA, 1962: interest paid on loans drawn down for business or professions deductible providing interest is related to funding assets for use in extending existing businesses or profession except for interest in the period from drawdown until first use.
383. Commissioner Of Income-Tax v. Hindustan Conductors Pvt. Ltd, 13 Jul. 1999.
384. Mittal Metal v. ITO (2008) 21 SOT 186 Del.

related party loan to be deductible even though interest on another related party loan had been set at 12%, because the 18% rate reflected a business purpose and fair market value. The IRD's approach was also rejected in *Besix Kier Dabhol*[385] where the Bombay High Court held that 284:1 leverage was acceptable in the absence of a specific thin capitalization rule.

The IRD has been materially disadvantaged in denying deductions for interest expenses both because there is no provision allowing it to convert debt into equity,[386] as *Ajinkya*[387] observes, and also because section 90(2) ITA[388] provides taxpayers with an election to apply either the DTC or India's domestic rules, whichever is the more favourable to it when calculating its taxable income. This makes any applicability of the ALS difficult for the IRD to sustain. However, taxpayers will cease having access to this election when India enforces its GAAR (first announced 2012/2103 Budget)[389] currently anticipated being from April 2017. India's adherence to the legal form (as a loan or equity) rather than adopting the economic substance of the financial accommodation was settled in *Zaheer Mauritius*[390] where the Court held gains on the disposal of compulsory convertibles to be interest rather than capital gain. This outcome may change once GAAR is introduced.

The thin capitalization discussion in the following sections of this study proceeds on the basis of India not having thin capitalization tax rules and for that reason, India is not referred to further in the sections unless there is a compelling reason for doing so.

4.2.3 Ratio or Arm's Length

Each of the BRICS,[391] except for SA and Brazil until 2010, adopt the fixed ratio approach to thin capitalization but the individual members have adopted different rules when implementing it. Prior to 2010, Brazil sought to counter excess leverage by applying its anti-avoidance rule[392] but because, as explained in Chapter 3, it had had little success in generally applying its anti-avoidance rule, in 2010 it introduced a 2:1[393] fixed ratio. In cases prior to 2010, the CARF had supported the RFB's application of the

---

385. Director of Income-Tax, International Taxation-II, Mumbai v. Besix Kier Dabhol SA IT Appeal No. 776, 2011, 30 Aug. 2012.
386. Zaheer Mauritius v. DIT [2014] 47 taxmann.com 247 (Delhi), held gains on the disposal of compulsory convertibles were interest rather than capital leaving it clear the instrument was debt.
387. The debt-equity conundrum- India, IFA Cahiers 2012 – Volume 97B, p. 336/346.
388. Majumdar, Tax Treaties and Tax avoidance: application of anti-avoidance provisions – India, IFA Cahiers 2010 – Volume 95A, p. 376; Datta, TP – A Retrospective Analysis, Asia-Pac. Tax Bull, 2010 (Volume 16), No. 1, p. 39; Bohra, New tendencies in tax treatment of cross-border interest of corporations – India, IFA Cahiers 2008 – Volume 93B, p. 353.
389. Dash, India-TP Regulations – A Comparative Study on the Confluence and Conflict between India, the OECD and Other Countries, Asia-Pac. Tax Bull, January/February 2010, p. 34; section 92B(i); Shome Expert Committee Final Report on GAAR, September 2012.
390. [2014] 47 taxmann.com 247.
391. Without a fixed ratio there is no reason to consider India.
392. Article 116, BTC; Articles 167(1), 187 Civil Code; Article 72, Law 4502/64, defining shams, abuse of right, tax fraud.
393. Law No. 12, 249/2010, preceded by Articles 24/25, PM 472/09 and NI 1,154, May 2011.

Chapter 4: Countering Avoidance: SAARs

anti-avoidance rules to thin capitalization *(16327.001870)*[394] but the RFB had been unable to convince the CARF to apply the anti-avoidance rule except to artificial financings. In *9101-00287*,[395] the CARF preserved the interest deduction but rather than relying on the 'legality principle' to do so, it relied on the financing being neither a simulation nor because any of the financing steps had been concealed. In preserving the interest deduction in *Colgate v. Kolynos*[396] (2009), the CARF relied on the leverage being a vendor requirement which meant that the borrower had not designed the financing's terms and conditions in a format to give it a tax benefit. In any event, structuring leverage in a form which provides an excessive deduction should not be seen as a tax device in Brazil because interest and dividends ('interest on equity')[397] are both deductible in Brazil, a position supported by *Dib and Piltz*.[398] They argued that 'interest on equity' made debt economically similar to equity. This position conflicts with that of *Rolim*[399] who argued that the interest on equity deduction was not like interest because it was constrained by the interest rate limitation. The rational way of reconciling these views is by agreeing that a thin capitalization rule is unnecessary to counter actual interest up to the interest on equity deduction, which means that *Dib and Piltz* are wrong when the actual interest expense exceeds that amount

Russia introduced the fixed ratio (3:1 for trading groups and 12.5:1 for banks and leasing companies) in 2001 and before then had not restricted interest deductibility for related party loans even though the Central Bank controls were loosened in 1992. Currently there is a requirement for domestic securities issued abroad to first have exchange control approval.

China introduced the fixed ratio (5:1 for financial companies and 2:1 for trading companies) in the 2008 EITL.[400] Before then China had tools[401] to control excess leverage but had little reason to apply them because the available tax incentives for enterprises meant little enterprise tax was paid regardless of the group financing structure adopted. *Dongmeu*[402] argued that this led to an indifference in China between debt and equity financing from a tax perspective to the extent the foreign debt did not

---

394. Decision 16327.001870 / 2001-42, 15 Jun. 2005.
395. Decision 9101-00287; Case No. 16327.001870 / 2001-42; Appeal No. 101-138101; Special Prosecutor, 24 Aug. 2009.
396. Colgate v. Kolynos (2009).
397. At juros sobre o capital próprio, Law 12, 973/2014.
398. Brazilian Thin Capitalization Rules and How Other BRICS Approach the Subject, Bull. Intl. Taxn, 2010 (Volume 64), No. 6, p. 337/338/339; General Report for the 50th IFA Congress, based on the Brazilian National Report of de Camargo; Utumi, Brazil: debt-equity conundrum, IFA Cahiers 2012 – Volume 97B p. 136/139/150/151; Oliveira, Brazil: Taxation of Foreign Passive Income for groups of companies, IFA Cahiers 2013 – Volume 98A, p. 170.
399. Prof Rolim, research conducted for this Thesis.
400. September 2008, MOF/SAT; Cai Shui [2008] No.121 (*Circular 121*); KPMG, China Alert-TP Focus, January 2012, p. 2.
401. Chapter 6, Article 46, *supra* n. 35; before 2008, thincap relied on total investment to registered capital for foreign investment enterprises, debt to registered equity for domestic enterprises and ALS, primarily governing interest rate, Dongmeui, Thin Capitalization Rules in China, Tax Notes Int'l, January 2010, p. 279; deductible interest on non-financial institution loans capped at same rate payable to financial institution, Article 38, EITIR.
402. *Supra* n. 401, at p. 279.

exceed capital subscribed[403], a position not accepted by the LTB in 2002 in *Procter and Gamble*.[404] The LTB partially denied deductions for interest incurred on that locally drawn loan, because the principal had been used to fund an interest free loan granted by the enterprise to a related foreign person. SA introduced the fixed ratio (3:1) in 1995[405] and more recently, both the ALS and the interest limitation.[406] *Hattingh*[407] observed that the fixed ratio had been assumed to represent the ALS, but when SARS[408] agreed to accept ratios other than the 3:1 should they meet the ALS, it indirectly acknowledged that the fixed ratio was not necessarily arm's length. However, adopting the fixed ratio had led to certainty and speed for both SARS and taxpayers: if not accuracy but, unfortunately, certainty was removed in April 2012 when SARS[409] announced the prospective replacement of the fixed ratio with the ALS[410] (effective 31 January 2016).[411] *Mazansky*[412] noted that the confusion amongst taxpayers arising from the deferred implementation of the ALS was compounded by the withdrawal of PN2 (covering thin capitalization) at the same time while the taxpayers continued to use the fixed ratio. Complexity increased because interest deductions were now to be limited[413] to approx. 40% of the borrower's EBITDA, when the debt was owed to foreign creditors holding at least 50% of the borrower's equity, or at least 50% of the

---

403. Article 36, Measures for Pre-Tax Deductions from Enterprise Income Tax, SAT May 2000 applicable to domestic loans while EITL applied to foreign loans. Article 36 repealed by EITL, statement by Miao Huipin, SAT Vice Director, April 2009, http://www.chinatax.gov.cn/n480462/n552873/ n1285478/index.html.
404. Guangzhou Tax Bureau, 2002.
405. Section 31, ITA 58 of 1962; Second Interim Report Katz Commission suggested flexible system but was ignored. Where non-resident granted financial assistance to connected resident or where finance was provided to other non-natural resident persons and lender owned plus 25% of the recipient's voting equity.
406. Section 23M, ITA: interest not exceeding approx. 40% of borrower's EBITDA.
407. *Supra* n. 3, Chapter 8, p. 255.
408. SARS Practice Note 2 (PN2), 14 May 1996.
409. SARS: Draft Interpretation Note (DIN): Determination of Taxable Income of Certain persons from International Transactions: Thin capitalization, http://www.drtp.ca/wp-content/uploads/2015/02/South_Africa_Draft_Thin_Capitalisation.pdf, last visited 1 Jan. 2016, p. 4.
410. Section 31, ITA, 1 Oct. 2011; para. 5, SARS Practice Note 7 (PN7), August 1999, where providing finance was seen as services for section 31 purposes; Dachs, SA, New Thin Capitalization Rules, International Tax Review, August 2014; SARS no longer accepts notional interest allocated to PE as deductible (continues to adopt version 7), OECD Commentary, Kadar, SA issues thin capitalization guidance – U.S. businesses financing SA operations should review compliance https://tax.thomsonreuters.com/wp-content/pdf/transfer-pricing/South-Africa-Issues-Thin-Capitalization-Guidance.pdf; SARS, DIN, *supra* n. 409, para. 9 when computing a PE's chargeable profits; New thincap rules, August 2011 – Issue 144, EY: Rules require functional analysis (DIN, *supra* n. 409, para. 5.2): requiring comparable data, allowing for quantitative and qualitative factors which third-party lenders use when making lending decisions. SARS considers taxpayer thinly capitalized where some of following present: greater interest bearing debt than sustainable in own right, term exceeds arm's length arrangement and repayment term is not arm's-length, considering whether finance provided was debt or equity, the economic substance (DIN, *supra* n. 409, para. 5.3) http://www.saica.co.za/integritax/2011/1983._New_thin_capitlisation_rules.htm.
411. Musviba, Where to with thin capitalization, SA Tax Guide, July 2014, http://www.sataxguide.co.za/where-to-with-thin-capitalisation/ adopted ALS for countering thincap.
412. Hybrid debt and hybrid equity Instruments and the interest limitation rule in SA, Bull. Intl. Taxn, 2015 (Volume 69), No. 3, p. 182.
413. *Supra* n. 404.

voting rights over the borrower's shares, while at the same time the ALS was to apply to the debt. As *Mazansky*[414] observed, SA now had two overlapping regimes seeking to validate the deductibility of related party interest without a hierarchy, which, according to *Oguttu*[415] resulted in SARS having additional options for denying deductions.

4.2.4 Associates

The first step in working out whether, and if so, how much of a taxpayer's deduction for interest is to be denied is to determine whether the interest was paid/accrued to an 'associate' and for this purpose the developed world deems enterprises to be 'associates' where 'one ...... directly or indirectly controls the other or where both .... are directly or indirectly[416] controlled by a third party'.[417] In the BRICS the widening of the meaning of associates, potentially increases the number of financing transactions where deductions can be denied. Adopting the fixed ratio simplifies the management of determining which relationships and which loans are to be scrutinized, which is beneficial for those tax authorities with constrained manpower capacity.

The developed world has not published a firm percentage ownerships which establishes parties as having the requisite 'associate'[418] status but the developed world generally accepts that enterprises having more than 50% common ownership are associates. Enterprises with lower common ownership may still be 'associates' depending on the nature and extent of the participation in the management, control or capital by one enterprise of the other, or by another in both. *Baker*[419] states that this uncertainty leaves 'a number of major issues open for debate' and it is some of these issues which the BRICS sought to clarify by establishing shareholding percentages (each of which is at the lower end of the developed world's scale) and describing fact patterns for other forms of participation (but which would not typically be seen as being 'participation' by the developed world).

With entities being 'associates' for Brazil[420] purposes when the common ownership threshold is as low as 10% and with the entities to which the test is applicable including individuals as well as legal entities, and with 'companions' of company officers or of other individuals or legal entities domiciled in Brazil acting as exclusive agents, distributors or concession holders for the non-resident also included, it seems that almost any non-passive relationship gives rise to associate status in Brazil.

---

414. *Supra* n. 412, at p. 183.
415. Curbing Thin Capitalization: A Comparative Overview with Reference to SA's Approach – Challenges Posed by Amended Section 31, ITA 1962, Bull. Intl. Taxn, 2013 (Volume 67), No. 6, p. 311/312/314/319; Challenges of Taxing Profits Attributed to PEs: A SA Perspective, Bull. Intl. Taxn, 2010 (Volume 64), No. 3, p. 170.
416. *Supra* n. 365, at p. 18.
417. *Ibid.*, at p. 24.
418. Transfer Pricing Guidelines, p. 11, p. 21/371, http://www.keepeek.com/Digital-Asset-Management/oecd/taxation/oecd-transfer-pricing-guidelines-for-multinational-enterprises-and-tax-administrations-2010_tpg-2010-en#.V81hEPkrLIU#page21 and Glossary, p. 23.
419. Double Taxation Conventions, p. 9B.17.
420. Article 23, Law 9430/1996; Article 243(1)/(2), Law No. 6404, 15 Dec. 1996.

Russia establishes a 20% threshold (increased to 25%[421] from 2015) of the borrower's authorized capital. In relation to participation, Russia treats as relevant, the influence[422] which an individual has on a company's behaviour[423] where the individual is an employee. It also treats as being relevant, structural relationships including counterparties resident in a Russian SEZ[424] (reflecting *Yukos*) where subject to special tax regimes[425] or entities having aggregate annual tainted turnover exceeding R100m. These widen the relationships which are associates. From 2015 'sister' companies (within the meaning of *Naryanmarneftegas*)[426] are also 'associates'. With Russia excluding from associate status a Russian PE[427] of a foreign legal entity[428] or the entity's debt other than the amount outstanding on the last day of the Accounting Period,[429] it narrows the entity or debt amount subject to the rule. The object behind clarifying the structural relationships which were 'participation' in Russia was to dispel scholarly[430] uncertainty arising from many sources, such as *Letter No.03-01-18/38106-2013*[431] that individuals were excluded from 'associate' status, even though the law included them. This was also the reason for the *MOF*[432] extending associate status to Russian resident (but foreign affiliated) lenders guaranteed by third Russian residents even though there was statutory support[433] for it doing so but that support had not been applied. The *MOF's* position on the guarantee was subsequently confirmed in *Distillery Topaz*.[434]

---

421. PwC, Tax Flash Report, Upcoming changes in thincap rules, February 2015 / Issue No. 3, Amendments to Article 269, RTC regarding controlled debt definition, Bill No. 675906-6.
422. Section 2(2)(b) refers to one party possessing the practical ability to control the business decisions of the other, *supra* n. 365.
423. MOF Letter, 22 Apr. 2010 N 03-02-07/1-182.
424. MOF Letter No. 03-01-18/38106; Federal Law No. 379-FZ, 29 Nov. 2014.
425. Unified tax on imputed income or agricultural tax regime.
426. Letter 22 Jun. 2015 No. 4-3/10807; Confirmed in May 2014 Revised Draft RTC, withdrawn in October 2014 and reinstated in 2015 draft RTC but already legally treated as associate because it had been MOF's (Letter No. 03-08-05/9669, 6 May 2014) position from 2014.
427. Russian real estate usually owned by PEs rather than Russian company.
428. Bruk, debt to equity Conundrum, Cahiers- Volume 97b, 2012, p. 622; Sychev, Russia, Derivs. & Fin. Instrums, 2013 (Volume 15), No. 5a/Special Issue, pp. 82, 83; Bruk, Russia Supreme Arbitration Court Adopts 'Disregard of Legal Entity' Approach to Combat Tax Fraud, Eur. Taxn, 2010 (Volume 50), No. 12, p. 573; Bruk, Russian Thin Capitalization Rules: Are They Compatible with Russian Tax Treaties?, Eur. Taxn, 2010 (Volume 50), No. 11, p. 506/508/509; Bruk, The taxation of foreign passive income for groups of companies – Russia, IFA Cahiers 2013 – Volume 98A, p. 638.
429. Section 269(2) RTC.
430. Veter, Russia New TP Rules, ITPJ, 2011 (Volume 18), No. 5; Gotovtseva, Russia New Rules on Allocation of Profits to PE in Russia: Threat or Opportunity? ITPJ, 2012 (Volume 19), No. 6, p. 458; Vakhitov, Non-Discrimination at the crossroads of International Taxation – Russia, Cahiers 2008 – Volume 93A, p. 517; Bruk, Tax Treaties and tax avoidance, *supra* n. 246, p. 692; *supra* n. 428, p. 640/642; Vinnitsky, *supra* n. 3, p. 102.
431. MOF excluding transactions entered into by individuals with corporates even though law establishes transactions as 'controlled'.
432. MOF Letter No. 03-08-05/23521-2013.
433. Law No. 58-FZ, 6 Jun. 2005 provides that relationship to be 'controlled'.
434. AP-58460/2014, January 2015.

China's[435] 25% threshold is also at the lower end of the developed world scale and in relation to indirect[436] voting interest holdings, a China enterprise is deemed to have a 100% ownership when the direct holding exceeds 25%.[437] China widens the other forms of participation giving rise to associate status by including situations in which one enterprise controls the appointment of senior executives (including senior managers[438]) of the other, or where senior managers of one enterprise act as the senior managers of the other.[439] It also treats entities as being associates when the lender to one enterprise receives 10% (or more) of the borrower's shares as security for the finance[440] or where a non-resident provides an arm's length loan to fund unpaid share capital.[441] A decision covering the latter situation is to be found in *Shaanxi*[442] where a LTB held the enterprises to be associates because while one continued to incur China losses the other foreign enterprise continued to provide share capital to fund them. China also treats enterprises as associates when the business operations (including production) of one enterprise are unable to function without using IP provided by the other, or where the proprietary knowledge of one enterprise or labour controlled by one enterprise, is also used by the other.[443]

SA's 20% threshold is also at the low end of the developed world's scale and its applicability to close companies[444] regardless of the putative associate's voting rights[445] further widens the meaning. By including persons as associates when they are neither named in a Trust Deed nor having had income or gains appointed to them by the Trustee but are named as contingent beneficiaries in a 'Letter of Wishes', it widens associate status to persons who are potentially discretionary trust beneficiaries.

The author concludes in this subsection that the BRICS both lower the threshold at which participating in capital constitutes 'associate' status and that by including a wider range of commercial arrangements which qualify as 'participation in

---

435. Article 109, REIT; Article 51, Tax Collection Law Implementation Rules; Related Party Transaction Forms under Guoshuifa (2008) No. 114, December 2008; Implementation Requirements on 2008 Annual Reporting Forms for Related Parties Transactions, Guoshuihan [2009] No. 72, February 2009; Treated as 'round tripping' counter: DeSouza, Structuring an Appropriate TP Policy, Asia-Pac. Tax Bull July/August 2008.
436. Unrelated third party or where unrelated party loan was guaranteed by related party or where finance which 'in substance' was debt was indirectly provided: Chen, Financing: a global survey of thincap and TP rules in 35 selected countries: China, International TP Journal, November/December 2008, p. 297, Article 119, EITL.
437. Article(9)(1), *supra* n. 200, http://www.kpmg.com/CN/en/IssuesAndInsights/Articles Publications/Documents/special-tax-adjustements.pdf.
438. General Director, Vice-General Manager, in charge of business sections or staff, Chapter 1(E), SAT Draft Implementation Measures, 17 Sep. 2015.
439. Article(9)(3)/(4), *supra* n. 200.
440. Article(9)(2), *supra* n. 200.
441. Guoshuihan [2009] No. 312, Notice Regarding Pre-tax Deduction of Asset Losses,' 4 Jun. 2009; Guoshuihan [2009] No. 777; SAT Ruling, June 2009 [2009] No. 68.
442. *2011*.
443. Article (9)(7), *supra* n. 200.
444. Section 1(a)(4)(d)(vi), IN No. 67, November 2012.
445. Section 1(a)(d)(4), IN: No. 67, *supra* n. 444.

management or control', the consequence is that the rules apply to a wider range of relationships than would be the case were the BRICS to apply the developed world's associate definition.

4.2.5 Hybrids and Thin Capitalization

The developed world defines debt[446] and equity[447] very broadly for thin capitalization purposes and when determining whether a financing relationship is debt it generally applies 'substance over form'. This is not the situation in the BRICS, except for China and SA, which have published rules determining whether a financing is to be treated as debt or equity.

Brazil treats hybrid debt as debt for tax purposes because it is debt for GAAP purposes. This position was published in a 2015 *Private Letter Ruling*,[448] and later confirmed by *Monteiro*.[449] Itis to be contrasted with the earlier Spanish decision *(No. 232/2011)*[450] which held that payments on *Juros* were dividends for Spanish purposes because under Brazil's mercantile, accounting and tax laws (Article 9, Federal Law No. 9249, 26 December 1995), *Juros* are equity for Brazilian purposes. This decision was later distinguished by the Brazilian Supreme Court in *Refinaria de Petróleo Ipiranga*[451] when it held that interest on equity was financial income, potentially giving rise to a hybrid status. In Russia, as *Bruk* and *KPMG*[452] confirm, without legislation reclassifying interest on hybrid debt as dividends, the interest remains as interest for taxation purposes. However, it is arguable that where the substance of a hybrid loan is different from the form (as it surely would be) that the 'unjustified tax benefit' concept could apply to deny a deduction for the interest expense, but this is yet to be clarified in Russia.

China and SA are alive to the tax consequences of hybrid debt and have published positions. With China having developed an interest in both 'substance over form' and 'economic and business' purpose since 2008, as discussed in Chapter 3 of this study, it was not surprising that *Gong Gao [2013] No. 41*[453] listed the features[454] to be used when determining whether a financing was debt or equity. A review of *Circular 41* confirms the factors are generally aligned with those of the developed world. In practice, China

---

446. Loans, financial instruments, finance leases, financial derivatives, arrangements giving rise to interest, discounts or other charges deductible for taxable profit purposes; *supra* n. 365, p. 24.
447. Share capital, capital contributions, retained profits, interest free loans, revaluation reserves; *supra* n. 365, p. 14.
448. Private Letter Ruling 159/2015.
449. Brazilian Thin Capitalization Rules and Tax Treaties: A Critical Approach, Bull. Intl. Taxn, 2015 (Volume 69), No. 11.
450. 27 Feb. 2014.
451. Refinaria de Petróleo Ipiranga S/A, REsp *1.200.492*, 14 Oct. 2015.
452. The debt equity conundrum, IFA Cahiers 2012-Volume 97B p. 628; Taxation of Cross-Border Mergers and Acquisition, https://home.kpmg.com/content/dam/kpmg/pdf/2014/05/russia-2014.pdf, p. 8.
453. Gong Gao [2013] No. 41, Jul. 2013.
454. Interest paid periodically, specific term, obligation to redeem, investor has neither ownership in the borrower's net assets nor voting rights and cannot participate in company's ordinary activities.

applies *Circular 41* widely as was evident in *Shaanxi*[455] and in the Ruling of June 2009 [2009] No. 68 where SAT denied deductions for interest on loans financing an enterprise's called up but unpaid share capital. The *SA National Treasury*[456] has listed the features which determine whether a financing is debt or equity for tax purposes. As *Mazansky*[457] observed, the listing results in interest payable on non-redeemable debt, debt convertible into shares (at the issuer's request), debt with yields not interest-related and debt with repayment terms or yields conditional on the issuer's solvency, being treated as dividends both for the issuer and investor with the payment not being tax deductible to the issuer. Reflecting international trends, regulatory hybrid debt, such as Tier II Bank issuances and long-term subordinated hybrid debt are not reclassified as equity and therefore the payments are tax deductible to the issuer.

4.2.6 Lender's Residence

The OECD[458] does not consider the lender's country of tax residence to be relevant when determining whether the thin capitalization rules apply (but does consider it relevant for WHT purposes) even if the place of residence offers attractive tax incentives to the lender. The developed world's position is to be contrasted with that of Brazil[459] and SA, because they treat the lender's residence as being relevant. In Brazil's case, even for non-associated lenders, where a lender is tax resident in a tax preferred jurisdiction[460] (corporate rate less than 20%, now 17%)[461] it is liable to the higher 25% WHT on interest expense and the interest deductibility is limited when the borrower's indebtedness to all tax preferred jurisdiction lenders exceeds 30% of its aggregate equity. The lender's country of tax residence [462] is not always punitive, such as where a domestic loan is guaranteed by a Brazil resident which is associated with a non-resident. In SA's case, there is a widening of the deductibility limitation when the lender is neither 'subject to tax' in its country of residence nor when the interest expense is included in an SA controlled foreign company's (CFC)[463] net income. The introduction in SA of interest WHT from January 2015 will in the author's opinion, mean that the interest is 'subject to tax' so that it will not matter that the interest is not subject to a CFC attribution for SA purposes. The consequence of this should be that the

---

455. 2011.
456. SA National Treasury, Request for Public comment for Incorporation into Forthcoming 2013 Tax laws Amendment Bill: Proposed limitations against Excessive Interest Deductions, 29 Apr. 2013, p. 2.
457. Hybrid debt and hybrid equity instruments and the interest limitation rule in SA, Bull. Intl. Taxn, 2015, Volume 69, No. 3.
458. *Supra* n. 365, at p. 3.
459. Article 25, PM No. 472, 15 Dec. 2009: Sections 24/ 25, Law 12,249/2010.
460. PM 22, 2000; Normative Instruction 1,037/2010.
461. Ordinance 488/2014, 4 Dec. 2014, *supra* n. 160.
462. Normative Instruction 1,154/2011.
463. Section 23M https://www.saica.co.za/integritax/2015/2395._Thin_capitalisation_and_section_23M.htm; Treasury argued change has broader objective than thincap which only determines debt pricing.

interest will not be subject to the interest limitation rule in SA which means the full deduction for the interest will not be disturbed by the limitation rule, a position supported by *Rood*.[464]

4.2.7 Safe Harbours

Until recently, the OECD[465] saw little merit in including safe harbours in the thin capitalization[466] rules but as *Feinschreiber*[467] has asserted there was much merit in the simplicity and certainty they offered for limited capacity tax authorities. The BRICS, except for China, have adopted safe harbours and with the Brazil, Russia and SA safe harbours depending neither on the borrower being small, nor on the situation being complex, they therefore do not confine the simplification to MNE groups which facilitates administration for undermanned tax authorities.

Brazil's safe harbour for loans drawn down before 31 December 2012 was a simple registration with the Central Bank, while the interest deductibility on loans not registered with the Central Bank was confined to interest calculated by using the LIBOR dollar rate for six-month loans plus a 3% pa margin. For loans drawn down from 1 January 2013, regardless of registration, the safe harbour depended on the lending currency. When the loan was advanced in $US, it was the LIBOR dollar rate plus a spread determined by the *MOF*. Russia's initial safe harbour was set at a spread of 20% either side of a comparable loan rate[468] which made it very generous. When it was extended in December 2012 for non-comparable loans to the Central Bank refunding rate (8.25% at December 2012) adjusted by 1.8 for rouble debt and 0.8 for other currencies,[469] it became complex to administer. The January 2015[470] variation to substitute a 'key rate' for the Central Bank rate led to a further option being available which gave rise to increased complexity. With the comparable loan basis requiring the completion of a TP study to be acceptable, (even for small-scale loans), as *Baker and Mckenzie*[471] observed, this resulted in further uncertainty for both the tax administrations and taxpayers, which of course was what safe harbours were intended to avoid.

---

464. Rood, Werksmens Attorneys, EBulletin, September 2014, http://www.werksmans.com/virt_e_bulletins/new-interest-limitation-rules-non-resident-creditor-subject-tax/.
465. *Supra* n. 365; Revised Section E on Safe Harbours in Chapter IV of Transfer Pricing Guidelines, 16 May 2013.
466. Transfer Pricing Guidelines, section A, para. 4.9.4; section E2, 4.100, which for a defined category of taxpayers or transactions avoid the TP rules through simplified administration or exempting a category of taxpayers or transactions. One consequence is compliance relief from documentation rules benefiting from certainty and administrative simplicity, especially for small taxpayers and others with less complex situations. The fixed ratio could be a safe harbour for those countries asserting the ratio to be a representation of the ALS.
467. Updating the OECD's Safe Harbour TP Provisions, http://www.oecd.org/tax/transfer-pricing/48330739.pdf.
468. Section 269(1) RTC; Vinnitskiy, Thin Capitalisation Rules and Non-Discrimination Clause, Chapter 28, p. 1/16.
469. Section 269(1) RTC.
470. Law No. 32-FZ, 8 Mar. 2015; Letter No. 03-03-06/1/46209, 11 Aug. 2015.
471. Tax Russia-Legal Alert, March 2015.

SA's safe harbour which was set at the prime rate or an interbank rate plus a 2% margin[472] was straightforward but when the 30%[473] interest limitation was introduced, this gave rise to uncertainty.

4.2.8 Exemptions

The OECD does not recommend members provide exemptions from the ALS for thin capitalization purposes, while the BRICS, other than Brazil, have provided them. However, while they exist in the BRICS they are of limited usefulness, except possibly for the SA exemption. Russia exempts 'back to back' loans granted by arm's length Russian banks where the deposited security with the Russian bank represents not less than 50% by value of the loan principal,[474] which as the author argues is intended to drive business to Russian banks. According to the MOF, thin capitalization is exempted from the ALS because the ALS applies to the supply of 'goods or services'[475] and loans involve the granting of finance rather than the supply of goods or services. China exempts domestic loans except for loans drawn down by borrowers having an effective tax rate greater than the lender's effective tax rate.[476] This carve to the exemptions is designed to limit the exemption's effectiveness China also exempts loans advanced by non-resident lenders where the borrower has satisfied the China tax authority that its actual ratio (even if exceeding the fixed ratio)[477] is compatible with the ALS. *Jinyan Li*[478] asserts that this process leaves the exemption having limited effectiveness while *DeSouza*[479] adopts the contrary view on grounds of the exemption being a taxpayer protection. In the SAT requiring the enterprise to self-certify its leverage level through completing detailed documentation,[480] it effectively outsources the administration of its thin capitalization rules to the enterprise in order to compensate for the limited capacity tax authority. SA's exemptions are driven by its domestic policy of encouraging SA's position as a regional investment hub for providing funding into southern Africa. SA has two exemptions, the first applicable for interest payable on loans drawn down to finance an OHQ entity investment providing the funding was invested (directly or indirectly) into qualifying shares[481] while the second is for interest payable

---

472. SA prime rate weighted average for rand loans, weighted average of relevant interbank rate for foreign currency loans.
473. SA National Treasury, Request for Public comment, *supra* n. 456, p. 6.
474. Bill No. 675906-6, Amending Part Two, RTC.
475. MOF March 2007.
476. Caishui [2008] No. 121.
477. Interest, guarantees or mortgage fees or other expenses in nature of interest: Article 87, *supra* n. 200.
478. Brief overview of Chinese thin-capitalization rules, August, 2011, http://www.taxindiainternational.com/columnDesc.php?qwer43fcxzt=NTQ=.
479. Structuring an Appropriate TP Policy, *supra* n. 435, p. 311.
480. Ability to repay; financing applications; registered capital movements; nature/purposes of debt and market conditions; currency, amount, interest rate, term; security and guarantees, comparable interest rates, convertible terms and other documents confirming debt to be arm's length: Article 89/90, *supra* n. 200; Thin capitalisation, *supra* n. 401, p. 287.
481. Least 10% of equity shares and voting rights (*supra* n. 409, para. 10.1/13) of foreign company.

on loans drawn down to finance highly taxed controlled foreign companies.[482] The author concludes the BRICS exemptions are intended to facilitate tax authority administration of the rules bearing in mind the level of manning within the tax authorities.

4.2.9 Excess Interest: Deemed Dividend

The OECD does not recommend how the non-deductible interest should be dealt with but in practice it is treated as interest rather than equity[483] and liable to interest WHT rather than dividend WHT, although this is not a universally agreed practice. This study reveals that the BRICS treat the excess in the manner best facilitating their charging and collection of additional taxation. Brazil treats the excess as interest liable to interest WHT and that means that tax is levied at the 15% or 25% WHT rate when WHT could not be charged if the excess were dividends because Brazil does not levy WHT on dividends. Russia treats the excess as dividends[484] and taxes it at the 15% WHT[485] or lower DTC rate which raises more tax because Russia's dividend WHT rate is generally greater than its interest[486] WHT rates. China re-characterizes *(Circular 2)*[487] the excess into dividends[488] and applies the CIT to the excess but does not refund any of that CIT[489] should there ultimately be no or lesser tax payable in China than that deductible under the CIT.[490] The author's theory is that China pursues this approach because the dividend WHT rates to be found in China's bilateral DTCs with the major providers of inbound FDI,[491] are generally less than the interest WHT rates levied under those DTCs. SA treated the excess as a dividend liable to the 10% STC until 2012 (when dividend WHT was introduced) and from then has treated the excess as a dividend liable to the 15% DWT.[492] Were the excess to have remained interest then no WHT would have been levied in SA because at that juncture SA did not impose IWT.[493] With dividend and interest WHT both now deducted at 15%, SARS should be indifferent between treating the excess as dividends or interest for WHT purposes, except for

---

482. *Supra* n. 409, at para. 11.
483. Commentary, Article 11(6), para. 79, *supra* n. 124.
484. Section 269(4); MOF Letter No. 03-08-05, December 2009; MOF Letter No. 03-03-06/1/435, July 2009. Foreign lenders can access DTC rates but Russia's DTCs do not override the RTC treating excess as dividends.
485. Section 269(4) and 284(3) RTC; Federal Law No. 25-FZ, 12 Feb. 2016.
486. Dividend/Interest WHT rates for major investor countries: Dividend WHT first: Austria (5/0); Cyprus (5/0); France (5/10-0); Germany (5/0); Luxembourg (10/0); Netherlands (5/0); UK (10/0); US (5/0).
487. Article 88, *supra* n. 200.
488. *Ibid.*
489. *Ibid.*
490. *Ibid.*
491. Dividend WHT first: HK (5/7); BVI (10/10); Japan (10/10); Singapore (5/7-10).
492. Section 31(3): Tax on dividends to shareholders declared/paid from 1 Apr. 2012 and STC on dividends declared before 1 Apr. 2012, regardless of payment date.
493. Introduced March 2015.

lenders tax resident in developed countries[494] (or in intermediate countries)[495] where SA would prefer treating the excess as dividends because the dividend WHT rates are generally higher than the interest WHT rates. With *SARS*[496] now treating the excess as a loan subject to TP adjustments, CIT will be payable each year on the deemed interest instead of a one-off WHT liability which likely increases the SA tax take.

4.2.10 Treaty Override

This subsection discusses whether the BRICS DTCs override their thin capitalization rules. A fundamental function of a DTC is the allocation of the right to tax income or profits between the contracting states covered by the bilateral DTC. That allocation requires an interpretation of the DTC's terms which, can be a complicated procedure, because of the necessity to first apply domestic tax law and then second, consider the international law. The allocation of the taxing right also involves interpreting provisions in the bilateral DTC itself and doing this may require relying on Article 3(2) of the DTC[497] to determine which contracting state's definition is to be used. This procedure may lead to the bilateral DTC overriding the domestic taxing provision ('DTC override') even if the right to make that override is not specifically mentioned in the DTC. Each of the BRICS provides for their bilateral DTCs to override the domestic tax law provisions to the extent of a conflict, a principle further discussed in later pages.

Public international law assists the parties in interpreting the provisions of a bilateral DTC and for this purpose, the *Vienna Convention*, which establishes that treaties are to be interpreted in 'good faith' (*pacta sunt servanda*), without retroactivity and with the benefit of general and supplementary provisions and materials[498] is helpful. *Engelen*[499] confirms this in detail in his well thought through Doctoral thesis. As *Vogel*[500] also explains, interpreting bilateral DTCs based on the *OECD Model Convention* is facilitated through using materials published by the OECD as to do so supports the Principle of Common Interpretation.[501]

The principle of non-discrimination (ND) is generally found in modern form bilateral DTCs[502] and while the developed world believes that a bilateral DTC's ND

---

494. Dividend WHT rate first: France (5/0), Germany (7.5/0), Netherlands (5/0), UK (5/0) and US (5/0).
495. Dividend WHT first: Mauritius (5/0); Seychelles (5/0).
496. *Supra* n. 409, at para. 6.2; Deloitte, 'SA TP: the new thin cap rules – an ongoing area of uncertainty', February 2014.
497. Article 3(2) provides for a DTC Article to be interpreted in accordance with the meaning of the concept in the State applying the provision when the parties to the DTC conflict in their interpretation.
498. Articles 31 and 32.
499. Interpretation of Tax Treaties under International law, IBFD Volume 7 Doctoral Series, 2004.
500. Double Tax Treaties and Their Interpretation, 4 Int'l Tax & Bus. Law 1 (1986) p. 37.
501. Scott, Codified Canons and the Common Law of Interpretation, The Georgetown Law Journal, Volume 98, 341/430.
502. Article 11(6), para. 32/36, *supra* n. 483.

Article should not provide for an override of the thin capitalization rules,[503] it is not to say that the ND Article may not override those rules as *Baker*[504] explains, and as the Court in *SA Andritz*[505] confirms. Sometimes the ND Article[506] in the DTC (or indeed in a Protocol) directly provides for it not to override an application of the thin capitalization rule while in other DTCs that position is arrived at indirectly by the ND Article being prevented from overriding the application of a domestic anti-avoidance provision, assuming that thin capitalization rule is such an anti-avoidance rule. The author returns to consider in later paragraphs whether the thin capitalization rule is a piece of anti-avoidance legislation.

While the BRICS generally do not provide for the ND Article in their bilateral DTCs to override the thin capitalization rule, there are limited instances where it does. Brazil provides neither a specific practice nor precedent for allowing the ND Article override while the Russian judiciary had for many years applied the override directly or indirectly, by adopting a specific provision in a bilateral DTC (or in a Protocol) to override the rule. One such example was *Swedwood Tikhvin*[507] where the Court held the interest to be fully deductible (even though the debt exceeded the fixed ratio) because the Protocol to *Russia/Netherlands* DTC provided for the interest to be deductible. The override was also applied in *A26-6967*[508] under the *Finland/Russia* DTC and in *KA40 / 9453-09-2*[509] under the *Cyprus/Russia* DTC. The *Severny Kuzbass*[510] decision under the Russia/Cyprus bilateral DTC reversed the override and, as *Wilson*[511] observed, represented a watershed in Russian tax jurisprudence. Subsequent decisions of the lower Regional Commercial Courts were, as observed by *Alexandrova*[512] influenced by *Severny Kuzbass* so that by the time *Aluplast*,[513] was decided, the override of the thin capitalization rule by the ND Article had finally been stopped. The grounds in *Aluplast* for the decision was that the thin capitalization rule was an anti-avoidance rule even though the *German/Russian* DTC Protocol specifically provided that the interest in such situations would be deductible. The Russian approach of the ND Article not overriding the thin capitalization rule is now aligned with the OECD[514] notwithstanding that many of Russia's bilateral DTCs and Protocols contain provisions which conclude to the contrary. China's DTCs generally do not provide for

---

503. Whether it applies to excess interest determined by the ratio instead of ALS is questionable because excess interest arises from a formula rather than from a special relationship. 11B-16, *supra* n. 419 raises the question but does not comment.
504. *Supra* n. 503, 24B.25.
505. SA Andritz, Case No. 233,894, 6 ILTR, 604, 2004.
506. Article 24(6), para. 73/74, potentially inapplicable where country has non-resident rules but not resident rules, *supra* n. 483.
507. A56-19578, Swedwood Tikhvin, April 2007.
508. A26-6967, September 2009.
509. KA40 / 9453-09-2, September 2009.
510. A27-7455/2010, November 2011, Northern Kuzbass, 15 Nov. 2011, No. 8654/11.
511. *Supra* n. 66, Part II p. 3.
512. Alexandrova, Tax Discrimination Against Foreign Investors in Russia, Newsletter-TerraLex Connections, http://www.terralex.org/publication/57939f6942, March 2012.
513. Case A41-21630, Aluplast, September 2014.
514. OECD Model Commentary Article 24(4), para. 74.

the ND Article to override the rule with the *China/Portugal*[515] Protocol in particular, specifically providing for the thin capitalization rule not to be overridden by the ND Article. Since SA's DTCs and Protocols do not contain an ND Article, a ND override of the thin capitalization rule on that basis is not possible.

4.2.11 Thin Capitalization: Anti-avoidance Rule?

The developed world asserts that provisions within bilateral DTCs should not overrule domestic anti-avoidance provisions and it suggests that thin capitalization is one such provision. Procedurally this analysis is made under Article 3(2) of the Model DTC.[516]

This subsection investigates whether the BRICS regard thin capitalization rules as an anti-avoidance provision and the outcome of this research is important for those DTCs which provide that domestic anti-avoidance provisions cannot to be overridden by a DTC provision. The author has conclude that Brazil and Russia do not have an 'avoidance' concept, because in Brazil's case the 'legality principle' is superior to 'substance over form' and misusing loopholes while in Russia's case, 'avoidance' essentially refers to administrative breaches with other abuse constituting evasion. The author therefore deduces that traditional thin capitalization cannot amount to avoidance in Brazil or in Russia. China and SA both treat transactions, structures or behaviour devoid of a 'reasonable business purpose' or involving misusing loopholes as avoidance. For this reason, the author deduces that traditional thin capitalization cannot be 'avoidance' in China or in SA where the financing form and terms exhibit a reasonable business purpose for the excess leverage or where the fixed ratio is not a loophole within the definitions of the respective countries' GAARs. Therefore, where an ND Article in a BRICS bilateral DTC overrides an application of the thin capitalization rule which has denied a deduction for excess interest under the fixed ratio, then in the BRICS, this ND override cannot be reversed where the DTC saves for an anti-avoidance provision (because the rule is not an anti-avoidance provision), except when the excess leverage is subject to either China or SA's GAAR.

4.2.12 Thin Capitalization and GAAR

This subsection studies whether GAAR would save the rule where an ND Article in a DTC would otherwise apply to override a country's application of its thin capitalization rule. While Brazil's GAAR[517] remains ineffective it cannot constitute an anti-avoidance provision to save the rule and although Russia's 'unjustified tax benefit' concept is a GAAR it is designed to counter evasion rather than avoidance and for that reason should not save in Russia except where a Russian bilateral DTC or Protocol saves for evasion. Also both China and SA's GAARs would not likely counter thin capitalization where the excess leverage was commercially justified and providing the main purpose

---

515. Zhu, Europe-China DTCs, Kluwer 2010, p. 256.
516. Article 3(2), para. 11, *supra* n. 514; *supra* n. 499, p. 477.
517. Article 116, National Tax Code.

for the excess leverage was the obtaining of finance for use in the business and not the obtaining of tax benefits. However, should the excess leverage transaction create rights not normally attributable to parties in arm's length transactions, then the GAAR would likely save the thin capitalization rules in China and SA. For these reasons, the author concludes that the probability of the BRICS' GAARs saving the rule when faced with an ND Article override is not axiomatic and he also further concludes that in his opinion the Russian cases overriding the ND Article were wrongly decided except for those cases where the relevant bilateral DTC or Protocol save specifically for the rule.

4.2.13 BRICS DTCs: Affirmative Savings

In the immediately preceding subsection, it was concluded that unless a DTC affirmatively saves for the rule, grounds exist for an ND Article which counters the thin capitalization rule not to be overridden, certainly in the Brazil and Russia DTCs, and subject to the facts in the China and SA DTCs. Based on the author's research, it can be concluded that a limited group of DTCs entered into by Brazil,[518] Russia,[519] China[520] and SA[521] provide a specific saving to counter the override. In China's[522] case, the DTC which specifically saves for 'special adjustments', would also save for thin capitalization because thin capitalization is such an adjustment. The author also concludes that the DTCs entered into by Russia,[523] China[524] and SA[525] which save for an 'avoidance' rule would not likely be effective. Additionally, he concludes that where the DTCs[526] entered into by China save for avoidance or evasion and the DTCs[527] entered into by Brazil save for evasion or treaty abuse, each of those DTCs would be ineffective because thin capitalization is neither evasion nor treaty abuse. In relation to GAAR, this study has not identified any BRICS bilateral DTC which save for GAAR.

4.2.14 BRICS and Coordination

The author's research found no evidence of the BRICS coordinating the shaping of their thin capitalization rules.

4.2.15 Thin Capitalization: Significance of Widening the Rules

The author concludes that the BRICS have widened the group of relationships constituting 'associate' and deduced from this conclusion that the widening allows the

---

518. SA (2003P), Turkey (2010P), Peru (2006P), Venezuela (2005P), Russia (2004NR), Israel (2002).
519. Malta (2013P), Italy (2009P), Brazil (2004NR), Portugal (2000), Spain (1998P).
520. Mexico (2005).
521. Brazil (2003P).
522. Switzerland (2013).
523. HK (2016).
524. HK(2015), Belgium (2009), Botswana (2012), Malta (2010), Singapore (2007), Finland (2010).
525. HK (2014).
526. Germany (2014), Bahrain (2013), Netherlands (2013), UK (2011), Denmark (2012), Barbados (2010P), Czech (2009).
527. Venezuela (2005), Russia (2004NR), Israel (2002), Chile (2001P).

BRICS to apply the 'fixed' ratio test to a wider group of lending transactions, which likely means that they can raise additional taxation. This conclusion is supported by their deeming the excess interest to either be a dividend, interest or an additional loan depending upon which results in the greater tax take. The author has also concluded that the BRICS have de-emphasized the importance of the tax based thin capitalization rules because their exchange controls continue to perform a supervisory function.

In relation to simplicity and certainty, the BRICS continued adoption of the fixed ratio recognizes the benefit for both taxpayers and the tax administration as does their application of safe harbours, but because the exchange control authorities continue to review in-bound related party loans, the necessity for the tax authorities to deal with the base erosion consequences of thin capitalization is less significant.

With India neither introducing a fixed asset ratio nor having an effective ALS for countering thin capitalization, the importance to India of exchange controls is elevated as is the need that other SAARs can counter the abuse.

4.3 TRANSFER PRICING

4.3.1 Background

This subsection focuses on whether the BRICS TP[528] procedures have been widened from those of the developed world[529] and if so, whether that widening is in response to

---

528. *Brazil*: Law 9, 430/96 Articles 18/24 and 28, modified by Law 9.959/2000, Law 10.451/2002, Law 11.727/2008, PM478/2009, PM 563/2012, converted into Law 12.715; NI 243/02; *Russia*: Central Bank limited corporate outbound FDI and capped personal FDI at US$75,000pa pre liberalization; Article 20/40, RTC, Law No. 227 – FZ, effective 1 Jan. 2012; *India*: Post liberalization applied section 92, ITA which apportioned profits using 'close connection' test established in Anglo-French Textile Co. Ltd v. Commissioner Of Income-Tax,1953 AIR 105; section 92A /92F, ITA and section 10A/10E, Income Tax Rules, Circular 14, 2001, issued by CBDT; *China*: Shenzhen 1988 temporary regulations for transactions with SEZ associates; 1990 Provisional Regulations; Article 13, FEITL; Article 52/58, FEITL Regulations applying 'fair price' from independent enterprises in same/similar transactions adjusted for reasonable costs/actual margins on non-connected transactions, management fees from foreign-invested enterprises to foreign associates disallowed except for expenditures deductible under different provisions. 1991 Regulations require documentation based on 'same dealings' with independent enterprises, Article 41(1) EITL 2008; Guo Shui Fa 237, 29 Oct. 1992; Tax Administration Rules and Procedures for Transactions between Associated Enterprises (Trial)-TP Circular (Guo Shui Fa) [1998] No. 59; Detailed Implementation Regulations, Administrative Regulations on Special Tax Adjustments; Yuan, China TP Under the New law, PwC, Shanghai, http://www.pwchk.com/webmedia/doc/633281271237582380_tp_cit_law_aug2007.pdf, p. 3;SAT, Implementation Measures for Special Tax Adjustments, October 2015; SAT, Announcement No. 16, 2015; *SA* section 31, ITA 1962, ALS for international disposals of goods/commodities only (Lategan, TP in the absence of comparable market prices, SA, IFA Cahiers 1992 – Volume 77a.p. 585) between related persons on basis equivalent to Article 9, DTC and denied deductions for 'grossly' excessive expenditure, section 103(1) ITA 1962 (*ITC 569 13 SATC 447*) or deemed donation rule, section 58, ITA 1962 (Tobacco Father v. CoT 17 SATC 39513); SARS PN2, *supra* n. 408.
529. Transfer Pricing Guidelines; September 2009 Draft revised Chapters I-III TPG-CFA response to comments received (2010);September 2008 discussion draft TP aspects of business restructuring-CFA response to comments received (2010); Transactional Profit Split methods-discussion draft (2008); Comparability Issues: series of draft issue notes- Public Invitation to

TP[530] having been identified as the major device facilitating the substantial illicit outflow of funds from the BRICS or whether the divergences reflect a UN[531] influence on the BRICS or arise from cooperation amongst the BRICS. Also studied is whether the divergences are a consequence of the BRICS treating mispriced transactions as evasion and a response to problems faced by the limited tax authority manpower in identifying, investigating and prosecuting mispriced transactions.

The author has identified that the BRICS TP rules have much in common[532] with, and many divergences from the developed world's core TP rules and he has also concluded that the BRICS tax authorities have identified a need to widen the rules.[533] The author has also concluded, rationally, that the need to widen the rules in the BRICS has arisen from a realisation by the tax authorities of the substantial number of mispriced transactions having been entered into, the volumes involved, the differing commercial facts and circumstances[534] and their limited manpower numbers to counter the abuse. He has also concluded that rationally, these factors have helped to shape the format of the divergences.

---

comment (2006); Paper on TP Methods (2010); Paper on Arm's Length Range (2010); Paper on Location Savings (2010); Paper on Comparability Adjustments (2010); Timing issues relating to TP-WP6, request for comments (2012);White Paper on TP Documentation- for public consultation (2013); July 2013 revised discussion draft on TP aspects of Intangibles – for public comment (2013); Paper on TP Legislation (2013); Handbook on TP Risk assessment- draft, for public consultation (2013); OECD Model Convention (2014); Integrated texts of the OECD Commentaries of 1997/2014.

530. *Supra* n. 31; Vakhitov, Recent Developments Regarding Judicial Anti-Tax Avoidance in Russia, Eur. Taxn, April 2005, p. 163, Matchekhin, Trends in company shareholder taxation: single or double taxation? – Russia, IFA Cahiers 2003 – Volume 88a, p. 767.
531. Practice Manual on TP for Developing Countries (2013); Model Tax Convention between Developed and Developing countries (1980/2011).
532. Vinnitskiy, p. 102/103, *supra* n. 3; Linklaters, May 2003, TP Rules, Practice, and Potential Development; A03104480/0.0/19 May 2003, p. 5; Akchurina, FBK Lawyers, http://fbk-legal.com/services_rule/transfertnoe-tsenoobrazovanie/; SARS confirms OECD Guidelines should be followed in absence of guidance, PN7, section 31 or SA's DTC: TP Country Profile, SA, January 2013, p. 3.
533. Pre 2001 rule inapplicable to transactions where price exceeds ALP (CBDT Circular 14, 2001); absence of TP case law upto June 2001 indicative of TP's then low priority to IRD (Verma, Limits on the use of low-tax regimes by multinational businesses: current measures and emerging trends – India', IFA Cahiers 2001 – Volume 86b, p. 567/571); pre 2001 rules ill-defined and seldom used (Govind, 'TP' Asia-Pac. Tax Bull, 2003), generally circumvented unless agent constituted PE (Desai, Tax Aspects of Transfer of Technology including Software, Asia-Pac. Tax Bull, 1999); India applied own interpretation of comparables (Hong, Impact of TP on Tax Planning, Asia-Pacific Tax Bulletin, 2003); management fees and similar administrative/shared service charges of foreign providers (Mukherjee, 'TP-A Practitioner's View, Asia-Pac. Tax Bull, 2006) to counter abuse. Rules were time consuming and costly to administer (Govind, *supra* n. 533). New rules gave IRD tools to counter 'base erosion' caused by round tripping; Finance Minister, para. 176, Budget Speech (2001); 248 Income Tax Reports (ITR) p. 34 Statutes (St.); Aztec Software, *supra* n. 186; section 92A.
534. Vora, TP and its Applicability to Domestic Transactions, EY 2012; Ostwal, Overview of TP, Indian and International, November 2014, http://cas.ind.in/knowledgecenter/cnsupdates/Session-IX.pdf, p. 6.

4.3.2 Associates

While the BRICS have adopted the broad core concepts and meanings of the *OECD Model Convention, Commentary* and *Transfer Pricing Guidelines*,[535] the constituents of 'associate' in the BRICS for TP purposes are essentially the same as those considered in the discussion on thin capitalization. Since India does not have tax based thin capitalization, the previous subsection did not consider the meaning of 'associate' for Indian purposes, but there is a definition for TP purposes and with thirteen sections and four subsections[536] the definition is extremely complex, as *Ostwal*[537] confirms. This complexity is indicative of the importance which India attaches to bringing within 'associate' as many relationships as possible in order that the tax take can increase. The Indian enterprise control threshold is set at not less than 26% (direct and indirect) voting power, while participation in management extends to relationships where more than 50% of the directors or governing members, or where one or more executive directors or members of one enterprise are appointed by the other enterprise. Structural relationships constituting participation include those where one party can, or is able to control the manufacturing, processing or intangibles[538] used by the other. This was considered in *Diageo India*[539] where the Court held decision making at the sub-board level focusing on the manufacturing process or supply chain of another constituted control of the decision making process and led to 'associate' status. Further broadening of participation is evident for enterprises controlled by individuals or those enterprises drawing down financing arrangements where the loan principal is not less than 51% of the borrower's aggregate book value or guarantees representing not less than 10% of the other enterprise's total borrowings. Relationships constituting participation include those where one enterprise controls not less than 90% of the other enterprise's purchases or sales of goods, together with the supply of goods used by one enterprise in the manufacturing or processing business of the other. Relationships where a first enterprise's purchases of goods can be directed by the second enterprise (i.e. the enterprise from whom the first enterprise purchases goods), also constitutes 'associate' status as are relationships between non-corporate entities which own not less than a 10% interest in another non-corporate entity. The detail of definition confirms how in India, 'associate' is an important concept.

---

535. Transfer Pricing Guidelines, para. 12; *supra* n. 503, 9B.16 observes the definition to be wide but does not extend beyond the enterprise to the business which it carries on.
536. Section 92A(1) and (2)(a) to (m), ITA.
537. Ostwal, *supra* n. 534, p. 6.
538. Manufacturing/processing of goods for others, business carried on by one enterprise wholly dependent on intangibles (knowhow, patents, copyrights, trademarks, licences, franchises, other business/commercial rights of a similar nature or data, documentation, drawings or specification relating to patents, invention, models, designs, secret formula, processes) of another; 2015 (9) TMI 438 – ITAT Punedcit, Circle-7, Pune v. W.B. Engineers International Private Limited.
539. Diageo India Private Limited v. ACIT [ITA No. 8602/Mum/2010, ITAT, 7 Sep. 2011 (AY 2006-07).

4.3.3 Transactions

While the *Transfer Pricing Guidelines* apply to transactions failing the ALS, in order to avoid narrowing the range, the developed world does not list transactions to be tested. In Brazil, India and Russia publishing lists of potentially proscribed transactions they potentially narrow the field, while China and SA adopt the developed world's approach.

With Brazil's list covering all imports and exports it would be difficult to be wider. India's list is based on the section 92B(1)[540] core principle[541] that to be a 'transaction' an arrangement must 'bear on the profits, income, losses or assets of such enterprises', which makes it broad. That core principle was fleshed out by the section 92B(2) Explanation[542] together with the definition of 'intangible property',[543] which was widened in 2012[544] and then again in 2014.[545] The requirement to identify income (profits or income) as a precondition to find a 'transaction' was considered in *Vodafone India Services ('Vodafone IV')*.[546] In that case, the Court rejected the IRD's[547] assertion that it found income to exist when an Indian company issued shares at a discount to foreign shareholders, because the discount was income. Delineating the boundaries of a 'transaction' has proven to be difficult in India as *Perot Systems*[548] confirms. In that case, the Court rejected the IRD's assertion that debtor amounts which had passed their due date and on which the recipient had decided not to charge interest became 'transactions'. In arriving at its decision, the Court relied on the fact that in this instance not charging interest was commercially expedient: a principle confirmed in the later *Pegasystems Worldwide*.[549] This position of 'commercial expedience' was not universally adopted as *Dinurje Jewellery*[550] confirms. In that case, below market lending arrangements were adjusted to reflect the creditor's actual costs, as *Sanghavi*[551] confirmed. The core principle has been further widened to treat as transactions, any

---

540. Transactions other than 'international', involving expenditure to persons covered by sections 40A(2)(b); 80A; 80-IA(8); 80-IA(10), Chapter VI-A or section 10AA, covered by section 80-IA(10)(8), or other transactions in previous year exceeding £600,000: section 92BA.
541. Transactions between atleast two associates where one or both are non-residents involving purchasing, sales or leasing of tangible or intangibles, or providing services, or lending or borrowing money, or any other transaction impacting the profits, income, losses or assets of associates including mutual agreements or arrangements where contributions to, costs or expenses incurred or to be incurred concerning a benefit, service or facility provided or to be provided to any one or more of such enterprises are allocated or apportioned.
542. Explanation i(a) to (e).
543. Explanation ii(a) to (l).
544. Finance Act 2012, backdating to 2002.
545. India entity or associate non-resident transaction will be 'international' regardless of other persons being non-resident. According to Novo Nordisk India Private v. DCIT, 30 Jul. 2015, ITAT, IT(TP)A No.146/Bang/2015 the 2015 extension was intended to provide clarity.
546. Vodafone India Services Pvt. Ltd v. Union Of India, on 10 Oct. 2014, WP-871-14.
547. Question No. 836, Parliament, 5 Mar. 2013, MOF confirmed for 2009/10 year 27 share adjustments including Shell (INR 152bn), Essar (INR 80bn), Vodafone (INR 13bn) and HSBC (INR9.35bn).
548. Perot Systems TSI (India) Ltd. v. DCIT (ITA Nos. 2320, 2321 and 2322/Del/2008).
549. Pegasystems Worldwide India v. ACIT, ITAT, 16 Oct. 2015, I.T.A. No. 1936/HYD/2014.
550. Dinurje Jewellery Pvt. Ltd, DCIT, ITAT, MA No. 419/Mum/2014, 20 Feb. 2015.
551. India/International TP or Not TP, Bull. Intl. Taxn, 2013.

agreements between arm's length persons which were entered into prior to an agreement entered into between associates, as in *Kodak India*.[552] The breadth of this decision was narrowed in the later cases of *Swarnandhra IJMII* and *Novo Nordisk*[553] where it was established that for this principle to apply, the associate must be non-resident. While *Ostwal*[554] and *Kumar*[555] have both observed that the list is unimportant from a practitioner's perspective, in the author's opinion, this fails to recognize the clarity and certainty benefits which a list brings to both the taxpayer and the administration, especially considering the limited tax authority capacity to identify, investigate and prosecute TP offences

Russia's listing, as *Narinyan*[556] argues, was narrow before 2012 because at that juncture it was confined to four categories[557] but, the subsequent widening into five categories with further subsections, the list became more relevant. This is especially so, considering its strict applicability to cross-border transactions with face values exceeding RUB60m (approx. $1.8m) entered into by Russian enterprises with 'black-list' residents. Similarly to India, delineating the boundaries of the list has led to uncertainty in Russia as evident in *Sun Inbev*[558] where the Court prevented TP adjustments being made in relation to license fees for technology which did not involve sufficient know-how features, while also preventing TP adjustments from being made in *Suzuki Rus*[559] on the grounds that the mere expectation of income was an insufficient reason to raise an adjustment.

While China's approach is similar to that of the developed world, *Circular 2*[560] widens by including deferred payment arrangements[561] and *draft Circular 2*[562] proposes that arrangements between China enterprises and foreign associates involving work carried out in China on improving foreign owned intangibles should be arrangements subject to TP adjustments where a portion of the intangible's value should be attributed to the China enterprise, where the foreign person resides in a tax haven.[563]

---

552. Kodak India Pvt. Ltd v. ACIT (ITA No. 7349Mum/2012).
553. Swarnandhra IJMII Integrated Township Development Company Pvt. Ltd. v. DCIT, in ITA no. 2072/Hyd/2011; Novo Nordisk India Private v. DCIT, 30 Jul. 2015, ITAT, IT(TP)A No.146/Bang/2015.
554. Ostwal, *supra* n. 534.
555. Judge Kumar confirmed to author in email 1 Dec. 2015.
556. New TP rules in Russia, September 2012, p. 35, http://www.offshoreinvestment.com/media/uploads/narinyan229(1).pdf.
557. Related domestic and cross-border; barter; foreign trade and where pricing within the short period of time deviated by more than 20% either way from the price set by taxpayer for identical or similar goods.
558. Sun Inbev, The Moscow Arbitration Court, Court of Appeal, 10 Feb. 2014.
559. Suzuki Rus, Moscow Arbitration Court, 19 Mar. 2013, Case No A40-111951/2012.
560. Article 10, *supra* n. 200.
561. Article 10(IV), Draft Implementation Measures, *supra* n. 438.
562. Consultation draft circular 'Implementation Measures for Special Tax Adjustments' to replace the existing Guoshuifa [2009] No. 2 (Circular 2), 17 Sep. 2015, draft Circular 2.
563. Person making substantial contributions to intangible's value through functions, investment and risks when developing, upgrading, maintaining, protecting, exploiting or promoting: Chapter VI, Articles 70 and 76, *supra* n. 562.

SA's approach conforms to the developed world but widens for arrangements entered into by a foreign person's SA PE with that foreign person's head office.[564]

The research allows a conclusion to be drawn that while the listing format adopted by the Brazil, India and Russia is intended to provide certainty for both taxpayers and the tax authorities, it establishes a basis for the very opposite outcome due to the difficulties in delineating the boundaries of the listed items.

4.3.4 CCAs

CCAs are becoming more important as MNEs see the cost and management benefits arising from sharing across the group of the finance, risks and costs associated with developing intangibles across the group companies' participating in the value chain. In relation to how to apportion values to the enterprises contributing the resources, the developed world[565] asserts that the ALS is to be applied. It has also resolved that the payments borne by each associate through this apportionment should not be treated as royalties[566] by the remitting country Both China[567] and SA[568] broadly agree with this approach but China widened its practice in 2015[569] when it began to require enterprises making such payments to non-residents, to make full disclosure to SAT for pre-approval. The obligation to notify SAT enabled the China's limited tax authority manpower to focus on the analysis instead of the identification.

Brazil and Russia have adopted a different approach by denying deductions for cross-border payments under CCAs. In Brazil's case, according to *Utumi*[570] deductions are denied when the payee is tax resident in 'tax preferred jurisdictions' while Russia (from 2014) denies deductions for all CCA payments made to related non-residents regardless of the payee's country of residence, according to *Variychuk*.[571] India has begun to pursue a similar approach for intra-group technical and management services, as *Fosroc Chemicals*[572] confirms, but when the Tribunal overrode the IRD's rejection of the deduction on the grounds that the cost of services had been reimbursed without mark-up, the IRD then shifted its focus to consider whether the reimbursed costs had been inflated.

---

564. Murphy, TP and intangibles – SA, IFA Cahiers 2007 – Volume 92A, p. 518; Hattingh, *supra* n. 3, Chapter 8, p. 239/256/257 arguing not appropriate for rules to apply to expenditure allocated to the PE by persons connected to the foreign head office; Oguttu, Challenges of Taxing Profits Attributed to PE, *supra* n. 415, p. 170/172.
565. Paragraph 8.23, *supra* n. 418.
566. *Ibid.*
567. Chapter 7, Article 64/7, *supra* n. 200.
568. PN7, *supra* n. 410, para. 19.1.
569. Public Notice 2015, No. 45.
570. Substance over Form and GAAR Rules in Brazil, International Taxation, 36/44, January 2013.
571. Russia, in Search of Effective Regulation: Draft Bill on TP, Bull. Intl. Taxn, 2011 (Volume 65), No. 2, p. 108/112.
572. Fosroc Chemicals India Pvt. Ltd. v. DCIT [IT(TP)A No. 148/Bang/2014 – AY 2009-10] – Taxsutra.com.

4.3.5 Excessive Leverage

The thin capitalization subsection of this study researched the limitation on interest deductibility using the fixed ratio, and while the developed world has argued that thin capitalization can also be countered by applying the ALS,[573] and China and Brazil have systems in place to replace the fixed ratio with the ALS, there is no published evidence of either Brazil[574] or China ever actually having done so. SA however, includes both the ALS and the interest limitation principle in its toolkit which widens the options at its disposal for countering leverage, and as *Oguttu*[575] argues this, rather than logic is the reason for adopting both approaches.

4.3.6 Methods

Having identified which parties the ALS is to apply to, the next step in the TP decision chain is to determine how the ALP is to be calculated. For this purpose the *Transfer Pricing Guidelines* establish five methods[576] and provide for the most appropriate method[577] to be chosen. In applying the methods, the process relies on identifying the price which would be charged in the same or similar arm's length transaction/s ('comparable') and then for that comparable to be adjusted to reflect the facts and circumstances[578] including the differences[579] between the actual transaction and the comparable for the tested party.[580] If more than one method produces an acceptable ALP then working out how to determine which of them is used, requires the parties to use the range[581] methodology.

Russia,[582] India,[583] China[584] and SA[585] have broadly adopted the OECD's five methods[586] although, as the following discussion shows, this has not always been the case. Brazil's methods are different except for CUP, as *Carramaschi*[587] observes. Brazil

---

573. *Supra* n. 365, at p. 17.
574. Profs Schoueri and Valadao in research for this study.
575. Oguttu, Curbing Thin capitalisation a comparative view to SA's approach, Bulletin for International taxation (Volume 67), No. 6.
576. TP methods, July 2010, Centre for Tax Policy and Administration; CUP, Cost Plus (CPM), Resale Price (RPM), TNMM and the PSM, http://www.oecd.org/ctp/transfer-pricing/45765701.pdf, last visited 1 Jul. 2016.
577. Paragraph 2.2, *supra* n. 418.
578. Chapters II and III, Transfer Pricing Guidelines, *supra* n. 418, September 2009 draft revised Chapters I-III; TPM – Discussion draft 2008; Comparability issues – public invitation to comment, Paper on TP Methods; Paper on Arm's length Range; Paper on Comparability Adjustments.
579. OECD, Paper of TP Methods, July 2010.
580. Paragraph 3.18, *supra* n. 418.
581. Paragraph A.7, *supra* n. 418.
582. Chapter 14.3 (Articles 105.7-105.13 of the RF Tax Code) – TP Methods.
583. Section 92C(1), ITA.
584. *Supra* n. 200.
585. PN7, *supra* n. 410 describes five methods because the legislation fails to refer to them.
586. Chapter 14.3 (Articles 105.7-105.13 of the RF Tax Code) – TP Methods.
587. Brazil, TP rules amended – resale price method, IBFD, February 2008.

has separate methods for imports[588] from those for exports[589] and while the RFB has argued that the fixed margins[590] are compatible with Article 9(1), *OECD Model Convention*, they are not unless the fixed margin produces an ALP compatible with the ALS, or the RFB accepts a taxpayer's representations that the actual price charged in the contracts was compatible with the fixed margin price.[591] While *Valadao*[592] and *Schoueri*[593] confirm that the fixed margins represent a 'concession to practicality', this conclusion seems questionable, when in *Marcopolo*,[594] the re-invoicing of bus parts through a tax haven associate (which had been shipped directly to the end customer) was treated as a simulation when it was clearly a TP case. Considered in the round, Brazil's TP methods result in an increase in the export prices while reducing import costs and while the fixed margins are intended to limit the difficulties for the RFB when dealing with complex economic submissions on a time sensitive basis,[595] without

---

588. At December 2015, fair price for imports: Average price for identical/similar products/services in purchase /sale transactions entered into in Brazilian internal/external market with similar payment conditions, determined by reference to costs, margins and ultimate destination sector. PIC (CUP), PRL (resale price method plus 20/30 or 40% fixed margin), CPL (production costs in country of origin plus 20%) and PCI (commodity exchange important price).
589. At December 2015, fair price for exports: Using exports prices. CAP (production costs plus 15%), PVEX (sales price on exports), PVA and PVV (resale price minus 15% for whole and 30% for retail), PCEX (commodity exchange export price) as outlined in Normative Rulings 243/02; 382/03 and 1312/12.
590. CPM and RPM use predetermined fixed margins but scholars provide a range of opinions on the benefits (Munyandi, India; Brazil; SA discuss TP IBFD June 2008; Carramaschi, Brazil, TP rules amended – RPM, IBFD, February 2008; ICC, Roundtable in Rio de Janeiro to discuss Brazilian tax issues, IBFD, 21 Oct. 2011, Shah, BRICS Joint communiqué on BRICS meeting, IBFD, 23 Jan. 2013; da Silveira, International Tax Planning in Brazil: What to Expect Following Recent Case Law, Bull. Intl. Taxn, 2010 (Volume 64), No. 11, p. 572; Velloso, TP in the absence of comparable market prices – Brazil, IFA Cahiers 1992 – Volume 77a, p. 313; Machado, Cross-border business restructuring – Brazil, IFA Cahiers 2011 – Volume 96A, p. 151/152; DeOliveria, The Taxation of foreign passive income for groups of companies – Brazil, IFA Cahiers 2013 – Volume 98A p. 169) justifying on economic grounds while others saw merit on insufficiency of RFB resources (Compatible with FRS' inability to manage without properly trained and sufficient staff as justification for the territorial basis (Neviani, Transfer of assets into and out of a taxing jurisdiction – Brazil, IFA Cahiers 1986 – Volume 71a. p. 202); another group justified margins on certainty for taxpayers. Brazilian legal system rejects economic interpretation of tax law (Malaquias, The VII Latin America TP Summit, 5/6 Oct. 2006, São Paulo, Brazil; Brazil; Ruling on application of RPM on repackaging and labelling activities 27 Oct. 2006) meaning that ALS would not be effective. Legally can adjust margins but does not wish to on Constitutional grounds (Torres, *supra* n. 161, p. 163).
591. Profs *Schoueri* and *Valadao* (Administrative Rule 222: Profs Valadao and Schoueri informed writer in Brasilia and SP respectively on 25/26 Feb. 2015 that RFB not interested in variations as to do so may open floodgates and confirm they are unaware of this ever happening).
592. Prof Valadao argues: using previously consented to or FRB reviewed margins provides stability and expectations in economic and fiscal relations (UN TP Manual, *10.2.1.3*). In arguing for wider range of fixed margins should be allocated to sectors (UN TP Manual, *10.2.9.4*) Valadao is moving towards recommending adopting ALS based on a wider range of industry margins which Law 12,715 provided a step towards.
593. Prof Schoueri, *supra* n. 3, p. 63.
594. *Supra* n. 168.
595. Prof Schoueri advised the writer on 27 Feb. 2015 in SP that FRB's SP TP team contains just eighteen executives.

Chapter 4: Countering Avoidance: SAARs

sufficient comparables, and with limited tax authority capacity, as *Orsini* [596] confirmed, the result is a system designed to increase taxes.

With the CUP and RPM being the only methods available to the FTS in Russia before 2012, and because rather than adopting the most appropriate method the FTS selected the 'substantiated position',[597] this provided the FTS with the power to allocate income in the manner best protecting Russia's tax revenue. Further divergences from the *Transfer Pricing Guidelines* pre 2012 were in relation to the comparability adjustments[598] where the FTS focussed on transactions occurring in the same or nearest Russian geographical location[599] with Government statistics (SPARK or RUSLANA)[600] being used instead of actual comparable transactions. *DLP Piper*[601] observed that the FTS generally adopted the RPM as the method for long-term intra-group sales of goods when the OECD[602] generally supported the CUP for such transactions.

In order to provide the IRD with the most flexibility in allocating income between countries, India[603] established as a sixth TP method, 'any other method prescribed by the Board'.[604] The CBDT has also used the TP rules in a manner intended to maximize India's revenue base, and the research supports this conclusion by referencing to how India uses multi-year data,[605] range data and cherry picking. While the *Transfer Pricing Guidelines* permitted the use of this data to smooth out profit flows, India rejected doing so for many years and when it relaxed the rule (ostensibly to minimize disputation)[606] it did so by limiting the right to the use data to that available from the immediately preceding year only and then only when the current year's data was unavailable[607] and then only when used in conjunction with RPM, CPM or TNMM methods. In relation to the use of the range concept,[608] when the methods produce two or more ALPs in India, while the *Transfer Pricing Guidelines* allow the adoption of any

---

596. Orsini, First Head of TP audit, RFB.
597. Article 40(3) RTC.
598. Paragraph 3.3.5, *supra* n. 418.
599. Article 40(5), RTC.
600. Global Transfer Pricing Review, *supra* n. 531, p. 5.
601. DLA Piper, Comparison of new Russian TP rules with OECD Guidelines, May 2012; McDermott, Will and Emery, Russian TP Law, 26 Feb. 2013.
602. Section D, *supra* n. 418.
603. Sengupta, *supra* n. 3, p. 149; section 92.1; ALP standard-applies CUP, RPM, CPM, PSM or TNMM (TPO identifies whether actual price satisfies ALP: Sections 92CA; 92C) or other method (CBDT: Notification 18/2012, May 2012) such as DCF applicable to intra-group share transfers approved by RBI when transferred from resident to non-resident (Jhabakh, Determination of ALP for sale of Shares to an AE, ITPJ, Vol 20, p. 283/286) in an uncontrolled transaction.
604. Section 92C(1)(f) ITA.
605. Chapter 10, UN TP Manual, difficulty in obtaining reliable data on capacity and working capital for comparability purposes (10.4.6.8); obtaining specialized databases and comparable prices for complex inter-company loans and those embedded in merger/acquisition transactions (10.4.10.4).
606. Ostwal, Recent Developments in International and Domestic TP, November 2014, p. 24 https://www.bcasonline.org/onlinebackup/webadmin/res_material/resfiles/187-TPOstwalBCAS-InternationalandDomesticTransferPricing-RecentDevelopments-TPOstwal.pdf.
607. OECD permits multiple years data to be used, para. B.5, *supra* n. 418.
608. Finance Minister Budget speech, 2014: range rules align India with OECD but rules have not enacted that intent: Jain, TP Rules – Use of multiple year data, is it end of litigation?, June 2015, taxindiainternational.com; para A.7.1, *supra* n. 418.

point within the range,[609] the CBDT arrives at the weighted average and uses it. This means that the MNE loses the flexibility of choosing the one ALP which more closely resembles its actual price. In relation to the IRD 'cherry picking' comparables to support its position, this approach was rejected by the Court in *Fuchs Lubricants*.[610] Also supporting the IRD's approach to establishing the ALP is its assertion that it can reject the financial consequences of business risks (such as bad debts, market and contractual risks) from being included in costs for ALP purpose *(Glamour Enterprises)*.[611]

With respect to China, it focuses on which of the five methods it should use to best protect its tax base rather than the method which strictly follows the *Transfer Pricing Regulations*. China adopts the 'most appropriate method' but as *Yuan* and *Deloitte*[612] have observed, the actual method adopted by SAT may not be the 'most appropriate method' because SAT retains a right to select the 'best method' which, like Russia and India, allows it to establish an ALP which best suits China. One example is in *Suzhou*,[613] where the SAT applied CUP to value shares sold in a listed company's subsidiary. It used the listed company's CUP without discount to reflect the non-marketability of the subsidiary's shares.

Similar to the *Transfer Pricing Guidelines*, China does not establish any method hierarchy although it generally accepts that the traditional transaction methods provide the most direct comparison where data is available. In practice the TNMM is used both by the authorities and taxpayers as the 'most appropriate method'. In relation to dealing with on/offshore business restructurings (such as when full manufacturers are converted into limited risk manufacturers)[614] into foreign associates,[615] a practice which increased in prevalence after the EITL's introduction, and especially given the concern for the potential loss of China tax revenues from those restructurings, SAT's right to choose the 'best method' became especially relevant. *Su*[616] observed that CUP was usually chosen to value the shift but when inappropriate, one of CPM, MV or an

---

609. Actual price plotted against must involve 35th/65th percentile of data set which diverges from OECD average (para. 3.62) with the actual price then falling anywhere within the range (para. A.7.2), *supra* n. 418.
610. Fuchs Lubricants (I) P. Ltd. v. Department Of Income Tax, I.T.A. No.7629 /Mum/2010, 20 Nov. 2012.
611. Glamour Enterprises (P.) Ltd. v. Deputy Commissioner of Income-tax, Circle-6, Jaipur, 2015 (10) TMI 1387 – ITAT Jaipur.
612. Yuan, China TP, *supra* n. 528, p. 3; Deloitte Tax Analysis, The New Chinese Special Tax Adjustments Rules – What are Implications, NTC Tax Analysis, p. 49/2009, 11 Jan. 2009.
613. Jiangsu Province-2012.
614. Involving the transfer of customer relationships, trademarks, third-party dealer networks.
615. Valuation provided by a PRC licensed valuer supports price: Cao, China Clarifies Tax Rules for Enterprise Reorganizations, Jones Day Publications Beijing http://www.jonesday.com/china _clarifies_tax_rules/, October 2010; Establishing ALP for reorganization seen as difficult due to uncertainty of 'profit potential' of assets and comparables absence: Han, Cross-border business restructuring – China, IFA Cahiers 2011, Volume 96A, p. 213/216; SAT interested in adjusting for outbound reorganizations but not for inbound reorganizations; SAT, Measures on Administration of CIT Concerning Enterprise Reorganizations, SAT Public Notice [2010] No. 4, July 2010;Wang, China Business Restructurings: A Case Analysis and Regulations Applicable to Business Restructuring, ITPJ, 2013 (Volume 20), No. 5, p. 323.
616. TP Aspects of Business Restructurings, Asia-Pac. Tax Bull, May/June 2012, p. 265/266.

income based method was chosen. This observation conflicts with the SAT's general approach of using TNMM, (as was evident in *Shenzhen*[617]) when the shift was of tangibles, intangibles or services,[618] or PSM[619] when the shift was of non-limited risk businesses[620] and TNNM (with a full mark-up profit indicator)[621] when the shift was for contract manufacturing. The importance to SAT of using functional and risk analyses[622] to countering the tax effects arising when enterprises converted from full risk to limited risk was evident in *Guo Shui Han [2009] No. 363*.[623] Further confirmation is to be found in *Circular 4*[624] which, for function shifts, now requires a functions and risk analysis[625] rather than completing the domestic reorganization notification form. *Yuan*[626] observed that the difficulty in identifying the best method for valuing these restructures was understandable because of the then limited tax authority TP manpower to deal with the project, together with the absence of widespread relevant foreign comparables even though SAT sought to counter these deficiencies through using information directly obtained from companies identified by it through 'third-party consultation', as *Coronado*[627] observed. The growing sophistication of the tax authorities' ability to counter methods abuse is evident from the denial of deductions for license fee payments by enterprises to non-resident associates, especially where it had become apparent that the previously agreed percentage fee was no longer relevant because the enterprise had contributed to the intangible's enhanced value.[628] That growing sophistication is also evident from *draft Circular 2s* proposal to include two 'other TP methods', first, the value contribution allocation method (VCM) and second, asset valuation methods. Where enterprises chose to retain their existing structure (rather than convert to limited risk manufacturers) but pay fees cross-border to reduce

---

617. Shenzhen, STB; Transfer Pricing Guidelines, *supra* n. 418, para. 6.23/6.24.
618. Chapter VI, Article 33, Draft Implementation Measures, *supra* n. 438.
619. Ying, China's TP System, SAT, http://www.taxjustice.net/cms/upload/pdf/Zhang_Ying_120 6_Helsinki_ppt.pdf, p. 33: PSM is applicable to supply chains while OECD TP Guidelines recommend CUP or CPM, para. 9.156/9.157.
620. Guoshuihan (2007) No. 236, Guoshuifa (2004) No. 143.
621. UN TP Manual, para. 10.3.5.4 disclosure contradicts SAT's statement in 2012 APA Report that TNNM is preferred with CPM not then having been used in TP assessments, para. 10.3.5.5.
622. Guoshuihan [2007] No. 236: Functions and risks requiring analysis of cost savings, market premium and other factors: Chapter V, Article 57, Draft Implementation Measures, *supra* n. 438; Ying, China's TP System, *supra* n. 619, p. 4.
623. Notice on Strengthening Monitoring and Investigation of Cross-Border Related Party Transactions, Guo Shui Han [2009] No. 363, Article 1/2/3.
624. SAT Announcement [2010] No. 4 (Circular 4): Restructuring transactions discussing methods, background, timing, legal form/substance, potential changes in the parties' financial/tax positions, abnormal economic benefits, potential obligations; Cheng Chi, TP Forum BNA, August 2010, KPMG, Shanghai.
625. Cheng, TP Forum BNA, August 2010, KPMG, Shanghai.
626. SAT argued that TNMM better reflected where the work force and tangibles were China located with adjustments for comparables evolving from developed countries where both profit and inflation rates were low, due to low risk, seen as not relevant, Yuan, *supra* n. 528.
627. Asian Tax Authorities Grasp TP: is China leading the Way? Asia-Pac. Tax Bull, March/April 2009, p. 73.
628. Unofficial 5% cap, Guoshuifa (2005) No. 45; UN TP Manual, 10.3.4.3.

taxable profits (*Anshan STB of Liaoning*[629] being illustrative), the STB, by applying the six tests in *Bulletin 16*,[630] held the fees to be non-deductible on the grounds of the fees being neither warranted nor provided.

According to PN7 (6 August 1999), CUP is SA's choice of method because 'it looks to the product or service transferred and is relatively insensitive to the specific functions ...performed by the entities being compared'.[631] In order to deal with the relative absence of comprehensive local comparables on intangibles, the foreign person is treated as the tested party even if it does not own the intangible,[632] with SARS relying on using EU, Australia and US[633] comparables. Where the methods produce two or more ALPs, the adoption of the mid-point (similar to India's weighted average) within the range in the absence of a compelling reason to the contrary[634] represents a simple approach of overcoming the insufficiency of trained officials to deal with the complex issue. One divergence of interest though is that which requires the associate to actually participate in the price bargaining in order for the actual price to be accepted as arm's length.[635]

4.3.7 Safe Harbours

The early versions of the *Transfer Pricing Guidelines*[636] argue that safe harbours[637] were not compatible with the ALS but, by 2013, this position had been relaxed, in part as a response to their adoption by many developed countries, especially for the benefit of small taxpayers or those with less complex situations and in the interests of promoting certainty and administrative ease. However, this relaxation is to be seen against the background of the OECD's recommendations that all safe harbours should be included in bilateral instruments so that double taxation[638] would be avoided. With limited tax authority manpower in the BRICS, it is rational to conclude that administrative ease and certainty drove the BRICS' adoption of the TP safe harbours and also to conclude why, all bar a few of the safe harbours, apply to taxpayers regardless of size, complexity or situation. However, the reason that none of the safe harbours has been included in any of the BRICS bilateral DTCs is that the BRICS do not see the benefit

---

629. 22 Dec. 2015.
630. Bulletin on Enterprise Income Tax Issues Related to Outbound Payments by Enterprises to Overseas Related Parties, [2015] No. 16, 18 Mar. 2015.
631. *Supra* n. 410, para. 9.3.4.
632. *Ibid.*, para. 11.3.2.
633. Nyiri, TP in South Africa: 15 by 2015, BDO SA, http://www.bdo.co.za/resources/ShowItem. asp?ResourceSectionId = 3&ResourceSectionName = Press&ResourceId = 14&ResourceName = BDO%20in%20the%20Press&IssueId = 614, visited 20 Dec. 2015.
634. Stanley, TP: Comment on Revenue's New Practice Note, October/November 1999, Volume 4 No. 5, Executive Business Brief 21.
635. PN7, *supra* n. 410, para. 11.14.1.
636. Section A, para. 4.9.4, *supra* n. 418.
637. Section E2, 4.100 categories of taxpayers or transactions avoiding obligations imposed by TP substituting simpler requirements such as establishing ALP through simplified administration, exempting taxpayers or transactions where consequence may be relief from documentation rules, *supra* n. 418.
638. Section E, para. 4.1.27, *supra* n. 418.

Chapter 4: Countering Avoidance: SAARs

of their sovereign right to tax being negotiated away to a counterparty in a TP matter, an issue discussed in the section of this study on APAs.

The BRICS have been selective in establishing their safe harbours in the expectation that their use will benefit domestic markets while not giving rise to tax avoidance opportunities. Brazil[639] has established a safe harbour for exports[640] but not for imports which is understandable because any import safe harbour would result in higher prices than the ALP and a reduced tax base. In designing the export safe harbour, Brazil shaped it so as to avoid shifting profits to tax havens. The actual price must be not less than 90%[641] of the average Brazilian sales price[642] and the safe harbour cannot be used when one of the counterparties is resident in a tax preferred jurisdiction. Export safe harbours apply also for goods[643] for sale as part of a programme to create new foreign markets. The effectiveness of Russia's safe harbour (plus/minus 20% of the ALP) has been reduced through it being applicable only for small taxpayers[644] from 2013. However, the 2014 removal of the minimum transaction value for transactions with associates' resident in tax preferred jurisdictions[645] or for import or exports of global exchange-traded commodities[646] also widens the safe harbour and facilitates profit shifting. With India devoid of a thin capitalization tax rule, there is much emphasis in India on countering TP and for that reason India's safe harbours[647] are complex and difficult to use but with them now having industry focus, they are intended to reduce disputation in key sectors. The original safe harbour legislation was based on the *Rangachary Committee's*[648] recommendations to 'simplify compliance, provide certainty ... thereby reducing disputes and relieving the tax administration of auditing taxpayers opting for safe harbours, thereby enabling better utilization of its resources'. However, in designing the safe harbours the CBDT wanted to avoid TP being used to facilitate offshore profit shifting so they prevented the safe harbours being used by counterparties resident in countries with corporate tax rates not more than 15%[649] or counterparties resident in notified countries.[650] In recent times, the establishment of the industry focussed safe harbours[651] have encouraged the channelling of FDI. The

---

639. Brazil Treasury Ruling 243/02, Article 32/37.
640. RFB can reject a safe harbour on audit.
641. Brazil Treasury, *supra* n. 639, subsection III.
642. Average sales price for same goods, services or rights in Brazilian market for same taxable year and similar payment conditions.
643. Exports representing less than 5% (Brazil NI 1.312/12; NI 243/2011) of exporters total turnover with profitability (*supra* n. 639, subsection VII) from those exports being less than 5% (10%) of the exporter's turnover with a 20% overall cap (Brazil N1 1.312) on total net export transactions.
644. Federal Law N 227-FZ, July 2011 for 2012 transactions with value less than RB1bn, Article 105.14(2), RTC.
645. +R60m/R100m turnover including transactions with 'blacklist' companies or UBOs residing in 'blacklist' territories. Article 105.14(9), MOF Letter No. 03-01-18/53941.
646. Oil products, metals, fertilizers and stones not less than R60mpa, MOF No. 03-01-18/35774.
647. MOF Notification, 18 Sep. 2013, Rules 10TA to Rule 10TG in Income-Tax Rules, 1962.
648. Second Report of Committee to Review Taxation of Development Centres and IT Sector, Safe Harbours, para. 2.9, p. 6, 13 Oct. 2012.
649. Rules 10TF and 10TA(i) leave unclear whether headline or effective.
650. Section 94A, ITA 1961.
651. CBDT Notice 73/2013, September 2013.

safe harbour focus on the automotive industry[652] is understandable given the high level of employment (approx. 20% of India's manufacturing base is connected to the automotive industry) it attracts, a fact confirmed in the *World Investment Report*[653] (2015). However, with the safe harbours being based on minimum operating margins rather than on the ALS and with the margins generally being higher than those established under the ALS,[654] taxpayers who adopt them do so in the knowledge that the certainty they provide may come at a cost of additional taxation. This is especially relevant because when a taxpayer elects to adopt a safe harbour it also opts out of being able to access MAP[655] to resolve cross-border tax disputes arising when the counter-party country refuses to accept the price established under the India safe harbour. However, the BITs and WTO dispute settlement procedures may then be one solution to deal with disputes arising from the MAP opt-out, and this is discussed in Chapter 8 of this study. These problems support *Ostwal's*[656] questioning of whether the safe harbours can be successful, especially where the interest[657] rate and guarantee fee[658] safe harbours establish rates below the market.

The simplicity and certainty which *Rangachary* sought to achieve from the safe harbours seems largely unobtainable today since the safe harbour rates have been set generally at a disadvantage to the ALP. It seems evident from *Aztec Software*[659] that, according to the Court, India's TP rules were intended to counter transactions breaching predetermined pricings (rather than transactions which were avoidance) even when the actual pricing met the ALS (paragraphs 17 and 22 of the judgment). This position then prevents the TP rules from simply being anti-avoidance[660] rules and supports the hypothesis that an Indian TP rule is intended to counter evasion, and that any transaction with an actual price set outside of the ALS, even if it fell within the safe harbour, would still be evasion.

---

652. 12% margin, manufacture and export of core auto components providing at least 90% of sales in testing year reflect related parties; 8.5%, manufacture and export of non-core auto components providing at least 90% of sales in testing year reflect related parties.
653. Table A, p. 47/49, *supra* n. 31.
654. 20% (20.47% OM applied in Philips Software Centre (P.) Ltd. v. ACIT [2008] 26 SOT 226 (Bang-Trib)for sales less than INR5bn with actual OM in 5%/10% range, *supra* n. 388) and 22% (sales over INR5bn with 'insignificant risk') for software development (Indian Rule:10TD(2)) and IT services (15 sub-class listing); 25% (IRD has adjusted BPO using 37% NP benchmark and 25% for IT companies providing software development/services and justifies margins by location savings), potentially 80%, from transferring businesses to India (Patel, Evolution of TP Jurisdiction in India, ITPJ, 2010) for knowledge process outsourcing services business with aggregate sales less than INR1bn; 30%, contract research and development business for software development with 'insignificant risk'; 29%, generic pharmaceutical drugs with 'insignificant risk'.
655. Rule 10TG.
656. *Supra* n. 534, p. 56.
657. SBI Base Rate +150bppa for Loans less than INR500m and SBI +300bppa for loans exceeding INR500m.
658. 2%, aggregate corporate guarantee not exceeding INR1bn and atleast 1.75%, aggregate guarantee loans where borrower has SEBI accredited credit rating as 'adequate to highest' safety, exceeding INR1bn.
659. *Supra* n. 186.
660. Developed world treats TP as counter avoidance as did Indian Government in 2001 (CBDT, Circular No. 14, 2001).

Chapter 4: Countering Avoidance: SAARs

The traditional view in China is that China has not established safe harbours, as *Tianlong*[661] observes. However, it can be argued that China does have safe harbours because transactions between China resident enterprises are exempted from TP where both enterprises have the same tax rate or where both enterprises do not to have the same rate but directly or indirectly the transaction lowered the national tax revenue (*Circular 2*)[662] or for transactions having reasonable commercial purposes (*draft Circular 2*).[663] The design of these so-called safe harbours has in part been shaped by the need to avoid their use for shifting profit offshore so their inapplicability to tax haven counterparty associates having profits of not less than RNB5m[664] is understandable. Also, China does not limit these safe harbours to small taxpayers or those with less complex situations.

The SA safe harbour[665] in place before April 2012 did not provide certainty because it was a SARS' discretion allowing it to refrain from applying the rules for taxpayers having conscientiously sought to comply[666] or for those where the comparability differences were minor.[667] The discretion was available for SARS to apply whether the taxpayer was small or the circumstances less complex. The RHQ safe harbour for interest expense on loans[668] drawn to finance foreign associates was compatible with SA's foreign policy but that concession was expanded from January 2013[669] to interest expense providing, and to the extent, that the borrowed funds were on-loaned to a foreign company in which the RHQ owned not less than 20% providing that company had a FBE.[670] The National Treasury, Media Statement, April 2013[671] confirmed that the safe harbour for interest on non-Rand financing could not be less than the interest rate on the foreign equivalent of the SA prime rate.

The information in this subsection confirms that the design of the safe harbour in the BRICS has in part been shaped by the need to counter offshoring profits and partly by the intention to channel investments. Further, since India's safe harbours generally fall outside the ALS, this supports the theory that mispriced transactions in India constitute evasion.

4.3.8 Documentation

Documentation is a fundamental feature of TP compliance and an important method used in identification of breaches, which means that the *Transfer Pricing Guidelines* guidance on disclosure and transparency are integral to the process. Those *Guidelines*

---

661. Tianlong, *supra* n. 3, p. 205.
662. *Supra* n. 200, Article 30.
663. Chapter V, Article 37(9), Draft Implementation Measures, *supra* n. 438.
664. Guoshuifa (2008) 114, (Circular 114).
665. *Supra* n. 410, para. 11.16.4.
666. *Ibid.*, para. 21.2.
667. *Ibid.*, para. 8.1.
668. Providing interest on loan does not exceed interest income from the foreign subsidiary.
669. Assessment years commencing from January 2013 but for 2012 assessment, 10% interest was required, section 31(5).
670. Section 9D(1), ITA 1961.
671. National Treasury, Media Statement, April 2013.

recommend disclosure[672] and transparency[673] but concede that the disclosure must be proportional to the nature of the business and the potential tax liability.[674] This proportionality test therefore means that it is unnecessary to attach all information on cross-border transactions with associates to the annual tax return[675] nor is it necessary for the contemporaneous preparation[676] and delivery to the tax authority of all information which the tax authority may require at a later enquiry stage. The importance of documentation is clear from BEPS Action Reports 13 which is discussed in Chapter 7 of this study.

This subsection concludes that the BRICS, bar SA, require contemporaneous preparation (Brazil,[677] Russia,[678] India,[679] China)[680] and that they also require delivery to the tax authority of significant volume of information, which potentially is all the information the tax authority requires to rule on the actual pricing. Adopting this approach represents a widening of the *Transfer Pricing Guidelines*, and seems likely to have been adopted by the BRICS in order to both encourage compliance and enable the tax authority to quickly commence investigations where it identifies breaches, and in this way, limit the illicit outflows through the use of mispriced transactions. It also has the consequence of allowing more cases to be investigated and compensates for the limited tax authority manpower.

The format for the contemporaneous preparation of documentation varies as does how it is provided to the tax authority. Brazil requires the information to be included in an annually filed return *(DIPJ)*[681] with both the taxpayer's preparation and the RFB's vetting facilitated through the information on stock management codes[682] covering both import and export transactions,[683] being available online. Russia's notification is annual and more mechanical while India, as *Shah*[684] observes, adopts a sophisticated and complete system designed to encourage compliance and penalize severely for failure to comply. The information to be supplied in India to the IRD is to be confirmed in an annual Independent Accountant's Report.[685] Where that Report is

---

672. Chapter V, para. 5.18/5.27, *supra* n. 418.
673. Chapter V, para. 5.2, *ibid*.
674. Chapter V, para. 5.7, *ibid*.
675. Chapter V, para. 5.15, *ibid*.
676. Chapter V, para. 5.4, *ibid*.
677. EY, Brazil, 2013 TP Global Reference Guide http://www.ey.com/GL/en/Services/Tax/International-Tax/Transfer-Pricing-and-Tax-Effective-Supply-Chain-Management/2013-Transfer-pricing-global-reference-guide--Brazil.
678. Article 105.16, RTC; *No. OA-4-13/14433*, 30 Aug. 2012-FTS.
679. Rule 10D, section 92D ITA.
680. Commencing August 2002, Shenzhen LTB required FIEs and FEs to file 'Annual Disclosure Form for Related Party Transactions' (40 pp.) for years 1998/2001; SAT Bulletin (2016) No. 42.
681. Means Statement of Economic and Tax Information of Legal Entities, disclosing information on import and export transactions on five forms.
682. Customs authorities' SISCOMEX and Foreign Service Trade's SISCOSERV.
683. PwC, International TP Policy, 2013/2014, p. 295; Ayub, Navigating Brazil's TP Complexity, International Tax Review, September 2015.
684. Workshop on TP, Drafting of Study Report & Accountant's Reporthttps://www.wirc-icai.org/(X(1)S(nkov2m3byv3isii42n4cjw45))/material/Drafting-of-TP-Study-Report-and-Accountants-Report.pdf, last viewed 14 Jul. 2016.
685. Form 3CEB.

neither lodged nor discloses[686] all associated transactions, the breach is deemed to be evasion with deductions denied for the payments made to the non-resident under the relevant transaction. Also any otherwise available DTC benefits are denied unless the foreign associate waives its rights to the DTC protection.[687] China requires the details[688] of foreign associate transactions[689] to be provided annually[690] to the local tax authority and should one of the relevant transactions be an inbound loan from a foreign associate then a TP study covering the loan must be lodged. This approach compensates for the limited tax authority manpower. While SARS[691] neither requires the contemporaneous preparation of information nor the lodgement of an Annual Report, it encourages taxpayers to do both by publishing that increased audit risk[692] follows when the information is not available promptly on enquiry.

4.3.9 APA

One consequence of TP adjustments is double taxation (unless relieved by DTC or unilateral concessions) while another is prolonged disputation with the tax authority. The former potentially leads to an environment not conducive to FDI while the latter consumes scarce tax authority manpower. In order to avoid these problems an APA provides the mechanism for the CAs to agree on the ALP.[693] It also improves administration and helps to contain taxpayer costs.[694] The developed world also argues that by improving tax authority[695] interdependency, resolution of open disputes[696] will be accelerated and integral to dispute resolution is an acceptance that the APAs should be bilateral or multilateral rather than unilateral.[697]

The consequences from both Brazil and SA not having APA programmes is first, no compromise on their sovereign right to tax (which is a benefit to the Government), which is important since mispriced transactions contribute to illicit offshoring of funds

---

686. Disclosure of ownership structure (individuals/entities owning plus 10% directly/indirectly, name, address and whether resident of notified jurisdiction, group profile), group entities entering into international transactions with Indian payer (ownership linkage, name, address, legal status, tax residence), business description and industry together with relevant information, data or documents (S.O. 1856(E)-June 2013).
687. India Form No. 10FC, Rule 21AC.
688. Ying, China's TP System, SAT, http://www.taxjustice.net/cms/upload/pdf/Zhang_Ying_120 6_Helsinki_ppt.pdf, p. 15/18; Peng, Structuring an Appropriate TP Policy', Asia-Pac. Tax Bull, November/December 2005, p. 479/483; gathering and processing relevant data was then unimportant: Jinyan, Li, TP in China, IBFD Bulletin, November 2000, p. 568/570.
689. *Ibid.*, p. 38, together with intensive auditor training and while strategy is aligned with developed world, China's administration method based on limited resources.
690. Yang, Structuring an Overseas Investment – What Do We Need To Know?, Asia-Pac. Tax Bull, September/October 2011, p. 351; *supra* n. 688, p. 479/483; Bulletin 42 requires fourteen forms completing on associate transactions increased from nine.
691. Paragraph 10, *supra* n. 410.
692. SARS, TP: Addendum to PN7: Submission of TP document, September 2005.
693. Paragraph 4.163, *supra* n. 418.
694. Paragraph 4.123, *ibid.*
695. Paragraph 4.168/4.174, *ibid.*
696. Paragraph 4.145, *ibid.*
697. Paragraph 4.162, *ibid.*

and second, double taxation or double non-taxation which is a problem for taxpayers. In relation to Brazil, *Pinto*[698] sought to explain the absence of an APA programme by the necessity for simplicity and certainty but the more likely explanation is the RFB saw no need for it because the fixed margins were clear. SARS' explanation for the absence[699] of an APA programme is 'depends on various factors' but then fails to elaborate but *Honibell's*[700] observation that the more likely explanation is an insufficiency of administrative capacity is a part explanation. The more likely reason, in the author's opinion, is SARS' inability to obtain suitable comparables. Sovereignty protection to counter mispriced transactions and double taxation also are consequences of the Russian and China APA programmes being limited respectively, to large resident companies[701] or companies with turnovers exceeding RMB40m.[702] TP is now extremely litigious[703] in India, which, follows from India's need to counter illicit outflows with limited available tax tools, i.e. without a thin capitalization rule or a GAAR. This has resulted in India introducing additional compliance procedures. Although the APA[704] programme (which was designed to complement the DRP,[705]) was seen as assisting in resolving disputes, it has been relatively unsuccessful, especially for US MNEs which ultimately enlisted the IRS and others lobbyists[706] to

---

698. Advance rulings – Brazil, IFA Cahiers 1999 – Volume 84b, p. 272.
699. Paragraph 16.2, *supra* n. 410.
700. *Supra* n. 212, at p. 638.
701. Russian PE's of non-residents also excluded: Article 115.19.
702. APA originally TP method: Article 28, Guo Shui Fa (1998) No. 59, from 2002 commencement was relatively poor with 67 unilateral and 37 bilateral APAs (*supra* n. 688, p. 14) with 110 yet to be concluded.
703. Number of TP cases more than 700 in IBFD Tax Case Database 19 Dec. 2014 and more than 1300 at 31 Jul. 2016. Adjustments of $846m for 2004 year, $605m for 2003 and $290m for 2002 (Chaudhury, India-Structuring an Appropriate TP Policy, Asia-Pac. Tax Bull, 2006; *supra* n. 655) trend is otherwise with adjustments increasing from 25% in 2010 to 59% cases and with collections from $1.1bn to more than $2bn (*supra* n. 388), 2011 approx. $8.5bn (Supekar, India- Development of TP Jurisprudence, Asia-Pac. Tax Bull, Volume 19, No. 1,2013), 2012 approx. $9bn (Chakravarty, India – BEPS Impact on TP – Relevance of Current Actions on India, Asia-Pac. Tax Bull, (Volume 20), No. 4, 2014).
704. MOF in 2001 refused to implement an APA programme because of IRD's so-called inadequate data and experience but 'may reconsider' a programme after three years. Introduced voluntary APA to complement the Dispute Resolution Panel (Rules 10F/10T) formed to reduce disputation (Para. 37, Explanatory Circular for Finance (No. 2) Act, 2009 which did not reduce disputation.
705. DRP focus changed from resolving disputes to increasing tax as evidenced GE India Technology Centre Private Limited v. DRP, TS-462-HC-2011(KAR) (when power to increase did not exist) but by M/s.Hamon Shriram Cottrell Pvt. Ltd. v. Income Tax Officer Ward 8(2), Mumbai. 400 065 Pan: AAACT2254Q, ITAT, Mumbai, 19 Apr. 2013 it existed and by Ranbaxy Laboratories Ltd v. Deputy Commissioner Of Income Tax W.P.(C) 6728/2011, 24 Jan. 2013 only the disclosure by company prevented DRP reopening assessment.
706. Disputation increased for US companies resulting in them supporting neither bilateral APAs nor India's approach to TP leading to double taxation for US MNEs in large number of cases and Investment Company Institute letter to India and US CA, February 2013; CBDT: India/US Bilateral relationship, letter dated 18 Apr. 2013 describing steps taken by India to reduce double taxation; Danilack, Deputy Commissioner (International), IRS reported Tax Notes Int'l, 4 Feb. 2013, criticized India's CA and described India's audit process as 'irrational' but disagreements resolved January 2015 when US and Indian CAs agreed way forward (Hindu, 6 Aug. 2015, 'India, U.S. resolve 35 TP disputes in IT sector' http://www.thehindu.com/business/india-us -resolve-35-transfer-pricing-disputes-in-it-sector/article7508664.ece).

Chapter 4: Countering Avoidance: SAARs

produce a way forward. However, even for MNEs with an APA there has not been much in the way of significant reduction in compliance because the *Annual Compliance Report*[707] remains still to be filed and the IRD's right to audit the MNEs compliance[708] with the APA continues to be unfettered. Furthermore, with the IRD possessing a right to cancel[709] the APA without appeal (except to a Constitutional Court)[710] as a consequence of failing to file that *Report* on time or for the *Report* containing material breaches, India's rights to cancel the APA are wider than those available in the developed world. India's compliance also seems wider than that of the developed world and certainly wider than China where SAT[711] possesses a right to cancel[712] an APA but only for enterprises which have operating results falling outside of the ALP or profits agreed in the APA. Whether enterprises can resort to the dispute settling procedures in BITs, WTO or under human rights legislation, to overturn the cancellations of an APA is considered in Chapter 8 of this study.

The decision by Russia, India and China to issue unilateral APAs (even though India and China can issue bilateral APAs and India multilateral APAs)[713] breaches the developed world's recommendations, but the author concludes that this approach supports the importance to them of their tax sovereignty when allocating income between countries. India's reluctance to fully participate in the programme is clear from the *CBDT Press Release (2016)*[714] which confirmed that only 41 APAs (including three bilateral APAs with Japan and the UK) had been agreed but with a mammoth 581[715] applications waiting to be considered. The position is a little better in China but still one of general disinterest by the China tax authorities, as is evident during the 2015/2014 period,[716] where 113 APAs (with a further seven concluded but not signed) were agreed and with 249[717] pending. Maybe the limited number of APAs in India and China is partly explained by manpower limitations but is more likely explained by a reluctance to give up tax sovereignty to a foreign country. This position is to be contrasted with that in Russia where of the approx. fifty APA applications received during 2013/2014 only approx. twenty remain to be processed.[718]

The other side of the APA programme is the TP method which the CAs adopt in the APA and except for China, little information is publicly available on which method

---

707. Form 3CEF.
708. CBDT, Rules 10 O/P, 36/2012.
709. CBDT, Rule 10R (1)(iii/iv).
710. ITD, APA Guidance with FAQs, p. 74.
711. Chapter 6, *supra* n. 200 Article 42, EITL; Article 113 Implementation Rules; Article 53, TCALAR.
712. Article 56(3), *supra* n. 200.
713. EY, Global TP Tax Authority Report, 2014, http://www.ey.com/Publication/vwLUAssets/EY-global-transfer-pricing-tax-authority-survey/$FILE/ey-2014-global-transfer-pricing-tax-authority-survey.pdf.
714. 1 Feb. 2016.
715. Investment advisory services, software development services and IT-enabled services.
716. China APA Annual Report, p. 20 http://www.chinatax.gov.cn/n810219/n810724/c1951566/part/1951585.pdf.
717. *Supra* n. 716, p. 22.
718. *Supra* n. 713.

they adopt. China has mainly adopted the TNMM[719] (74%) method[720] and this confirms a divergence from the developed world's preference for CUP. Asserting that TNMM is the most used method is difficult to reconcile with *Shenzhen*[721] where CUP was the preferred TP method for the sale of tangible goods.

4.3.10 Audit Selection

Using the available information to determine which enterprise to audit is a complicated process and one requiring the risks to be matched with available resources. For this reason, it is not surprising that the developed world[722] recommends adopting a flexible approach to audit selection.

This study concludes that Brazil, Russia and India now use automated systems in audit selection while it is difficult to know what is done in China and SA because they are yet to publish on the topic. The author also concludes that there is a wide range of issues which India and China test for, and that the Indian audit selection criteria has proven to be incompatible with the tax authority's manpower levels leading to an explosion in disputation. The study also concludes that with China having dramatically increased manpower levels in recent years, (a fundamental requirement to the working of its system of negotiating settlements), rationally, this has resulted in a quicker resolution of disputes.

Brazil's approach to audit selection, according to EY,[723] has been to establish a Special Delegacy for Largest Taxpayers (DEMAC) based in São Paulo with branches in Rio de Janeiro and Belo Horizonte and to interrogate the sophisticated IT system which enterprises log information into when fulfilling their disclosure obligations, as *Ayub*[724] observes. This approach compensates for the limited tax authority manpower. EY[725] has confirmed that in recent years audits have focussed on the automotive, pharmaceutical, chemical and oil, gas industries together with intra-group services. Russia has established in Moscow an interregional[726] TP team which undertakes analytical work on TP and together with a team of approx. forty professionals not only leading the TP

---

719. **CPM** preferred for tangibles because it avoids consequences of few comparables for products sold overseas. APA Report describes **TNNM** as most used method a view supported by the absence of **CPM** in TP assessments, *supra* n. 688, Article 53, Guo Wu Yuan Ling No. 362; CPM (15%), CUP (4%), PSM (3%) RSM (1%) and 3% other (SAT 2013 APA Report, p. 27). OECD believes CUP is most appropriate for intangibles where comparables exits and PSM otherwise, CFA, Revised Discussion on Intangibles, para. 164/166.
720. 65% of APAs relate to tangibles so China prefers TNMM over CUP (15% intangibles, 20% services, SAT 2013 APA Report, p. 24) in tangibles transactions.
721. Shenzhen-STB.
722. Chapter IV, section B1, *supra* n. 418.
723. *Supra* n. 713, p. 16/38/40/102.
724. Navigating Brazil TP complexity, September 2015.
725. TP Global Reference Guide, 2013, http://www.ey.com/GL/en/Services/Tax/International-Tax/Transfer-Pricing-and-Tax-Effective-Supply-Chain-Management/2013-Transfer-pricing-global-reference-guide---Brazil, last visited 20 May 2016.
726. Created in April 2012 to employ plus 200 specialists, PwC, Russia's new TP Rules, Overview and Practical Aspects, http://www.pwc.com/gx/en/tax/publications/transfer-pricing/perspectives/assets/tpp-russiasnewrules.pdf.

Chapter 4: Countering Avoidance: SAARs

audits, but also negotiating APAs and enforcing Russian TP legislation. The interregional team collects, processes and analyses intercompany data and by comparing that data with market data, selects cases to audit. Adopting this approach results in a more precise audit selection and compensates for the relatively few TP officers to identify, audit and resolve. With India employing approx. 252 TP auditors in 2016 (70 from around 2012) it is unsurprising they have been unable to resolve the disputes leading to an almost 100% increase in litigated cases in the eighteen months to July 2016. While identifying TP problems to audit initially focussed on 'close connections',[727] as in *Anglo-French Textile*,[728] it became evident from *Kusum Products*[729] that this approach was not sustainable. Remembering that India neither had a rule to counter thin capitalization nor a GAAR, by 2003, it established as its audit selection criteria all transactions with foreign associates on the basis of values and frequency thresholds[730] without regard to risk. This confirms that India does not see TP as being avoidance because it did not establish avoidance as precondition for deciding to audit. This approach resulted in a substantial increase in the number of audits[731] even though there was no high probability that all (or any) of the enterprises audited had breached the rules. In response to what was seen as over auditing and the failure to sensitize for risks, in 2015, the audit guidance[732] was further updated with from 2016[733] the strict thresholds being augmented by a Computer Assisted Scrutiny Selection (CASS) risk factor system. While CASS risk factors have not been published, *EY*[734] believes they would likely include payments for intra-group services and using intangibles, significant transactions with related parties in low tax jurisdictions, intangible transfer transactions, business restructurings, loss making operations, significant advertising, marketing and promotional spend, excessive debt and entities characterized as limited risk. These are the classic risk factors and should result in fewer but more intense audits. With audits also triggered because of compliance failures, such as not filing the Accountant's Report or the Report's failure to include all transactions, this further increases the work load of the small tax authority team. Enterprises are also audited where, in prior years, they had been subject to a TP adjustment of approx. $1.5m. Unless the audit thresholds are substantially increased in India and without a

---

727. Sengupta, BRICS and Emergence, p. 126; International transaction's profit determined by applying ratio of total business profits to total business receipts (Desai, Tax Aspects of Transfer of Technology, Asia Pacific Bulletin, 1999); Dinoida, TP Demystified, Bharat Law House, New Delhi 2014/2015, p. 16; AO could determine profits using Rule 10/11, Income Tax Rules, 1962 for 'business connection' principle and had power to apply the same test when calculating resident's profit.
728. *Supra* n. 528.
729. Kusum Products Ltd, IT Reference No. 288 of 1987.
730. Section 119, Instruction No. 3, 20 May 2003, Computation of Income from International Transactions-associates exceeding INR50m and in 2006/2007 increased to plus INR150m without risk profiling for tax avoidance (Ramanujan, Rolls Royce Decision: Income Attribution to PE's, ITPJ, May/June 2008; *supra* n. 533).
731. IBFD DTC database lists 1086 TP cases, (25 Nov. 2015) with 10 cases predating 2006.
732. No. 15 of 2015.
733. Instruction No. 3 of 2016.
734. Indian tax administration issues revised guidance on TP audit procedures, 15 Mar. 2016, http://taxinsights.ey.com/archive/archive-news/indian-tax-administration-issues-revised-guidance-on-transfer-pricing.aspx, last visited 15 Jul. 2016.

substantial increase in the IRD manpower and with a backlog and relative disinterest to agree to APAs and with the substantial illicit outflows being structured through mispriced transactions, the probability for a certain and simple TP system in India is not high.

The published information does not disclose the China TP manpower numbers but according to *Jinyan Li*[735] approx. 100 officers were employed in 2012 on TP issues which increased to approx. 1,000 by 2014, of whom 200 were SAT based with the remainder based in the LTBs. She argues a further 20% increase was to take place by 2016 which large percentage increase is, according to *Yuan*,[736] explained by the relatively few TP disputes before 2008[737] resulting in the then need for few officers. The subsequent wide range of TP issues which China now focusses on in audits is giving rise to a greater manpower requirement. China acknowledges that even these numbers may be insufficient and should that be the case, one way of dealing with capacity shortage would be through industry wide or enterprise group audits.[738] This approach potentially mirrors Brazil's system of applying different fixed margins for different industries and could foretell China's future adoption of a TP system based on Brazil's fixed margins. As *Tang*[739] observed, the wide range of audit issues now focussed on by China includes offshoring of profits especially to havens,[740] as in *Chengdu*[741] where deductions for license fees were denied solely because the payee was a BVI resident, to enterprises receiving losses from non-resident associates and where payments were made to foreign licensors not owning the intellectual property, as in *Xiamen*.[742] It also included China enterprises incurring on-going losses (in related party transactions) or having low or fluctuating[743] profitability. Further, audit items for potential audit include non-deductible payments for fees paid to foreign associates[744] which were

---

735. Reinforcements from new review panel for substantial cases and National database (Eighth Session, UN Committee of Experts on International Cooperation in Tax Matters, 15/19 Oct. 2012 Geneva).
736. MNEs conducted business for years without audit: Yuan, China Changing TP Landscape: Like It or Not, ITPJ, 2013 (Volume 20), No. 4, p. 259/260/261.
737. Fewer than 233 TP audits conducted until recent years partially explained by limited resources, SAT 2013 APA Report: 6 officials in APA programme and 2006/2011 audits increased from 177 to 207.
738. UN TP Manual, para. 10.3.7.3.
739. *Supra* n. 515, at p. 46.
740. *Supra* n. 683, at p. 332.
741. 14 May 2014.
742. 20 Jan. 2014.
743. Article 29, *supra* n. 200.
744. *Ibid.*; Location of production and management decisions, investment returns and profits compared to similar companies, losses continue for atleast two years while business expands: Guoshuifa [1998] No. 59 (Circular 59); Guoshuifa [2004] No. 143 (Circular 143); Guoshuifa [2004] No. 118 (Circular 118); Guo Shui Han [2009] No. 363, Article 3; Bulletin 16 denies deductions for payments to foreign associates regardless of commercial circumstances where neither functions, risks nor substantive activities conducted; Guo Shui Fa (2008) No. 86; Payments for duplicative activities denied where enterprise's management decisions are controlled by foreign associate, per SAT or where they relate to shareholder activities little different from OECD 'no benefit' test. SAT agrees with Transfer Pricing Guidelines, (Chapter VII) for intra-group services but disagrees with deductibility of service fees where subsidiary may benefit if it does not require service, e.g. strategic management, group accounting and legal.

bundled[745] into other apparently deductible payments to camouflage them and mechanical matters, such as where enterprises failed to file, or filed incomplete forms[746] or failed to contemporaneously prepare documentation.

SARS' approach to audit for many years was a 'light touch' which resulted in few litigated TP disputes and the need for relatively few tax officials to administer the disputes. However, with *EY*[747] confirming that with more than thirty TP audits having been concluded in SA in recent years and more than thirty cases under investigation,[748] the 'light touch' is being abandoned. The increase in TP audits has arisen because SARS is now focussing on transactions entered into with foreign associates liable to lower taxes than those applicable to the SA counterpart[749] or companies which have long-term low or no SA profits.[750] It is also focussing on companies which make year-end 'true-up' payments as *KPMG*[751] observes.

4.3.11 Burden of Proof

Another important feature of the *Transfer Pricing Guidelines* is determining who has the burden of proving whether the actual price is the ALP. In the developed world, the policy is for the burden of proof[752] to remain with the tax authority except for taxpayers which fail to act in good faith or those where false or misleading returns are filed (*Transfer Pricing Guidelines* may reflect the civil law burden of proof, but not the common law, where it sits with the taxpayer). A dramatic divergence and one rationally driven both by limited manpower and the volume of the mispriced transactions to be countered, sees Brazil, India and China automatically shifting the burden of proof to the taxpayer for all TP disputes, while SA shifts the burden where the taxpayer fails to complete a TP Study. Given the developed world's acceptance that the burden can be shifted only in the event of evasion, and because Brazil, India, China and SA shift the burden, this supports this study's hypothesis that mispriced transactions are, for the BRICS, evasion. Russia does not shift the burden to the taxpayer from the FTS.

4.3.12 UN Transfer Pricing Manual[753]

With the developing countries a growing FDI focus for MNEs and because of their market size and due to their being at a different stage of the economic cycle to the developed countries, they present different issues on TP matters to those of concern to

---

745. Deductions for management and license fees through misdescription. SAT argues it is disadvantaged because services are provided beyond its borders resulting in difficulties identification unless enterprises describe the transaction in Annual Reports.
746. Article 115, FEITL Regulations.
747. EY, Global Tax Alert News from TP, December 2014.
748. *Supra* n. 747.
749. Paragraph 12.6.1, *supra* n. 410.
750. TP Associates, SA, p. 2, file:///C:/Users/Peter%20Wilson/Downloads/SouthAfrica_Country_Summary.pdf, 13 Jun. 2011.
751. *Supra* n. 531.
752. B2, para. 4.11, *supra* n. 410.
753. ST/ESA/347, NY, 2013.

the developed countries. As a consequence of canvassing these issues, the UN published a *UN Transfer Pricing Manual*[754] for use by developing countries to better understand the policy and administrative practices which those countries can use to counter MNE[755] TP strategies. In that Manual (Chapter 10),[756] the UN permitted the BRICS to outline the problems they have had to deal with in TP disputes and each, bar Russia, provided an outline. The main issues which they canvassed related to valuing intangibles (including location benefits, marketing intangibles and market premium), business reorganizations (shifting offshore functions and risks) resulting in full risk manufacturers converting into low risk and R&D Centres. Dealing with the insufficiency of comparables was also discussed. While the UN outlined that the BRICS simply presented their experiences, the more accurate description of what occurred is that they outlined their approaches for countering MNE strategies which result in value not being taxed in the country where it was created, a taxation[757] problem of major focus to the BRICS. The significance of the BRICS then having policies for dealing with these problems is that many of those policies were subsequently incorporated in the BEPS recommendations, discussed in Chapter 7 of this study.

4.3.13 Compensatory Adjustments and Double Taxation

Where one jurisdiction unilaterally makes TP adjustments or an enterprise elects a safe harbour (not incorporated in a bilateral DTC), then the likely outcome is that the enterprise or its counterparty will face economic double taxation.[758] The developed world recommends that foreign tax authorities allow secondary adjustments to reflect the additional (primary) tax, or in the case of a safe harbour, a different tax, to the other counterparty, but the provision does not require that adjustments be made. Additionally, secondary adjustments[759] can be made reflecting the notional economic consequences of the primary adjustment such as the additional benefit amount for the foreign enterprise being treated as dividend, equity or debt. This may give rise to WHT or a portion of the constructive equity or debt becoming liable to tax in some other manner, undefined by the *Transfer Pricing Guidelines*. The *OECD Model Convention* provides that 'compensatory adjustments' can be made under Article 9(2) to reflect the primary adjustment, in the related party's tax affairs but, as *Baker*[760] observes, this perception of Article 9(2) is not universally held. While Article 9(2) provides that the corresponding adjustments[761] '*shall*'[762] be made, the right to make that adjustment is limited when the primary adjustment is found by the counterparty tax authority, not to

---

754. Preamble to Chapter 10, *supra* n. 753, p. 357.
755. *Supra* n. 753, at p. iii.
756. *Ibid.*, Chapter 10.
757. *Supra* n. 17.
758. *Supra* n. 418, C2, para. 4.32.
759. *Ibid.*, para. 4.66.
760. *Supra* n. 419, 9B.05.
761. *Supra* n. 418, C5.
762. The term 'shall' first appeared in the 1977 Model.

Chapter 4: Countering Avoidance: SAARs

be acceptable,[763] i.e. secondary adjustments are non-mandatory.[764] In the absence of bilateral DTC compensatory relief, double taxation can only be avoided where the counterparty State offers unilateral relief or the parties gain relief through the MAP. Where disputes fail to settle within two years,[765] the taxpayer can request the dispute be settled by Arbitration.

None of the BRICS specifically provides in their domestic tax law for compensatory adjustments, an approach which aligns with their policy of not compromising their sovereignty on TP tax issues. Neither Brazil nor Russia provides for compensatory adjustments (broadly) in their DTCs even though the Russian Model[766] establishes such adjustments as policy. Decisions such as *United-Bakers Pskov LLC/ Kellogg Group*[767] confirm that absent compensatory adjustments, double taxation results in Russia but the question then is whether relief from that double taxation is available under the MAP. In Brazil, as *PwC*[768] observed, 'few taxpayers have tested this course (*MAP*) and none successfully because Brazil's TP rules were enacted after the DTCs became effective'. The better view, according to the author is that where the DTC does not contain an Article 9(2) based on the *OECD Model Convention*, there can be no legal basis for MAP.[769] Since the Russian MAP policy, according to *Deloitte*,[770] does not *require* the CAs to consult to avoid double taxation, this creates uncertainty but should the counterparty reside in one of the three DTCs[771] containing an Arbitration Clause, then double taxation may be avoided this way. The Indian approach is clearer even though also unhelpful, because the CA[772] has confirmed that where the DTC does not contain an *OECD Model Convention* Article 9(2), MAP cannot apply. With approx. thirty Indian bilateral DTCs[773] not containing Article 9(2), the prospect of economic double taxation for counterparties relying on those DTCs is high. In China, as *Tang*[774] argues, the CAs are '*not obliged*' to follow MAP[775] but merely to use their 'best

---

763. *Supra* n. 418, para. 4.35.
764. *Ibid.*, para. 4.35.
765. *Ibid.*, para. 4.40.
766. 24 Feb. 2010, No. 84, Russian Model DTC; *supra* n. 66.
767. Federal Commercial Court of the North-West Region 18 Sep. 2013, United-Bakers Pskov LLC/ Kellogg Group, A52-4072/201218 September 2013.
768. *Supra* n. 683, at p. 296.
769. OECD Model Commentary, Positions, para. 5.
770. Deloitte, Global TP Country Guide, 2015, p. 188; Russia reserves the right to replace 'shall' with 'may'.
771. Netherlands (1996), Belgium (2015), Switzerland (2011).
772. India Rule 44H(2).
773. Non-OECD: Armenia (2003), Azerbaijan (1988), Bangladesh (1991), Belarus (1997), Brazil (1988), Bulgaria (1994), Kuwait (2006), Libya (1981), Malaysia (2001), Mauritius (1982), Moldova (1988), Mongolia (1994), Oman (1997), Russia (1997), Sierra Leone (1956), Ukraine (1999), Slovak (1986), Singapore (1981), UAE (1992), Uzbekistan (1993), Vietnam (1994) and Zambia (1981). OECD: Belgium (1993), Czech (1998), Germany (1995), Greece (1965), France (2000), Korea (1985), Spain (1983), Sweden (1997).
774. *Supra* n. 515, at p. 45.
775. Relief can be claimed where the bilateral DTC contains an Article 9(2) as Tiaonlong, p. 207, *supra* n. 3; MAP Procedures (7 Jul. 2005) observed.

endeavours' and because of this, with approx. eighteen DTCs[776] not containing an *OECD Model Convention* Article 9(2), relief seems unlikely in those DTCs. SA includes the *OECD Model Convention* Article 9(2) in all but a few of its DTCs,[777] which means that taxpayers faced with double taxation in SA should be able to access MAP. *Hattingh*[778] argues though that SA's approach generally gives rise to economic double taxation, but with just a few DTCs not offering compensatory relief, his observation seems too broad. With economic double taxation in the BRICS (bar SA) on TP matters a real possibility, the rights of taxpayers to resolve such disputes under either a BIT, WTO or Human Rights Conventions needs to be considered and Chapter 8 outlines the issues involved.

In relation to secondary adjustments, the BRICS take different approaches in that neither Brazil nor India make them, while Russia[779] makes them only for domestic transactions. In India, it requires a Court decision *(Vodafone India Services)*[780] to reject the TPO's assertion that such adjustments could be made. China and SA are able to make secondary adjustments with China levying dividend WHT[781] on the adjustment and SARS', prior to January 2015, levying interest[782] WHT on the adjustment. Since then, because of calculation and enforcement problems, SA now treats the adjustment as a distribution 'in specie' liable to 15% dividends tax without DTC relief.[783]

With each of the BRICS adopting various forms of safe harbours and without any of those safe harbours being included in bilateral DTCs[784], economic double taxation can arise, as *Vinnitskiy*[785] has argued for Russia. With many of the BRICS DTCs failing to include an Article 9(2) modelled on the *OECD Model Convention* and with their policies not encouraging MAP participation, the ability to resolve that double taxation is limited. The author therefore concludes that for Brazil, Russia and India the simplicity and cost advantages the tax authorities sought from granting safe harbours are likely to be swept away by the double taxation and the costs of resolving it which

---

776. OECD: Austria (1991), Belgium (1988T), Canada (1986), France (1984), Germany (1985T), Hungary (1992), Korea (1994), Italy (1996), Japan (1983), Slovenia (1988), Spain (1990), Switzerland (1990T), UK (1984T), Non-OECD: Bosnia (1988), Croatia (1988T), Macedonia (1988T), Malaysia (1985), Thailand (1986).
777. OECD: Article 9(2): Germany (1965), Israel (1978), Italy (1996), Sweden (1955T), Switzerland (1967T), UK (1968T); Non-OECD: (Brazil 2003), Malawi (1968), Sierra Leone (1951), Swaziland (1972T), Tanzania (1959T), Trinidad (1960T), Uganda (1959T), Zambia (1956T), Zimbabwe (1965)). SA obliged not to make corresponding adjustments in DTCs with Canada (1997), Mexico (2009) and Seychelles (1998) and only for fraud, wilful default, or gross negligence.
778. Key practical issues to eliminate double taxation of business income – SA, IFA Cahiers 2011 – Volume 96B, p. 578.
779. Federal Law No. 150-FZ, June 2015.
780. Vodafone India Services Pvt Ltd. V. Union of India & Ors, Writ Petition No. 1877, 2013; Itra, Undervaluation of Shares and Secondary adjustments: Next wave of TP litigation in India, TPIJ, 2013, International Tax Centre.
781. Wong, China-International Tax Review, February 1999, p. 251.
782. Section 31, ITA.
783. EY, Global Tax Alert: SA amends law on TP Secondary adjustments, March 2015.
784. Paragraph 4.102/4.109, *supra* n. 418.
785. *Supra* n. 3.

follows from adopting the safe harbour. With most of China's DTCs containing compensatory adjustment provisions, double taxation can be reversed if the China CA agrees to the adjustment, since it is not obliged to allow the adjustment. Any economic double taxation in SA is likely to be resolved under the compensatory adjustment provisions.

4.3.14 Transfer Pricing: BRICS Cooperation

While cooperating on countering TP is an objective of the BRICS Revenue Heads[786] and cooperating on ensuring value is taxed in the country of creation and where the services were performed, is a Leader's objective, it is difficult to find much evidence of the members' actual cooperation in developing TP policy. It is evident that India[787] has provided both China and SA with assistance in developing their TP regime, but there is no published evidence on the form or content of that assistance. However, this study concludes there is evidence of common a position on where value creation should be taxed as well as compliance matters, including contemporaneously prepared and annually delivered documentation and penalties for failing to prepare or deliver. The study also concludes that there is evidence of common positions on reversing the onus of proof, compensatory adjustments and on the establishment of safe harbours. As the BRICS have announced the establishment in each tax authority of a point of contact for the other BRICS' tax authorities, and because there is much similarity in the broad thrust of their TP rules and having regard to the existing cooperation between India, China and SA, the author s deduces that there has been cooperation in the development of policy because coincidence seems unsupportable.

4.3.15 BRICS: Significance of Widening of TP

With countering mispriced transactions viewed as being integral to stemming illicit outflows but constrained by limited TP tax authority manpower, the BRICS have by widening the definitions included additional relationships within the rules. The consequence of these widened definitions when working in tandem with difficult to avoid documentation requirements has been an explosion in disputation, certainly in India, where audit criteria until recently covered all transactions exceeding thresholds. While safe harbours have apparently been designed to both lessen the disputation and channel investment, they come at a cost to the ALS especially in India, and in the absence of compensatory adjustments to avoid economic double taxation, have resulted in the development of a system which is contrary to the objectives of certainty

---

786. New Delhi, 17/18 Jan. 2013.
787. Transfer Pricing – India experience, March 2014 – Issue 174 https://www.saica.co.za/integritax/2014/2290._Transfer_pricing_-_India_experience.htm.

and predictability. Reflecting on the BRICS reversing the onus of proof in TP matters from the developed world's approach, and relying on the developed world's acquiescence that reversal is indicative of evasion, the author concludes, that this supports his hypothesis that in the BRICS, mispriced transactions constitute evasion.

4.4 CFC RULES

4.4.1 Background

This subsection researches whether the BRICS CFC rules have been widened from those of the developed world[788] and if so, whether the widened format can be effective in countering the accumulation of passive income in lowly taxed foreign entities and whether the tax authority manpower limitation was relevant in the shaping of the rules. This subsection also searches for evidence confirming whether the widened format results from cooperation amongst the BRICS.

The relevance of the rules is to be determined against the background of outbound FDI flows[789] and the author concludes that the widening for China and Russia[790] (and the proposed Indian format) is designed to simplify the rules. SA's divergence responds to the need to support the Government's RHQ[791] focus while Brazil's widening is designed to ensure that both individuals and enterprises are taxed on a level playing field basis. There is little evidence of coordination between the BRICS in developing their CFC policies or law.

Having regard to the volume of OFDI (*see* Chapter 1 Table 1.1), the rules have the most significance for Russia, China and SA, because the Russia and SA OFDI exceeds the inflow into those countries and has done so in each of the 2014 and 2015 years and for China because outflow and inflow are essentially in balance, but very substantial. The OFDI in both India and Brazil is small in comparison to the inbound FDI.

4.4.2 Exchange Controls and OFDI

In the absence of much OFDI in the pre-liberalization and immediate post liberalization periods, there was little need for a rule designed to tax at residence, passive income derived in a foreign controlled enterprise which had been lowly taxed at source. The need for such rules was also lessened because OFDI was controlled by exchange

---

788. OECD, International Tax Avoidance and Evasion, Four Related Studies, Paris: OECD, 1987; OECD, CFC Legislation: Studies in Taxation of Foreign Source Income (1996); OECD, Harmful Tax Competition-An Emerging Global Tax Issue (1998).
789. *Supra* n. 31, at p. 8.
790. China and Russia are two of the world's top six investor countries in 2013 and 2014 with China and India (*supra* n. 31, p. 26) expected to be two of the top twelve investor countries in the near future, with the other BRICS members not placed in the top twenty OFDI.
791. *Supra* n. 31, at p. 9.

controls. Brazil,[792] China[793] and SA[794] all eventually established the rules with China being the last of this three to do so in 2008. Russia[795] established its rules from 2015. India's[796] rules are yet to be enforced ostensibly, as the *Financial Express*[797] asserts, because of an expectation that as currently drafted they may not be compatible with the *BEPS Action Report 3* recommendations,[798] but should be.

Brazil's exchange controls impacted OFDI as *Goldfajn*[799] observed, not by preventing capital flight, but by establishing a 40% 'black market' premium during the 1980s which peaked at 170% by May 1989. This premium lead to import over-invoicing and export under-invoicing as the means to accumulate profits offshore. The Russian[800] and Indian[801] exchange controls were intended to prevent the formation of foreign entities but Russian persons circumvented them by using nominees to form tax haven companies, trusts or foundations on their behalf. Relatively few Indian owned foreign companies were formed, and those which were 'close',[802] were taxed in India

---

792. Ordinary Law No. 9,249-1995 taxes residents on foreign subsidiary/affiliate's profit as asset in the balance sheet regardless of dividends paid; NI No. 38/1996 (followed by Ordinary Laws No. 9,532/1997 and 9,959/2000) taxes available profits after payment of dividends. Complementary Law No. 104-2001 (amended Article 43, BTC) made taxing independent of the CFCs location, legal status and source (para. 1) and determined timing and conditions for when foreign income was deemed available (para. 2). PM No. 2,158-35/2001 established principle of profits deemed available when deemed distributed i.e. year end.
793. China implemented limited rule in January 1991 applying to transactions between China residents and associates. This required them to transact on a reasonable commercial basis: Article 54, (1991 Rules) to counter the accumulation of profits in offshore connected entities but EITL (Chapter 6 of the EITL, Article 45) extended application.
794. Absence of rules to counter the accumulation of passive income in lowly taxed neighbouring countries (Danziger, The disregard of a legal entity for tax purposes – SA, IFA Cahiers 1989 – Volume 74a, p. 126) observed, justified the 'source plus' rule (introduced 1997, Taxing of items arising from SA sources plus limited categories of foreign source items, Engel, National Treasury's Detailed Explanation to section 9D of ITA (June 2002), Preface, http://www.treasury.gov.za/divisions/tfsie/tax/legislation/Detailed%20Explanation%20to%20Section%209D%20of%20the%20Income%20Tax%20Act.pdf) which taxed foreign source income but by 2001/2002, in tandem with further loosening of exchange controls and the Katz Commission's recognition of growing outbound FDI (Katz, section 1.9, http://www.polity.org.za/polity/govdocs/commissions/katz1-2.html), the 'residence minus' system (Engel, *supra* n. 794 explained the 'residence-minus' system of taxing on a worldwide basis less limited categories of foreign source items) was implemented to tax a foreign entity's non=business income (section III, p. 7 and following, Engel, *supra* n. 794; Eskinazi, Source And Residence: A New Configuration Of Their Principles – SA, IFA Cahiers 2005 – Volume 90A p. 586) except for business income diverted from SA which too became taxable.
795. Bill introduced into Duma, October 2014, enacted in November 2014, signature by Federal Council, December 2014 (Law No. 630365-6), effective 1 Jan. 2015 http://base.consultant.ru/cons/cgi/online.cgi?req=doc;base=LAW;n=180884;fld=134;dst=1000000001,0;rnd=0.5458116580266505.
796. India published a draft in 2010 DTC (section 58(2)(u) and Clause 5(a), Twentieth Schedule) later expanded in 'Second Schedule', DTC 2013.
797. Prasad, Financial Express, 20 May 2015.
798. Issued 11 Oct. 2015.
799. Capital Flows and Controls in Brazil What Have We Learned?, National Bureau of Economic Research, May 2007, p. 372.
800. Belyakova, Draft Law Would Introduce New CFC Regime in Russia, 2014 WTD 218-5.
801. *Supra* n. 533.
802. Section 104/109, ITA 1961, withdrawn Finance Act, 1987.

on the shareholder level to the extent of the distributions being insufficient.[803] Consequent to the 2001 exchange controls relaxation, Indian OFDI[804] increased and by 2003, the *Mathur Committee*[805] recommended the introduction of CFC rules which, as explained above, are yet to become effective. With China encouraging OFDI since 1979, its exchange controls had little impact in preventing the outflow, but as Davies[806] observes, the amount of OFDI was not significant before 2002 because it was only from 2000 that the 'Going Global' policy became effective. Of major difference though for China was that most providers of OFDI were SOEs which had little reason to illicitly move money offshore or to avoid repatriating profits. SA[807] exchange controls however have limited OFDI and continue to do so, especially where it is detected that a tax haven is to be used as a conduit for the OFDI into third countries.

4.4.3 Evolution of the Rules

A combination of exchange controls and the volume of OFDI were instrumental in shaping the evolution of the BRICS CFC rules and while the early intention of the BRICS, bar Brazil, was to tax income accumulating in tax havens, Brazil's approach was designed to tax resident companies and individuals on a world-wide basis leaving investors indifferent to the structure adopted for foreign investment. Brazil' rules were also different to those of the developed world because they were designed tax Brazilian controllers of foreign companies on their foreign income whether the foreign companies were subsidiaries or affiliates, as in *Eagle Distribuidora de Bebidas*.[808] Of much relevance to the effectiveness of the rules in Brazil was the debate on whether or not they were constitutional, with Brazil enterprises maintaining that they were unconstitutional because the rules taxed active foreign income in the same way as passive income. The MNEs argued that this gave rise to a competitive disadvantage for Brazilian MNEs. Of the many reasons advanced supporting the rules' unconstitutionality, some which resonated most, were their taxing of income (deemed dividends) before realization *(Torres* and *Oliveira)*,[809] their failure to exclusively apply to abusive transactions *(Rolim*[810] and *Bocachica)*[811] and being contrary to the policy of encouraging Brazilian MNE's international growth *(Pires)*.[812] Of the reasons supporting their constitutionality, the two of most relevance were that they countered abuse *(da Silveira*

---

803. Sections 92 and 93, ITA 1961.
804. Direct/portfolio: US$ 44.80bn (2008); US$77.50bn (2009); US$80.32bn (2010) per RBI.
805. Report of Working Group on Non Resident Taxation, January 2003, para. 3.3.2.
806. China Investment Policy, OECD Working Papers on International Investment 2013/01, p. 34.
807. F.6 Capital transactions, 6.1 Foreign investment by SA residents, SA Foreign Exchange Manual.
808. No. 16327.000530/2005-28, Sentence No. 101-97070, 17 Dec. 2008.
809. At p. 150/157/159, *supra* n. 161; *supra* n. 398.
810. Rolim, Tax Treaty Disputes: Global Theory and Practice: The BRICS World, LSE, October 2012, p. 24.
811. Constitutionality of the Brazilian CFC Legislation, Bull. Intl. Taxn, 2013 (Volume 67), No. 10, p. 567.
812. Brazil/International/European Union, The Brazilian CFC Regime: A Comparative Analysis from an International Tax Law Perspective, Bull. Intl. Taxn, 2013 (Volume 67), No. 6, p. 295/297.

Chapter 4: Countering Avoidance: SAARs

and *D'Éça*)[813] and they resulted in companies and individuals being taxed on a like basis *(Guerra)*.[814] It was not until *National Industry Confederation and Direct Action of Unconstitutionality* 2,588[815] that the rules were held to be unconstitutional for foreign affiliates not resident in tax preferred jurisdictions and for the purpose of retroactivity to 2002, as in *Embraco Empresa*[816] and constitutional, for profits of tax haven controlled entities as in *Coamo Agroindustrial*.[817] The constitutionality for CFCs resident in countries being not tax preferred jurisdictions nor for foreign affiliates was left undecided. In order to provide some guidance through this maze, the RFB[818] amended the rules, which according to *Ronsenblatt*[819] resulted in them aligning with the developed world.

The Russia and China rules evolved from limited provisions countering foreign profit accumulation which were simple to circumvent. In Russia's case, the early approach of countering 'round tripping' by taxing in Russia foreign dividends[820] (sourced in profits shifted offshore) through reversing the dividend exemption, was found to be ineffective because MNEs simply ceased paying dividends, and instead granted loans back, as *Bruk* and *Matchekhin*[821] explain. They also explained that reversing the dividend exemption did not counter international avoidance structures or indirect disposal of Russian assets, as *Boltenko*[822] confirmed. All this resulted in the 2013[823] proposed Russian CFC[824] rules which became effective from January 2015.

In China's case, the limited provisions before 2008 taxed the profits of so-called non-independent business dealings[825] but since these were 100% foreign ownerships, it was as *de Ridder*[826] observed, simple to restructure the shareholding so that the China

---

813. *Supra* n. 590; Trends in company shareholder taxation: single or double taxation? – Brazil, IFA Cahiers 2003 – Volume 88a, p. 213.
814. Tax treatment of corporate losses – Brazil, IFA Cahiers 1998 – Volume 83a p. 352.
815. National Industry Confederation, 2011; Direct Action of Unconstitutionality 2,588, 10 Apr. 2013.
816. Embraco Empresa Brasileira de Compressore, April 2013.
817. Coamo Agroindustrial Cooperativa Extraordinary Appeal 611, 586 April 2013.
818. Law 12,973, May 2014 and NI 1520, December 2014.
819. O'Shea, London Conference Debates, International Tax Issues, Tax Notes Int'l, 28 Nov. 2011, p. 627.
820. Exempt for Russians owning plus 50% of foreign company's capital for 365 or more continuous days when invested amount was plus $US17m.
821. *Supra* n. 246, at p. 690; *supra* n. 428, p. 641; EOI and cross-border cooperation between tax authorities – Russia, IFA Cahiers 2013 – Volume 98B p. 659.
822. Russia's 2015 Tax Revolution, 2015 WTD 209-14.
823. President Putin, December 2013, transactions which should be taxed in Russia include sale of TNK-BP occurring outside Russia even though sellers and buyers were Russian residents; atleast $111bn of Russian goods (20%, total exports) were sold through foreign companies; atleast 50% of $50bn Russian OFDI invested into offshore entities and revenues of companies organized in offshore jurisdictions belong to Russian beneficiaries; Committee of Federation Council for Budget and Financial Markets, 16 Dec. 2013 approved twelve proposals for de-offshorization.
824. First draft changes to Part 1/Part 2, RFTC introduced 18 Mar. 2014, Second 27 May 2014; Third 26 Jun. 2014.
825. Article 54, *supra* n. 793.
826. China International Tax Considerations, November/December 2005, Asia-Pac. Tax Bull, p. 469.

enterprise no longer owned 100% of the foreign company.[827] Regardless of the simplicity in circumvention, the real question for China was whether it was necessary to implement any CFC rules[828] when the preponderance of OFDI was made by SOEs[829] which, as *Yang*[830] and the *World Bank*[831] observed, regularly distributed profits to their Government shareholders. SA's rules for taxing foreign income which arose from OFDI made in the post apartheid era, were shaped first by the *Franzen Commission* and then later by the *Margo Commission*,[832] but how foreign passive income was taxed was uncertain. Active foreign income was generally untaxed in SA.

It is clear that the BRICS CFC rules developed in response to their growing OFDI, round tripping, international trade and the accumulation offshore of passive income.

4.4.4 Control

The developed world requires a 'control' relationship to be established between the resident and non-resident before the rules can apply and the BRICS, except for Brazil, followed suit.

The developed world's definition of 'control' for CFC purposes mirrors the developed world's definitions of 'associate' for thin capitalization and TP purposes, which results in a control relationship being established even in the absence of legal control, i.e. de-facto control. Legal 'control' generally but not always, requires more than 50% ownership and it is most unusual for the qualifying percentage to fall to 10%.

As is evident from the thin capitalization and TP discussion in this study, the BRICS' have widened the meaning of legal and de-facto 'control' and for CFC purposes they again reduce the legal threshold to 20% and 25% respectively in Brazil [833] and Russia[834] and by including additional legal and de-facto relationships. India's draft provisions[835] also widen the net by not setting a threshold above which control exists. China[836] and SA[837] both leave the legal control constituting ownership at 50%, but

---

827. Article 52, *supra* n. 793 (Article 13, FEITL limited the investment to wholly owned subsidiaries) referred to 'control'.
828. Article 45 EITL; Implementing Rules and *supra* n. 200.
829. Huffpost Politics, China 'Going Out, 2.0: Dawn of a New Era for Chinese Investment Abroad, June 2015 http://www.huffingtonpost.com/china-hands/china-going-out-20-dawn-o_b_7046 790.html; CSIS, 'Freeman Briefing, China's Going Out investment Strategy, 27 May 2008, last visited 10 Jul. 2016 http://csis.org/files/publication/080527_freeman_briefing.pdf, p. 3.
830. *Supra* n. 378.
831. SOE Dividends: How Much and to Whom?, p. 2, October 2005.
832. First taxed by the *Franzen Commission*, Appointed November 1967 and then not taxed by the *Margo Commission*, *supra* n. 292.
833. Includes ventures controlled jointly with non-related parties; Rosenblatt, Brazil: Recent case law and new CFC rules, Queen Mary, University of London, 3rd Annual BRICS Conference.
834. Law 376-FZ, Article 25:13 and Law 150-FZ.
835. De-facto test of 'dominant influence' in relation to a foreign company with a 'special contractual relationship' (Schedule Twenty, Direct Taxes Code 2010, section 5(b)(iii) and Schedule Two, Direct Taxes Code 2013, section 5(b)(iii)) with an Indian company is also unclear and is likely to lead to substantial administrative complexity for both the IRD and taxpayers without better definition.
836. Article 115(A), *supra* n. 200.
837. Section 9D, *supra* n. 670.

widen the constituents of de-facto control. Illustrative of Brazil's extension of de-facto control is its inclusion of relationships which exert influence (but at a level lower than the 'top level' decisions) over the non-resident's 'financial and operating policy' even where the resident does not actually control the company.[838] Russia has widened the group of persons accounted for in the 25% legal threshold by including individuals (as well as companies) holding interests in foreign foundations, foreign partnerships, trusts and other collective investments. In relation to the 'concentration test' (aggregating each resident's participation exceeding 10% to accumulate to Russian shareholding exceeding 50%) the aggregation of spouses and minor children holdings aligns with the developed world, while the absence of a concentration test for non-corporate structures represents a potential loophole. In extending control to persons exercising, or having the right to exercise a 'decisive influence'[839] on 'profit distributions' regardless of the legal basis for doing so, control is widened from the developed world's right to influence a 'company's affairs'. China widens the legal and de-facto tests by, in relation to the legal test, including individuals when applying the concentration test (aggregating residents owning at least a 10%[840] interest contributing to the 50% test)[841] and in treating a more than 50%[842] second tier holding as being 100% ownership at the first tier (same as for thin capitalization and TP). In relation to de-facto control, its extension to residents exerting substantial influence over the foreign person's purchases or sales[843] also widens the net. SA[844] legally widens by including in the concentration test, persons with rights to participate or vote[845] from as little as 1%.

4.4.5 Potentially Attributed Income

Having established the basis for determining which foreign enterprises can be 'controlled', the next step is to work out which income or gain amount of the CFC is potentially attributed income to the controller because, depending on classifications, the controller's country of residence may seek to tax it. In working out the potentially attributed amount, the developed world normally requires the foreign person to rework its 'taxable profits' assuming it is tax resident in the controller's country, and then by reference to the person's jurisdiction profits[846] or transaction profits, such as those referable to holding, financial/banking, sales invoicing, IP assets, digital goods and

---

838. Effective 1 Jan. 2015, taxpayers elect to apply from 2014 year.
839. Provision of, or ability to exercise decisive influence on asset manager's decisions for distribution of profit (income) between participants (shareholders, principals or others) or other beneficiaries as prescribed by foreign legislation or agreement governing the entity.
840. Article 116, Consultation Draft Circular 'Implementation Measures' to replace Circular 2, *supra* n. 455.
841. Article 115(A), *supra* n. 200.
842. Article 77, *supra* n. 200.
843. Article 117(2), PRC Regulations on Implementation of EITL.
844. Section 9D, *supra* n. 670.
845. Section 9D, *supra* n. 670. Shares representing equity capital, including non-participating preference shares but excluding convertible debentures, options and similar interests until converted into shares; *supra* n. 794, p. 3.
846. Designing Effective Controlled Foreign Company Rules, Action 3 – 2015 Final Report, para. 95.

services, captive insurance or reinsurance.[847] The portion attributed to the controller is then calculated using its controlling percentage.

The BRICS adopt different approaches to the calculation with some widening the developed world's approach while others narrowing it. All bar SA adopt the CFC's 'undistributed profits' as the starting point instead of the jurisdiction or the transaction approach. Brazil however, treats the CFC's year end[848] 'undistributed profits'[849] (converted into reais) as if it were a dividend, as in *Eagle 2*,[850] and attributes it, leaving both the jurisdiction and transaction bases ignored. This means that for Brazil, by including both active and passive income in the potentially attributed amount there is no exemption from attribution. For foreign affiliates,[851] the actually distributed or accrued amount becomes the potentially attributed amount unless the controller elects[852] that the CFC rules should apply to the affiliate. Russia's approach to the undistributed profits[853] depends upon whether the company has been audited and tax resident in a country with which it has a DTC. As a concession and narrowing from the developed world, in such cases, the undistributed profits (converted into Roubles) listed in the foreign company's financial statements[854] would be accepted as the potentially attributed amount. Where the concession is inapplicable, the undistributed profits must be recalculated using Russia's corporate tax rules including the complex and unclear definitions of passive income,[855] which as *Davies*[856] observes, leaves much to the FTS' discretion, especially given the catch-all 'other income'[857] definition and results in a widening. Dividends paid by the foreign resident reduce the attributed amount. Two aspects of India's proposed calculation suggest it may intentionally lead to double taxation which would widen from the developed world. The first is India's proposal to adopt the CFC's book profits[858] as the potentially attributed income but to require adjustments for general provisions, interim dividends[859] and previously undeducted losses[860] but to retain capital gains in accordance with the *Standing Committee of Finance's*[861] recommendations. This calculation may prove to be difficult because it

---

847. *Supra* n. 846, para. 74.
848. NI 1520/2014; Law 12973/2014; Yolanda Participações s/a, Recurso Especial N° 1.211.882 – RJ (2010/0159996-0), 5 Apr. 2011.
849. CFC losses can be consolidated until 2022 providing not resident in tax haven, controlled by a privileged country resident, taxed at an effective rate less than 20% or less than 80% of profits are from active income.
850. Eagle Distribuidora de Bebidas S/A v. No. 16327.000530/2005-28, Sentence No. 101-97070, 17 Dec. 2008.
851. Jeffrey, New regulations for Brazilian CFC rules, International tax review, January 2015.
852. Law 13,259/2016.
853. Article 309.1.3(1-12), RTC.
854. Article 309, RTC but converted into roubles, Article 309.1(2), RTC.
855. Article 309.1 (4)(1-12), RTC.
856. CFC rules: towards the de-offshorisation of the Russian economy, Financier Worldwide, March 2015.
857. Article 309.1(4) (13), RTC.
858. Section 4, Schedule 2, India DTC 2010.
859. Standing Committee on Finance (2011/2012) Fifteenth Lok Sabha MOF, DTC Bill, 2010, 49th Report, p. 179.
860. If apportionable amount negative then not attributed to residents.
861. *Supra* n. 859.

presupposes access to information which may not be available to third party shareholders. Second, in relation to adjustments for mispriced transactions[862] made by the IRD which have increased the controller's Indian income, there is no proposal to reduce the CFC's book profits for the same amount in order to avoid double taxation. This potential double taxation serves to increase the deterrent and compliance obligations where both TP and CFCs are being used by Indian MNEs. China's approach is both concessionary and widening. It is concessionary in that it defines the potentially attributable amount as being the CFC's undistributed profits (converted into RMB) including passive income,[863] and in so doing avoids the obligation for widespread recalculations. It widens by requiring China's complicated passive income rules to be accounted for. SA[864] recalculates the CFC's book profits using SA's tax rules and includes passive income and widens by including capital gains.[865] As a further widening, it includes in undistributed profits, a portion of the CFCs adjusted book profits representing its period of ownership, should it leave the group before year end. This requirement presents administrative difficulties unless the company is sold at year end.

4.4.6 Substance

The developed world generally excludes the CFC's potentially attributed amount from attribution when its source country presence is of such substance with respect to functions, assets and risks that it can justify having earned the income itself, especially where the income has not been derived from an associate. This test is usually expressed either as a threshold above which the income is no longer attributed or by reference to specific activities.[866]

The study confirms that each of the BRICS, other than Russia, provides some form of substance exemption or relief and while Brazil does not provide an active income exemption, substance became relevant from January 2015[867] as a precondition for both the granting of a fictitious 9% tax credit for business undertakings in the oil/gas sector (e.g. production, chartering boats or services) and for consolidating[868] different CFC's financial results. Substance is of most importance in India and China and to a lesser extent in SA, because while each of India and China establish a proportional test for exemption, SA uses a nexus test. India exempts income from active trades or businesses[869] and in determining which activities satisfy the test, factors such as how local employees or other personnel are *used* in the CFC's industrial, commercial or financial undertakings or how the company fits into the *'economic life of*

---

862. Section 3(2) Schedule 2, *supra* n. 858.
863. Articles 76 and 80, *supra* n. 200.
864. Section 9D(2A), ITA 1962, *supra* n. 670.
865. Paragraph 2(1)(a), Eighth Schedule.
866. *Supra* n. 846, para. 4.2.2.
867. MOF 427/2014, 29 Sep. 2014; NI 1,520/2014, regulates taxing foreign income under Law 12,973/2014 and Law 13,043/2014.
868. Consolidation available until 2022, *supra* n. 867.
869. Section 5(a)(iv), Twentieth Schedule, Taxes Act 2010.

the territory' of which it is tax resident[870] are relevant. With these tests being subjective and devoid of explanation they are likely to give rise to disputation. *Sanghvi*[871] observes that the test can only be satisfied when activities are conducted in the CFC's residence country but if this were correct then it would exclude active foreign branches, which on a rational basis, seems incorrect. Therefore, the better view is that the exemption applies when activities are conducted in third countries from a fixed presence because those activities contribute to the 'economic life of the territory'. Substance is also key in India exempting passive income (a concept very widely defined)[872] because for the income to be exempt it must be derived from a base capable of generating the income, providing that the passive income is less than 50% of the potentially attributed amount. In relation to China, a CFC's potentially attributed amount will not be attributed where the CFC has substance providing the passive income represents less than 50% of the CFCs profits. Determining the meaning of substance in China is difficult but *Circular 2*[873] linked '*mainly*' and 'generated from active business operations'[874] but then failed to define the link. *Draft Circular 2*[875] explained the link as being the *contribution* to the CFC's income from the efforts of the resident country's employees, the assets it naturally uses for those efforts and the risks it assumes, a position *Dongmeui*[876] confirms and one supported by *Jinyan Li's* [877] observation that the decision of whether a CFC is engaged in 'active business operations' is made having regard to functions, risks, assets, personnel and the relevant business environment at its disposal. *Sharkey* and others[878] have recommended further clarification of the meaning of 'active' and 'mainly'. SA's position on substance[879] is similar to that of both India and China, but differently focusses on whether there is a 'nexus' between the foreign business establishment[880] (FBE) and the CFC's country of residence which confirms the activities as having a bona fide non-tax

---

870. Section 5(e)(I and ii), *supra* n. 869.
871. Proposed CFC Regime, Asia-Pac. Tax Bull, 2012 (Volume 18), No. 1, p. 57/58/61/62.
872. Dividends, interest, residential property rentals, capital gains, annuities, royalties, revenue from sale or licensing of intangibles for industrial, literary or artistic property, income from sale of goods or services (including financial services to persons directly or indirectly controlling the company or controlled by the company, or associated enterprises), income from managing, holding or investing in securities, shareholdings, receivables or other financial assets or other residuary sources providing less than 25% of total income.
873. *Supra* n. 200.
874. Article 84(ii), *supra* n. 200.
875. Article 119, *supra* n. 562.
876. CFC rules and the latest developments in the PRC, Xiamen University, PRC, http://www.law.hku.hk/aiifl/wp-content/uploads/ppt/TLRP-DoreenQiu-ppt.pdf.
877. China's CFC Regime existing Rules and improvement Suggestions, Bulletin for International Tax, Volume 68 No. 10, p. 537/538/540.
878. Sharkey, China's Income Tax Concept of 'Enterprise' and Concept of 'Company' – Interaction with the Australia/China Tax Treaty, IBFD Bulletin April 2005, p. 160/161; Lin, China Foreign Tax Credit and Global Investment Structures, Asia-Pac. Tax Bull, 2010 (Volume 16), No. 3, p. 223; Tang, China, Country Survey: Derivatives & Financial Instruments, 2013 (Volume 15), No. 5a/Special Issue, p. 92; Hou, China The Taxation of Partnerships Asia-Pac. Tax Bull, September/October 2014, p. 333; SAT website: http://202.108.90.175/fangtan/templates/n5/interviewlog.html.
879. Katz Fifth Report, p. 17/18, http://www.treasury.gov.za/publications/other/katz/5.pdf.
880. Sections 9D(9)(b) and 11, *supra* n. 670.

business usage,[881] a position which *Honibell*[882] confirms. Having regard to these factors, it is clear that the substance tests are subjective, even though the parameters are objective, and since the manpower at the tax authority to conduct the investigations is limited, the substance test will be difficult to administer in a certain and predictable manner.

4.4.7 Exemptions

The developed world acknowledges that some countries provide exemptions from the rules because they believe that avoiding stalling OFDI is important and reducing complexity encourages compliance and assists administration. However, the OECD's policy is to discourage exemptions being granted since doing so results in business fragmentation and increases administrative complexity.[883] The OECD acknowledges that the options for exempting the potentially attributed amount, includes the situation where that amount had been taxed at rates comparable to the rates applicable in the controller's country, or where the amount had been earned by a foreign entity established in a 'white list'[884] jurisdiction or where the amount falls below a de minimis threshold.

In each of the BRICS (except Brazil) providing exemptions, they diverge from the developed world and while Brazil chose not to provide exemptions in the belief that doing so would conflict with its policy of taxing individuals and companies on a comparable global basis, this resulted in Brazil's MNEs adopting business structures which they believed would qualify for the exemption. The Brazil MNEs did this by establishing companies in countries having DTCs with Brazil which contained an Article 7 (BPA) modelled on the *OECD Model Convention* Article 7, because they believed doing so would exempt the foreign company's potentially attributed amount from Brazilian taxation. This strategy is considered further below.

Each of Russia, India, China and SA included in their CFC rules comparable tax rate exemptions but the Russian and Indian formats suggests a less than wholehearted attitude to providing this exemption because of the confines established in which the exemption may apply. In Russia and SA both setting the exemption rate at not less than 75% of the comparable rate, it seems not to be very concessionary, but in Russia's case, the 75% must first, reflect the Russian effective rate[885] and second, the CFC must be incorporated in a country having a DTC with Russia, and, most importantly, the DTC must contain an information exchange Article and the FTS must believe that information will be exchanged by the counterparty state. Chapter 5 of this study confirms that most of Russia's DTCs contain an information exchange Article, but the FTS' long list

---

881. *Supra* n. 794, at p. 11/13.
882. *Supra* n. 210, at p. 581/583.
883. *Supra* n. 846, para. 3.2.
884. *Supra* n. 846, para. 3.1.
885. Article 25.13(7)(3), RTC.

of countries not exchanging information[886] gives reason to doubt the likely effectiveness of the exemption. As *Lungi*[887] observes, this provides the FTS with a route to override the exemption at will. In SA's case, the 75% rate must reflect the tax otherwise payable by the CFC[888] on that income. The comparable rate exemption for India is set at 50% of India's rate while the exemption rate for China cannot be set at a rate 'distinctly lower' than the China rate[889], which has been taken to be not less than 50%[890] of the China 'effective' rate, as confirmed in *Shandong*.[891] However, the usefulness of India's exemption for CFC foreign branches is questionable because the exemption is inapplicable where the CFC is neither taxed at the place of incorporation nor at the place of central management.[892]

Each of Russia, India and China has established threshold exemptions, with Russia's at R10m,[893] INR25lacs[894] for India and RMB5m[895] for China. China has in *draft Circular 2*[896], proposed adjusting the RMB5m to be net of any distributions during the year. SA's exemption applies only to passive income[897] not exceeding 5% of the CFCs total gross receipts, and according to the *National Treasury*[898] was established solely in the interests of administrative convenience.[899]

Russia, India, China and SA have included in their CFC rules exemptions designed to avoid stalling targeted OFDI. Russia exempts Russian controllers of CFCs resident in Member States of the Eurasian Community.[900] India exempts controllers of CFCs producing 'commercial benefits' such as from share trading on any recognized foreign stock exchange, while China exempts CFC's profits to the extent required[901] to finance viable foreign business needs[902] as was referenced in the 'Going-Out' Strategy.[903] SA exempts the profits of FBEs[904] (except for SA profits diverted to FBEs) and

---

886. At https://www.pwc.ru/en/tax-consulting-services/assets/legislation/tax-flash-report-2016-3 7-eng.pdf, while the MOF's tax preferred countries for dividend exemption purposes is limited to forty countries (Order No. 108n of 13 Nov. 2007).
887. Russia Updates List of Countries That Do not Exchange Information, World Tax Daily, February 2016.
888. Section 9D(2A), *supra* n. 670.
889. *Jinyan Li* (*supra* n. 877) observed that Circular 2 failed to confirm whether the 'profit' for the comparable rate test was gross or net, but with the draft *revised Circular 2* adjusting the exemption to profit after distributions, the inference is that it is net because distributions are most likely made from 'net' profits.
890. Article 76, *supra* n. 200.
891. June 2015.
892. Clause 5(d), Schedule Twenty, *supra* n. 835 and Clause 8, Schedule 2 of 2013 DTC.
893. Article 15.15(7), RTC.
894. Clause 5(a)(ii), Schedule Twenty, *supra* n. 835.
895. Article 84(iii), *supra* n. 200.
896. *Supra* n. 438.
897. Section 9D(9)(b)(iii)(aa), *supra* n. 670.
898. *Supra* n. 794, at p. 18.
899. *Ibid*.
900. Article 25.13(7)(2)RTC.
901. Concept is not defined in *Circular 2* nor in the draft *Circular 2*, *supra* n. 562.
902. Article 77, Circular 2, *supra* n. 200.
903. Yelery, China's 'Going Out' Policy, Sub-national Economic Trajectories, Institute of Chinese Studies, 2014.
904. Section 9D(9)(b), *supra* n. 670.

RHQs (investees not exempt FBEs) but if, as *ENSAfrica*[905] suggests, calculating the SA hypothetical tax for the exemption is difficult and if as *Honibell*[906] suggests, the FBE exemption is complicated to administer, then this leaves the exemption as being hollow.

Brazil, Russia and China have established 'list' exemptions. Brazil's blacklist[907] is used to determine whether profits of affiliated companies are taxed on a paid or accrual basis while Russia's list is used to determine whether the comparable rate exemption applies. With China's 'whitelist'[908] having remained unchanged since 2009 and with many countries having introduced tax concessions since then, such as the 'patent box' incentives, *Jinyan Li's*[909] observation that the SAT does not treat the list seriously seems plausible.

Table 4.1 BRICS 'Blacklist' Countries

Country	Regime and Countries
Brazil	**Low-tax jurisdictions:**[1] Payments of interest (thin capitalization), royalties and capital gains earned by entities resident in 'low-tax jurisdictions' are subject to a final Brazilian 25% withholding tax rather than the generally applicable rate (Administrative Rule 1,037/2010, issued 7 June 2010). Transactions between a Brazilian tax resident and a low-tax jurisdiction tax (countries which do not tax income or levy income tax at a top rate lower than 20%,[2] or have laws restricting access to shareholding and beneficial ownership of investments) resident are subject to TP rules, irrespective of the two parties being associates. Payments by a Brazilian entity to a legal entity resident in a low-tax jurisdiction are deductible only when the payment's beneficial owner is identified; proof of the foreign legal entity's operational capacity has been provided and the goods and services were actually sold/provided to the Brazilian entity. The new CFC rules introduced by Provisional Measure 627 provide for different tax treatments depending on the location of the parent company. **Privileged Tax regimes (Article 24A of Law 9,430 as expanded by Article 23, Law 11727/08)**: A jurisdiction is privileged if it does not tax income or taxes it at a top rate lower than 20%;

---

905. Simplifying the CFC legislation, March 2011, https://www.ensafrica.com/news/simplifying-the-controlled-foreign-company-legislation?Id=201&STitle=tax%20ENSight, last visited 31 may 2016.
906. *Supra* n. 210, at p. 581.
907. Table 4.1.
908. Australia, Canada, France, Germany, India, Italy, Japan, New Zealand, Norway, SA, UK and USA: *Guo Shui Han* [2009] No. 37.
909. *Supra* n. 877.

Country	Regime and Countries
	grants tax advantages to a non-resident entity or individual not required to carry on 'substantial economic activity' in the country or a particular territory or where the privileges are conditional on the company not exercising any substantial economic activity in the country or a particular territory; does not tax or taxes foreign source income at a top rate less than 20% or fails to grant access to information related to the composition of shareholders of its legal entities, title or beneficial ownership of earnings attributed to non-residents and to economic transactions performed. Thin capitalization also applies to interest payable to privileged tax regime persons. **Low-tax jurisdictions**: American Samoa; Andorra; Anguilla; Antigua and Barbuda; Aruba; The Ascension Islands; Bahamas; Bahrain; Barbados; Belize; Bermuda; British Virgin Islands; Brunei; Campione D'Italia; Cayman Islands; Channel Islands (Jersey, Guernsey, Alderney and Sark), Cook Islands; Costa Rica; Cyprus; Djibouti; Dominica; French Polynesia; Gibraltar; Grenada; Hong Kong; Isle of Man; Kiribati; Lebanon; Labuan; Liberia; Liechtenstein; Macau; Madeira Island; the Maldives; Malta; Marshall Islands; Mauricio Islands; Monaco; Montserrat; Nauru; Netherlands Antilles; Niue Island; Norfolk Island; Panama; Pitcairn Islands; Queshm Island; Saint Helena; Saint Lucia; Saint Kitts and Nevis; Saint Vincent; Samoa; San Marino; Seychelles; Singapore; Solomon Islands; St. Peter and Miguelão Island; Oman; Swaziland; Switzerland (suspended in view of a revision request filed by the Swiss government); Tonga; Tristan da Cunha; Turks and Caicos Islands; United Arab Emirates; US Virgin Islands and Vanuatu. NB: Normative Ruling No. 1,474/2014, published in the Official Gazette, 20 June 2014, converts the provisional exclusion of Switzerland from the list of tax havens (black list), in force from 25 June 2010, into a permanent ruling out. **Privileged Tax regimes:** Denmark holding companies without substantial economic activity; Netherlands holding companies without substantial economic activity; Iceland International Trading Companies; Hungarian companies incorporated as offshore KFT's; United States state Limited Liability Companies controlled by non-residents which are not subject to the federal income tax; Spanish companies incorporated as Entidad de Tenencia de Valores Extranjeros (ETVEs); Malta International Trading and International Holding Companies. The same Normative Ruling has included in the list of privileged tax regimes (grey list), the Swiss regimes which are applicable to legal entities incorporated as a holding company, domiciliary company, auxiliary company, mixed company

Chapter 4: Countering Avoidance: SAARs

Country	Regime and Countries
	and administrative company, whose tax treatment result in the imposition of Corporate Income Tax at a rate lower than 20%, as provided for by the federal, cantonal and municipal legislation.
	Normative Ruling No. 1,474/2014 has also grey-listed any Swiss tax regime applicable to other types of legal entities by means of the issuance of rulings by the tax authorities, which results in the levy of the Corporate Income Tax at a rate lower than 20% as provided for by the federal, cantonal and municipal legislation. Consequent to the inclusion of these entities and regimes in the Brazilian grey list, transactions involving Switzerland will trigger the Brazilian TP and thin capitalization rules.
Russia	**Blacklist Law**: Decree of the Ministry of Finance No. 108n,10.12.2007 covering countries providing low tax rates and (or) not disclosing information (i.e. has not entered into an agreement with Russia) and is relevant for TP rules (in accordance with effective TP rules in Russia, those transactions with parties incorporated in a state or territory included on the Ministry of Finance's tax haven blacklist are subject to TP controls whether the parties to such transactions are related or not (subject to a threshold of RUR60 million set for 2013, with no minimum threshold established for 2014 onwards). Dividends from blacklist country companies do not qualify for the participation exemption. The CFC list is tied to the list. The new CFC rules have encouraged some countries, including BVI and Malta (proposal dated 4 August 2014 by Russian Ministry) to be excluded from blacklist to negotiate EOI Agreements. Note, Cyprus' listing reversed from 1 January 2013, after amendments to the Russia/Cyprus DTC.
	Blacklist Countries: Anguilla; Andorra; Antigua and Barbuda; Aruba; Bahamas; Bahrain; Belize; Bermuda; Brunei-Darussalam; Vanuatu; British Virgin Islands; Gibraltar; Grenada; Dominica; Hong Kong; Macau; Comors: Anzhuan's Island; Liberia; Liechtenstein; Mauritius; Malaysia: Labuan Island; Maldivian Republic; Malta; Marshall Islands; Monaco; Montserrat; Nauru; Netherlands Antilles; Niue; United Arab Emirates; Cayman Islands; Cook Islands; Turks and Caicos Islands; Palau; Panama; Samoa; San-Marino; Saint Vincent and the Grenadines; Saint Kitts and Nevis; Saint Lucia; Isle of Man, Jersey, Guernsey, Alderney, Sark; Seychelles.
India	**Notified jurisdictional area Law**: Section 94A was introduced in the Income-tax Act, 1961, through the Finance Act, 2011, and applies to transactions with persons located in notified jurisdictions, 'Notified' having regard to the lack of effective EOI with India even if the parties have entered into a DTC containing an EOI Article. A notification causes all parties to the transaction being treated as 'associated' enterprises resulting in the TP regulations applying including maintenance of documentation; deductions not being allowed in India

Country	Regime and Countries
	for payments made to a financial institution in the notified territory unless the Indian payer provides an authorization allowing the Indian tax authority to obtain information from the that financial institution on the payee; deductions denied to the Indian payer for other expenditure or allowance from the transaction with a person located in the notified territory unless the Indian taxpayer maintains and furnishes the prescribed information; if any sum is received from a person located in the notified territory, the onus is on the Indian taxpayer to satisfactorily explain the source of the payer or beneficial owner's money, with failure resulting in the amount being treated as income of the Indian recipient; any payment made to a person located in the notified territory is subject to 30% Indian WHT or as otherwise prescribed.
	Notified Jurisdictional Countries: On 1 November 2013 India 'notified' Cyprus for not disclosing information on money transferred by Indian citizens conducting business in Cyprus who were suspected of evasion. Following the notification, every payment made to any person in Cyprus by an Indian taxpayer is liable to 30% WHT and not 15% Indian DTC WHT. Switzerland, United Arab Emirates, Hong Kong, Singapore, Samoa and Seychelles are countries potentially to be notified because despite requests to do so, information has not been shared properly with India. On 13 March 2014, India advised the Swiss Finance Minister of a pending notification.
China	**White List Law**: China has a 'whitelist' applicable to CFCs where the CFC is tax resident in a country listed as a 'non-low tax' country by the SAT, or where the income is mainly generated from active business operations or where the annual amount of profits is less than CNY 5 million (Article 84 (Guo Shui Fa [2009]) No. 2)
	White List Countries: USA; UK; France; Germany; Japan; Italy; Canada; Australia; India; South Africa; New Zealand and Norway (Guoshuihan [2009] No. 37, January 2009)
South Africa	South Africa does not have a 'Blacklist' nor a 'Whitelist' for taxation purposes.

1. The Brazilian tax administration can allow for the general income tax rate applying in the jurisdiction as well as for taxes imposed on income from labour, capital and regional concessions so that a jurisdiction can be a low or nil-tax jurisdiction when it taxes individuals but not companies or grants regional tax relief resulting in those corporations paying income tax at a rate of less than 20%. (Provisional Measure 22, 2000).
2. MOF Ordinance 488/14, dated 4 December 2014 reducing to 17%.

4.4.8 Notification

The developed world has identified the importance of notification to compliance and detection and recommends that resident controllers are required to notify the tax authority of their CFCs and of the undistributed profits of each company.

Each BRICS member has established a notification process but for some this is through exchange control while for others the notification is through the tax system. Also some tax authorities require early notification while another provides for non-disclosure being a strict liability and yet another extends the Statute of Limitations on CFC audits. The author deduces from this that the BRICS notification procedures have been designed to force compliance by substantially increasing the penalties for failure to comply.

Brazil and India both currently notify through the exchange controls with Brazil requiring disclosure to the Central Bank on both acquisition[910] of a foreign company and annually thereafter, for assets valued at more than $100,000 or quarterly for assets valued at not less than US$100m. Since Brazil's notification to the Central Bank is early and annual and independent of the filing tax returns, it provides the authorities with early notice. Were an Indian investor to acquire a foreign investment without first obtaining RBI approval, he would be in breach where the investment was in a Joint Venture or in a wholly owned subsidiary providing the financial commitment exceeds 100% of the Indian company's net worth calculated on the last audited balance sheet date.[911] For investments of this nature the RBI's early notification complements the information provided under the *Black Money Act*.[912] The proposed Indian rules also require notification of 'investments and interests in any entity outside India in such form and manner as may be prescribed' and the provisional notification arrangements are to be found in the Direct Tax Code.[913] Russia, China and SA rely on notification through taxation procedures with Russia requiring further notification separate to lodging the annual return. Since that separate notification[914] is to be made by 20 March following the end of the Accounting Period in which the controller acquires any (plus) 10% participations, the FTS possesses information on which to assess whether an audit should commence. Additionally, with the onus of proof being reversed so that it is the controller who is required to justify[915] why it has not included any potentially attributable amount in its notification return, and by establishing non-disclosure[916] as a criminal offence,[917] compliance is encouraged. China's annual 'Statement of External Investments'[918] (attached to the annual return) requires the controller to disclose all plus 10% (direct and indirect) participations together with all increases or decreases in

---

910. Declaration of Brazilian Capital Abroad, Resolution 3.854/2010, Article 8.
911. RBI (Foreign Exchange Department) Central Office, Mumbai-400 001 Notification No. Fema 120/ rb-2004 dated 7 Jul. 2004.
912. *Supra* n. 258.
913. Twentieth Schedule, section 7, p. 288.
914. Notification made to the controller's (Article 25.14(5)(4), N376 FZ) local tax office covers acquisitions and disposals of business entities and non-formal structures (Article 25.14(5), N376 FZ) together with increases or decreases in participations (Article 25.14(3), N376 FZ) and information on founders and beneficiaries' interests in distributed income (by 20 March of year following year in which undistributed profits were earned by the CFC, first notification by 20 Mar. 2017).
915. Article 25.14(6)(9), N376 FZ.
916. Article 25.14(8), N376 FZ.
917. Penalties for the 2015/2017 years can be waived providing controller reimburses the Russian Budget for the taxes and interest.
918. Article 78, *supra* n. 200.

those participations during the year. The Statement also requires the inclusion of information on whether the business is 'active'. Consequent to both *Gong Gao [2014] No. 38*[919] and *Shui Zong Han [2015] No. 327*, information on linked investments[920] is now disclosable as are both the CFC's annual audited financial statements and the China GAP auditor's report. With this information, the tax authority can make calculations and work out whether exemption claims should be accepted. One would expect that possessing this volume of information should satisfy the tax authority's thirst for detail because it has not because it has extended the *Statute of Limitation* so that tax audits may now commence within ten years from the relevant return date. As *Jinyan Li*[921] observed, this extension recognizes the difficulties for the tax authority in both obtaining and processing the information due to the limited manpower constraints. In SA, the notification is provided annually to SARS through *Form IT10B*[922] which is attached to the annual tax return. This form discloses information on whether the investment is 'active or passive', taxes paid and the other shareholders. Separate disclosure to satisfy the RHQ policy is required on *Form RCH01*.[923]

4.4.9 Tax Credits

With attribution potentially leading to economic double taxation, the developed world recommends credits be allowed against the domestic tax liability, with the credit amount being calculated by reference to the foreign tax on the attributed amount i.e. essentially the underlying[924] taxation. While the BRICS policy is to allow the credits, it is questionable whether the law effectively provides for them in China and in India, while Russia limits credits when the CFC does not reside in a DTC country.

With Brazil's domestic law allowing unilateral credits for the CFC's corporate tax on its undistributed profits, together with a 9% fictitious credit (upto 2022), there is likely to be little double taxation. Where affiliates[925] are liable to the CFC tax, then the credits are also available for WHTs, leaving double taxation on the dividends to the extent of the CFC's unrelieved underlying taxes. Russia's position is different because it provides that the tax credit will only be available for a CFC's underlying taxes where the CFC is resident in a country having a DTC with Russia where the CFC's financial statements are audited. The policy here is to drive investment away from tax preferred jurisdictions to countries with information exchanging provisions with Russia, which actually will exchange with Russia. SA's legislation provides credits[926] for a CFC's underlying taxes.

---

919. Supplemented by Shuizonghan [2015] No. 327 ('Circular 327'), 18 Jun. 2015.
920. *Article 79, Guo Shui Fa [2009] No. 2*.
921. *Supra* n. 877.
922. Controlled Foreign Company, 2012 Onward, http://www.sars.gov.za/Pages/Forms.aspx?pageid=C18A.
923. Schedule for Company electing to be a HC, http://www.sars.gov.za/Pages/Forms.aspx?pageid=C18A.
924. *Supra* n. 846, at p. 65.
925. *Supra* n. 851.
926. Sections 6quat(1)(b) and (1A)(b), ITA 1962, SARS Interpretation Note: No. 18 (Issue 2), 31 Mar. 2009, para. 3.2, p. 6.

In relation to India and China, the generally accepted view is that they allow credits for underlying taxes but, as the author concludes, this is not free from doubt. The proposed Indian law attributes under the CFC rules 'specified profit', a concept defined in the Second Schedule[927] as being the CFC's 'net profit after tax'. That definition should mean credits are allowed for the tax[928] but if the 'tax' referred to in the definition is the book tax rather than the actual tax paid to the Government, and where the latter exceeds the former, then double taxation will remain unrelieved to that extent. The excess tax is not likely to be relieved by Article 23 of India's DTCs because that Article does not provide for a CFC's corporation tax to be creditable. According to Yang,[929] Jinyan Li[930] and Deloitte[931] the plain words of the *EITL* and China's DTCs confirm the creditability of the underlying taxes for China purposes but with both the *EITL* and *RET* allowing credits for 'underlying taxes' in respect of *'derived income'*[932] while the controllers are attributed on *'deemed dividends'*,[933] the terms do not align. This argument is supported by the *Article 82, Circular 2* stipulation that credits for underlying taxes *'can'* but not *'will'* be granted. If the *EITL* does not provide for the creditability of underlying taxes, then Article 22 of China's DTCs will not likely relieve the tax because it credits underlying taxes on *'dividends paid by'* a foreign person when attributed amounts are not dividends paid.

4.4.10 BPA Override

4.4.10.1 *What Is the Argument?*

In this section, the research considers whether the BRICS DTCs override the CFC rules so resulting in a potentially attributed amount not being taxed. The developed world asserts that the rules can neither be overridden by an Article 7 in a DTC based on the *OECD Model Convention* (BPA) nor by the ND Article found within a DTC, because to do so would frustrate one of the DTC main objectives, namely countering avoidance and evasion, and preventing double taxation.[934] Arnold[935] confirms that neither a BPA nor an ND Article should override the rule since tax is not being levied 'on such profits', a position which *Bricom Holdings*,[936] *Re A Oyj Abt*[937] and *Gyo-Hi*[938] confirm. However,

---

927. Section 4(1), DTC 2013.
928. DTC 2013 confirmed taxes paid by foreign company in third countries, treated as comparable where credit given in residence country.
929. *Supra* n. 690.
930. *Supra* n. 877.
931. Guide to CFC regimes, p. 12, http://www2.deloitte.com/content/dam/Deloitte/global/Documents/Tax/dttl-tax-guide-to-cfc-regimes-14-july-2015.pdf, last visited 1 Jul. 2016.
932. Article 22, EITL provides for tax credits but not specifically underlying tax credits but Article 23(1) provides for credits except that it requires the resident *derives income*.
933. Article 80, *supra* n. 200 treats the attributable amount as deemed dividend.
934. OECD Commentary, Article 1, paras E.1/7 and 23.
935. International Tax Treaty Case Law News, Bull. Intl. Taxn, 2012 (Volume 66), No. 1, 24 Nov. 2011, p. 55/56.
936. Bricom Holdings Limited v. The Commissioners of Inland Revenue, IRC 1997, STC 1179.
937. A Oyj Abp, Case. No. KHO:2002:26, 20 Mar. 2002.
938. Gyo-Hi, Case No. 2008, No. 91, 29 Oct. 2009.

the French Court upheld the BPA override in *Schneider Electric*,[939] an outcome which *Sandler*[940] supports when observing that the CFC rule may be incompatible with DTCs.

4.4.10.2 Treaties and Interpretation

In an earlier subsection of this study, the author outlined the circumstances in which a BRICS member's domestic tax law may override a DTC and in that discussion the relevance of Article 3(2) of the *OECD Model Convention*, the *VCLT* and the OECD interpretation materials, together with other supplementary materials is considered. It is sufficient for the moment to summarize that with Brazil, Russia and China all acceding[941] to the *VCLT*, it follows that they should cede priority to DTCs over their domestic law (where there is a conflict) and while neither India nor SA has acceded to the *VCLT*, India's High Court in *AWAS Ireland*[942] confirmed that Article 27 applies in India while SA's *Chief Law Officer*[943] confirmed that even though SA is not a party to the *VCLT*, it is bound by the *VCLT* because it codifies customary law. Following from this therefore, is that the BRICS should be bound by the *VCLT* sections 31 (good faith) and 32 (supplementary means), when interpreting treaties.

4.4.10.3 BRICS and BPA Override

The developed world does not agree that the BPA overrides the rules even though exceptions exist (*see* section 4.4.10.1), but the Brazil Courts have confirmed that it can. The main consequence of Brazil's position is that it compensates Brazil MNEs for the absence of an active income exemption. Over the years, many scholars,[944] including *Torres*, have argued that the BPA could override the rule but it was not before *Vale*,[945] *Petrobras*[946] and now *Curitaba*[947] that the position was clarified by the Courts, both under the old and now the new Brazil CFC law. In those cases, the Courts held that the

---

939. Societe Schneider Electric, Case No. 232276, RJF 10/2002, 28 Jun. 2002.
940. Interaction Between DTCs and CFC legislation Pushing the Boundaries, 2nd ed. Kluwer, London 1998.
941. Brazil (2009); Russia (1986); China (1997).
942. Directorate General of Civil Aviation (W.P.(C) 671/2005, 19 Mar. 2015).
943. Office of the Chief State Law Adviser, http://www.dfa.gov.za/chiefstatelawadvicer/general.html, last visited 20 Jun. 2016.
944. *Supra* n. 161, p. 150/157/159; Violin, The Brazilian CFC Regime: Recent Developments, Bull. Intl. Taxn, 2014 (Volume 68), No. 4/5, p. 269; Violin, Brazil-The Brazilian CFC Regime: Update on Recent Developments, Bull. Intl. Taxn, 2014 (Volume 68), No. 9 p. 508/509/511; Xavier, Principles for the determination of the income and capital of PEs and their applications to banks, insurance companies and other financial institutions – Brazil, IFA Cahiers 1996 – Volume 81a, p. 308; Branco, Source and Residence: A New Configuration of Their Principles – Brazil, IFA Cahiers 2005 – Volume 90A, p. 206; *supra* n. 398, p. 173/175; Carvalho, Cross-border outsourcing – issues, strategies and solutions – Brazil, IFA Cahiers 2014 – Volume 99A, p. 174; Rolim, Brazil Tax Treaty Disputes, isabel.calich@lhm.com.br and j.d.rolim@rolinvlc.com, p. 24.
945. Companhia Vale do Rio Doce v. Federal Union – Appeal 1,325.709 24 Apr. 2014.
946. CARF, Petrobras, 21 Oct. 2014.
947. Process No. 5005596-52.2015.4.04.7000/PR, Federal Court of Curitiba, May 2016.

Chapter 4: Countering Avoidance: SAARs

DTCs should be interpreted on a 'good faith' basis *(pacta sunt servanda)*[948] and because international law generally overrides Brazilian domestic law to the extent of any inconsistency,[949] the BPA should override the rules. In finding for the taxpayers, the Court rejected the RFB's *18/2013* position that potentially attributed amounts were calculated by reference to the CFC's profits rather than the CFC's profits themselves being taxed for a second time, a position which *Arnold*[950] believes is compatible with the *OECD Model Commentary*. In rejecting the RFB's position, the Courts argued that Brazil neither followed the developed world's approach to interpreting DTCs nor did it rely on the *'lex specialis'* approach to establish the hierarchy between domestic and international law. Also relevant to this debate is the Federal Judge's explanation in *Curitiba*, that when the counterparty is resident in a country having a DTC with Brazil containing an Article 7 based on the OECD Model Convention, that Brazil's CFC rules are unconstitutional. It is unnecessary to rely on the BPA override in four of Brazil's DTCs[951] because those DTCs automatically exempt controllers from attribution, while a second group of four Brazil DTCs[952] prevents Brazil resident controllers from being taxed on foreign source dividends, also effectively overriding the rules, based on Brazil treating attribution as if a dividend.

With the other BRICS acknowledging the supremacy of international law, the question arises as to whether their Courts would adopt the Brazil approach. With CFC laws in India yet to become effective, it is not timely to answer the question although if one was to predict the outcome, the analysis would need to recognize that India generally follows the *OECD Model Commentary* as evident in *Girish*[953] *(Azadi, British Airways and Aztec Software)*[954] even though cases exist where it does not *(VR SRM firm).*[955] With the OECD asserting that the CFC rule is a calculation method, it is unlikely that the Indian Courts would find for a BPA override but the contrary argument can be made based on the rule being incorporated in the ITA Part taxing 'residuary income'[956] rather than the Part countering avoidance.[957] If it is not taxed as if resulting from avoidance, can it be saved by a DTC which saves for anti-avoidance provisions? If it is not avoidance then the Indian DTCs containing a BPA modelled on the *OECD Model Convention* would override the rule except for the DTCs specifically

---

948. Article 26 VCLT.
949. Min. Xavier de Albuquerque, 1 Oct. 1977, DJ PP-09433, 29 Dec. 1977; Vale, *supra* n. 899, where VCLT influenced the decision to hold a DTC superior where conflict exists even though Article 98, BTC cedes authority to international treaties.
950. *Supra* n. 935.
951. Article 23(5): Denmark (1974), Czech Republic (1986), Norway (1982) and Slovakia (1986).
952. Austria (1980), Article 23(2), 25%; Ecuador (1988) Article 23(2), 10%; India (1988) Article 23(3) and Spain (1974), Article 23(4) providing dividends are liable to respectively Indian or Spanish tax (Article 10(1)).
953. India's position on OECD Model Convention and Commentary, p. 7, http://www.fitindia.org/downloads/Girish_Dave_2009.pdf.
954. Azadi, *supra* n. 123; British Airways Plc v. DCIT [2002] 80 ITD 90 (Del); Aztec Software, *supra* n. 186; 294 ITR 32 Bang, 12 Jul. 2007.
955. Commissioner of Income-Tax v. Vr. S.R.M. Firm and Others on 15 Mar. 1994, para. 22.
956. Section 58(2)(u), *supra* n. 796.
957. Part F: Prevention of Abuse of the Code, Chapter X1 Special Provisions Relating to Avoidance of Tax.

saving for the rule, a position supported by *Besix Kier Dabhol*.[958] Following on from this conclusion therefore is the question whether the two Indian DTCs[959] specifically saving for the rule, the four saving for evasion,[960] the four saving for avoidance and evasion[961] and the further five[962] saving for 'evasion or avoidance, whether or not described as such', are of sufficient force to counter a BPA override. The author discusses this question in a following section of this study. Since the current Russian position on the ND[963] Article in its DTCs is that it does not override the thin capitalization law because, based on the OECD position,[964] to do so would frustrate a main objective of the DTC (i.e. countering avoidance or evasion), the author predicts the Russia Courts would not likely follow the Brazil precedent. China's position is that the BPA in its DTCs does not override the rules, because were it to do so, it would counter an anti-avoidance or evasion rule, but the author concludes that the evidence supports the contrary position.[965] China's accession to the *VCLT* results in its DTCs overriding domestic law to the extent of any conflict, but having regard to *Circular 75*[966], (which interpreted certain Articles in the Singapore/China DTC, in relation to PEs, and which interpretation has since become the generally accepted position on interpreting other China DTCs), the author concludes that China views its DTCs as being interpreted by domestic rather than international concepts, in other words there is no override. If it is correct to assume that it was China who requested the insertion in the Mexico/China DTC[967] of the specific saving provision for the CFC rules and also in the ten DTCs[968] which save for provisions countering avoidance, evasion or for special adjustments, then the rational conclusion is that China had decided, absent the specific savings provisions, that the BPA would override.[969] A simpler explanation could be that the provisions resulted from counterparty requests, but when reviewing the DTCs[970] where the saving has been included, the author finds the contrary position to be supported because those countries include HK, the principal beneficiary country of China OFDI. In SA, the *National Treasury*[971] has confirmed that the BPA would not override the rule because the CFC rules are a calculation tool for working out the controller's share of the

---

958. Director of Income-tax, International Taxation-II, Mumbai v. Besix Kier Dabhol SA IT Appeal No. 776 OF 2011, 30 Aug. 2012.
959. Canada (1996), Mexico (2007).
960. Luxembourg (2008), Malta (2013), Saudi Arabia (2006).
961. Estonia (2001), Georgia (2011), Uruguay (2011).
962. Ethiopia (2011), Fiji (2014), Indonesia (2012, NIF), Malaysia (2012), Uzbekistan (1993).
963. Article 24(6) Russia MDTC 2010.
964. Russia's tendency to follow the OECD Model Commentary (the Federal Arbitration Court North-West Region No. A45-3310/2011, 31 Jan. 2012; No. A56 23858/2011, 8 Feb. 2012 and Superior Court of Arbitration No. 8654/11, 15 Nov. 2011 confirmed Russia follows the OECD Commentary), although not universally so (Moscow Arbitration (Commercial) Court No. A40-60755/2012, 29 Aug. 2012 confirms that Russia does not follow the OECD Commentary).
965. Article 58 EITL provides the DTC prevails to the extent of any inconsistency.
966. Guoshuifa [2010] No. 75 (Circular 75), 26 Jul. 2010.
967. Mexico (2005).
968. Bahrain (2002), HK (2006), Belgium (2009), Finland (2010), Germany (2014, NIF), Malta (2010), Netherlands (2013), Switzerland (2013), UK (2011) and Finland (2010).
969. Li Na in in GAARs, *supra* n. 164, p. 198.
970. HK, Netherlands, Switzerland, Belgium.
971. National Treasury, 2002, p. 2.

Chapter 4: Countering Avoidance: SAARs

CFE's 'net income'[972] (i.e. the OECD approach), a position supported by *AM Moola*.[973] However, there is a position to the contrary following the judgment in *Tradehold*,[974] and bearing in mind *HogansLovells*'[975] argument that international agreements take precedence over domestic legislation (a position confirmed by *Oguttu*[976]), because the DTCs are *lex specialis*, except where savings provisions have been included in the DTC. With just four of the more than twenty SA DTCs entered into since the CFC rule became effective specifically saving for the CFC rule[977] and with none of the counterparty countries immediately thought of as major recipients of SA OFDI, the author concludes it to be more likely for the saving request to have been made by the counterparty than by SA giving rise to the conclusion that SA believed that the BPA override does not exist.

The author concludes that were the tax authorities in the BRICS (bar Brazil) to narrow their active income exemptions, then in India and perhaps less likely in China, the override may apply. Its application in India would require the Court to reject the force of OECD materials when interpreting DTCs and in China, would require the SAT accepting that absent a savings provision in a DTC that the CFC rule is not generally saved by a DTC.

4.4.11 CFCs: Anti-avoidance Rule?

Determining whether the DTCs which save generally for avoidance would be effective against the CFC rules, requires analysing whether the rule counters 'avoidance' and for DTC purposes the answer to this question, depends on the DTC containing an Article 3(2) modelled on the *OECD Model Convention* which allows for the BRICS' definitions to be determinative. Based on the analysis in Chapter 3 of this study, the conclusion is that grounds exist to support the argument that the rule does not counter 'avoidance' as the BRICS define that concept, With the position in Brazil due to the 'legality principle' ensuring little qualifies as 'avoidance' and in Russia because the 'unjustified tax benefit' concept countering evasion and not avoidance because avoidance in Russia is limited to relatively minor administrative matters. The China and SA position is more difficult to conclude on because while both countries deem structures devoid of reasonable business purpose to constitute avoidance, for those structures which accumulate passive income derived from trading businesses inside a structure supported by reasonable business purpose, that accumulation is arguably not avoidance. The position in India is different again because potentially attributed amounts is to be taxed under the 'residuary' income section of the Code and not in the 'avoidance' section which supports the conclusion that the CFC rules does not counter avoidance

---

972. *Supra* n. 971, p. 5.
973. AM Moola Group Ltd v. C: SARS [2003] 65 SATC 414.
974. SARS v. Tradehold Ltd [2012] 3 All SA 15(SCA).
975. The Impact of International Development, February 2015, http://www.hoganlovells.com/en/publications/the-impact-of-international-developments, last visited 15 May 2016.
976. Resolving conflict between CFC legislation and tax treaties: a SA perspective, XLII CILSA 2009.
977. HK (2014, NIF) refers to tax avoidance; Canada (1995) refers to amounts included in income rather than direct CFC reference; Brazil (2003) and Mexico (2009) directly refers to rule.

4.4.12 CFCs and GAAR

In this subsection, the author considers whether a specific saving in the relevant DTC for GAAR would be effective and in the author's opinion it is unlikely to be effective for Brazil, India and SA but likely would be effective for Russia and China. With Brazil's GAAR[978] still ineffective the question does not arise, but were it to become effective, he predicts it is unlikely to apply to offshore accumulations because the CFC rule constitutes a self-contained taxing rule, or as *Schoueri*[979] explains nothing in Law No. 9,249/95 'leads to the conclusion that it was specifically drafted to counter abusive behaviour'. With both GAAR and the rules yet to become effective in India, the question does not yet arise but were both effective, it would unlikely counter the BPA override because the proposed 'impermissible avoidance arrangements' definition excludes arrangements covered by SAARs and the CFC rule is a SAAR, or for CFCs formed for non-tax reasons as *Mehrotra*[980] confirms. In relation to SA, the author deduces that GAAR would be inapplicable were the offshore structure supported by commercial substance because such arrangements are unlikely to constitute 'impermissible arrangements'. *Oguttu's*[981] assertion that the CFC rule is an 'impermissible arrangement' because SA follows the *OECD Model Convention* is questionable because that approach pre-supposes a conflict with domestic law which cannot be the case for a CFC law because that rule is a domestic law. China's GAAR saves the rule because accumulating foreign passive income through offshore corporate structures reduces China tax while Russia's 'unjustified tax benefit' concept saves the rule because accumulating income offshore through foreign entities sits comfortably within the definition of 'unjustified tax benefits'.

4.4.13 CFCs: DTCs and BPA Override

As concluded in the previous subsections of this study, arrangements covered by the rules are unlikely to constitute arrangements countered by GAAR in Brazil, India (when it becomes effective) and SA and by arrangements constituting avoidance in Brazil, India and Russia. Based on these conclusions, it can be deduced that the anti-avoidance savings provisions in each of those countries DTCs are ineffective except for the specific DTCs entered into by Brazil,[982] Russia,[983] India[984] and SA[985] which refer to the CFC rule itself as a reason to save.

---

978. Schoueri, *supra* n. 164, p. 131 confirms that GAAR does not exist because Article 116 of the Tax Code is disputed.
979. *Supra* n. 164, at p. 136.
980. GAAR in India, CBD MOF India, Fourth IMF-Japan High-Level Tax Conference, Tokyo, 2013 https://www.imf.org/external/np/seminars/eng/2013/asiatax/pdfs/india.pdf, p. 5 last visited 15 May 2016.
981. Oguttu, *supra* n. 164, p. 630.
982. Peru (2006), Turkey (2010P), Russia (2004P), SA (2003).
983. Brazil (2004P), Canada (1994).
984. Canada (1996P), Mexico (2007), Spain (2012P).
985. Brazil (2003), Mexico (2009), Canada (1995).

4.4.14 BRICS: Cooperation and CFC Rules

Notwithstanding the BRICS Revenue Heads[986] agreeing to 'develop a BRICS mechanism to facilitate countering abusive tax avoidance transactions, arrangements, shelters and schemes', the author concludes that there is no readily obtainable information confirming any coordination between the BRICS tax authorities in formulating their CFC rules.

4.4.15 Significance: Divergences from the Developed World

While the BRICS have widened the rules' applicability by including additional relationships in the controller definition, lowering the control threshold, when viewed against their DTCs, the rules' effectiveness is questionable having regard to members own domestic law definitions of avoidance and evasion together with the applicability of GAAR when the foreign person resides in specified countries having DTCs with the relevant BRICS member. In order to encourage compliance to compensate for the limited tax authority manpower to identify and audit, the BRICS have established procedures requiring early notification of foreign investments.

They have widened the notification procedures by continuing to use exchange controls in Brazil and India and complex returns in Russia, China and SA and indicative of the importance of the rules to Russia and China is Russia's reversal of the burden of proof for failure to notify and China's extension of the Statute of Limitations to ten years for commencing CFC audits and its requirement for the disclosure of information linking together all the potential controllers. While some of the BRICS have adopted rule simplifications, including using the CFC's undistributed profits as the starting point (rather than re-computing those profits using domestic rules), Russia's tough stance is evident from its failure to agree to this simplification except for CFCs resident in countries having DTCs with Russia which exchange information.

One looming cloud over the rule's effectiveness is the potential for a BPA in a DTC to override it and while this position now applies only in Brazil, the potential for it to apply exists in other member countries. The problem for the BRICS from the override is that any relevant avoidance, evasion or GAAR savings provisions in the DTCs may be ineffective because the domestic definitions of those concepts do not cover arrangements which the rule is typically designed to cover. Since Russia has already considered and dispensed with similar arguments for thin capitalization, its Courts would not likely support a BPA override. Should taxpayers argue that the CFC rule is ineffective for any one of the reasons in this section then there is very real potential for complex disputes exacerbating the manpower capacity problems which gives rise to the necessity for dispute resolution procedures including MAP and others discussed in Chapter 8 of this study to be available and effective.

---

986. New Delhi, 17/18 Jan. 2013.

4.5 NEXT CHAPTER

Chapter 4 concludes that the BRICS' approach to countering thin capitalization, TP and controlled foreign corporations is wider than the developed world's and that in formulating the divergences they have sought to increase the deterrent to overcome the MNEs transactions, structures and behaviour resulting in substantial illicit outflow. An elevated deterrent has been required in the BRICS to counteract their relatively small manpower capacity to deal with the problems and for this reason, the BRICS have also imposed strict notification requirements and in the circumstances of non-compliance, substantial penalties. Also except for TP, the author concludes there is no publicly available evidence of the BRICS having coordinated their CFC approach.

In the circumstances in which the deterrent fails to be effective, it is axiomatic that countering transactions, structures or behaviour requires access to information describing what the taxpayer has done. In Chapter 5, the author researches whether the BRICS approach to the information exchanging architecture is compatible with both their need for information to stem those illicit outflows and with the developed world's architecture. Also studied is in the next Chapter is whether the BRICS have sought to influence the design of that global exchanging architecture in order that the final form compensates their tax authorities' small manpower capacity and if such influence exists, whether it indicates that there has been BRICS coordination.

CHAPTER 5
Information Exchange

> One of the main challenges for international tax law nowadays is how to ensure full effectiveness of domestic tax law regarding transactions with other countries and the consequent movement of capital.
>
> – Heloisa Estellita[987]

5.1 INTRODUCTION

Gathering information on transactions and structures is fundamental to identifying instances of evasion and avoidance. Therefore, it is unsurprising the developed world is building an international architecture to facilitate and accelerate the exchange by one tax authority of information on taxpayers' transactions, entity ownership, assets, financial accounts and private tax rulings, with other tax authorities whether in response to specific queries, events or simply automatic. With cross-border mispriced transactions including financings and the use of tax havens being significant contributors to evasion and avoidance, the developing architecture is focussing much on them. In this Chapter, therefore, the research is on whether the BRICS approach to exchanging information is compatible with their need to obtain information and whether the BRICS have sought to influence the design of the developed world's exchanging architecture in order that it provides them with information they must have to counter the transactions, structures or behaviour facilitating illicit outflows or investment of funds into tax preferred jurisdictions. The research also focuses on whether that influence is designed to compensate for their limited tax authority capacity to deal with evasion or avoidance.

---

[987]. Tax EOI and international cooperation in Brazil, rev. direito gv Volume 11 No.1 são Paulo jan./june 2015, http://www.scielo.br/scielo.php?script=sci_arttext&pid=s1808-24322015000100013.

5.2 EXCHANGING ARCHITECTURE

For many years, countries have sought the assistance of other countries and third persons in collecting information for use in pursuing tax claims, but both the *OECD*[988] and those relying on the *Revenue Rule*[989] recognized that doing so was a complicated procedure and even more so, when countries or third persons refused to provide assistance.[990] Globalization brought FDI into developing countries, including those previously closed off to the western world, and many of the formats adopted for structuring that FDI were new to the BRICS tax authorities. This massive amounts of FDI and the newness of the structural format resulted in increased opportunities for MNEs to implement mispriced, sham or to involve themselves in evasion practices. The first serious steps taken to share tax based information across borders were taken by the *OECD*[991] when it strengthened Article 26 of the *Model Convention,* and Article which was reflected in Article 26 of the *UN Model Convention.*[992] The strengthened Article 26 was a useful tool where the counterparties trading patterns warranted a DTC, but when the trading patterns did not warrant a DTC or where one country was a tax haven, the OECD had no solution before recommending the countries enter into bilateral agreements based on its *Model TIEA.*[993] In more recent times, various Multilateral and Mutual Assistance Agreements have been introduced including the *Common Reporting Standard*[994] and the *Country-by-Country Reporting Standard*[995] with the objective of strengthening the existing architecture supporting global information exchange and widening it to encompass more countries and more information.

The BRICS have joined this growing international process by strengthening their domestic information gathering rules and procedures, incorporating the strengthened *OECD Model Convention* Article 26 into their bilateral DTCs and by entering into TIEAs

---

988. Transparency and Global Tax, Clearing the Way, http://www.oecdobserver.org/news/fullstory.php/aid/4118/Transparency_and_Global_tax.html.
989. AG v. Lutwydge (1729) 145 eng. rep 674 (ex.div) where the English Court refused to enforce in England bonds due to Scotland because Scotland was a foreign country.
990. Article 26, *supra* n. 132.
991. Preliminary remarks OECD Model Commentary, Article 26.
992. Article 26, UN Commentary 2011, at 1.1.
993. April 2001, with 2015 Protocol for use by parties wishing to extend an effective TIEA to automatic and/or spontaneous exchange.
994. MAC; Standard for Automatic Exchange of Financial Account Information in Tax Matters, 2014 including proposed Common Reporting Standard; Extended to British Overseas Territories, June 2013, FATCA (reporting to IRS by Foreign Financial Institutions holding non-US accounts for US Citizens and Green Card Holders) with Models 1 and 2 IGA signatory countries (http://www.treasury.gov/resource-center/tax-policy/treaties/Pages/FATCA-Archive.aspx).UK has entered into FATCA style agreements with Crown Dependencies. Supporting DTCs and TIEAs is Global Forum (restructured in September 2009). Directives, Agreements and Co-operation arrangements (EU Directive on Administrative Cooperation in Taxation (Council Directive:2011/16/EU, February 2011 on administrative cooperation on taxation); Council of Europe/OECD 1988 Convention on Mutual Administrative Assistance in Tax Matters (Concluded on January 1988, amended by Protocol, Paris in 2010); Council Directive 2010/24/EU, 16 Mar. 2010 concerning Mutual Assistance for the Recovery of Claims relating to taxes, duties and other measures) between EU MS' with third countries and between non-EU MS' and non-OECD members (including developing countries).
995. BEPS Action 13: Country-by-Country Reporting Implementation.

Chapter 5: Information Exchange

and the Multilateral and Mutual Assistance Agreements. Their commitment to the coordination amongst the BRICS of the promotion and facilitation of an effective exchange of information policy is clear from the *Hangzhou* Leaders Statement[996] (September 2016) and *Heads of Revenue*[997] announcements.

5.3 EXCHANGING INFORMATION

Accessing accurate and complete statistics on the nature and extent of BRICS exchanged information is difficult to come by, but statistics on BRICS exchanging can be found at a wide range of sites, including the *Automatic Information Exchange*[998] and *Global Forum*[999] portals and through the *Peer Review Reports*[1000] together with reports of the OECD,[1001] *IDB*,[1002] *Indian Finance Ministry*[1003] and scholars such as *Vinnitsky*.[1004] From this information, we know the BRICS have been exchanging information for many years through the bilateral DTCs and in more recent times through their TIEAs.

The author concludes from his study of the BRICS *Peer Review Reports* that the BRICS have been receiving spontaneous requests for information since at least 2009 while China, India and Russia have been automatically sharing information outbound from 2004, 2009 and 2000[1005] respectively. Of the spontaneous requests received during the 2009/2011 period, Russia received most (approx. 8,000 on corporation taxation[1006] and VAT data, split evenly)[1007] with the other BRICS receiving relatively few requests: China received 296, 221 and 345; Brazil received 89 requests from 18 DTC partners; India received 97[1008] requests between July 2009 to June 2012 primarily from the US, UK, Ukraine and Japan and SA received 221 requests from 25 jurisdictions during 2007/2010. In relation to the automatic exchange of information, China has

---

996. 'Corruption, illicit cross-border financial-flows, and ill-gotten wealth derived from illegal activities, stashed in foreign jurisdictions, adversely impacts institutional capacities and effectiveness and (they) called for enhanced cooperation and effective measures among G20 economies', http://www.brics.utoronto.ca/docs/160904-hangzhou.html.
997. New Delhi, 17/18 Jan. 2013; Moscow November 2015.
998. At https://www.oecd.org/tax/automatic-exchange/.
999. At http://www.oecd.org/tax/transparency/automaticexchangeofinformation.htm.
1000. Peer Review Phases 1 and 2: Brazil April 2012, July 2013; Russia October 2012, October 2014; India November 2010, November 2010; China Phases 1 and 2 Jun. 2012; SA Phase 1 and 2 Oct. 2012.
1001. OECD 2012, AEOI, What is it, How it Works, Benefits, What Remains To Be Done, p. 16.
1002. State of Taxation Administration In Latin America, 2006/2010, 2013, p. 502.
1003. SIT, designated for the task and placed under CBDT.
1004. 2014 EATLP Congress RUSSIAN NATIONAL REPORT, p. 6, http://www.eatlp.org/uploads/public/2014/National%20report%20Russia.pdf.
1005. According to *Zolotoryova* (Deputy Head of the Office of International Cooperation and Information Exchange of Russian MO Taxes and Charges) more than 2,000 requests in 2,000 growing to approx. 5,000 by 2003 with most from Belarus and Kazakhstan.
1006. Most requests for bank account information, Peer Review Report, Phase 1, p. 76.
1007. Russia Phase 2 Peer Review, p. 389.
1008. Twenty-five, owning companies, trusts, partnerships; fifty-five, accounting information and thirteen, banking information, Peer Review Report, Phase 2, p. 23.

exchanged approx. 10,000[1009] pieces annually, India approx. 2m pieces between 2009/2012 with more than fifty partner countries while Russia has been testing automatic exchange with OECD members since 2013.[1010] The high level of requests to Russia for information likely indicates Russian resident subsidiaries of foreign MNEs participating in transactions avoiding resident country tax.

The OECD has not disclosed any statistics on inbound exchanging into Brazil, Russia or SA but according to the OECD, with India and China inbound exchanging just 7 and 5 cases respectively, nothing of substance can be learned from these statistics. The picture is similar for OECD disclosure on outbound exchanging for Russia, China, India and SA where 13, 7, 9 and 8 cases respectively are mentioned. Statistics on Brazilian outbound exchanging within Latin America for 2008/2010 obtained from the *IDB*[1011] confirm exchanges during that period of 12, 6 and 2 cases respectively with inbound exchanging of 9, 20 and 29 cases respectively. The *2014 SIT Report*[1012] disclosed that Indian exchanging in 2012 consisted of just 333 outbound requests received from 85 DTC partners. This is indicative of relatively little actual exchange interest from a wide range of international tax authorities. India's receipt of information on 9,743 cases from those partners in 2012 and by 2013, on 24,085 cases (New Zealand (10,372), Spain (4,169), UK (3,164), Sweden (2,404), Denmark (2,145), Finland (685), Portugal (625), Japan (440) and Slovenia (44)), is indicative of India being an early exchanging adopter. Further statistics on requests received by Russia were published by *The Inter-Parliamentary Assembly of the Eurasian Economic Community*, which confirmed that during 2008/2011 information was requested on 460, 286, 252 and 128[1013] cases respectively, indicative of a declining interest by international authorities in the Eurasian community obtaining information from Russia. With Russia's requests for information during 2009/2013 from foreign tax authorities being respectively, 1,069, 975, 669, 898 and for the first six months of 2013, just 469 requests and with an increasing proportion of those requests not being responded to (22.6%, 28.8%, 24%, 30.8% to 47% respectively),[1014] evidences that the number of cases which Russia could pursue based on exchanged information has been declining.

The conclusion based on this analysis is that the BRICS have been exchanging information for many years. The patchy statistics however paint a picture of more data being exchanged automatically than spontaneously, and in relation to Russia, a pattern of declining requests with an increasing percentage of requests remaining unsatisfied. The author's deduction from this (tiny) sample is that the existing architecture is yet to contribute substantial information for use in countering evasion and avoidance and in relation to China, for example, forcing the tax authorities to resort to reviewing MNE websites (as in *Qidong, 2012*) in order to obtain relevant information.

1009. China Combined Phases 1 and 2 Peer Review Report, p. 87, dividends, interest, royalty, salary and pension.
1010. *Supra* n. 1004, at p. 10.
1011. *Supra* n. 1002, at p. 502.
1012. India Economic Times, 10 Aug. 2014, http://articles.economictimes.indiatimes.com/2014-0 8-10/news/52648254_1_income-tax-department-tax-matters-alleged-tax-evasion.
1013. *Supra* n. 1004, at p. 6.
1014. *Ibid.*, at p. 10.

These statistics paint a picture of little real success by the international community in exchanging with the BRICS, which supports the policy decision of the BRICS Leaders and Revenue Ministers to commit to improving the exchanging architecture.

5.4 DTCS-ARTICLE 26

In this subsection, the research is on the BRICS approach to the information exchanging provisions of the OECD and the UN Model Conventions and the conclusion is that the Russian and SA[1015] published Model Conventions include exchanging provisions modelled on the *OECD Model Convention* but it is not apparent whether other BRICS follow suit in the absence of their Models or information on their policies being publicly available. Having regard to the following summary, it is evident that the BRICS' Article 26 is converging with the developed world's Article 26. With Russia setting the connection between taxpayers and information at the 'essential'[1016] level rather than the developed world's 'foreseeably relevant'[1017] level, it establishes a point of potential conflict with the exchanging countries on specific exchanges, which may lead to the truncation of information received by Russia. The Russian Model's proposed sharing of information obtaining through exchange with the 'Federal Executive Committees' could also further truncate that availability. With the SA Model Convention Article 26 mirroring the OECD Model's Article 26, few problems are expected.

Since neither Brazil, China nor India publish Model Conventions, identification of their policy is available only through studying Article 26 in their DTCs, considering their reservations and positions to the OECD Article 26 and the Commentary on that Article (if any), Government Reports[1018] and multilateral agreements which have been entered into. In relation to Reservations and Positions on exchanging, none have been taken by Brazil, Russia or SA from the Model Article 26 except for Russia's use of 'essential', India's reservation on the necessity for documents to be certified and China's position on whether information arising from transactions entered into before the DTC became effective can be exchanged, which China argued it could not. This position is relevant because, as *Swiss Federal Administrative Court*[1019] confirms, identifying the effectiveness guides the parties on which information can be used in investigations.

In relation to how the BRICS approach to Article 26 has changed since liberalization, the author notes that the BRICS did not incorporate the entire OECD or the UN Model Convention Article 26 into their DTCs before liberalization, but since liberalization the trend[1020] has been to follow the OECD Article 26, as *Jianwen*[1021] observes. One

---

1015. 24 Feb. 2010, N84, p. 4.
1016. 'Absolutely necessary' per Oxford Dictionary.
1017. 'Reasonable possibility… that requested information will be relevant: Article 26, para. 1. 5, *supra* n. 483.
1018. RFB 2008 issued Manual on Information Exchange; Indian Manual on Exchange, 2015; SARS, Automatic Exchange of Information, February 2016.
1019. Swiss Federal Administrative Court 17 Dec. 2013.
1020. BRICS Members Peer Review Reports; SA para. 184.
1021. *Supra* n. 515, at p. 281.

example is that soon after liberalization, the India and China DTCs[1022] referred to Article 26 as a device to 'counter evasion and avoidance' but the later India and China DTCs[1023] no longer contain that reference even though the UN Commentary[1024] argues that exchanging is designed to facilitate countering evasion and avoidance. Another example of how India's use of Article 26 has changed since liberalization is India's notification of Cyprus as a non-exchanging (section 94A) counterparty for Article 26 purposes *(Expro Gulf)*[1025] which resulted in Cyprus residents having tax deducted in India at the Indian domestic rates even though they were treaty resident. India's approach was driven by the IRD's frustration at the Cyprus Tax Department's refusal to provide, or the delays in it providing information to the IRD on Cyprus business entities or bank accounts owned by Indian tax residents.

The OECD Model Convention stipulates that to be exchangeable, the information must be 'foreseeably relevant', 'sufficiently dependable' and not be seen as simply a 'fishing exercise'.[1026] In this study, the author has identified the published views of India and Russia on this issue, and to be 'foreseeably relevant' in India, there must be a clear and specific request for the information as *AZP*[1027] confirms, while the consequences from the information must be clear as *BJY & Ors*[1028] confirms. That is, the information's failure to reveal a non-resident's liability to Indian tax meant that the information was not 'foreseeably relevant'. In relation to 'sufficiently dependable', *Mitsui*[1029] confirms that information received from a foreign tax authority is 'sufficiently dependable' while *Mammen*[1030] confirms that the IRD's conclusion that a foreign foundation was established by an Indian taxpayer merely on the basis that the person had signed the declaration was not 'fishing'. In relation to Russia, the FTS has received information from the Cyprus,[1031] Luxembourg[1032] and the Netherlands[1033] CAs which it has used in investigations. The OECD[1034] argues that information can be available for transactions entered into before the DTC became effective providing the request is made after the DTC became effective, a position supported by *Mark Krok*,[1035] but is a position which India rejects.[1036]

1022. India: Italy (1981), Libya (1981), UK (1981), Singapore (1981); China: Japan (1983), US (1984), France (1984) and UK (1984).
1023. India: Japan (2015P), Thailand (2015), Belarus (2015P) and Croatia (2014); China: Zimbabwe (2015), Chile (2015), HK (2015) and Estonia (2014).
1024. UN 2001 Model DTC Commentary, General Considerations, p. 2.
1025. Expro Gulf Limited v. UOI (Writ Petition No. 2871/2014, 22 Jan. 2015.
1026. *Supra* n. 514.
1027. Comptroller of Income Tax v. AZP, 2012, SGHC 112, 23 May 2012.
1028. .Comptroller of Income Tax v. BJY & Ors, 2013 [2013] SGHC 173.
1029. .Mitsui and Company India Pvt. Ltd. v. ITO - WPC No. 1121/2012 & CM No. 2447/2012, 26 Sep. 2012.
1030. .Mammen v. DCIT (ITA No. 870/Mds/201) 21 Jan. 2013.
1031. Moscow Arbitrazh Court, Case No. A40-4757/14 75-1, 15 Apr. 2014.
1032. North-West District FAS, Case No. A52-4072/2012, 6 Jun. 2014.
1033. North-West District FAS, Case No. A21-2110/2005-C1, 9 Jan. 2007.
1034. OECD 2014 Model Commentary, Article 26, para. 10.3.
1035. Commissioner for the SA Revenue Service v. Mark Krok, 31 Jan. 2014.
1036. *Supra* n. 1019.

Chapter 5: Information Exchange

5.5 TIEAs

Superficially, it seems the BRICS have been less enthusiastic about signing and enforcing TIEAs than they have been about bilateral DTCs because less than 50% of their signed TIEAs have been enforced, except for those entered into by China where the proportion of enforced TIEAs is far greater. An alternative explanation for the BRICS failure to enforce many of the TIEAs is that each of the BRICS tax authorities (bar China) limited manpower had been unable to progress enforcement due to more pressing matters, including their participation in the BEPS programme. Were the former view correct then it would question the BRICS commitment (except for China) to exchanging information with tax preferred jurisdictions. Having researched the question, the author concludes that there is no one approach amongst the BRICS. Brazil's failure to enforce any of its TIEAs (except for the US)[1037] has not proven to be materially disadvantageous because Brazil obtains information on foreign payees[1038] before payments to them are made by the Brazil counterparty. Russia's failure results from a legal concern which is that until Russia published its Model TIEA[1039] in 2014 its negotiators argued that they did not have a template to work from. While India's policy is to exchange information[1040] its failure to ensure that more than 50% of its TIEAs[1041] were enforced, according to the *Indian SIT*,[1042] was due to the IRD's belief that the TIEAs were focused on collecting documents when they should be focused on collecting tax. It is difficult to identify any reason justifying SA's failure to enforce the few TIEAs it has entered into.

5.6 MULTILATERAL AGREEMENTS

Together with bilateral agreements, the evolving exchanging architecture is being built on multilateral agreements on Mutual Assistance and on Financial Account Exchange. The potential benefits to the BRICS which the designers of these Agreements assert, include the speedy effectiveness, fewer debatable issues, reduced administrative costs[1043] and the reduction in outside distractions to the legal enforcement process.

With each of the BRICS having signed and enforced the *MAC*[1044] they have fulfilled the BRICS Leaders requirement that they participate in the G20 led exchanging process. FATCA is US led and bilateral (and works on mirror agreements) and without the BRICS entering into FATCA Agreements or coming to another form of

---

1037. 19 Mar. 2013.
1038. Brazil, Phase 1 Peer Review Report.
1039. Decree No. 805, August 2014, based on the OECD Model Agreement on EOI on Tax Matters (2002).
1040. Manual on Exchange of Information, Government of India, MOF, Department of Revenue, CBRT confirms intention to exchange information.
1041. In 2015 India was negotiating TIEAs with thirty countries, *supra* n. 1040, p. 115.
1042. Rediff Business: India signs info exchange pact with two tax havens, November 2014.
1043. At http://www.oecd.org/ctp/exchange-of-tax-information/conventiononmutualadministrativeassistanceintaxmatters.htm, February 2016.
1044. Sign: Brazil (2011), Russia (2015), India (2012), China (2016), SA (2014); Enforce: Brazil (2016), Russia (2016), India (2013), China (2017), SA (2015).

accommodation with the IRS, their financial institutions with US taxable presences or income, would have been become liable to US penalties. While Russia was a late *TIEA* starter it confirmed early starter status on the *MAC*[1045] (1 January 2016) for both administrative and criminal matters. In relation to the Cayman Islands, Russia has agreed to exchange information from 1 January 2012 for both administrative and criminal matters and it intends to use the meaning of those concepts under Russian laws rather than under Cayman island laws. The choice of Cayman is difficult to comprehend because it is not on the listing of major providers to, or recipients of FDI from Russia (*see* Chapter 1 Tables 1.2 and 1.3) while the BVI, which is on that list, is yet to arrive at any published understanding with Russia on this process. Russia's agreeing on exchanging back to 2012 is understandable because it allows Russia to obtain information on a wider group of mispriced transactions and the ownership of parties involved because such transactions and (hidden) ownership constitute evasion and potentially criminal evasion in Russia and constitute a Russian focus. Any decision by the Cayman Islands to reject Russian requests for that information would not likely be supported under *Article 3(2)* of the *MAC* because Russia's enforcement of the *MAC* 'as a whole' would, as *Engelen*[1046] asserts, justify supporting a meaning of criminal evasion in the Convention different to that in Cayman. The *MAC* also acts as the basis for other forms of exchange and assistance and the BRICS[1047] (other than Brazil which signed in September 2016) have, by entering into the CRS *MCAA* [1048] to automatically exchange financial account information, aligned themselves with the developed world. Brazil's earlier failure to sign the MCAA when taken with its failure to enforce any of its TIEAs may be indicative of a policy to prevent ownership of foreign entities and of foreign bank account information by Brazil tax residents from being shared back to Brazil for investigation. In relation to the *CbC MCAA* Reports[1049] which, broadly, provide for automatic exchange of information on the global allocation of income between jurisdictions, other than for Brazil and Russia, the BRICS have entered into it. The failure by Brazil and Russia to sign the CbC MCAA is, in Brazil's case, not a policy failure because information on foreign associates' profits is neither required for the smooth functioning of its ALS (because fixed margins are used) nor for its CFC rules (because undistributed profits are attributed), while Russia's failure to sign is arguably due to its relative lower importance following from the comparatively few Russian outbound MNEs and a current focus on administering the relatively recently introduced de-offshorization (including the CFC) rules. In relation to FATCA, the BRICS (other than China and Russia)[1050] have entered into FATCA Agreements, and while a proposed Russian FATCA Agreement stalled, Federal Law No. 173-FZ[1051] authorized

---

1045. FTS Letter No OA-4-17/22482, 22 Dec. 2015.
1046. *Supra* n. 499, at p. 482.
1047. India (2017), China (2018), SA (2017).
1048. Covering financial account information from financial institutions.
1049. Reporting firstly 2018 for 2016 year information.
1050. Brazil (NF), India (F) and SA (F) entered in Model 1 FATCA Agreement with China's Model 1 pending. Russia proposed February 2014 to commence FATCA negotiations but agreement yet to emerge.
1051. 28 Jun. 2014, law 'On Specifics of Conducting Financial Transactions with Foreign Nationals and Legal Entities, Amendments to the Russian Code of Administrative Offences and

Chapter 5: Information Exchange

Russian financial institutions to register for FATCA, which according to *Kuznets*[1052] resulted in Russian banks avoiding penalties from what they saw as the inevitable disclosing of confidential information, as *Thomson Reuters*[1053] observed. A similar position prevails for China where *Xiangmin*[1054] confirmed 'China's banking and tax laws and regulations do not allow Chinese financial institutions to comply directly with FATCA.

5.6.1 Exchanging Prior Information

In relation to transactions entered into before the *MAC* and the *MCCA* became effective, it is anticipated that the developed world will respond in the same manner as it did for Article 26 *OECD Model Convention*[1055] which is by allowing the information to be exchanged on transactions entered into before the *DTC* was enforced providing the exchange request was made after enforcement. In relation to Article 26, SA follows the developed world *(Mark Krok)*[1056] as does India (*Exchanging Manual* reproducing the entire OECD Article 26 Commentary) and for those reasons, they both would be expected to respond similarly under *MCCA*. In relation to China, its Article 26 'position' is to exchange information only relating to taxable periods after the agreement comes into operation and from this it can be deduced that China will follow the same approach for *MCCA*. Russia's Article 26 position is to exchange widely, and on that basis it will likely adopt the same position for *MCCA* purposes. For these reasons, the author concludes that the BRICS, other than China, will exchange under the MCAA information relating to periods before its enforcement (providing request is after enforcement) but that Brazil will not exchange and therefore concludes that China and Brazil are not fully cooperating in the exchange of information, which contradicts their Leaders proposal.

5.7 FINANCIAL ACCOUNT INFORMATION

This subsection researches whether the BRICS' existing procedures for gathering information on the entity[1057] to be disclosed, such as its name, address, jurisdiction of residence and TIN are compatible with the developing world's architecture and in relation to persons controlling that entity, whether the procedures for gathering information on it including the name, address, jurisdiction of tax residence, TIN and

---

Invalidation of Certain Provisions of Russian Legislative Acts' permits Russian financial organizations to register for FATCA and directly report information on clients to IRS.
1052. Compliance of Russian financial institutions with FATCA rules: U.S. requirements versus national legislation, November 2014, Thomson Reuters; Vitko, FATCA compliance for National banks – Central Bank clarifications, IBFD, November 2015, Letter No. 1245/2568.
1053. *Ibid*.
1054. Deputy Director, People's Bank of China, http://www.reuters.com/article/us-asia-regulation-china-idUSBRE8AR0N720121128, last visited June 2016.
1055. *Supra* n. 1034.
1056. *Supra* n. 1035.
1057. Legal person or arrangement such as a company, partnership, trust, foundation, CRS Miscellaneous, E3, p. 60.

date and place of birth, for reportable persons[1058] are compatible with that architecture. The rules confirm that information on the entity's controllers collected by financial institutions through the AML/KYC process[1059] can be used and that the persons controlling[1060] the entity are the natural persons exercising control[1061] over it. Clarity on where ultimate control sits is to be found in the *FATF* 'look through' recommendation.[1062]

Summaries of countries existing systems and procedures for collecting the information and their rights to legally exchange it are published as Reports of the *Peer Review Group*.[1063] The Reports published on the BRICS represent a unique resource to assist it identifying the compatibility of the BRICS architecture with the procedures being developed by the G20.

5.7.1 BRICS and Peer Reviews

In this subsection, the focus is on the nature and extent of the BRICS involvement in the *Global Forum* and in the *Peer Review Reports* and the author concludes that they have established themselves in positions of influence on the Global Forum, which rationally, enables them to influence the design of the global exchanging systems and procedures. The author also concludes that the evolving procedures are compatible with the existing exchanging procedures in Brazil, India, China and SA (but for different reasons) but not with the Russian procedures.

5.7.1.1 Global Forum: Roles of Influence

Each of the BRICS (except for Russia) is represented on the *Global Forum's Steering Group* and on the *Peer Review Group* and with SA and China holding the roles of Chairman and Vice Chairman, respectively of the *Steering Group* and with India holding the Vice Chair role of the *Peer Review Group*, they are in positions which influence the 'preparation and guidance of the *Steering Group's* future work'[1064] and 'developing the methodology and detailed terms of reference for...., transparent and accelerated *Peer Review* process'.[1065] This influence is supported by each of the BRICS being a member of the *AEOI Group*[1066] which 'monitors the implementation, and helps developing countries benefit from it'. The importance with which India holds its ability to devise and monitor a workable AEOI architecture, one which is compatible with

---

1058. Section 2(a), Section 2, Model CAA.
1059. CRS, 2(b), p. 42.
1060. CRS, Reportable Persons, D6, p. 57.
1061. Includes settlors, protectors, beneficiaries and trustees together with any natural persons owning ultimate effective control in trusts and for any other legal person, the persons holding the same roles.
1062. Transparency and Beneficial ownership, October 2014, p. 8.
1063. *Supra* n. 1000.
1064. At http://www.oecd.org/tax/transparency/steeringgroup.htm.
1065. At http://www.oecd.org/tax/transparency/about-the-global-forum/peerreviewgroup.htm.
1066. At http://www.oecd.org/tax/transparency/about-the-global-forum/#d.en.341948.

Chapter 5: Information Exchange

India's procedures is evident from its holding the AEOI Group Vice Chair, and its representative's (Monica Bhatia)[1067] appointment as Head, *Global Forum Secretariat* and through its contribution to the cost of a Secretariat[1068] administrator, which as *Bhatia*[1069] observes further cements 'India's ... lead in the (Global Forum) work'. The author deduces from this information that India, China and SA, and especially India, are in positions which allow them to participate in shaping the evolving global exchanging system's design in a manner suitable to their countries' requirements for information which facilitates their investigating mispriced transactions and use of tax havens.

5.7.1.2 AEOI: Legal Basis for Exchange

In this subsection, the study focuses on whether each member has the legal right to exchange information and concludes that they do and in Brazil's case, it evolves from the Constitution[1070] and the BTC[1071] while Russia's authority derives from its Constitution, Civil Code and Tax Code.[1072] India's right to exchange is based on section 90(1) ITA while China relies on its DTCs and TIEAs and *Guo Shui Fa (2006) No. 70*. SA's right to exchange emanates from its Constitution (section 231(4)), Tax Administration Act (section (3)) and ITA (section 108(2)).

5.7.1.3 AEOI: Procedures Facilitating Exchange

This subsection researches the compatibility of the BRICS exchanging procedures with the obligation to exchange information on ownership and financial accounts with the procedures being developed by the G20/OECD and conclude that the Brazil, India, China and SA procedures are compatible but for different reasons, while the Russian procedures are not.

In relation to exchanging entity ownership information, the effectiveness of the CRS depends upon the establishment of an AEOI system in each country to collect ownership information which is then linked to other agencies and foreign governments through an international sharing architecture. That architecture requires common data forms and a common software to enable the exchange to be effective. The data must be collected into a public register to facilitate the exchange, but the procedures currently available in the BRICS for collecting entity ownership information into public registers are deficient other than for China, and when that data is collected through the tax system, it is deficient in Russia and SA. On this basis, it can be deduced that entity ownership collection procedures in Brazil, Russia, India and SA are not compatible

---

1067. Previously Indian Revenue Service, International Tax Review, December 2014.
1068. Global Forum 2015 Annual Report, p. 26.
1069. *Supra* n. 1067.
1070. Sections 49, 59 and 84.
1071. Sections 194/5 and 9. Ordinance RFB/PGFN 1,427/2015, effective 8 Oct. 2015 regulating cooperation between RFB and General Office of National Treasury's Attorney for promoting EOI on international mutual assistance.
1072. Russia Phase 2 Peer Review Report, p. 8.

with the evolving architecture but China's public registrars are compatible because they contain information on all China enterprises.[1073]

Collection by the exchanging architecture of ownership information in Brazil is deficient because the access of ownership information placed on the public register is subject to attorney/client privilege. In Russia[1074] and in India, information collected is limited: in Russia to large companies (a company with more than fifty shareholders) and in India to public companies or members of a chain of companies and then only collected annually. In SA, ownership details on close companies are only filed with SARS as there is no requirement for that information to be publicly registered. From this information, it is deduced that except for China, ownership information on all companies in the other BRICS' is not publicly available. Tax returns in Russia and in SA do not contain ownership information so the system cannot pick up ownership information that way.[1075] Also Russia's right to exchange is fettered first, by a taxpayer's right of appeal to higher tax officers before it can be exchanged and then to Courts and second, because of an inability to exchange information obtained from an 'audit service', which is defined to include tax consulting. Brazil has since 2011 annually collected ownership information on resident companies, but this information was initially quarantined on constitutional grounds, but since *ADIN No. 2386,2389*[1076] sharing has become permitted. Indian tax returns only contain information on plus 10% voting interest owners. Ownership information[1077] of China enterprises is included in China tax returns as is information on any enterprise which is obligated to pay its China taxes from a China bank account.

With the BRICS financial institutions using the international AML/KYC procedures when opening financial accounts to obtain ownership information on the owner of the new account, it is rational to conclude that they retain records on the entity's controllers. This means that the financial institutions most likely have this information to exchange. However, with Russia's legal right to exchange on Russian individuals restricted by both secrecy provisions[1078] and by law, financial account information cannot be automatically assumed to be exchangeable except for individuals having dual citizenship or those with foreign residence permits or, on Russian companies having more than 90% equity directly/indirectly controlled by Russian citizens.[1079] A further deficiency before January 2013 in the Russian system was the absolute prohibition of sharing ownership information[1080] on individuals held by financial institutions before January 2013.

1073. State Administration for Industry and Commerce.
1074. Common State Register, http://www.chinacheckup.com/questions/china-company-registration-search-website, last visited 21 Jul. 2016.
1075. EOI devolves from the Constitution and Article 7, RTC and Article 93.1 RCC.
1076. Extraordinary Appeal 601,304, with Direct Actions for Unconstitutionality 2390, 2386, 2397e 2859 (24 Feb. 2016).
1077. Bank account number plus owner's name, nationality, address, TIN.
1078. Article 857, RCC.
1079. Federal Law No. 173-FZ, effective 30 Jun. 2014.
1080. Article 86(2), RTC.

Chapter 5: Information Exchange

5.8 BRICS AND COORDINATION

The Heads of Revenue[1081] agreed in Moscow to exchange information with each other and globally subject to resolving legal issues and resolving either domestic or international issues which may delay the CRS implementation. The foregoing information describes the legal impediments to each member's pursuit of compliance. The author concludes that because of the BRICS' participation on committees influencing the architecture's design, it is rational to assume they have coordinated their approach to those Committees but there is little evidence on which to base a conclusion that in determining how their individual country legal systems and procedures should be amended to ensure compatibility with the developing architecture, that they have coordinated. Also concluded is that Russia's absence from positions of influence in the committees designing the exchanging architecture is premised on its Constitutional limitations to outbound exchanging, and the author also concludes from the publicly available information that there is little progress on Russia's rules becoming compatible. The available published information is inconclusive on whether the BRICS are sharing amongst themselves their ideas for how the exchanging system should be developed.

5.9 BRICS: CONSEQUENCES OF EXCHANGING

This Chapter has identified that the BRICS approach to exchanging information is broadly compatible with that of the developed world's existing exchanging architecture but that while the BRICS have included normal exchanging language in DTCs and in TIEAs, their slowness to enforce most of their TIEAs is counterproductive to their obtaining information from entities in tax havens. It is evident also that the BRICS are exchanging under DTCs but in a limited manner under the TIEA architecture. The BRICS are clearly supportive of the AEOI process as beholds countries commanding positions of influence in its design but Brazil's failure to sign the *MCAA* together with its failure to enforce the TIEAs represents a failure to implement the BRICS cooperation agenda. The evidence also supports the conclusion that the procedures for collecting and exchanging ownership in place in Russia and SA require upgrading. This therefore leaves both China and India at the forefront of the BRICS exchanging architecture which is to be expected given their leading roles in designing and managing the process which is developing the architecture and also because of the very substantial of value amounts involved in China mispriced transactions which requires access to substantial amounts of information to counter while. In India's case, countering mispriced cross-border transactions has become the main focus of dealing with illicit flows having regard to it not having rules countering thin capitalization, CFCs and GAAR. Being at the centre of designing the new architecture also provides the BRICS with the opportunity of minimizing the risk that other countries recommendations may result in

---

1081. *Supra* n. 997.

the need for the BRICS to substantially vary their own systems and procedures, which were they to implement those recommendations, would further constrain their limited tax authority manpower.

5.10 NEXT CHAPTER

In this Chapter, the author has considered the BRICS participation in the existing and evolving architecture providing them with information for use in countering international tax abuse. In the next Chapter, the effectiveness of their methodology for countering taxpayers' claims for DTC benefits, and whether their divergences from the developed world's approach reflects their limited tax authority capacity, are studied. Included in this investigation is whether declaring countries to be non-cooperative or applying indirect asset disposal rules, widens the options available to the BRICS to counter DTC abuse. The research also considers the existence of any evidence of coordination amongst the BRICS on their approach to denying DTC benefits.

CHAPTER 6
Countering Treaty Benefits

6.1 INTRODUCTION

Tax authorities struggle to deny benefits in the absence full information detailing the circumstances of the claim and the foreign person's rights to the benefits under domestic law or DTC. In the previous Chapter, it was concluded that, first, the BRICS approach to exchanging information is broadly compatible with that of the developed world's exchanging architecture and second, that the BRICS have sought to influence that architecture's design in order that it complements their tax authority manpower capacity. Once in possession of that information, the tax authority can work out whether the DTC benefits should be denied and if so why. In this Chapter, the study concerns whether the BRICS approach to some of the concepts used by source country tax authorities to deny the benefits is wider than that of the developed world and to determine whether their approach on those concepts is influenced by coordination amongst them or by their limited tax authority manpower capacity. The concepts researched in this Chapter are POEM, comprehensive liability (*CLT*), beneficial ownership, limitation of benefit *(LOB)* and main purpose tests *(MPT)*. Also studied is whether the BRICS approach to denying the DTC benefits by declaring the counter party country to be non-cooperative or by applying indirect asset disposal rules, is wider than the approaches of the developed world which deal with similar problems.'

6.2 RESIDENT

6.2.1 Introduction

In this subsection, the research considers the differences in the BRICS definitions of 'resident' to those of the developed world and concludes that the developed world determines an enterprise's place of residence to be either the place of incorporation

(Louisville v. Letson),[1082] a test the OECD believes to be unacceptable[1083] or the place from where the central management and control (CMC) abides *(De Beers Consolidated Mines*[1084] and *Wood v. Holden)*[1085] which, according to *Bullock v. Unit Construction*[1086] is the place where the 'highest level' of control of the business is to be found. *Laerstate*[1087] helpfully explains that 'top level' decisions are neither ministerial matters' nor matters of 'good housekeeping'. The research concludes that when the ostensible 'top level' decision makers have been usurped by 'outsiders', such as in *Smallwood Trustees*[1088] or *Laerstate*,[1089] that the place where the usurper makes those decisions becomes the place of CMC. Until 1983 the HMRC argued a company's POEM abided where the CMC was sited, but in *SP1/90* it conceded that when the top level decisions were made at a place different from that where the ultimate control or major policy decider abided, then POEM and CMC would abide at different places.

In relation to the BRICS, the reason for the initial reliance by Brazil, Russia, India and China on the country of incorporation for an entity being its place of residence was that doing so simplified administration for the manpowered constrained tax authorities and that in pre-liberalisation period, it would not likely have occurred to a tax authority that a foreign company could be owned by domestic resident because of the exchange control and associated difficulties confronting a resident who wished to establish a foreign company. The author deduces that the subsequent realization by tax authorities that foreign companies, nominally foreign owned, were actually owned or controlled by residents of the domestic country, led them to consider whether other factors (such as management and control) established tax residence at a place other than the place of incorporation.

Brazil retains the place of incorporation test for residence but has extended it to include Brazilian branches, agents or representative offices of foreign companies while India[1090] treats domestic incorporated companies as Indian tax resident (and until April 2017[1091]) as well as all foreign incorporated companies unless the 'control and management'[1092] of that foreign company wholly resides outside India. From April 2017, India has adopted POEM as the determining test of residence and when announcing the adoption of POEM the Government[1093] published it's expectation that the change would result in foreign 'shells' becoming Indian tax resident because their POEM will be seen to be located in India. China treats enterprises formed under its laws[1094] as being China tax resident as it does for those enterprises formed under the

---

1082. Louisville v. Letson Louisville, C. & C.R. Co. v. Letson, 2 How. 497, 558, 11 L.Ed. 353 (1844).
1083. 2014 OECD Model Commentary, Article 4(3), para. 22.
1084. De Beers Consolidated Mines Ltd v. Howe [1906] AC 455.
1085. Wood v. Holden [2006] EWCA Civ 26.
1086. Unit Construction v. Bullock, [1960] AC 351.
1087. News Datacom Ltd and another v. Atkinson (Inspector of Taxes) [2006] STC (SCD) p. 732, which the Special Commissioners' decision in First-Tier Tribunal in Laerstate agreed with.
1088. Smallwood Trustees Anor [2010] EWCA Civ 778.
1089. Laerstate v. HMRC, [2009] UKFTT 209.
1090. Section 6(3), ITA, 1961, prior to Finance Act, 2015 amendment.
1091. Proposed start date per 2016 Budget.
1092. Section 6(3)(i) and (ii), ITA, 1961.
1093. India Finance Minister Budget Speech 2015, p. 32.
1094. Article 2, *supra* n. 35.

laws of Hong Kong or Macau where they have an 'actual/effective management organ' in China, as *Guo Shui Fa [2009] No. 82 (Circular 82)* prescribed. *China Mobile Vodafone*[1095] is an illustration. *Sharkey*[1096] has observed that neither CMC nor POEM is the same as 'actual/effective management' but having regard to *Article 2, Circular 82*,[1097] the author concludes that it is much closer to POEM than to CMC. Russia changed its approach in January 2015 from the place of incorporation test to POEM as part of the de-offshorisation rules, while SA continues to treat companies incorporated in SA as resident, with as *Majachani*[1098] observes, foreign companies being deemed SA resident where their POEM is in SA or, as in *Tradehold*,[1099] where the company was not exclusively resident elsewhere because of a DTC.

6.2.2 POEM

The Commentary to both the UN[1100] and OECD[1101] Model Conventions defines POEM and while they are similar, there are important differences. The OECD concludes that POEM subsists where key management and commercial decisions... necessary for the conduct of the entity's business *as a whole* are in substance made,[1102] and this includes the place where the Board meets (CMC test) and where the CEO and other senior executives meet to carry on the activities. This means that the test essentially focusses on the place where *the company's top decision makers meet to transact the company's business*. This conclusion has been arrived at bearing in mind the place where the company's senior day-to-day management is carried on, the place where the company's headquarters is located and the country's laws governing the company's legal status. The UN[1103] definition mirrors the OECD's at the core, but then diverges by arguing that the place where the company's books are kept is an important[1104] factor to be included in the discussion, as is *the place where the company's economic activities and functional management takes place*. So, while the UN considers the place where the business happens to be relevant, the OECD[1105] does not. In researching which POEM meaning the BRICS adopt, the author has conducted his analysis by considering

---

1095. 2011.
1096. Correctness of Chinese Position of Enterprise Residence in Chinese Law: Institutional and Treaty Implications, Bull. Intl. Taxn, 2014 (Volume 68), No. 11, 22 Oct. 2014, p. 619/620.
1097. Senior executives and management responsible for daily business operations; the financial and personnel decisions or must be approved by persons or departments in China; are main property, ledgers, corporate seals and Board meeting and shareholders minuted are kept and not less than 50% of the directors or senior executives with voting rights are located principally in China.
1098. Residence of Entity for Tax purposes – SA: a review of the concept 'place of effective management' University of Cape Town, A Minor Dissertation Presented Partial Fulfilment of requirements for the Degree of Master of Laws in Taxation, February 2010.
1099. *Supra* n. 974.
1100. UN Model DTC between Developed and Developing Countries, p. 94/96.
1101. OECD Technical Advisory Group 2001, Discussion Document, p. 88/89, *supra* n. 483.
1102. Paragraph 24, *Supra* n. 1101.
1103. Paragraph 4(3), para. 10, *supra* n. 1100.
1104. Paragraph 24.1/3, *supra* n. 1101, UN refers to 'where most important accounting books are kept'.
1105. Paragraph 10, p. 94, *supra* n. 1100.

how each BRICS member views the importance of the place where the *highest decision making takes place,* or the *place where economic activities* occur.

6.2.2.1 Highest Decision Making

The significance of this place to the BRICS is gradually reducing, except for SA. It is not important to Brazil because Brazil relies on the incorporation test but it was important to Russia until June 2015[1106] from when the place where Board meetings take place has been downgraded. This place became important in SA from 2011 because before then *(SARS Discussion Paper on IN6)*[1107] SA had relied on the place where the 'lower decision making' took place *(ENSafrica)*[1108] which, according to *SARS,*[1109] was the place where the company's regular day-to-day management implemented decisions and not the place where the directors or senior managers made them. SARS decided[1110] that because both *Tradehold*[1111] and *Oceanic Trust*[1112] had rejected the importance of the 'lower place', it should adopt as the place, the place where the persons actually calling the shots and exercising realistic positive management on the company's business, *as a whole,* were substantively located.[1113] This place, according to SARS, was where the company's head office was located and when any delegation of that decision making took place, it was that place and the place where the Board substantively made the decisions. SARS no longer saw as being important both the place where the shareholders met (unless the shareholders usurped the directors' powers) and the place of incorporation. The place where the higher decisions are taken is important for both India[1114] and for China but with India's POEM (effective April 2017) to be found at the 'place where key management and *commercial decisions* necessary for the conduct of the business of the entity as a whole are in substance made',[1115] India is likely to apply focus on foreign companies engaged in non-Indian active businesses which have the majority of their Board meetings outside India,[1116] but only when there is an Indian resident usurper.[1117] China relies on the place of higher decision making[1118] as *Heilongjiang*[1119] confirms.

1106. Federal Law No. 150–FZ, June 2015.
1107. At http://www.sars.gov.za/AllDocs/LegalDoclib/DiscPapers/LAPD-LPrep-DP-2011-02%20-%20Discussion%20Paper%20POEM%20on%20IN6.pdf, dated 2011.
1108. Pinch, https://www.ensafrica.com/news/revised-draft-interpretation-note-regarding-place-of-effective-management?Id=1950&STitle=tax%20ENSight; 19 Aug. 2015.
1109. Interpretation Note 6 (IN6), issued 2002.
1110. *Supra* n. 1107.
1111. *Supra* n. 974.
1112. Oceanic Trust Co Ltd NO, V SISM, Case No. 2011/2255556/09, 13 Jun. 2011.
1113. *Supra* n. 1107, para. 8.1.
1114. Foreign persons are unlikely to being deemed Indian resident when atleast one Board meeting occurs in the foreign place each year.
1115. F. No. 142/11/2015-TPL, CBDT, para. 2.
1116. *Supra* n. 1115, para. 7.
1117. *Ibid.*, para. 8(2)(a).
1118. RET, 2008, Article 4.
1119. Heilongjiang Province 2013.

Chapter 6: Countering Treaty Benefits

6.2.2.2 Economic Activities

The place where a person's economic activities occur is gradually becoming more significant to the BRICS as a determining factor of POEM, even if it is of no relevance to Brazil and of little relevance to SA.[1120] This place is a significant factor when Russia determines where POEM is 'located and therefore should these activities take place exclusively outside Russia then the foreign company's POEM cannot be found in Russia. In deciding where those activities take place, Russia considers the location of the qualified personnel *using the company's assets to transact the company's business* and takes into account whether or not those personnel are permanently located outside Russia. With India recognizing the importance of *the location at which the 'main and substantial' activity of the company is carried on (Ruling F No. 142/11/2015-TPL 2015)*,[1121] a principle confirmed in *Shaan Marine Services*,[1122] the place where economic activities occur has assumed significance. India has also recognized that because the facts and circumstances required to make this decision are complex, it has established a safe harbour POEM[1123] to reduce the administrative complexity for the resource constrained IRD. In determining whether the taxpayer meets the safe harbour, the IRD has regard to the place at which the foreign company's people, assets and payroll are located and if less than 50% of each occurs in India then the person will not have an Indian POEM. With China locating POEM at the place where management, business organization and representative offices are located and *at the place where labour services are provided*,[1124] foreign enterprises engaged in China production or other business operations can become China tax resident.

This study concludes that residence for Brazil relies exclusively on the place of incorporation while Russia now relies on the place of economic activities. Residence for India allows for the place of higher decision making for foreign companies with foreign Board meetings and together with China, treats as being very important the place where economic activities take place. China also finds relevant for the place of highest decision making which is the place SA almost exclusively focusses on for residence purposes.

6.2.3 Residence and DTCs

The developed world provides DTC benefits when the foreign person satisfies the residence test in the DTC and does not fail the so-called comprehensive liability[1125] test (CLT). The CLT is designed to prevent foreign persons, which are residents under the law of the country of incorporation, from qualifying as a resident of that Contracting State for DTC purposes, resulting in the forfeiture of the DTC benefits. The CLT does

---

1120. *Supra* n. 1107, at p. 13.
1121. F. No. 142/11/2015-TPL, *supra* n. 1073, para. 8(2)(f).
1122. Shaan Marine Services Private Limited v. IRD, 27 May 2014.
1123. Paragraph 5(a) and p. 7, *supra* n. 1115.
1124. Article 4, *supra* n. 1118.
1125. Paragraph 4B.01, 4B.05, *supra* n. 503; *supra* n. 483, para. 8.2, p. 84.

not exclude foreign persons from being DTC resident, merely because that foreign person is liable to tax in that State on a territorial basis.[1126] According to *Baker*,[1127] the CLT also does not exclude foreign persons from qualifying as DTC resident merely because they derive income or capital which is tax exempt because of a special privilege granted to attract FDI[1128] (excluding conduits)[1129] or because that person is a pension fund, charity or an entity of a similar nature.[1130] This means therefore, that companies not liable to tax *(Baker)*[1131] because of the absence of an attachment to a State[1132] of a kind discussed in *Crown Forest*,[1133] such as the absence of an *'effective connection'* (or nexus), would not qualify as a DTC resident and because of that failure would lose the DTC benefits.

While this is the approach of the developed world, this study concludes that it is not policy for Brazil because Brazil does not include a CLT[1134] in many of its DTCs nor is it the policy for India, even though a CLT is incorporated in approx. 65%[1135] of India's DTCs. This conclusion follows from foreign residence, for Indian purposes, being largely determined by whether the relevant person possesses a COR issued by the counterparty State's tax authority. A CLT has also been included in Russia's DTCs from the late 1990s, but with the Russian DTCs with both Cyprus and The Netherlands including a territorial CLT, and with The Netherlands being Russia's largest provider of FDI, the CLT of little practical relevance in rejecting DTC benefits in Russia. China began to include CLTs in its DTCs[1136] from around 2008 but with no CLT included in the DTCs with HK[1137] and Singapore[1138] (as *SingStat*[1139] confirms), and with both

---

1126. *Supra* n. 514, para. 8.3, p. 84.
1127. *Supra* n. 419, para. 4B.05.
1128. Article 4, para. 8.2, *supra* n. 514.
1129. OECD, Conduit Companies Report, 1987, Article 1.
1130. *Supra* n. 1129, para. 14(a).
1131. *Supra* n. 419, 4B.07.
1132. *Ibid.*, 4B.07.
1133. Crown Forest Industries Limited, 1995 2 SCR 802.
1134. Volvo Brasil v. RFB 457.228, 18 Mar. 2004, Superior Court held 'liable to tax' meant susceptible to taxation.
1135. OECD: Belgium (1993), Canada (1996), France (1992), Ireland (2000), Israel (1996), Italy (1993), Japan (1989), Malta (1994 which adopted provision in 2013), Netherlands (1998), Slovak (1986), Sweden (1988 which adopted new provision in 1997), Switzerland (1994), Turkey (1985), UK (1981 adopted new provision in 1993), Non-OECD: Azerbaijan (1988), Bangladesh (2013), Brazil (1988), Bulgaria (1994), China (1994), Egypt (1969), Kenya (1985), Malaysia (2001 adopted provision in 2012), Mauritius (1982), Moldova (1988), Namibia (1997), Oman (1997), Russia (1997), Singapore (1994), Tanzania (1979 adopted new provision in 2011), Thailand (1985), Trinidad (1999), Uzbekistan (1993), Vietnam (1994), Zambia (1981).
1136. OECD: Czech (1988), Denmark (2012), Estonia (1988), Finland (2010), France (2013, not in 1984 DTC), Germany (2010-NIF not in 1985 DTC), Greece (2002), Ireland (2010), Latvia (1996), Lithuania (1996), Netherlands (2013 not in 1983 DTC), Switzerland (2013 not in 1990 DTC), UK (2013 not in 1984 DTC), Non-OECD: Albania (2004), Azerbaijan (2005), Bahrain (2013), Cuba (2001), Ecuador (2013), Ethiopia (2009), HK (2010), Kuwait (1989), Malta (2010), Morocco (2002); Russia (2014-NIF but not in 1994 DTC), Saudi Arabia (2006), Syria (2010), Turkmenistan (2009), Uganda (2012-NIF), Zambia (2010).
1137. HK/China DTC, Article 4(2).
1138. Singapore (2007/2010), Article 4(1).
1139. At http://www.tablebuilder.singstat.gov.sg/publicfacing/sortByTime.action.

countries being significant contributors of China inbound FDI, the absence of the test is likely explained as a policy initiative not to disturb inbound FDI to China. SA began to include a CLT in its DTCs[1140] from around 2000 but with the test not included in the DTC with the UK,[1141] this is likely explained by the UK being the largest provider of FDI to SA.

This study concludes that the CLT is of little practical relevance to the BRICS when working out whether their DTCs should reject the DTC benefits, and further concludes that this is so because the DTCs, with the main providers of inbound FDI into the BRICS, do not contain a CLT. Also concluded is that the similarity of the CLT relevance to the BRICS is unlikely to derive from actual coordination between the BRICS officials because there is no published information that such coordination has taken place.

6.2.4 BRICS: DTC Residence and POEM

The reason that the developed world includes POEM[1142] in Article 4 of *the OECD Model Convention* is to use it as a tie-breaker when determining which of the two DTC States is the State of residence for purposes of the DTC. Accessing a tie-breaker can become necessary when each of the States, applying their own domestic residence definition, conclude that the one person is resident in their own State, making the person a dual residence at the domestic level. This situation may arise when one State relies on the place of incorporation test to determine residence while the other State uses POEM, CMC or some other concept to determine residence. While Article 3(2) of the Model Convention, as *Engelen*[1143] envisages, allocates the right to determine the meaning of residence to the State applying the law, where POEM is used as the 'tie-breaker' and the two States adopt different POEM meanings then DTC benefits may be rejected even though both States use POEM as their test.

The author concludes that the answer depends on whether the counterparty resides in a developed country and if it does, which POEM meaning it adopts. However, Brazil should not reject DTC benefits for a foreign person, because of a dispute over the location at which that foreign person's POEM is to be found, since Brazil uses the place of incorporation test to establish tax residence. The same outcome would have followed in Russia before January 2015. While POEM was formally incorporated into the RTC from January 2015 (even though Russia's 1992 Model DTC[1144] referred to it), POEM should have no relevance to Russia's DTCs[1145] which cede the country of

---

1140. OECD: Sweden (signed 1995 not amended in 2010 Protocol), UK (2002), Non-OECD: China (2000), Congo (2005), India (signed in 1996 not amended in 2013 Protocol), Malaysia (2005), Nigeria (2002), Oman (2002).
1141. At https://en.santandertrade.com/establish-overseas/south-africa/foreign-investment.
1142. *Supra* n. 483, at p. 88; *supra* n. 1100, p. 94/96.
1143. *Supra* n. 499, p. 486/487.
1144. N352, Article 1(3).
1145. OECD: Canada (1995), Chile (2004), Non-OECD: Kuwait (1999), Laos (1999), Macedonia (1997), Mongolia (1995), Thailand (1999), Turkey (1997).

residence to the country of incorporation but it will be relevant for those DTCs[1146] requiring the CAs to consult, assuming that in those consultation, the FTS use its POEM to determine the place at which residence is to be found. It will also be relevant in Russia's DTCs[1147] where POEM is used as a 'back stop' for dealing with unclear fact patterns or definitional conflict. However, it can be deduced that were the counterparty to be a developed country resident relying on POEM to be found at the place where the highest decisions were taken, when Russia relies on POEM to be found at the place where economic activities take place and assuming the foreign person's Board meets in the foreign location but the activities are located in Russia, then it will be difficult to avoid dual resident status and the resulting forfeiture of the DTC benefits. In relation to India, were a company having a foreign place of incorporation to have not less than one Board meeting each year outside India then it would not be Indian tax resident before April 2017, resulting in it being most unlikely that the DTC benefits would be disturbed. But with POEM effective in India from April 2017 and with approx. 60% of India's DTCs including POEM as the 'tie breaker' for situations where the CAs are unable to establish the place of residence through consultation,[1148] then, were the counter party resident in a developed country, the DTC benefits could be denied because India would likely rely on the location where the economic activities occur to be the place where residence is to be found. The same outcome should ensue for the DTCs[1149] which require the CAs to consider POEM as part of the consultation process, but POEM will not be relevant in the DTCs[1150] requiring the CAs by 'mutual agreement' to determine residence when at least one Board meeting occurs outside India. This analysis is complicated but it can be concluded that unless the Indian DTCs are amended, India's practical solution to the problem of relying on a COR[1151] to establish residence should avoid the rejection of DTC benefits and complex administrative consultations involving tax authority limited manpower, unless India disputes that the preconditions for issue of a COR were met. Were that to be the case, then POEM would become relevant in that instance. In relation to China, POEM became the exclusive tie-breaker in its DTCs from around 2004,[1152] and by 2008 it had been included as the tie breaker in twenty-seven DTCs. But with the CAs also required to mutually consult on the location of residence

---

1146. OECD: Canada (1984), Estonia (2002), Finland (2000), Iceland (1999), Norway (1996), US (1992); Non-OECD: Argentina (2001), Belarus (1995), Egypt (2001), Indonesia (1999), Kazakhstan (1996), Latvia (2010), Lithuania (1999), Sri Lanka (1999).
1147. OECD: Israël (1994), Luxembourg (2011); Non-OECD: Cyprus (1998), Malta (2013), Singapore (2002). Cyprus and Luxembourg DTCs refer to POEM factors.
1148. Neither aligned to OECD nor UN.
1149. OECD: Estonia (2011), Finland (2010), Non-OECD: Indonesia (1987), Latvia (2013), Lithuania (2011).
1150. OECD: Canada (1996), Japan (1989), Mexico (2007), Turkey (1997), US (1989) Non-OECD: Colombia (2011).
1151. Notification No. 39/2012, 17 Sep. 2012; Effective March 2013 the probability of losing benefits increased for those holding CORs because the MOF confirmed that while CORs (Circular No. 789, 13 Apr. 2000 continues pending discussions between India and Mauritius) were 'necessary they were not sufficient' to perfect DTC benefits and to police this test, *Rule 21AB* (Notification No. 57/2013 [F.NO. 142/16/2013-TPL]/SO 2331, 1 Aug. 2013) requires non-residents to detail the foreign person's status, country of registration, TIN and foreign address.
1152. OECD: Denmark (2012), Finland (2010), France (2013), Germany (1985), Netherlands (2013), Switzerland (1990), UK (2011); Non-OECD: Albania (2004), Algeria (2006), Armenia (1996),

in a further twenty-nine DTCs, POEM would have become relevant to a determination of residence under those DTCs too were the SAT to use it in the consultations. Were the counter party to be resident in a developed country then forfeiture of the DTC benefits would be possible should China rely on the location of the economic activities in that instance for determining POEM, even though it had not dispensed with using the place of highest decisions to determine residence. Since POEM is included as the 'tie-breaker' in approx. forty-seven SA DTCs and with SARS using the place of highest decision as the place at which POEM is to be found, it is unlikely SARS would reject the DTC benefits were the counterparty to be resident in a developed country. However, with seven DTCs allocating residence to the place where the Head Office is located and with a Head Office place considered by SARS to be an indicia of POEM, it is unlikely where these DTCs to apply that the benefits would be denied. In relation to the sixteen DTCs requiring the CAs to consult in the event of uncertainty over where POEM is to be found, it is considered unlikely that SARS would agree to a compromise because doing so would fetter its sovereignty. From the research in this subsection, it can be concluded that the trend is for the BRICS to establish the place at which economic activities are carried out as the taxing jurisdiction and this approach accords with that recommended by the BRICS Leaders.

6.2.5 Residence: Effectiveness in Denying DTC Benefits

The author concludes in this subsection that the BRICS domestic definitions of residence and the implications from those definitions for DTC residence and the relevance of CLT and POEM to that definition, is that there is unlikely to be any significance of the CLT for DTC benefits purpose, but there is the potential for DTC benefits to be rejected by Russia and China should the counterparty be a developed country person but not if a developing country person. In relation to Brazil, India and SA, using POEM is unlikely to give rise to a rejection of DTC benefits. Therefore, with the 'residence' concept not giving rise to a clear pathway for the BRICS to deny DTC benefits, they need to adopt other concepts to counter the DTC abuse.

6.3 BENEFICIAL OWNERSHIP, LIMITATION OF BENEFITS, PRINCIPAL PURPOSE

6.3.1 Introduction

In this subsection, the research examines whether the BRICS use the beneficial ownership test or the LOB and MPT to overcome the deficiencies identified in the

---

Azerbaijan (2005), Botswana (2012), Ethiopia (2009), Hong Kong (2010), Jamaica (1996), Malta (2010), Saudi (2006), Tajikistan (2010), Uganda (2012), Zambia (2010), 15 of 20 DTCs from 2004.

preceding subsection. Also the focus is on whether there is evidence of the BRICS coordinating their approach to counter treaty abuse, a programme agreed by the BRICS in the *Heads of Revenue*[1153] meetings.

6.3.2 Beneficial Ownership

The developed world[1154] requires the foreign recipient of dividends, interest and royalties to establish beneficial ownership as a precondition for accessing the lower DTC WHT rates.

Much scholarly research has been directed at defining beneficial ownership both in the contractual and trust contexts but the contractual context is seen to be the more pertinent for interpreting DTCs. In this respect, *Vogel*[1155] described beneficial ownership as representing the rights possessed by the foreign person to freely decide whether returns on the asset should be used by it or made available for use by others while the *OECD*[1156] defined it as being the foreign person's unfettered right to pass the dividends, interest or royalties to third persons of its choice except when acting as an agent, nominee or conduit for the real owner. With the *OECD R6*[1157] and *Partnership Reports*[1158] asserting a meaning for settlors, beneficiaries and other ultimate controllers, a position reinforced in the *FATF Report*,[1159] it represents a different approach to that of the contractual meaning of beneficial ownership. With *Baker*[1160] arguing that beneficial ownership for DTC purposes establishes an 'international fiscal meaning', for the purpose of facilitating DTC interpretation, he proposes a middle approach and his assertion is supported by precedent including *Indofood*.[1161] In that case, beneficial ownership was held to arise from the contractual relationship because those arrangements had substance in practical and commercial terms. Also relevant is *Prevost Car*,[1162] which held beneficial ownership to be found in the person having a degree of freedom to deal with the receipt and where that degree of freedom could be identified having regard to the recipient's degree of possession, use, risk and control. Were the recipient to be a conduit, agent or nominee devoid of a discretion to retain the funds *(Skat)*,[1163] then the foreign person would lack beneficial ownership, unless the

---

1153. *Supra* n. 997.
1154. Formed part of OECD DTCs since 1940s and before then the lower rates applied to payments.
1155. *Supra* n. 419.
1156. Articles 10, 11/12, UN and OECD Models.
1157. R(6) DTCs and use of Conduit Companies Report, November 1986.
1158. The Application of the OECD Model Tax Convention to Partnerships, 26 Aug. 1999 asserts 'beneficial ownership' is used to counter avoidance.
1159. FATF Recommendation 24: the natural person(s) ultimately owning or controlling the customer and/or the person on whose behalf a transaction is conducted while extending to persons exercising ultimate effective control over legal person or arrangement through the use of 'ultimately owning or controlling' traceable through entity chains.
1160. *Supra* n. 419, 0B-14.
1161. Indofood International Finance Limited v. JPMorgan Chase Bank NA, London Branch, A3/2005/2497, 2 Mar. 2006.
1162. Prevost Car 2004-2006(IT)G and 2004-4226(IT)G, 22 Apr. 2008.
1163. SS A/S v. Skat, B-2152-10, December 2011.

distribution obligations were narrow. *Velcro*[1164] refocussed the discussion back to beneficial ownership being be found at the person assuming risks and control and in doing so, limited the relevance of the contractual obligation test, a position supported by *6537/2010*[1165] which was decided at a similar time. However, in 364 / 2012 / 2C_377 / 2012,[1166] beneficial ownership was held to be found at the person having the right to decide on whether to surrender the capital or asset for use or, usages, and in so doing this merged the owner's contractual right test with the owner's obligation to bear losses from how the money was disbursed. The *HMRC*[1167] furthered the debate on the meaning of beneficial ownership by establishing as a practical guide, that beneficial ownership could be found at the person who did not have specific obligations (documentary or commercial) to pass the income (not necessarily immediately) to another person (either as interest or dividend) and in determining whether any such obligations existed, the presence and nature of the recipient's commercial purpose[1168] was important as was the degree of substance.[1169]

The next section considers the beneficial ownership meaning in the BRICS and the relevance to that consideration of the *contractual obligations* and the *possession, use, risk and control* tests.

6.3.2.1 *Contractual Obligations*

There is neither a clear nor a consistent approach in the BRICS to the significance of contractual obligations to beneficial ownership. With Brazil[1170] and Russia both being civil law countries neither had historically recognized the separation of ownership into beneficial and legal, and this led to some opportunities for DTC abuse. In seeking to counter that abuse Brazil, as confirmed by *Torres*,[1171] relied on the disclosures of beneficial ownership given to the Exchange Control authority at the time when

---

1164. Velcro v. Queen, 2012 TCC 57.Court rejected CRA's argument that Dutch licensor was a collection agent inserted into the in order to avoid the NA deriving the income because it did not have a DTC with Canada, leaving 25% WHT to be deducted on payments to the NA licensor.
1165. Switzerland - Case No. 6537/2010, 7 Mar. 2012.
1166. Switzerland - Case 2C_364 / 2012 / 2C_377 / 2012, 5 May 2015.
1167. Recent updates to International Manual, 12 Jun. 2012, Reinforcing position of Dutch Parliament, Van Raad, Intertax (1988) 241 at p. 245.
1168. HMRC establishes connection between 'beneficial ownership' and 'conduits' from reviewing commercial agreements linking income received to amounts paid (arrangements entered into under direction), whether local tax rules render it impossible (or unlikely) for foreign company to be beneficial owner, income traced through intermediary to territory without DTC with the UK or having a UK DTC not reducing withholding taxes.
1169. Employees, offices and activities within residence territory and whether responsibilities are discharged by other persons (group companies or third parties). Insufficiency of employees not necessarily fatal to beneficial ownership where holding company established for commercial purpose.
1170. Rocha, Treaty Shopping and Beneficial Ownership under Brazil's Tax Treaties, Bull. Intl. Taxn, 2012 (Volume 66), No. 7 and Transparency International, http://download.uol.com.br/fernandorodrigues/2015-Nov-9-Brazil-BO-country-report-final.pdf, p. 1, last viewed 14 Jun. 2016.
1171. *Supra* n. 161, at p. 166.

approval was sought to introduce the FDI into Brazil. The absence of a general statutory beneficial ownership concept in Brazil did not mean one did not exist because in 2010, one was specifically enacted for thin capitalization purposes,[1172] a position confirmed by *Bichara*.[1173] Law 12249/2010 established that beneficial ownership resided with the individual or legal entity *receiving the interest* unless received under a structure which was solely or mainly designed to save tax and only then, when the recipient received the interest as agent, trustee or nominee for third parties. *Rocha*[1174] has suggested that the beneficial ownership meaning for thin capitalization should be adopted widely in Brazil, but doing so would infringe the 'legality principle' and therefore should be rejected. Russia began to recognize beneficial ownership as a formal concept from December 2014 even though that concept had existed informally from 2003.[1175] Under that informal rule, a person qualified as the beneficial owner of dividends when it both received them and was the registered shareholder, an outcome which led to DTC abuse. The MOF[1176] recognized the abuse in rulings from 2004 and in one ruling, denied beneficial ownership to a Depository while in a later ruling[1177] accepted the 'actual income recipient' as being the beneficial owner providing it was not contractually obligated to dispose of the right to third parties to receive that income.[1178] This discord was clear in *Eastern Vale Partners*[1179] where the Court held that the party bearing the contractual obligations of the transaction was irrelevant but then decided to align with the MOF in a *Cassational Judgment*[1180] and in *Yanden*.[1181] Following these decisions, the MOF reinforced the contractual obligations test in an April 2014[1182] ruling. In that ruling, the MOF asserted that conduits owning limited income retention rights should not be treated as beneficial owners unless the recipient controlled the income's 'economic destiny'.

Beneficial ownership had not been relevant for China before 2008, in the absence of WHT nor for SA[1183] before 2012, in the absence of a WHT on dividends and royalties and before 2015 in the absence of a WHT on interest. This position changed when WHTs were introduced in China and in SA because accessing the lower DTC rate took on enhanced importance, which caused the tax authorities to increase scrutiny. *SAT's*[1184] approach to beneficial ownership had evolved from that of 2008 to the point

---

1172. Article 26(1), Law 12249/2010.
1173. Conflicts in attribution of income to persons – Brazil, IFA Cahiers 2007-Volume 92B p. 136.
1174. *Supra* n. 1170, at p. 357.
1175. From 2003 foreign companies were treated as 'beneficial' owners when both 'legally entitled' to the income and the registered shareholder.
1176. Private Ruling No. 2004-11-16:RU-1, 8 Nov. 2004.
1177. Private Ruling No. 03-08-02, 21 Apr. 2006.
1178. Sychev, Derivatives and Financial Instruments, Special issue, September/October 2013 p. 81.
1179. Eastern Value Partners Limited, Ninth Arbitrazh Appellate Court Resolution No. 09AP-33421/2012-AK of 5 Dec. 2012.
1180. Moscow Municipal Court Cassational Judgement No. 4g/2-12260/12 of 25 Dec. 2012.
1181. Yanden Enterprises Limited, Federal Arbitration Court of the East, 6 Feb. 2014, the Judgment No. A19-2735/2013.
1182. MOF Letter No. 03-00-RZ/16236, 9 Apr. 2014.
1183. Section 64D, ITA. New dividend tax defines 'beneficial owner' as 'person entitled to the benefit of the dividend attaching to the share' but definition only applies for dividends tax.
1184. Guoshuihan [2009] No. 81; Guoshuifa [2009] No. 124 (Administrative Measures on Non Residents Enjoying Treaty Benefits (Trial)); Guoshuihan [2009] No. 601 (notice regarding the

Chapter 6: Countering Treaty Benefits

where by 2014 it was seen as being more of an economic or substance[1185] test than one determined by the nature of the contractual relationships between the parties. This realisation led to the tax authority requiring notification of fact patterns, as is discussed in detail below. Since there were many different views in SA on beneficial ownership, the position was complicated. For example, SARS adopted the contractual obligations test and considered the person having 'ultimate control' to be the beneficial owner (*FATF*[1186] recommendations of rights and entitlement for use and enjoyment and to whom the duty of care was owed on income and property)[1187] while *ACAMS*[1188] explained that beneficial ownership resided with the person possessing the power (exercisable directly/indirectly) to vote on, or influence the transaction. Further opinions on the meaning can be found at *Ensight*[1189] which argued that absent a different approach under SA's tax laws, *Velcro* would be persuasive. While the contractual obligations approach is simpler for SARS to manage, assuming transparency on the legal relationships, *Velcro* was complicated because of its requirement that there be full information available on all the economic factors.

India's approach to beneficial ownership was for many years, seen as not relying on either the contractual obligations or on the functional performance but on whether the foreign person possessed a COR[1190] issued the foreign person's country of residence tax authority. This approach was simple for the tax authority to administer. It was also an approach confirmed by *Azadi Bachao Andolan*[1191] as being acceptable when the Court overturned the IRD's rejection of CORs issued by the Mauritius tax authority for Mauritian companies investing in India, funded by third country residents. The author deduces that one reason the Court protected the COR was Mauritius'[1192] significance to India as a provider of inbound FDI. The Court also rejected the IRD's assertion that 'treaty shopping' was illegal.[1193] The *Azadi* principle was subsequently confirmed in

---

interpretation and determination of beneficial owner under DTCs); SAT Announcement [2012] No. 30 (notice regarding the determination of beneficial owner in DTCs); SAT Announcement [2014] No. 24 ('Announcement 24'), 21 Apr. 2014, elaborating on beneficial owner.
1185. Recipient's constitution, cash flows, directors meetings, functional analyses, legal agreements, assets ownership and revenue records, employees, expenditures, IP licenses, patent and agency/nominee agreements.
1186. Natural person at end of chain, owning or controlling customer, 'Ultimate Beneficial Ownership: Developments in international standard setting' Republic SA, Financial Intelligence Centre; Makhetha, Comparative Analysis of usage of Concept 'Beneficial Owner' in SA DTCs, Minor Dissertation, University of Johannesburg, October 2013, p. 6/25/77.
1187. Investors register securities under nominee arrangement with broker's name as owner of record with the investor as beneficial owner.
1188. SA Chapter, Ultimate Beneficial Ownership, March 2011.
1189. At https://www.ensafrica.com/news/the-concept-of-beneficial-ownership-Velcro-Canada-v-The-Queen?Id=610&STitle=tax%20ENSight, 24 Apr. 2012.
1190. Beneficial owner established in Circular No.682, 30 Mar. 1994 and Circular No. 789, 13 Apr. 2000; Butani, India-Tax Treaty Interpretation, Asia-Pac. Tax Bull, January/February 2004.
1191. *Supra* n. 189.
1192. Fact Sheet on FDI: April 2000 to December 2011 http://dipp.nic.in/English/Publications/FDI_Statistics/2011/india_FDI_December2011.pdf.
1193. To stem these structures IRD terminated the ruling (Business entities not 'managed and controlled' from Mauritius. Report of Working Group on Non-Resident Taxation, 3 Jan. 2003, para. 3.3.1, argued DTCs should include provisions countering treaty shopping and conduits.

E-trade[1194] and later in *Universal International*.[1195] In *E-trade*, a Mauritian entity was held not to be a conduit even though its US shareholder funded the purchase of the intermediary's Indian shares, participated in the sale process and ultimately received the surplus funds as dividends. In *Universal* the intermediary royalty structure which the IRD rejected had been approved by the Indian Government for FDI purposes.

However, the *Azadi* principle does not mean that indirect owners of Indian assets cannot be held to be the beneficial owners, as evident from *Tata Industries*[1196] and from *Vodafone International*.[1197] In *Tata*, the Mauritian intermediary was confirmed to be a nominee and not a beneficial owner of the shares which it held on behalf of joint venture parties and from *Vodafone International*, where the Court held that possessing a COR might not establish beneficial ownership when the structure was a colourable device. *Korde*[1198] has confirmed that the IRD retains the right to ignore CORs when it believes the foreign tax authority should not have issued it or, as in *P*,[1199] when the income recipient was an agent even though it possessed a COR. The position has been further complicated by the Indian Government's *2013 Finance Bill*[1200] decision to continue the COR's relevance for establishing tax residence but ceased possessing a COR as being sufficient to establish beneficial ownership.

6.3.2.2 *Possession, Use, Risk and Control*

The person having possession, use, risk and control of the (recipient's) funds has been found to be relevant in the BRICS, bar Brazil, when determining who has beneficial ownership, even though the concept's meanings adopted by each BRICS member have subtle differences. This has resulted in complex fact patterns presenting particular difficulties for undermanned tax authorities because much of the required information was shrouded by the taxpayers. As discussed in the previous section of this study, beneficial ownership as a concept is legislated in Brazil only for thin capitalization purposes and therefore the person with possession, use, risk and control of the funds for Brazil purposes may not be relevant when determining who is entitled to the DTC

Indian Comptroller argued Mauritian conduits were used by third country investors to avoid Indian taxation, *Report No. 13, 2005)* but following the withdrawal of funds from India by Mauritian investors CORs were reinstated as beneficial ownership test in *Circular 789* (13 Apr. 2000). When the appeal by the IRD of *Circular 789* to the Delhi High Court was upheld, it was done so principally, but not wholly, on the grounds of it facilitating 'treaty shopping'(Seen as illegal in absence of commercial benefits for Mauritius or India) which was reversed on appeal.

1194. E*Trade Mauritius Ltd, AAR 826 of 200922 March 2010.
1195. ADIT v. Universal International Music BV, 2011-TII-22-ITAT-MUM-INTL.
1196. Tata Industries Ltd. v. DDIT. (Mum)([2011] 12 Taxmann.com 141).
1197. Vodafone International Holdings B.V. v. Union of India, Civil Appeal No. of 2012 (arising out of S.L.P. (C) No. 26529 of 2010) 20 Jan. 2012.
1198. Commissioner-Indian Revenue Service, Beneficial Owner – the debate continues, Tax Planning International Review, June 2013.
1199. XYZ, P No. 9 of 1995, 22 Dec. 1995.
1200. Zobalia, Anti-Avoidance Regime and Shome Committee Recommendations, Asia-Pac. Tax Bull, 2013 (Volume 19), No. 3, p. 177.

benefits. However, with the Supreme Court in *Brasil Volvo*[1201] deciding that DTC benefits were not available for interest paid to the Panama branch of a Japan bank because the Bank's head office had not *used the funds,* (i.e. the funds remained in Panama), the author deduces that Brazil treats the person having the right to use, and in fact uses the funds as the person entitled to the DTC benefits even though a specific Brazil beneficial ownership test does not formally exist. In the Russian legislation[1202] introducing beneficial ownership for DTC purposes, the necessity to identify the 'controlling' person was established as a precondition and fundamental to that task was a consideration of the functions and risks[1203] assumed by the foreign person. This supports the conclusion that there is much similarity between Russia's beneficial ownership process and the *Prevost Car* and *Velcro* principles, and further supports the conclusion that Russia has codified *Prevost Car* and *Velcro* into its beneficial ownership test. For this reason, Russia is able to 'look through'[1204] the legal owner's[1205] residence for DTC purposes to find the residence of the ultimate owner by considering factors such as the risks assumed and the functions performed by each person in the chain, with the controlling person's residence being the same as that of the legal owner's residence when they are the same person. In India, possession, use, risk and control is translated into the recipient's freedom to deal with the moneys, as *Bamford Investments*[1206] concludes and the relevance of the person's responsibility for his own transactions, as in *Yum Restaurants.*[1207] With the IRD continuing to look both for ways to distinguish *Azadi* and for grounds to establish that the foreign tax authority's issuance of the COR was inappropriate, it can be concluded that relying on these beneficial ownership principles should be acceptable. Establishing the meaning of beneficial ownership in China after the EITL had been introduced became fundamental, and by 2009 (*Circulars 601*[1208] and 81)[1209] China had established the meaning by reference to substance, as *Dongmei*[1210] observed. How relevant possession, use, risk and control became was evident when a person was denied beneficial ownership because he was under an obligation to transfer all, or substantially all (deemed to be more than 60%) of the income received to a third country resident within twelve months from receiving it, especially when the recipient had substantially no business operations, other than the rights giving rise to the income. SAT's approach to beneficial ownership in these Circulars was contradicted by *Cao*[1211] who believed that beneficial ownership having an 'international meaning' (like Baker's *international fiscal*

1201. Volvo Brasil Veículos Ltda v. Federal Revenue Service, 457.228, 18 Mar. 2004.
1202. Law 376-FZ, Article 7.
1203. Law, *supra* n. 1162, Article 7(3).
1204. *Ibid.*, Article 7(2).
1205. Actual owner can request refund of excess tax withheld on foreign company's income. When actual owner is Russian resident it must notify the tax authority at the foreign company's place of registration.
1206. JC Bamford Investments, ITA No. 80/Del/2013, 4 Jul. 2014.
1207. Yum Restaurants (India) Pvt. Ltd, ITA No. 1097/Del/2014.
1208. Guo Shui Han [2009] No. 601.
1209. Guoshuihan [2009] No. 81.
1210. China's Capital Gains Taxation of Non-residents and Legitimate Use of Tax Treaties, Tax Notes Int'l, November 2010, p. 621.
1211. *Supra* n. 515, p. 90/91.

meaning) for DTC purposes, but the *Yangzhou*[1212] and *Xinjiang*[1213] decisions support SAT's substance approach. While SAT introduced a safe harbour beneficial ownership test (namely retention of 40% or more and for twelve months) to simplify administration, other factors which could not be simplified such as whether 'sufficient' persons were employed to manage the assets generating the business, whether those persons had 'sufficient' discretion to invest the income and whether an appropriate level of tax was paid in the foreign person's residence country, made the substance test subjective and difficult to administer. With the decisions on beneficial ownership in *Jiangdu*,[1214] *Chongqing*,[1215] *Mudan*,[1216] *Shenzhen*[1217] and Qinghai[1218] made on the basis of substance, beneficial ownership had become one of China's most important weapons for denying DTC benefits. The application of the substance test led to much concern, as observed by *Jiang Bian*[1219] *and Dongmei*,[1220] (especially in Hong Kong where many China SOEs had listed), that pure intermediary holding companies[1221] would be denied DTC benefits, as seen in *Fujian*.[1222] In response, China published *Announcement 30*[1223] which applies specifically to publicly listed companies or for publicly listed company subsidiaries resident in listed DTC countries when that person would otherwise fail the substance test. With most China inbound FDI[1224] emanating from Hong Kong, it was not surprising when *Circular 165*[1225] publicized a further relaxation to the substance policy for companies resident in Hong Kong receiving dividends from China enterprises. This concession applied even were the Hong Kong company to be obligated to pass more than 60% of their receipts to other persons providing they were Hong Kong residents or were the Hong Kong company a holding company, provided those companies were not excluded from beneficial ownership for other reasons. SA applies the possession, use and risk of loss and control test, as *Makhetha*[1226] confirms.

The author concludes in relation to Russia and China, that substance is the most important criteria for establishing beneficial ownership, and that substance is to be found by applying a range of factors which reduces to who possesses, uses and loses or controls. Brazil however, considers who uses the funds while India focusses on the

---

1212. May 2010.
1213. December 2008.
1214. 2010.
1215. June 2010.
1216. July 2010.
1217. 2011.
1218. September 2014.
1219. Taxation of Dividends, Interest and Royalties and Technical Service Fees, Asia Pacific Tax Bulletin, 2013, Volume 19, No. 4 p. 236/240.
1220. Interpretation of Tax laws in China, *supra* n. 77.
1221. SAT instructed LTB to examine foreign dividends paid in 2012 and 2013 (*Shui Zong Han [2014] No. 317*) and report to SAT (*Shui Zong Ji Bian Han [2014] No. 207*) on action taken to apply beneficial ownership test.
1222. June 2010.
1223. Subsection (3).
1224. Approx. 75% of inbound FDI came from Hong Kong in 2015, https://en.santandertrade.com /establish-overseas/china/foreign-investment.
1225. Shuizonghan [2013] No. 165, 12 Apr. 2013.
1226. Comparative Analysis of usage of Concept 'Beneficial Owner', *supra* n. 1146.

Chapter 6: Countering Treaty Benefits

level of recipient freedom to deal with the moneys and the relevance of the recipient's responsibility for his own transactions. SA follows the possession use and risk test.

In relation to coordination between the BRICS, the *Heads of Revenue*[1227] on this concept, while the BRICS have published an intention to counter DTC abuse and while there are similarities in the beneficial ownership definitions of Russia and China, there is also no published evidence that this similarity follows from actual coordination between their officials.

6.3.3 BRICS: DTCs and Beneficial Ownership

This subsection researches on whether the different approaches of the BRICS to the developed world[1228] on the meaning of beneficial ownership may result in qualification conflicts for WHT purposes. In relation to Brazil, both its early DTCs[1229] and many of its later DTCs[1230] include the beneficial ownership precondition for accessing the lower DTC rates, but this requirement had little impact on the actual amount of WHT deducted on dividends, because Brazil does not levy WHT on dividends. In relation to WHTs on interest and royalties, in the absence of a widely applicable beneficial ownership definition, Brazil's thin capitalization definition would not be relevant because the developed world requires definitions to apply for all tax laws.[1231] This view is disputed by *Utimi*[1232] on the grounds of the RFB being able to interpret beneficial ownership 'as it sees fit'. The better view though is that the RFB could not adopt the thin capitalization definition for beneficial ownership purposes because to do so would be arbitrary. There would unlikely be any qualification conflicts in SA arising from the definition because while most of its DTCs[1233] contain a beneficial ownership precondition, the definition is based on the developed world's. In India, while not all its bilateral DTCs include beneficial ownership as a pre-condition for the lower WHT, beneficial ownership is essentially irrelevant for foreign persons possessing a COR[1234]

1227. *Supra* n. 997.
1228. OECD Model Commentary, Article 4, para. 13.1.
1229. 1970s DTCs not using beneficial ownership, OECD: Austria (1975), Denmark (1974), Finland (1972), Italy (1978), Japan (1976), Sweden (1975). 1970s DTCs using beneficial ownership, OECD: Belgium (1972), Luxembourg (1978) but only royalties, Spain (1974). Non-OECD 1970 DTCs do not contain the test.
1230. OECD: Turkey (2010), Mexico (2003); Non-OECD: Trinidad (2008), Peru (2006), Venezuela (2005), Russia (2004), SA (2003).
1231. Article 4, para. 13.1, *supra* n. 514.
1232. At http://tozzinifreire.com.br/blog/tax/2016/02/03/treaty-series-the-bilateral-income-tax-treaty-between-brazil-and-spain/#.VxyItfkrLIU.
1233. All bar eight of SA's DTCs – OECD: Germany (1973), Israel (1978), Poland (1993), Non-OECD: Grenada (1960), Malawi (1971), Sierra Leone (1960), Zambia (1956) and Zimbabwe (1965) where residence is sufficient (Germany is SAs fourth largest inbound FDI provider, https://en.portal.santandertrade.com/establish-overseas/south-africa/foreign-investment).
1234. Consequence of adopting this approach is the unlikelihood of qualification conflict denying DTC benefits, a position reaffirmed by 2013 Finance Act Amendments: Narvekar, Tax residence certificates: The road ahead for foreign companies in India, International Tax Review, 19 Jun. 2013. OECD: Germany (1973), Israel (1978), Poland (1993).

and currently absolutely irrelevant for Mauritius residents[1235] unless the recipient is an agent for a non-Mauritian or the usage of the COR, according to the IRD, is a colourable device. For this reason, while possessing a COR may result in a qualification conflict it is not likely to be one which results in the application of a non-DTC WHT rate in India. With beneficial ownership for China and Russia[1236] based on substance rather than on contractual relations the author foresees the potential for qualification conflicts. China has anticipated this problem by carving out from the beneficial ownership provisions, their applicability to foreign persons resident in countries from which much of its inbound FDI emanates, including Hong Kong. Russia is different again for DTC claims made before the introduction of the beneficial ownership definition because before then, Russia's domestic meaning arose from its Model DTCs, MOF rulings and precedent which can only be used for DTC purposes, if constituting 'applicable tax laws', which as the author concludes, they do not. o. The author has formed this view on the basis that neither MOF rulings nor Presidential Decrees (as the Russian Models are) constitute 'applicable tax law'[1237] and so prevents their adoption for Article 3(2) purposes. This means that in the absence of a definition there could be no qualification conflicts. However, for payments made after December 2014 the qualification conflicts would allow Russia to levy WHT at the non-DTC rate.

6.3.4 Limitation of Benefits (LOB)

In previous subsections of this study, it has been concluded that DTC benefits were unlikely to be forfeited by the major providers of FDI to the BRICS under the CLT but these benefits were likely to be rejected by Russia, SA and China applying their beneficial ownership tests, except in China's case for qualifying FDI providers resident in Hong Kong. Also concluded was that DTC benefits were unlikely to be denied by Brazil or by India under the beneficial ownership test because Brazil does not have such a provision while India relies on the COR to establish ownership. Also concluded was that DTC benefits may be denied by Russia and by China when applying their POEM but not for Brazil, India and SA.

In order to reinforce these provisions and to widen the anti-abuse provisions in the DTCs, the developed world acknowledges that DTC benefits claimed by

---

1235. Protocol varies for capital gains.
1236. Beneficial ownership found in all Russia's DTCs bar five (four signed around 1997 (Kazakhstan (1996), 'actual owner'; Korea (1997), 'resident', interest and royalty, Lebanon (1997), effective owner; Syria (2000), 'resident', dividends;) and fifth (UAE (2011), resident, dividends and interest) signed in 2011.
1237. 1993 *Russian Federation Constitution* stipulates that *Ukases* (Presidential Decrees), have the power of law but neither alter the Russian Constitution nor Regulations and may be superseded by laws passed by the *Federal Assembly*.

Chapter 6: Countering Treaty Benefits

conduits[1238] in 'treaty shopping' situations, as *Borrego*[1239] observes, should be denied through the application of an LOB or an MPT,[1240] provided the relevant bilateral DTC contains the provisions. This explanation is supported by *Avi-Yonah's*[1241] assertion that LOBs and MPTs are required in the DTCs to counter the so-called channel approach to base erosion which uses cross-border payments to a controller or to an associate, of interest or royalties or payments discharging other obligations, which may include associates one step removed from the controller or associates residing in a third country. He also explains[1242] that many countries fail to include the provisions in their DTCs because of the vagueness of the developed world's LOB and MPT[1243] provisions even though the *OECD Model Commentary*[1244] recommends their inclusion. Strangely, the *OECD Model Convention* is yet to include them but this will change as part of the BEPS recommendations[1245] which are discussed in the following Chapter.

6.3.4.1 *BRICS and LOBs*

In this subsection, the research considers whether the BRICS include LOBs and MPTs in their DTCs and if, so the significance of those inclusions. Brazil does not have a domestic LOB and as a consequence relies on the simulation test (essentially an MPT) to counter DTC abuse, as *Marcopolo*[1246] shows. In that case, the Court found the nature of the substance of the two intermediaries' not sufficient to establish a real business

---

1238. 1987 CFA Report, DTCs and Use of Conduit Companies, established that when a company's main function is the holding of assets or rights then that by itself is insufficient to categorize it as an 'agent or nominee', but a company cannot be the beneficial owner when it has narrow powers, performs fiduciary or administrative functions or acts on account of the beneficiary. OECD observes such companies have title to property, but neither economic, legal nor practical ownership attributes; Formal residence in one State solely to benefit from that State's DTC (Article 1 paras 7/10 (11 Apr. 1977), *supra* n. 514; de Broe, International Tax Planning and Prevention of Abuse, section 7.1, IBFD 2007; Beneficial ownership requirement introduced in Article 10(2) when benefits not available for direct investments (Pistone, El Abuso de los Convenios Internacionales en Materia Fiscal, in Uckmar; V. Uckmar, Introducción, Curso de Derecho Tributario Internacional, (translated by C.J. Billardi & J.O. Zanotti Aichino) at Volume II, p. 122) Rosembuj, Fiscalidad Internacional, Marcial Pons 1998, p. 111.
1239. LOB Clauses in DTCs, EUCOTAX Series on Eur. Taxn., p. 94, Kluwer L. Intl. 2006.
1240. 1988 OECD Conduit Report argued that where DTCs fail to contain provisions safeguarding the availability of benefits, then they should be granted relief on a 'good faith' basis.
1241. Rethinking Treaty Shopping: Lessons for the European Union, 2 Pub. L. & Leg. Theory Working Paper Series, Working Paper No. 182, p. 11 (January 2010), p. 12.
1242. *Supra* n. 1241, at p. 20.
1243. Beneficial ownership, look-through, channel approach (ownership of entity), limitation on residence, exclusion and subject-to-tax: Article 1, para. 13/19; main purpose of entering into transaction or arrangements was to secure DTC benefits, general DTC abuse covered by substance over form, economic substance, and general abuse rules, Article 1 paras 9.5, 22, 22.1/2.
1244. Article 1, para. 19; Reports on DTC and Use of Base companies and DTC and Use of Conduit Companies, published at R(5)-1 and R(6)-1; UN, 'Department of International Economic and Social Affairs, Contributions to International Co-operation in Tax Matters: Treaty Shopping, Thin Capitalization, Co-operation between Tax Authorities, Resolving International Tax Disputes, New York 1988.
1245. Discussion in Chapter 7 on BEPS Action Deliverable 6.
1246. *Supra* n. 168.

purpose for the intermediary's role in the transaction. This means that Brazil's approach to countering treaty shopping is to use an MPT, a position which *Torres*[1247] and *Castro*[1248] confirm. This leads to the conclusion that Brazil has merged the developed world's LOBs and MPTs into a general anti-abuse concept. Russia did not formally publish an LOB policy before its 2010 Model DTC,[1249] but that Model lays out an LOB which is designed to counter conduiting but only when the CAs form the view that the DTC had been abused. The importance for the CAs 'to consult' is evident from A40-60755/12-20-388[1250] where the Court confirmed the availability of the DTC benefits even though the conduiting structure was clearly abusive, but did so because the CAs had failed to consult. According to *Wilson*,[1251] the LOB included in the 2010 Russian Model LOB is comparable to the OECD's approach in the types of income which it is designed to counter, including conduits and income from maritime transport or from banking, finance, insurance, investment or the like. However, the Russian Model widens the structures constituting conduits by including those where foreign persons provide headquarters activities or administrative services when the profits derived from those activities are not liable to tax in the foreign person's state of residence or, are taxed at a rate substantially lower than the rate applicable to those profits were the foreign person be a source country resident. It also widens the LOB by including a 'qualifying person' test, broadly one where 50% or more of the intermediary's share capital is held (directly/indirectly) by third state residents providing the intermediary was not carrying on significant (non-passive)[1252] businesses in the State in which the intermediary was resident. The breadth of Russia's LOB suggests that in concept it effectively merges the OECD's LOB and MPT but from a practical perspective, the LOB's effectiveness remains questionable since in *Eastern Value Partners*,[1253] the Court refused to deny DTC benefits even though the intermediary's ultimate owner participated directly in the intermediary's transactions by signing both the loan agreement and the lease purchase. LOBs are intended to provide a 'backstop' counter when taxpayers satisfy the beneficial ownership test, but with China's beneficial ownership[1254] test being based4 on substance, it is difficult to conceive of circumstances in which an LOB may be required to apply to a foreign person and China,

---

1247. International Tax Law: Tax planning and transnational operations, São Paulo: Journal of the Courts, 2001, p. 327.
1248. Brazil Anti-Treaty Shopping Measures: Current and Future Developments regarding Beneficial Ownership and LOB Clauses in Tax Treaties, Bull. Intl. Taxn, 2011 (Volume 65), No. 12, p. 665.
1249. February 24, 2010 N 84, Articles 10/11/12. Not referred to in the Russian 1992 Model DTC (Russian MDTC, May 28, 1992 N352, Articles 7/8/11).
1250. A40-60755/12-20-388 (Eastern Value Partners Ltd), 28 Nov. 2012.
1251. *Supra* n. 66, at p. 5/6.
1252. Ownership of securities, passive subsidiaries or similar activity with related parties.
1253. A40-60755/12-20-388, 28 Nov. 2012.
1254. Guo Shui Han [2009] No. 601; Wei Cui, China/UK DTC(2011), Bull. Intl. Taxn, 2013 (Volume 67), No. 6, p. 278; Jiang Biang, Taxation of Dividends, Interest, Royalties and Technical Service Fees, Asia-Pac. Tax Bull, 2013 (Volume 19), No. 4, pp. 238, 239; Finnerty, Structures Lacking Substance and Business Purpose Come under Further Challenge, Asia-Pac. Tax Bull, 2009 (Volume 15), No. 6 p. 394; Baker & Mckenzie, China Tax Monthly, Beijing/Hong Kong/Shanghai, September/October 2014.

Chapter 6: Countering Treaty Benefits

except perhaps for an abusive Hong Kong structure which on first principles, qualifies for the permitted carve-outs. This conclusion has become clear for DTC benefits for dividends, interest, royalties and capital gains as discussed in *Shenzen*.[1255] However, should a structure satisfy the beneficial ownership then, according to *Yang*,[1256] GAAR would be available to counter the DTC abuse. For this reason, China's approach is more reflective of an MPT than of an LOB, but having regard to the risk factors[1257] set out in *Shui Zong Han [2014] No. 317*,[1258] it is suggestive that China also has merged the OECD's LOB and MPTs concepts. India does not have a domestic LOB test even though it requires one in the absence of tools to counter residence and beneficial ownership abuse and faced with both the *Azadi* rule and the taxpayer's right to elect a domestic provision[1259] over a DTC. In an effort to overcome these difficulties, according to *Malik*,[1260] a line of thinking has developed based on tax motivated treaty shopping being countered, but the probability of a Court distinguishing *Azadi* has proven to be low as is evident from *Intertek Testing*.[1261] In that case, the Court held the intermediary to be *capable of providing* a service even though it did not do so and in *International Global Networks*[1262] the Court held the structure's form and business purpose were sufficient even though the intermediary was an agent for the Indian company in placing advertising and in *Ardex Investments Mauritius*[1263] where *the many years of ownership* were held not to be indicative of treaty shopping. These decisions support *Bajpai's*[1264] lament that India can only counter treaty shopping where the structure represents fraud or evasion *(Juggi Lal Kamlapat)*[1265] in which case a 'look through' should apply. One significance of *Azadi* is that it has contributed to the IRD, from around 2005, incorporating LOBs into India's DTCs which arguably is the reason the OECD[1266] believes that India is an LOB leader, but, in practice the OECD is mistaken, because India has not translated the LOBs into denying DTC benefits because first of enforcement problems stemming from *Azadi* and second, in the absence of a GAAR. With Mauritius being the largest contributor of FDI to India and because of India's substantial reluctance to amend the India/Mauritius DTC due to the real commercial concerns

---

1255. 2011.
1256. Tax treaties and tax avoidance: application of anti-avoidance provisions – China, IFA Cahiers 2010 - Volume 95A, p. 216.
1257. Declared but unpaid distributions, distributions paid to foreign shareholders without deducting taxes, distributions to foreign persons disguised as loans, converting retained profits into capital for reinvestment without deducting tax, obtaining DTC benefits through agents or conduits residents in favourable tax rate countries.
1258. LTBs used when determining whether DTC benefits should be allowed for dividends or disguised dividends during 2012 and 2013.
1259. Section 90(1)(a)(ii), ITA.
1260. Investing into India, Asia-Pac. Tax Bull, 2014 (Volume 20), No. 4, p. 239.
1261. Intertek Testing Services v. AAR No. 751 of 2007, 7 Nov. 2008.
1262. International Global Networks ITA No. 2865/Mum/2008, 23 Jul. 2010.
1263. Ardex Investments Mauritius Ltd, A.A.R. No. 886 of 2010, 14 Nov. 2011.
1264. Piercing the corporate veil in taxation matters: India and International Transactions, with Special Reference to Direct Tax Code 2010, Bull. Intl. Taxn, 2012 (Volume 66), No. 10, para. 3.2.
1265. Juggi Lal Kamlapat v. Commissioner Of Income-Tax, U.P, 1969 1 SCR 988.
1266. Deliverable six explains that the US together with a few DTCs entered into by Japan and India contain LOB's, para. 16, p. 24.

for how doing so may impact the long-term economic relationship between the countries, the options for the IRD to successfully deny DTC benefits for structures involving the Mauritius DTC[1267] are extremely limited. In the author's opinion, because the recently signed Protocol[1268] denies DTC benefits only on capital gains, its significance for the potential forfeiture of DTC benefits on dividends, interest and royalties will be low. However, India's DTC with Singapore (also a significant FDI provider to India) protects India's right to reject DTC benefits[1269] but with the test expressed in monetary terms (Singapore based annual expenditure SGD 200,000 in the immediately preceding twenty-four months) the test removes the requirement to deal with subjective intentions and simplifies administration. The Singapore approach reflects a substance test, constituting more of an MPT than of an LOB, but in doing so provides a simpler tool for the tax authority to deal with. In the absence of WHTs before April 2012 for dividends and before March 2015 for interest, SA had little reason for a need to counter conduiting[1270] even though the *Davis Tax Committee*[1271] and *Blerck*[1272] confirmed that rules should be included in the Tax Act to do so. However, this explanation does not explain why SA had not enacted an LOB to counter royalty conduiting but, if as *Mazansky*[1273] asserts, SA has broadly abrogated its taxing rights on foreign persons to foreign tax authorities' where doing so encourages inbound FDI, then this is the explanation. However, the more likely explanation though is the long standing existence in SA of a GAAR[1274] which applies to conduits even though there has been a need to expand the GAAR in recent years.[1275] Following on from the introduction of WHTs, according to the *Davis Tax Committee*,[1276] SA has been renegotiating DTCs rather than introducing LOBs but *West*[1277] confirms there is little evidences of LOBs having been included in SA's DTCs which gives rise to some doubt over the *Davis Tax Committee's* conclusion.

1267. Hamzaoui, IBFD, reported in July 2013 Mauritius proposed a Singapore replicating LOB; Protocol denies CGT relief to Mauritius companies.
1268. Signed 11 May 2016.
1269. 2005 *Protocol* to Singapore/India DTC included an LOB.
1270. ENSafrica, International Tax, 2406. Treaty shopping, April 2015 – Issue 187 https://www.saica.co.za/integritax/2015/2406._Treaty_shopping.htm.
1271. Interim Report Action Plan 6: Addressing BEPS in SA, http://www.taxcom.org.za/docs/New_Folder/5%20DTC%20BEPS%20Interim%20Report%20on%20Action%20Plan%206%20-%20Treaty%20Abuse%202014%20deliverable.pdf.
1272. Company-Shareholder Taxation in SA: Single or Double Taxation?, 2003 International Bureau of Fiscal Documentation, p. 572 para. 6.2 and para. 2.1.3.
1273. SA's Treaty Network –Why is SA the Meat in the Sandwich, Bull. Intl. Taxn, April 2009, p. 149.
1274. Section 90, amended to section 103 and later section 80.
1275. Mazansky, Duke of Westminster still lives in SA (but is very careful when he crosses the road), Bulletin for International Fiscal Documentation, 2005 at p. 116.
1276. *Supra* n. 1271, at p. 6.2.1.
1277. Tax Avoidance Revisited: Exploring the Boundaries of Anti-Avoidance Rules in the EU BEPS Context Report, Tax Institute for Fiscal Research University of Cape Town South Africa, EATLP 2016, http://www.eatlp.org/uploads/public/South%20Africa%20(6%20Feb%2020 16).pdf, p. 14.

6.3.5 MPT

The MPT is a general anti-abuse test designed to counter DTC abuse of a kind not easily subject to the LOB and the MPT usually found in the dividend, interest and royalty Articles of a bilateral DTC. In relation to the BRICS, the Brazil and Russia[1278] DTCs generally include an MPT in those Articles and Brazil did so, according to *Torres*,[1279] in order to be able to counter artificial transactions creating, or associated with the creation or assignment of property rights. While *Gomez*[1280] argues that including MPTs into Brazil's DTCs has been a priority, the author's review of its DTCs concludes that the practice is yet to become widespread. In relation to Russia, while an MPT has been policy since the 2010 Russian Model, as *Wilson*[1281] observes it was left undefined until the MOF's explanation rulings including *Letter 2011 N-03-08-13*. One ruling confirmed that dividends paid by Russian companies to Cyprus shareholders would not benefit from the Russia/Cyprus DTC when the dividends received by the Cyprus intermediary were immediately distributed to the Dutch parent because doing so indicated that the Cyprus company was not in 'control of (its) economic destiny'. The explanation is helpful, but it can be deduced from the MOF using words more closely resembling beneficial ownership, that the MOF was unclear of the difference between an MPT and beneficial ownership. With neither India, China nor SA including MPTs into their domestic law each remains able to potentially counter the DTC abuse only by applying a GAAR, but in India's case, this can only be possible from April 2017 when it's GAAR[1282] becomes effective. As *Shome*[1283] observes, abusing DTCs[1284] is intended to be treated as 'impermissible'[1285] and therefore will enable the Courts to reject DTC benefits. China's GAAR[1286] is already applicable to the DTC abuse which an MPT is intended to cover, but there is insufficient information, according to *West*[1287] on the potential applicability of SA's GAAR to such abuse.

6.3.6 DTCs: LOB and MPTs

Even though the OECD *Model Convention* does not contain LOBs or MPTs, the OECD[1288] acknowledges that different formats have been employed by members and non-members in their DTCs. The broad range of LOB's includes 'qualified persons',

---

1278. Chapter 3, Articles 10(8), 11(9) and 12(8), Russian Model DTC.
1279. *Supra* n. 161, at p. 168.
1280. BRICs: Tax Treaty Policy Regarding Dividends, Bull. Intl. Taxn, August 2012, p. 404.
1281. *Supra* n. 66, p. 7.
1282. International Taxation Volume 13 October 2015, No. 71, 361–365.
1283. Expert Committee on GAAR, 9 Oct. 2012, p. 7.
1284. Section 90A(2A) ITA will allow GAAR to work in a DTC context.
1285. Section 96, ITA establishes arrangements with 'main purpose' of obtaining tax benefits as arising from rights or obligations not ordinarily created between arm's length persons or those resulting in misuse or abuse of the Act or lacking commercial substance or carried out by non-bona fide means.
1286. Article 47, *supra* n. 35, Article 120, EITL Implementation Rules.
1287. *Supra* n. 1277, at p. 14.
1288. Article 1 Commentary, para. 20 through to 21.

'preferential tax' regimes or 'special income' tests, while the MPTs includes 'general anti-abuse' or rules specifically targeting 'dividends, interest, royalties and capital gains'. In this subsection, the research focuses on whether the BRICS approach to LOBs and MPTs in their DTCs conforms to these options, and if not why.

6.3.6.1 LOBs

This study concludes that each of the BRICS include LOBs in their bilateral DTCs, even though the LOBs are found in a relatively small number of their DTCs. In relation to Brazil, only six contain of its DTCs contain LOBs with four[1289] focussing on countering treaty abuse and two[1290] taking the qualified person form (which is reversed in one[1291] DTC when substantial business reasons justify the structure or transaction). With Brazil's four most recent DTCs[1292] applying the so-called special income approach, this leads to the conclusion that this is Brazil's current LOB format. Many of Russia's pre-2010 DTCs contain LOBs with two[1293] adopting the qualified person approach, three[1294] treaty abuse and a further three[1295] the preferential tax regime. Of the eight DTCs (and Protocols) signed since 2010, five[1296] contain the anti-abuse test and one[1297] the qualified person test. From this it can be concluded that Russia's current LOB is the general anti-abuse format, which sits comfortably with its 2010 DTC policy. India has included LOB's in its DTCs from around 2003[1298] with the qualified person test adopted in nine DTCs,[1299] treaty abuse in two[1300] and preferential tax regimes in a further two.[1301] From this it can be concluded that India's current format is the qualified person test. China includes LOBs in only seven DTCs with four[1302] adopting the qualified person test and three[1303] the anti-abuse test. This therefore means that China's current format is the qualified person test. SA has included LOBs in seven DTCs with one DTC[1304] using the qualified person approach while two old DTCs[1305] adopt the specific

---

1289. Mexico (2003), Russia (2004), Venezuela (2005), Turkey (2010).
1290. Israel (2002), Trinidad (2008).
1291. Israel (2002).
1292. SA (2003), Russia (2004), Venezuela (2005), Peru (2006) applicable to shipping, banking, financing, insurance, investment or similar activities or from headquarters, co-ordination centre or similar entities providing administrative or support services to group companies carrying on business primarily in third States.
1293. US (1992), China (2014).
1294. Israel (1994), Brazil (2004), Chile (2004), Cyprus (2010), Malta (2013).
1295. UK (1994), Indonesia (1999), Mexico (2004), Singapore (2015P).
1296. Singapore (2015P), Belgium (2015), Malta (2013), Cyprus (2010), Luxembourg (2011).
1297. China (2014).
1298. LOBs in the earlier US and Namibia DTCs.
1299. US (1989), Armenia (2003), Mexico (2007), Iceland (2007), Tajikistan (2008), Tanzania (2011), Uruguay (2011), Sri Lanka (2013), Albania (2013).
1300. Kuwait (2006), Poland (2013).
1301. Namibia (1997), Singapore (2011).
1302. US (1986P), Ecuador (2013), Russia (2014), Chile (2015).
1303. US (1984), Israel (1995), Czech (2009).
1304. Mexico (2009).
1305. Sweden (1995), Denmark (1995).

Chapter 6: Countering Treaty Benefits

income test and a further three old DTCs[1306] follow the preferential tax regime approach. One Protocol[1307] counters structures where more than 50% of the foreign person's shareholders are third country residents.

The current approach in China and India is the qualified person and special income, respectively while it is anti-abuse in Brazil and Russia, respectively. The qualified person approach is adopted by SA (one suspects at Mexico's request). Based on this information, it can be concluded that there is an inconsistency of approach amongst the BRICS, but with a broad trend in India and China's DTCs towards the qualified person test.

6.3.6.2 MPT

The author has identified that while the BRICS include MPTs in their DTCs, they are to be found in a very small number of DTCs, except for India's DTC network. Brazil began including MPTs in its DTCs and Protocols from around 2001 but they are found in only eight DTCs[1308] of which seven apply solely to dividends, interest and royalties (current policy) and with one applying solely to dividends.[1309] This data confirms *Torres'*[1310] observation. Russia has included MPTs in DTCs for many years and of the six[1311] signed before 2010, two were framed as a general anti-abuse provision and a further two[1312] are applicable solely to dividends, interest and royalties and a further two[1313] applicable to interest and royalties. One earlier DTC[1314] focusses on whether the foreign person was subject to preferential tax rates. Including MPTs in the DTCs from 2010 (second Russian Model DTC) has been policy, with four[1315] (current policy) applicable to dividends, interest and royalties (one[1316] which reverses the MPT for a business purpose explanation of the structure or transaction), four applying to DTC abuse[1317] providing the CA's consult beforehand and a further four[1318] providing the FTS with a right to reject the benefits even without consulting the other CA when it identifies DTC abuse. Complicating the position is the inclusion of an MPT in the Other Income Article in one DTC[1319] and also countering for entities or structures established for tax purposes, in the Cyprus Protocol.[1320] India has included MPTs in its DTCs since 2007

1306. Norway (1996), UK (2002), Ghana (2004).
1307. Spain (2006P) and capital gains.
1308. Ukraine (2002), SA (2003), Russia (2004), Venezuela (2005), Peru (2006), Trinidad (2008).
1309. Chile (2001).
1310. Tax Treaties and Tax Avoidance, *supra* n. 161.
1311. Brazil (2004), Chile (2004), Lithuania (1999), Estonia (2002).
1312. Chile (2004A), Brazil (2004A).
1313. UK (1994), Mexico (2004).
1314. UK (1994).
1315. HK (2016A), Malta (2013A), China (2014A), Singapore (2015PA).
1316. Singapore (2015P).
1317. Luxembourg (2011), Switzerland (2011), Latvia (2010P), UAE (2011).
1318. Malta (2013), Switzerland (2011), Cyprus (2010PR), Belgium (2015).
1319. China (2014).
1320. Cyprus (2010P).

but with little consistency of approach. Twelve DTCs[1321] extend the provision beyond that applying to dividends, interest and royalties to covering general DTC abuse associated with the formation of the foreign person, sixteen[1322] apply to transactions arranged for the main purpose of obtaining the DTC benefits, two[1323] apply to dividends, interest or royalties and one[1324] applies to interest and royalties. Further complexity evolves from the forfeiture of DTC benefits where the foreign person is subject to preferential tax regimes,[1325] when used as a conduit[1326] or controlled by non-residents[1327] in a further DTC. Thus, it can be concluded that India's current MPT policy is that of general abuse. China has included MPTs in only three DTCs[1328] entered into since 2009 and while each applies to dividends, interest, royalty, its applicability is extended to capital gains with one[1329] DTC containing a general treaty abuse provision. The lack of MPTs in China's DTCs could be seen as insubstantial focus but with MPTs included in the Hong Kong and Singapore (the two significant inbound China FDI providers) DTCs, the better view is that it represents a targeted focus of countering structures satisfying the relaxation of the beneficial ownership test for Hong Kong residents when the foreign person should not qualify for that relief. SA has included MPTs in nine DTCs since 2003 with dividends, interest and royalties covered in eight[1330] with one (Netherlands)[1331] applicable to dividends only (Netherlands does not levy interest or royalties WHT), one[1332] to situations where more than 50% shareholding of the intermediary resides in a third country and one[1333] where the foreign person qualifies for a preferential tax regime. With the current MPT approach in Brazil, Russia and SA being that of applying to dividends, interest and royalties with an extension to include capital gains in China and with India to apply a general anti-abuse concept, it suggests a similar policy amongst Brazil, Russia, China and SA (with a China extension) but a different approach in India.

1321. UAE (2007P), UK (2012P), Luxembourg (2008), Norway (2011), Colombia (2011), Lithuania (2011), Georgia (2011), Romania (2013), Malta (2013), Latvia (2013), Macedonia (2013), Israel (2015P).
1322. Poland (2013P), Mexico (2007), Iceland (2007), Myanmar (2008), Tajikistan (2008), Finland (2010), Ethiopia (2011), Uruguay (2011), Nepal (2011), Malaysia (2012), Indonesia (2012), Sri Lanka (2013), Bhutan (2013), Albania (2013), Fiji (2014), Korea (2015).
1323. UK (2012P), Uzbekistan (2011P).
1324. Ukraine (1999).
1325. Singapore (2012P).
1326. Switzerland (2010P).
1327. Korea (2015).
1328. HK (2015P), Belgium (2009P), Singapore (2010P).
1329. Singapore (2010P).
1330. Brazil (2003), Bulgaria (2004), Australia (2008P), UK (2010P), Oman (2011P), Chile (2012), HK (2014), Qatar (2015).
1331. Netherlands (2005P).
1332. Brazil (2003).
1333. UK (2010).

6.3.6.3 Significance of LOB and MPT Approach

Since a small the proportion of DTCs entered into by the BRICS embrace either an LOB or an MPT, it can be deduced that they have not established a comprehensive approach for countering DTC abuse. This means that the DTCs do not compensate for the deficiencies identified in their residence and beneficial ownership tests. Their policies are reflective of a tax authority with limited manpower which must focus on countering mispriced cross-border transactions because doing so leads to a greater financial benefit for the economies.

While there is a trend for the adoption of a qualified person test as an LOB (except for Russia and SA) and a dividend, interest and royalty test as an MPT with an extension for general DTC abuse (and with China extending for capital gains), this could be construed as misleading because few of the BRICS DTCs contain either test, except for India where a general anti-abuse provision is widely adopted. India's adoption of that general anti-abuse provision however, is likely to be hollow in the absence of a GAAR and while section 90(2) continues to apply.

6.3.6.4 Coordination: LOB and MPT

The previous subsections confirm that the BRICS, to the extent they adopt LOBs and MPTs, have similar approaches to their LOBs and MPTs and while the *Heads of Revenue* and *Leaders' Communiques* do not specify the particularity of coordination of their response to DTC abuse, the author has identified that the recently adopted LOBs confirm a trend to using 'qualified person' test while the recently adopted MPTs confirm a trend to the 'dividend, interest and royalties' test. While this is suggestive of coordination, the absence of published information confirming that to be so prevents that conclusion being drawn.

6.3.7 Non-cooperative Countries and Indirect Transfers

6.3.7.1 Introduction

In this subsection, the research is on the techniques available for the BRICS to deny DTC benefits when the first country tax authority concludes that the second country tax authority has not exchanged information under their bilateral DTC which the first requires to determine whether DTC abuse has taken place in the first. Also considered is the BRICS response to MNEs using DTCs to prevent profits on indirect asset transfers from being liable to tax at source and whether the BRICS responses evidence coordination amongst the tax authorities.

6.3.7.2 Non-cooperative Countries

The BRICS generally apply higher withholding tax rates for foreign persons resident in 'blacklist countries'[1334] as a standard approach in common with the developed world. India widened this approach in November 2013 when declaring Cyprus[1335] to be a non-cooperative jurisdiction because of its failure to freely exchange information with India. This declaration[1336] was later the subject of *Expro Gulf*[1337] which confirmed the IRD's right to withdraw the 10% Cyprus/India DTC rate for dividends paid by Indian companies to Cyprus shareholders, leaving the application of the domestic maximum 30% and in *T. Rajkumar*,[1338] where a capital gain was taxed at 30% even though the foreign person was a Cyprus resident. The declaration was significant to the Indian Treasury for two reasons, first, because Cyprus then was the seventh largest source of inbound Indian FDI (tenth in 2012) and second, it resulted in a Protocol to the Cyprus/India DTC retro-active to November 2013 under which Cyprus agreed to accelerate exchanging. Indicative of another approach taken by India to countering what was believed to be an insufficiency of information exchange, is India's representations to the *Swiss Government*[1339] for a swift completion of a facility for enhancing information exchanging.

India's notification to Cyprus was intended to transfer specific data collection responsibility from India to Cyprus leaving India's tax authority manpower conserved and also establishing a deterrent against similar behaviour by other countries, including Switzerland.[1340] Brazil's 2009 decision to treat all counterparty transactions and behaviour as evasion when the counterparty fails to exchange information with Brazil also is a deterrent and also compensates for the little tax authority manpower in Brazil available to focus on this issue.

6.3.7.3 Indirect Asset Transfers

In this section, the author researches whether rules exist to tax in one country ('source') the profits from transactions arising in another country relating to assets (immoveable or moveable) residing in the source country, even when the assets were disposed of indirectly. The core developed world principle[1341] is that when immoveable property[1342] owned by a non-resident is alienated, the profits from that alienation are taxed in the country where the property is situated. In order to circumvent this charge, non-residents establish ownership either through resident or non-resident companies

---

1334. *See* Chapter 2 Table 2.6.
1335. Section 94A, Notification No. 86/2013, 1 Nov. 2013.
1336. Higher WHT, disallowed deductions for expenditures or payments to financial institution resident in those countries.
1337. Expro Gulf Limited v. UOI, Writ Petition No. 2871/2014, 22 Jan. 2015.
1338. T. Rajkumar & Others v. UOI, Writ Petition Nos. 17241/2015.
1339. At http://www.business-standard.com/article/economy-policy/india-swiss-agree-to-speed-up-tax-info-exchange-116061501334_1.html, 16 Jun. 2016.
1340. June 2016 meeting required experts to meet by September 2016.
1341. Article 13(1), *supra* n. 132.
1342. Article 6(1), *ibid*.

and take the profit by selling the shares. When the company sold is non-resident, the argument is that the gain cannot be taxed in the 'source' country, because it was extra-territorial. Should the foreign company be resident in a DTC country with the 'source' country, then the source country's liability is potentially removed,[1343] even if more than 50% of the value of the shares alienated (directly or indirectly) represents that immoveable property.[1344] With the operability of Article 13(1) of the Model DTC not subject to a beneficial ownership[1345] precondition under the developed world's policy, land owning conduit companies may be effective loopholes. In this subsection, it is considered whether the BRICS approach to indirect asset transfers compensates for these deficiencies. The subsection also researches for evidence of co-ordination amongst the BRICS in the development of their responses and whether the BRICS response has been shaped by tax authority manpower limitations.

6.3.7.4 Domestic Rule

Both Russia and SA tax these indirect gains but limit the gains to be taxed those arising on the disposal of immoveable property. In Russia's case, the rule became effective from January 2015[1346] for gains arising on the direct or indirect disposal of Russian situated immoveable property[1347] providing the value of that property represented not less than 50% of the value of the shares alienated. In order to simplify administration by the tax authority, the tax liability was a final 20% of the gross proceeds[1348] deducted at completion. In extending the charge to profits on the alienation of financial derivatives covering Russian immoveable property, the range of alienations has widened but because the rule is inapplicable to indirect disposals of movable property, such gains may only become taxable in the source country, were an anti-abuse provision to apply. SA also has extended the right to tax to indirect disposals[1349] but only for alienations where the asset's value 'primarily' subsists in SA immoveable property or assets representing a right or interest in that property, unless the immoveable property is trading stock. With 'primarily' established for SA purposes at 80%, circumvention is feasible.

Both India and China extend the taxing of indirect alienations to moveable property and establish procedures by which the tax authority must be given notice of

---

1343. UN, Attachment to UN Coordinator Paper: (2) Note on Capital Gains Taxation and Taxation of Indirect Asset Transfers, 15 Oct. 2015 para. 1.1.
1344. OECD Report on Developing countries (Part 1, Report to G20 Development Working Group on Impact of BEPS in low income countries, July 2014, p. 20) explains the problem as being particularly relevant for mineral licence transfers.
1345. Relevance of beneficial ownership when taxing non-residents capital gains is questionable in its absence in Article 13, Model DTC; Arnold, India Tax Treaty News, Bull. Intl. Taxn, Volume 65 (2011) No. 2, p. 650/654.
1346. Federal Law 24.11.2014, N 376-FZ.
1347. Consistent with Russia's 2010 Model DTC, Article 13(4).
1348. At http://www.consultant.ru/document/cons_doc_LAW_171241/.
1349. Foreign companies which together with connected persons, directly or indirectly own at least 20% of the rights being sold (SARS, http://www.sars.gov.za/TaxTypes/CGT/Pages/default.aspx) are liable to the tax.

an indirect ownership change. In India's case[1350] the extension became effective in 2012 but excluded from the charge all profits on the indirect alienation of both residential and agricultural land or profits arising from compulsory acquisitions. Prior to 2012, the absence of an indirect transfer provision had not prevented the IRD from seeking to tax such gains[1351] as is evident in *KSPG Netherlands*[1352] where the AAR rejected the IRD's assertion that the gain was taxable, relying on the foreign person being a separate entity neither to be disregarded nor to be 'looked through'. In *Marcel Dassault*,[1353] the AAR held the gain to be taxable on the grounds that the structure holding the assets was a 'colourable device' used to avoid Indian taxation when a reorganization which sat inside a French group was followed by an arm's length alienation of the French holding company. However, as *Jhabakh*[1354] explains this decision should be treated with care as it was very much fact specific. The IRD assessed *Vodafone*[1355] on the indirect purchase of the Hutchison Indian mobile network and on appeal, the profit was held not taxable in India because India did not apply a 'look through' when the five 'look at'[1356] tests were met. In response the *Indian Finance Act, 2012*[1357] introduced a right to retroactively tax gains from indirect asset transfers of Indian assets but limited the provision to foreign shares with values derived (directly or indirectly) 'substantially' from Indian located assets, regardless of whether the asset was immoveable or movable property.[1358] In defining 'substantially', the *Shome Expert Committee*[1359] recommended that it meant situations in which at least 50% of the value was attributable to Indian tangible and intangible assets (but with a US$1.67m floor). This recommendation was broadly supported in *Copal Research*[1360] and subsequently legislated in the *Finance Act 2015*. In order to simplify tax authority administration and increase the deterrent, Form 49D[1361] was created for providing the IRD with details of any indirect ownership changes. In order to avoid stalling inbound FDI, Form 49D was confined to sellers 'controlling' foreign companies or those holding more than 5%[1362] in the intermediary. In China's case, countering indirect asset transfers is provided for

---

1350. Section 45, ITA which is not limited to immovable property.
1351. By applying section 9(1)(i), ITA.
1352. KSPG Netherlands Holding v. Director of Income Tax International, Mumbai, 25 Feb. 2010.
1353. Marcel Dassault, AAR No. 846 & 847 of 2009, 28 Nov. 2011.
1354. Recent Case Law: Indirect Transfer of Interest and Controlling Stake in Indian Companies Held Taxable, Derivs. & Fin. Instrums, March/April 2012, p. 92.
1355. Civil Appeal No. of 2012.
1356. Participation in investment, duration of time period for which the holding structure exists, period of business operation in India, generation of taxable revenues in India and timing of exit and continuity of business on exit.
1357. Section 5(4)(g).
1358. Mehta, Vodafone, Hydra and Hercules, Second labour revisited, GITC Review Volume xi No. 2, December 2012.
1359. *Supra* n. 1283.
1360. DIT v. Copal Research Limited, Mauritius [2014] 49 Taxmann 125.
1361. CBRT, Manner of determination of fair market value and reporting requirement for Indian concern-Indirect transfer provisions-section 9(1) of the Income-tax Act, 1961-Draft Rules-reg, F No. 142/26/2015-TPL, 23 May 2016, para. 4.
1362. Expert Committee suggested excluding shareholders of less than 26%.

Chapter 6: Countering Treaty Benefits

through the GAAR (established in 2008), the associated RET[1363] together with SAT rulings and Announcements[1364] describing the implementation procedures. China's GAAR was established to counter transactions essentially devoid of 'reasonable commercial purpose' and by way of illustration, this covered those where the main purpose was reducing, exempting or deferring tax payments or involving intermediaries with insufficient 'economic substance' as *Zhang*[1365] confirmed. *Lampreave*[1366] explained this included structures such as tax preferred jurisdiction companies. One case illustrating GAAR's application to indirect asset transfers is *Guizhou*,[1367] which involved the profits on sale of a BVI being taxable in China when the BVI, as a shell, failed to exhibit sufficient substance in the BVI (place of incorporation), even though it had sufficient substance in Hong Kong. Difficulties arose in China with what 'economic substance' meant, so *Circular 698* and the later *Circular 24* were published to clarify and by way of illustration, *Heilongjiang*[1368] confirmed that *economic substance existed at the place where company officers were located who were responsible for conducting the foreign company's business operations*. The connection between GAAR and indirect asset transfers was reaffirmed in *Announcement 7* which confirmed that the GAAR procedures were to be followed by the tax authorities when investigating indirect transfers. The Announcement set out factors indicative of structures which were 'commercially acceptable' and those which were not and also published safe harbours. Some examples include group reorganizations,[1369] listed shares[1370] and direct DTC exemptions.[1371] Structures not 'commercially acceptable' included those devoid of the necessary commercial purpose and *foreign companies with 75% or more of their value deriving directly or indirectly from China taxable properties*, which meant both moveable and immoveable i.e. indirect transfers. Also treated as not being 'commercially acceptable' were structures with 90% or more of the foreign person's total assets (cash excluded) directly or indirectly, derived from China investments, or those where 90% or more of the foreign person's income, directly or indirectly, derived from China at any time in the year preceding the indirect transfer. Other illustrations of not 'commercially acceptable' transactions included foreign companies having *functions performed and risks assumed in the foreign country not proportional to the alleged substance or where the foreign person's tax liability on the indirect transfer profit was less than the amount*

1363. Section 47, *supra* n. 35(the GAAR principle) and Article 120 DIR to reduce, eliminate, or defer China tax.
1364. Guoshuihan [2009] No. 698 (Circular 698); Announcement (2011) No. 24, (Circular 24): Shui Zong Han [2013] No. 82; SAT Gong Gao [2015] No. 7, (Announcement 7).
1365. China: taxing offshore transactions, Practical law, March 2011, http://uk.practicallaw.com/5-505-6503#a666693.
1366. Anti-tax avoidance measures in China and India, an evaluation of Specific decisions, Bulletin for International Tax, Volume 67, No. 1,49/60.
1367. 2011.
1368. 2013.
1369. Purchaser and transferee having at least 80% commonality of shareholding, with 50% or more of the shares value deriving directly or indirectly from China real properties and the consideration in transferee shares.
1370. Open market purchases.
1371. Article 5, Announcement 7.

which would have been paid in China. With *Jiandu*,[1372] *VodafoneChina Mobile*,[1373] *Fuzhou*,[1374] *Tianjin*,[1375] *Xuzhou*,[1376] *Luohe City*,[1377] *Guizhou*[1378] and *Heilongjiang*[1379] as illustrations of GAAR's applicability to indirect disposals, it is clear that this indicates a focus of the China tax authorities. While publishing a list of non-acceptable indirect asset transfer structures simplified administration, it gave taxpayers an understanding of how to structure their disposals to lessen the probability of China imposing taxation.

Brazil does not tax indirect asset transfers but taxes profits on the direct alienation of shares in Brazilian companies[1380] including those owning Brazilian immoveable property.[1381] It is unlikely indirect asset transfers would be taxed in Brazil due to the 'legality principle' generally overriding 'substance over form'.

6.3.7.5 Indirect Transfers and DTCs

In this subsection, there is consideration to whether the BRICS DTCs can reverse an application of the domestic indirect asset transfer rule and if so, whether a domestic provision can reverse that DTC override.

The relevant provision in the *OECD Model Convention* is Article 13(4) which allows the 'source' country to tax gains from the alienation of shares deriving more than 50% of their value (directly or indirectly) from immoveable property situated in the 'source' State. Therefore, where parties include in a DTC an Article 13(4) modelled on the *OECD Model Convention* it is clear that should the immoveable property's value represent less than 50% of the company's assets, the DTC would override a gain to be taxed under the domestic transfer rule. It is also clear that the DTC would override the taxing of any gain arising under a domestic law on the indirect disposal of moveable assets. With each of the BRICS adopting a 50% value (except for SA which established an 80% test), it is unlikely a gain taxed under a domestic rule would be reversed for this reason, while any gains taxed in China or India on the indirect disposal of moveable property would be reversed providing the Article 13(4) included in the relevant DTC had been modelled on the developed world's provision. The provisos to these conclusions are that the intermediary company had not become a treaty resident in the source country or another DTC anti-abuse provision was not applicable. Another proviso for China is that the intermediary must be the beneficial owner.

1372. 2010.
1373. 2011.
1374. 2010.
1375. 2010.
1376. 2010.
1377. 2010.
1378. 2011.
1379. 2013.
1380. Latin Lawyer, published 19 Aug. 2014.
1381. 15% rate on shares sold on SE by registered investors, Resolution No. 2,689/00; 25% rate for tax preferred jurisdiction residents (Article 18, Law 9,249) except assets held through funds not resident in tax preferred jurisdictions, where each member holds individually/together, not more than 40% of aggregate Fund shares or receives not more than 40% of the aggregate Fund distributions.

Chapter 6: Countering Treaty Benefits

In relation to anti-abuse provisions, with China taxing indirect gains under its GAAR, the conclusion is that it would be difficult to sustain a DTC override and that should the intermediary be tax resident in one of the three countries where Protocols[1382] (with China) include a beneficial ownership test then it should also be difficult to sustain a DTC override. While *KPMG*[1383] has observed that beneficial ownership has been widely applied by China when denying DTC relief for indirect asset transfers when the substance is not reflective of the legal owner being the beneficial owner, it is arguable that KPMG misses the point because China counters indirect asset transfers by applying GAAR leaving beneficial ownership irrelevant except for the three Protocols. In any event, with the indirect gain being taxed by GAAR it is difficult to reconcile *Announcement 7s* confirmation that DTC benefits for indirect asset transfers are preserved by DTCs, especially considering *Jiandu*[1384] and *Luohe*[1385] where the China/HK DTC was ignored in favour of the China/US DTC to reveal the US Co as the ultimate owner thereby allowing China to apply the less concessionary US/China DTC.

In relation to the other BRICS, with India not having an effective GAAR to override an Article 13(4) application to profits on the indirect transfer of moveable property, India would be left to apply an anti-abuse (MPT) provision should the intermediary be resident in a country having a DTC with India containing such a provision. While SA's GAAR is thought to extend to international transactions and DTCs, a position confirmed by *Oguttu*,[1386] should it not do so then an indirect asset transfer could only be countered if the intermediary resided in a DTC containing an MPT anti-abuse provision. However, with SA's MPTs almost exclusively applying to dividends, interest and royalties only such an application is unlikely. Russia's 'unjustified tax benefit' doctrine extends to international transactions and from that, it can be deduced that that concept should override a DTC to preserve any gain taxed in Russia under its indirect asset transfer rule providing the structure or behaviour constituted evasion. Were that not the case then this would be limited with only two of Russia's DTCs containing an anti-abuse provision.

6.3.8 BRICS and Coordination

With the BRICS taking the position at the *Leaders* and *Heads of Revenue*[1387] meetings that profits should be taxed in the country where the value is created and activities performed, their (except for Brazil) adoption of the indirect asset transfer rule for immoveable property examples this policy. The extension by India and China of taxing indirect transfers to moveable property is another application of this policy. While

---

1382. HK (2015P), Belgium (2009P), Singapore (2010P).
1383. Taxation of Cross Border M&A, p. 3.
1384. 2010.
1385. 2010.
1386. *Supra* n. 164, at p. 629.
1387. *Supra* n. 997.

there is no publicly available information supporting actual coordination between the tax authorities, the author believes, rationally, that with it being an application of group policy, that co-ordination is likely.

6.3.9 Significance: Non-cooperative and Indirect Asset Transfers

The significance of the BRICS approach to non-cooperation and indirect asset transfers is that in relation to the former, India has encouraged Cyprus and Switzerland to participate more widely with India in exchanging information (and likely indirectly other countries through India taking this aggressive stance) and Brazil has encouraged a wider exchange of information. It can therefore be deduced that both India and Brazil have established procedures designed to provide additional information when pursuing mispriced international transactions and tax haven usage. In relation to indirect asset transfers, the significance is both the potential for additional revenue as well as evidencing further implementation of their policy of taxing profits in the country where the value had been created and activities performed. It can also be concluded that little in the LOB/MPT procedures compensates for the limited authority manpower but that both the non-cooperative rules and the indirect asset notifications should simplify administration.

6.4 NEXT CHAPTER

In this Chapter, the conclusion is that the BRICS have adopted additional methods for countering mispriced transactions and tax havens but that situations of abuse, not countered by their domestic rules and DTCs remain. Therefore, in the next Chapter, the research focuses on whether were the BRICS to implement the *BEPS Action Plan* recommendations that their procedures for countering that abuse would be strengthened and in doing so, reduce the significance of the limited tax authority capacity as a factor contributing to the difficulties in countering abuse. Also researched in the next Chapter is whether were the BRICS to sign the *Multilateral Instrument*[1388] that doing so would improve their ability to counter DTC abuse.

1388. Developing a Multi-lateral Instrument to Modify Bi-lateral DTCs, Action 15.

CHAPTER 7
BEPS Final 2015 Reports

> Cross-border tax evasion and avoidance undermine our public finances and our people's trust in the fairness of the tax system. Today, we endorsed plans to address these problems and committed to take steps to change our rules to tackle tax avoidance, harmful practices, and aggressive tax planning.
>
> – G20 Leaders' Declaration, Saint Petersburg Summit, 5–6 September 2013.

7.1 INTRODUCTION

The conclusion in Chapter 6 was that even though the BRICS approach to the concepts relied on to deny DTC benefits is wider than that of the developed world's, gaps remain in their international tax systems which allow foreign persons to qualify for DTC benefits when the spirit of law probably suggests that they should not. In this Chapter, the research investigates whether were the BRICS to localize the *BEPS Final Action Reports*[1389] recommendations that their procedures for countering DTC abuse would be strengthened and whether the formulation of their localization proposals (published or enacted to date) have been influenced by coordination amongst their tax authorities or by the limited tax authority manpower. This Chapter also studies whether their signing of the *Multilateral Instrument*[1390] would improve their capacity to counter DTC abuse.

The background to the production of the *Final Reports* is the G20 leaders request that the G20 and the OECD provide an international integrated methodology for countering the growth in so-called base erosion and profit shifting.[1391] This abuse has been encouraged by investment liberalization together with MNEs globalizing to take advantage of that liberalization. These reasons have been complemented by Governments' requirements for additional revenue after the 2008 global financial crisis

---

1389. At http://www.oecd.org/ctp/beps-2015-final-reports.htm.
1390. Developing a Multi-lateral Instrument to Modify Bi-lateral DTCs, Action 15.
1391. OECD/G20 BEPS Project Explanatory Statement, p. 4.

severely depleted the Treasury. The BRICS leading role in formulating the Reports[1392] is in part due to India, Brazil, China and SA being elected to participate in the eight non-OECD G20 countries in the *Bureau Plus*[1393] which oversaw the BEPS Project. Participating in the decision making process gave them the opportunity to influence.

While the BRICS have not individually formally responded to all of the recommendations, Brazil, India and China have presented responses in the *UN BEPS Questionnaire*[1394], a document which was published before the *Final Reports* and, subsequently in different fora. For instance, the *SAT Beijing Conference,* 10 October 2015[1395] (a few days after the release of the *Final Reports*) announced SAT's intention to localize some of the recommendations[1396] and confirmed its decisiveness to act. India's 2016/2017 Finance Bill[1397] which also introduced some of the recommendations confirmed India's decision to implement. SA's *Davis Tax Committee*[1398] telegraphed its likely responses to some of the draft Action Plans as did SA's *Finance Minister Gordhan's*[1399] subsequent publication on the Final Reports. The *Committee's* Second and Final BEPS report is due for submission to the Minister of Finance by the end of September 2016.[1400] This open approach has not been replicated in Brazil or in Russia where neither Government has published any wide ranging response to the recommendations. Brazil's Professor *Valadao's*[1401] publication is seen as nearest available representation of the RFB's views, because of his close working relationship with the RFB.

In relation to the SAT's priorities, the October 2015 Conference focussed on policies strengthening the administration of its anti-tax avoidance,[1402] rules requiring the LTB to increase its investigations on the level of economic substance associated with cross-border service fees and of royalties[1403], while continuing the monitoring of administrative procedures, rights and liabilities of taxpayers and self-adjustment

---

1392. India MOF Annual Report, 2014/2015, p. 216.
1393. CFA consists of twelve members, expanded to sixteen.
1394. At http://www.un.org/esa/ffd/tax/Beps/index.htm, last visited 31 May 2016.
1395. Liao Tizhong, Director General, SAT International Taxation Department, announced the draft Circular 2, *supra* n. 562, and listed fifteen unacceptable MNE practices. China at the Forefront of BEPS Implementation, International Tax Review, 4 Dec. 2015, http://www.taxcom.org.za/docs/New_Folder/1%20DTC%20BEPS%20Interim%20Report%20-%20The%20Introductory%20Report.pdf, last visited 20 Jun. 2016.
1396. Members of SATs BEPS Task Force and 50 SAT officials participated in the Task Force with over 1000 submissions.
1397. Equalization levy (*BEPS Action 1*), patent box incentive regime (*BEPS Action 5*), country-by-country (CbyC) reporting (*BEPS Action 13*) and deferral of POEM from April 2016 to April 2017.
1398. *Supra* n. 1271.
1399. 2016/2017 Budget Speech, 24 Feb. 2016.
1400. At http://www.taxcom.org.za/, last visited 31 Aug. 2016.
1401. TP in Brazil and Actions 8, 9, 10 and 13 of the OECD BEPS Initiative, Bull. Intl. Taxn, 2016 (Volume 70), No. 5 p. 304.
1402. SAT Notice on Effectively Conducting Collection of Tax Revenues, (No. 78 [2014]), 20 Jun. 2014.
1403. Notice of SAT General Office on Conducting Anti-Tax Avoidance Investigations on Outbound Payments of Large Amounts of Expenses (No. 146 [2014]), 29 Jul. 2014.

practices.[1404] Xing[1405] confirmed that China's rules countering indirect asset transfers (an abuse not specifically subject to the recommendations) had been considered by the SAT as being integral to the recommendations countering DTC abuse. SA's SARS3 *February 2016 Notice*[1406] confirmed its ongoing prioritization of investigating both the deductibility of fees payable for intragroup services[1407] rendered by non-resident associates (whether physically present in or anticipated being physically present in SA) and whether non-resident service providers had conducted business in SA through an SA PE. The *Minister of Finance*[1408] also announced that the Government's focus continues to be on countering '*MNEs evasion through TP practices*, DTC misuse and illegal money flows'[1409] (a statement which is supportive of one of this study's hypotheses that mispriced transactions constitute evasion) in SA while focussing on the inappropriate use of hybrid instruments and adopting other BEPS recommendations.[1410]

7.2 STRENGTHENING ANTI-ABUSE RULES

In the following subsections, the research considers whether were the BRICS to implement the *BEPS 2015 Final Reports* recommendation, that their procedures for countering abuse would thereby be strengthened resulting in more effective use of the limited tax authority manpower.

7.2.1 Introduction

Since each of the BRICS is at a different stage of the economic and political development cycle (different political systems, different trends in inbound and OFDI and different levels of tax authority manpower and dispute resolution procedures) there can be no single response to the question posited in 7.2. This is especially so since the research described in previous Chapters identified methodologies of some BRICS which, as concluded in this Chapter, either pre-empts some of the BEPS recommendations or renders their adoption redundant for that particular BRICS member. In researching the question, the author decided on a logical and rational approach: one which makes the research in this Chapter manageable. This he did by grouping the major recommendations of each Action Plan under 'like' groups. The recommendation groups he chose were those impacting domestic rules (hybrid mismatches, CFC rules, interest deductibility and harmful tax practices), international rules (digital economy,

---

1404. Announcement on Monitoring and Administration of Special Tax Adjustment, ([2014] No. 54), 29 Aug. 2014.
1405. *Supra* n. 1395.
1406. Public Notice, Listing Arrangements for Purposes of Sections 35(2)/36(4), Tax Administration Act, 2011 with a threshold exceeding $US667,000.
1407. Consultancy, engineering, installation, logistical, managerial, supervisory, technical or training.
1408. 2016/2017 Budget Speech, 24 Feb. 2016.
1409. *Supra* n. 1408, at p. 16.
1410. *Supra* n. 1404, at p. 16/17.

abuse of DTCs and PEs), value creation (Action 8/10) and information gathering (disclosure of aggressive tax planning, TP documentation and Country-by-Country (CbyC) Reporting). The dispute resolution (mandatory and binding dispute resolution and MAP) recommendations are considered in Chapter 8, with that Chapter's research centring on whether the methodology (outside of the normal processes) adopted by the BRICS for resolving international tax disputes reflects the importance of countering mispriced transactions.

7.2.2 Domestic Actions

In this subsection, the research is on whether the BRICS methodology for dealing with the domestic recommendations is compatible with the Action Plan recommendations and whether localizing the recommendations would strengthen their current methodology for countering the abuse.

7.2.2.1 Hybrid Mismatches

None of the BRICS[1411] have publicly confirmed a response to the hybrid recommendations. China has confirmed that it is continuing to review the hybrid rule[1412], while in SA the *Davis Tax Committee*[1413] has recommended changes in line with the BEPS hybrid recommendations and the *Finance Minister* has asserted that SA needs to counter hybrids.

In a nutshell, the hybrid recommendations[1414] deny deductions for payments made by the issuer of a hybrid instrument where the payment is not taxable to the recipient or is also deductible to the recipient in its country of tax residence. The recommendations also prevent the DTC overriding the domestic provisions denying deductions for payments on hybrids. Having regard to the recommendations, they are unlikely to be relevant for Brazil because Brazil neither recognizes hybrids as constituting anything different from the form nor does it legislate to counter them, as *Bon*[1415] confirms. The recommendations will neither be relevant for Russia nor for India because both countries follow the legal form for granting tax relief for payments in financing arrangements. This conclusion potentially could change for India should its GAAR become effective in 2017. In relation to each of China and SA, since both have had anti-hybrid rules[1416] since 2013, it can be deduced that neither country would

---

1411. Brazil, BEPS Implementation by Country, February 2016, Russia, BEPS Implementation by Country Report, February 2016, India, BEPS Implementation by Country, April 2016, China, BEPS Implementation by Country, February 2016, SA BEPS Implementation by Country, May 2016.
1412. *Supra* n. 1395.
1413. Addressing BEPS in SA, Action 2: Neutralize the Effects of Hybrid Mismatch Arrangements, Interim Report, p. 30.
1414. *Supra* n. 1413, at p. 11/12.
1415. BEPS knocking on Brazil's doors, Tax Notes Int'l, 21 Dec. 2015, p. 1039.
1416. Gong Gao [2013] No. 41, July 2013.

materially benefit from localization on deductibility, a position confirmed by *Xing*[1417] for China and the *Davis Tax Committee*[1418] for SA. However, because there are uncertainties in SA surrounding the applicability of GAAR to countering DTC abuse, it can be deduced that localizing the DTC override recommendation would strengthen SA's methodology for dealing with hybrids.

7.2.2.2 CFC Rules

The reason for none of the BRICS[1419] having published a response to the CFC recommendations, except for China's confirmation that it continues to actively review its CFC rule, is that the recommendations have been pre-empted by the BRICS members (including a new rule in Russia). In some instances, the BRICS CFC rules are wider than the recommendations.

With Brazil's CFC rules excluding a mainstream active income exemption they are already broader than the recommendations, and for this reason it is deduced that any localizing would narrow Brazil's taxing right giving rise to a conflict with a major tenet of Brazil's international tax policy. The main recommendations[1420] cover the CFC definition, exemptions and threshold requirements, income definition, computation of income, income attribution and prevention and elimination of double taxation and in the author's opinion neither Russia, China nor SA would likely localize the recommendations because doing so would not strengthen their rules because their rules on these issues are wider than the developed world's approach.

In relation to defining the controller, the recommendation proposes a not less than 50% test but with China, India and SA already adopting the 50%[1421] threshold, it is deduced that there would be no reason for them to change. With Brazil and Russia having established, 20% and 25% (respectively) thresholds, localizing the recommendation would weaken their rules. As for the exemption recommendations[1422] for CFC profits taxed at an effective tax rate 'sufficiently similar' to that applicable in the controller's country of residence, Brazil's rule would be weakened were it to localize this recommendation. With the existing rules in Russia, SA, India and China already containing an exemption for CFC's paying tax at not less than 75% of the resident rate for Russia and SA and 50% of the rate for India and China, these rates are clearly 'sufficiently similar' rate. Should India and China localize the recommendation each would need to factor in any net impact on OFDI. The recommendations define the income to be attributed[1423] as being income from holding companies, financial and

---

1417. *Supra* n. 1395.
1418. *Supra* n. 1271, at p. 30.
1419. Brazil, BEPS Implementation by Country, February 2016, Russia, BEPS Implementation by Country Report, February 2016, India, BEPS Implementation by Country, April 2016, China, BEPS Implementation by Country, February 2016, SA BEPS Implementation by Country, May 2016.
1420. Designing Effective CFC rules, 2015 Final Report, p. 9/10.
1421. *Supra* n. 1420, para. 2.1.
1422. *Ibid.*, para. 3.1.
1423. *Ibid.*, para. 4.1.

banking services, sales invoicing, IP services, digital goods and services, captive insurance and reinsurance. With each of the BRICS currently defining income to be attributed more widely than the recommendation, localization of this recommendation is unlikely to strengthen their rule. The recommendation for calculating[1424] income to be attributed is to use the controller's country's laws and with each of the BRICS, bar Brazil and Russia (providing the CFC is located in a DTC country and the books are audited) already adopting this approach, it is deduced that there is no benefit for them from localizing. With Brazil booking the CFC's year end retained profit as a single profit figure, this simplifies the rules' administration for both the taxpayer and the RFB, and for that reason it is deduced that Brazil will not localize this recommendation because doing so would result in a forfeiture of these benefits.

In relation to the proportion of attributable income to be attributed, the recommendation[1425] requires reflecting in the to be attributed amount, both the controller's proportionate ownership and the period of ownership. Since the BRICS, except for Brazil and SA, currently attribute income on this basis, they will not benefit from localizing. Since the attribution of income in Brazil and SA requires the resident to be the controller on the last day of the income year (prorated for SA where it is not), this simplifies the rules' administration for both taxpayers and the tax authority and therefore were this recommendation to be localized in Brazil and SA, it would likely result in the forfeiture of this benefit. The recommendations[1426] propose the elimination of double taxation through the granting of tax credits for direct and underlying taxes and the current laws in Brazil, Russia and SA grant these credits even though Russia, according to *CMS*,[1427] establishes as a precondition for the credit, the acceptance by the FTS of documentation justifying that the foreign taxes had been paid. With the granting of credits in India not being integral to India's proposed CFC rule and their availability in China unclear, localizing in India and China would benefit taxpayers but weaken the rules effectiveness as a deterrent.

7.2.2.3 *Interest Deductibility*

The recommendations[1428] establish a methodology which, when applied, deny deductions for excessive interest both on a single country and group wide basis and fundamental to that methodology is identifying which payments constitute interest[1429] even if the finance form is a profit participating loan, notional amount under a derivative, arrangement fees in connection with borrowings or other payment. The recommendations establish deminimis, fixed and group ratios and rules for carrying forward unused interest.

1424. *Ibid.*, para. 5.1.
1425. *Ibid.*, para. 6.1.
1426. *Ibid.*, para. 7.1.
1427. Update on Russian CFC rules: further tightening of the de-offshorisation policy or a positive development for taxpayers?, Tax Connect Flash, March 2016.
1428. Limiting Base Erosion Involving Interest Deductions and Other Financial Payments, Action 4-2015 Final Report, p. 26.
1429. *Ibid.*, at p. 29/30.

Chapter 7: BEPS Final 2015 Reports

None[1430] of the BRICS has published on whether it proposes to localize the interest deductibility recommendations but it is likely none will localize a deminimis exemption[1431] for entities with low net interest because doing so would weaken the rule as a deterrent against excessive leverage and encourage fragmentation. The recommendation that interest deductibility should relate to the nature of the borrower's business, on an EBITDA basis (e.g., interest falling within a 10%–30%[1432] EBITDA[1433] tolerance), while not currently applicable in any of the BRICS except SA, would likely strengthen the deterrent and for that reason, it is deduced that it should be localized. Currently SA is the only BRICS member adjusting deductions for net third party interest expense[1434] on an EBITDA basis and it can be deduced that were the other BRICS to localize the EBITDA recommendation that doing so would strengthen the rule as a deterrent. In relation to how unused interest under the EBITDA test is dealt with, SA currently prevents its carry forward[1435] which means that were it to localize the recommendation, the SA rule would be weakened.

7.2.2.4 Harmful Tax Practices

The recommendations[1436] to counter harmful tax practices (which is one of the four minimum standards to be localized) includes a so-called nexus substance requirement as a pre-condition for tax incentives (whether they apply to intangible or tangible property) to be allowed. Managing the nexus is expected to be facilitated by the compulsory spontaneous exchange of tax rulings[1437] where two or more jurisdictions are involved.

None[1438] of the BRICS has included a spontaneous exchange of rulings provision in its existing law except for India in its *2016 Finance Bill*.[1439] Both China and SA have announced an ongoing review of their tax incentives. The nexus[1440] recommendation requires the identification of a 'physical connection' between the place where the asset is created and the place where it is owned, as a prerequisite for the deductibility of

---

1430. Brazil, BEPS Implementation by Country, February 2016, Russia, BEPS Implementation by Country Report, February 2016, India, BEPS Implementation by Country, April 2016, China, BEPS Implementation by Country, February 2016, SA BEPS Implementation by Country, May 2016.
1431. *Supra* n. 1428, at p. 34/35.
1432. *Ibid.*, at p. 50.
1433. *Ibid.*, at p. 43/44.
1434. *Ibid.*, at p. 57.
1435. *Ibid.*, at p. 67.
1436. Countering harmful tax practices more effectively, taking into account transparency and substance, Action 5 Final Report, p. 9/10.
1437. CAN (Guidance in Applying the 1998 Report on Preferential Tax regimes, OECD 2004) OECD 2004, Mutual Administrative Assistance.
1438. Brazil, BEPS Implementation by Country, February 2016, Russia, BEPS Implementation by Country Report, February 2016, India, BEPS Implementation by Country, April 2016, China, BEPS Implementation by Country, February 2016, SA BEPS Implementation by Country, May 2016.
1439. Phasing out deductions and exemptions measures, p. 7/8.
1440. *Supra* n. 1436, at p. 24, benefit relates to both expenditure and proportion of activities relating to expenditures.

expenses paid cross border. With the Brazil *(Siqueira)*,[1441] India and SA *(Deloitte)*[1442] tax law already including such a nexus, it is unlikely that these countries will need to localize the recommendation to strengthen their laws. However, with China currently permitting 40% of the activities to be foreign *(Deloitte)*[1443] and Russia yet to establish any nexus test (because it is not an international IP hub), it seems likely that localizing recommendation in China and Russia would strengthen their tax laws.

The recommendation[1444] requiring the compulsory exchange of tax rulings applies to rulings granted for preferential regimes, unilateral APAs, downward adjustments of taxable profits, PEs, conduits and other transactions giving rise to base erosion or profit shifting. While localizing this recommendation would be compatible with the BRICS *Heads of Revenue*[1445] commitment to reducing base erosion, doing so seems unlikely to generate substantial information of benefit for third countries from Brazil and little from both Russia and China because the RFB does not issuing rulings, the FTS has only recently agreed to issue reasoned opinions[1446] and then only for MNEs subject to the FTS' tax monitoring (which *Dentons*[1447] suggests is currently applicable to just ten companies) and China does not issue rulings except for APAs. Localization would, however, strengthen the BRICS access to information which they require to counter international abuse by their resident MNEs. While the *Davis Tax Committee's*[1448] preliminary recommendation was for SA to spontaneously exchange rulings but only when SARS believed[1449] the ruling allowed foreign persons to benefit from downward adjustments in the foreign tax, and with SARS yet to issue APAs,[1450] it is unclear which information SARS would have on hand to exchange to the benefit of the foreign tax authority. The author deduces that localizing would strengthen both SA and India's tax laws because doing so would provide SARS with access to information on its resident MNEs international abuse and would build on India's 2016 decision[1451] to exchange high level conclusions from future APAs with the relevant foreign CAs. The recommendation also requires countries agreeing to continue the periodic review of their tax incentives. The reviews have been an integral feature of the OECD[1452] work programme to date on harmful tax practices and now include considering reviews on both intangible property and non-property incentives. Since most of the BRICS'

1441. *Siqueira Castro Advogados*, R&D Tax Incentives in Brazil, 15 Feb. 2016.
1442. 2015 Global Survey of R&D Incentives, p. 20/45.
1443. *Ibid.*, at p. 12/42.
1444. *Supra* n. 1436, at p. 46.
1445. *Supra* n. 997.
1446. Effective 2 Jun. 2016.
1447. Federal Law No. 130-FZ.
1448. *Supra* n. 1413, at p. 18.
1449. Potentially impractical because it calls for SARS to have knowledge of the foreign tax system.
1450. *Supra* n. 410, para. 6.2.
1451. EY Global Tax Alert News from TP, 2 Mar. 2016.
1452. OECD'S Project on Harmful Tax Practices: 2006 Update on Progress in Member Countries, https://www.oecd.org/tax/harmful/37446434.pdf; Germany/UK Joint Statement Proposals for New Rules for Preferential IP Regimes, https://www.gov.uk/government/uploads/system/uploads/attachment_data/file/373135/GERMANY_UK_STATEMENT.pdf.

incentives have been found to comply[1453] (although some have not),[1454] it seems probable that localizing this recommendation would unlikely strengthen the BRICS laws but would facilitate their participation in reviewing other countries practices which the BRICS may consider to be harmful to them.

7.2.3 International Actions

7.2.3.1 *Digital Economy*

It is well known that the number of business transactions generated using digital means in the last twenty years has grown dramatically, leaving distinguishing between the 'cyber' and 'land based' economies[1455] somewhat difficult. With this conclusion as the background,[1456] the recommendations acknowledge that concepts designed to counter BEPS in the 'land based' economy, such as PEs, TP and CFCs are equally applicable to the 'cyber' economy.[1457] The means that any recommendation localizing should be applicable to both components of the economy. Other subsections of this Chapter, consider whether the BRICS will strengthen their laws through localizing these recommendations. The recommendations also postulate alternative suggestions[1458] for dealing with the digital economy, partly because of the necessity to apply (as soon as possible) some form of control over the digital economy and partly because the format adopted for that early control may become a permanent basis for countering abuse, peculiar to digital transactions. These early control suggestions include levying indirect taxes, requiring the foreign provider to have a significant economic presence in the source country, applying WHTs to certain kinds of income and equalization levies.[1459]

In relation to the alternative suggestions, both Brazil and SA have pre-empted the recommendations and in Brazil's case (40% growth in 2013)[1460] this was done by

---

1453. Brazil's PADIS semi- conductor regime; China's reduced rate for advanced technology services; India's offshore banking, SEZs, tonnage tax shipping schemes and insurance business arrangements and SA's international shipping incentive.
1454. Potentially non-complying incentives include China's reduced rate regime (*supra* n. 1436, p. 63) for new and hi tech enterprises although SAT (SAT Beijing 10 Oct. 2015 Conference) signalled intention to contest because of the incentive's pre-conditions being more stringent than recommendation. SA's HQ exemption and SEZs are potentially but not actually harmful which allowed Davis Tax Committee, p. 17 to preliminarily recommend elevation of the substance to their minimum (required level of substance for HQ concessions, *supra* n. 1436, p. 38) to reflect place where management decisions are taken and expenses incurred on behalf of companies and coordinating group activities.
1455. Addressing Tax Challenges of the Digital Economy, Action-1, Final Report 2015, p. 11/12.
1456. Jinyan Li, Papers on Selected Topics in Protecting the Tax Base of Developing Countries, Paper No. 9, June 2014 Protecting the Tax Base in the Digital Economy, UN p. 14/18.
1457. *Supra* n. 1455, at p. 65.
1458. *Ibid.*, at p. 115.
1459. *Ibid.*
1460. IDG Connect, Ecommerce in Brazil: Ways to overcome the obstacles, 24 Jun. 2015, http://www.idgconnect.com/blog-abstract/10091/ecommerce-brazil-ways-overcome-obstacles.

slowing the delivery of offshore online purchases resulting in the online retailers dramatically reducing their offerings which led to a reduction in the potential for tax abuse. SA implemented a VAT from July 2014 to reflect its long-held concern[1461] that the digital economy was a tool facilitating evasion and avoidance. In levying VAT on persons making payments through SA bank accounts even if not SA residents (the *Davis Tax Committee's*[1462] preliminary response to the draft recommendation), the law substantially increased the catchment even if it was a preliminary response. China and India responded to the suggestions by introducing additional charges and in China's case, because offshore online purchases had reached approx. 20% of foreign trade it had become a serious problem. China's April 2016 response[1463] was to increase taxes for online imports while India introduced an equalization levy[1464] in the 2016 Finance Act, which is payable by the foreign suppliers of the digital transactions. With the additional charges in India and China not being corporation tax, the result is much difficulty in obtaining refunds under a DTC. Russia[1465] is proposing to introduce a VAT from January 2017 on digital services provided by foreign suppliers to Russian consumers.

7.2.3.2 DTC Abuse

These recommendations[1466] are designed to counter a wide range of DTC abuse (second of the four minimum standards).In this subsection, the focus is on the LOB recommendations designed to counter abuse arising from the nature of the legal entity, its ownership and general activities. The MPTs recommendations considered in this subsection are intended to counter DTC shopping and other situations which the LOBs historically have been unable to counter, such as general DTC abuse. With China[1467] publishing an intention to include LOBs in its DTCs and with SA's *Davis Tax Committee's*[1468] recommending that its GAAR be used more widely to counter DTC abuse, the BRICS have only scratched the service on dealing with DTC abuse.

1461. *Supra* n. 405.
1462. *Supra* n. 1413, at p. 40/41.
1463. At http://www.offshore-e-com.com/asp/story/Chinas_eCommerce_Tax_Changes_Come_Into_Effect____70928.html, variable tariffs, a general 17% import VAT and a consumption tax on luxury or non-essential items, including alcohol, petrol, jewellery and cars.
1464. Chapter VIII, 2016/2017 Finance Bill: Memorandum: Provisions Relating to Direct Taxes, p. 5/6, 6% on gross payments exceeding INR100,000pa to non-residents without India PE but applicable to business-to-business online advertising.
1465. Duma approved December 2015, https://www.taxamo.com/blog/russia-digital-vat/.
1466. Preventing Granting of Treaty Benefits in Inappropriate Circumstances, Action 6, 2015 Final Report, p. 8/11.
1467. Brazil, BEPS Implementation by Country, February 2016, Russia, BEPS Implementation by Country Report, February 2016, India, BEPS Implementation by Country, April 2016, China, BEPS Implementation by Country, February 2016, SA BEPS Implementation by Country, May 2016.
1468. *Supra* n. 1413.

7.2.3.2.1 LOB

In section 6.3.6.1, it was concluded that relatively few of the BRICS DTCs included LOBs, with the bulk of those LOBs being included in the Brazil, Russia, India and China DTCs being based on the qualified person test while the LOB formats used by SA in its DTCs have differed widely. It is deduced that while these four members have pre-empted the recommendations to the extent of the LOBs included in their DTCs which are based on the qualified person test, their laws would be strengthened by localizing the LOB recommendations to all their DTCs and especially for SA[1469] which is yet to develop a preferred approach to the LOB format and for India[1470] where the residence principle is deficient. It can be deduced that solely with respect to uniformity and simplicity, China would not likely benefit from localizing the LOB recommendation because its beneficial ownership test is currently effective and because it believes LOBs to be of secondary *(UN)*[1471] importance. Even allowing for this, the SAT has confirmed that the LOB format incorporated in the China/Chile DTC[1472] represents its post BEPS Model, but it seems likely that the SAT means that it is an LOB format which the SAT will accept rather than one which it requires.

7.2.3.2.2 MPT

In section 6.3.6.2, it has been concluded that relatively few of the BRICS DTCs included MPTs but in relation to the DTCs where they were included, the bulk of the Brazil, Russia, SA and China MPTs are applicable to the dividends, interest and royalty Articles alone, with China extending this applicability to the capital gains Article. India's MPTs are based on an anti-abuse test. From this it is deduced that Brazil, Russia and SA will strengthen their right to deny DTC benefits with respect to dividends, interest and royalties by localizing the recommendations. In relation to India,[1473] it is deduced that by including in its DTCs the MPT for dividends, interest and royalties, this will assist in establishing uniformity and consistency but will not likely assist in establishing a basis to deny DTC benefits once GAAR has been implemented. With China countering the abuse covered by MPTs either by applying GAAR or by its beneficial ownership test, it is deduced that localizing the MPT recommendation is

---

1469. Action Plan 6: Prevent Treaty Abuse, p. 71 *recommended* SA includes LOBs in its new DTCs and when amending older treaties, *supra* n. 1413.
1470. *Baxi*, Mauritius No Longer A 'Sweet Spot'?, Khaitan & Co, May 2016, confirmed India committed to localizing, but because of Mauritius' importance to inbound FDI, India and Mauritius inserted a 'bright line' LOB (Total expenditure on Mauritius based operations of atleast $US40,000 in immediately preceding twelve months) into bi-lateral DTC(Protocol, 10 May 2016) modelled on the India/Singapore Protocol LOB (Article 3, 2005 Protocol, total annual expenditure on Singapore based operations of atleast S$200,000 or INR50,00,000 in immediately preceding twenty-four months period).
1471. China's response to UN BEPS questionnaire, points 5/6 http://www.un.org/esa/ffd/wp-content/uploads/2014/10/ta-BEPS-CommentsChina.pdf, last visited 20 Jun. 2016.
1472. Article 26.
1473. India, points 5/6, *supra* n. 1471.

unlikely to strengthen China's right to reject DTC benefits, even though adopting the format widely in its DTCs would establish conformity and consistency with the developed world's international tax law.

7.2.3.3 PEs

The PE recommendations[1474] are intended to counter strategies designed to avoid tax accruing on income in the country where the income was created and in reality, is sourced. None[1475] of the BRICS has commented publicly on the PE recommendations but both China and India have pre-empted them through, in China's case, *Circular 75*[1476] and in India's case, legislation and judicial decisions on TP disputes. Therefore, neither China nor India need to localize the recommendations to strengthen their rights to tax the income in the country where it was created.

7.2.3.3.1 Commissionaire Agreements: Business Presence

The recommendation is to establish provisions countering profits not being liable to tax in the source country when the MNEs earn the profits under commissionaire agreements or by establishing local presences which fall short of constituting a PE.

India has for many years taxed income attributable to a 'domestic business connection'[1477] (something wider than the OECD PE)[1478] when there was a 'nexus', as explained in *Aggarwal*,[1479] between that business and India, providing that the business was ongoing, as explained in *Fried Krupp*.[1480] This position was supported by Ms. *Saksena*[1481] at the *UN Tax Committee* Meeting Geneva, October 2015, when she stated that India should be allowed to tax income arising from Indian customers, without limitation, a position generally rejected by the developed world, as explained by Mr *Louie*[1482] at that same *UN Tax Committee*. Were the Indian position as explained by Ms Saksena to be correct, then the 'domestic business connection' test would not always control the right to tax because of the limitations to that test exposed in

---

1474. Preventing Artificial Avoidance of PE Status, Action 7, 2015 Final Report p. 9.
1475. Brazil, BEPS Implementation by Country, February 2016, Russia, BEPS Implementation by Country Report, February 2016, India, BEPS Implementation by Country, April 2016, China, BEPS Implementation by Country, February 2016, SA BEPS Implementation by Country, May 2016.
1476. Guoshiufa [2010] No. 75, Circular 75.
1477. Section 9(1), ITA: Relationship between businesses carried on by non-residents yielding profits or gains where some Indian activity contributes to profits or gains and requires continuity between non-resident's business and Indian activity. Isolated transactions are not normally regarded as business connections. CBDT Circular No.: 23, 23/7/1969 extends definition to forming local subsidiaries to sell the foreign company's goods.
1478. Article 5, OECD Model.
1479. C.I.T. v. R.D. Aggarwal and Co, Civil Appeals Nos. 808/809, 1963, 6 Oct. 1964.
1480. CIT v. Fried Krupp Industries Tax Case Nos. 357/360, 1976 Reference Nos. 256/259, 1976, 2 May 1980.
1481. Joint Secretary, Tax Planning and Legislation, at CBDT.
1482. US International Treaties Division, Deputy Director.

Interroute Communications[1483] where the Court denied the existence of a 'domestic business connection' when neither the activities nor the equipment were located in India. It is therefore deduced that were India to localize the business presence recommendation, it would likely weaken its position to tax profits arising under commissionaire arrangements. With China already countering commissionaire arrangements[1484] by applying the 'establishment or places of business' test and *Circular 75*,[1485] a Circular which arose out of deeming non-residents working in China for a foreign parent to constitute a PE of the foreign parent (but not those working for the China subsidiary) under the Singapore/China DTC, localization is not required to strengthen China's rules for countering commissionaires. Neither Brazil nor SA will benefit from localization because Brazil does not recognize the PE[1486] concept nor does SA[1487] recognize commissionaire arrangements. Russia has recently adopted the PE concept *(Deloitte)*[1488] and therefore it would benefit from localization.

7.2.3.3.2 Dependent Agency PEs

The recommendations[1489] provide that where an intermediary's activity on behalf of a foreign person regularly results in the conclusion of contracts to be performed by that foreign person, a PE arises unless the intermediary performs those activities as an independent business.

SA acknowledges that dependent agents are persons who are subject to the principal's *detailed instructions* and *comprehensive control*[1490] and for that reason localization would not likely strengthen its laws. *Oriflame*[1491] has held in Russia that when a Luxembourg company uses the Russian company's staff in Russia that doing so constitutes a dependent agency in Russia, and for that reason localization would not likely strengthen its laws. Under *Circular 75,* China has already determined that the *nature of negotiations carried out* by the so-called agent are indicative of whether the relationship amounts to a dependent agency, but those negotiations do not automatically determine the position when the foreign person directs and uses in China, the China company's human and material resources. Therefore, localization would benefit China. With *Amadeus Global*[1492] confirming that in India the local company constitutes a dependent agent of the foreign company when the foreign company is totally

---

1483. Interoute Communications Ltd v. Assessee, I.T.A. No. 2284/Mum/2014, 31 Mar. 2016.
1484. *Supra* n. 1474.
1485. Guoshuifa [2010] No. 75 ('Circular 75').
1486. Brazilian Chamber of Commerce in Gt Britain, International Aspects of Brazilian Taxation, http://brazilianchamber.org.uk/committees/article/international-aspects-brazilian-taxation, last visited 20 Jun. 2016.
1487. Deloitte TP Guide, 2015, p. 199.
1488. BEPS Actions Implementation by Country.
1489. *Supra* n. 1474, at p. 10.
1490. Steenkamp, The PE Concept In DTCs Between Developed And Developing Countries: Canada/SA As A Case In Point, International Business & Economics Research Journal – May/June 2014 Volume 13, No. 3, p. 544.
1491. *Supra* n. 248.
1492. Civil Appeals Nos. 808/809, 1963, 6 Oct. 1964; Tax Case Nos. 357/360, 1976, 2 May 1980; ITA No. 2433/ 2145/Del/2000, 1022/1024/Del/2005, 30 Nov. 2007.

dependent on the subsidiary for the rendering of services and because in *Aspect Software*[1493] local subsidiary constituted a dependent agent of the foreign parent when the subsidiary acted as a communication channel between the Indian customers and the foreign parent, it seems that localization would not likely strengthen India's laws to deal with dependent agent PEs. Also, localization would be academic for Brazil pending establishment of the PE concept.

7.2.3.3.3 Excluded Activities

The developed world excludes certain activities of a foreign person from giving rise to a PE in the source country and the nature of those activities are set out in Article 5(4) of the *OECD Model Convention*. The recommendation proposes that each Article 5(4) activity be qualified by inserting in each subsection the 'preliminary and auxiliary qualification'[1494] which is not how the Model Article 5(4) is currently drafted. That recommendation has begun to be incorporated into the Russia, India and China DTCs and therefore the localization is already underway. The Russian judiciary's confirmation in *Bloomberg*,[1495] *NA40-58575/11-129-248*[1496] and *Astellas Pharma*[1497] that the conduct of preliminary activities by local presences constitutes a PE when the activities are 'core', evidences Russia's pre-empting of the recommendation as does the recently concluded *India/Thailand*[1498] and *India/Korea*[1499] DTCs, for India which is indicative of India already localizing the recommendation. In China, the *Circular 75* requirement that each sub-paragraph in Article 5(4) of its bilateral DTCs be qualified by inserting the 'preparatory and auxiliary' test *(see China/Chile DTC)*,[1500] confirms the pre-emption by China of the recommendation. In the absence of the PE concept in Brazil, localization is academic while the failure of the *Davis Tax Committee* to comment on excluded activities in SA supports the author's deduction that localization would benefit SA.

7.2.4 Value Creation Actions

The recommendations[1501] in Report 8/10 focus on the methodologies for improving the right to tax value in the jurisdiction in which the value was created and contain revised and new guidance on specific aspects of the ALP for commodity transactions, transactional profit split methods, intangibles, intragroup services and CCAs. With the BRICS (other than Russia) publishing their views on some of these concepts in Chapter 10 of

---

1493. Aspect Software Inc v. IRD, ITA Nos. 1124 & 1125/Del/2014, 18 May 2015.
1494. *Supra* n. 1474, at p. 28.
1495. Bloomberg v. Tax Inspector, Federal Arbitration Court Moscow District, No. A40-94391/10-142-134, 8 Dec. 2010.
1496. A40-58575/11-129-248 v. Federal Arbitration Court, 2 Aug. 2012.
1497. Astellas Pharma Europe BV v. Federal Tax Service A40-155695/12, 6 Feb. 2015.
1498. Signed 29 Jun. 2015, effective 1 Apr. 2016.
1499. Signed 18 May 2015, not effective at 19 Jun. 2016.
1500. Concluded 25 May 2015, yet to be enforced.
1501. Aligning TP Outcomes with Value Creation, Action Reports 8/10, 2015 Final Report.

the *UN TP Manual*[1502] in 2013, the research in this subsection is on whether the recommendations reflect the substance of those Chapter 10 views. In order that the research task is manageable, the focus in this subsection is on the recommendations for location savings and other local market features, work force and MNE strategies but does not focus on PSMs or commodity transactions, which are left for another time.

7.2.4.1 Location Savings and Other Local Market Features

Both China and India have long asserted that the comparability analysis described in the *Transfer Pricing Guidelines* does not adequately provide for the identification, quantification and allocation of location-specific advantages, so when *Tizhong Liao*[1503] and the (unnamed) *Indian* representative[1504] discussed this at length in the *UN TP Manual*, it was no surprise. Following on from this, it is unsurprising that in approx. 36% of all TP audits,[1505] the SAT and the IRD have asserted that benefits from location savings should be allocated and taxed in the source country.

Following on from the China and India *UN TP Manual* discussion and having regard to the Tribunal's decision in *Mitsubishi Corporation*[1506] where it found 'locational savings' existed on the procuration of goods for the real purchaser, it is unsurprising that the recommendation[1507] acknowledges the importance of how to allocate the cost savings and local market advantages or disadvantages. China's allocation basis set out in the *UN TP Manual* was to apply the full cost-mark up percentage to the savings[1508] while India's asserted that the savings should be allocated in a manner benefitting both parties with neither party receiving all or none of the savings.[1509] China further considered the issues in *Draft Circular 2*.[1510] With the recommendation proposing that the benefits be apportioned by reference to functions, risks and assets, it is deduced, rationally, that this represents the essence of the Indian and China representations from the *UN TP Manual* and for China, additionally, from the *draft revised Circular 2*, and therefore need not be further localized. Brazil did not discuss location savings in the *UN TP Manual*, and this was because it considers that they are accounted for in the fixed margins so localization is not warranted. With neither Russia nor SA presenting a position on location savings in the *UN TP Manual* nor publishing any substantial thought on the issue since, it seems probable that localization would strengthen their respective laws, but, on the basis of both countries markets offering fewer location savings than those in India and China, the benefits from localization in Russia and SA would be small.

1502. Chapter 10, UN Practical Manual on TP for Developing Countries, Department of Economic & Social Affairs, ST/ESA/347, p. 367/415.
1503. *Ibid.*, at p. 375.
1504. *Ibid.*, at p. 394.
1505. ThomsonReuters webinair: https://tax.thomsonreuters.com/wp-content/pdf/transfer-pricing/China-Asserts-Location-Savings.pdf with 2100 participants, last visited 15 Jun. 2016.
1506. Mitsubishi Corporation India Pvt. Ltd v. IRD, No: 5042/Del/11, 21 Oct. 2014.
1507. *Supra* n. 1501, at p. 43.
1508. *Supra* n. 1502, at p. 379.
1509. *Ibid.*, at p. 395.
1510. *Supra* n. 562.

7.2.4.2 Assembled Workforces

The recommendation stipulates that access to uniquely experienced or qualified employees will likely influence the ALP for services[1511] or enhance intangibles values,[1512] and because India[1513] and China[1514] set out in the *UN TP Manual* that access to skilled workforces constituted a location benefit, a rational explanation for the shape of the recommendation is that the Indian and China representations successfully influenced the OECD to adopt their formulation. For that reason, localization would not likely strengthen their laws. Also it is unlikely Brazil would localize the recommendation because it believes these benefits are reflected in the fixed margins while localization will strengthen the Russia and SA laws.

7.2.4.3 MNE Group Synergies

The recommendation requires benefits arising from accessing group companies or synergies (including combined purchasing power, economies of scale, combined and integrated computer systems, integrated management and elimination of duplication, increased borrowing capacity) which are not available to independent parties, should be allocated between the parties except where the benefit results purely from group membership (passive association). Where the benefit arises from concerted group actions cost allocation is required.[1515] With each of India[1516] and China[1517] asserting in the *UN TP Manual* that group synergies can constitute a location benefit, a rational explanation for the shape of the recommendation on this point is that the Indian and China representative again influenced the OECD. For these reasons, localization by India and China would be unnecessary while localizing would benefit SA and Russia. As explained earlier in this subsection, Brazil has no need to localize.

7.2.4.4 Intangibles

7.2.4.4.1 Identification

The recommendations[1518] provide that the use of one person's intangible[1519] by a related person must be compensated for on the same basis which would apply in an independent transaction in comparable circumstances with the costs incurred on

---

1511. *Supra* n. 1501, at p. 46.
1512. *Ibid.*
1513. *Supra* n. 1502, at p. 394.
1514. *Ibid.*, at p. 376.
1515. *Supra* n. 1501, at p. 47.
1516. *Supra* n. 1502, at p. 391.
1517. *Ibid.*, at p. 383.
1518. *Supra* n. 1501, at p. 67.
1519. Neither physical nor financial but capable of being owned or controlled for use in commercial activities including patents and know how secrets, trademarks, tradenames and brands, rights

research, development and advertising being accounted for in that allocation, even when expensed to the creator's profit and loss.[1520] The recommendation asserts that compensation is necessary when the work generates value.

The contributions to the *UN TP Manual* by China, India and SA on this point explained different positions on the nature of the asset arising from incurring the costs and while China[1521] explained that the costs could generate global brand names, technical know-how and business processes intangibles, India[1522] argued that brands, trademarks, know-how, design technology and local marketing attribute intangibles[1523] could arise from the expenditures. SA[1524] asserted that the costs could generate local marketing intangibles but it seems likely that the absence of further comment from SA was because the deductibility of cross-border intangible payments in SA has been controlled by the *Exchange Control*[1525] ceiling of 6%, or exceptionally 8%, of the SA licensee's turnover. A similar position arises in Brazil where deductions for payments in respect of the use of, or the transfer of patent licenses and technical, scientific, administrative or similar assistance fees are 'capped' and 'collared' at 1%-5%[1526] of net sales, subject to prior Brazilian Patent and Trademark Office approval. While similarities exist between the recommendations shape and the China and India positions, their laws would be strengthened by localizing the recommendations. There seems little benefit for Brazil and SA from localizing providing their deductions continue to be subject to local exchange controls, but this position conflicts with *Valadao's*[1527] assertion that the recommendation is irrelevant for Brazil, because imports are not subject to TP adjustments.

7.2.4.4.2 DEMPE

In working out how the benefit is to be allocated, the recommendation[1528] requires considering the duties performed, assets used and risks assumed and is also to reflect the level of participation in the development, enhancement, maintenance, protection and exploitation (DEMPE) of the intangible. China has confirmed that value should also be allocated for managing customer relationships and localizing products *(draft*

---

under contracts and government licences, licenses and similar limited rights, goodwill and going concern value, group synergies and market specific characteristics *(supra* n. 1501, p. 70/73).
1520. *Supra* n. 1501, at p. 67.
1521. *Supra* n. 1502, at p. 380.
1522. *Ibid.*, at p. 396.
1523. Establishing 'bright line' test for persons bearing no or limited risk with costs confined to routine expenditure on advertisement, marketing and sale promotion, para. 10.4.8.16, *supra* n. 1502.
1524. *Supra* n. 1502, at p. 414.
1525. *Ibid.*, para. 10.5.5.2.
1526. Finance Minister Ordinance No. 436, 1958.
1527. *Supra* n. 1401, at p. 305.
1528. *Supra* n. 1501, at p. 73.

Circular 2 and *Ms Wang)*[1529] as well as when[1530] a source country enterprise participates in the group 'value chain'.[1531] The importance to China of allocating value to the country where both assets are sited and people reside became clear in *Chengdu*[1532] when the STB required the enterprise retain profits referable to the matched expenditure and a profit margin. Both China[1533] and India[1534] in the *UN TP Manual* asserted that where licensed IP is involved, the value to be allocated for the source country person's assistance in the value creation, out of the foreign licensor's profits, should reflect the expenditures incurred when providing the skilled staff to improve the intangible. India[1535] and SA[1536] conclude that the profits referable to the work undertaken on improving marketing intangibles should be allocated, with India requiring the allocation to reflect routine expenditures on advertising, marketing and sales promotion (AMP), a position supported by *LG Electronics*,[1537] *Maruti Suzuki*,[1538] *BMW India*,[1539] *Discovery Communications*[1540] and *CanonSony*.[1541] It also asserted[1542] that value should be allocated to enterprises which provided strategic advice, monitoring, use of the assets and controlling risk with the amount to be allocated reflecting the economically significant risks borne by it. India also argued that using a low cost plus basis to calculate the value to be allocated would not likely be arm's length.[1543] SA explained that the allocation should reflect the economic ownership as having remained with the SA person, even when the legal ownership was transferred to a foreign person, but with the intangible's maintenance continuing to be undertaken by the SA person. In these circumstances, the abuse would be countered by rejecting SA deductions claimed for payments made to the new owner on the grounds that the SA person retained economic ownership.[1544] From this analysis it is clear that, rationally, the shape of the recommendations has been formulated having regard to the India and China positions, and therefore there is no need for their countries to localize. Having regard to the different approaches adopted by SA and Brazil when dealing with unrepresentative value allocation, it is unlikely localization would strengthen their laws.

1529. 10 Oct. 2015 Conference.
1530. *Supra* n. 1502, at p. 385.
1531. China equates value chain analysis with global formulary method.
1532. May 2014.
1533. *Supra* n. 1502, at p. 380.
1534. *Ibid.*, at p. 397.
1535. *Ibid.*, at p. 401.
1536. *Ibid.*, at p. 414.
1537. LG Electronics India Pvt. Ltd v. IRD, ITA No. 3823/Del/2009, 17 May 2013.
1538. Maruti Suzuki India v. IRD, ITA No. 5237/Del/2011, 2 Aug. 2013.
1539. BMW India Pvt. Ltd v. IRD, ITA No. 5354/Del/2012, 16 Aug. 2013.
1540. Discovery Communications India v. IRD, ITA No. 1297/2010 and ITA No. 1101/2011 24 Nov. 2014.
1541. Canon, Sony & Others v. ADIT, 55 Taxmann.com 240 (Delhi) 2015, 16 Mar. 2015.
1542. *Supra* n. 1502, at p. 397.
1543. *Ibid.*, at p. 399.
1544. *Ibid.*

7.2.4.4.3 Cost Contribution Agreements (CCA)

The recommendations[1545] require the 'value' of members' contributions to be in proportion to their benefits from the expenditure, having regard to similar arrangements with arm's length persons [1546] with annual adjustments balancing out unequal sharing[1547] using hindsight.

Allocating profit under CCAs was addressed by India,[1548] China[1549] and to a lesser extent SA[1550] in the *UN TP Manual*. In that Manual, India argued that Indian R&D centres were being used by MNEs in creating intangibles which were then transferred to the MNEs non-Indian group without the R&D Centre being (fully) compensated for the risks it had borne.[1551] China asserted that the activities carried out by China enterprises for the foreign MNEs in developing intangibles were often (miss) described as contract R&D services for which a small margin was attributed to the China enterprise for its work. China wrote[1552] that its initial counter for these transactions was to require an ALP based on material costs and a mark-up, a basis reinforced in the later *Draft Circular 2, Chapters 6* and *9*. However, in practice, this basis conflicted with *Shenzhen*[1553] where the authority used the PSM to allocate the net profits arising from the related party transactions. SARS' explained in the *UN TP Manual* that the intangible transactions it had identified involving SA companies seemed to show the SA companies as 'low value' contributors when they were not, but deferred finding its own solution to the problem in favour of studying the India and China[1554] proposed solutions. Russia's response for dealing with cost sharing has been to deny deductions for payments made by the Russian enterprise.[1555] It can be deduced therefore that because China and India's solutions are substantially similar to the recommendations[1556] that rationally, both countries representatives contributed to the formulation of the recommendations. As further support of China's influence in the design of those recommendations is *Deloitte's*[1557] observation that when the draft Action 8 required the allocable value to be the 'economic value' this conflicted with the *Draft Circular 2s* use of 'value' which was later adopted in the Final Report.[1558] Localization in SA would strengthen its law but would not in Brazil because of its different approach and would also not strengthen the Russia law.

1545. *Ibid.*, at p. 166.
1546. *Supra* n. 1501, para. 8.13.
1547. *Ibid.*, at p. 172.
1548. *Supra* n. 1502, at p. 399.
1549. *Ibid.*, at p. 381.
1550. *Ibid.*, at p. 413.
1551. The foreign parent's remoteness made risk control unlikely.
1552. *Supra* n. 1502.
1553. January 2016.
1554. *Supra* n. 1502, at p. 414.
1555. 2015 Global TP Guide, p. 187.
1556. *Supra* n. 1501, at p. 166.
1557. China Tax Alert: SAT issues draft guidance on TP rules and BEPS initiatives, 21 Sep. 2015.
1558. *Supra* n. 1501, para. 8.13.

7.2.4.4.4 Intra-group Services

In the *UN TP Manual*,[1559] India acknowledges that mispriced intra-group service transactions were one of the major contributors to base erosion. It identified transactions involving the provision of services to foreign MNEs by Indian companies being priced on a 'cost' basis without there being mark-up while the provision of services by the foreign MNE to the Indian company were charged with a mark-up within the 5%–10% range. India concluded that the former was not likely to constitute arm's length while the latter would be. When considering methods which could produce an ALP, it confirmed that the percentage of sales was one which would not, as the Tribunal approved in *Nalco India*.[1560] It also confirmed that charges for inbound services from related persons would not be deductible where the service was duplicative, shareholding related and of any other nature where only incidental benefits were provided to the Indian customer. China did not comment on the question in the *UN TP Manual* but did so in *draft Circular 2* and *Bulletin 16*[1561] by confirming that deductions for intra-group service fees would be denied where the service did not provide economic benefits to the customer i.e. duplicative, shareholder or those where compensation had already been paid or which were unrelated to the function and risk profile. SAT also confirmed than when benefits were provided, the deductible payment would be limited to the ALP as in *People's Daily, 2013* where deductions for royalties were denied on the grounds that one of the main purposes for granting the licence was to generate losses in China. In *Xiamen*,[1562] it was held that because costs[1563] charged to a Singapore global centre by the group were differently calculated to the basis applied by that centre to the China enterprise, that the China enterprise deduction was limited to that extent. Since these transactions are complex and considering the 'real' transactions are extra-territorial, China's *(draft Circular 2)* chose to require enterprises to populate a special file to be retained for audit. That file contained the relevant agreements, costs documentation, allocation keys and evidence confirming the actual benefits. This approach recognizes the difficulty that the transaction presents for the limited tax authority manpower to administer. While China simplifies administration through denying deductions (*draft Circular 2*) for management, control and oversight activities ('shareholder activities'), it also faces complicated compliance in countering payments for these activities where the payments were merged into payments for other

---

1559. *Supra* n. 502, at p. 402.
1560. Nalco India Ltd v. DCIT, on 3 I.T.A No.529/Kol/2008, 3 Feb. 2016.
1561. SAT Public Notice [2015] No. 16 nominates non-deductibles to include payments to related foreign persons not carrying on functions, risks or owning or operating substantial operations or activities (Article 3), service fees to related foreign persons where the enterprise does not directly or indirectly own economic benefits (Article 4), royalties to foreign related persons not compatible with the ALP when the foreign person is holding legal ownership without contributing to the IP's value creation (Article 5), royalties payable to related foreign persons as compensation for incidental benefits arising from financial or listing activities, where the holding or financing company is established offshore for the main purpose of financing or listing (Article 6).
1562. 20 Jan. 2014.
1563. Reflects reasonable costs and allocation keys based on sales, operating assets, headcount, staff salaries, facility utilization, data flow, working hours.

acceptable intra group services. SARS adopts the different approach of shifting the onus for determining deductibility to the Exchange Control, which authority according to ENSAfrica[1564] generally approves payments considered to be market-related. Russia and Brazil, however, allow deductions only when the payments are economically justified and based on documentation, and in Brazil's case, this may include stock exchange or information generated from other reputable institutions.

7.2.4.4.4.1 Benefits Test

The recommendation confirms that fundamental to determining the deductible amount is an identification of the 'benefit' obtained by the customer from the service and because each of the BRICS already broadly follows the recommendation[1565] further localization is unnecessary. However, with Brazil requiring customers to demonstrate the payment to be a 'necessary' business operating cost *(Valadao)*[1566] and because China requires enterprises confirm the 'linkage' between the service and marginal profits, their methodologies are wider than the recommendations.[1567]

7.2.4.4.4.2 Shareholder Activities and Duplication

In relation to fees payable by the source country for shareholder[1568] and duplicative[1569] services provided offshore, the recommendation is that deduction for these payments should be rejected, but China's approach is wider because it excludes from deductible stewardship expenditure[1570] any payments for management, control and oversight activities. It seems probable therefore that China will not localize the recommendation because doing so would weaken its laws. In the absence of any material published by SA, Brazil and Russia on payments for such services, it seems likely that their laws would be strengthened by localizing the recommendation.

7.2.4.4.4.3 Centralized Services

With available skills to manage widespread MNE groups not easily obtainable and in order to cost effectively facilitate the organization of the personnel, centralizing

---

1564. International Tax, Cross-border Service Arrangements, September 2015, Issue 192, https://www.saica.co.za/integritax/2015/2445._Cross-border_service_arrangements.htm, last visited 20 Jun. 2016.
1565. *Supra* n. 1501, at p. 144.
1566. *Supra* n. 1401, at p. 307.
1567. Cheng, China's New TP Guidelines and BEPS, International Tax Review, 4 Dec. 2015.
1568. *Supra* n. 1501, at p. 144.
1569. Where costs arise from activities undertaken by companies for themselves or incurred by other companies not to be re-charged, *supra* n. 1501, p. 145.
1570. Stewardship, including coordination centres as described in 1979 Report, falls outside definition of non-recoverable shareholder costs, i.e. costs of parent's juridical structure, parent's reporting requirements, raising funds for acquisitions, parent's compliance with tax laws and ancillary to MNE group governance.

services has become integral to effective global MNE management. The recommendation[1571] lists services normally found to exist in centralized platforms as including planning, coordinating budgeting, financial advice, accounting, auditing, legal and computer services. It recommends that the pricing[1572] for these services satisfies the ALS, unless they constitute 'low value', in which case a simplified 5% mark-up[1573] (WHT limited to mark-up)[1574] is recommended. If the costs were 'passed through' then the recommendation is for no mark-up.

In relation to the 'pass through no mark-up' approach, Brazil mirrors *(COSIT 23/2013)*[1575] it and India potentially mirrors,[1576] it but the other BRICS fails to express an opinion. For this reason, it can be deduced that localizing the recommendation for the BRICS, other than for Brazil, would clarify their laws. Localization would also protect the tax base for out-bound fees, except potentially for China, because in China deductions are denied for certain stewardship costs, a position which conflicts with the recommendation which allows them.

The 'simplified' approach, defines qualifying 'low value' intra-group services as being supportive non-core, not involving unique intangibles and, where there is neither control nor risk assumption.[1577] It also requires that the group does not provide the services to arm's length parties. Examples include accounting, processing receivables, human resources, monitoring health and safety, IT and legal.[1578] In relation to the BRICS, *Valadao*[1579] believes the recommendation is generally in line with Brazil's approach even though one is yet to be legislated, but the author concludes Brazil's position is actual to the contrary. Since Brazil has not limited the margin to 5%, localization would not be in Brazil's interests because doing so would potentially weaken its tax base. India has confirmed that making payments for 'low value services' which are not marked up is unacceptable and therefore localization will clarify and strengthen its law and with China denying deductions for certain low value services,[1580] its right to tax would be weakened by localization. Since deductibility in SA is determined by the Exchange Control using market rates, localizing the 5% mark-up potentially compromises SA's right to tax and for that reason it seems that localization in SA would not protect SA's tax base. In relation to non-low value services, China and India currently require an ALP mark-up on the costs which reflects the benefits obtained by the customer, with the cost base being built on allocation keys. In adopting this basis, they have pre-empted the recommendations. However, it can be deduced that neither Brazil, Russia nor SA would be likely to localize this recommendation

---

1571. *Supra* n. 1501, at p. 145.
1572. *Supra* n. 1502, at p. 143.
1573. *Ibid.*, at p. 158.
1574. *Ibid.*, at p. 160.
1575. Issued 23 Sep. 2013.
1576. *Supra* n. 1502, at p. 404.
1577. *Ibid.*, at p. 153.
1578. *Ibid.*, at p. 155.
1579. *Supra* n. 1401, at p. 308.
1580. *Supra* n. 1567.

because in Brazil and Russia the deductibility already depends on there being a 'necessary business' test while in SA the deduction depends on the Reserve Bank pre-approving payments.

7.2.5 Information Gathering Actions

7.2.5.1 Disclosure of Aggressive Tax Planning

The recommendation requires public disclosure of tax authority rulings approving aggressive tax planning strategies and with *JITSIC*,[1581] now having thirty-six members, may be the forum for the exchange, especially since each BRICS member, bar Brazil, is a *JITSIC* member. By introducing *Provisional Measure 685*,[1582] Brazil proposed supporting the exchange of the rulings but the Measure failed to be converted into law because, as *Rubinstein*[1583] argued, it was unclear which rulings should be exchanged. While *Utimi*[1584] suggested that the Measure was in line with the recommendation,[1585] it seems that it was not because the recommendation proposed countries develop their own 'hallmarks' of schemes for disclosure but the Measure did not do this. It can therefore be deduced that Brazil's proposed approach is considered to be wider than the recommendation. Having regard to Brazil's broad TP, thin capitalization and CFC rules and its adoption of fixed margins and its lateral approach to WHTs, the author deduces that there would be no significant strengthening of its laws by localizing the recommendation. In relation to Russia, *Deloitte*,[1586] asserts that it has localized the recommendation by ratifying the *MAC*, but the author deduces this to be an oversimplification because while Article 4(1) *MAC* requires the exchange of 'foreseeably relevant' materials, these rulings do not sit easily within that concept.[1587] The author also deduces that localization would strengthen the operation of Russia's de-offshorisation laws. India has not published on whether it will localize the recommendation but because India is a leader in developing the global exchanging architecture and because its laws establish severe penalties for failure to disclose information, it is deduced that its laws would be strengthened by localization. With China having published a *SAT Task Force*[1588] on the recommendation, it has explained that should it decide to exchange these rulings it would first be required to adjust the compliance

---

1581. At https://www.oecd.org/tax/forum-on-tax-administration/ftajitsicnetwork.htm, last visited June 2016.
1582. Provisional Measure No. 685 (2015) thttp://idg.receita.fazenda.gov.br/noticias/ascom/2015/novembro/nota-sobre-a-medida-provisoria-no-685-1, last visited 1 Jun. 2016.
1583. Closing Brazilian Tax Gap: Public Shaming, Transparency and Mandatory Disclosure as Means of Dealing with Tax Delinquencies, Tax Evasion and Tax Planning, Derivs. & Fin. Instrums, 2016 (Volume 18), No. 1, 7 Mar. 2016.
1584. Brazil and BEPS Action 12, 7 Aug. 2015.
1585. Mandatory Disclosure Rules, Action 12, Final Report 2015, p. 10/11.
1586. Russia: BEPS Actions Implementation, February 2016.
1587. Commentary to Convention p. 36, para. 13 recognizes necessity for new convention or Protocol to exchange material not covered by it.
1588. 2015 SAT BEPS Conference.

burden threshold[1589] in the *Law on Tax Collection and Administration*.[1590] The author deduces that making this change would provide China with information supporting its industry wide audits but due to China's legislative approach, the change is likely to be delayed for some years. SA has not published a policy on this recommendation, but it can be deduced that localization would strengthen its laws because access to this information should partially compensate for the deficiencies in its TP law arising from the insufficiency of arm's length comparables. The SA *TP Reporting* rules[1591] should be the mechanism to introduce the change.

7.2.5.2 Country-by-Country (CbyC) Reporting

The recommendation[1592] (third of the four minimum standards) requires MNEs with global turnover exceeding €750m to make available specified information to tax authorities for Accounting Periods commencing 1 January 2016. The *CbyC Report*[1593] is to disclose the MNEs (aggregate and per jurisdiction) revenue, profit (loss) before income tax, income tax paid, income tax accrued, stated capital, accumulated earnings, number of employees and tangible assets (other than cash or cash equivalents) together with for each MNE entity, the country of tax residence and where different from the place of organization, then that place. Also required is a description of the main business activity or activities of each company.[1594] In establishing an €750m floor, which according to the OECD exempts atleast 85% of the world's MNEs, *Brennan*[1595] and the *TJN's*,[1596] 'game changer' may prove to be hollow in countering evasion and avoidance in all bar the largest MNEs.

However, should the BRICS tax authorities' manpower in TP continue to be constrained, it is probable that localization at the €750m floor will produce information which may remain unused for many years. This also means that while the information exists waiting to be reviewed, it is not being used to counter evasion and avoidance but the mere fact that it is given, potentially acts as a deterrent. This concern has not stopped the BRICS from localizing the recommendation with Russia, India and SA[1597] having done so, respectively in a draft bill,[1598] *2016 Finance Bill*[1599] and

---

1589. EY, China Tax & Investment News, p. 8, 21 Jan. 2015.
1590. 5 Jan. 2015.
1591. December 2015, Draft Notice, section 29 of Tax Administration Act, 2011.
1592. Guidance on TP Documentation and Country-by-Country Reporting, BEPS Final Report, Action 13.
1593. Implementation is based on the CbC MCAA.
1594. Article 4(1), Model CbyC Legislation.
1595. BEPS CbyC Reporting: Practical Impact for Corporate Tax Departments, http://www.thetaxadviser.com/issues/2015/jun/brennan-june15.html, 1 Jun. 2015, The Tax Adviser.
1596. At http://www.taxjustice.net/topics/corporate-tax/country-by-country/, last visited 10 Jun. 2016.
1597. Each having ratified MCAA, https://www.oecd.org/tax/automatic-exchange/about-automatic-exchange/CbC-MCAA-Signatories.pdf, last visited 8 Apr. 2016.
1598. Draft Bill April 2016.
1599. Finance Bill, 2016 Provisions relating to Direct Taxes, p. 25/26.

Regulations,[1600] while China's *draft Circular 2*[1601] pre-empted the recommendation. In relation to Brazil, with *Valadao*[1602] confirming that Brazil's TP legislation already facilitates access to such information[1603] for inbound MNEs, there is no need to localize in Brazil other than for avoiding the obligation to file in each jurisdiction in which trade takes place. *Valadao* did not explain the recommendations' relevance to outbound MNEs, but this can be deduced as being nil based on the absence of an active exemption in Brazil's CFC rules, which results in global income being taxed in Brazil.

7.2.6 MAP and Mandatory and Binding Dispute Resolution

The recommendation[1604] (fourth of the four minimum standards) requires the effective and good faith implementation of MAP in order that DTC disputes can be quickly resolved and also includes the requirement to establish administrative procedures for this purpose. It also acknowledges that resolving DTC disputes will be facilitated by those countries which adopt the proposed binding and mandatory arbitration. The recommendation also confirms that a group of countries had agreed to include this provision in their DTCs.

The BRICS have not adopted a uniform approach to MAP in that while Brazil and Russia have both tentatively established MAP as policy for their DTCs and Russia, has in its Model DTC, their domestic methodology for MAP's operation and access leaves unanswered questions. *Gomes*[1605] explains the lack of public awareness of the MAP process is the reason that it is yet to be formally used by the Brazil tax authorities, which means that localizing would strengthen Brazil's laws, while *Dzhalchinov*[1606] has observed in relation to Russia, that because the MOF[1607] has published a limited explanation of MAP's taxpayer rights, which publication *Wilson*[1608] observes as being modelled on the *MAP Manual*,[1609] a fuller explanation of the MAP would arise from localization and doing so would strengthen the laws. In acknowledging that there are issues, it is to be noted that MAP has been used by the FTS in resolving disputes with

---

1600. MOF regulations, draft section 257 TAA published 11 Apr. 2016.
1601. *Supra* n. 562.
1602. *Supra* n. 1401, at p. 307.
1603. MNEs operating through Brazil resident companies disclose taxable profits by country, profits of foreign subsidiaries and foreign investments and detailed information on imports and exports.
1604. Making Dispute resolution mechanism more effective, Action 14, 2015 Final Report.
1605. Dispute resolution procedures in international tax matters – Brazil, FA Cahiers 2016 - Volume 101A, p. 156.
1606. *Ibid.* 1605, at p. 586.
1607. At http://www.minfin.ru/common/img/uploaded/library/2012/03/Provedenie_vzaimoso glasitelnoy_protsedury.pdf, last visited April 2016.
1608. *Supra* n. 66, at p. 4.
1609. At http://www.oecd.org/ctp/dispute/manualoneffectivemutualagreementprocedures-index.htm.

Belarus,[1610] German[1611] and Netherlands[1612] residents on service fee income and DTC benefits on dividends, interest, royalties and capital gains. SARS has published a basic MAP access procedure[1613] as *Roeleveld*[1614] confirms, but access continues to be difficult because of the limited tax authority manpower capacity. Even allowing for this, SARS has used MAP in disputes on double taxation, TP, PE profit attribution, dual residence and WHT and the SA taxpayers would benefit from the greater awareness which localization brings. With India and China some years ago publishing MAP guidelines,[1615] they do not now need to localize. The CBDT issued MAP instructions[1616] in 2002 with the process having been used to resolve Indian tax disputes from 2001, according to Agarwal.[1617] The current position, as disclosed in the *MOF 2014/2015 Report*,[1618] is that India is in MAP discussions with the UK, Japan, Switzerland, Netherlands, China and Australia. SAT first issued the MAP procedures in *Guo Shui Fa [2005] No. 115*, which were updated in *Gong Gao [2013] No. 56* but because the rulings do not cover thin capitalization, CFC, TP and GAAR (Special Tax Adjustments), SAT argues its sovereignty on international tax disputes remains uncompromised. Consequently, taxpayers disputing with China such adjustments cannot resolve them through MAP except where the dispute applies to residence (an important concept for availing of DTC benefits), PEs and profit attribution, CGT exemptions or lower rates and non-discrimination *(Gong Gao [2013] No. 56)*. With SAT retaining a right to reject MAP applications (except those involving serious double taxation or infringing rights) or terminating those already commenced when it believes inadequate information had been provided, it retains much control over the process and confirms that the only real way of resolving tax disputes in China is negotiating with the tax authorities.

In relation to the proposal for binding and compulsory Arbitration, none of the BRICS has agreed to the policy and it seems none is likely to do so as *Owens*[1619] confirms. *Deloitte* asserts that the reason that none of the BRICS will adopt the recommendation is that their legal systems are incompatible, especially those of India[1620] and China,[1621] but it seems the better explanation is that none is prepared to cede sovereignty to the counterparty State on a revenue raising matter,[1622] especially in relation to a policy matter which aligns with *BRICS Leaders* policy.

1610. MOF Letters No. 03-08-13/9297, 25 Feb. 2015 and No. 03-08- 05/8995, dated 3 Mar. 2014 referring to MAP conducted 29 Mar. 2011.
1611. MOF Letter No. 03-08-05/1412, 20 Jan. 2014 referring to an MoU dated 26 Sep. 2001.
1612. MOF Letter No. 03-08-13, 26 Jun. 2012 referring to an MoU signed before 2013.
1613. At http://www.sars.gov.za/Legal/International-Treaties-Agreements/DTA-Protocols/Pages/Mutual-Agreement-Procedure.aspx, last visited 15 Jun. 2016.
1614. *Supra* n. 1605, at p. 623.
1615. China and SA publish MAP statistics and only through OECD. By the end of 2014, there were fifty-five and eight respectively for 2013 and 2014. China reported twenty-three and twenty-nine new disputes in 2013 and 2014, respectively while SA reported two and four new disputes respectively for 2013 and 2014.
1616. Instruction No. 12, 1 Nov. 2002.
1617. *Supra* n. 1605, at p. 313.
1618. At p. 224/225, http://finmin.nic.in/reports/AnnualReport2014-15.pdf.
1619. Prof Owens, email 16 Sep. 2016.
1620. BEPS Action Plans by Country, India, April 2016.
1621. China, February 2016, *supra* n. 1619.
1622. India MOF 2014/2015 Annual Report, p. 214.

Chapter 7: BEPS Final 2015 Reports

7.3 MULTILATERAL INSTRUMENT ('MI') AND THE BRICS

7.3.1 Introduction

The speed with which countries implement wide ranging changes to their DTC networks is limited by the capacity of the team negotiating the treaties and the domestic approval procedures, These issues contribute to countries failing to quickly adapt their treaty networks to changing international recommendations. The slower the countries are to adapt their DTC networks the longer it takes to stop the bleed from evasion or avoidance. As a solution, the recommendation[1623] proposes countries entering into an *MI* which will automatically incorporate into their DTC network, the provisions dealing with MAP, dual residence, hybrid mismatch, abuse of third state PEs and general treaty abuse. This position is supported by *Owens*.[1624] Recognizing that some countries may have difficulties with this broadbrush solution, the recommendation proposes incorporating 'opt-outs' from certain of the provisions, perhaps modelled on the opt-outs included in the *ILCA*.[1625] With the BRICS participating in the Ad Hoc group shaping the *MI*, they are in a position of influence over its design and the opt-out terms. In this subsection therefore the research considers whether the BRICS tax laws would be strengthened by their signing the *MI* and in order to ensure researching this question is manageable, the author confines himself to considering whether the *MI* would assist the BRICS in countering DTC abuse and restricting the potential loss of sovereignty under binding MAP.

7.3.2 DTC Abuse

With China having both an effective beneficial ownership test and a GAAR, its entering into the *MI* is unlikely to strengthen its laws for countering DTC abuse. However, the remaining BRICS would benefit from adopting the *MI* because only a small number of their DTCs contain LOBs or MPTs and fewer DTCs contain general anti-abuse provisions. Adopting the *MI* should also compensate for the deficiency or absence of the GAARs in Brazil, Russia and India.

7.3.3 Binding MAP

In relation to the binding MAP, with India and China having long established procedures for its application and with Russia and SA having begun to use it, while Brazil believes it to be unnecessary, it is deduced that were the BRICS to adopt the *MI* without effective opt-outs, that their tax laws would be weakened. This conclusion is based principally on the author's assumption that a binding MAP would be seen by the BRICS as a restriction on their policy for taxing profits in the jurisdiction in which the

---

1623. Multi-lateral Instrument to Modify Bi-lateral DTCs, Action 15, p. 24/25.
1624. Dispute Resolution: The Next Frontier, Issues Paper, International Tax and Investment Center, October 2015.
1625. *Supra* n. 1622, at p. 43.

profits were created and activities performed, even though the BEPS recommendations have skewed the developed world's approach nearer to the BRICS as this study concludes in relation to TP issues, but still not totally aligned with India and China. While gaps remain, so does the concern that should counterparty CAs take positions conflicting with the BRICS then the BRICS policy on sovereignty would be frustrated should they agree to resolve a cross-border tax dispute through binding and compulsory MAP.

7.3.4 Opt Out

Were the BRICS to sign the *MI*, then shaping the opt-out in a way which respects their sovereignty policy would be a pre-condition for their adoption.

7.4 RECOMMENDATIONS: BRICS COORDINATION

In this study it has been concluded that evidence exists of the BRICS co-ordinating[1626] their policy for countering evasion, avoidance, DTC abuse and encouraging information exchange but practical evidence confirms the most active area of coordination to be in TP, which supports the *Leaders* objective of profits being taxed in the jurisdiction where created and activities performed.

Considering the BEPS recommendations, it is evident that many reflect existing BRICS policy as discussed in the previous subsections of this Chapter. Having regard to the contents of Chapter 10 of the *UN TP Manual*, responses provided by Brazil,[1627] India[1628] and China[1629] to the 2014 UN BEPS questionnaire, cooperation between Jiangsu Provincial Office (2014/2015 Plan)[1630] and the Indian Government concerning India's TP safe harbour rules, together with the literature, it is possible to conclude that the BRICS focus on TP and particularly in shaping the recommendations on location benefits, savings and other intangibles, which is unsurprising given the use by MNEs of mispriced transactions to facilitate illicit flows. *Ms Wang's*[1631] assertion that BEPS has allowed China to participate in reshaping the world's international tax law evidences China's involvement in the process, a position confirmed by *Desouza's*.[1632]

1626. December 2015 meeting focussed on BEPS cooperation (Third BRIC Country Taxation Leader Conference was Convened and China will Take a Zero-tolerance Stance on Cross-border Tax Evasion, People's Daily: 28 Dec. 2015.
1627. At http://www.un.org/esa/ffd/tax/Beps/CommentsBrazil_BEPS.pdf, last visited 21 Jun. 2016.
1628. At http://www.un.org/esa/ffd/tax/Beps/CommentsIndia_BEPS.pdf, last visited 21 Jun. 2016.
1629. At http://www.un.org/esa/ffd/tax/Beps/CommentsChina_BEPS.pdf, last visited 21 Jun. 2016.
1630. Jiangsu Province Issues Country's First Official View of BEPS, 23 TP Report 274, 6 Dec. 2014.
1631. SAT Beijing BEPS Conference 10 Oct. 2015.
1632. Administrative Measures on Tax Compliance for 2014/2015, issued 29 Apr. 2014 *see* http://www.jsgs.gov.cn/art/2014/4/29/art_55_212500.html, last visited on 18 Jun. 2016 explains BEPS Project and China's policy response. Represents first Chinese tax authorities official position on BEPS.

The *People's Daily* quote also supports China's major role in influencing the shape of the recommendations:[1633] *'The Chinese side pointed out that, BRIC countries shall, by means of responding to the BEPS project, strengthen cooperation in such fields as TP ..., adopt a zero-tolerance stance on cross-border tax evasion and "grey profit" of enterprises, and jointly combat ...transferring profit to tax havens and... concealing income to evade tax payment obligations ...through leveraging ... tax information asymmetry. "Grey profits" of enterprises ... (refers) to MNCs leaving large ...profits in tax havens ...with taxes not paid on the profits in any country'.*

The extent of individual BRICS member manpower commitment to the BEPS process is unclear and whether that commitment was limited by tax authority manpower constraints. We do know that China's manpower commitment to BEPS through a SAT BEPS Task Force was approx. 50 SAT officials who contributed more than 1,000 submissions to the process.

7.5 NEXT CHAPTER

In this Chapter, it is concluded that the BRICS positioned themselves at the centre of the BEPS process where decisions on formulating the recommendations were made. Also, it is concluded that were the BRICS to localize the recommendations then, generally, the rules of Brazil, Russia and SA would more likely be strengthened than those for India and China (they having pre-empted many of the BEPS recommendations) with the latter two countries having contributed to shaping the relevant provisions in the image of their own laws lessening the requirement to change their laws. Brazil's different approach was not likely to be conducive to localization of many of the recommendations. The formulation of the BRICS localization proposals published to 23 September 2016, while being coordinated at the political level fail to evidence any tangible coordination at the tax authority level other than for TP. While signing a *MI* would likely improve their ability to resolve international tax disputes, the BRICS reluctance to adopt compulsory and binding MAP discourages its adoption without a wide ranging opt-out.

The next Chapter researches the existence of methodologies other than MAP for resolving cross-border tax disputes and considers whether adopting those methodologies would be compatible with the BRICS reluctance to compromise their sovereignty, especially when resolving disputes concerning the location of profit derivation and activity.

1633. At http://www.chinatax.gov.cn/2013/n2925/n2953/c1962901/content.html.

CHAPTER 8
Dispute Resolution

8.1 INTRODUCTION

The previous Chapter concluded that localizing the BEPS recommendations would generally more likely strengthen the international tax law of Brazil, Russia and SA than that of India and China because the latter two countries had pre-empted many of the recommendations. The previous Chapter also deduced that based on the research, the BRICS were unlikely to localize the compulsory and binding MAP recommendation without opt-outs being included in the *MI*, because to do otherwise would potentially compromise their sovereignty over international tax law. In this Chapter, the focus is on whether the BRICS failure to embrace arbitration as a tool to be used when resolving international tax disputes can be explained by each Member's reluctance to compromise their tax sovereignty or instead by their adoption of other dispute resolution procedures instead of Arbitration.

8.2 ARBITRATION

Loeb[1634] questions whether arbitration is an efficient mechanism for the developed world to resolve disputes which MAP cannot resolve, or whether it is a broader and alternative means by which cross-border tax disputes can be resolved. The same questions can be asked of the BRICS. Whichever of these is correct, it is evident that using arbitration in resolving international tax disputes is in its infancy, as *Owens*[1635] observes, even though the first important treatise on how arbitration can be used to resolve such conflicts was written by *Mattson* and *Lindencrona*,[1636] 'Arbitration in

---

1634. International Arbitration in Tax Matters, European and International Tax Law and Policy Series, p. 5.
1635. Dispute Resolution: The Next Frontier, Issues Paper, International Tax and Investment Center, October 2015.
1636. Arbitration in Taxation, Stockholm, Norstedt, 1982.

Taxation', 1981. At that juncture, arbitration had for this purpose, little relevance to the BRICS because liberalization was recent which meant that FDI (both inbound and outbound) was minimal. However since 1981, the steady growth in knowledge from the *ICC's*[1637] 1999 confirmation of its commitment to 'encourage governments to accept compulsory and binding arbitration in international tax conflicts' (based on a 1984 position paper)[1638] during the years to the 2004 OECD[1639] Report on cross-border[1640] dispute resolution tools (MAP, arbitration and 'supplementary'[1641] mechanisms including the JWG thirty-one Proposals), has given rise to the OECD Model Tax Convention's Article 25(5)) which provides for the arbitration of disputes which MAP has been unable to resolve during a reasonable time period. In more recent years, it has been asserted[1642] that were a permanent tax experts' arbitration panel[1643] to be established to resolve cross-border tax disputes then the countries which agreed to submit disputes to the panel would benefit from the resulting increase in FDI, as *Mooji*[1644] confirms. *Baker*[1645] supports the panel proposition because it circumvents *MAP*, which he believes 'breach(es) virtually every requirement of the fair trial standards'. The author believes that the establishment of an expert panel by itself, would not be the reason for an acceleration in the resolution of such disputes, but rather the establishment of a timetable within which the disputes must be resolved. In contrast to *Baker*, the author believes that *MAP's* failure to comply with the human rights principle of a fair trial is not the cause of MAP being unfair, but rather the slow decision making resulting from the absence of a timetable and suitable procedures which the CAs must adhere to.

In relation to the BRICS and arbitration, the previous Chapter concluded that Brazil, Russia and SA's participation in MAP was in its infancy and for that reason it is premature to conclude on whether the members had developed a clear position to arbitration were MAP unsuccessful. This theory was supported by the Brazil, India and China DTCs generally not including arbitration provisions while the Russia and SA DTCs do. As for Brazil, *Gomes*[1646] explained that it does not support arbitration as the method for resolving tax disputes which MAP cannot resolve, although constitutionally

---

1637. ICC, Policy Statement Arbitration in international Tax Matters Commission on Taxation, 3 May 2000.
1638. At http://www.iccwbo.org/Advocacy-Codes-and-Rules/Document-centre/2000/Arbitration-in-international-tax-matters/.
1639. Improving the Process for Resolving International Tax Disputes, http://www.oecd.org/tax/treaties/33629447.pdf.
1640. Oortjiwn, Dispute Resolution in Cross-Border Tax Matters, European Taxation, April 2016, p. 165.
1641. Supplementary means to those in OECD Model: Commentary on Article 25 (2014).
1642. Fourth Meeting of the Platform for Tax Good Governance, Aggressive Tax Planning and Double Taxation, May 2014.
1643. Tribute is supported by PCA, Peace Palace, The Hague, since 1913.
1644. Tribute, the permanent tax arbitrational tribunal, International Tax Review, February 2015.
1645. *Supra* n. 1634, at p. 469.
1646. IFA Cahiers 2016 - Volume 101A: Dispute resolution procedures in international tax matters – Brazil, p. 156.

it is not prohibited from doing so. *Castro*[1647] explains that without an arbitration Article in Brazil's DTCs, a basis for resolving tax disputes which MAP cannot resolve does not exist. There is however a contrary view which says that Brazil does have a legal basis for arbitration and that it is to be found in Brazil's *BITs* and *CIFAs*,[1648] especially since the *CIFAs* resolve disputes through Joint Committees, the absence of which in MAP is the source of one of the main complaints against MAP.

The Indian system for resolving cross-border tax disputes is faced with an ever increasing number of MAP cases,[1649] and *Vohra*[1650] has explained that being able to access arbitration would be beneficial for both the IRD and taxpayers. However, this is disputed by *Kapoor*[1651] (CBDT Chair) who wrote that *'One must understand that if MAP works, there is no need for arbitration. Because taxation is a sovereign right and when the two CAs who represent the two sovereigns cannot resolve a dispute how would you ensure the arbitration award will be fair? I think we need to live with MAP and also the domestic legal system. The Indian jurisprudence fortunately has world recognition of being fair. So if MAP cannot resolve an international tax dispute and if Indian jurisprudence is not able to respond, then arbitration is not the answer'*. As an arbitration clause is not included in India's DTCs, *Kapoor's* explanation may be the reason, or at least establish Indian policy on the matter. Notwithstanding Kapoor's statement, the evidence is of a changing trend because the Government[1652] has agreed to abide by the BIT arbitration procedure to resolve the cross-border tax disputes in *Vodafone, Cairn* and *Nokia India.*[1653] However, in order to avoid losing control of the arbitration process (or put differently to protect India's tax sovereignty), India has prescribed that its Arbitration Act[1654] is that Act which should be applied. The Indian arbitration system historically has been very slow (with short and intermittent hearings, *Parekh*),[1655] which means the probability of a quick resolution of these disputes is low. The 2015 amendments[1656] to the Indian Arbitration Act sought to accelerate the conduct of the arbitration procedures, and should those changes

---

1647. Brazil's Anti-Treaty Shopping Measures: Current and Future Developments regarding Beneficial Ownership and LOBs Clauses in Tax Treaties, Bulletin For International Taxation, December 2011, p. 663.
1648. Cooperation and Investment Facilitation Agreements (CIFAs) focus on cooperation and investment facilitation as methodology for promoting ways of preventing and settling disputes and state/state dispute settlement as a backup but do not provide for investor/state arbitration.
1649. *Supra* n. 1634, at p. 224.
1650. Litigation Strategies, Options and Solutions, 68 Bull. Intl. Taxn. 4/5 (2014), p. 211.
1651. Chair of CBDT, http://www.newindianexpress.com/business/news/Arbitration-not-Way-to-Settle-Tax-Issues/2015/10/14/article3079197.ece, 14 Oct. 2015.
1652. Prakash, Emerging TP and International Tax Issues, 20 Intl. Transfer Pricing J. 6 (2013).
1653. Nokia India Private Ltd v. Deputy Director of Income Tax, International Taxation, New Delhi, ITA 3532/Del/2013, May 2015, suing the Government over retrospective application of existing provision.
1654. Arbitration Act governs arbitration in India, including statutory arbitration while UNCITRAL Model Law on International Commercial Arbitration 1985 forms the basis for the Arbitration Act, recent amendments to the Arbitration Act depart from UNCITRAL Model Law in order to deal with archaic provisions found in the operation of the law.
1655. Indian Arbitration Law: A roundup of the year 2015, p. 2.
1656. *Ibid.*, at p. 3.

successfully achieve that objective then they would predicate arbitration as the means in India for resolving international tax disputes.

China's policy of settling tax disputes by negotiation means that a right to resort to arbitration need not be included in the China DTCs, which both *Eichelberger*[1657] and *Vanistendael*[1658] confirm. This conclusion though is subject to the negotiation process producing a result which is fair to be sides. However, with 'finance' now having become one of *CIETAC's*[1659] sectors of expertise and because *CIETAC* since 2012 has been authorized by China's BITs[1660] to use arbitration when resolving investor/state disputes, this should mean that taxpayers can apply to CIETAC to resolve a tax dispute. With arbitration not to be found in the 2010 Russian Model and because the practice and public discussions in Russia concerning resolving international tax disputes rarely focus on arbitration and with *Dzhalchinov*[1661] observing that only three Russian DTCs[1662] contain a right to arbitration, it is clear that an effective Russian tax arbitration system is embryonic[1663] as *Wilson*[1664] confirms. Since only three SA DTCs[1665] contain an arbitration clause for use in resolving tax disputes which MAP cannot resolve, it is also clear that the use of arbitration in SA is embryonic, a position supported by *Roeleveld*[1666] on capacity limitation grounds.

8.3 INVESTMENT TREATIES

Since the BRICS, other than India (and potentially China) have not developed systems for resolving cross-border tax disputes through arbitration which MAP cannot resolve, the question is whether such disputes can be resolved by the dispute settling procedures in a relevant BIT (*UNCTAD* database)[1667] or in a relevant other Investment Treaty. The UNCTAD *Investment Dispute Settlement Navigator*[1668] details the disputes settled by arbitration in a BIT and by another relevant investment agreement but it is generally accepted that those treaties were not entered into principally to resolve cross-border corporate tax disputes because that function was reserved primarily for the bilateral DTCs. However, with *UNCTAD*[1669] confirming that investment agreements are designed to avoid conflicts of competence arising from one government agency applying a BIT in a different way from that applied by another for a DTC and

---

1657. Tax Litigation, 18 Asia-Pac. Tax Bull. 2 (2012), p. 150.
1658. Taxation, Tax Avoidance and the Rule of Law, 16 Asia-Pac. Tax Bull. 3 (2010), p. 212.
1659. At http://www.cietac.org/index.php?m = Page&a = index&id = 34&l = en.
1660. Including the Cross-Strait Investment Protection and Promotion Agreement, Article 7, Expropriation of investment and returns.
1661. IFA Cahiers 2016 - Volume 101A: Dispute resolution procedures in international tax matters – Russia, p. 583.
1662. Netherlands (1996), Belgium (2015P, NIF), Switzerland (2011P).
1663. *Supra* n. 1640, at p. 584.
1664. *Supra* n. 66.
1665. Canada (1995), Netherlands (2005), Switzerland (2007).
1666. SA, *supra* n. 1661, p. 623.
1667. At http://investmentpolicyhub.unctad.org/IIA.
1668. At http://investmentpolicyhub.unctad.org/ISDS/FilterByCountry.
1669. BITS 1995/2006: Trends in investment rulemaking, http://unctad.org/en/docs/iteiia20065_en.pdf, p. 82/83.

because the BIT dispute resolution procedure can be used to resolve disputes limiting States rights to pursue their own 'fiscal' policies, it is clear that BITs can resolve cross-border tax disputes.

The author has reviewed typical BITs[1670] and from that review has been able to conclude that tax may be considered in one of the three options. One option is that the BIT does not apply to tax disputes of any matters (laws or regulations, regardless of the degree of inconsistency) and if that position were correct then a BIT cannot resolve tax disputes. Another option is for the BIT to exclude all tax matters except for specified situations[1671] included in a specific investment agreement entered into between the investor and the State.[1672] The third option is for the BIT to apply to decisions of a tax authority [1673] (other than those matters on offer to nationals alone or to third parties under a MFN clause in the BIT) giving rise directly/indirectly to expropriation ('confiscatory tax measure') of the taxpayer's assets. *Park*[1674] has observed that the BITs should resolve tax disputes when 'the investment dispute *(goes to)* the very legitimacy of the tax' or, as *Gregoire*[1675] wrote, the State's confiscation amounted to expropriation.

The author has tested the BRICS BITs and investment agreements by reference to the tax options set out in the previous paragraph. In relation to Brazil, the absence of its BITs being enforced seems, prima facie, to prevent their use in resolving tax disputes but relying on the Hague District Court's decision in *Yukos*,[1676] it is possible to conclude that the BITs signed by Brazil which are yet to become effective can protect inbound FDI investors in the same way that any Brazil Provisional Measure can be effective for Brazil tax purposes. The author has also identified that for the many effective Russian BITs which contain expropriation provisions of a kind relied on by the Tribunal in Yukos, as *Renta 4*[1677] confirms, they establish a legal basis for claims against Russia when Russia imposes taxes in a manner contrary to the BIT. This, according to the author, constitutes a dispute settling regime. A small group of Russia's BITs contain exclusions for specific tax matters, such as countering double taxation or other fiscal matters (except for the Russia/Canada BIT),[1678] but with the expropriation clause in those BITs being found in *Veteran Petroleum*[1679] (a Yukos shareholder) to technically applicable (later reversed by The Hague Court's finding that investor protection in signed but unenforced BITs is only available for BITs compatible with the Russian

---

1670. Argentina/New Zealand BIT (1999) is an example.
1671. Canadian Model BIT (2004) embodies the first approach.
1672. BIT would not, in principle, apply to taxation measures unless the State's CAs disagreed the measure taken amounted to expropriation or violated the investment contract.
1673. Protocol of Germany/Mexico BIT (1998) typifies this approach.
1674. Arbitrability and Tax, Chapter 10, http://studylib.net/doc/8931722/chapter-10-arbitrability-and-tax, p. 183.
1675. Taxation and expropriation under BITs: setting the standard, Butterworths Journal of International Banking and Financial Law, November 2015.
1676. At http://globalarbitrationnews.com/the-hague-district-court-sets-aside-yukos-awards-2016 0426/.
1677. Renta 4 SVSA v. Russian Federation, award on jurisdiction in Stockholm under auspices of Arbitration Institute of Stockholm Chamber of Commerce, 20 Mar. 2009.
1678. 27 Jun. 1991.
1679. Russian Federation vs Veteran Petroleum Limited, C/09/477160 / HA ZA 15-1, 20 Apr. 2016.

Constitution or other laws), it seems likely that the BITs can resolve tax based expropriations because Yukos involved a tax dispute. The tested Indian BITs contain the expropriation and MFN Articles but not specific taxation provisions even though India's *Model BIT*[1680] (Article 11) reserves on taxing rights to the host State. Until recent years, few foreign persons resorted to BITs to resolve Indian tax disputes because it was not seen that BITs could be a viable option to resolve the dispute, but as *Prakash*[1681] observes the BIT notifications by *Vodafone*[1682] (Netherlands/India BIT does not exclude taxation measures *in toto* but limits the exclusion to national treatment, MFN and expropriation) and by *Cairn*[1683] (under the UK/India BIT), both of which are currently in consultations may prove that the disputed retroactive application of tax laws can be resolved by a BIT. *Nokia*[1684] has notified India under the Finland/India BIT that the retroactive application of WHT on cross-border software payments is contrary to a BIT. Since each of the MNEs indirectly owned Indian assets, the taxpayers are relying on *Walde and Kolo's*[1685] explanation that expropriations can be indirect, to support their claim under the BIT. China's BITs contain the expropriation and MFN provisions but not general provisions protecting foreign investors from China taxation but this did not prevent *Tza Yap Shum*[1686] (a China resident) being compensated under a BIT for indirect expropriation in Peru. It was held that the expropriation resulted from unfair taxation,[1687] arbitrarily imposed on a presumed basis. From this, it can be deduced that the China BITs can be used to resolve cross-border tax disputes. This case is additionally noteworthy because, as *Smith*[1688] observes, it is illustrative of China's new liberalized[1689] BIT (1998) policy which requires protection for China OFDI under the 'Going Out' Policy, a policy which focusses on developing countries,[1690] where the risk of economic loss is higher. The new approach was designed to improve China OFDI providers' rights when seeking to settle disputes with a foreign Government by arbitration, especially increase the compensation where expropriation or nationalization was involved, as *Berger*[1691] observes. China now applies the *ICSID* international

---

1680. Model Text for the Indian BIT, https://www.mygov.in/sites/default/files/master_image/Model%20Text%20for%20the%20Indian%20Bilateral%20Investment%20Treaty.pdf.
1681. India and BITs—A Changing Landscape, http://icsidreview.oxfordjournals.org/content/29/2/419.abstract.
1682. Review of claims in investment Arbitration – Vodafone and India, Student Initiative to Promote Legal Awareness, National Law School of India, University, Bangalore, p. 16.
1683. Cairn Energy PLC v. India http://investmentpolicyhub.unctad.org/ISDS/Details/691.
1684. Nokia India Private Ltd v. Deputy Director of Income Tax, International taxation, New Delhi, ITA 3532/Del/2013, May 2015.
1685. Coverage of Taxation under Modern Investment Treaties, Oxford Handbook of International Investment Law, p. 305/307.
1686. Tza Yap Shum v. Republic of Peru (ICSID Case No. Arb/07/6) award, 7 Jul. 2011.
1687. Imposed by Peru on Peruvian company indirectly 90% owned by China investor.
1688. Smith, Chinese BITs: Restrictions on International Arbitration, (2010) 76 Arbitration 58/69, p. 58.
1689. Berger, China's new BIT programme: Substance, rational and implications for international investment law making, German Development Institute, https://www.die-gdi.de/uploads/media/Berger_ChineseBITs.pdf, p. 7, China/Barbados BIT, July 1998, was the first BIT to offer foreign investors unrestricted access to international arbitration.
1690. Three out of twenty-two BITs with liberal investor-state dispute settlement provisions signed with developed countries.
1691. *Supra* n. 1689, at p. 11.

arbitration model as *Shan*[1692] observes, for all/any (investor-state) disputes, when previously that basis applied on an 'ad hoc' basis and only for expropriation claims. The significant growth in China inbound and OFDI since 1998 has surprisingly not resulted in the growth in BIT cases (two where China is host and four where it is claimant) being used to settle investment disputes. The reason for this is China's preference for disputes to be resolved through bilateral negotiation a process which allows it to control sovereignty. In relation to SA, *Peterson*[1693] observed that the BIT programme which began in the immediate post-Apartheid era (approx. 1994) and included expropriation and MFN provisions, changed from approx. 2010[1694] partly because SA realized that it had become a capital exporting country (into southern and near Africa)[1695]. Also relevant was SA's expectation of increased expropriation claims due to the BEE programme (which the Government[1696] could have argued supported human rights) which reflected previous compensation payments,[1697] as *Sclemmer*[1698] observes. SA's new approach resulted in its BIT programme stalling both because just one of the twenty BITs signed since 2000 (Nigeria) has been enforced and because nine BITs[1699] enforced before 2000 were terminated. *Hunter*[1700] observes that the termination timings closely followed the 2012 adoption of the ANC's proposal for increased natural resources taxation.

Owens[1701] has observed that the rise of the BRICS together with the consequences from the strengthening of international tax law by BEPS will contribute to a tsunami in cross-border tax disputes requiring resolution: the question is whether the BITs can resolve those disputes?

It can be concluded that except for China and India, foreign investors are not applying to resolve cross-border tax disputes under BITs, which according to *Lennard*[1702] has been due to the BRICS' reluctance (except for China)[1703] to apply the *ICSID*

1692. China's Investment Treaty Policy-Recent Changes and Future Direction, Xi'an Jiaotong University, China.
1693. SA's BIT Implications for Development and Human Rights, Dialogue on Globalization, 26 Nov. 2006, p. 6.
1694. Columbia FDI Perspectives on topical FDI issues by the Vale Columbia Centre on Sustainable International Investment No. 109 25 Nov. 2013 Editor-in-Chief: Karl P. Sauvant, Managing Editor: Shawn Lim; Lessons from SA's BITs review by Xavier Carim, p. 2.
1695. SA, BIT Policy Review, Framework, Review Government Position Paper, June 2009, p. 7.
1696. *Ibid.*, at p. 30.
1697. *Ibid.*, at p. 8.
1698. Overview of SA's BITs and Investment Policy, http://icsidreview.oxfordjournals.org/content/early/2015/11/22/icsidreview.siv040.
1699. Austria, BLEU, Denmark, France, Germany, Netherlands, Spain, Switzerland and UK.
1700. At http://www.rh-arbitration.com/south-africa-terminates-bilateral-investment-treaties-with-germany-netherlands-and-switzerland/.
1701. Arbitration in International Tax Matters, featured perspective, Reprinted from Tax Notes Int'l, 30 Mar. 2015, p. 1189.
1702. *Supra* n. 1634, at p. 440.
1703. Relied on ICSID since February 1993, Russia since in 1992 but yet to ratify. Neither Brazil, India nor SA have signed, https://icsid.worldbank.org/apps/ICSIDWEB/about/Pages/Database-of-Member-States.aspx?tab = AtoE&rdo = BOTH.

Convention's[1704] arbitration provision. It seems that in relation to India a different cause is the reason, and that is because India now uses the Indian Arbitration Act in BIT disputes. *Lennard* supports his conclusion by reference to Brazil and India having signed but not acceded to the ICSID Convention with neither Russia nor SA having signed the ICSID but in reality neither Brazil nor India has signed, while Russia has signed but not yet enforced. It seems evident that the reason that they are reluctant to work with the ICSID is their general distaste in working with an arbitration system which forces the adoption of a decision because that arrangement is contrary to their policy of not ceding sovereignty when resolving international tax disputes. Following on from this therefore is that their failure to adopt arbitration is not due to any limited capacity in the tax authority, but because of the expectation that BITs arbitration will result in an increase in compensation awards against them due to the BRICS widened approach for both TP and denial of DTC benefits being seen as unacceptable internationally, and as an expropriation when the quantum of disputed tax potentially results in the sterilisation of the business.

8.4 WTO

If ICSID based arbitration is unacceptable to the BRICS other than for China for settling cross-border tax disputes then is the WTO's DSU[1705] acceptable? Working out whether it is acceptable depends on whether the WTO Agreements influence corporation tax provisions and whether the DSU process can resolve disputes over those provisions. The first part of that question was considered in Chapter 2 of this book and the second part is now considered.

The *TPRM* process provides WTO members with the opportunity of reviewing and questioning other members' tax incentives and through this, all WTO members can discuss and review whether their own tax incentives comply as well as whether the incentives of other WTO members comply. This process encourages self-compliance in the interests of minimizing the potential for disputes to arise.

While the WTO package contains procedures for formally resolving[1706] disputes between sovereign states, those procedures are on the surface not relevant for resolving Investor/State disputes, including cross-border tax disputes. However, because *'the Members[1707] recognize the DSU serves to preserve the rights and obligations of Members under the covered agreements'*, and because the DSU rules[1708] and procedures *'apply to consultations and settlement of disputes between Members <u>concerning their rights and obligations under the WTO Agreements</u> taken in isolation or in combination'*

1704. Confirmed from review of ICSID listing of cases on 21 Jul. 2016, https://icsid.worldbank.org/apps/ICSIDWEB/cases/Pages/AdvancedSearch.aspx?cs = CD28&cte = CD18&cntly = ST30;S T113;ST157&rntly = ST30;ST157.
1705. At https://www.wto.org/english/tratop_e/dispu_e/dsu_e.htm.
1706. Article (1) Annex 2, WTO Agreement, https://www.wto.org/english/thewto_e/whatis_e/tif_e/disp1_e.htm.
1707. Article 3(2), DSU, https://www.wto.org/english/tratop_e/dispu_e/dsu_e.htm.
1708. Article 1(1), *ibid.*

and with tax disputes impacting on the money available for a country's budget *(a right)*, it is arguable that investors' cross-border tax disputes can be resolved through the DSU.

Facilitating its use as a dispute resolution method is the absence of many of the *ICSID* arbitration provisions which the BRICS believe fail to preserve members' sovereign rights, as *Bello*[1709] observes. Examples include injunctive relief, incarceration, damages for harm or police enforcement, but legal consequences do exist, including compensation or retaliation when the party fails to promptly comply[1710] with a Panel decision. The contrary position can be taken, as *Jackson*[1711] asserts.

With the DSU providing the parties with a relatively brief period to resolve disputes by negotiation (managed by DSB)[1712] or where by negotiation, a Panel[1713] fails to resolve the dispute within fifteen months for a disputed settlement or twelve months for one which is not, the process can be quick. However, according to *Seda*,[1714] the process may be prolonged for developing countries should the *DSU* begin to be used for resolving tax disputes if their lack of tax authority capacity for creating and implementing strategies for concessions before the Panel causes delays or frustrates the process.

Determining whether the BRICS would respond positively to a proposal for using the DSU in resolving cross-border tax disputes when arbitration had failed is difficult to judge, but the author deduces that Brazil, India and China would respond positively. In relation to China, this likely positive outcome follows from *Wenhua's*[1715] explanation of its successful participation in *Steel Safeguards*[1716] and its participation in M*exico against China*[1717] and in *Argentine and Panama.*[1718] According to *Wenhua*, *Steel Safeguards* left China confident[1719] that the DSU would be fair, objective and effective, while in *Mexico against China* (consultations on China's direct taxation law),[1720] China chose to remove that law when it was identified as breaching both SCM and GATT and

---

1709. WTO DSU: less is More, American Journal of International Law, Volume 90, No. 3, July 1996, p. 416/418.
1710. Grace is provided for implementation where immediate compliance is impractical.
1711. WTO DSU--Misunderstandings on the Nature of Legal Obligation, The American Journal of International Law, Volume 91, No. 1 (January 1997), p. 62.
1712. At https://www.wto.org/english/tratop_e/dispu_e/disp_settlement_cbt_e/c3s1p1_e.htm.
1713. Panels normally consist of three people possessing relevant background and experience from Members independent of the dispute. Panellists usually chosen in consultation with countries in dispute and only selected by the WTO Director-General when parties fail to agree.
1714. Published by Sida 2004 Department Infrastructure and Economic Cooperation Authors: Busch and Reinhardt, printed by Edita Sverige AB, 2004, p. 6/7.
1715. China's Experience in Dealing with WTO Dispute Settlement: A Chinese Perspective, Journal of World Trade 45, No. 1 (2011), p. 5.
1716. US – Definitive Safeguard Measures on Imports of Certain Steel Products ('US – Steel Safeguards') Case 252, initiated 2002.
1717. WT/DS451/1, G/L/1004, G/SCM/D94/1G/AG/GEN/103, 18 Oct. 2012.
1718. Argentina – Measures Relating to Trade in Goods and Services, WT/DS453/AB/R. 14 Apr. 2016.
1719. China fully participated into the DSU by making written submissions, preparing legal arguments, appearing before the Panel and Appellate Body and received a quick positive outcome.
1720. Exemptions, reductions, offsets, refunds for enterprise groups including FIEs and HNTEs and enterprises located in designated geographic areas and SEZs and those generating income from producing certain agricultural goods including cotton.

did so within the required seven years. In *Argentine and Panama* where China became a third party, the DSU considered Panama's allegation that various Argentine tax measures[1721] were applied exclusively to 'blacklist' countries and the Appeal Body decided that Argentina's blacklist was not inconsistent with GATS. The outcome should be the same for Brazil and India since they were third parties in *Argentine and Panama*. Therefore, were the WTO DSU provisions to be incorporated into the BITs, Brazil, India and China would likely increasingly use the BITs in the resolution of BRICS cross-border tax disputes. There is insufficient evidence to draw a conclusion on how Russia and SA would react.

8.5 HUMAN RIGHTS

With the BRICS at the date of this study not adopting binding and mandatory arbitration, this results in the BITs not being able to constitute a suitable basis for resolving Investor/State cross-border tax disputes. While the author concludes the DSU can be used for resolving Investor/State disputes, this is not a universally held opinion. Therefore, this leaves to be researched whether provisions within the Human Rights Conventions[1722] can fill the vacuum, or alternatively whether those Conventions can influence the formulation of BRICS corporation tax laws.

While the *OECD* is at the centre of developing the world's international tax governance, the *UN* has led the development of human rights laws *(International Covenant)* and with the UN's membership being considerably greater than that of the OECD, the question is whether the *International Covenant* has shaped international corporation tax laws, or as *Baker*[1723] questions, whether it can support a defence to a cross-border tax dispute. In order to keep the study of these questions manageable, the research is confined to the *International Covenant*. In relation to whether it can support a defence, *Baker* answers his own question in the negative when concluding that the right to a fair trial[1724] is not to be found in the arbitration procedures available for resolving cross-border tax disputes. Other human rights, including the right to protect private property and the right to fair treatment in the event of criminal charges, are also not reflected in arbitration.

In relation to whether the *International Covenant* has or can shape international corporation tax laws, the UN *Special Rapporteur's 2014 Report*[1725] confirms that it can.

1721. Capital gains taxes, WHT, TP and EOI.
1722. 2005 World Summit Outcome, U.N. GAOR, 60th Session, p. 138/139, U.N. Doc. A/60/L.1, at http://www.who.int/hiv/universalaccess2010/worldsummit.pdf.
1723. *Supra* n. 1634, at p. 467.
1724. European Convention on Human Rights, Article 6, Right to Fair Trial together with 1952 Protocol Article 1, Protection of Private Property; Article 14(1) International Covenant on Civil and Political Rights; Article 8(1), American Convention on Human Rights; Article 16/17/47 European Charter on Rights and Freedoms.
1725. Promoting and protecting of human rights, civil, political, economic, social and cultural rights, including right to development: Report of Special Rapporteur on Extreme Poverty and Human Rights, Magdalena Sepúlveda Carmona, A/HRC/26/28; IOB Study, Evaluation of Issues in Financing for Development, Analysing effect of Dutch corporate tax policy on Developing Countries, November 2013 policy on developing countries.

She responds that in order to fund the improvements in human rights, members need to widen their corporate tax base and improve efficiency by countering tax abuse including evasion, fraud and other illegal practices such as losses arising from other illicit financial flows and bribery, corruption and money laundering. With her confirmation that the States which take coordinated action against evasion are best placed to protect human rights while those which allow tax abuse[1726] and other illicit financial flows through secrecy and other policies are not, she confirms the influence.[1727] Tax authority influence is also important here with her arguing that without the tax authorities being appropriately resourced[1728] members face difficulties in pursuing human rights compatible corporation tax initiatives. Taking her recommendations forward has so far seen them being incorporated in the *Lima Declaration*,[1729] which acknowledged that 'tax revenue is the most important, most reliable and most sustainable instrument to resource human rights' and, in the *UN Human Rights Council's* [1730] confirmation of a linkage between international tax abuse and human rights, consisting of the duties to respect, protect, be accountable and an effective remedy. The BRICS founding *Leaders' Summit Statement*[1731] also committed each member to improving human rights, and each BRICS member has sought to establish a basis for doing so through adhering to human rights agreements[1732] or participating on international human rights committees.

From this, it can be deduced that the BRICS agree that by strengthening their international tax law, they establish a basis for improving their citizens' human rights.

In relation to whether the *International Covenant*[1733] is an influencing factor in resolving BRICS international tax disputes, it is relevant that each member (other than for China) has ratified the Covenant and therefore each member (other than China)[1734] has by definition, agreed to the principles of fair trial and protection of property. In relation to resolving Brazil and SA cross-border tax disputes, with there being no cases

---

1726. Tax abuse by corporations and HNWIs forces Governments into raising revenue from other sources, often regressive taxes falling hardest on poor.
1727. A/HRC/25/52, para. 42.
1728. VIA, p. 14, para. 57.
1729. Experienced advocates, practitioners, activists, scholars, jurists, litigators committed to advancing tax justice through human rights and realizing human rights through just tax policy. http://www.taxjustice.net/2015/06/24/the-lima-declaration-on-tax-justice-and-human-rights/, 24 Jun. 2015.
1730. Advisory Committee, 9 Aug. 2016.
1731. Article 10, Joint Statement of BRIC Countries Leaders, 16 Jun. 2009, Yekaterinburg, Russia.
1732. Working Group on the UPR, Brazil, A/HRC/WG.6/1/BRA/1 7, March 2008; Chapter 2 and Article 15(1) Russian Constitution; Summarized in the UPR National Report at A/HRC/WG.6/13/IND/1, March 2012; *see* Indian Human Rights Commission at http://nhrc.nic.in/; A/HRC/WG.6/17/CHN/1, August 2013 and Compilation of the China position in A/HRC/WG.6/17/CHN/2, August 2013; SA Constitution through the Bill of Rights (Chapter 2).
1733. Brazil (http://tbinternet.ohchr.org/_layouts/TreatyBodyExternal/Treaty.aspx?CountryID=24&Lang=EN); Russia (http://tbinternet.ohchr.org/_layouts/TreatyBodyExternal/Treaty.aspx?CountryID=24&Lang=EN); India (http://tbinternet.ohchr.org/_layouts/TreatyBodyExternal/Treaty.aspx?CountryID=24&Lang=EN); China (http://tbinternet.ohchr.org/_layouts/TreatyBodyExternal/Treaty.aspx?CountryID=24&Lang=EN) and SA (http://tbinternet.ohchr.org/_layouts/TreatyBodyExternal/Treaty.aspx?CountryID=24&Lang=EN).
1734. Conforms with China's approach for negotiated rather than imposed settlements.

for those countries incorporating human rights principles into the defence that the author is aware of, and because very few human rights related international tax cases have been heard, the author is unable to draw a conclusion for Brazil and SA. The position in India is different though because of the substantial number of published cross-border tax cases (substantially focussing on TP) and with none, to the author's knowledge relying on human rights grounds, he deduces that those grounds are not relevant factors for resolving in India such disputes. The position in Russia is different because in many cases taxpayers have incorporated human rights grounds in defences such as in *Labushev*,[1735] where the Court struck out a defence against evasion on the grounds of the applicant failing to have responded in time to an opportunity to rebut the tax authority's assertion and by so doing, confirmed that Russia had complied with the *International Covenant's* procedures. In *Timinskiy*,[1736] the Court held the *International Covenant* not to have been breached because when charging the taxpayer with evasion, the explanation provided was clear and straightforward. A breach of the *International Covenant* by Russia was incorporated into a defence into a series of cases associated with *Yukos*,[1737] where in *Khodorkovskiy and Lebedev*[1738] the Court held the human rights of both persons had been violated when as shareholders of the Yukos group, which had been charged with Russian tax evasion,[1739] they were imprisoned. In *Reznik*[1740] another case associated with Yukos, the individual relied on a human rights defence in support of not having made a defamatory statement pertaining to the *Lebedev* case, and the Court concurred, based on the *International Covenant*. Another example is that of *East West Alliance*[1741] (a Ukrainian case) which successfully incorporated human rights grounds into a defence against a charge of carrying out an evasion scheme involving an allegedly fraudulently changed document to avoid declaring income at completion. *Magnitsky*[1742] also evidences an individual's human rights not being protected by the *International Covenant* in resolving tax disputes.

8.6 HUMAN RIGHTS DEFENCE

This book has described circumstances in which by law or through tax authority action, taxpayers can be held to have participated in evasion or avoidance and resulting

---

1735. Labushev v. Russia, No. 4144/06, ECTHR (First Section), Decision of 11 Dec. 2007.
1736. Timinskiy v. Russia, No. 74947/01, ECTHR (Fifth Section), Decision of 11 Sep. 2007.
1737. ECHR and Grand Chamber held Yukos' right to a fair trial in tax matters was violated and Russia's enforcement proceedings and penalties were disproportionate.
1738. Khodorkovskiy and Lebedev v. Russia (applications nos. 11082/06 and 13772/05), 25 Jul. 2013, Final 25/10/2013.
1739. TP between Russian producing oil company and SEZ associates where substance was held not to exist in associates.
1740. Reznik v. Russia, ECHR 102 (2013) 4 Apr. 2013, Case 4497/05.
1741. East West Alliance Limited v. Ukraine, No. 19336/04, ECTHR (Fifth Section), Judgment (Merits and Just Satisfaction, Strasbourg, 23 Jan. FINAL, 2 Jun. 2014. Court awarded €5m compensation as the market value for aircraft confiscated by the tax police.
1742. February 2012, Russian police announced intention to resubmit charges of evasion against Magnitsky for second trial. 11 Jul. 2013, Moscow Court posthumously found Magnitsky guilty of evasion.

Chapter 8: Dispute Resolution

in a freely negotiated agreement with a tax authority being cancelled without a right of appeal. The book has also identified instances of retroactive law, especially in India.

The Indian *2015 Black Money Act* provides the Indian tax authority with a right to determine whether a taxpayer's explanation for holding foreign income and assets, or its failure to disclose the assets or income, is acceptable. The IRD is also given the right to cancel an APA without appeal, except by the taxpayer appealing to a Constitutional Court in the event of a failure to file on time an *Annual Compliance Report* or the *Report* contains material breaches. Article 14 of the *International Covenant* establishes that *'all persons shall be equal before the courts and tribunals. In the determination ...of his rights and obligations in a suit at law, everyone shall be entitled to a fair and public hearing by a competent, independent and impartial tribunal established by law'*. Guidance on Article 14 in the *1994 US Report on Human Rights*[1743] establishes it as a defence for an individual faced with serious 'hardship' in civil cases involving governmental action which *Goldberg*[1744] confirms. From this it can be deduced that the rights given to the Tax Authority under the *Black Money Act* should be overridden by the *International Covenant* but not when there is a right of appeal to a Constitutional Court, unless requiring such an appeal is disproportional *(Louloudakis)*.[1745] In relation to retroactively taxing *Vodafone* and *Cairn* for capital gains tax in India, the question is whether doing so breaches the right to a fair trial. The Indian Constitution[1746] prevents retroactive imposition or increasing penalties under criminal laws but allows them under civil laws *(Shiv Dutt)*[1747] such as a taxing legislation. Accordingly, because back-taxing is a civil penalty, it is unlikely a human rights defence would protect these companies. SAT can cancel an APA based on the enterprise's operating results being materially different to the anticipated prices or the profits established in the APA. Since China has not signed the *International Covenant*, a human rights defence would not likely be sustained. It therefore can be deduced that both India and China have protected their right to tax profits where created or where the activity is performed and would not likely be successfully challenged under human rights law.

8.7 CONCLUSION

In this Chapter, the conclusion drawn is that the supplementary methods for resolving international tax disputes, including arbitration, are neither widely applied in the BRICS nor have the BRICS established legal systems widely supporting their application. Also concluded is that he BRICS failure to embrace arbitration for resolving international tax disputes can be explained by their reluctance to compromise their right to sovereignty over international tax dispute resolution. This chapter also concludes that international tax disputes have been resolved under BITs and the DSU

1743. Civil and Political Rights in the US, Report of the USA to the UN Rights Committee under the International Covenant on and Political Rights, 111 1994, p. 118/119.
1744. Goldberg v. Kelly, 397 U.S. 254 (1970).
1745. Louloudakis v. Greece (2002) ECR I-5447I.
1746. Article 20(1).
1747. Shiv Dutt Rai Fateh Chand v. Union of India, AIR 1984 SC 1194.

and that the BITs could form the basis of an acceptable format for resolving disputes providing procedures such as from the DSU, which are protective of the BRICS requirement of sovereignty over international tax, were included in the BITs. Also concluded is that little evidence exists of human rights considerations being incorporated into the defence of an international tax dispute except for Russia and India but not in China which is yet to sign the *International Covenant*. It is also clear that there is no evidence of cooperation between the BRICS on using the BITs, DSU or human rights as defences to tax disputes even though, at the *Leaders Meetings*, they agreed to participate in, and cooperate on WTO and human rights issues. Limited manpower capacity in the BRICS tax authorities is not relevant for this reason.

In the next Chapter, the link between inbound FDI and countering DTC abuse and supplementary methodology for resolving cross-border tax disputes is investigated.

CHAPTER 9
BRICS and FDI: DTC Anti-abuse and Dispute Resolution

9.1 INTRODUCTION

This Chapter investigates the link, if any, between the level of BRICS inbound FDI and their methodology for countering DTC abuse and supplementary methodology for resolving cross-border tax disputes, or put differently, whether the BRICS approach to dealing with these issues, if more closely aligned with the developed world's approach, would clear the way for an increase in inbound FDI.

In answering these questions, it is helpful to consider the commercial background. Until 2014,[1748] the BRICS received considerably more inbound FDI than they invested outbound (except for Russia where geopolitical considerations led to higher outflow[1749] in earlier years) with substantial amounts of the Brazil, Russia, India and China inbound FDI being received through intermediate companies' resident in tax preferred jurisdictions,[1750] most of which had entered into bilateral DTCs with the BRICS. The sheer volume of inbound FDI, the use by investors of tax preferred resident intermediaries to funnel that FDI, the implementation by MNEs of structures and transaction forms designed to exit profits with limited BRICS source taxation (principally using mispriced related party trade transactions, intangibles and financings),[1751] the relatively few in number tax authority manpower available to investigate and counter that tax abuse have all contributed to the intensification of BRICS efforts to counter DTC abuse. One consequence from this has been an increasing number of disputes on cross-border transactions, structures or behaviour which have failed to quickly resolve through traditional procedures in part because the assigned manpower

---

1748. See Chapter 1 Table 1.1.
1749. UNCTAD, World Investment Report 2016, Investor Nationality: Policy Challenges, p. 15, http://unctad.org/en/PublicationsLibrary/wir2016_Overview_en.pdf.
1750. See Chapter 1 Table 1.2.
1751. Supra n. 29, 31, 33.

to resolve the disputes was few in number as well as because their apparent reluctance to fully embrace the developed world's supplementary dispute resolution mechanisms (i.e., MAP and arbitration in DTCs and BITs). The outcome of this disputation can include double taxation.

Whether the BRICS approach to dealing with these problems has contributed to a stalling of FDI, or merely a reduction in the proportional increase is difficult to determine, especially in the absence of empirical studies, but it can be concluded that FDI into Russia[1752] and into SA[1753] has been effected by geopolitical and governance issues for the former and investor protection uncertainty for the latter, but that with inbound FDI into the other members increasing it is difficult to sustain the argument that their approach to countering DTC abuse and dispute resolution is linked to inbound FDI. The author comes to this conclusion for Brazil,[1754] despite a 'heavy and complicated tax system', because its FDI drivers are its large population (approx. 200 million), proximity to raw materials, protection from international crises through diversification and facilitating access to Latin American countries. There is evidence that the reduction in Russia inbound FDI can be traced back to the geopolitical tensions between it, the Ukraine and the West together with the economic crisis. Even though Russia has in recent times sought to reverse the trend through implementing economic reforms, the administrative problems, corruption, uncertainties about the rule of law and the establishment by Russia of a right to seize Russian sited foreign owned assets (in response to the *Yukos* related European confiscations), this plan has failed. SA's free-market economy has encouraged FDI but the failure of its inbound FDI to substantially increase can be traced to stalled investor protection[1755] rules. The economic opportunities speak for themselves in India and China[1756] but based on the ever-increasing inbound FDI, the author does not believe the rapid increase in cross-border taxation disputation has had a material impact[1757] on inbound FDI into either country.

For these reasons, it is difficult to sustain the argument that were the BRICS to align themselves with the developed world's approach to countering DTC abuse and improving resolution of cross-border disputes that it would clear the way for increased inbound FDI. However, should investors take the view that were the BRICS to improve

---

1752. At https://en.portal.santandertrade.com/establish-overseas/russia/foreign-investment, last visited February 2017.
1753. At https://en.portal.santandertrade.com/establish-overseas/south-africa/foreign-investment, last visited February 2017.
1754. At https://en.portal.santandertrade.com/establish-overseas/brazil/foreign-investment, last visited February 2017.
1755. Gosling, What comfort does SA's Protection of Investment Act provide to foreign investors?, Norton Rose Fullbright, April 2016, http://www.insideafricalaw.com/blog/what-comfort-does-south-africa-s-protection-of-investment-act-provide-to-foreign-investors, last visited January 2017.
1756. State Council, New policy on foreign investment (Guo Fa [2017] No. 5) attracting more foreign investors includes opening more sectors or industries to foreigners, improving FDI environment and relaxing government interventions.
1757. At https://en.portal.santandertrade.com/establish-overseas/india/foreign-investment; https://en.portal.santandertrade.com/establish-overseas/china/foreign-investment, last visited January 2017.

Chapter 9: BRICS and FDI: DTC Anti-abuse and Dispute Resolution

investment protection rights, specifically in relation to preventing material tax changes amounting to expropriation[1758] and were they to improve the rule of law and good governance that FDI would increase, then that would establish a linkage, but, this theory is likely only to be relevant for Russia and SA. Therefore, the more persuasive argument to put to each BRICS member is that were they to more closely align their international tax law to that of the investor country group (assumed to be OECD members) that this would contribute to a 'level playing field' for inbound FDI purposes.

9.2 DTC ANTI-ABUSE

In this section, the investigation is on whether the BRICS approach to countering DTC abuse has been established in a manner designed to confirm a level playing field with the investor group, and for that purpose, this subsection considers the position against the constituents of DTC abuse in the BRICS and in the developed world for transactions, structures and behavior. In this Chapter, the author assumes that DTC abuse is that which arises from transactions, structures or behaviour established or entered into, where the obtaining of a favourable DTC[1759] treatment was a principal purpose of the establishment or the transaction, structure or the behaviour.

In relation to structures, DTC abuse exists when the FDI provider establishes an intermediary in a third country (where little pre-existing business or commercial nexus exists) solely or mainly in order that the source country's DTC benefits can be obtained. The BRICS conclude on this by testing the nature of the economic substance and business purpose attaching the intermediary to its jurisdiction. The BRICS also contend that when the intermediary economically carries on business in the source country through an arrangement not giving rise to a tax presence (PE) in that country (except for Brazil where PEs are not recognized) because the legal arrangements are fragmented into discrete arrangements, that this constitutes abuse. In relation to transactions (such as providing finance, intangibles or services through an intermediary), they too can be abusive when the intermediary is unable to substantiate for DTC purposes its beneficial ownership[1760] in the interest, licence fees or service fees which pass through the structure onto the ultimate beneficiary.

9.2.1 Application

The issue for FDI providers, whether residing in a developed or developing country, is how the BRICS apply their rules to counter the abuse from MNEs using structures or transactions to channel inbound FDI. Much uncertainty arises from the absence of

---

1758. EnCana Corporation v. Ecuador, LCIA Case No. UN3481, Award, 3 Feb. 2006, section 177; Starrett Housing Corporation, Starrett Systems, Inc., Starrett Housing International, Inc., v. Government of Islamic Republic of Iran, Bank Omran, Bank Mellat (Case No. 24).
1759. Paragraph 9.5, Article 1 OECD and para. 24, Article 1 UN.
1760. Brazil and Russia, beneficial ownership (broadly) resides with the person receiving the payment providing it is the registered owner, in China and SA it (broadly) resides in the person possessing economic control and substance. In India, beneficial ownership (broadly) depends upon the issuance of a COR by the foreign tax authority (Chapter 6, section 6.3.2).

uniformity between the BRICS or between the BRICS and the developed or developing worlds (except for SA) on how they apply their DTCs. Judicial examples of the uncertainty include *Volvo*[1761] (Brazil) where the Brazil Court decided that the DTC could only apply where double taxation arose, and it did not in this case because the interest was tax exempt in Panama or in *Swedwood Tikhvin*[1762] and *Severny Kuzbass*[1763] (Russia) where the ND Article in the Russia DTC was in the first case held to override Russia's thin capitalization rules while it did not in the second case. In *Yangzhou*[1764] and *Xinjian*[1765] (China) the uncertainty centred on what substance was required to meet the very high beneficial ownership threshold. Much uncertainty exists in India because of the potential application of India's retroactive legislation (*Vodafone*[1766] and *Copal Research*).[1767] While there is no empirical evidence linking the quantum of FDI into the BRICS and uncertainty surrounding the DTC applicability, rationally, any uncertainty about the availability of those benefits should cause a prudent investor to think twice about making the investment or more likely to change the investment terms by say, channelling the investment through a jurisdiction where the DTC network was clearer or where the BIT provides more protection from expropriation. This makes these issues more relevant for FDI providers considering investing in Russia or in SA where governance and the rule of law have more connection with investment decisions than they do in the other BRICS while they are relevant for FDI providers considering investing in India where the connection between tax and investment protection has become more apparent.

This absence of a uniform approach stands as the norm and is contrary to both the *Leaders*[1768] and the *Revenue Ministers*[1769] communiques requiring coordination between the BRICS' tax authorities, but this study does not set out to criticize the lack of coordination, but, were those authorities to provide clear explanations and administrative guidelines in both a transparent and reasonable format, that doing so would facilitate investment decisions, especially for providers considering investing in Russia, SA and India where investment protection is of a higher relevance. This criticism is not fair for China which has issued Circulars and established procedures dealing with its anti-DTC abuse rules, but the criticism is relevant for arbitrary decisions, such as in *Heilongjian 2013*[1770] where because the tax authority had been unable to deny DTC benefits as the investor was publicly listed, it chose to arrive at essentially the same economic outcome by concluding the non-resident to be China tax resident.

Discussed, in the following subsections, is the relationship between countering abuse and investment decisions and to facilitate this analysis, the author has

---

1761. *Supra* n. 1201.
1762. *Supra* n. 507.
1763. *Supra* n. 510.
1764. *Supra* n. 1212.
1765. *Supra* n. 1213.
1766. *Supra* n. 333.
1767. *Supra* n. 1360.
1768. 8th BRICS Summit: Goa Declaration, Goa, India, 16 Oct. 2016, para. 53.
1769. Communiqué of BRICS Heads of Revenue Meeting, Delhi, 18 Jan. 2013.
1770. *Supra* n. 1119.

aggregated into one group the rules which counter international abuse domestically (domestic rules) and into a second group the rules incorporated in DTCs (international rules).

9.2.2 Domestic Rules

9.2.2.1 *Transfer Pricing*

We know that in the developed world TP adjustments are a creature of domestic law and that those adjustments can be overridden when not consistent with any relevant DTC (Article 9). We also know that working out whether the adjustment is consistent is conducted by applying the interpretation to be found in the law of the country which is to make the adjustment (Article 3(2)). Therefore, because DTCs make up part of the rules which regulate TP adjustments this links them to inbound FDI which means that where TP adjustments amount to expropriation, by deduction the DTCs are linked to expropriation.

The BRICS and the developed world have yet to formalize a level playing field across all aspects of the ALS but with their *Leaders* and *Heads of Revenue* focussing on ensuring that profits are taxed in the country where the activities take place giving rise to the profits and with this objective particularly relevant in India and China in relation to intellectual property and value chains, much scope exists for disputation. However, it is generally difficult to conceive of intellectual property and value chain disputes amounting to expropriation but not so difficult when investors rights had been materially disadvantaged, such as when an APA is cancelled because TP notifications were not lodged on time or worse still, when treated as evasion, because related party transactions were not included in the Annual Notification to the IRD (India). For either of these actions to amount to expropriation, they must constitute an 'abusive undertaking'[1771] which reduces the investment's value.

Looking then more generally at the core features of the BRICS' TP rules designed to counter mispriced related party transactions, it is clear that because the core approach to counter them in the BRICS (except for Brazil) is very similar to that of the developed world, the core concepts should not amount to expropriation. However, the widening of the range of relationships,[1772] intensification of the taxpayer notification obligations[1773] and the broadening of the rights to sanction senior company executives[1774] of the offending companies, gives rise to major differences between the BRICS and the developed world's approach to the counter. While each of these differences has the potential to generate double taxation, only the breaching of the notification provisions amounts to an 'abusive undertaking'.

1771. Link-Trading Joint Stock Company v. Moldova, UNCITRAL, Final Award dated 18 Apr. 2002, section 64.
1772. Chapter 4, section 4.3.2.
1773. Chapter 4, section 4.3.8.
1774. Chapter 3, section 3.3.4.

9.2.2.1.1   APA Programme

The developed world has recommended that states adopt procedures which minimize arm's length pricing disputes before they occur, and one of the procedures is the APA programme for agreements on arm's length prices to be entered into between taxpayers and tax authorities on a unilateral, bilateral or multilateral basis. Since the BRICS have only partially embraced this concept, the likelihood for disputation from conflicting ALPs remains high in the BRICS relationship with the developed world, but pricing disputes are unlikely to constitute abusive undertakings. The failure by Brazil and SA to implement APA programmes results in the providers of FDI to both countries having to rely on their DTCs with the respective countries to avoid double taxation arising from pricing disputes. This is an unsatisfactory outcome for providers of FDI to Brazil where the TP provisions in its DTCs do not include compensatory adjustments[1775] and without a dispute resolution process, such as MAP, it is difficult to see how double taxation can be avoided. This means it would constitute an abusive undertaking. Further, it is unlikely the provider of FDI to Brazil could be compensated under a BIT for the loss, with few, if any of Brazil's BITs providing a right to receive such compensation having become effective but with tax considerations not seemingly a relevant factor when FDI decisions are taken, it has little practical relevance. Since the potential for double taxation in Russia is high because Russia's APA programme is limited to large Russian resident companies[1776] and is unilateral only and because its DTCs do not provide for compensatory adjustments, this leads to the conclusion that the resulting double taxation is an abusive undertaking which potential foreign FDI providers factor in when making investment decisions. The potential for double taxation in India from TP disputes is also high with India having entered into just 111 unilateral and bilateral APAs over the programme's so far for four years (November 2016)[1777] and because the counter party is tax resident in one of the countries (approx. one-third) with which India has a DTC and which does not contain the Article 9(2) provision. This leads to the conclusion that the resulting double taxation is an abusive undertaking which potential FDI providers consider.

The absence of an APA programme in SA is countered by it including an Article 9(2) in all but a few of its DTCs, leading to the conclusion that double taxation arising from pricing differences should not likely be relevant for potential providers of FDI to SA. China has adopted an APA programme (it is bilateral)[1778] but because it applies only to companies with turnovers exceeding RMB40m (approx. GBP 4.6m),[1779] its applicability is limited. This limitation though is not considered to be important to the decision making by potential providers of inbound FDI because they factor into their consideration China's abundant commercial opportunities.

1775. Chapter 4, section 4.4.13.
1776. *Supra* n. 701.
1777. CBDT, Press Release, Signing of APAs, 18 Nov. 2016.
1778. 2005/2014, 43 bilaterals (170 pending) and 70 unilateral (12 pending), China APA Annual Report (2014).
1779. *Supra* n. 702.

Since the double taxation arising from the failure to resolve pricing disputes in advance amounts to an abusive undertaking in Brazil, Russia and India (for some counterpart countries) of a kind likely to affect potential inbound FDI, the rational approach for the potential FDI providers to those countries would be to channel the transactions through intermediaries' resident in countries having an Article 9(2) in the DTC with the respective BRICS member. Adopting this restructure, potentially facilitates FDI into India but is unlikely to do so for Brazil or Russia because neither of the latter's DTCs contain Article 9(2). Providers of FDI into SA and China do not evidently focus on the same concern.

Were Brazil, Russia and India to establish widely applicable bilateral and multilateral APA programmes then that would likely reduce the potential for abusive undertakings reducing impediments to inbound FDI. It seems probable that the BRICS introducing such broad APA programmes is currently unlikely while they continue to believe that limiting their tax sovereignty through APAs is counterproductive but this conclusion does not seem rational because an APA is a negotiated agreement in the same way as are the bilateral DTCs. It is also irrational by reference to the BRICS' trend of writing savings provisions (including GAAR) into their domestic tax law and into their DTCs.

In the author's view, the BRICS have concentrated their energies on establishing 'safe harbours' instead of the APA programme, because doing so shifts the onus to the taxpayers and compensates for the BRICS limited tax authority manpower. The safe harbours are a relatively recent phenomenon and therefore cannot be the reason that Brazil, Russia and part of India's DTCs[1780] do not contain Article 9(2). One reason for the absence is the increased importance that foreign investors comply with those countries' TP rules if they wish to avoid uncompensated double taxation. This reason is less important in China because approx. 80%[1781] of its DTCs contain an Article 9(2) and in SA[1782] where substantially all of its DTCs contain the provision. A different explanation for the absence of Article 9(2) in most of Russia's DTCs is that the DTCs were irrelevant to FDI because many of the FDI providers reside in jurisdictions not having DTCs with Russia and many were 'round tripping' Russians. This explanation is supported by Russia's de-offshorisation rules which have focussed on tax preferred jurisdictions and round tripping.

While the absence of compensatory adjustments in Brazil, Russia and part India might be viewed as being less conducive for inbound FDI, it is only Russia where FDI is sensitive to the country's level of governance and confiscatory behaviour, as evidenced in the *Yukos* expropriation.

1780. *Supra* n. 773.
1781. *Supra* n. 776.
1782. *Supra* n. 777.

9.2.2.1.2 Safe Harbours

If safe harbours[1783] are included in TP legislation it is because Governments have decided to reduce disputation, but when they are not included in the bilateral DTCs and do not apply to all fact patterns rather than those which simply are complex or involve substantial sums, they diverge from the OECD's recommendations. In the BRICS widely adopting safe harbours, the question is whether they have done so primarily to encourage inbound FDI or to compensate for the shortage of manpower to negotiate APAs or investigate taxpayer's TP. It is not likely that safe harbours avoid abusive undertakings nor do they give rise to good governance or promote the rule of law and for that reason they do not encourage FDI (unless industry targeted as in India) and must therefore be seen as an approach designed to shift the onus to taxpayers and replace widespread APA programmes.

The BRICS approach to safe harbours increases the potential for double taxation because in shaping their safe harbours none follows the OECD's recommendations. One reason for the safe harbours not being included in the DTCs is that it obviates the need to defend its terms with the DTC counterparty negotiating teams and another is that it avoids fettering the BRICS sovereignty over its TP tax policy.

The difference from the developed world's approach is not a negative for inbound FDI since much of that FDI emanates from tax preferred jurisdictions. It is relevant though that the BRICS diverge by preventing their safe harbours (except for SA) from applying to transactions with tax preferred jurisdiction counterparties, or with other persons who have shifted profits to tax preferred jurisdictions residents through mispriced transactions. With much of the BRICS inbound FDI being channelled through tax preferred counterparties the failure of the safe harbours to apply to such counterparties should theoretically represent a disincentive for their FDI but the recent years FDI trends do not disclose any real shift from the countries which have provided FDI in the past. These safe harbour constraints seem inevitably to drive counterparties to use intermediaries' resident in DTC jurisdictions giving rise to DTC abuse when that intermediary is a conduit or fails to beneficially own the structure or the transaction. In relation to India, whether a taxpayer adopts its 2013 safe harbours (even when channelling through a DTC intermediary) depends upon the outcome of complex cost benefit studies since many of the safe harbours, which are industry specific, are positioned outside of the ALP. Some taxpayers may agree to pay higher taxes at the benefit of saving the costs of a dispute.

Were the BRICS to incorporate their 'safe harbours' into their bilateral DTCs, Protocols or MOUs, this would counter the absence of an Article 9(2) for both Brazil and Russia but not likely improve them as places for FDI because safe harbours are not a governance, rule of law or expropriation issue arising from an abusive undertaking. Therefore in India's safe harbours being positioned outside the ALP this could mean that the safe harbours are an abusive undertaking because of the additional (tax) expense incurred in adopting them.

1783. Chapter 4, section 4.3.7.

9.2.2.1.3 Country-by-Country Reporting

Both the developed and developing worlds have decided that receiving information as early as possible contributes to countering mispriced related party transactions. While many forms of notification exist, such as APAs and annexures to annual tax returns, what has been recommended[1784] is a breakdown of MNE's profits and activities giving rise to those profits, between the corporate entities. In relation to the BRICS, with each having committed to CbyC reporting[1785] (India and China having already implemented the CbyC rules) it is clear they believe this will assist in deterring mispriced transactions and for those entered into, providing information to counter them. Unfortunately, in the absence of fine tuning of the CbyC rules, this will not be the case in the medium term[1786] for all bar the largest of the BRICS outbound MNEs because the €750m threshold[1787] eliminates most of them in the medium term. Therefore, this leaves old fashioned in-depth analysis of MNEs financial affairs by the tax authorities[1788] as the only realistic alternative.

With SARS[1789] already recognizing this €750m threshold as being too high to produce meaningful information it has required additional disclosure be included in the *ITR14*[1790] for all SA companies owning gross assets in excess of R10m[1791] or gross income exceeding R20m ('medium to large businesses') on intra-group interest, royalties and service fees, which is to be prepared by jurisdiction. The failure to share this information with the foreign parent of the inbound FDI (because it is not included in the CbyC Report) provider may lead to double taxation because of an adjustment made in SA for which there is no compensatory adjustment in the counterpart. This wider disclosure of mispriced transactions is likely to encourage SA companies to shift to structural transactions to avoid SA taxation when in the other BRICS members', it is definitional conflicts (such as what constituents a 'group' for accounting purposes under CbyC and 'control' for TP purposes) which will be the reason for structural transactions to be entered into to shift profits. Where the intermediary established because of the restructure is a conduit or does not have beneficial ownership, then DTC abuse is likely.

The CbyC reporting is unlikely to be relevant to an FDI provider considering investing in the BRICS because, except for the largest of projects, it will have little disclosure relevance. This is not the position in SA where the threshold is far lower,

---

1784. BEPS Final Report 13.
1785. Brazil, Public Consultation RFB No. 11/2016; Russia, http://regulation.gov.ru/projects#npa =41254; India, section 286 Income Tax Act, 1961; China, SAT Public Notice (2016) No. 42; SA, Draft Regulations Pursuant Tax Administration Act 28, 2011, 11 Apr. 2016.
1786. Reporting threshold at €750m: OECD/G20 estimates that approx. 85/90% (*supra* n. 1784, para. 53) of MNEs would be excluded but reporting would cover approx. 90% of corporate revenues. If correct then the possibility remains of many transactions shifting profits by abusing DTCs being undisclosed.
1787. OECD's 2020 threshold review, *supra* n. 1784, para. 54.
1788. *Supra* n. 1784, para. 25.
1789. At https://www.ensafrica.com/news/new-ITR14-requires-country-by-country-reporting-in-company-tax-returns?Id=2272&STitle=tax%20ENSight.
1790. 18 Apr. 2016.
1791. R10bn (equivalent) OECD threshold.

and, in any event, that lower threshold does not constitute a governance concern or expropriation since it does not constitute an abusive undertaking. If the disclosed information had been used by the BRICS' tax authority to assert that the MNE group had undertaken evasion then where that decision resulted in expropriation it would be relevant for FDI, but this is likely only to be the case in Russia and SA when investor protection is considered to be relevant by FDI providers.

9.2.2.2 Thin Capitalization

With excessive leverage granted by related lenders to borrowers' resident in, or trading in a BRICS member countered by the borrowing country's thin capitalization rule, the role of the DTC is limited to examining whether it overrides the domestic rule and overrides how the excess interest is treated for withholding tax purposes. The DTC does not override the rejection of an interest deduction on debt provided by arm's length tax preferred jurisdiction lenders nor does it apply to hybrid debt. In this subsection, the investigation is on whether these features are relevant to potential providers of FDI to the BRICS.

9.2.2.2.1 ND Article Override

The BRICS, other than for India which is yet to implement tax based thin capitalization,[1792] have widened the developed world's thin capitalization 'relationship'[1793] definition from that of the developed world. While this by itself does not result in DTC abuse, it leads to it when the loan is channelled through an intermediary principally for the purpose of overriding the rule or reducing withholding tax on the excess. For this reason, it becomes important to determine whether the relevant DTC ND Article can override the rule and where that is possible, whether that DTC includes a provision saving for the domestic rule.[1794]

This gives rise to complex interrelationships between the DTC and domestic law which may be difficult to administer as a series of Russian decisions evidences. The Russian courts firstly held that the ND Article could override the thin capitalization rule *(Swedwood Tikhvin)*[1795] and then later decided that it could not *(Severny Kubass)*[1796] when the transaction or structure providing the debt constituted avoidance or evasion. The problem with this decision is the potential for double taxation since Russia's definition of evasion and avoidance con be distinguished from that of the developed world[1797] (as can the meanings in the other BRICS except for SA) and leaves open the

---

1792. Included EBITA rule in 2017 Budget to restrict deductibility of associated enterprises' interest expense to 30% of EBITDA, or actual interest paid/payable to the associate, whichever is less, Mr Jaitley, Finance Minister.
1793. Chapter 4, section 4.2.4.
1794. Chapter 4, section 4.2.10.
1795. *Supra* n. 507.
1796. *Supra* n. 510.
1797. Chapter 3.

possibility that a Russian Court or one from another member may reject a savings provision on the grounds that thin capitalization constitutes neither avoidance nor evasion,[1798] but simply a Government tax policy on the level of debt which is acceptable for tax purposes. In order for the BRICS to avoid this, the author recommends they include provisions in their DTCs or Protocols specifically preventing the ND Article from overriding decisions on 'thin capitalization'. Leaving unclear whether the override applies is contrary to good governance and because potential providers of Russian inbound FDI (of the BRICS) focus on governance, amending its DTCs to confirm that the override does not counter 'thin capitalization' would increase Russia's friendliness for potential FDI providers.

9.2.2.2.2 Arm's Length Lenders Resident in Tax Privileged Countries

Other than the WHT on interest payable to non-resident lenders, the developed world generally does not apply different thin capitalization rules by reference to whether the lender resides in a tax preferred jurisdiction. This is not the case in Brazil and SA[1799] which extend the rules to loans provided by arm's length lenders resident in tax preferred jurisdictions. Circumventing this rule induces the lender to treaty shop the finance through countries not considered to be tax preferred by Brazil or by SA, which potentially gives rise to DTC abuse. Were Brazil and SA to reverse this approach then the resulting simplification would better position them both for obtaining arm's length finance. One potentially acceptable approach would be to prevent the rule applying to commercial loans provided by a lender who could meet a functions, assets and risks test. Since the probability of expropriation would be considered by the potential provider of FDI into SA, treating arms length's lenders differently would only constitute expropriation if it were an abusive undertaking which, rationally, it is not.

9.2.2.3 Hybrid Debt

With Brazil and Russia not formally establishing procedures which determine the level of economic substance the deductibility of payments made on 'hybrid debt' depends on, the potential for non-resident lenders to abuse the withholding tax provisions in both Russia's and Brazil's DTCs, is left open. In Russia, the abuse from the absence of hybrid rules follows from, were the thin capitalization to apply, the excess being treated as dividends liable to dividend withholding tax with that percentage generally exceeding the percentage for interest.[1800] In Brazil, were the thin capitalization rules to apply, the excess would continue to be treated as interest liable to interest withholding tax because were the interest to be deemed a dividend, no additional tax would be levied because the withholding tax deducted from dividends is nil. Therefore, with

---

1798. Chapter 4, section 4.2.11.
1799. Chapter 4, section 4.2.6.
1800. Chapter 4, section 4.2.9.

governance and investor protection relevant considerations for potential providers of Russian FDI, the absence of hybrid rules would be conducive to attracting FDI.

9.2.2.4 Residence

When considering whether the benefits on offer by one state to the providers of foreign FDI located in another jurisdiction have been abused, it is necessary to determine if that foreign person had artificially arranged to be tax resident in that state in order that it could claim the benefits. This then raises whether the measures adopted by the states to counter that artificiality could constitute a breach of governance or investor protection, or expropriation.

9.2.2.4.1 Place of Incorporation and POEM

Rationally, over the years, many MNEs abused the BRICS DTCs by being able to rely on outdated corporate residence definitions to qualify for the benefits, with one such example being that of both Brazil and Russia which established tax residence at the place of incorporation even if the foreign person had neither a presence nor central management and control at that place. This incorporation test continues to apply in Brazil, while Russia abandoned it from January 2015 when POEM became effective. India's use of the place of incorporation test for foreign companies ceases from April 2017 when the POEM test becomes effective. Until then foreign 'shell' companies effectively controlled in India have been able to benefit from the DTC benefits simply by ensuring that atleast one Board meeting took place outside India[1801] each year. In reality, this outcome should continue once POEM becomes effective as long as the foreign person possesses a COR validly[1802] issued by the tax authority at the place of incorporation. China has since 2008 determined foreign companies tax residence by the location of the company's 'real administrative organ'[1803] and for this purpose the place at which substantial and comprehensive management and control over production and operations of the enterprise's personnel, accounts and property[1804] was to be found has been important. It is not clear whether 'real administrative organ' and POEM are identical, but because the 'real administrative organ' test recognizes the importance of where personnel are controlled, accounts kept and property located, it is broader than POEM and therefore results in more foreign companies being deemed China tax resident than would be under POEM. Also by adopting a derivative benefit approach to residence, such as in *Tianjin 2010*,[1805] China has applied its DTC with the country of tax residence of the ultimate controller, to the intermediary's profits or income,

---

1801. Foreign company is Indian resident only when that company's 'control and management' is wholly within India.
1802. Not validly issued when Indian tax authority concludes the certificate should not have been issued.
1803. Article 2, EITL.
1804. Article 4 Order No. 512 State Council, EITL Implementing Regulations.
1805. *Supra* n. 1375.

resulting in benefits lost to the extent of that excess. SA aligns with the developed world by denying benefits where the non-resident's POEM is located in SA or, as in *Tradehold*,[1806] where that was not conclusively located outside of SA under a DTC.

Brazil's place of incorporation test provides clarity, simplicity and certainty resulting in the protection of foreign investors rights and because that objective is relevant to attracting FDI into SA, that Government would be well served by resolving the uncertainty from *Tradehold*. It is unlikely that either India or China would be required to modify their approaches to countering residence artificiality, because neither represents a breach of investor rights of such magnitudes that it constitutes expropriation.

9.2.2.4.2 POEM Tie-Breaker: Decision Makers' Location v. Economic Activities Location

Disputes between states on where POEM is located should not amount to expropriation although they could where the conflict leads to unrelieved double taxation of such magnitude rendering the investment (almost) worthless. In practice, obtaining a DTC's benefits requires the foreign company to be 'resident of the Contracting State'[1807] which is the counterparty to the DTC. Therefore, when country A deems the foreign company to be tax resident in country A while country B deems it also to be resident of country B, then unless the DTC between A and B provides a methodology (usually POEM) for ceding residence to one of A or B, the DTC benefits on payments from A would be unavailable. In working out which of A or B the foreign company is resident for DTC purposes, Article 4(3)[1808] of the DTC provides that it will be the country in which POEM is to be found while Article 3(2)[1809] of the same DTC instructs that in applying the rules, the POEM meaning in the country applying the DTC is the meaning to be used for this purpose.

In relation to the BRICS, except for Brazil, foreign persons can shift their tax residence from one state to another by artificially relocating POEM from one state to another (except if the other state is an incorporation state), and in doing so abuse the benefits on offer under the BRICS DTCs. Potentially double taxation may arise from this abuse for foreign persons based in developing or developed countries investing in Russia or China (little relevance to SA)[1810] because both countries work out where the POEM is located by focussing on both the place at which major economic activities are located[1811] (UN[1812] basis) and the place at which the highest decisions[1813] are taken (OECD[1814] basis), in the absence of rules determining which of the two tests is the more

---

1806. *Supra* n. 974.
1807. Defined in Article 4(1) *OECD Model Convention*.
1808. *OECD Model Convention*.
1809. *Supra* n. 499.
1810. *Supra* n. 1107.
1811. Chapter 6, section 6.2.2.2.
1812. *Supra* n. 1103.
1813. Chapter 6, section 6.2.2.1.
1814. *Supra* n. 1102.

important. POEM is effectively irrelevant in India providing the FDI provider possess a valid COR because the foreign company may be tax resident in a country at which neither the highest decision makers are located nor are economic activities to be found. If these were the facts, then India could rightly argue[1815] that the COR should not have been issued, but its current rules (absent a GAAR effective April 2017) do little to counter such abuse. Resolving where POEM resides becomes more difficult for MNEs which have created additional abuse by breaking their value chains into discrete functions, because doing so results in a narrowing of economic activity in each country.

It is not likely that double taxation arising from disputes over where POEM or tax residence is to be found would rise to the level of an expropriation and therefore clarifying the issue would not likely improve the landscape for inbound FDI in Russia especially because approx. 75% of inbound FDI emanates from tax preferred jurisdictions.

9.2.2.5 Beneficial Ownership

Whether a foreign intermediary is entitled to DTC benefits on dividends, interest and royalties received from a counterparty depends on whether the intermediary can satisfy the beneficial ownership test without failing a limitation of benefits or main purpose test. This subsection investigates whether there is a relationship between the BRICS meaning, DTC benefits and inbound FDI.

9.2.2.5.1 DTCs: Contractual Control v. Economic Control

Historically there was little need to consider whether foreign FDI providers into the BRICS abused the withholding tax benefits under DTCs benefits because few of the members imposed such taxes but this has changed in recent years and has led to consideration of whether abuse has arisen from different approaches.

The developed world's approach to identifying the beneficial owner of the income or gain has largely been driven by considering whether the contractual arrangements entered into between the intermediary and third party left the intermediary contractually in control of the funds[1816] received from the source country. This is different from the BRICS where neither the contractual obligations test nor the possession, use, risk and control test[1817] solely applies. This uncertainty has fed the perception that MNEs have abused the rights offered in the BRICS DTCs but this is neither the case for Brazil nor for India. In relation to Brazil, abusing beneficial ownership in order to pay less taxes on dividends[1818] is irrelevant firstly, because there is no dividend withholding tax and secondly, as Brazil is a civil law jurisdiction, there

---

1815. *Supra* n. 1151.
1816. Chapter 6, section 6.3.2.1.
1817. Chapter 6, section 6.3.2.2.
1818. *Supra* nn. 1229 and 1230.

is no broadly discernible beneficial ownership test except for the narrow test applicable to thin capitalization.[1819] As for India, it is difficult to abuse the DTC beneficial ownership test when the shareholder's beneficial status is settled squarely by the possession of a COR[1820] as evident in *E-Trade[1821] and Universal International.[1822] In relation to Russia, while it is too early to conclude that MNEs have abused beneficial ownership[1823] in the DTCs, it is likely they have done so because Russia's economic substance approach does not likely sit comfortably well with the developed world's contractual approach which is relevant since FDI providers from the developed world make up more than 70% of Russian's inbound FDI. It is also too early to determine whether the beneficial ownership concept which is contained in most of SA's DTCs is being abused since withholding tax became effective in SA only from 2012 for dividends and royalties and from 2015 for interest and, consequently, SARS has yet to develop a single approach to the concept and identified if and so how its DTCs have been abused. In China's case, beneficial ownership has become an extremely important concept for countering DTC abuse since 2008 but is now much less likely to be abused in the DTCs because more than 73% of China's inbound FDI has been provided by developing countries, predominantly Hong Kong where special arrangements are in place for China. With the connectivity between POEM and beneficial ownership in China being evident from the tax authority holding that foreign persons cannot be beneficial owners in the absence of economic substance *(Circulars 601, 82 and Announcement 30)*[1824] and in *Yangzhou*[1825] and *Xinjiang*[1826] and because POEM is found at the place where economic activities take place, this evidences the importance of substance rather than form in China.

The different approaches adopted by the BRICS to countering the abuse of beneficial ownership in their DTCs could not have had any impact on the levels of inbound FDI in Brazil or in India and while it is too soon to identify in Russia and SA it is not likely to have done so because it neither impacts good governance, the rule of law nor of investor protection. The different approach by China likely has impacted inbound FDI by encouraging it to be channelled through Hong Kong which has been given some carve outs from the normal China beneficial ownership rulings.

9.2.3 International Rules

9.2.3.1 *Limitation of Benefits*

Another approach used by many countries to counter DTC abuse is the limitation of benefits provision to cap or eliminate DTC benefits when the intermediary fails to meet

---

1819. *Supra* n. 1231.
1820. *Supra* n. 1234.
1821. *Supra* n. 1194.
1822. *Supra* n. 1195.
1823. Tax concept from December 2014, previously MOF concept.
1824. *Supra* nn. 1208, 1209, 1223.
1825. *Supra* n. 1212.
1826. *Supra* n. 1213.

specific or general tests. This subsection investigates whether there is a relationship between the BRICS meaning, DTC benefits and inbound FDI and includes a consideration on whether the BRICS adopting the BEPS LOB recommendation would facilitate inbound FDI.

9.2.3.1.1 BRICS and Treaty Shopping

The BRICS have been slower to adopt the LOB as a concept to counter DTC abuse than the developed world. Since Brazil has not generally included LOBs into its DTCs (six DTCs[1827] contain them) this has resulted in the RFB relying on simulation to counter the abuse,[1828] but this has not produced a coherent policy because of the disagreement between the Courts and advisers on the legality of simulation. China has refrained from including LOBs in more than a handful of its DTCs[1829] because its approach to dealing with beneficial ownership abuses, as in *Shenzen*[1830] indicated that it did not need an LOB, and in default China could rely on GAAR. India has taken a different route since *Azardi's* [1831] (2003) confirmation of the legality of treaty shopping and India's failure to counter this outcome due to the taxpayer's section 90(a)[1832] election enabling it to adopt domestic rules when doing so provides a more favourable DTC outcome. This has led the IRD to begun including LOBs in DTCs and, in the Mauritius and Singapore Protocols,[1833] the LOB is not defined by general concepts but rather by monetary considerations which provide a more transparent and simpler landscape for investors to manage. In relation to SA, treaty shopping was historically not of much significance because of the absence of WHT on dividends and royalties (before 2012) and on interest (before 2015) together with SA continuing to allocate the taxing right on these payments to non-residents as an inducement to attract FDI.[1834] Russia's approach to LOBs is different to the other BRICS in that not only was it established some years ago, (2010)[1835] but it was based on the CAs consulting on whether the MNE had abused the DTC. The fallacy of this approach was evident in *A40-60755/12-20.388*[1836] when the CAs failure to consult resulted in the FTS denying the benefits.

In relation to the impact on potential FDI of the BRICS approach to LOBs, because their approach is in its infancy it is unlikely that any of the BRICS (except possibly Russia) constitutes it as a rule of law or governance breach nor is it likely to amount to an abusive undertaking resulting in an expropriation (especially in SA) of a kind which

---

1827. *Supra* n. 1289.
1828. Chapter 6, section 6.3.4.1.
1829. *Supra* nn. 1302 and 1303.
1830. *Supra* n. 1255.
1831. *Supra* n. 1259.
1832. *Ibid.*
1833. *Supra* n. 1268 for Mauritius and *supra* n. 1269 for Singapore.
1834. *Mazansky.*
1835. *Supra* n. 1249, even though a selection of DTCs before then contained LOBs.
1836. *Supra* n. 1250.

could impact FDI. Therefore, only for Russia is it possible that FDI could be effected because potential FDI providers would prefer that the CAs consult if it is a requirement to do so, for confirming the DTC benefits.

9.2.3.1.2 BEPS Recommendation

With the BRICS existing approach to LOBs having limited effect on inbound FDI, the question is whether that outcome would change were the BRICS to adopt the *BEPS Action Plan 6* recommendation. With one of the more likely recommended formats for an LOB being the 'qualified person' test, this is unlikely to result in any FDI changes since that format (albeit a much simplified version)[1837] is the LOB format most recently adopted in the Brazil, Russia, India and China DTCs. SA's DTC LOB format has no single form.[1838] However, the more likely outcome of the localization would be an increase in the tax authorities' success in countering the abuse except for India unless section 90(a) is abandoned. Potentially there is room for definitional conflict to impact the FDI levels arising from the meaning of the 'active conduct of a business' test[1839] because paragraph 47 of the Plan explains that the constituents of a 'business' has been left to the country interpreting the rules to determine, and in China's case, the inevitable conflict from the interrelationship between 'substance and economic importance' in its beneficial ownership test and whether an active business is carried on. Whether an active business is carried on rests in part on determining whether the persons running the business 'conducted the substantial managerial and operational activities'. The author does not envisage these conflicts amounting to breaches of governance rule of law or investor protection and for that reason does not expect any link between the recommendation and FDI in the BRICS.

9.2.3.2 Main Purpose Tests

The main purpose test is used by many countries to counter DTC abuse which MNEs achieve by limiting source country WHTs on dividends, interest and royalties, principally. This subsection investigates whether there is a relationship between the BRICS meaning, DTC benefits and inbound FDI and includes a consideration on whether the BRICS adopting the BEPS MPT recommendation would facilitate inbound FDI.

9.2.3.2.1 BRICS and MPTs

MNEs may abuse DTCs by using intermediaries established with little or no substance, but they may also abuse DTCs by channelling equity, loans or intellectual property

---

1837. Members adopted the 'qualified person' format, except India where the recommendation's format were partly modelled on the Indian (*supra* n. 1466, para. 25) provision, none had adopted a format consistent with the recommendation.
1838. Chapter 7, section 7.2.3.2.1.
1839. *Supra* n. 1466, p. 36.

transactions through controlled intermediaries, when the intermediary has no real connection with the country in which it has been established. Other than China, the BRICS have done relatively little to widely counter this abuse and between them, there is no single format used to counter it. Brazil includes MPTs in a small number of DTCs[1840] but the format adopted focuses on countering the artificial receipt by the intermediary of property rights through assignment or by creation. SA includes MPTs in a wide group of DTCs but there is neither consistency of approach nor of format, which is reminiscent of the Russian approach included in its pre-2010 DTCs (new Model). Since then Russia's MPT policy has centred on countering benefits where the DTC has been abused and because the only potentially reliable definition of abuse in Russia is 'unjustified tax benefit', the probability that this provision could be successfully applied to counter DTC abuse has become dependent on *Resolution 53* being widely understood and applicable. China has included MPTs[1841] in only a few of its DTCs because of its belief that the beneficial ownership test was its main tool for countering DTC with fall back to GAAR. India has included MPTs in many DTCs[1842] but the failure to adopt a consistent or uniform format together with the powerful section 90(a) results in little abuse being countered this way. The BRICS current format is unlikely to have given rise to a problem for inbound FDI except perhaps for SA, where the uncertainty of approach could be viewed as giving rise to a governance concern.

9.2.3.2.2   BEPS Recommendation

With the BRICS existing approach to MPTs having little effect on inbound FDI, the question is whether that would change were the BRICS to adopt the *BEPS Action Plan 6* recommendation.[1843] In relation to Brazil and SA, simply including the test in more DTCs is unlikely to improve the FDI landscape but more likely to generate additional tax authority disputation. The position in Russia would differ because localizing would constrain the FTS' current right to reject the benefits where the CAs simply decided to do so and consequently would improve governance leading to an increase in inbound FDI. Were India to localize the recommendation little would change in taxation unless section 90(a) was withdrawn or GAAR becomes effective and unless those changes were made there would be little impact on FDI. Any China localization would not likely improve the SAT's powers to counter the DTC abuse because its current 'beneficial ownership' test is powerful which means that were it to be diluted by localization, there would be less disputation. This would unlikely result in any impact on FDI.

1840. *Supra* n. 1308.
1841. *Supra* n. 1328/1329.
1842. Chapter 6, section 6.3.5.2.
1843. *Supra* n. 1466, pp. 54 and et seq.

9.2.3.3 Indirect Asset Transfers

Structuring the FDI requires MNEs to focus on the tax consequences from both receiving periodic returns on the investment and the profit, if any, when the investment is exited. Typically this leads MNEs to channel the FDI through intermediaries when doing so provides the opportunity to minimize or avoid the exit profits being taxable in the source or resident country. This becomes especially relevant in relation to immoveable property because the source of both the periodic and exit taxes is the country where the property sits. Using an intermediary resident in a DTC country having neither a nexus with that source country nor economic substance can be viewed as abusing the DTC.

9.2.3.3.1 Domestic Rules

The developed world (before BEPS) did not generally recommend rules countering such structures unlike the BRICS (other than Brazil)[1844] which had done so. Russia sought to counter the abuse when at least 50% of the company's assets represented Russian sited immoveable property[1845] and widened the applicability by extending the rules to disposals of derivative transactions written over Russian sited immoveable property. SA countered the abuse when atleast 80% of the company's assets represented SA located immoveable property. China also widened the applicability to indirect disposals of movable property as well as immoveable property, but then narrowed the impact by exempting profits when less than 75% of the assets owned by the company in which shares were being sold represented China immoveable property. This rule has applied since 2008, allowing China to counter the abuse by applying its GAAR to indirect transfer arrangements which are devoid of 'reasonable commercial purpose justifying the existence of the structure' *(Guizhou).*[1846] This approach required further clarity which came in *Circulars 698, 24* and *Announcement 7*, especially in relation to the meaning of 'reasonable commercial purpose'. The rulings also confirmed that gains arising on group reorganizations, disposal of listed shares and where DTCs exemptions[1847] were applicable could not be reversed by the rule. The absence of a rule in India turned out to be telling as *Vodafone*[1848] evidences, because it resulted in India introducing an indirect transfer rule in the *2012 Finance Act*[1849] which was made retroactive to 1962! *Vodafone* and *Cairn* (also an indirect asset transfer case) have argued that the retroactivity was an abusive undertaking and as such, have claimed

---

1844. Brazil taxes gains on alienation of resident company's shares allowing the rule to be abused through disposal of shares in intermediaries, especially the ineffectiveness of Brazil's simulation rule partly due to the legality principle.
1845. Russian Model DTC is unclear whether this is a reference to the number of properties or value of assets, Wilson, *International tax Report, June 2012.*
1846. *Supra* n. 1367.
1847. *Supra* nn. 1369, 1370 and 1371.
1848. *Supra* n. 1355.
1849. *Supra* n. 1357.

compensation from India under the Dutch and UK respective Investment Treaties on the grounds of the retro-activity amounting to expropriation.[1850]

As these rules stand today, it is clear that India's use of retroactive legislation is a relevant factor for existing FDI providers but its retroactive application to indirect disposals should not affect the position of potential FDI investors because they are aware the law exists. With SA's rule applying to companies only with more than 75% (a high percentage) SA sited immoveable property, this does not disincentivise foreign persons from providing FDI.

9.2.3.3.2 BRICS and DTCs

Stuffing the property owning companies with moveable property might have circumvented the rule but when the immoveable property had substantial value, the financial cost of the additional investment may have outweighed the costs of doing so, and in any event, may have been overridden by a GAAR. Where a country does not have a GAAR, one benefit from using an intermediary to own the property which is tax resident in a DTC country is that (regardless of whether the DTC was modelled on the OECD[1851] or the UN[1852] Model Conventions) a 50% test is applicable. While the 50% ceiling overrides the China and SA ceilings it has little or no impact because the gain remains not taxable due to the actual percentage falling below the 75%/80%. The second benefit is that the DTCs do not include moveable assets and therefore where a gain on the indirect disposal of moveable assets is taxed, (India and China), the DTC will override. These benefits have contributed to MNEs, particularly those investing into China or India, channelling their FDI through intermediaries. This has led to DTC abuse in the absence of a real connection with the intermediary country. For this purpose, China has countered this intermediation by including a 'beneficial ownership' test in the Protocols with the three countries[1853] (including Hong Kong) providing much of China's inbound FDI.

Russia's extension of the test to derivatives over immoveable property gives rise to uncertainty but it is unlikely to negate potential inbound FDI because neither gives rise to governance or rule of law problems. The extended indirect transfer rules in China and India (except for the retroactive application) would also not likely negate inbound FDI because they too neither breach the rule of law or governance nor do they amount to expropriation.

9.2.3.3.3 BEPS Recommendation

With both the UN and OECD Model Conventions together with the BRICS domestic rules leaving unclear when the percentage test was to be measured, the

---

1850. *Chakrabarti*, India: BITS and Pieces - India's BIT revisited, Indus Law, March 2016.
1851. Article 13(4) OECD Model Tax Convention; *supra* n. 1344.
1852. *UN Model Tax Convention Commentary*, p. 233/234.
1853. *Supra* n. 1382.

recommendation that it be made at any time[1854] during a 365-day period prior the sale constitutes a welcome clarification. The localization of this recommendation by both India and Russia strengthens their domestic rules but not so for China or SA because they each have a GAAR. The recommendation's extension to the countering of indirect transfers through partnerships or trusts[1855] would not strengthen the rules if localized by China or India because China pre-empted that extension in *Announcement 7* and India also did so in section 9(1)(i), ITA, 1961. The localization of the recommendation would not likely therefore pave the way for any greater FDI because the clarification and certainty provided amounts to neither an improvement in the rule of law or governance neither does it improve investor protection which avoids an expropriation.

9.2.3.4   Third Country PEs

The developed world has become concerned in recent years that structures owning shares, debt claims, rights or other property owned by a country A resident deriving income or gains from country B, give rise to DTC abuse when the assets generating the income or gain have been transferred to a third country PE (C) of the country A resident, which lightly taxes the income or gains (so-called triangular structures).

9.2.3.4.1   Domestic Rules

Triangular structures are unlikely to create abuse within the BRICS since profits of foreign PEs of resident enterprises are taxed on a worldwide basis, except for investments in countries where the BRICS provide tax sparing relief, which economically provides the resident with the same or similar net of tax profit as would apply should the resident be granted a PE exemption. Accordingly, it is unlikely triangular structures would encourage inbound FDI to the BRICS unless the funds were to be invested into a third country where tax sparing with the BRICS was granted so that the localization of a rule to deal with the so-called DTC abuse would not likely negatively impact FDI.

9.2.3.4.2   BEPS Recommendation

The *BEPS Action Report 6* recommended that triangular abuse be countered except for income taxed at not less than 60% of the tax ordinarily applicable in country C or where the income had been derived through the conduct of an active business (broadly something other than a financial business) in the third country PE.[1856] Were this recommendation to be localized in the BRICS, it would not reverse the current position and provide opportunities for DTC abuse since as a policy, the BRICS DTCs do provide foreign branch exemptions. Nor would the recommendation counter tax sparing

---

1854. *Supra* n. 1466, p. 72.
1855. *Ibid.*
1856. *Ibid.*, p. 75.

benefits because as drafted, it does not apply to sparing and this is relevant because at the date of writing the BRICS (other than Brazil) have sparing with small groups of counterparties (Russia,[1857] India, China[1858] and SA).[1859]

Since the BRICS have no need to counter this kind of DTC abuse it is irrelevant to their attractiveness as FDI locations and with it also being inapplicable for tax sparing it is not a relevant factor for that purpose either.

9.2.3.5 DTCs and Business Purpose

BEPS Action Plan 6 acknowledged that rather than the DTCs being used to avoid double taxation and prevent avoidance and fiscal evasion, they have been used by MNEs to create double non-taxation[1860] which had not been contemplated by the *OECD* nor by the *UN Model Conventions* as an acceptable purpose of the DTC. In order to counter that outcome, the recommendation[1861] provided that by including the purpose in the DTC's title and in the Preamble, that both statements would be taken into account when interpreting the DTC because of Article 31(1) and (2) of the *VCLT*. The recommended expanded Preamble provides that avoidance or evasion should not be created through treaty shopping.[1862]

Prior to the recommendation's publication, few, if any of the BRICS DTCs contained such specificity in the Title or in the Preamble and at the date of writing, none has published an intention to localize the recommendation but the recent Indian, SA DTCs and one China DTC have included the recommendation or phraseology broadly similar to it in the DTC. The recent Indian DTCs[1863] with Cyprus, Kenya, Thailand, Korea and Croatia have adopted the phraseology similar to the recommendation with only Cyprus[1864] contributing FDI of significance (approx. 2%) to India. SA's recent DTCs[1865] with the UAE and Qatar, neither country of which contributes significant FDI to the BRICS, also have adopted wording similar to the recommendation. These DTCs contain the expanded Title and a reference in the Preamble to the importance of economic cooperation between the parties. Variation in China's DTCs to reflect the recommendation has been confined to the Chile (2015) DTC where both the Title and the Preamble closely mirror the recommendation. In the author's opinion,

---

1857. Algeria, Argentina, Cuba, Saudi Arabia, Thailand and Vietnam, all income and dividends, interest and royalties on Mongolia.
1858. Cai Shui [2009] No. 125; Brunei, Bulgaria, Cuba, Cyprus, Ethiopia, India, Italy, Jamaica, Kuwait, Macedonia, Malaysia, Mauritius, Morocco, Nepal, Oman, Pakistan, PNG, Seychelles, Sri Lanka, Switzerland, Thailand, Trinidad, Tunisia, Vietnam, Yugoslavia on all income, dividends interest or royalties depending on the country.
1859. Algeria, Botswana, Egypt, Ethiopia, Greece, Israel, Mozambique, Pakistan, Romania, Seychelles, Swaziland, Thailand, Tunisia and Uganda.
1860. *Supra* n. 1466, section B, p. 91.
1861. *Ibid.*, section B, p. 91, p. 72.
1862. *Ibid.*, p. 92.
1863. 18 Nov. 2016, 11 Jul. 2016, 29 Jun. 2015, 18 May 2015, 12 Feb. 2015.
1864. *See* Chapter 1 Table 1.2, position 10.
1865. 23 Nov. 2015, 6 Mar. 2015.

Chapter 9: BRICS and FDI: DTC Anti-abuse and Dispute Resolution

this was initiated by the Chile negotiator, Liselotte Kana[1866] (who has negotiated Chile's DTCs and is a participant in the BEPS process) because the same wording is found in other Chile agreements but not in other China DTCs. None of the recent Russian DTCs[1867] nor the Brazil DTCs contains the recommendation.

If this is the BRICS current position, then what is the justification for it? In the author's opinion, it is driven by their belief that their respective GAARs and 'unjustified tax benefit' rules represent suitable deterrents for DTC abuse. In relation to India, the inclusion in the DTCs of the economic cooperation objective is an acknowledgement that until section 90(a) is repealed any provision purporting to counter DTC abuse is unlikely to be effective while Brazil's position is an acknowledgement that in the absence of an anti-abuse provision and its reluctance to follow the developed world's meanings, it would be difficult to give meaning to the provisions for Brazil tax purposes.

Were the BRICS to fail to widely implement the recommendation then it is unlikely to constitute a failure of governance or the rule of law and neither is it likely to constitute a failure to protect investors amounting to expropriation. For that reason, it should not disadvantage the BRICS in relation to potential inbound FDI.

9.2.3.6 *DTC and Savings Provisions*

Savings provisions are perhaps the most important feature of any DTC because they preserve the Government's sovereign right to tax or to exempt taxpayers (residents or non-residents), where it chooses to do so. BEPS Action Plan 6 recommends that this sovereign right be formally incorporated into DTCs as a 'saving clause' which overrides the DTC except for nominated exceptions[1868] which the State intends the DTC should apply to. For this Chapter's purposes, the exceptions to the saving's clause are those reflecting business profit and TP corresponding adjustments, double taxation relief, non-discrimination and MAP. This subsection therefore investigates the link, if any, between the savings provisions and inbound FDI.

9.2.3.6.1 *BEPS Recommendation*

While neither the *OECD*[1869] nor the *UN*[1870] *Model Tax Conventions* contain general savings clauses designed to override DTC abuse, the Commentaries to the Conventions discuss how domestic law provisions or the Convention itself may counter that abuse. In order to clarify whether Contracting States have rights to override the DTC, *BEPS Action Plan 6* recommended broadening of the domestic provisions and including the

---

1866. At http://www.nacchamber.com/?events&ID = 348, last viewed 5 Feb. 2017, who requested the inclusion of similar clauses in two recent Chilean DTCs, Japan (January 2016), Uruguay (2016).
1867. HK (2016), Singapore (Protocol 2015), Belgium (2015), China 2015.
1868. Articles 7(3), 9(2), 19, 20, 23, 24, 25 and 28.
1869. Paragraph E, Article 1.
1870. Para 42 to 79, Article 1.

guiding principle into the DTCs[1871] (paragraph 63) as a specific savings clause. The recently published UN proposal[1872] aligns. While a savings provision is designed to protect the state's sovereign right to tax, in this section, the discussion is confined to the state's rights in relation to business profit and TP corresponding adjustments, non-discrimination and MAP, for each is relevant for inbound FDI. Of these features, uncompensated TP adjustments (subject to quantum) can constitute expropriation while the failure to implement MAP constitutes a failing to protect investor rights.

9.2.3.6.2 BRICS and DTCs Savings Clauses

At the time of writing none of the BRICS has included a general savings provision in Article 1 of any of their DTCs and subject to the available information read by the author, none has been proposed,[1873] let alone has a provision based on the recommendation or the UN proposed savings clause been incorporated into any of the BRICS domestic policy. Consequently, the BRICS DTCs continue to be weak in countering DTC abuse except where they specifically incorporate provisions saving for avoidance or evasion or when specifically saving for specific anti-avoidance rules. The problem with this approach for the BRICS (discussed in Chapter 4) is that many of the transactions, structures or behavior constituting DTC abuse fail to fall within the BRICS' meaning of avoidance or evasion, leaving questionable their effectiveness. Therefore, were they to include the recommended savings clause in Article 1 of their DTCs much additional comfort would be provided.

Having regard to the discussion in the immediately foregoing paragraph, and the BRICS DTCs stand today, where uncompensated TP adjustments (subject to quantum) is not resolved by MAP or by Arbitration, it can constitute expropriation while the failure to provide a taxpayer with a right to access MAP constitutes a failing to protect investor rights.

9.2.3.7 Contract Splitting

Where a foreign investor carries on a long-term business (particularly construction contracts) within a country the nature of its business activities may leave it with a local tax presence giving rise to a source country tax liability unrelieved by a DTC exemption, unless it splits its single contract or functions into discrete components each of which is then treated as a carve out from a DTC PE. This is intended to avoid that local tax presence arising. Where this disaggregation represents an artificial barrier, the DTC will have been abused.

1871. *Supra* n. 1466, para. 58.
1872. E/C.18/2016/CRP.10, p. 15/16.
1873. SA entered into DTC with UAE, which saves for hydrocarbon taxing rights.

9.2.3.7.1 BRICS and Contract Splitting

Since the *UN Model Convention's* duration is six months and the *OECD Model Convention's* period is twelve months, adopting the UN approach makes it more likely that MNEs would abuse the DTC by disaggregation. With Brazil's DTCs mostly adopting the UN approach this suggests that MNEs investing into Brazil are more likely to disaggregate in Brazil as they are in SA, although in that country's case, the duration in part depends upon the industry in which the FDI investor participates, e.g. six months for non-residents exploring or exploiting natural resources[1874] but generally extending to twelve months[1875] in SA's older DTCs which then reduces to more than six months[1876] in later DTCs. Providers of FDI into Russia are less likely to disaggregate because its *Model Convention's* duration is twelve months while MNEs investing into China are likely to disaggregate since the duration period depends upon the foreign investor's tax residence. Where the FDI provider is Hong Kong tax resident, it is likely to disaggregate because the China/Hong Kong DTC provides for a six-month period.[1877] Other China DTCs favour more than twelve months[1878] with one establishing nine months[1879] and another an eighteen-month[1880] period. This absence of consistency is indicative of the absence of a policy. It is difficult to draw a conclusion on whether inbound Indian investors would disaggregate since the recent DTC with Mauritius provides for a nine-month period[1881] (where disaggregation may be less likely) while the Singapore DTC provides for a six months' duration[1882] (where disaggregation is more likely). Other DTCs with India adopt twelve months[1883] with one exception being when the project together with other sites continues for more than six months.[1884]

9.2.3.7.2 BEPS Recommendation

The recommendation's main purpose test[1885] is intended to counter the abuse as shown in Example J to the proposed Commentary in the *Action Report 7*[1886] on the PE Commentary. This Example focusses on projects (not exclusively natural resources contracts) being combined when the separate projects represent a 'coherent whole commercially and geographically'. Were the BRICS to localize the aggregation principle only Russia would potentially be materially impacted, because inbound Russian

---

1874. Singapore (2015); Cameroon (2015).
1875. Singapore (2015); UAE (2015); Mauritius (2013); Cyprus (2015).
1876. Zimbabwe (2015); Brazil (2003); Qatar (2015); Cameroon (2015); HK (2014); Lesotho (2014).
1877. Malaysia (1985); Macau (2003); Chile (2015); HK (2015); Indonesia (2015); Austria (1991).
1878. Pakistan (2007); Romania (2016); Zimbabwe (2015); Estonia (2014); Germany (2014); France (2013).
1879. Cambodia (2016).
1880. Russia (1994).
1881. Mauritius (2016); Armenia (2003).
1882. Singapore (2011); Cyprus (2016); Vietnam (1994); Kenya (2016); Japan (2015); Israel (1996); Thailand (2015); Belarus (2015).
1883. Kuwait (2006); Slovenia (2003); Kazakhstan (1996); Tajikistan (2008).
1884. New Zealand (1999).
1885. *Supra* n. 1466, para. 29/30 p. 69.
1886. At pp. 42 et seq.

investors which had not disaggregated because the twelve-month period did not warrant doing so, would suffer. However, with aggregation likely neither to constitute an abusive undertaking nor a breach of governance or of the rule of law, it is unlikely to negate inbound FDI into Russia.

9.2.3.8 Multilateral Instrument

BEPS[1887] acknowledged that countering the abuses covered by the various recommendations could only be quickly and effectively achieved through each state entering into a Multilateral Instrument[1888] which would automatically modify each of the DTCs networks[1889] which the states had entered into. This global approach would compensate for the few officials employed by each state to renegotiate new DTCs or Protocols incorporating the recommendations. However, the *MI* would not directly amend the state's domestic laws and for that reason each state would be required to make those changes.

9.2.3.8.1 Changes and Sovereignty

An instrument which automatically changes a state's DTC obligations needs to be considered against that state's right to sovereign control of its taxing policy applicable to taxing or exempting of residents or non-residents otherwise coming within its tax net. This is especially relevant to the BRICS because their *Leaders Statements* reinforced the principle of sovereign right to tax profits in the country where they were sourced and where the activities took place which gave rise to them. While identifying the profits to be taxed under this policy sounds simple, but in practice it is not, because of definitional conflicts, MNEs abuse of domestic provisions and of the DTCs coupled with the few officials to resolve disputes when they arise.

Therefore, the challenge for the BRICS from having broad DTC networks (Brazil's network is relatively small), relatively small tax treaty negotiating teams, substantial inbound FDI and unacceptable levels of illicit outflows in part structured as being abusive of the DTCs, is whether and if so how to quickly adapt their DTC networks to counter that abuse. In that debate they needed to consider whether the benefits of quickly stemming the outflows through adopting the *MI* were justified against the costs from losing some of their sovereign taxing right[1890] because such Instruments ordinarily bind all the signatories to a 'one size fits all' unless opt out provisions[1891] are included.

1887. Action 15, p. 11.
1888. Concept is not new, Avery Jones and Baker, *The Multiple Amendment of Bilateral Double Taxation Conventions*, Bulletin for International Taxation, January 2006, p. 19/22; Convention on Mutual Administrative Assistance in Taxation Matters.
1889. *Supra* n. 1623, p. 16/17.
1890. *Ibid.*, p. 17.
1891. *Ibid.*, p. 43.

9.2.3.8.2   The Instrument

While the *MI*[1892] is intended to modify dispute resolution provisions within the DTCs (including Multilateral MAP and binding and compulsory arbitration) it is also intended to strengthen the provisions countering DTC abuse such as dual residence, transparent entities' hybrid mismatch arrangements and triangular PEs. The *Draft Instrument*[1893] achieves these objectives by including Multilateral MAP[1894] and mandatory and binding arbitration[1895] provisions as well as by including provisions countering corresponding adjustments,[1896] hybrid mismatch,[1897] dual resident entities,[1898] LOBs,[1899] indirect asset transfer capital gains,[1900] triangular PEs[1901] and strategies avoiding PE status such as specific activity exemptions[1902] and contract splitting.[1903] It also includes an interpretation rule[1904] and a rule providing for the enforcement of earlier provisions on the 'later in time'[1905] concept.

To be effective the *MI* must also be signed by a significant number of countries and with a 100-member Ad Hoc group having worked on the Instrument, this should be possible and there must also be few as possible countries reserving their positions (opt-out)[1906] on the provisions.

9.2.3.8.3   BRICS and the Instrument

This subsection discusses the relevance of the *MI*'s provisions to countering DTC abuse which the BRICS encounter while the following section considers the applicability of the *MI*'s provisions to dispute resolution.

It is rational to conclude that the BRICS will sign the *MI* because each was a member of the 100 Ad Hoc group and in China's case, its representative was the Group's Vice Chair. However, with little comment from the BRICS (other than from Russia's MOF[1907] and SA's Prof Hattingh)[1908] on the *Draft Instrument* it is difficult to be

---

1892. *Ibid.*, p. 24/25.
1893. At   http://www.oecd.org/tax/treaties/multilateral-convention-to-implement-tax-treaty-related-measures-to-prevent-BEPS.pdf.
1894. *Supra* n. 1893, Article 16.
1895. *Ibid.*, Article 19.
1896. *Ibid.*, Article 17.
1897. *Ibid.*, Article 3.
1898. *Ibid.*, Article 4.
1899. *Ibid.*, Article 7.
1900. *Ibid.*, Article 9.
1901. *Ibid.*, Article 10.
1902. *Ibid.*, Article 13.
1903. *Ibid.*, Article 14.
1904. *Ibid.*, Article 32.
1905. Article 30(3) VCLT.
1906. *Supra* n. 1893, Article 28, Final Provisions, structured by granting signatories the right to reserve positions on a wide range of provisions.
1907. 5 Oct. 2016, will sign during the 2017/2019 Budget period.
1908. OECD Official outlines challenge for the Instrument, Tax Notes, 5 Dec. 2016 including SA's Parliament will require an analysis of the *Instrument's* impact on trade and investment prior to entering into it.

sure whether they will sign and if so, which positions they will reserve on, if any. That having been said, India's likely position can be determined from the *Confederation of Indian Industry (COI)*[1909] comments that the *MI* would be compatible with India's DTCs based on the *UN Model Tax Convention* and the e-commerce rules would be compatible with sovereignty issues. The COI also recommended that monetary thresholds should form part of the *MI's* LOB provisions which should be modelled on the provisions now forming part of the Mauritius and Singapore Protocols but *Article 7* of the *MI* fails to include such a provision. It also confirmed that in order to facilitate interpretation, the *VCLT* should be referred to in the *MI* as the guide. The earlier SA *Davis Tax Committee*[1910] recommended that any *MI* should be supported as a general principle but subject to such amendments in the context of SA's own laws.

The absence of comment from the other BRICS members should not be taken as indifference because each has a system and procedures designed to counter DTC abuse. The absence may be symptomatic of either uncertainty of what the response should be or an intention to avoid 'showing their hand' before the BRICS as a whole have marshalled a common approach or it could represent indecision on how best to deal with losing tax sovereignty through enforced multilateralism[1911] should many opt-outs not be elected. In the author's view the latter cannot be the case because Article 11 of the draft *MI* establishes a saving for a state's sovereignty except in specific circumstances from which a state may opt-out, and therefore, the more likely answer is that the BRICS are preparing responses which will see Brazil, India and China adopting many reservations to reflect the differences between their provisions and those of the OECD but with Russia and SA having fewer reservations. This conclusion is based on Brazil's international tax law having diverged substantially from that of the developed world while China's approach to countering DTC abuse is sophisticated does not need to rely on the *MI* to be effective while India focusses on protecting its sovereignty. With Russia having announced its intention to sign the Instrument to counter DTC abuse, fewer reservations are expected as for SA because it generally adopts the OECD approach. This debate is considered further in section 9.3.1.

Were the BRICS to sign the *MI* then FDI investors would view this as improving their rights but the reality would depend on the opt out adopted by each Member. That having been said, were SA and Russia to sign with few reservations as is expected to be the case, then doing so would improve investor protection, governance and the rule of law and improve the landscape for inbound FDI in those countries.

1909. OECD/G 20, Comments received on public discussion draft, BEPS Action 15, 30 Jun. 2016, http://www.oecd.org/ctp/treaties/public-comments-received-discussion-draft-Development-of-MLI-to-Implement-Tax-Treaty-related-BEPS-Measures.pdf, p. 67.
1910. At p. 4.
1911. Vinnistkiy, Action 15, Multilateral Instrument, p. 21, http://ibdt.org.br/material/arquivos/Biblioteca/SLIDES/Danil%20Vinnitskiy.pdf.

9.3 SUPPLEMENTARY DISPUTE RESOLUTION

One probable outcome of the BEPS process is the increasing amount of relevant taxpayer information coming to the tax authorities' attention which will inevitably lead to increased disputation with tax authorities, which when compounded by the increasingly sophisticated tax authority[1912] computerized matching software will be more difficult for taxpayers to refute. This growing web of interlocking data sharing has the potential to create disputation gridlock and, if in Russia or SA, and were it to rise to the point of breaching investor protection or governance then it would negatively impact potential FDI providers. In order to minimize these consequences, increasing taxpayer sophistication is required when planning transactions and structures, as is proper advice and documentation.

While disputes arising from cross-border transactions and structures have traditionally been resolved through discussion with the tax authority on the merits of the case or, when that failed through formal appellate (administrative or judicial) procedures, the question is whether the existing procedures are sufficiently robust to deal with the increasing number of disputes and the increasing complexity through the localization of BEPS recommendations. The then question which potential FDI providers must answer in relation to a proposed BRICS investment is whether their procedures can effectively function in this new environment. While this question is more relevant for FDI purposes for potential providers into Russia and SA, it is relevant to the other members simply in relation to the likely level of management time to be committed to resolving tax disputes. This section therefore considers the likely BRICS response to the supplementary dispute resolution procedures included in the existing DTCs and proposed by the *MI*.

9.3.1 MAP

9.3.1.1 *MAP and BRICS Dispute Resolution*

In the absence of much published information it is difficult to conclude on whether MAP[1913] has significantly contributed to the resolution of BRICS cross-border tax disputes and whether it will be able to cope with the anticipated increase in disputes. Drawing a conclusion on those questions may have been facilitated had the *BEPS* regularly published MAP statistics[1914] but based on the available information it is evident that Russia, India and SA[1915] have sparingly resolved disputes through MAP

1912. See https://www.gov.uk/government/uploads/system/uploads/attachment_data/file/580534/aeoi_uk_submission_schema_set_v2.0.zip.
1913. Chapter 7, section 7.2.6.
1914. BEPs Final Report 14, para. 1.5, p. 18.
1915. OECD MAP Statistics report thirteen new MAP cases, SA and twenty-five for China in 2015 with a year-end inventory of eighteen cases in SA and ninety-nine in China, http://www.oecd.org/tax/dispute/map-statistics-2015.htm.

with Brazil's[1916] MAP being only rudimentary and without any publicly available information on China's use of MAP. The use of MAP though has begun with India's[1917] objective of quickly resolving cross-border disputes and China's[1918] recently expanded team focussing on resolving TP disputes.

Looking closely therefore at the nature of disputes resolved so far by Russia, India and SA using MAP, it is evident that Russia's focus has centred on service fees and WHTs on dividends, interest, royalties and capital gains while SA has focussed on TP, PE profit attribution, dual residence and withholding taxes generally. India[1919] has focussed its MAP (since 2001)[1920] on disputes centring on TP[1921] (approx. 120 TP disputes), DTC and domestic anti-abuse[1922] when not in accordance with the DTC. Taking these areas of settlement as indicative of policy, it is rational to conclude those countries have decided that using MAP did not compromise their taxing sovereignty[1923] in those particular areas except SA, where it refused permission for domestic anti-abuse disputes to be resolved through MAP. Assuming China's use of MAP to resolve TP, DTC abuse and domestic abuse leading to double taxation or taxation not in accordance with the DTC and disputes over residence, PEs and profit attribution, CGT exemptions or lower rates and non-discrimination is indicative of its policy, then the rational conclusion would be that China accepts MAP as not compromising its sovereignty[1924] in these areas.

9.3.1.2 *The MI and Sovereignty*

How then does the *Instrument* provide for a state to maintain its tax sovereignty on those subject matters which the BRICS have refused to be resolved by MAP? The answer to this is in two parts: the first being the direct reservation to the MAP Article (Article 16) and the second being the savings clause (Article 11). The Article 16 reservation is that the state must have met the minimum standard for improving dispute resolution under the OECD/G20 BEPS Package which is firstly, the state's DTCs must provide that the person can present the case to the CA of the state of which the person is a resident, while the second part, is that for cases where the taxpayer is

---

1916. At https://www.oecd.org/tax/dispute/Brazil-Dispute-Resolution-Profile.pdf, September 2016.
1917. India 2015/2016 MOF Report, p. 204(f), http://finmin.nic.in/reports/AnnualReport2015-16.pdf.
1918. China agreed to increase focus on MAP and has done so through establishing in the International Department an anti-avoidance team to hire many TP experts. EY, Global Tax Alert News from TP, October 2016.
1919. *Supra* n. 1618.
1920. *Supra* n. 1617.
1921. *Supra* n. 1917, p. 213.
1922. Including thin capitalisation and CFC.
1923. At http://www.oecd.org/tax/dispute/Russia%20Dispute-Resolution-Profile.pdf, December 2016; http://www.oecd.org/tax/dispute/India-Dispute-Resolution-Profile.pdf, November 2016; http://www.oecd.org/tax/dispute/South-Africa-Dispute-Resolution-Profile.pdf, September 2016.
1924. At http://www.oecd.org/tax/dispute/China-Dispute-Resolution-Profile.pdf, September 2016.

claiming ND Article protection and the CA considers that MAP is inapplicable in that instance, that bilateral notification or consultation with the CA of the other state has been implemented (Article 16(5)(a)) to deal with the situation. Article 11 stipulates that the state's right to tax may not be compromised except in specified circumstances, such as when it reserves (Article 11(3)(a)) on a resident's right to request the CAs (i.e., MAP) to consider a case of taxation not in accordance with the DTC (Article 11(1)(f)). Within the boundaries of these two rights, the room for a state to reserve is limited because that reservation would be applicable to the entire savings clause and not simply to MAP.

9.3.1.3 BRICS, MAP and Sovereignty

Considering then how the BRICS may deal with their need to reserve on certain subject matters and not on others they find themselves in a very difficult position. They either reserve on MAP as a whole, which rationally is not likely to be their preferred position or do not reserve at all, which also would not be their preferred position. For this reason, rationally, the BRICS will not reserve on MAP but instead tactically, will refuse to agree a settlement through MAP on subject matters where they believe their sovereignty is, or maybe compromised leaving their sovereignty to be protected through options available to them contained within the mandatory and binding arbitration provisions. Agreeing for all matters to be referred to MAP would provide a level playing field for potential FDI providers.

9.3.2 Binding and Mandatory Arbitration

This leads to investigating the scope for the BRICS to protect their sovereignty through this process.

9.3.2.1 BEPS Recommendation

The germ for the mandatory and binding recommendation was formulated by the OECD more than twelve years[1925] ago but because before BEPS, the BRICS had little formal status within the OECD's infrastructure for developing tax policy, they had little opportunity to formally comment on it. This changed with their admission as associate members for BEPS and with the BEPS *Action Plan 14's* proposal for binding and compulsory arbitration to be included in the *MI* because the 'business community and a number of countries consider … (said that the) best way to resolve disputes was through MAP'.[1926]

1925. Improving the Resolution of Tax Treaty Disputes p. 14, Report adopted by the Committee on Fiscal Affairs on 30 Jan. 2007, http://www.oecd.org/ctp/dispute/38055311.pdf; http://www.oecd.org/ctp/dispute/oecdaimstoimproveinternationaltaxdisputesmechanisms.htm.
1926. Final Report 14, para. 62.

The *MI* provides for a state to *choose to apply* compulsory and binding arbitration and when it does so to notify the Depositary (Article 18). In relation to those matters which MAP failed to resolve, the *person who presented the case to the CA* for MAP[1927] shall be the person who can request[1928] the case be submitted to arbitration *according to any rules or procedures agreed* upon by the CAs (Article 19(1)). It is possible to divine from these provisions how a member could frustrate the mandatory and binding process to protect its sovereignty. First, it may decide not to elect that the process applies to any of its disputes, which, rationally, is a decision none of the BRICS is likely to take. Second, since it is the person who presented the case to the CA who has the right to apply for mandatory and binding arbitration, members where the taxpayer has no right to present the case to MAP, as in China, or in SA or where a taxpayer does not have a right request MAP to deal with domestic anti-abuse provisions, will protect their sovereignty.

The *MI* (Article 19) allows persons not to accept the arbitration decision ((4)(b)(i)), where that decision is found to be invalid by the final decision of a court of one of the contracting states ((4)(b)(ii)) or when a person directly impacted by the case pursues litigation in any court or administrative tribunal on issues already resolved by the arbitration ((4)(b)(iii)). Therefore, states desiring to protect sovereignty could simply refuse to accept the decision or they establish within their domestic laws' provisions that decisions of their courts or of administrative tribunals (either as a matter of law or as a matter of administrative policy or practice) would override the MAP decision. They could also reserve on the right to transfer a dispute to arbitration when domestic litigation (either before submission to arbitration or during the arbitration process) had considered the issue ((12) (a)).

These provisions present to the BRICS many opportunities to frustrate the implementation of a mandatory and binding arbitration decision and because of that it becomes relevant to investigate whether their existing law already provides for the opportunities to do so. Brazil[1929] does not allow a matter to progress to MAP when the taxpayer has previously sought to resolve the dispute through administrative or judicial process. China[1930] prevents taxpayers from claiming MAP when a dispute is being heard by a Court or Tribunal or has been decided by a Court or Tribunal. SA[1931] allows MAP to be accessed at the same time as the matter is proceeding through the Courts or administrative tribunal but disallows MAP when a decision has been determined by a court. Russia[1932] allows MAP to proceed at the same time as the dispute is proceeding through the Courts or Administrative Tribunal but it is unclear whether MAP can be applied when a decision has been finally determined by a court or administrative tribunal. India[1933] allows MAP both where the taxpayer has sought to resolve the dispute through a domestic court or tribunal and where that court or tribunal has

---

1927. *Supra* n. 1893, Article 19(4).
1928. *Ibid.*, Article 19(1).
1929. *Supra* n. 1916.
1930. *Supra* n. 1924.
1931. *Supra* n. 1923.
1932. *Ibid.*
1933. *Ibid.*

already decided the case. Therefore, Brazil, Russia, China and SA are able to frustrate an arbitration decision under Article 19(4)(b)(ii) or (iii) of the *MI* while India seems it cannot. In order to strengthen their protection of the sovereign right to tax, each of the BRICS should include in their domestic laws a provision reflecting Article 19(4)(b)(i).

In the *MI* also allowing the states to ignore the arbitration decision when within three months from the decision being delivered to them, the CAs agree on a different resolution of the unresolved issues (Article 24(2), it provides further opportunities for sovereignty to be protected in direct negotiations).

9.3.2.2 Arbitration Rules

The question then is whether the rules of international arbitration could be adopted by the CAs as the rules for use in a mandatory and binding arbitration. This is possible where a state reserved on the *MI's* default rules[1934] and is relevant because the *MI* provides flexibility in the rules by which the arbitration is conducted. The flexibility is further extended by allowing the chosen rules to apply to all cases or simply the one case under consideration. Should the member choose rules which protects its sovereignty then this supports its weaponry to minimize the probability of the arbitration arriving at a decision not in the interests of its sovereignty. The related question is whether were the BRICS to adopt flexible rules instead of the default rules that the landscape for increased inbound FDI would improve.

UNCTAD[1935] has explained that those developing countries which improve their rules and regulatory transparency stand the best chance of maintaining or even increasing their inbound FDI when current economic predictions expect a negative influence on inbound FDI[1936] for a protracted period. While countries traditionally focus on investment incentives as devices to encourage FDI, facilitating new investment treaties which establish 'predictability' as a focus is seen as being important in 23%[1937] of cases.

Predictability covers anticipating and dealing with in the Investment Agreement, those matters which could give rise to disputes as well as agreeing the procedures for use when resolving the dispute.[1938] Investment disputes include excessive corporation tax charges amounting to expropriation.[1939] From a review of the BITs and similar investment agreements entered into by the BRICS, it is evident that only Brazil's new investor treaties focus on that facilitation which means it is as a country, improving the perceptions of the FDI providers of it as a place to invest.

1934. *Ibid.*, Article 23(1).
1935. UNCTAD Global Action Menu, September 2016.
1936. UNCTAD, Global Investment Trends Monitor, No. 25, February 2017, p. 7.
1937. *Supra* n. 1936, p. 4.
1938. Mediation and regular consultation between the regulators on investors' specific investment concerns.
1939. Chapter 8, section 8.3.

Brazil's new arrangements for resolving investment disputes[1940] are based on a process similar to mediation and this new process is potentially a model which the other BRICS could follow as alternative rules to those proposed in the *MI's* binding and mandatory arbitration Article. Another alternative could be the rules provided by Canada[1941] where the arbitration can be concluded by abandonment[1942] (one of the parties walking away) and which are flexible on location, language and settlement offers. Either the rules of Brazil or of Canada could represent the arrangements which the CAs adopt when beginning a mandatory and binding arbitration covering an expropriation tax dispute.

9.3.3 Human Rights

Were the BRICS to adopt these rules would it be relevant to whether the investor's human right to a fair trial[1943] had been breached, an important issue considering that protecting human rights is a core principle of the *BRICS Leaders*.[1944]

Relevant to this consideration is the *European Court of Human Rights* acknowledgment that 'matters outside the scope of Article 6 include tax proceedings: tax matters still form part of the hard core of public-authority prerogatives, with the public nature of the relationship between the taxpayer and the community remaining predominant'.[1945] This may explain the existence of little evidence of the BRICS Courts' specifically citing an investor's right to a fair trial as having been breached as a factor when resolving cross-border tax disputes (section 8.5), except in *Yukos*.[1946] A right to a fair trial is not relevant in China. Therefore, were the BRICS to adopt the binding and mandatory arbitration proposal and were they to adopt alternative arbitration rules, such as the Canadian or the Brazil rules, it would be difficult to sustain an argument that the investor had not received a fair trial. Were the rules adopted by the CAs to permit one of the parties to 'walk away' as constituting the conclusion of the arbitration, then this too would not constitute a breach of the right to a fair trial because both states had agreed to the rules. Therefore, were the BRICS to reserve on the *MI's* own rules and adopt the alternative rules discussed in this Chapter, then it is unlikely this represents an impediment to inbound FDI on human rights grounds, because the right to a fair trial is not a right conferred on investors.

1940. Martin, Brazil's New Investment Treaties: Outside Looking … Out?, University of California, Berkeley, 16 Jun. 2015, http://kluwerarbitrationblog.com/2015/06/16/brazils-new-investment-treaties-outside-looking-out-2/, last visited 10 Feb. 2017.
1941. At http://adric.ca/wp-content/uploads/2015/11/ADRIC_Arbitration_Rules_Booklet.pdf.
1942. ADR Institute of Canada, Inc. Rules, 5.5.1(b).
1943. Right to fair trial provides fairness and certainty of the judicial process and prevents Governments from abusing their powers and is enshrined in legislation in each of the BRICS except for China (*supra* n. 1733).
1944. *Supra* n. 1731.
1945. Guide on Article 6 of the Convention – Right to a fair trial (civil limb), 2013, p. 12/66.
1946. *Supra* n. 1737.

9.4 CONCLUSION

This Chapter set out to identify whether a link exists between the level of BRICS inbound FDI and their methodology for countering DTC abuse and their approach to supplementary methodology for resolving cross-border tax disputes and if so, whether more closely aligning with the developed world's approach to both would clear the way for an increase in inbound FDI at the expense of a materially adverse reduction in their tax sovereignty.

The research has concluded that only in relation to Russia and SA may it be asserted with some justification that an improvement in geopolitical and governance issues for the former and investor protection for the latter, would lead to an increasing FDI and that to link in how the BRICS counter DTC abuse it would be necessary to conclude that their approach to countering those abuses was either a matter of governance or of investor protection (i.e., expropriation). This Chapter has also concluded that the adoption of the *MI's* mandatory and binding arbitration would improve the landscape for inbound FDI by improving governance and investor protection (but only where excessive taxation amounted to an abusive undertaking) but again with those features relevant to Russia and SA only. Were the BRICS to adopt the mandatory and binding arbitration provisions in the *MI* they would align with the developed world and in doing so would not give rise to a material reduction in the right to tax sovereignty because the proposed arbitration rules build in flexibility to protect that sovereignty.

CHAPTER 10
Summary of Conclusions

10.1 RESEARCH PROBLEMS AND HYPOTHESES

The problem researched in this study is whether the shape of the BRICS international tax law has diverged from the core of the developed world's international tax law and, if so, whether that divergence reflects the necessity to counter an elevated level of evasion and avoidance in the BRICS, resulting from MNEs international transactions or behaviour or adopting tax haven structures to facilitate illicit outflows. This study also researches whether the form taken by their international tax laws has been influenced by their, in the main, limited tax authorities' manpower to identify and counter those transactions, structures or behaviour and whether the formulation of those procedures has been influenced by coordination between their tax authorities or international governance institutions. The study also researches whether were the BRICS to adopt the BEPS recommendations that they would become more attractive jurisdictions for inbound FDI.

In considering the problems, the author established two hypotheses. The first is that the BRICS tax authorities have responded to the substantial increase in cross-border transactions and structures used to facilitate illicit trade flows resulting in evasion or avoidance, by increasing the deterrents included in their international tax law through widening its coverage and increasing notifications, because the absolute manpower numbers and competency were incompatible with the task. The second hypothesis is that outside of TP, there is little evidence of coordination between the BRICS in formulating their international tax law even though there is political agreement at the *BRICS Leaders'* level for this to happen.

10.2 TAX AUTHORITY CAPACITY

The author has deduced that the BRICS tax authorities' manpower available to counter evasion and avoidance was limited in the immediate post-liberalization period and had not during the 2009–2013 period for which published statistics are available shown a material increase in numbers except for China. This deduction is based on the published statistics for audit and investigation manpower confirming that the author believes to be relatively small manpower numbers in Brazil, India and SA both on an absolute and relative basis, while the limited information available on the manpower employed in TP teams between 2011/2014 confirms fewer than 100 persons except for China where around 1,000 officers are projected. Rationally therefore, it can be deduced that the BRICS' tax authorities have had to formulate their international tax law for countering the abuses in the knowledge that limited manpower requires systems and procedures which outsources the obligation to disclose to the taxpayers and leaving the tax authority less reliant on its own staff.

10.3 TAX COORDINATION AND COOPERATION

The *BRICS Leaders* and the *Heads of Revenue* have agreed on the need for cooperation and coordination of their systems and procedures for countering evasion and avoidance, taxing of income in the jurisdiction where the economic activity occurred and value created, exploration of enhanced cooperation towards countering base erosion and promoting information exchange amongst their tax authorities' including localizing the *BEPS Action Plans* and the *Common Reporting Standard*. This agreement amongst the BRICS conflicts with *Pistone's*[1947] question of whether the BRICS will 'meaningfully organize'. The author also concludes that the *Heads of Revenue* have agreed that coordination and cooperation should occur, but deduces from the practical coordination and cooperation coverage being limited to mispriced intangible transactions and the constituents of intangibles (especially in China and India) such as location specific benefits, indirect asset transfers and exchanging information, that these are the three policy areas where the BRICS are jointly shaping their international tax law. This deduction describes a trend between China and India to mutually assist which is an evolution from the position which *Pistone*[1948] explained.

10.4 INTERNATIONAL TAX LAW

Having identified the relevance in shaping their international tax law of limited manpower capacity and the agreement between the *Heads of Revenue* to concentrate on countering mispriced intangible transactions, indirect asset disposals and exchanging information, the author now summarizes his conclusions and answers the problems set for this study.

In relation to why the BRICS adopted the developed world's core international tax policy in the immediate post-liberalization period, he concludes that none of the tax authorities' limited manpower capacity, their cooperation, the volume of illicit outbound flows or the global financial governance institutions was the most significant

---

1947. *Supra* n. 3, p. 505.
1948. *Ibid.*, p. 502.

reason for the BRICS adopting the OECD core. The major reason the author believes, in that period was the BRICS realization that because the FDI provider investor countries were predominantly developed world resident, adoption of the investor countries core international tax law and policy was unlikely to deter them from providing FDI. In relation to later times, the author has concluded that the 'prisoner's dilemma' and the 'lock-in' are the reasons that Russia, China and SA have broadly followed the *OECD Model Convention* but the 'political clout' theory explains the reason that Brazil and India continue to closely follow the UN approach to DTCs. Also, it can be deduced that Accession to the WTO has materially influenced the shape of Russia and China's international tax law and while the *BITs* and *TIPs* influence has been to a lesser extent, they explain the inclusion in the BRICS international tax policy and law of provisions designed to counter the MNEs who ignored the request for the FDI not to be provided in transactional or structural formats which artificially reduced the source country's tax base (Chapter 2).

In relation to whether the BRICS have widened the constituents of evasion and avoidance from that of developed world, the conclusion arrived at is that they have when treating mispriced cross-border transactions and using tax havens without commercial substance, as evasion and potentially criminal evasion. These countries have taken this approach because, having identified them as the principal transaction and structure forms which facilitated the illicit offshore flow of funds, treating those transactions or structures as evasion allowed for the potential imposition of sanctions on company officers: an approach designed to deter these people from adopting the transactions or structures. The widening also compensates for the limited tax authority manpower to identify and audit the transactions. With the tax laws of neither Brazil nor India containing a GAAR, this gave rise to an onus on their tax authority manpower to pursue of procedures to counter these transactions (Chapter 3).

With respect to why the BRICS widened the approach from that of the developed world in countering thin capitalization, TP and CFC strategies, the question was in doing so they intended to increase the deterrent, or, as the author deduces, that it was because by widening the range of relationships subject to the rules (which is relevant with the BRICS definition of evasion), increasing the notification obligations and in certain instances, treating the failure to correctly notify as evasion, this encouraged the MNEs to comply with provisions not generally applicable in the developed world. Also, deduced is that the nature of the MNEs notification obligations was tightened, reversing the onus of proof and Brazil's exclusion of an active income exemption from its CFC rules and its fixed margin approach to TP, are all designed to compensate for the limited tax authority manpower. The widened TP rules, particularly in India and China, and Brazil's different TP rules, represents the embodiment of the *BRICS Leaders* policy of ensuring profits (including those from intangibles) are taxed in the jurisdiction where they were created and activities performed which gave rise to the income or gain. The author deduces this policy is relevant for India in the absence of thin capitalization and CFC rules as the main tool at the IRD's disposal to counter mispriced transactions and structures without substance. The applicability of the BPA DTC override in Brazil represents a serious flaw in Brazil's CFC rules while it is deduced from certain of the DTCs and concepts of the other BRICS that except for Russia, the

BPA DTC override may also be sustainable in those States for certain DTCs. This override is potentially secure from savings provisions in the relevant DTCs because of definitional conflicts. The author believes that the failure to rectify these conflicts could lead to unwarranted consumption of limited tax authority manpower (Chapter 4).

The *BRICS Leaders* have confirmed the importance of cooperation and coordination in designing and operating the exchanging architecture, and from this confirmation the author deduces that the BRICS, particularly, India and China, because of their positions of influence in the committees designing and monitoring the adoption of the emerging architecture systems and procedures, have positioned themselves to shape the procedures to the extent possible, to minimize divergences from their own arrangements. In relation to that emerging architecture, the India and China existing systems and procedures are broadly compatible while changes are required in SA and especially in Russia, where constitutional changes are required to allow free outbound exchange. With the India and China systems being compatible with the new architecture, few constraints exist on their tax authorities' manpower (but some constraints in Russia and SA exist) when facilitating the receipt of information for use in pursuing mispriced transactions and non-substantiated tax haven use. In relation to the traditional exchanging architecture, with the BRICS' Article 26 now largely modelled on the developed world's Article 26, the impediments for free exchange under their DTCs are now t limited but their capacity for exchanging with the tax preferred jurisdictions is limited with approx. 50% of the BRICS signed TIEAs currently enforced except for China where most TIEAs are enforced. The limited available statistics on information exchange is evidence of the existing DTCs and TIEAs having failed to produce but a trickle of exchanged information which, rationally, supports the BRICS' decision to adopt positions of influence in designing the new system to ensure that, where possible, an increase in their access to the information to counter international tax abuse producing illicit outflows from their countries. With Brazil failing to enforce any TIEAs, its small DTC network and its failure to enforce the MCAA, it seems that it has decided it does not need to implement the BRICS agenda for information sharing because the information it requires to enforce its SAARs is available in Brazil already and because its expects foreign tax authorities to exchange when the failure to do so constitutes evasion in Brazil (Chapter 5).

The *BRICS Leaders* and the *Heads of Revenue* have confirmed an intention to cooperate and coordinate in the design of DTC provisions countering benefit abuse but the author deduces the absence of a consistent approach to do so. China broadly deals with DTC abuse through its beneficial ownership test, the meaning of which is wider than that in the developed world and the BRICS can deny DTC benefits through asserting the foreign person is not DTC resident by applying POEM, a new concept in Russia and in India, because a qualification conflict exists between the BRICS and the developed world in relation to what each believes POEM means. The BRICS' POEM (except for Brazil which is confined to incorporation) is more influenced by the place where economic activities are undertaken than the developed world which relies on the place where the highest decisions are made as the place where POEM is to be found. The BRICS have limited opportunities to reject DTC benefits by applying an LOB or an MPT because only a small proportion of their DTCs contain those provisions, but in order to avoid conflicts through the divergences with the developed world, their trend for LOBs is the 'qualified person' and for MPTs is the dividend, interest and royalty approach except for China which extends to capital gains, although anti-abuse, especially in India is important. In relation to denying DTC benefits, the author concludes that India and Brazil have increased the deterrent, in India's case, by being able to declare a country as being non-compliant (Cyprus) when not fully exchanging or in Brazil, by treating the failure to exchange as evasion. Also concluded is that in the BRICS taxing profits from the indirect transfer of immoveable property in the country where the profit was created (situs of the immoveable property) and with China and India extending this to the indirect transfer of moveable property, that this approach embodies the *BRICS Leader's* requirement to tax profits in the country where they were created (Chapter 6).

In order to arrange, where possible, that the BEPS recommendations reflected the BRICS positions, the BRICS positioned themselves as influencers such as by joining the *Bureau Plus* committee formulating the recommendations. With China making in excess of 1,000 representations on the formulation and drafting of the recommendations and having established a BEPS Task Force with more than fifty members, it had a clear commitment to influence and one consistent with the growth in its tax authority manpower. Without publicly available information on the other BRICS' level of influence outside of the *Bureau Plus*, the author is unable to deduce the level of commitment to influence. In relation to the recommendations covering TP and particularly intangibles and location benefits, the author believes that the BRICS influence has contributed to shaping the recommendation in a form compatible with the policy outlined by China, India and SA in Chapter 10 of the *UN TP Manual*, a Chapter which as the author believes evidences the 'proper dialogue' which *Pistone*[1949] was calling for. So far as the BRICS localizing many of the other recommendations, it is deduced that doing so in Brazil, Russia and SA would strengthen their international tax law while those for India and China would not be strengthened in some instances because the recommendations were, in those cases, reflective of pre-existing policies of India and China. Also, concluded is that Brazil's different approach was not likely to be compatible with localization. In relation to coordination, it seems likely that confirmatory evidence exists at the political level that coordination is taking place, but that while the BRICS agreed to localize the recommendations, especially those covering evasion, avoidance, DTC abuse and exchanging information, there is little evidence of any significant coordination at the administration level outside of TP described in the *UN TP Manual* and exchanging of information. In relation to the *MI*, it is likely the BRICS would not localize unless doing so includes an opt-out from the binding and mandatory MAP because of the concern that agreeing to binding MAP would compromise sovereignty over the taxing of profits at the place where they were created (Chapter 7).

The differences the author has identified in this study between the BRICS and the developed world's international tax law have the capability of translating into

---

1949. *Ibid.*, p. 502.

disputation and much of it. Outside of the traditional methods for resolving cross-border tax disputes, supplementary dispute resolution procedures exist, including arbitration but these are currently neither widely applied in the BRICS nor have the BRICS included provisions in their international tax law which encourage their use. The BRICS failure to embrace arbitration for tax purposes, including the BITs provisions (except for India), is explained by the reluctance to compromise their right to sovereignty over the tax dispute resolution procedure, except in India's case, but then the safety latch comes from the Indian Arbitration Act being used. There is no publicly available evidence of constraints from tax authority manpower in using Arbitration. The WTO DSU has been used by China, Brazil and India in resolving State/State international tax disputes even though its use has been limited to a few cases involving taxation. Since China generally is in agreement with the DSU process, the author deduces that were the BIT or MAP dispute resolution procedures to include the WTO DSU procedures then the BRICS would have less reason to abstain from MAP and Arbitration. While protecting human rights is an objective of the *BRICS Leaders* agenda, little evidence exists of this translating into that factor being an influencer of their international tax law or into the dispute resolution provisions, except for Russia and India. With China yet to sign the *International Covenant,* human rights issues are irrelevant (Chapter 8).

Further, the author concludes that there is little probability of inbound FDI increasing were the BRICS to adopt the BEPS measures to counter abusive transactions (except for Russia and SA) and there are, relying on sovereignty grounds, few reasons for the BRICS to reject the Instrument's proposed binding and compulsory arbitration provisions (Chapter 9).

Finally, the author's answer to the research questions are that the shape of the BRICS international tax policy and law has diverged from the developed world's core international tax law with the divergences strengthening the BRICS rights to counter mispriced transactions and unsubstantiated use of tax havens. In shaping their international tax laws, the limitations arising from tax authority manpower capacity have been relevant and also that while there is political agreement for the coordination of the BRICS approach to countering the abuse and adopting the *Common Reporting Standard,* the coordination focus has been squarely on mispriced transactions, indirect asset transfers and the exchanging information architecture. With their divergences from the developed world's international tax policy and law to DTC benefits potentially leading to double taxation because of definition conflicts, the author proposes the *Heads of Revenue* adopt the Annex A recommendations which would both strengthen their international tax policy law and avoid DTC abuse while conserving manpower and improving the dispute resolution procedures.

ANNEX
Communiqué of BRICS, Heads of Revenue Meeting

We, the Heads and Representatives of the Revenue Administrations of the Federal Republic of Brazil, the Russian Federation, the Republic of India, the People's Republic of China, and the Republic of South Africa being committed to a globally fair and modern tax system, hereby agree to incorporate the following policies into our taxation laws in order that income is taxed in the country of source, conflict between our tax authorities is avoided and little materially adverse consequences arise from the small number of manpower in our tax authorities to counter abuse:
Conserving Manpower:

1. Training

Within five years all our officers focusing on countering mispriced trading, financing or intangible transactions shall have been fully trained on the relevant international tax law and policy in conjunction with international governance institutions.

2. Notifications

In relation to all transactions entered into by one of our residents with a foreign associate or with companies controlled by such residents, that documents fully and accurately describing those transactions shall be contemporaneously prepared and in a form acceptable to our tax authorities and provided to our tax authorities in an independently certified Annual Report, within 45 days from the end of the Accounting Period in which the transaction occurs. Should the taxpayer's disclosure be incorrect, misleading or late, our tax authorities shall deem that to be evasion with sanctions applicable to members of the Enterprise's Board which provided the incorrect, misleading or late disclosure.

Annex

3. Information Exchange

We acknowledge the importance of the exchanging information architecture for countering mispriced trading, financing or intangible transactions or the use of structures in tax preferred jurisdictions lacking substance, and require that the exchanging provisions in all our DTCs be modelled on OECD Article 26 and all our TIEAs be expeditiously enforced and our legal systems be compatible with the computer systems sharing information under the *Common Reporting Standard*.

Strengthen International tax law:

1. Evasion

We confirm that materially mispriced trading, financing or intangible transactions or the use of structures in tax preferred jurisdictions lacking substance, constitutes evasion with sanctions being applied to members of the Enterprise's Board which entered into the transaction or established the structure with 'materially' for this purpose being an atleast 5% deviation from the ALP.

2. BEPS

We confirm that profits should be taxed in the jurisdiction in which they were created and for group intangibles the allocation must reflect functions, assets and risks of the respective group members' contributions in the creation or development with the Notification requirements set out above being applicable.

3. Treaty Abuse

That beneficial ownership shall be the main factor determining whether foreign persons qualify for DTC benefits and for this purpose, the foreign person shall be the beneficial owner, when its use of functions, assets and risks was the main reason for its receipt of the amount on which the treaty claim is made. We agree that where it is not the main reason, but the foreign person satisfies the qualified person test then DTC benefits will be granted.

Dispute Resolution:

1. Common definitions

We agree that without savings provisions in DTCs being based on common interpretations, the prospect for double taxation is increased and therefore require our tax authorities to limit double taxation by adopting common terminology and meanings.

2. MAP

We confirm we adopt MAP for resolving international tax disputes but providing MAP incorporates the arbitration dispute settling procedures of the WTO DSU. Where our tax authorities are unable to resolve the dispute using MAP we agree to accept notification from an investor under a BIT providing the BIT incorporates the WTO DSU settling procedures and providing the method of arbitration is one chosen by our respective tax authority.

3. Human Rights

We acknowledge the importance of human rights in the design and implementation of our international taxation laws and require our taxation authorities to respect the right to a fair trial.

FDI

We confirm that our Members shall adopt dispute resolution procedures, which, shall avoid discouraging the provision by MNEs of FDI to our members.

Bibliography

(2014 (Volume 68), No 2). *Report of the Proceedings of the Fourth Assembly of the International Association of Tax Judges.* Bulletin for International Taxation

(2014). *India's Response to UN BEPS Questionnaire.* www.un.org/esa/ffd/wp-content/uploads/2014/10/ta-BEPS-CommentsIndia.pdf

(May 2012). *Black Money: White Paper.* Minister of Finance, Department of Revenue and Central Board of Direct Taxes

(May 2015). *Manual on Exchange of Information.* Government of India, Ministry of Finance Department of Revenue Central Board of Direct Taxes Foreign Tax & Tax Research Division

Abreu, J. (November 2010). *A Suggested Interpretation Note for Section 9D of the Income Tax Act.* Potchefstroom Campus of the North-West University

ACAMS. (March 2011). Ultimate Beneficial Ownership. *ACAMS South African Chapter*

ADB. (September 2013). *Tax Policy and Administration Research and Capacity Development, Project Number: 47231-001 Research and Development Technical Assistance (RDTA)*

Advisors, B. (5 July 2013). 'Permanent Establishment' Needs to Be Long Term Nature-CESTAT, Dehli Bench Order. *BMR Edge, Tax & Regulatory*, Doc 2013-16275

Advisors, B. (6 January 2013). Asia Pacific Performance SICAV Ruling. *BMR Edge Tax & Regulatory*, Doc 2013-232

Agarwal, A. (2013). The Taxation of Foreign Passive Income for Groups of Companies – India. *IFA Cahiers - Volume 98A*, 359–375

Agarwal, A. (2016). Dispute Resolution Procedures in International Tax Matters – India. *IFA Cahiers- Volume 101A*, 303–317

Agarwal, A. (March 2014). Thin Capitalisation in India. *www.lowtax.net/articles/Thin-Capitalization-in-India*

Agrawal, K. (2013). *Transfer Pricing in India: Government Guidance Note on Report Under Section 92E, Indian ICAEW.* Indian Chartered Accountants

Ainsworth, R. (3 December 2013). UN Transfer Pricing Guidelines: Brazil's Contribution to Chapter. *Tax Notes International*, Doc 2013-24905

Ajinkya, B. (2012). The Debt-Equity Conundrum- India. *IFA Cahiers- Volume 97B*, 329–349

Alexandrova, J. (2012, March). *Tax Discrimination Against Foreign Investors in Russia.* Retrieved 28 December 2015, from www.terralex.org/publication/57939f6942

Bibliography

Allen, C. (2001–2002). The Effective Role of the United States International Tax Law in Dismantling Apartheid in the Union of South Africa and in the Rebuilding of South Africa after the Demise of Apartheid. *27 T. Marshall L. Rev. 165*, pages 167–182

Alvarrenga. (2013, Volume 67, No 7). International/European Union/Brazil/Spain/United Kingdom/United States Preventing Tax Avoidance: Is There Convergence in the Way Countries Counter Tax Avoidance? *Bulletin for International Taxation*, 348–363

Andref, W. (October 2014). Outward Foreign Direct Investment by Brazilian and Indian Multinational Companies: Comparison with Russian and Chinese Multinationals. *International Conference "The BRICS Countries: International Instability, Growth Trajectories and Structural Transformations", People's Friendship University of Russia*, (pp. 1–44)

Andref, W. (Vol. 12, No 2). Outward Foreign Direct Investment from BRIC Countries: Comparing Strategies of Brazilian, Russian, Indian and Chinese Multinational Companies. *The European Journal of Comparative Economics*, 79–131

Arner, D. (2011). Redesigning the Architecture of the Global Financial System. *Faculty of Law, University of Hong Kong*, Law Research Paper 2011/008

Arnold, B. (2011). India, Tax Treaty News. *Bulletin for International Taxation, Vol 65, No 2*, 650–654

Ashley, S. (January 2013). How BRICS Can Influence Tax Policy. *International Tax Review*

Ault, H. (1990). Taxing International Income: An Analysis of the US System and its Economic Premises. In a. e. Razin, A., *Taxation and the Global Economy*. Chicago: University Press of Chicago

Austin, J. (1832). *The Province of Jurisprudence Determined*

Auyeung, P. (June 2008). Taxation Trends and Issues in the People's Republic of China: 1949 to 2006. *Bulletin For International Taxation*, pp. 248–258

Avdonina, E. (2008). Financing: a Global Survey of Thin Capitalization and Transfer Pricing Rules in 35 Selected Countries: Russia. *International Transfer Pricing Journal November/December 2008*, 336

Avi-Yonah, R. (2004). International Tas as International Law. *University of Michigan, Public Law and Legal Theory*, Research Paper No 41

Avi-Yonah, R. (3 August 2004). Bridging The North/South Divide: International Redistribution and Tax Competition. *University of Michigan Law School*, www.SSRN.com

Avi-Yonah, R. (6 January 2014). Transfer Pricing is Still Dead: Reviving Enforcement. *Tax Notes International*, Doc 2013-28162

Ayub, C. (September 2015). Navigating Brazil's TP Complexity. *International Tax Review*

Azevedo, R. (2010). *Tax Avoidance and Evasion: A Comparative Study of the Brazilian and American Legal Systems*. The George Washington University

Badenhorst, M. (2007). Conflicts in the Attribution of Income to a Person – South Africa. *IFA Cahiers- Volume 92B*, 549–566

Bagchi, A. (1994). *Tax Policy and Planning in Developing Countries*. Oxford: Oxford University Press

Baistrocchi, E. (No 4 2008). Use and Interpretation of DTCs in the Emerging World: Theory and Implications. *British Tax Review*, 352–391

Baistrocchi, E. (Vol. 33, No. 4 (2013)). The International Tax Regime and the BRIC World: Elements for a Theory. *Oxford Journal of Legal Studies*, pp. 733–766

Baistrocchi, E. Resolving Transfer Pricing Disputes: A Global Analysis, Cambridge University Press. December 2012

Bajpai, P. (2012). 'Piercing the Corporate Veil' in Taxation Matters: India and International Transactions with Special Reference to the Direct Tax Code 2010. *Bulletin for International Taxation*

Baker & McKenzie. (March 2015). *Tax Russia-Legal Alert*

Baker, P. (2000). *A Short Paper on Tax Avoidance, Tax Mitigation and Tax Evasion*. www.taxbar.com,

Baker, P. (2016). *International Arbitration in Tax Matters*. IBFD and Institute for Austrian and International Tax Law

Baker, P. (February 2007). Beneficial Ownership: After Indofood. *www.taxbar.com*

Baker, P. (June 2014). Some Recent Decisions of the European Court of Human Rights on Tax Matters. *European Taxation*, 250–252

Baker, P. (May 2013). Improper Use of Tax Treaties, Tax Avoidance and Tax Evasion. *Paper No 9-A in Papers on Selected Topics in Administration of Tax Treaties for Developing Countries for the United Nations*

Baker, P. *Double Taxation Convention and International tax law*. Sweet and Maxwell, Loose Leaf

Bal, A. (2014). Tax Incentives: Ill-Advised Tax Policy or Growth Catalysts? *European Taxation*, 63–70

Bank, W. (1990). *Report No. 8147-R Brazil, An Agenda for Tax Reform (In Three Volumes) Volume Ill: Assessment of the Brazilian Direct Taxes*. Country Operations Division Brazil Department Latin America and the Caribbean Region

Bank, W. (2013). *Financing For Development, Post 2015*

Bank, W. (October 2011). *Tax Transparency Raising Government Revenue Through Responsible Tax Administration*. International Finance Corporation

Bank, W. (October 2013). *Financing For Development Post-2015*. World Bank

Bao, L. (November 2001). Several Issues at the Forefront of the Current Tax Theory Debate. *Asia-Pacific Tax Bulletin*, 288–296

Barandt, P. (last visited 15 September 2015). German Criminal Tax Law from an American Perspective Including Criminal Evasion of German Inheritance Tax, http://www.barandt.com/e_german_criminal_tax_fraud_law_from_an_american _perspective_including_criminal_evasion_of_german_inheritace_estate_tax.html

Baxi, D. (May 2016). Mauritius No Longer A 'Sweet Spot. *Mondaq*

Bellaver, R. (17 November 2014). Tax Planning and Treaty Shopping in Brazil. *Tax Notes International*, 627–632

Belyakova, M. (2014). Draft Law Would Introduce New CFC Regime in Russia. *Worldwide Tax Daily*, 21805

Bibliography

Benshalom, I. (No 08: 43). The New Poor at Our Gates: Global Justice Implications of International Trade and Tax Law. *Northwestern University School of Law*, Public Law and Legal Theory Series

Berger, A. (2008). China's New Bilateral Investment Treaty Programme, Substance, Rational and Implications for International Investment Law Making. *Paper Prepared for the American Society of International Law International Economic Law Interest Group*

Berger. https://www.die-gdi.de/uploads/media/Berger_ChineseBITs.pdf). China's New BIT Programme: Substance, Rational and Implications for International Investment Law Making. *German Development Institute*

Bergsman, J. (November 1999). Improving Russia's Policy on Foreign Direct Investment. *World Bank*

Besada, H. (March 2013). South Africa in the BRICS-Opportunities, Challenges and Prospects. *Africa Insight*, Vol 42(4), pp. 1–15

Bevan, A. (October 2000). The Determinants of Foreign Direct Investment in Transition Economies. *William Davidson Institute Working Paper No 342*

Bhatia, M. (July/August 2012). How the OECD Is Promoting Tax Transparency. *www.internationaltaxreview.com*, 27–28

Bian, J. (2013). China (People's Rep.) – Taxation of Dividends, Interest, Royalties and Technical Service Fees. *Asia-Pacific Tax Bulletin, Volume 19, No. 4*, 236–240

Biang, J. (2013 (Volume 19, No. 4). Taxation of Dividends, Interest, Royalties and Technical Service Fees. *Asia-Pacific Tax Bulletin*, 236–240

Bird, R. (2012, No 6). Subnational Taxation in Large Emerging Countries: BRICS Plus One. *Institute on Municipal Finance and Governance*, 1–50

Bispo, R. (2013) Volume 67, No. 7. Cross-Border Intra-Group Hybrid Finance: A Comparative Analysis of the Legal Approach Adopted by Brazil, the United Kingdom and the United States'. *Bulletin For International Taxation*, 364–378

Blerck, M. (December 2003). Company-Shareholder Taxation in South Africa: Single or Double Taxation? *International Bureau of Fiscal Documentation*, 567–573

Blouin. (January 2014). Thin Capitalization Rules and Multinational Firm Capital Structure. *IMF Working Paper, WP/14/12*

BMR. (6 January 2013, Volume 8 Issues 1.1). BMR Edge: Tax and Regulations: Asia Pacific Performance SICAV. *BMR Edge*, Doc 2013-232

Bocachica, E. (2013). Constitutionality of the Brazilian CFC Legislation. *Bulletin for International Taxation, Volume 67, No. 10*, 565–567

Bohra, V. (2008). New Tendencies in Tax Treatment of Cross-Border Interest of Corporations – India. *IFA Cahiers - Volume 93B*, 343–364

Boolell, S. (June 2013). Tax Crimes, Money Laundering Offences and International Cooperation. *Mauritius 7th IFA Conference* (pp. 647–657). Mauritius: International Taxation

Borodin, V. (March 2005). Russia: Tax and Currency Control Aspects of Outbound Investments. *IBFD Bulletin*, 121–126

Bowler, T. (2009). *Countering Tax Avoidance in the UK: Which Way Forward, The Institute for Fiscal Studies, TLRC Discussion Paper No. 7.* Tax Law Reform Committee

Bibliography

Branco, R. (2005). Source and Residence: A New Configuration of Their Principles – Brazil. *IFA Cahiers – Volume 90A*, 205–219

Branston, T. (2013). *Comments on the Discussion Document of 30 July 2013 on the OECD Guidelines (Chapter VI)*. Gazprom Marketing & Trading Ltd

Brauner, Y. (2003). An International Tax Regime in Crystallization—Realities, Experiences and Opportunities. *56 Tax Law Review*, 259

Brauner, Y. (Vol. 25). International Trade and Tax Agreements May Be Coordinated, But Not Reconciled. *Virginia Tax Review*, pp. 252–311

BRICS Communique. (23 January 2013). BRICS Countries to Jointly Develop Tax and Transfer Pricing. *Tax Notes International*, Doc 2013-1540

BRICS Communique. (5 February 2013). BRICS Countries Dissatisfied with OECD and UN Tax Policy. *Tax Notes International*, Doc 2013-2623

BRICS Report. (2012). Oxford University Press

BRICS. (July 2015). Strategy for BRICS Economic Partnership. *Ufa Summit*

BRICS. (November 2015). Communique of BRICs Heads of Revenue Meeting, pp. 1–3

Brondolo. (November 1999). Organisation Options For Tax Administration. *International Bureau of Fiscal Documentation Bulletin*, 499–512

Brooks, K. (Spring 2009). Tax Sparing: A Needed Incentive for Foreign Investment in Low Income Countries or an Unnecessary Revenue Sacrifice. *Queen's Law Journal*, 1–38

Bruk, B. (2009). New Protocol to the Russia-Cyprus Tax Treaty Initialled: End of the "Cyprus Era" in Russian Tax Planning? *European Taxation, (Volume 49), No. 10*, 464–470

Bruk, B. (2010 Volume 50, No. 12). Supreme Arbitration Court Adopts 'Disregard of Legal Entity' Approach to Combat Tax Fraud. *European Taxation*, 573–577

Bruk, B. (2010). Russia Supreme Arbitration Court Adopts 'Disregard of Legal Entity' Approach to Combat Tax Fraud. *European Taxation, 2010 (Volume 50), No. 12*, 573–577

Bruk, B. (2010). Russian Thin Capitalization Rules: Are They Compatible With Russia's Treaties. *European Taxation, November*, 506–510

Bruk, B. (2010). Tax Treaties and Tax Avoidance: Application of Anti-Avoidance Provisions – Russia. *IFA Cahiers - Volume 95A*, 685–700

Bruk, B. (2011). Key Practical Issues to Eliminate Double Taxation in Russia. IFA

Bruk, B. (2012). The Debt Equity Conundrum. *IFA Cahiers-Volume 97B*, 615–631

Bruk, B. (2013). The Taxation of Foreign Passive Income for Groups of Companies – Russia. *IFA Cahiers - Volume 98A*, 623–643

Bruno, A. (December 2007). Bringing Uniformity to Brazilian Court Decisions: Looking at the American Precedent and at Italian Living Law. *Electronic Journal of Comparative Law, vol. 11.4*

Butani, M. (2007). Transfer Pricing and Intangibles – India. *IFA Cahiers – vol. 92A*, 319–340

Butani, M. (January/February 2004). India-Tax Treaty Interpretation. *Asia-Pacific Tax Bulletin*, 56/69

Butani, M. (July/August 2014). India-Permanent Establishment Concept – An Indian Perspective. *Asia-Pacific Tax Bulletin*, 247–254

Bibliography

Butler, R. (July 2000). Taxation of Global E-Commerce. *Asia-Pacific Tax Bulletin*, 220–227

Calderón, A. (July 2014). Outward FDI in Brazil: A Matter of Economic Growth and Institutional Configuration. *Prepared for the FLACSO-ISA Joint International Conference in Buenos Aires*, pp. 1–28

Calich, I. (September 2011). *(PhD Thesis) The Impact of Globalisation on the Position of Developing Countries in the International Tax System.* London: London School of Economics

Canto, C. New Tendencies in Tax Treatment of Cross-Border Interest of Corporations, Brazil. *IFA Cahiers 2008. vol. 93B*, 151–171

Cao. (August 2010). China Clarifies Tax Rules for Enterprise Reorganizations. *Jones Day Publications*

Carmona, M. *Report of Special Rapporteur on Extreme Poverty and Human Rights.* A/HRC/26/28

Carrero. (June 2013). Transfer Pricing Disputes, Abusive Tax Schemes and the Protection of the European Convention on Human Rights Against Oppressive Tax Actions: The Yukos Case. *Bulletin for International Taxation*, 283–293

Carvalho, J. (2014). Cross-Border Outsourcing – Issues, Strategies and Solutions – Brazil. *IFA Cahiers - vol. 99A*, 155–177

Casley, A. (2011). India-Marketing Intangibles: The Latest Controversy. *ITPJ, (vol. 18), No. 3*, 165–170

Cassiolato, J. (2011). *BRICS and Development Alternatives, Innovative Systems and Policies.* London: European Communities

Castro. (December 2011). Brazil's Anti-Treaty Shopping Measures: Current and Future Developments Regarding Beneficial Ownership and Limitation on Benefits Clauses in Tax Treaties. *Bulletin for International Taxation*, 662–673

CBDT. (April 2013). *India-US Bilateral Transfer Pricing Relationship.* Government of India

Centre for Budget and Governance Accountability. (March 2013). *Tax Dodging: An Overview.* India

CFA. (2013). *Transfer Pricing Aspects of Intangibles, Revised Discussion Draft.* OECD

CFA. (July 2010). *Paper on Location Savings.* OECD

Chakravarty, A. (2012). India-Transfer Pricing Aspects of Business Restructurings. *Asia-Pacific Tax Bulletin, (vol. 18), No. 3*, 267–270

Chakravarty, A. (2013). India - Circulars on Transfer Pricing of Contract R&D Centres: The Road Ahead. *ITPJ, (vol. 20), No. 6*, 404–406

Chakravarty, A. (2014). India - BEPS Impact on TP – Relevance of Current Actions on India. *Asia-Pacific Tax Bulletin, (vol. 20), No. 4*, 269–275

Chaudhury, I. (2006 November/December). India-Structuring an Appropriate Transfer Pricing Policy. *Asia-Pacific Tax Bulletin*, 484–489

Chawla, A. (2013). Exchange of Information and Cross-Border Cooperation Between Tax Authorities – India. *IFA Cahiers 2013 - vol. 98B*, 339–358

Chawla, A. (29 July 2013). A Passage from India: Does the Convergys Judgment Demystify Profit Attribution? *Tax Analysts*, 449, 450

Chawla, A. (June 2013). Tax Residency Certificate Prescription: Whether There Is Any Certainty. *International Taxation*, 736–737

Chawla, A. (November 2013). Tax Transparency-Whether Perfect Communication under Indian Tax Framework. *International Taxation*, 531–534

Chawla, A. (September 2013). Revised Tax Compliance Procedures-Foreign Remittances. *International Taxation*, 367–368

Chen, X. (September/October 2013). Behavioural Game Split: The Arm's Length Principle and Highly Integrated Enterprises. *International Transfer Pricing Journal*, 339–353

Chen, Y. (2008). 'Financing: a Global Survey of Thin Capitalization and Transfer Pricing Rules in 35 Selected Countries: China. *International Transfer Pricing Journal, November/December*, 295–297

China. (2014). *China's Response to UN BEPS Questionnaire, Points 5/6.* www.un.org/esa/ffd/wp-content/uploads/2014/10/ta-BEPS-CommentsChina.pdf

Chmelev, A. (1999). Russia's New Transfer Pricing Rules. *IBFD Bulletin, November*, 481–485

Chou, S. (2007). Unified Enterprise Income Tax Law and Its Impact on Transfer Pricing. *ITPJ, July/August*, 246–248

Chrishty, M. (2009). Royalties and Fees for Technical Services in International Trade. *Asia-Pacific Tax Bulletin*, 40–50

Christian, A. (2011). A Toolkit for Civil Society. *Tax Justice Advocacy*, pp. 1–138

Christians, A. (2010). Networks, Norms and National Tax Policy. *University of Wisconsin Law School,Legal Studies Research Paper Series*, Paper No. 1078

Christians, A. (2010). Taxation in a Time of Crisis: Policy Leadership from OECD to G20. *University of Wisconsin Law School, Legal Studies Research Paper Series* Paper No. 1107

Christians, A. (2011). How Nations Share:The Role of Law in Creating and Resolving International Tax Disputes. *University of Wisconsin, Legal Studies Research Paper Series* Paper No. 1159

Christians, A. (2014). Avoidance, Evasion, and Taxpayer Morality. *Washington Journal of Law & Policy*, 39–59

Christians, A. (August 2008). Sovereignty, Taxation, and Social Contract. *University of Wisconsin Law School,Legal Studies Research Paper Series*, Paper No. 1063

Christians, A. (May 2007). Hard Law & Soft Law in International Taxation. *University of Wisconsin Law School, Legal Studies Research Paper Series*, Paper No. 1049

Christians, A. Case Study Research and International Tax Theory. *University of Wisconsin Law School, Legal Studies Research Paper Series* Paper No. 1110

Christians, A. Fair Taxation as a Basic Human Right. *University of Wisconsin Law School, Legal Studies Research Paper Series*, Paper No. 1066

Christians, A. Global Trends and Constraints on Tax Policy in Less Developed Countries. *University of Wisconsin Law School, Legal Studies Research Paper Series*, Paper 1086

Christians, A. Global Trends and Constraints on Tax Policy. *Legal Studies Research Paper Series, University of Wisconsin, Law School*, Paper No. 1086

Bibliography

Church, N. (October 2013). Double Taxation Agreement Between South Africa and Mauritius

CI, R. (2013). Agreement for the Exchange of Information Relating to Tax Matters, (pp. DOC 2013-26524)

Cockfield, A. (19 September 2011). Introduction: The Last Battleground of Globalization. *Tax Notes International*, 867

Coe. (1995). *Macroeconomic Crises, Policies, and Growth in Brazil, 1964–1990.* World Bank, Comparative Economic Studies

Commerce, J. (6 March 2013). *Suggestions for the Government of India by JCCH 2013.* Worldwide Tax Daily

Committee. (2014). Addressing BEPS in SA, Interim Report Action 8: Assure TP Outcomes Are in Line with Value Creation with Regard to Intangibles

Committee. (2014). Addressing BEPS in SA, Interim Report, Action 15: Develop a Multinational Instrument

Cooper. (2014). Papers on Selected Topics in Protecting the Tax Base of Developing Countries Draft Outline - Paper No. 5 May 2014, Preventing Tax Treaty Abuse. (pp. 1–7). New York: UN

Co-operation. (21 September 1947). *vol. 1 General Report.* Committee of European Economic Co-operation

Coronado, L. (2009). China-Asian Tax Authorities Firmly Grasp Transfer Pricing: is China Leading the Way? *Asia-Pacific Tax Bulletin, March/April*, 72–75

COT. (May 2000). Arbitration in International Tax Matters, Document No. 180/438. *International Chamber of Commerce*

Cotrut, M. (2014). CFE Forum 2014: Policies for a Sustainable Tax Future' European Taxation. *European Taxation, June*, 264–269

Cui, W. (2010 (Volume 64), No. 11). Tax Classification of Foreign Entities in China:The Current State of Play. *Bulletin for International Taxation*, 559–565

Cui, W. (2011). Two Paths for Developing Anti-Avoidance Rules. *Asia Pacific Tax Bulletin, vol. 17, No. 1*

Cui, W. (2013 (vol. 67), No. 6). China/United Kingdom Double Taxation Convention (2011). *Bulletin For International Taxation*, 271–279

Cui, W. (2014). Taxing Indirect Transfers: Improving an Instrument for Stemming Tax and Legal Erosion. *Virginia Tax Review, vol. 33, No. 4*, 1–49

D'Éça, F. (2003). Trends in Company Shareholder Taxation: Single or Double Taxation? – Brazil. *IFA Cahiers vol. 88a*, 207–233

Dagan, T. National Interests in the International Tax Game. *18 Virginia Tax Review*

Dagan, T. The Costs of International Tax Cooperation. *University of Michigan Public Law and Legal Theory*, Research Paper 02-13

Dalal, K. (January/February, 2005). Planning Inbound and Outbound Transactions with OECD and Non-OECD Countries. *Asia-Pacific Tax Bulletin*, 36–55

Daly, M. (2005). The WTO and Direct Taxation. *WTO,Geneva, Switzerland*

Danziger, E. (1989). The Disregard of a Legal Entity for Tax Purposes - South Africa. *IFA Cahiers- vol. 74a*, 121–134

Dash, S. (2010). India-Transfer Pricing Regulations – A Comparative Study on the Confluence and Conflict Between India, the OECD and Other Countries. *Asia-Pacific Tax Bulletin, January/February*, 24–34

Datta, P. (2010). India, Transfer Pricing – A Retrospective Analysis. *Asia-Pacific Tax Bulletin, (vol. 16), No. 1*, 36–41

Daurer, V. (2014). *Tax Treaties and Developing Countries.* The Hague: Kluwer Law International BV

Dave, K. (2005). Source and Residence: A New Configuration of Their Principles – India. *IFA Cahiers - vol. 90A*, 339–365

Davies, N. (March 2015). CFC Rules: Towards the Deoffshorisation of the Russian Economy. *Financier Worldwide*

Davis Tax Committee. (2015). Addressing Base Erosion and Profit Shifting in SA, Action 2: Neutralise the Effects of Hybrid Mismatch Arrangements, Interim Report

DeBroe, L. (2008). *International Tax Planning and Prevention of Abuse'.* IBFD Online Books

Delal, K. (1999). International Restructurings: Tax Consequences for Operations in India. *1999 International Bureau of Fiscal Documentation*, pp. 560–565

Deloitte. (11 January 2009). *The New Chinese Special Tax Adjustments Rules - What Are the Implications?.* NTC Tax Analysis Issue P49/2009

Deloitte. (February 2014). South African Transfer Pricing: The New Thin Capitalisation Rules – An Ongoing Area of Uncertainty. *http://pressoffice.mg.co.za/deloitte/ PressRelease.php?StoryID = 246366*

Dentons. (May 2016). Advanced Tax Rulings In Russia: Tax Administration Rules Have Changed. *http://www.dentons.com/en/insights/alerts/2016/may/10/advance-tax -ruling_russia_moscow*

DeOliveira, A. (2013). The Taxation of Foreign Passive Income for Groups of Companies – Brazil. *IFA Cahiers - vol. 98A*, 159–180

De Ridder, P. (2005). China International Tax Considerations. *Asia-Pacific Tax Bulletin*, 467–470

Desai, D. (12 December 2013). Force of Attraction Rule Not Applicable if Services Are Rendered Outside India. *Worldwide Tax Daily*, Doc 2013-28579

Desai, N. (1999). Tax Aspects of the Transfer of Technology (Including Software). *Asia Pacific Tax Bulletin*, 40–46

DeSilveira. (2010). International Tax Planning in Brazil: What to Expect Following Recent Case Law. *Bulletin for International Taxation, vol. 64, No. 11*, 566–576

DeSouza, G. (2008). China-Structuring an Appropriate Transfer Pricing Policy. *Asia-Pacific Tax Bulletin, July/August*, 308–311

Diaz, O. (2006). Punishment under Criminal Tax Law in Argentina. *IBFD Bulletin*, 399–406

Dib, R. (2010). The New Brazilian Thin Capitalization Rules and How the Other BRICs Approach the Subject. *Bulletin for International Taxation, (vol. 64), No. 6*, 336–341

Dinoida, P. (2014/15). *India Transfer Pricing Demystified.* New Delhi: Bharat Law House, New Delhi

Bibliography

Dixon, M. (2013). *Textbook on International Law*. Cambridge: Oxford University Press

Dobinson, I. (2002). The Criminal Law of the People's Republic of China (1997): Real Change or Rhetoric? *Pacific Rim Law and Policy Journal*, 1–65

Dongmei, Q. (2014). Interpretation of Tax Laws in China: Moving Towards the Rule of Law. *Hong Kong Law Journal, vol. 44, Issue 2*, 589–620

Dongmei, Q. (November 2010). China's Capital Gains Taxation of Nonresidents and the Legitimate Use of Tax Treaties. *Tax Notes Int'l*, 593–621

Dongmeui, Q. (18 January 2010). Thin Capitalization Rules in China. *Tax Notes Int'l*

Dua, A. (2004). Group Taxation – India. *IFA Cahiers - vol. 89b*, 341–365

Dunbar, D. (2010). Taxation of Inward Investment – Treaty Shopping, Taxation of Capital Gains, and Dividends: Innovative Solutions to an Old Problem. *Asia-Pacific Tax Bulletin, (vol. 16), No. 6*, 447–463

Dunbar, D. (December 2008). Statutory General Anti-Avoidance Rules: Lessons for the United Kingdom from the British Commonwealth. *Bulletin For International Taxation*, 529–550

DuPlessis. (2012). Some Thoughts on the Interpretation of Tax Treaties in SA. *SA Merc LJ 24*

DuToit, C. (1 March 1999). *Beneficial Ownership of Royalties in Bilateral Tax Treaties Hardcover*

Dwarka-Canabady, U. (January 2013). Mauritius: A Well Reguldated International Financial Centre Lifting New Global Challenges. *International Taxation*, 9–13

Dzhalchinov, D. (2016). Dispute Resolution Procedures in International Tax Matters - Russia. *IFA Cahiers - vol. 101A*, 575–588

Easson, A. (2004). *Tax Incentives for Foreign Direct Investment*. The Hague: Kluwer Law International

Edgar, T. (2008) vol. 56). Foreign Direct Investment, Thin Capitalization and The Interest Expense Deduction. *Canadian Tax Journal*, pp. 803–869

Eichelberger, J. (2012). China: Tax Litigation. *Asia-Pacific Tax Bulletin, (vol. 18), No. 2*, 147–151

Elliott, A. (23 September 2013). ABA Meeting: Tech Company Tax Directors Defend International Tax Structures. *Tax Notes International*, Doc 2013-22376

Engel, K. (June 2002). National Treasury's Detailed Explanantion of Section 9D of the Income Tax Act. *Tax Policy Chief Directorate, National Treasury*, pp. 1–25

Engelen, F. (2004). *Interpretation of Tax Treaties under International Law*. IBFD vol. 7 Doctoral Series

EnsAfrica. Simulated Transactions: Welcome Clarification from the Supreme Court of Appeal. *ENSafrica Tax Team, Simulated Transactions: Welcome Clarification from the Supreme Court of Appeal, https://www.ensafrica.com/news/simulated-transactions-welcome-clarification-from-the-Supreme-Court-of-Appeal?Id = 1389& STitle = tax%20ENSight*

Eskinazi, R. (2005). Source and Residence: A New Configuration of Their Principles - South Africa. *IFA Cahiers- Vol. 90A*, 571–595

Essers, P. (February 2014). International Tax Justice Between Machiavelli and Habermas. *Bulletin for International Taxation*, 54/66

Etsebeth, V. (2010). The International Exchange of Information: Realising the Promise and Managing the Threat. *Stellenbosch Law Review*, pp. 45–66

Ettinger, B. (1959). Law of Taxation-Income Tax Act,1959. *Ann. Surv. S. African L*, pp. 302–307

EY. (3 June 2013). Global Tax Policy in 2013. *Tax Analysts*, 979–988

EY. (February 2011). *China: Tax Policy and Controversy*

EY. Issue 2013002, (21 May 2013). Further Updates on Indirect Transfer Public Cases. *China Tax and Investment News*, 1–12

EY. Issue No. CTIN2015003, (7 February 2015). China SAT Refines the Tax Matters Related to Non- Residents' Indirect Transfer of China Taxable Assets. *China Tax and Investment News*

EY. Issue No.CTIN2014001, (25 July 2014). China GAAR is under Way – China Releases Discussion Draft of Administrative Measures of General Anti-Avoidance Rules for Public Solicitation. *China Tax and Investment News*

EY. Issue No.CTIN2014002, (19 December 2014). China Released Administrative Measures for General Anti-Avoidance Rules (GAAR). *China Tax and Investment News*, 1–5

Fazelbhoy, A. (June 2013). Indirect Transfer of Assets: An International (Indian) Perspective. *Mauritius 7th IFA Conference* (pp. 679–683). Mauritius: International Taxation

Feinschreiber, R. Updating the OECD's Safe Harbour Transfer Pricing Provisions. http://www.oecd.org/tax/transfer-pricing/48330739.pdf

Ferreira. (2003–2004). Form versus Substance: A Comparison of Brazil's Tax System to the Tax System of the United States of America. *U. Miami Inter-Am. L. Rev.*, 311–343

Filho, G. (1983 - vol. 68a.). Tax Avoidance/Tax Evasion – Brazil'. *IFA Cahiers*, 285–293

Finance, I. (22 January 2013). BRICS Countries Agree Further Tax Policy Cooperation Needed. Tax Notes International

Finance, M. (14 August 2013). *Tax Administration Reform Committee Set-Up*. ITAT Online.org

Finance, M. (18 July 2013). *Press Information Bureau: Shome Committee on Tax Related Disputes*. Ministry of Finance, Government of India

Finance, S. (27 November 2013). *South Africa Complies with Global Transparency Standards*. Worldwide Tax Daily

Finnerty, C. (2009 (vol. 15), No. 6). Structures Lacking Substance and Business Purpose Come under Further Challenge. *Asia-Pacific Tax Bulletin*, 394–399

Finnerty, C. (2012 (vol. 18), No. 5). Strengthening Cross-Border Tax Enforcement and the Evolving (China) General Anti-Avoidance Rule. *Asia-Pacific Tax Bulletin*, 239–246

Fisher, J. (2014). Fairer Shores: Tax Havens, Tax Avoidance Corporate Social Responsibility. *Boston University Law Review*, 337–366

Fonseca. (2011). Brazil: Key Practical Issues to Eliminate Double Taxation of Business Income. *IFA Cahiers- vol. 96B*, 165–179

Ford, D. (August 2013). Private International Law. *Amercian Society of International Law*

Franklin, J. (1997-1998). Tax Avoidance by Citizens of the Russian Federation: Will the Draft Tax Code Provide a Solution? *Duke Journal of Comparative and International Law*, 135-174

Freedman, J. (2004). Defining Taxpayer Responsibility: In Support of a General Anti-Avoidance Principle. *British Tax Review 4*

Freedman, J. (2010). Improving (Not Perfecting) Tax Legislation: Rules and Principles Revisted. *British Tax Review*, Issue 6

Freedman, J. (2014,vol. 20, No. 3). Designing a General Anti-Abuse Rule: Striking a Balance. *Asia-Pacific Tax Bulletin*, 167-173

Friedlander, L. (2006). Policy Forum: The History of Tax Treaty Provisions And Why It Is Important to Know About It. *Canadian Tax Journal*, vol. 54, No. 4 pp. 907-921

Frolova, M. (22 July 2013). News Analysis: Do Recent Amendments to Russian Law Signal Enactment of FATCA. *Worldwide Tax Daily*, Doc 2013- 17518

FRS. (2014). *Comments from Brazil Subcommittee on Base Erosion and Profit Shifting Issues for Developing Countries.* UN

FRS. (August 2002). Tax System and Administration in Brazil-Tax Study 08. *Ministry of Finance, Federal Revenue Service, General Coordination of Tax Policy*

Fullbright, Norton Rose. (November 2013). Registration of Foreign Loans in Brazil

Fussi. (Fall of 2009). *A Legal and Economic Analysis of the Effects of the Savings Tax Directive-Combating International Tax Avoidance.* Aarhus School of Business

G-20. (6 September 2013). G20 Leaders' Declaration. *St Petersburg Summit* (pp. Doc 2013-21295). St. Petersburg: Worldwide Tax Daily

G8. (18 June 2013). G-8 States Action Plan Principles on Company Ownership Transparency, (pp. DOC 2013-14838)

Gada, V. (2014). Cross-Border Outsourcing – Issues, Strategies and Solutions - India. *FA Cahiers - vol. 99A*, 365-384

Gao, F. (2011). *Corporate Income Tax Law and Practice in PRC.* Oxford University Press

Geng, X. (July 2004). Round-Tripping Foreign Direct Investment and the People's Republic of China. *ADB Institute Research Paper Series No. 58*

GFI. (2004-2013). *Illicit Financial Flows*

Gidirim, V. (2006). Judicial Challenge of Cross-Border Royalty Fee Structure by Tax Authorities. *ITPJ, July/August*, 208-210

Girish, K. (January 2016). LOB provisions in DTCS- Indian Experience. *International Tax Research and Analysis Foundation, Occasional Paper No. 5*, 1-37

Gladie, L. (vol. 21 No. 1, February 2014). Tax Issues in China for Secondment Arrangements in MNCs. *Proceedings of ASBBS Annual Conference*, (pp. 443-448). Las Vegas

Glenn, D. (30 December 2013). India Clarifies Administration of Transfer Pricing Safe Harbor. *Worldwide Tax Daily*, Doc 2013-29754

Godfrey, D. (June 2013). Exchange of Information: Update on the Work of the Global Forum. *Mauritius 7th IFA Conference* (pp. 658-674). Mauritius: International Taxation

Goldfajn, I. (May 2007). Capital Flows and Controls in Brazil What Have We Learned? *National Bureau of Economic Research*

Gololbov. (vol. 17, 2008). The Yukos Tax Case or Ramsay Adventures in Russia. *FSU Business Review*, 166–253

Gomes, G. (2015). Tax Incentives on Research and Development (R&D) – Brazil. *IFA Cahiers, vol. 100A*, 169–191

Gomes, M. (2016). Dispute Resolution Procedures in International Tax Matters – Brazil. *IFA Cahiers - vol. 101A*, 156–175

Gómez, M. (August 2012). The BRICs: Tax Treaty Policy Regarding Dividends. *Bulletin for International Taxation*, 401–419

Gonnet, S. (5 March 2012). *China's SAT Gives Overview of Anti-Avoidance Initiatives.* Nera Economic Consulting

Goradia, S. (September 2013). Recent EU Cases/Developments and Compaeison with Indian Judicial Precedents. *International Taxation*, 325–336

Gorbunova, L. (26 February 2013). Moscow Tax Inspectorate Announces 2012 Reporting. *Worldwide Tax Daily*, Doc 2013-4327

Gorodnichenko, Y. (February 2008). *Lessons from the Russian 2001 Flat Tax Reform.* Vox

Gosai, N. (June 2013). Transfer Pricing: A South African Perspective. *Mauritius 7th IFA Conference* (p. 702). Mauritius: International Taxation

Gotovtseva, N. (2012). Russia New Rules on Allocation of Profits to Permanent Establishments in Russia: Threat or Opportunity? *International Transfer Pricing Journal, (vol. 19), No. 6*, 457–458

Government, A. (July 1999). *Final Report of the Review of Business Taxation, A Tax System Redesigned.* Canberra: Australian Government Printing Service

Govind, H. (January 2003). Transfer Pricing. *Asia-Pacific Tax Bulletin*, 14/21

Govind, H. (October 2000). Employees' Stock Option Plans-Developments to Finance Act 2000. *Asia-Pacific Tax Bulletin*, 319–322

Graetz, M. (2001). Taxing International Income: Inadequate Principles, Outdated Concepts, and Unsatisfactory Policies. *26 Brooklyn Journal of International Law*, pp. 1357–1361

Gravelle, J. (January 2015). Tax Havens: International Tax Avoidance and Evasion. *Congressional Research Service*, 1–55

Greco. (2011). Crise do formalismo no direito tributario brasileiro. *1 Revista da PGFN*, 9–18

Gregoire, M. (November 2015). *Taxation and Expropriation under Bilateral Investment Treaties: Setting the Standard.* Butterworths Journal of International Banking and Financial Law

Grinberg, I. (October 2013). Taxing Capital Income in Emerging Countries: Will FACTA Open the Door?' Word Tax Journal. *World Tax Journal*, 325–367

Guerra, J. (1998). Tax Treatment of Corporate Losses – Brazil. *IFA Cahiers - vol. 83a*, 351–363

Guo Shui Fa. [2001] No. 3

Guo Shui Fa. [2010] No. 75

Guo, W. (2013). China -Corporate Loss Utilization Through Aggressive Tax Planning. *ITPJ, (vol. 20), No. 1*, 35–41

Bibliography

Gupta, A. (6 January 2014). Transfer Pricing is Still Dead: But It Is Feeling Much Better Every Day. *Tax Notes International*, Doc 2013-29156

Gupta, S. (2013, vol. 19, No. 2). The General Anti-Avoidance Rule – An Indian and International Perspective. *Asia-Pacific Tax Bulletin*, 97–107

Gurria, A. (24 March 2013). Fiscal and Taxation Reforms for a More Inclusive Growth in China. *China Development Forum*, (pp. Doc 2013-7025)

Gutlev, T. (27 February 2013). News Analysis: Russia's IKEA Tax Case on Inseparable Improvements. *Worldwide Tax Daily*, Doc 2013-4329

Gutuza, T. (2010). Tax and E-Commerce: Where is the Source. *127 S. African L.J*, pp. 328–338

Gutuza, T. (2010). Tax and E-Commerce: Where is the Source. *127 South African Law Journal*, 328–338

Gutuza, T. (May 2013). *PhD Thesis: An Analysis of the Methods Used in the South African Domestic Legislation and Double Tax Treaties Entered into by South Africa for the Elimination of Double Taxation.* Capetown: University of Cape Town

Gutuza, T. (vol. 125, No. 3, 2008). Taxing the Partner of a Foreign Partnership. *The South African Law Journal*, 514–520

Guzman, A. (1997).Why LDCs Sign Treaties That Hurt Them: Explaining the Popularity of Bilateral Investment Treaties. *Berkeley Law Scholarship Repository*, 639–688

Guzman, A. (1998). Why LDCs Sign Treaties That Hurt Them: Explaining the Popularity of Bilateral Investment Treaties. *38 Virginia Journal of International Law*

Han, A. (January 1982). People's Republic of China Foreign Enterprise Income Tax Law and Regulations. *Santa Clara Law Digital Commons, 6 Hastings Int'l & Comp. L. Rev. 716 1982–1983*, 689–717

Han, M. (2011). Cross-Border Business Restructuring – China. *IFA Cahiers- vol. 96A*, 209–218

Hann, A. (January 1982). People's Republic of China Foreign Enterprises Income Tax Law and Regulations. *Santa Clara Law Digital Comms*, 689/717

Hansen, I. (January 2008). *(LLM Thesis) China - The New Corporate Income Tax Law and Its Effect on Transfer Pricing.* Jönköping: Jonkoping International Business School

Harteveld, P. (2014 (vol. 54), No. 62). Fiscal Monitoring of Assets and Properties Held Abroad by Italian Resident Individuals, Non-Commercial Entities, Simple Partnerships and Similar Entities. *European Taxation*, 240–249

Hattingh, J. (2011). Key Practical Issues to Eliminate Double Taxation of Business Income - South Africa. *IFA Cahiers- vol. 96B*, 575–597

Hattingh, J. (Bulletin for International Taxation, November). *South Africa - The Volkswagen Case and the Secondary Tax on Companies: Part 2 – The Effect on the Taxation of Dividends with Emphasis on Deemed (Constructive) Dividend.* 509–533: 2009

Hattingh, J. The Tax Treatment of Cross-Border Partnerships under Model-Based Tax Treaties: Some Lessons from *Grundlingh v. SAARS. The South African Law Journal*, pp. 38–50

Hearson. (November 2011). *The G20's Convention on Fighting Tax Evasion: Three Reasons to Be Sceptical.* Actionaid

Hegde, N. (June 2013). Delhi Tribunal Decision in Convergys Customer Management Group Inc. Does It Reignite Some Contentious Tax Issues. *International Taxation*, 730–735

Hellevig, J. (May 2015). Transfer Pricing in Russia. *Awara*

Hines, J. (May 1996). Tax Policy and the Activities of Multinational Companies. *National Bureau of Economic Research, Working Paper Series*, Working Paper 5589

Hoaglund, L. (30 January 2013). Jersey Signs TIEA with Brazil, Latvia. *Tax Notes International*, Doc 2013-2029

HOC. (Ninth Report of Session 2013–2014). *Committee of Public Accounts, Tax Avoidance- Google.* House of Commons

Hoffmann, R. (1990). International Mutual Assistance Through Exchange of Information – Brazil. *I FA Cahiers vol. 75b*, 245–254

Holmes, C. (2007). A Comparative Survey of Cost Contribution Agreements - China and International Best Practices. *Asia-Pacific Tax Bulletin, July/August*, 299–313

Hong, F. (2003). Impact of Transfer Pricing on Tax Planning. *Asia-Pacific Tax Bulletin, November/December*, 359–363

Honibell, M. (2011). *International Tax: SA Perspective.* SiberInk

Honibell. (2011). *International Tax, A SA Perspective.* Capetown: SiberInk

Hoogland, W. (23 October 2013). News Analysis: BEPS Dominates Discussions at International Tax Summit. *2013 International Tax Summit and International Fiscal Association China Conference* (pp. Doc 2013-24397). Beijing: Tax Notes International

Hou, J. (2014). China the Taxation of Partnerships. *Asia-Pacific Tax Bulletin, September/October*, 331–336

Hsu, S. (November 2014). Chinese Direct and Financial Outbound Investment. *The Diplomat*

Hung-Gay, F. (2011). Reported Trade Figuring Discrepancy, Regulatory Arbitrage and Round-Tripping: Evidence from the China-HK Trade Data. *Journal of International Business Studies*

Hutchinson, A. (2014). Simulated Transactions and the Fraus Legis Doctrine. *The South African Law Journal*, 69–87

ICC. (2011, October 21). Roundtable to Discuss Brazilian Tax Issues. Rio de Janeiro

Illouz, A. (3 July 2009). Allocation of Jurisdictional Power and Institutional Choice in the International Trade Regime and International Tax Regime-A Game Theory Analysis. *SSRN: http://ssrn.com*

IMF. (11 October 2013). *Statement by Vice Minister Zhu Guangyao to the Plenary Session of the 2013 Annual Meetings of the World Bank Group and International Monetary Fund*

IMF. (2011). *Determinants of Development Financing Flows from Brazil, Russia, India, and China to Low Income Countries.* IMF Working Paper WP/11/255

IMF. (2014). *Rising BRICs and Changes in Sub-Saharan Africa's Business Cycle Patterns.* IMF Working Paper WP/14/35

Bibliography

IMF. (2015). *Coordinated Direct Investment Survey Guide-2015, Pre-publication Draft*

IMF. (2015). *Fiscal Affairs Department, At a Glance*

IMF. (January 2011). *New Growth Drivers for Low-Income Countries: The Role of BRICs*

IMF. (July 2011). *FDI from BRICs to LICs: Emerging Growth Driver.* IMF Working Paper WP/11/178

IMF. (June 2015). *South Africa: Technical Assistance Report-Revenue Administration Gap Analysis Program—The Value-Added Tax Gap.* IMF Country Report No. 15/180

IMF. (March 2004). *China: International Trade and WTO Accession.* IMF Working Paper WP/04/36

IMF. (March 2012). *BRICs' Philosophies for Development Financing and Their Implications for LICs.* IMF Working Paper WP/12/74

IMF. (May 2014). *Policy Paper Spillovers in International Corporate Taxation*

IMF. (May 2014). *Spillovers in International Taxation*

IMF. (11 November 2009). *Report on the Technical Assistance Evaluation Mission to the People's Republic of China*

IMF. (November 2011). *Low-Income Countries' BRIC Linkage: Are There Growth Spillovers?* IMF Working Paper WP/11/267

IMF. (September 1998). *Energy Tax Reform in Russia and Other Former Soviet Union Countries.* IMF-Finance and Development, September 1998, vol. 35, No. 3

IMF. (September 2000). *Statement by the Hon. Aleksei Kudrin, Governor of the Fund for the Russian Federation, at the Joint Annual Discussion.* IMF Press Release No. 23

Immerman, E. (2004). Group Taxation - South Africa. *IFA Cahiers - vol. 89b*, 595–605

India, P. (24 December 2013). *Sharing Insights, News Alert, LG Electronics.* www.pwc.in

India, P. (October- November 2013). *Be in the Know: India Spectrum.* www.pwc.in

Indian, F. (22 January 2013). BRICS Countries Agree Further Tax Policy Cooperation Needed, (pp. DOC 2013-1498)

India-Russia. (1997). *India-Russia, Income Tax Treaty*

Industry. (4 February 2013). *Align Indian Transfer Pricing Regulations with OECD Guidelines.* New Delhi: Tax Analysts

Internationaltaxreview. (September 2012). The Future for BRICS Tax Policy. *23 Int'l Tax Rev. 25*, 25–26

Investigations. (21 May 2013). *Hearings Offshore Profit Shifting and the U.S. Tax Code - Part 2 (Apple Inc.)*

Investment Agreements

IOB. (November 2013). *Evaluation of Issues in Financing for Development, Analysing Effect of Dutch Corporate Tax Policy on Developing Countries*

Jackson, A. (January 1997). WTO DSU--Misunderstandings on the Nature of Legal Obligation. *The American Journal of International Law, vol. 91, No. 1*

Jackson, R. (12 July 2013). Russian Court Convicts Dead Whistleblower of Tax Evasion. *Worldwide Tax Daily*, Doc 2013-16730

Jackson, R. (15 November 2013). Companies Must Engage with Local Tax Officials to Expand Investment in China. *Worldwide Tax Daily*, Doc 2013-26429

Jackson, R. (26 November 2013). GAAR Casting Shadow Over India-Mauritius Tax Treaty. *Worldwide Tax Daily*, Doc 2013-27177

Jain, A. (2003, April). Tax Evasion and Corruption: Indian Perspective. *Asia Pacific Tax Bulletin*, pp. 124–127

Jain, A. (June 2013). Guidance Note on APA: Making Process More Transparent. *International Taxation*, 705–708

Jain, A. (June 2015). TP Rules - Use of Multiple Year Data - Is It End of Litigation? *Taxindiainternational.com*

Jain, J. (June 2013). Buy-Back Tax: A New End to an Old beginning. *International Taxation*, 720–724

Jain, K. (October 1999). Tax Incentives – A Critical Appraisal. *Asia-Pacific Tax Bulletin*, 333–338

Jain, R. (2007). Conflicts in the Attribution of Income to a Person – India. *IFA Cahiers - vol. 92B*, 291–309

Jaitley, A. (10 July 2014). *India Budget 2014–2015*

James, G. (July/August 2011). Beware of China's Tax Avoidance Stance. *www.internationaltaxreview.com*, 34–35

James, S. (18–22 October 2010). *Committee of Experts on International Taxation, Item 3 (o) of the Provisional Agenda: Tax Competition in Corporate Tax: Use of Tax Incentives in Attracting Foreign Direct Investment*. UN

James, S. (2001). Developing a Tax Compliance Strategy for Revenue Services. *IBFD*, 158–164

Jeffrey, P. (January 2015). New Regulations for Brazil CFC rules. *International Tax Review*

Jha, R. (November 2013). Transfer Pricing Safe Harbour Rules: Avoidable Defects. *International taxation*, 567–572

Jhabakh, K. (December 2010). Has the AAR Put the Mauritius Saga to Rest? *Bulletin For International Taxation*, 626–635

Jhabakh, K. (March/April 2012). Recent Case Law: Indirect Transfer of Interest and Controlling Stake in an Indian Company Held Taxable. *Derivatives & Financial Instruments*, 89–92

Jhabakh, P. (2013). India-Determination of Arm's Length Price for Sale of Shares to an Associated Enterprise. *ITPJ (vol. 20), No. 4*, 283–286

Jhabakh, P. (October 2013). The Kodak(2013) Case: The Applicability of the Indian Transfer Pricing Provisions. *Bulletin For International Taxation*, 560–564

Jianxiong, Z. (1998). Tax Legislation of the People's Republic of China and Its Information Sources. *Revenue Law Journal, vol. 8, Issue 1*, 207/215

Jinyan, L. (2000). Transfer Pricing in China. *IBFD Bulletin, November*, 565–576

Johnson, A. (2006). *Russia Tax, Law and Business Briefing*. World Trade Executive

Johnston, S. (13 December 2013). Indian Court Releases Nokia Assets Frozen in $335m Royalty Tax Dispute. *Worldwide Tax Daily*, Doc 2013-28563

Johnston, S. (19 March 2013). Indian Budget Delivers Surprise Retroactive Tax Amendments. *Tax Notes International*, Doc 2012-5561

Johnston, S. (2 April 2013). MNE's In India With Tax Haven Links Pay 30% Less Tax, Report Says. *Tax Notes International*, Doc 2013-7760

Johnston, S. (2 May 2013). India to Slash Withholding Tax on Bonds to Attract More Foreign Investment. *Tax Notes International*, Doc 2013-10601

Johnston, S. (28 May 2013). *BRIC Practitioners Shine Spotlight on Important Tax Updates.* Doc 2013-12854: Worldwide Tax Daily

Johnston, S. (30 December 2013). Indian Tax Tribunal Stays $597m Vodafone Transfer Pricing Demand. *Worldwide Tax Daily*, Doc 2013- 29751

Johnston, S. (30 September 2013). Indian Government Releases Rules on Implementation Of GAAR. *Worldwide Tax Daily*, Doc 2013-22931

Johnston, S. (5 March 2013). India to Resolve Vodafone Case Before Changing Retrospective Tax Laws. *Worldwide Tax Daily*, Doc 2013-5042

Johnston, S. (7 August 2013). Vodafone in 'Talks About Talks' With India in Effort to Resolve Tax Dispute. *Worldwide Tax Daily*, Doc 2013-19121

Johnston, S. (8 February 2013). India's Cricket Governing Body Hit with $433m Tax Bill. *Tax Notes International*, Doc 2013-2910

Johnston, S. (9 December 2013). Brazilian Mining Giant to Settle Long-Running Tax Dispute for $9.5bn. *Tax Notes International*, Doc 2013-27868

Johnston, S. (March 2016). India's Equalization Levy Not Proposed as Income Tax. *World Wide Tax Daily, 2016 WTD 55–4*

Jones, J. (1999). The David R Tillinghast Lecture: Are Tax Treaties Necessary?". *53 Tax Law Review 1*

Jung, M. (2011 (Volume 51), No 6). Jung, 'Trends and Developments in Swiss Anti-Treaty Shopping Legislation and Treaty Shopping Case Law. *European Taxation*, 230–244

Kadar, Z. South Africa Issues Thin Capitalization Guidance – U.S. Businesses Financing South African Operations Should Review Compliance. *https://tax. thomsonreuters.com/wp-content/pdf/transfer-pricing/South-Africa-Issues-Thin-Capitalization-Guidance.pdf*

Kaka, P. (2013). India: Capital Gains and Tax Avoidance. In Lang, *Tax Treaty Case Law Around the Globe* (pp. 137–145). Tilburg

Kalgin, V. (29 July 2013). Russia's Supreme Arbitration Court Rules for Taxpayer in Dividend Tax Case. *Worldwide Tax Daily*, Doc 2013-17982

Kalotay, K. (8 J. World Investment & Trade 125 2007). The Rise of Russian Transnational Corporations. *The Journal of World Investment and Trade*, 126–148

Kamath, S. (1 March 2013). No Taxes Due in India on Gains from Sale of French Company That Held Shares in Indian Company. *Worldwide Tax Daily*, Doc 2013-4614

Kamath, S. (10 July 2013). No CGT Due on Sale of Shares in Nonoperating Subsidiary, Indian Court Rules. *Worldwide Tax Daily*, Doc 2013-16256

Kamath, S. (15 October 2013). No Withholding Due on Technical Fees Paid to Singapore Firm, Indian Advance Ruling Authority Says. *Worldwide Tax Daily*, Doc 2013-23814

Kamath, S. (16 October 2013). Payments for Offshore Design Services Taxable in India, Mumbai Tribunal Holds. *Worldwide Tax Daily*, Doc 2013-23898

Kamath, S. (16 September 2013). India Has Right to Tax Profits of Residents PE's in Other Countries, Mumbai Tribunal Holds. *Worldwide Tax Daily*, Doc 2013-21807

Kamath, S. (17 December 2013). Partnership's Management Fees Not Taxable in India, Mumbai Tribunal Holds. *Worldwide Tax Daily*, Doc 2013-28861

Kamath, S. (17 November 2013). Fees Paid to Foreign Sales Agent Not Indian Source Income, Tribunal Holds. *Worldwide Tax Daily*, Doc 2013-26033

Kamath, S. (2 April 2013). Payments for IT Services Not Taxable as Royalties, Indian Tribunal Says. *Worldwide Tax Daily*, Doc 2013-7576

Kamath, S. (2 December 2013). India Tax Tribunal Clarifies Source Rules, Taxing Rights in a Treaty Case. *Worldwide Tax Daily*, Doc 2013-27557

Kamath, S. (22 April 2013). India Rule on Dividend Deduction Does Not Violate Treaty With France. *Worldwide Tax Daily*, Doc 2013-9653

Kamath, S. (23 April 2013). No Taxes Due on Gain from Sale of Shares in Italian Company.Hyderabad Tribunal Says. *Worldwide Tax Daily*, Doc 2013-9655

Kamath, S. (24 January 2013). Chennai Tribunal Rejects Transfer Pricing Method in Share Sale by Unrelated Joint Venture Partners. *Worldwide Tax Daily*, Doc 2013-1446

Kamath, S. (24 June 2013). Representative Office in India Does Not Create a Tax Liability for Nike, High Court says. *Worldwide Tax Daily*, Doc 2013-15175

Kamath, S. (25 February 2013). Payments to Singapore Testing Lab Not Taxable in India, Dehli Tribunal Says. *Worldwide Tax Daily*, Doc 2013-4094

Kamath, S. (27 August 2013). Fees Paid to Access to Online Database taxable As Royalties, Mumbai Tribunal Holds. *Worldwide Tax Daily*, Doc 2013-20393

Kamath, S. (30 April 2013). Google and Yahoo Not Taxable in India on Ad Revenue,Tribunal Rules. *Worldwide Tax Daily*, Doc 2013-10356

Kamath, S. (4 June 2013). Delhi Tribunal Supports Taxpayers Formula for Cost Sharing Agreement With Parent. *Worldwide Tax Daily*, Doc 2013-13276

Kamath, S. (4 September 2013). Services Provided Outside India Are Not Attributable to Indian PE. Mumbai Tribunal Holds. *Worldwide Tax Daily*, Doc 2013-20981

Kamath, S. (7 May 2013). Transfer Pricing Rules Apply to Working Capital Loan to Offshore Subsidiary, Mumbai Tribunal Holds. *Worldwide Tribunal Holds*, Doc 2013-10913

Kamath, S. (9 December 2013). Mumbai Tax Tribunal Quashes Transfer Pricing Assessment Against Cadbury India. *Worldwide Tax Daily*, Doc 2013-28128

Kamdin, B. (November/December 2006). India-Foreign Institutional Investors – A Testimony to India's Progress. *Asia-Pacific Tax Bulletin*, 467–472

Kanamugire. (July 2013). A Critical Analysis of Tax Avoidance in the South African Income Tax Act 58 of 1962, as Amended. *Mediterranean Journal of Social Sciences*, 351–363

Kanwar, V. (2015). Treaty Interpretation in Indian Courts: Adherence, Coherence, and Convergence. in H. P. (eds.), *Domestic Courts and the Interpretation of International Law: Converging Approaches* (pp. 1–34). Oxford University Press

Kapadia, S. (January 2013). Extempore Speech in Tax Conference Organised by Foundation for International Taxation. *International Taxation*, 1–4

Kapadia, S. (June 2013). Ex-tempore speech. *Mauritius 7th IFA Conference* (pp. 637–641). Mauritius: International Taxation

Bibliography

Kapur, A. (13 May 2012). *Indian Transfer Pricing System.* Director General of Income Tax (Admn.), Personal Views

Kasipillai, J. (2012). *Tax Avoidance, Evasion and Planning in Malaysia.* Malaysia: CCH Asia Pte Ltd

Katz, M. (1995). *Katz Commission-Second Interim Report, Transfer Pricing.* South African Tax Commission

Keen, M. (16 November 2004). Information Sharing and International Taxation. *Tilburg University, Discussion Center*

Keen, M. (July 2012). The Theory of International Tax Competition and Coordination. *Max Planck Institute for Tax Law and Public Finance, Department of Business and Tax Law*, Working Paper 2012 – 06

Ketan, D. (May 2013, vol. 6, Issue 5). *Be in the Know: India Spectrum.* PwC

Ketan, D. October-November 2013: vol. 6, Issue 8. *Be in the Know: India Spectrum.* PwC

Ketan. (December 2012, vol. 5, Issue 12). *Be in the Know: India Spectrum.* PwC

Khaw, L. (November 2013). China: SAT Clarifies Meaning of Technical Services" Inseparable" from Transfer of Technology. *Deloitte Global Services Limited, World Tax Advisor*

Kinanis. (2009). Recent Development on the Double Tax Treaty Between Cyprus and Russia. *www.kinanis.com*

Knoll, M. (December 2006). Taxes and Competitiveness. *University of Pennsylvania Law School, Institute for Law and Economics*, Research Paper No. 06-28

Knoll, M. (May 2009). Reconsidering International Tax Neutrality. *University of Pennsylvania Law School, Institute for Law and Economics*, Research Paper No. 09-16

Kollman, J. (30 March 2015). Arbitration in International Tax Matters, Featured Perspective. *Tax Notes Int'l, 30 March 2015*

Kollruss, T. (2013) vol. 3, Issue 1. Foreign Direct Investment Decisions and Tax Planning. *Journal of Chinese Tax and Policy*, pp. 2–9

Kolo, W. (2008). *Coverage of Taxation under Modern Investment Treaties in Muchlinske, Ortino & Schreuer (eds.), The Oxford Handbook of International Investment Law*

Korde, A. (2013). Beneficial Owner – The Debate Continues. *Tax Planning International Review*

Korobelnikov, A. (26 October 2013). Russian Supreme Arbitration Court Delivers Landmark Ruling in Thin Cap Case. *Worldwide Tax Daily*, Doc 2013-24799

KPMG. (1 July 2013). Russian Legislation News

KPMG. (2013). *Global Transfer Pricing Review, SA*

KPMG. (May 2014). *Taxation of Cross-Border Mergers and Acquisition.* https://home.kpmg.com/content/dam/kpmg/pdf/2014/05/russia

Krever, G. (3 December 2012). The Missing Link in China's Tax administration. *TaxAnalysts, Tax Notes International*, 878

Krever, R. (28 August 2013). China Releases Fourth APA Report. *Worldwide Tax Report*, Doc 2013-20437

Krever, R. (vol. 1), No. 1, 30 June 2007. Managers and Their Lawyers: Minimising Tax, Maximising Ethics and The Business Decision Making Process. *Journal of Macau, Business of Science and Technology*, 93–99

Krishnamurthy, V. (2014). India Aims to Reduce Transfer Pricing Disputes Through Safe Harbour Rules. *Bulletin for International Taxation,(vol. 68), No. 1*, 47–52 *******

Krishnamurthy, V. (June 2013). Shell shocked! Companies Asked to Shell Out Taxes on Shares Allegedly Issued at a Discount to Their Parent. *International Taxation*, 709–719

Krishnamurthy, V. (September/October 2013). Transfer Pricing Adjustment on Issuance of Shares to Overseas Parents Leaves Companies Shell-Shocked. *International Transfer Pricing Journal*, 310–316

Krishnamurthy, V. (No 1-2014). India Aims To Reduce Transfer Pricing Disputes Through Safe Harbour Rules. *Bureau of International Taxation*

Kuijs, L. (October 2005). *SOE Dividends: How Much and to Whom?* World Bank

Kumar, A. (2011/2012). *India's Taxation Regime: Perspectives on the Proposed Changes' Fourth NLSIR Symposium Rapporteur Report.* 23 National Schedule India Rev

Kumar, A. (3 June 2013). *Mondaq.* Retrieved 8 16, 2016, from India: Tax Residency Certificate Requirement In India — Bumpy Road Ahead?: http://www.mondaq.com/india/x/238218/Income + Tax/Tax + Residency + Certificate + Requirement + in + India + Bumpy

Kumar, M. (January/February 2012). India-Taxation Aspects of Mergers and Acquisitions. *Asia-Pacific Tax Bulletin*, 71–75

Kumarasingam, S. (2015). Tax Avoidance and Tax Evasion Explained and Exemplified. *South African Tax Guide,http://www.sataxguide.co.za/tax-avoidance-and-tax-evasion-explained-and-exemplified/*

Kuptsove, A. (17 June 2013). Russia Publishes Final Tax Strategy for 2014–2016. *Worldwide Tax Daily,* Doc 2013-14542

Kurilina, O. (31 October 2013). Russia Enacts Regional Tax Incentives. *Worldwide Tax Daily,* Doc 2013-24798

Lampreave, P. (2013). Anti-Tax Avoidance Measures in China and India: An Evaluation of Specific Court Decisions. *Bulletin for International Taxation, (Volume 67), No. 1,* 49–60

Lategan, M. (1992). Transfer Pricing in the Absence of Comparable Market Prices - South Africa. *IFA Cahiers 1992 - Vol. 77a,* 585–597

Law, S. (No 1-2014). Base Erosion and Profit Shifting-An Action Plan for Developing Countries. *Bureau of International Taxation*

Lawson, K. (20 February 2013). *India-US Bilateral Tax Relationship.* Investment Company Institute

Lawson, K. (February 2013). *Letter to Indian and US Competent Authorities.* Investment Company Institute

Lazerow, H. (April 2005). Criteria of International Tax Policy. *University of San Diego School of Law, Legal Studies Research Paper Series*, Research Paper No. 06-08

Bibliography

Ledyaeva, S. (WP No 2013-05). If Foreign Investment Is Not Foreign: Round-Trip Versus Genuine Foreign Investment in Russia. *CEPII*, 1–66

Ledyaeva, S. *Round-Trip Investment Between Offshore Financial Centres and Russia.* www.smithschool.ox.ac.uk/events/Ledyaeva_Karhunen%202.pdf

Legwaila, T. (2012). Tax Characteristics of an Ideal Holding Company Location. *De Jure 45 Volume 1 2012*, pages 22–45

Lemos. (April 2013). The Non-Ratification of BITs in Brazil: A Story of Conflict in a Land of Cooperation. *Government of Brazil*, 1–29

Lennard, M. (January 2013). The New United Nations Model Double Taxation Convention and Related UN Tax Cooperation Work. *International Taxation*, 45–59

Lerner, D. (3 April 2013). Financial Transparency: Challenges And Opportunities for Developing Countries. *Worldwide Tax Daily*, Doc 2013-8016

Levy, M. (2003). Transfer Pricing in China. *Intertax, Volume 11*, 107

Li, J. (1995). China: Procedures for Tax litigation. *IBFD*

Li, J. (2008). Transformation of the Enterprise Income Tax in China: Internationalization and Chinese Innovations. *Bulletin For International Taxation*, 275–288

Li, J. (2010). Tax Transplants and Local Culture: A Comparative Study of the Chinese and Canadian GAAR. *11 Theoretical Inq. L. 655*, 655–685

Li, J. (2012). The Great Fiscal Wall of China: Tax Treaties and Their Role in Defining and Defending China's Tax Base. *Bulletin for International Taxation, (Volume 66), No. 9*, 452–479

Li, J. (2015). Tax Transplants and Local Culture: A Comparative Study of the Chinese and Canadian GAAR. Theoretical Inquiries in Law. *Osgoode Hall Law School, Research Paper No. 04 Vol. 11/ Issue*, 75–105

Li, J. (December 2007). Fundamental Enterprise Income Tax Reform in China: Motivations and Major Changes. *Bulletin For International Taxation*, 519–528

Li, J. (July 2008). Transformation of the Enterprise Income Tax in China: Internationalization and Chinese Innovations. *Bulletin For International Taxation*

Li, J. (June 2014). *Papers on Selected Topics in Protecting the Tax Base of Developing Countries, Paper No. 9, Protecting the Tax Base in the Digital Economy.* United Nations

Li, J. (24–25 November 2012). Keys to Successful Tax Transplants: Process, Process, Process. *Chinese Tax Conference.* Guangzhou: Osgoode Hall Law School, York University, Canada

Li, N. (2014). China's CFC Regime: Existing Rules and Improvement Suggestions. *Bulletin for International Taxation, Volume 68, No. 10*, 536–540

Lin, J. (2010). China Foreign Tax Credit and Global Investment Structures. *Asia-Pacific Tax Bulletin, Volume 16, No. 3*, 221–227

Lingguang, B. (2004). China, Transfer Pricing System: Rules and Procedures. *ITPJ, March/April*, 91–97

Linklaters. (May 2003). Russia: Transfer Pricing Rules, Practice, and Potential Development. *A03104480/0.0/*, 1–7

Lipsher, L. (16 July 2013). Asian Tax Review: A New Tax System For China. *Tax Notes International*, Doc 2013-15432

Lipsher, L. (19 August 2013). Asian Tax Review: India's Irrational Blacklisting Idea. *Tax Notes International*, Doc 2013-17729

Lipsher, L. (2 October 2013). Asian Tax Review: Tax Reform in China and India. *Tax Notes International*, Doc 2013-21012

Lipsher, L. (2 October 2013). Asian Tax Review: Tax Reform in India and China. *Tax Notes International*, Doc 2-13-21012

Lipsher, L. (25 June 2013). Asian Tax Review: China Opens the Tax Umbrella. *Tax Notes International*, Doc 2013-14374

Lipsher, L. (29 May 2013). Asian Tax Review: China Outlines Tax Goals. *Tax Notes International*, Doc 2013-11566

Lipsher, L. (4 February 2013). Asian Tax Review: Vodafone: India's Hunt For Tax Revenue. *Tax Notes International*, Doc 2013-1852

Liu, J. (2015) (Volume 22), No. 4. Bulletin 16: China Makes a Pre-Emptive Strike Against BEPS. *ITPJ*, 245–249

Louw, E. (1986). Currency Fluctuations and International Double Taxation - South Africa. *IFA Cahiers - Vol. 71b*, 135–148

Lui, J. (2003). Review the Legal Jurisprudence of Tax Avoidance. *Foreign Related Taxation Journal, Volume 8*

Lukov, V. (2012). A Global Forum for the New Generation: The Role of the BRICS and the Prospects for the Future. *Russian Ministry of Foreign Affairs Coordinator for BRICS Affairs*

Lungu, L. (1 August 2011). New Russian Transfer Pricing Rules To Take Effect in January 2012. *Worldwide Tax Daily*, Doc 2011-16260

Lungu, L. (10 December 2013). Russia Clarifies Taxation of Cross-Border Interest Payments Under Treaty with Germany *Worldwide Tax Daily*, Doc 2013-28227

Lungu, L. (10 July 2013). Russia Clarifies Taxation of Technical Services Under Indian Treaty. *Worldwide Tax Daily*, Doc 2013-16512

Lungu, L. (11 December 2013). Russia Clarifies Tax Treatment of Dividends, Bond Transactions. *Worldwide Tax Daily*, Doc 2013-28325

Lungu, L. (11 June 2013). Russian Court Rules on PE Determinations Under Tax Treaty With Cyprus. *Worldwide Tax Daily*, Doc 2013-14128

Lungu, L. (13 December 2013). Russian Finance Ministry Clarifies Recognition of Controlled Transactions. *Worldwide Tax Daily*, Doc 2013-28670

Lungu, L. (13 January 2014). Russia Clarifies Tax Treatment of Dividend Payments and Free Use of Equipment. *Worldwide Tax Daily*, Doc 2014-644

Lungu, L. (14 June 2013). Russia Clarifies Corporate Tax Regime for Capital Stake Sale by Nonresident. *Worldwide Tax Daily*, Doc 2013-14457

Lungu, L. (14 May 2013). Company Can Deduct Trademark Royalty Fees, Russian Court Says. *Worldwide Tax Daily*, Doc 2012-10059

Lungu, L. (14 November 2013). Russia Clarifies Reporting Requirements for Groups of Transactions. *Worldwide Tax Daily*, Doc 2013-26225

Lungu, L. (15 March 2013). Russia Clarifies Procedure for Concluding APAs. *Worldwide Tax Daily*, Doc 2013-6058

Lungu, L. (15 May 2013). Russia Clarifies Tax Regime for Foreign Income Gained by Consolidated Group Member. *Worldwide Tax Daily*, Doc 2013-11740

Bibliography

Lungu, L. (15 October 2013). Russia Clarifies Taxation of Foreign-Source Income Under French Treaty. *Worldwide Tax Daily*, Doc 2013-23875

Lungu, L. (17 July 2013). Russia Clarifies Nondiscrimination Provisions of Tax Treaties. *Worldwide Tax Daily*, Doc 2013-17031

Lungu, L. (18 March 2013). Brazil Ratifies TIE with the United States. *Tax Notes International*, Doc 2013-6215

Lungu, L. (18 October 2013). Russia Clarifies Interest-Free Loans Can Be Controlled Transactions for Transfer Pricing Purposes. *Worldwide Tax Daily*, Doc 2013-24060

Lungu, L. (19 August 2013). Russia Clarifies Tax Treatment of Non Residents Russian Source Capital Income. *Worldwide Tax Daily*, Doc 2013-19916

Lungu, L. (2 October 2013). Russia Clarifies Tax Obligations of Nonresidents with PEs in Russia. *Worldwide Tax Daily*, Doc 2013-23160

Lungu, L. (20 November 2013). Russia Clarifies Tax Consequences of Debt Forgiveness, Capital Contributions. *Worldwide Tax Daily*, Doc 2013-26639

Lungu, L. (21 May 2013). Russia Clarifies Applicable Treaty For Payments by Russian Bank to UK Branch of Turkish Bank. *Worldwide Tax Daily*, Doc 2013-12356

Lungu, L. (25 August 2013). Russia, PRC Discuss Tax Cooperation. *Worldwide Tax Daily*, Doc 2013-17774

Lungu, L. (27 August 2013). Russia Clarifies Reporting Requirements for Controlled Transfer Pricing Transactions. *Worldwide Tax Daily*, Doc 2013-20449

Lungu, L. (27 December 2013). Russia Clarifies Taxation of Non Residents Immovable Property and Branches in Russia. *Worldwide Tax Daily*, Doc 2013-29673

Lungu, L. (27 November 2013). Russia Clarifies Tax Treatment of Capital Increases and Share Buybacks. *Worldwide Tax Daily*, Doc 2013-27399

Lungu, L. (29 October 2013). Russia Clarifies Taxation of US Citizen Selling Immovable Property in Russia. *Worldwide Tax Daily*, Doc 2013-24972

Lungu, L. (3 July 2013). Russia Clarifies Application of Thin Capitalisation Rules Under US Tax Treaty. *Worldwide Tax Daily*, Doc 2013-16048

Lungu, L. (31 July 2013). Russia Explains Conditions for Controlled Transactions. *Worldwide Tax Daily*, Doc 2013-18342

Lungu, L. (31 October 2013). Russia Clarifies Taxation of Income From Capital Reductions Under Dutch Treaty. *Worldwide Tax Daily*, Doc 2013-25203

Lungu, L. (4 November 2013). Russia Clarifies Transfer Pricing Provisions. *Worldwide Tax Daily*, Doc 2013-25459

Lungu, L. (5 April 2013). Italian Consulting Company Did Not Have PE in Russia, Finance Ministry Says. *Worldwide Tax Daily*, Doc 2013-8041

Lungu, L. (5 December 2013). Russia Clarifies Recognition of Related Parties in Transfer Pricing Regime. *Worldwide Tax Daily*, Doc 2013-27935

Lungu, L. (5 November 2013). Russia Clarifies Application of Cyprus Treaty. *Worldwide Tax Daily*, Doc 2013-25582

Lungu, L. (6 December 2013). Russia Clarifies Tax Treatment on Outbound Royalties and Debt Forgiveness by Nonresident. *Worldwide Tax Daily*, Doc 2013-28042

Lungu, L. (6 March 2013). Russia Clarifies Tax Treatment of Fees For Services Provided by Luxembourg Intermediary. *Worldwide Tax Daily*, Doc 2013-5136

Lungu, L. (6 November 2013). Russia Clarifies Tax Liability Under Treaty with Norway on Sale of Immovable Property. *Worldwide Tax Daily*, Doc 2013-25695

Lungu, L. (7 January 2014). Russia Clarifies Application of Treaties to Foreign Subdivisions and Deductibility of Royalties. *Worldwide Tax Daily*, Doc 2014-257

Ma, S. (1 November 2012). *China: Administrative Review Committee of Appeal Established.* IBFD

Machado, R. (2011). Cross-Border Business Restructuring – Brazil. *IFA Cahiers - Volume 96A*, 149–167

Majachani, A. (2010). Residence of an Entity for Tax Purposes – South Africa: A Review of the Concept 'Place of Effective Management. *University of Capetown, Master of Laws in Taxation Thesis*

Majumdar, A. (2010). Tax Treaties and Tax Avoidance: Application of Anti-avoidance Provisions – India. *IFA Cahiers- Volume 95A*, 369–388

Majure, K. (November 2013). FATCA: Practical Issues for Non-financial Companies. *International Taxation*, 514–520

Makhetha, D. (October 2013). *A Comparative Analysis of the Usage of the Concept 'Beneficial Owner' in South African Double Tax Agreements, Minor Dissertation.* University of Johannesburg

Malaquias. (5/6 October 2006). The VII Latin America Transfer Pricing Summit. São Paulo, Brazil

Malik, G. (2010). Casenote – The E*Trade Decision. *Asia-Pacific Tax Bulletin*, 304–307

Malik, G. (2014 Volume 20, No. 4). Investing into India. *Asia-Pacific Tax Bulletin*, 237–241

Maraias, A. (November 2014). Kenya/Mauritius/Nigeria/South Africa,The Risk for Tax Treaty Override in Africa – A Comparative Legal Analysis. *Bulletin For International Taxation*, 604–611

Marchyshyn, M. (September 2011). *BRICS Conclusions on Financial Crises, 2008–2011.* BRICS Information Centre

Margalioth, Y. (10 January 2003). Tax Competition, Foreign Direct Investments and Growth, using The Tax System To promote Developing Countries. *Tax Competition. Doc*, 157–200

Markham, M. (2014). The Development of Transfer Pricing in China. *Australian Tax Forum, Vol. 29, 2014*

Martin, J. (21 June 2013). China Pushing Location Specific Advantage Profit Allocations, Practitioners Say. *Worldwide Tax Daily*, Doc 2013-11307

Martin, J. (23 May 2013). India Offers Detailed APA Programme Guidance. *Worldwide Tax Daily*, Doc 2013-12647

Martin, J. (30 April 2013). India Hits 27 Firms With Transfer Pricing Adjustments: Court Challenges Filed. *Worldwide Tax Daily*, Doc 2013010455

Martin, J. (9 May 2013). Expect More Aggressive Chinese Transfer Pricing Positions. *Worldwide Tax Daily*, Doc 2013-11307

Martin, J. (January 2013). BRICS Countries to Jointly Develop Tax and Transfer Pricing. *Tax Notes International*, DOC 2013-1540

Mason, R. (2005). U.S. Tax Treaty Policy and the European Court of Justice. *59 Tax Law Review 65*

Bibliography

Matchekhin, V. (2003). Trends in Company Shareholder Taxation: Single or Double Taxation-Russia. *IFA Cahiers, Volume 88a*, 767–782

Matchekhin, V. (2013). Exchange of Information and Cross-Border Cooperation Between Tax Authorities – Russia. *IFA Cahiers - Volume 98B*, 655–665

Mazansky, E. (2005). The Duke of Westminster Still Lives in South Africa (But Is Very Careful When He Crosses the Road). *Bulletin for International Fiscal Documentation*

Mazansky, E. (2012) (Volume 66), No. (2). Court Enforces EOI Request in Respect of a Non-Taxpayer. *Bulletin For International Taxation*, 91–92

Mazansky, E. (April 2001). South Africa Changes to a Worldwide Tax System. *2001 International Bureau of Fiscal Documentation*, pages 138–146

Mazansky, E. (April 2004). South Africa and its Worldwide Tax Regime: Have We (Almost) Come Full Circle? *IBFD Bulletin*, 151–157

Mazansky, E. (April 2007). South Africa's New General Anti-Avoidance Rule- The Final GAAR. *Bulletin For International Tax*, pages 159–166

Mazansky, E. (April 2009). South Africa's Treaty Network –Why Is South Africa the Meat in the Sandwich. *Bulletin For International Taxation*, 145–151

Mazansky, E. (June 1995). Residence Blurs South African Rules. *International Tax Review*, pages 31–34

Mazansky, E. Hybrid Debt and Hybrid Equity Instruments and the Interest Limitation Rule in SA. *Bulletin for International Taxation, 2015 (Volume 69), No. 3*, 178–185

Mazansky. (2011). South Africa New Headquarter Company Regime. *Bulletin for International Taxation, Volume 65, No 3*, 166–172

McClure. (1999). Tax Holidays and Investment Incentives. *International Bureau of Fiscal Documentation*, 326–339

McIntyre, M. (April 2006). Comments on the OECD Proposal For Secret and Mandatory Arbitration of International Tax Disputes. *Wayne State University Law School*, Legal Studies Research Paper Series, No 07-05

McKenzie, B. (2010). *Dispute Resolution Around the World, Brazil*

Medaglia, T. (June 2014). Brazil TP Rules. *International Tax Review*

Meena, S. (26 April 2013). *Income Tax Overseas Units*. Press Information Bureau, Government of India, Ministry of Finance

Mehta, N. (2006). India-An Integrated Approach to Formulating a Transfer Pricing Strategy Concerning Marketing and Distribution Affiliates. *ITPJ, May/June*, 124–143

Mehta, N. (December 2012). India Discussion in ICC-FICCI International Tax Roundtable

Mehta, N. (December 2012). Vodafone, Hydra and Hercules, Second Labour Revisited. *GITC Review Vol.xi No.2*, 83–95

Mehta, P. (December 2012). India Discussion in ICC-FICCI International Taxation Roundtable

Messere, K. (February 2003). Expansion of the OECD's Tax Activities. *IBFD Bulletin*, 75–81

Meyer, S. (September 2010). The Meaning of Beneficial Ownership and the Use Thereof for Treaty Shopping and Tax Avoidance. *University of Pretoria*, 1–63

Michel, B. (July 2013). IFA Turns 75! Proceedings of the IFA 75th Anniversary Jubilee Conference. *Bulletin For International Taxation*, 383–390

Miller, A. (Doc 2013-23821). South African Government Ratifies Mutual Assistance Convention. *Worldwide Tax Daily*

Mironov, M. (2010). *Tax Evasion and Growth: Evidence from Russia.* Madrid, Spain: IE Business School

Mitra, R. (2013). Undervaluation of Shares and Secondary Adjustments: Next Wave of TP Litigation in India. *Transfer Pricing International Journal, International Tax Centre*

Mitra, R. (January 2013). Transfer Pricing in India- Better and Sunny Days Ahead. *International Taxation*, 66–75

Mody, A. (12 August 2013). Emerging Trends in Indian Transfer Pricing. *Tax Analysts*, 633–635

Mohandas, T. (September 2013). Limited Incentives to Elect Safe Harbour Rules in India. *International Taxation*, 337–358

Monani, S. (October 2015). Tax Residence Certificate- Indian Perspective. *International Taxation Vol. 13, No 75*, 361–365

Monteiro, A. (2015 (Volume 69), No. 11). Brazilian Thin Capitalization Rules and Tax Treaties: A Critical Approach. *Bulletin for International Taxation*

Moran, T. (2008). The United Nations and Transnational Corporations: A Review and Perspective. *Transnational Corporations, Vol. 18, No. 2 (August 2009)*, 1–312

Moran, T. (20–21 September 1999). Foreign Direct Investment and Development: A Reassessment of The Evidence and Policy Implications. *OECD Conference on the Role of International Investment in Development, Corporate Responsibilities and the OECD Guidelines for Multinational Enterprises.* PARIS: OECD

Morgan, E. International Tax Las as a Ponzi Scheme. *Suffolk Transnational Law Review*, Vol 34, Book 1

Morisset, J. How Tax Policy and Incentives Affect Foreign Direct Investment. In B. Bora, *New Directions for Research in FDI* (pp. 1–30). Rutledge

Morozova, A. (2003). Recent Corporate Tax Changes in Russia: Something Old, Something New and Something Borrowed. *2003 International Bureau of Fiscal Documentation*, pages 59–93

Morriss, A. (27 October 2011). Cartelizing Taxes: Understanding the OECD's Campain Against Harmful Tax Competition. *The University of Alabama School of Law*

Mortier, F. (December 2015). The Russian Permanent Establishment: A Trap for Foreign Distributors? *European Taxation*, 554–565

Mukherjee, S. (19 April 2012). BRICS Finance Ministers Meeting in Washington, DC. *Worldwide Tax Daily*

Mukherjee, S. (19 February 2013). India- Australian Tax Treaty Shields IT Support Services Fees From Taxation in India. *Worldwide Tax Daily*, Doc 2013-3533

Mukherjee, S. (2005). Intra-Group Management Services: Learning from Transfer Pricing Audits. *ITPJ, November/December*, 314–316

Mukherjee, S. (2006). India-Transfer Pricing – A Practitioner's View. *Asia-Pacific Tax Bulletin, March/April*, 94–97

Bibliography

Mukherjee, S. (2008). Recent Judicial Pronouncements on Transfer Pricing. *Asia-Pacific Tax Bulletin, May/June*, 206–212

Mukherjee, S. (July/August 2014). Development of International Tax in India. *Asia-Pacific Tax Bulletin*, 228–229

Murphy, O. Transfer Pricing and Intangibles - South Africa. *IFA Cahiers - Volume 92A*, 505–525

Murray, R. (2012). *Tax Avoidance.* Sweet and Maxwell

Musviba, N. (July 2014). Where to with Thin Capitalisation. *SA Tax Guide*, http://www.sataxguide.co.za/where-to-with-thin-capitalisation

Naban, D. (December 2007). Tax Risk Management from a Legal Perspective. *Asia-Pacific Tax Bulletin*, 455–459

Nakayama, K. (March 2011). Tax Policy: Designing and Drafting a Domestic Law to Implement a Tax Treaty. *International Monetary Fund: Technical Notes and Manuals*

Narvekar, A. (June 2013). Tax Residence Certificates - Road Ahead for Foreign Companies in India. *International Tax Review*

Naskar, A. (March/April 2013). The General Avoidance Rule - An Indian and International Perspective. *Asia- Pacific Tax Bulletin*, 97–107

Natale, M. (7 January 2013). Brazil Amends Transfer Pricing Rules on Financial Transactions. *Tax Notes International*, Doc 2013-298

Nee, O. (1996). A Loss of Investor Privileges: China's Capital Equipment Import Duty Exemption. *China Business Review, 32*

Nelly, C. (2013). *Cyprus Braces for Russian Cash Exodus.* www.ekathimerini.com

Nelson, S. (August/September 2003). China: Tax Controversies. *Asia-Pacific Tax Bulletin*, 235–240

Network, T. (2011). *The Cost of Tax Abuse, A Briefing Paper on the Cost of Tax Evasion Worldwide*

Neviani, T. (1986). Transfer of Assets into and out of a Taxing Jurisdiction – Brazil. *IFA Cahiers- Vol. 71a.*, 197–207

Ni, P. (October 2013). What You Need to Know About Setting Up an Offshore Trust for a Chinese HNWI. *Offshore Investment.com*

Nieuwenhuizen, A. (16 July 2013). *Draft Handbook on Transfer Pricing Risk Assessment.* Grant Thornton

Norwood, B. (2013). China - Location Savings and Other Location-Specific Advantage. *Asia-Pacific Tax Bulletin, (Volume 19), No. 5*, 332–334

Nov, A. (Apr. 18, 2005). Tax Incentives For Foreign Direct Investments: The Drawbacks. *Tax Notes International*, p. 263

Novikov, D. (30 May 2013). Russian Finance Ministry Announces Tax Strategy for 2014 and Beyond. *Worldwide Tax Daily*, Doc 2013-13023

O'Connell, A. (April 2008). Combating Large-Scale Tax Evasion, Australia's Experience. *International Tax Bulletin*, 145–150

O'Donoghue, M. (3 December 2013). News Analysis: Another Adverse Shift In Russia's Tax Policy on Financing Structures. *Worldwide Tax Daily*, Doc 2013-27641

O'Donoghue, M. (30 December 2013). Recent Key Russian Developments. *Worldwide Tax Daily*, Doc 2013-29405

Bibliography

O'Donoghue, M. (31 January 2013). News Analysis: Is Russia's Stance on Foreign Courts' Tax Rulings a Warning to Investors. *Worldwide Tax Daily*, Doc 2013-1879

O'Donoghue, M. (4 January 2013). Russia: 2012 Year in Review. *Tax Notes International*, Doc 2012-23437

O'Neill, J. (2001). *Building Better Global Economies BRICs*. Goldman Sachs Global Economic Paper No 66, November 2001

OECD. (16 May 2013). Revised Section E on Safe Harbours in Chapter IV of Transfer Pricing Guidelines

OECD. (1987). *International Tax Avoidance and Evasion, Four Related Studies*. Paris

OECD. (1987). Thin Capitalisation; Taxation of Entertainers, Artistes

OECD. (1995/2013). *Transfer Pricing Guidelines for Multinational Enterprises and Tax Administrators*

OECD. (1996). *Controlled Foreign Company Legislation: Studies in Taxation of Foreign Source Income*

OECD. (1998). *Harmful Tax Competition, An Emerging Global Tax Issue*. OECD

OECD. (1998). *OECD Report on Harmful Tax Competition*

OECD. (2003). TAG Discussion Paper, 'Place of Effective Management' Concept: Suggestions for Changes to the OECD Model Tax Convention

OECD. (2006). *Comparability Issues; A Series of Draft Issue Notes-Public Invitation to Comment*

OECD. (2008). *Transactional Profit Methods-Discussion Draft*

OECD. (2010). *Paper on Arms' Length Range*

OECD. (2010). *Paper on Comparability Adjustments*

OECD. (2010). *Paper on Location Savings*

OECD. (2010). *Paper on Transfer Pricing Methods*

OECD. (2010). *September 2008 Discussion Draft on TP Aspects of Business Restructuring-CFA Response to Comments Received*

OECD. (2010). *September 2009 Draft Revised Chapters I-III TPG-CFA Response to Comments Received*

OECD. (2011). *Paper on TP Legislation*

OECD. (2012). *OECD's Current Tax Agenda*

OECD. (2012). *Timing Issues Relating to TP- WP6 Draft, Request for Comments*

OECD. (2013). *A Boost to Transparency and International Tax Co-operation*. OECD, Centre For Tax Policy and Administration

OECD. (2013). *Handbook on TP Risk Assessment-Draft, for Public Consultation*

OECD. (2013). *July 2013 Revised Discussion Draft on TP Aspects of Intangibles-for Public Comments*

OECD. (2013). *White Paper on TP Documentation-for Public Consultation*

OECD. (2014). *Model Agreement Between the Competent Authorities of [Jurisdiction a] and [Jurisdiction b] on the Automatic Exchange of Financial Account Information to Improve International Tax Compliance*

OECD. (2014). *Preventing the Granting of Treaty Benefits in Inappropriate Circumstances, OECD/G20, BEPS Project*

OECD. (2014). *Standard for Automatic Exchange of Financial Account Information*

Bibliography

OECD. (2015). *BEPS Action 4: 2015 Final Report, Limiting Base Erosion Involving Interest and Other Financial Payments*

OECD. (2015). *BEPS: Actions 8/10: Final Report 2015, Aligning TP Outcomes with Value Creation.* BEPS

OECD. (31 July 2013). OECD Announces Information Exchange Peer Review Reports. *Tax Notes International*, Doc 2013-18548

OECD. (April 2012). *The Global Forum on Transparency and Exchange of Information for Taxation Purposes: Information Brief*

OECD. (August 2012). Thin Capitalisation Legislation a Background Paper for Country Tax Administrations, Initial Draft

OECD. (August 2014). *Part 2 of a Report to G20 Development Working Group on The Impact of BEPS in Low Income Countries*

OECD. (February 2001). TAG Draft Discussion Paper, The Impact of the Communications Revolution on the Application of 'Place of Effective Management'

OECD. (January 2006). *Manual on the Implementation of Exchange of Information Provisions for Tax Purposes*

OECD. (July 2010). *Paper on Location Savings*

OECD. (No year). *Employee Stock Option Plans: Impact on TP- a Study*

OECD. (November 1986). R(6) Double Taxation Conventions and the Use of Conduit Companies Report

OECD. (November 1986). *R4: Thin Capitalisation: Adapted by the OECD Council*

OECD. *1979 Report on Transfer Pricing and Multinational Enterprises*

OECD. *Centre For Tax Policy and Administration, Glossary of Tax Terms.* wwww.oecd.org/document/29/ 0,3343,en_2649_34897_33933853_1_1_1_1,00.html

OECD/G20. (2015). *Action 13: Guidance on the Implementation of Transfer Pricing Documentation and Country-by-Country Reporting.* OECD/G20

Oguttu, A. (2009). Resolving the Conflict Between Controlled Foreign Company Legislation and Tax Treaties: A South African Perspective. *42 Comp. & Int'l L.J. S. Afr.*, 73–114

Oguttu, A. (2010). A Critique on the OECD Campaign Against Tax Havens: Has it Been Successful? A South Africa Perspective. *21 Stellenbosch L. Rev. 172*, 172–200

Oguttu, A. (2010).The Challenges of Taxing Profits Attributed to Permanent Establishments: A South African Perspective. *Bulletin for International Taxation, (Volume 64), No. 3*, 165–175

Oguttu, A. (2011). Developing South Africa as a Gateway for Foreign Investment in Africa: A Critique of South Africa's Headquarters Regime. *36 SAYIL*, 61–93

Oguttu, A. (2011). Exposing and Curtailing Secret Offshore Tax Shelters, the Tools and Enablers. A Call for Vigilance in South Africa. *44 Comp. & Int'l L.J. S. Afr. 30*, 30–58

Oguttu, A. (2011, Volume 65, No. 6). The Role of Tax Havens in the Global Financial Crisis: A Critique of International Initiatives and Measures to Curb the Resultant Fiscal Challenges and the Example of South Africa. *Bulletin for International Taxation*

Oguttu, A. (2013). Curbing Thin Capitalization: A Comparative Overview with Reference to South Africa's Approach – Challenges Posed by the Amended Section 31 of the Income Tax Act 1962. *Bulletin for International Taxation, (Volume 67), No. 6*, 311–326

Oguttu, A. (2013). International/South Africa - Curbing Thin Capitalization: A Comparative Overview with Reference to South Africa's Approach – Challenges Posed by the Amended Section 31 of the Income Tax Act 1962. *Bulletin for International Taxation, Volume 67, No 6*, 311–326

Oguttu, A. (2014). A Critique on the Effectiveness of Exchange of Information on Tax Matters in Preventing Tax Avoidance and Evasion: A South African Perspective. 1–18: *Bulletin for International Taxation, (Volume 68), No. 1*

Oguttu, A. (Bulletin for International Taxation, Volume 64, No. 3). *South Africa The Challenges of Taxing Profits Attributed to Permanent Establishments: A South African Perspective.* 165–175: 2010

Oguttu, A. (November 2007). *Curbing Offshore Tax Avoidance: The Case of South African Companies and Trusts, Doctor of Laws Thesis.* University of South Africa

Oguttu, A. (Vol. 4, Issue 3 (2009)). The Challenges E-Commerce Poses to the Determination of a Taxable Presence: The "Permanent Establishment" Concept Analyzed from a South African Perspective". *Journal of International Commercial Law and Technology*, 213–223

Okamura, T. (Vol. 11, Iss. 2 [1993], Art. 1). The Japanese Tax System: Due Process and the Taxpayer. *Berkeley Journal of International Law*, 125–158

Oliveira, A. (2013). The Taxation of Foreign Passive Income for Groups of Companies – Brazil. *IFA Cahiers- Volume 98A*, 159–180

Oliver, D. (2000). Beneficial Ownership. *International Bureau of Fiscal Documentation*, 310–325

Oliver, L. (1997). Tax Avoidance Options Available to the Commissioner for Inland Revenue. *4 South African Law Journal*, 725–745

Oliver, L. (2010). Tax Treaties and Tax Avoidance: Application of Anti-avoidance Provisions - South Africa. *IFA Cahiers- Volume 95A*, 719–729

Olivier, L. (2002). The 'Permanent Establishment' Requirement In and International and Domestic Context: An Overview. *119 South African Law Journal*, 866–873

Oortjiwn, H. (April 2016). Dispute Resolution in Cross-Border Tax Matters. *European Taxation*, 163–168

Orsini, EP. (September/October 2013). New Brazilian Supreme Court Decision on CFC Rules. *International Transfer Pricing Journal*, 336–338

Ostwahl, T. (2010). Anti-Avoidance Measures in India. *National Law School of India Review*, 59–103

Ostwal, T. (November 2014). *Overview of Indian TP*

Owens, J. (2013 Volume 67, No. 3). The Role of Tax Administrations in the Current Political Climate. *Bulletin for International Taxation*, 156–150

Owens, J. (October 2015). Dispute Resolution: The Next Frontier, Issues Paper. *International Tax and Investment Center*

Panse, A. (June 2013). Arms Length in Price Control Situations: Case of Royalty. *International Taxation*, 725–729

Bibliography

Parada, L. (30 June 2014). Lessons Learned From the Swiss Julius Baer Case. *Tax Notes International*, 1217–1224

Pardasani, M. (September 2013). Draft Indian Safe Harbour Rules- A Watershed. *International Taxation*, 359–364

Parillo, K. (5 February 2013). BRICS Countries Unsatisfied with OECD and UN Tax Policy. *Tax Notes International*, Doc 2013-2623

Passos, A. (1988). Recognition of Foreign Enterprises as Taxable Entities - South Africa. *IFA Cahiers- Vol. 73a*, 211–223

Patel, V. (2010). India - The Evolution of Transfer Pricing Jurisprudence in India. *ITPJ, November/December*, 402–416

Patel, V. (207). India- Information Technology Industry and Related Transfer Pricing Issues. *ITPJ, July/August*, 233–237

Patel, V. (January 2011). CBDT Sets Up Income Tax Overseas Units in Its Bid to Join Global Efforts to Increase Transparency in International Financial Matters. *International Transfer Pricing Journal, (Volume 18), No. 4*, 302–303

Pawar, B. (2013). India-Location Savings. *Asia-Pacific Tax Bulletin, (Volume 19), No. 5*, 336–339

Peng, T. (2005). China-Structuring an Appropriate Transfer Pricing Policy. *Asia-Pacific Tax Bulletin, November/December*, 477–484

Piening. (1997). *Global Europe: The European Union on World Affairs*. Lynne Rienner Publishers

Pinto, L. (1999). Advance Rulings-Brazil. *IFA Cahiers-Vol 84b*, 267–279

Pires, L. (2013). Brazil/International/European Union, The Brazilian Controlled Foreign Company Regime: A Comparative Analysis from an International Tax Law Perspective. *Bulletin for International Tax, Volume 67, No 6*, 295–300

Pistone. (2015). *BRICS and the Emergence of International Tax Coordination*. Amsterdam: IBFD

Pogorelov, R. (19 December 2013). News Analysis: Russia's Beneficial Ownership Concept. *Worldwide Tax Daily*, Doc 2013-29069

Pogorletskiy, A. (May/June 2002). The Russian Tax Reform. *Intereconomics*, pages 156–161

Politics, H. (June 2015). *China 'Going Out' 2.0: Dawn of a New Era for Chinese Investment Abroad*

Polivanova-Rosenauer. (June/July 2002). Review of the Corporate Income Tax Chapter of the Russian Tax Code. *European Taxation*, 228–239

Prakash, P. (2013). Emerging Transfer Pricing and International Tax Issues. *ITPJ, (Volume 20), No. 6*, 374–378

Prebble, J. (1996). 'Criminal Law, Tax Evasion, Shams, and Tax Avoidance: Part II – Criminal Law Consequences of Categories of Evasion and Avoidance. *New Zealand Journal of Taxation Law and Policy*, 59–74

Prebble, Z. (April 2008). Comparing the General Anti-Avoidance Rule of Income Tax Law with the Civil Law Doctrine of Abuse of Law. *Bulletin for International Taxation*, 151–170

Pustovalov, E. (2016): Tax Avoidance Revisited: The Russian Federation. http://www.eatlp.org/uploads/public/Russia%20(11%20Dec%202015).pdf, 1–13

Bibliography

PwC. (12 August 2013). Sharing Insights: News Alert:After Considering Divergent Judicial Views The Tribunal Upholds Selection of Foreign AE as Tested Party in Accordance With International Best Practices. *www.pwc.in*, 1–4

PwC. (17 June 2013). Sharing Insights: News Alert: Development Agreement. *www.pwc.in*, 1–4

PwC. (17 June 2013). Sharing Insights: News Alerts: Sale of a Company's Shares Cannot Be Treated As a Sale of Immovable Property Held By That Company Merely Because the Transaction Escaped Taxation. *www.pwc.in*, 1–5

PwC. (28 January 2013). South Africa Delays the WHT on Interest until 1 July 2013 and Increases the Rate to 15%. *African Tax Newsalert*

PwC. (8 July 2013). Sharing Insights: News Alert. *www.pwc.in*, 1–3

PwC. (November 2013). *Senate Finance Committee Chairman Baucus Releases International Tax Reform Discussion Draft.* Washington: www.pwc.com

Qin, X. China-New Advance Pricing Agreement Procedure. *ITPJ, March/April*, 69–72

Qiu, D. (2014 (Volume 68), No. 12). China/BVI/Cayman Islands/Hong Kong, Collecting Unpaid Tax Offshore: Caribbean Tax Havens and FDI in China. *Bulletin for International Taxation*, 648–659

Qiu, D. (2015). *CFC Rules and the Latest Developments in the PRC, Xiamen University, PRC.* http://www.law.hku.hk/aiifl/wp-content/uploads/ppt/TLRP-DoreenQiu-ppt.pdf

Qiu, D. (February 2013). The Concept of "Beneficial Ownership" in China's Tax Treaties- The Current State of Play. *Bulletin for International Taxation*, 98–104

Ramanujan, A. (2008). Rolls Royce Decision: Income Attribution to Permanent Establishments. *ITPJ, May/June*, 148–157

Rangachary, N. (September 14, 2012). *First Report of the Committee to Review Taxation of the Development Centres and the IT Sector.* Government of India

Rao, G. (October 2009). *Initiative for Policy Dialogue Working Paper Series-Tax System Reform in India.* Initiative for Policy Dialogue

Rao, K. (February 2011). India's FDI Flows:Trends and Concepts. *Institute for Studies in Industrial Development*, Working Paper 2011/01

Rao, M. (25 July 2005). Trends and Issues in Tax Policy and Reform in India. *paper Presented at India Policy Forum*

Rao, M. (October 2009). Tax System Reform in India. *Initiative for Policy Dialogue Working Paper Series*

Rao, S. (November/December 2002). India, Inbound Investments – Strategies and Challenges. *Asia-Pacific Tax Bulletin*, 356–364

Ray, R. (1998). Indian Society and the Establishment of British Supremacy, 1765–1818. In P. J. Marshall, *The Oxford History of the British Empire: vol. 2, The Eighteenth Century* (pp. 502–29)

RBI. (2013). *Master Circular No. 12/2012-13, External Borrowings.* Reserve Bank of India

Reuter, P. (2012). *Draining Development, Controlling Flows of Illicit Funds from Developing Countries.* World Bank

Rg, G. (1957). Taxation in Brazil. *World Tax Series, Little, Brown and Company*

Richardson, V. (1987). The Tax Residence of Companies. *IFA Cahiers - Vol. 72a*, 147–159

Richardson, V. (1998). Tax Treatment of Corporate Losses - South Africa. *IFA Cahiers 1998 - Vol. 83a*, 733–742

Ring, D. (14 April 2008). What's at Stake in the Sovereignty Debate? *Boston College Law School, Legal Studies Research Paper Series*, RESEARCH PAPER 153

Ring, D. (2007). International Tax Relations: Theory and Implications. *60 Tax Law Review 2*, 2

Ring, D. (July 2010). Who Is Making International Tax Policy? International Organisations as Power Players in a High Stakes World. *Boston College Law*, Research Paper 185

Ring, D. The Promise of International Tax Scholarship and Its Implications for Research Design, Theory, and Methodology. *Saint Louis University Law Journal*, Vol 55, pages 307–330

Rixen, T. (2011). Tax Competition and Inequality, The Case for Global Tax Governance. *Global Governance: A Review of Multilateralism and International Institutions*, Vol 17

Rocha, S. (July 2012). Treaty Shopping and Beneficial Ownership under Brazil's Tax Treaties. *Bulletin For International Taxation*, 351–360

Roeleveld, J. (2013). Exchange of Information and Cross-Border Cooperation Between Tax Authorities - South Africa. *IFA Cahiers 2013 - Volume 98B*, 687–704

Roeleveld, J. (2016). Dispute Resolution Procedures in International Tax Matters – SA. *IFA Cahiers - Volume 101A*, 623–633

Rohatgi, R. (2001). *Basic International Taxation.* Kluwer Law International

Rolim, J. ((2011) 96a 152). *Brazilian Report in International Fiscal Association-Studies on International Fiscal Law.* Cahiers de Droit Fiscal International

Rolim, J. (2014). Tax Treaty Disputes in Brazil. *London School of Economics (forthcoming)*

Rolim, J. Notes on Non Tax Avoidance Law Created by Complementary Law 104/2001. *O Planejamento Tributario E a Lei Complementar 104*

Ronsenblatt, P. (2014). Brazil: Recent Case Law and New CFC Rules. *3rd Annual BRICS Conference, Queen Mary, University of London*

Rosembuj. (1998). Fiscalidad Internacional' Marcial Pons. 111

Rosenblatt, P. (2012). Brazil: CFC Rules Update. *40 (4) Intertax 279*

Rosenbloom, H. (10 September 2007). The Tillinghast Lectuzre. *Harvard Law School, International Tax Program*

Rovnick, N. (2013, March). *Rovnick, Most Foreign Investment in BRICs Isn't Foreign at All—It's Tycoons Using Tax Havens.* Retrieved from Quartz: http://qz.com/66944/the-brics-biggest-investment-sources-are-tax-havens-which-mostly-shows-the-rich-stealing-from-the-poor/

Roxan, I. (2012). Limits to Globalisation: Some Implications for Taxation, Tax Policy and the Developing World. *LSE Law, Society and Economy Working Papers*, Working Papers 3/2012

RSA. (12 October 2013). *Statement of Auto Exchange Tax Information.* Ministry of Finance

RSA. (17 July 2013). *Terms of Reference for the South African Tax Review Committee.* South African National Treasury
RSA. (18 July 2013). *Moody's Investors Service Affirms South Africa's Credit Ratings and Maintains the Negative Outlook.* RSA National Treasury
RSA. (21 May 2013). *Budget Vote 10.* National Treasury
RSA. (27 February 2013). *2013 Budget Speech, Minister of Finance*
RSA. (27 February 2013). *South Africa Lists Tax Amendments in 2013 Budget Review.* South African National Treasury
RSA. (27 February 2013). *South Africa Releases Budget Review Tax Components for 2013.* South African National Treasury
RSA. (29 April 2013). *Request for Public Comment for Incorporation into Forthcoming 2013 Tax Laws Amendment Bill: Proposed Limitations Against Excessive Interest Deductions.* RSA National Treasury
RSA. 5th Report - Basing the South African Income Tax System on the Source or Residence Principle - Options and Recommendations. *National Treasury, Republic of South Africa (Katz Report)*
Rubinstein, F. (7 March 2016). Closing the Brazilian Tax Gap: Public Shaming, Transparency and Mandatory Disclosure as Means of Dealing with Tax Delinquencies, Tax Evasion and Tax Planning. *Derivatives & Financial Instruments, (Volume 18), No. 1*
Rubinstein, F. (July/August 2013). Tax Incentives for Investments in Brazilian Infrastructure Bonds. *Derivatives & Financial Instruments*, 154–155
Russia-India. (1988). *India-Russia Income Tax Treaty*
Samoletova, J. (26 April 2013). *Brazil Confirms 2004 Tax Treaty with Russia "Not in Force".* 2013 EYGM Limited
Samoylenko, V. (5 April 2004). Government Policies for Internal Tax Havens in Russia. *Tax Notes Int'l*, 77–86
Sancilo, P. Clarifying (or is it codifying) the notable abstruse, Step Transactions, Economic Substance and The Code. *J.D. Candidate 2013, Columbia Law School*
Sandler, D. (1998). *The Interaction Between DTCs and CFC Legislation Pushing the Boundaries.* London: Kluwer
Sanghavi, D. (2013). India/International TP or Not TP: Examining the Applicability of the Arm's Length Principle to Inter-Company Equity Financing Transactions. *Bulletin for International Taxation, (Volume 67), No. 9*, 497–505
Sanghavi, S. (18 January 2012). India, Proposed CFC Regime. *Asia-Pacific Tax Bulletin, 2012 (Volume 18), No. 1*, 56/63
Santos, R. (2013). Tax Treaty Qualification of Income Derived from Hybrid Financial Instruments. *Bulletin for International Taxation, 2013 (Volume 67), No. 10*
Santos. (2013). Tax Treaty Qualification of Income Derived from Hybrid Financial Instruments. *Bulletin for International Taxation, 2013 (Volume 67), No 10*
Sapire, M. (27 November 2013). Latin American Practitioners Discuss Tax Planning Challenges. *Tax Notes International*, Doc 2013-27307
Sapra, M. (18 April 2013). *India-US Bilateral Relationship.* New Delhi: Department of Revenue, Government of India

Bibliography

Sapra, M. (18 June 2013). Tax Court Judges Discuss Beneficial Ownership Questions at Miami Conference. *World Wide Tax Daily*, Doc 2013-14627

Saran, S. (26 November 2013). Foreign Companies' Sale of Shares in Indian Company Not Subject to Indian Tax. *Tax Notes International*, Doc 2013-24718

SARS. (10 September 2013). *SARS Enforcement and Customs Operations for August 2013*

SARS. (16 January 2013). *SARS Enforcement and Customs Operations for December 2012*. SARS

SARS. (1999). *Practice Note 7-Section 31 of the Income Tax Act, 1962, Determination of Taxable Income of Certain Persons from International Transactions: Transfer Pricing*. Republic of South Africa

SARS. (2 September 2013). *G 20 Summit: A Test for World Leaders*. South African Government News Agency

SARS. (2013). *Draft Comprehensive Guide to Dividends Tax*. www.sars.gov.za

SARS. (2013). *Strategic Plan-2013/14 - 2017/18*

SARS. (2013). *Transfer Pricing Country Profile*

SARS. (2014). *Guide on the Implementation of an Intergovernmental Agreement to Improve International Tax Compliance Requiring the Reporting of Financial Information for Exchange of Information Purposes, Draft*

SARS. (29 April 2013). *Annexure C: Draft Explanatory Memorandum: Anti-Hybrid Debt Instrument Recharacterisation*

SARS. (31 March 2009). *Interpretation Note: No. 18 (Issue 2)*

SARS. (5 August 2013). *SARS Enforcement and Customs Operations for July 2013*. South African Revenue Service

SARS. (7 February 2013). *South Africa Notes Tax Fraud Cases*. South African Revenue Service

SARS. (9 September 2013). *G20 Countries to Share Tax info to Curb Evasion*. South African Government News Agency

SARS. (Doc 2013-25767). *Media Statement: The Davis Tax Committee Calls for Contributions*. Worldwide Tax Daily

SARS. (February 2015). *Draft Interpretation Note: Determination of Taxable Income of Certain Persons*. http://www.drtp.ca/wp-content/uploads/2015/02/South_Africa_Draft_Thin_Capitalisation.pdf

SARS. (February 2016). *Automatic Exchange of Information (Includes FATCA and the Common Reporting Standard (CRS)*

SARS. (June 2014). *Business Requirement Specification, Automatic Exchange of Information (FATCA)*

SARS. (November 2005). *Discussion Paper on Tax Avoidance and Section 103 of the Income Tax Act, 1962 (Act No. 58 of 1962)*

SARS. (September 2011). *Discussion Paper on Interpretation Note 6 Place of Effective Management*

SAT. (10 December 2013). *Guoshuihan[2009] No. 698*. 2009-27725: Worldwide Tax Daily

SAT. (2012). *China Advance Pricing Arrangement Annual Report*, SAT, People's Republic of China

SAT. (2015). *China's International Tax Work Conference to Strengthen Global Cooperation and Continuously Develop Upgraded Version of International Tax Work, 2014/2016*

SAT. (24 August 2009). *Guo Shui Fa(2009), No 124 Documentation Requirements on Treaty Benefit claim*

SAT. (24 December 2013). Bulletin [2013] 72, China Releases Guidelines for Nonresident Companies' Tax-Free Reorganisations. *Worldwide Tax Daily*

SAT. (3 December 2013). Caishui [2013] 91, China Confirms Capital Gains Tax Deferral in Shanghai Free Trade Zone. *Worldwide Tax Daily*

SAT. (30 October 2013). Guoshuihan[2009] 212, Clarifying the EITL Treatment of Income from Technology Transfers. *Worldwide Tax Daily*

SAT. (5 December 2013). Guofa [2013] 46, China Provides Tax Exemption for Dividends From Preferred Stock. *Worldwide Tax Daily*, Doc 2013-27854

SAT. (9 September 2013). Conduct Taxation Analysis with Scientific Attitude and Focus on Serving Economic & Social Development. (pp. Doc 2013-21514). *Worldwide Tax Daily*

SAT. (9 September 2013). Reinforce Cross-Border Tax Source Risk Management & Improve Construction of Four Major Mechanisms. *Strengthening International Tax Administration of the Tax System* (pp. Doc 2013-21512). Worldwide Tax Daily

SAT. (December 2009). *Guo Shui Han (2009) No 698, Capital Gains*

SAT. (February 2009). *Guo Shui Han (2009) No 81, Dividends*

SAT. (July 2009). *Guo Shui Han (2009) No 395, Residence*

SAT. (July 2010). *Guo Shui Fa (2010) No 75, Comprehensive Document with Regards to General Application of Treaty Articles*

SAT. (June 2010). *Guo Shui Han (2010) No 266, Taxation of Interest Derived by Chinese Branches of Foreign Banks*

SAT. (October 2009). *Guo Shui Han (2009) No 601, Beneficial Owner*

SAT. (September 2009). *Guo Shui Han (2009) No 507, Royalties*

SAT. *Guo Shui Han (2008) No 955, Foreign Branch of Chinese Resident Bank*

Sauvant. (16 (2015) 11–87). The Negotiations of the UN Code of Conduct on Transnational Corporations. *The Journal of World Investment & Trade*, 11–87

Schachter. (1984). Compensation for Expropriation. *78 AM. J. INT'L L 121*, 121

Schneider, B. (24–25 November 2012). The Chinese Income Tax System and the Rule of Law. *International Conference on China Tax and Policy*. Guangzhou

Schoueri, E. (1995). 'Planejamento Fiscal Através dos Acordos de Bitributação: Treaty Shopping. *Editora Revista dos Tribunais*, 21

Schoueri, E. (2016). *GAARS- A Key Element of Tax Systems in Post BEPS World* (pp. 109–146). IBFD

Scott. (2010). Codified Canons and the Common Law of Interpretation. *The Georgetown Law Journal, Vol 98*, 341/430

Seldon, A. (1979). Tax Avoision. *The Institute of Economic Affairs*

Selig, M. (August/September 1999). Half Trust, Half Company, All Anstalt: The History and Possible Tax Consequences of the Liechtenstein Anstalt Down Under. *Bulletin*, 377–399

Bibliography

Shah, R. (2013). India-Transfer Pricing Issues Relating to Marketing Intangibles. *Asia-Pacific Tax Bulletin, (Volume 19), No. 2*, 42–45

Shah, R. (8 April 2013). Taxing the Cloud: India. *Tax Analysts*, 159–163

Shaheen, S. (September 2012). The Future for BRICS Tax Policy Coordination. *www.internationaltaxreview.com*, 25–26

Shan, W. China's Investment Treaty Policy-Recent Changes and Future Direction, Xi'an Jiaotong University, China. *Oxford Brookes University*

Shaoying, C. (December 2011). Denial System in Anti-avoidance. *East China University of Political Science*

Sharkey, N. (2005). China's Income Tax Concept of "Enterprise" and the Concept of "Company" – Interaction with the Australia–China Tax Treaty. *IBFD Bulletin*, 157–166

Sharkey, N. (2011). China's Tax Treaties and Beneficial Ownership: Innovative Control of Treaty Shopping or Inferior Law Making Damaging to International Law? *Bulletin for International Taxation, (Volume 65), No. 12*, 655–661

Sharkey, N. (2012). International Tax as International Law and the Impact of China. *British Tax Review 270*, 269–282

Sharkey, N. (22 October 2014). The Correctness of the Chinese Position of Enterprise Residence in Chinese Law: The Institutional and Treaty Implications. *Bulletin for International Taxation, 2014 (Volume 68), No. 11*, 617–626

Sharkey, N. (24 November 2011). Enterprise Income Tax in China: Simplicity to Complexity Through Institutional Context. In B. C(ed), *Commercial Law of the People's Republic of China, edn. 1st*, Sydney: Thompson Reuters

Sharkey, N. Forum: China's New Enterprise Income Tax Law: Continuity and Change. *UNSW Law Journal*, Vol. 30(3), pp. 836, 833–841

Sharma, D. (2013). India's Tax Treaty Policy for Taxation of Services and the OECD Principles: *University of Oxford*

Sharma, P. (December 2012). The International Use of the India- Mauritius(1982) and India-Singapore(1994) Tax Treaties to Promote Foreign Direct Investment in India. *Bulletin for International Taxation*, 632–636

Sharma, S. (2008). Attribution of Profits to Permanent Establishments-The Indian Experience. *Asia-Pacific Tax Bulletin, March/April*, 93–105

Sharma, S. (2013, Volume 19, No 2). Compatibility with the International Meaning of Beneficial Ownership. *Asia-Pacific Tax Bulletin*, 91–96

Sharma, S. (6 August 2015). Substantial Light on Indirect Transfer Provisions. *Asia-Pacific Tax Bulletin, Volume 21, No. 4*

Shatalov, S. (1988). Practical Issues in the Application of Double Tax Conventions – Russia. In *IFA Cahiers* (p. 603)

Sheppard, L. (28 August 2013). News Analysis: The OECD's Special Measures. *Worldwide Tax Daily*, Doc 2013-20588

Shome, P. (January 2013). Developments in International Taxation. *International Taxation*, 5–8

Shpak, A. (29 July 2013). News Analysis: The Application of Russia's Thin Cap Rules to Related-Party Loans. *Worldwide Tax Daily*, Doc 2013-17986

Shpak, A. (3 June 2013). News Analysis: Russian Lessons in Transfer Pricing. *Worldwide Tax Daily*, Doc 2013-13026

Sicular, T. (1998). Capital Flight and Foreign Investment: Two Tales from China and Russia. *World Economy, Vol. 21, Issue 5*, 589–602

Siegmann, T. (November 2007). The Impact of Bilateral Investment Treaties and Double Tax Treaties on Foreign Direct Investment. *University of St. Gallen Law School Law and Economics Research Paper Series*, Working Paper No. 2008-22

Silva, S. (12 April 2013). Brazilian Multinationals Are Not Protected by Tax Havens, Supreme Court Rules. *Tax Notes International*, Doc 2013-8754

Silveira, R. (2010). International Tax Planning in Brazil: What to Expect Following Recent Case Law. *Bulletin for International Tax Law, November 2010*, 566–576

Sinha, Y. (2012). *The Direct Taxes Code Bil 2010*. New Delhi: Ministry of Finance

Slemrod, J. (March 1994). *Free Trade Taxation and Protectionist Taxation*. Michigan: International Tax Policy Forum

Soares Da Silva, D. (17 July 2001). Proposed Tax Reforms Aim to End Brazilian States Tax Wars. *Tax Notes International*

Soares de Silva, D. (13 November 2013). Brazil's Revenue Department Accepts Outside Audit Reports in Transfer Pricing Case. *Tax Notes International*, Doc 2013-26124

Soares de Silva, D. (14 November 2013). Brazil Ends Transitional Tax Regime and Changes Corporate Tax. *Tax Notes International*, Doc 2013-26257

Soares de Silva, D. (15 January 2013). Brazil Confirms Tax breaks for 2016 Summer Olympic Games. *Tax Notes International*, Doc 2013-627

Soares de Silva, D. (17 December 2013). Brazil Establishes Criteria for Monitoring Large Taxpayers in 2014. *Tax Notes International*, Doc 2013-2885

Soares de Silva, D. (19 November 2013). Brazil Creates CFC-Type Rules for Personal Income Tax. *Tax Notes International*, Doc 2013-26579

Soares de Silva, D. (25 September 2013). Heavy Tax Fine Unconstitutional, Brazilian Supreme Court Justice Holds. *Tax Notes International*, Doc 2013-22589

Soares de Silva, D. (27 August 2013). Brazilian Government Looking Into Tax on Web-Based Businesses. *Tax Notes International*, Doc 2013-20516

Soares de Silva, D. (3 September 2013). Brazil's Revenue Department Clarifies Taxation of Foreign Subsidiaries. *Tax Notes International*, Doc 2013-20875

Soares de Silva, D. (31 July 2013). Brazil's Attorney General Trying to Limit Binding Higher Court Decisions. *Tax Notes International*, Doc 2013-18396

Soares de Silva, D. (6 September 2013). Brazil Confirms Tax Liability for Nonresidents' Capital Gains. *Tax Notes International*, Doc 2013-21139

Soares de Silva, D. (8 April 2013). Exemption for Dividend Distributions Applies Only to Adjusted Profits, Brazilain AG says. *Tax Notes International*, Doc 2013-8260

Sodhani, A. a. (2 October 2013). Indian GAAR: Rules Notified. *Nishith Desai, Legal and Tax Counselling Worldwide*, 1–4

Solovev, I. (2001). Tax Evasion and Tax Optimization. *Michigan Journal of International Law*, 711–764

Spencer, D. (May 2012). Transfer Pricing: Will the OECD Adjust to Reality. http://www.taxjustice.net/cms/upload/pdf/Spencer_120524_OECD_.pdf

Bibliography

Srinivasan, A. (2012). Piercing the Corporate Veil in Taxation Matters. *Asia-Pacific Tax Bulletin*, 45–55

Stanley. (October/November 1999,.Vol 4 No 5). *TP: Comment on Revenue's New Practice Note*. Executive Business Brief 21

Steenkamp, L. (May/June 2014). The Permanent Establishment Concept in Double Tax Agreements Between Developed and Developing Countries: Canada/South Africa As A Case in Point. *International Business & Economics Research Journal – Volume 13, Number 5*, 539–551

Steenkamp, L. (September 2013). Beneficial Ownership Provisions in Tax Treaties Between Developed and Developing Countries: The Canada/South Africa Example. *International Business & Economics Research Journal, Volume 12, Number 9*, 1107/1118

Stewart, M. ([2004] BTR: No.2). The International Monetary Fund and Tax Reform. *British Tax Review*, 146–175

Steyn, M. (2003). Foreign Branch Operations in a Globalised Environment: A South African Income Tax Perspective. *Southern African Business Review*, pages 56–69

Steyn, M. (2003). Foreign Branch Operations in a Globalised Environment: A South African Income Tax Perspective (part 2). *Southern African Business Review*, pages 46–55

Stroykova, S. (2012). Russia Introduction of APA Guidance. *International Transfer Pricing Journal, (Volume 19), No. 3*, 237–241

Stroykova, S. (September/October 2013). Recent Guidance on Filing the Notification on Controlled Transactions. *International Transfer Pricing Journal*, 352,353

Su, J. (2012). China -Transfer Pricing Aspects of Business Restructurings. *Asia-Pacific Tax Bulletin, May/June*, 263–266

Supekar, D. (2013). India- Development of Transfering Pricing Jurisprudence. *Asia-Pacific Tax Bulletin, Volume 19, No 1*, 44–50

Surtees, P. (24 December 2012). 2012 Year in Review: South Africa

Surtees, P. (25 February 2013). South Africa Clarifies Meaning of 'Substantially Similar Taxes' in Its Treaties. *Worldwide Tax Daily*, Doc 2013-4214

Surtees, P. (26 March 2013). South African Revenue Service Issues Thin Capitalisation Guidance. *Worldwide Tax Daily*, Doc 2013-7045

Sussman, L. (11 January 2013). China Issues Guidance on Treaties' Capital Gains Tax Provisions. *Worldwide Tax Daily*, Doc 2003-589

Sychev, I. (2013). Russia Country Survey. *Derivatives & Financial Instruments, (Volume 15), No. 5a/Special Issue*, 79–84

Taferner, A. (February 2001). Tax Reform – Act II. *European Taxation*, 46–60

Tang, G. (2010). *Europe-China Tax Treaties*. Kluwer

Tang, J. (2013). China, Country Survey, Special Issue. *Derivatives & Financial Instruments, Volume 15, No. 5a*, 92–104

Tang, J. (2014). Taxation of Hybrid Instruments in China: New Developments and Main Issues. *Derivatives & Financial Instruments January/February*, 28–32

Tax Justice Network. (2011). *The Cost of Tax Abuse, A Briefing Paper on the Cost of Tax Evasion Worldwide*

Taxanalysts. (2013). Measures Taken by Government (India) to tackle Black Money. *Worldwide Tax Daily*, Doc 2013-29820

Taxation and Expropriation under BITs: Setting the Standard. (November 2015). *Butterworths Journal of International Banking and Financial Law*

Taxes. (August 2013). *Safe Harbour Rules*. Government of India, Ministry of Finance, Department of Revenue

Teather, R. (2005). *The Benefits of Tax Competition*. London: Institute of Economic Affairs

Teather, R. (January 2013). Demonstrating Substance in Jersey. *International Taxation*, 92–97

Temple-West. (March 2013). *US-China Anti-tax Evasion Deal Seen as Crucial, but Elusive*. Reuters

Terhoeven, J. (September 2009). The Role of Taxation in Attracting Foreign Direct Investments to South Africa: A BRICS Comparison. *University of Pretoria*

Thacker, A. (January/February 2004). India–Mauritius Tax Treaty: The March of the Law. *Asia-Pacific Tax Bulletin*, 70–75

The, K. (26 December 2013). Reliance Infocomm: More Fuel for India's Hot Debate About Royalties and Software Purchases. *Worldwide Tax Daily*, Doc 2013-27655

Tianlong, H. (August 2013). China- Tax Treaty and Policy – Development and Updates. *Renmin University of China*, 1–52

Tiburcio, C. (2013). Private International Law in Brazil: A Brief Overview. *Panorama of Brazilian Law, Vol 1, no 1*, 1–37

Tickle, D. (2013). The Taxation of Foreign Passive Income for Groups of Companies - South Africa. *IFA Cahiers- Volume 98A*, 661–682

Tien, J. (2013). China-Landmark MAP and APA Case Concluded by Competent Authorities in 2012. *ITPJ, (Volume 20), No. 1*, 18–20

Tien, J. (3 December 2013). News Analysis: China's Implementation Measures for Treaty-Related MAPs. *Worldwide Tax Daily*, Doc 2013-27644

Tognetti, S. (November 2015). New Environment for Tax Planning in Brazil: BEPS Impact. *http://www.ttn-taxation.net/pdfs/Speeches_SaoPaolo_2015/SP01-SilvaniaTognetti.pdf*

Tognetti, S. (Sao Paulo, 2014). Changes in Brazilian CFC Rules. *TTN Conference*

Tolia, S. (2010). What's "Ruling" Indian Transfer Pricing? *ITPJ, May/June (Volume 17), No. 3*, 193–199

Tolia, S. (5 July 2013). India Transfer Pricing Perspective, Recent Judicial Developments on Significant Issues. *www.pwc.in/services/tax/news*

Torres, H. (2001). International Tax Law: Tax Planning and Transnational Operations. *São Paulo: Journal of the Courts*

Torres, H. (2002). Form and Substance in Tax Law-Brazil. *IFA-Cahiers 2002*, 175–185

Torres, H. (2010). Tax Treaties and Tax Avoidance: Application of Anti-avoidance Provisions-Brazil. *IFA Cahiers-Volume 95A*, 149–170

Treasury, R. (24 October 2013). *Explanatory Memorandum on the Taxation Laws Amendment Bill 2013*. Worldwide Tax Daily

Treasury, R. (DOC 2013-26387). *Inviting Technical Tax Proposals for Annexure C of Budget Review*. Worldwide Tax Daily

Bibliography

Tseng, W. (February 2002). Foreign Direct Investment in China: Some Lessons for Other Countries. *IMF Policy Discussion Paper PDP/02/3*

Tyutyuryukov. (July 2014). GAAR- A Key Element of Tax Systems in the Post BEPS Tax World. *WU, Rust*

UN. (2013). *Practical Manual on TP for Developing Countries*

UN. (2013). *United Nations Handbook on Selected Issues in Administration of Double Taxation Treaties for Developing Countries.* United Nations

UN. (October 1947). Documents on the Development and Codification of International Law. *Supplement to American Journal of International Law, Volume 41, No. 4*

UNCTAD. (1998). *World Investment Report.* New York and Geneva: United Nations

UNCTAD. (2000). Taxation. *Series on Issues in International* Union, D. (2011). *The EU Foreign Policy Towards the BRICS and Other Emerging Powers.* Directorate B, European Parliament

US Treasury. (20 March 2007). *Brazil-United States Tax Information Exchange Agreement*

USA. (1994). *Civil and Political Rights in the US, Report of the USA to the UN Rights Committee under the International Covenant on and Political Rights*

Utumi, A. (2012). Brazil: The Debt-Equity Conundrum. *IFA Cahiers - Volume 97B*, 135–155

Utumi, A. (January 2013). Substance over Form and General Anti-Avoidance Rules ("GAAR") in Brazil. *International Taxation*, 36–44

Vakhitov, R. (2008) Non-discrimination at the Crossroads of International Taxation – Russia. *IFA Cahiers - Volume 93A*, 498–518

Vakhitov, R. (AprilL 2005). Recent Developments Regarding Judicial Anti-tax Avoidance in Russia. *European Taxation*, 163–167

Vakhitov, R. (December 2015). Taxation of CFCs and other Anti-offshore Measures in Russia. *TaxAnalysts,1571*

Valadao, M. (May 2016). Transfer Pricing in Brazil and Actions 8, 9, 10 and 13 of the OECD Base Erosion and Profit Shifting. *Bulletin for International Taxation*, 296–308

Valadao. (2011). *BRIC, Tax System Structures and the Effects on Development and Foreign Trade Performance-Lessons and Solutions.* ABDI

Valeeva, A. (2 December 2013). Russia May Return to Riskier Procedure for Initiating Tax Crime Cases. *Worldwide Tax Daily*, Doc 2013-27569

Van den Hurk, H. (January 2014). Starbucks versus the People. *Bulletin for International Taxation*, 27–34

Van Os, R. (October 2011). *Dutch Bilateral Investment Treaties- a Gateway to Investment Protection by Multinational Companies.* Amsterdam: SOMO

VanderWolk, J. (2002). Purposive Interpretation of Tax Statutes: Recent UK Decisions on Tax Avoidance Transactions. *International Bureau of Fiscal Documentation, Bulletin*, 70–76

Vanderwolk. (April 2000). Direct Taxation in the Internet Age-A Fundamentalist Approach. *IBFD*, 173–180

Vanistendael, F. (18 May 2010). China (People's Rep.) - Taxation, Tax Avoidance and the Rule of Law. *Asia-Pacific Tax Bulletin*

Vann, R. (2010, Volume 2, No 3). Taxing International Business Income: Hard-Boiled Wonderland and the End of the World. *World Tax Journal*, 291–346

Varansi, S. (September 2013, Vol 9). Dispute Resolution in Tax Matters: An India-UK Comparative Perspective. *International Taxation*, 313, 324

Variychuk, E. (16 September 2013). Russian Tax Authorities Issue New Guidance Letters to Address Ongoing Transfer Pricing Questions. *Worldwide Tax Daily*, Doc 2013-21765

Variychuk, E. (2011). Russia, in Search of Effective Regulation: Draft Bill on Transfer Pricing. *Bulletin for International Taxation, (Volume 65), No. 2*, 107–112

Variychuk, E. (2012). Russia Consolidated Groups of Taxpayers: A New Concept in Russian Tax Law. *Bulletin for International Taxation, (Volume 66), No. 2*, 100–103

Vasutin, R. (2015). *Vasutin, New Russian De-Offshoring Rules—Impact on Foreign Investors and Russian Businesses, DLA Piper,https://www.dlapiper.com/~/media/Files/Insights/Publications/2015/01/New_Russian_deoffshoring_rules.pdf, p10*. Retrieved from www.dlapiper.com

Vega. (2011). Explaining Reservations to the OECD Model Tax Convention: An Empirical Approach. *www.indret.com Barcelona*, 1–19

Vehorn, C. (November 1999). Organizational Options for Tax Administration. *IBFD Bulletin*, 499–512

Velloso, F. (1992). Transfer Pricing in the Absence of Comparable Market Prices – Brazil. *IFA Cahiers - Vol. 77a, p313*, 313–320

Verma, D (2001). India-Transfer Pricing Rules. *ITPJ, November/December*, 229–232

Verma, D. (2001). India-New Transfer Pricing Regulations. *ITPJ, May/June*, 74–79

Verma, M. (2001). Limits on the Use of Low-Tax Regimes by Multinational Businesses: Current Measures and Emerging Trends-India. *IFA Cahiers - Volume 86b*, 567–581

Veter, E. (2011). Russia New Transfer Pricing Rules. *International Transfer Pricing Journal, (Volume 18), No. 5*, 337–342

Vinnitskiy, D. (2014). *The Sources of the Exchange of Information in Russia.* EATLP Congress

Vinnitskiy, D. (n.d.). Russia: Thin Capitalisation Rules and Non-Discrimination Clause. *Chapter 28*, 1–16

Vinnitskiy, D. The Approach of the Russian Federation to Separation of Powers in Taxation Matters

Violin, P. (2014). Brazil, The Brazilian CFC Regime: Recent Developments. *Bulletin for International Taxation, (Volume 68), No. 4/5*, 269–272

Violin, P. (2014). Brazil-The Brazilian CFC Regime: Update on Recent Developments. *Bulletin for International Taxation, (Volume 68), No. 9*, 508–511

Violin, P. (January 2012). Brazil's Controlled Foreign Company Regime in Question. *Bulletin for International Taxation, (Volume 66), No 2*

Vogel, K. (Volume 4, Issue 1 1986). Double Tax Treaties and Their Interpretation. *Berkeley Journal of International Law*, 1–85

Vogel, K. *Double Taxation Conventions-A commentary to the OECD, UN and US Model Conventions for the Avoidance of Double Taxation on Income and Capital with*

Bibliography

Particular Reference to German Tax Treaty Practice. 3rd Edition, Kluwer Law International 1997

Vohra, A. (May 2014). Litigation Strategies, Options and Solutions. *Bulletin for International Taxation*, 207–211

Vora, R. (2012). *Transfer Pricing and its Applicability to Domestic Transactions*

Waal, M. (November 2010). The Abuse of the Trust or Going Behind the Trust Form, The South African Experience with Some Comparatives file:///C:/Users/Peter%20Wilson/Downloads/dewaal_abuse_2012.pdf, 1/23

Wadhwa, S. (2002 Volume 87a). Form and Substance in Tax Law - India. *IFA Cahiers*, 337–356

Wakhinstaya, E. The Role of OECD Commentary in Tax Treaty Interpretation www.academia.edu/3802841/Status_of_OECD_Commentaries

Wang, H. (March 2016). A Deeper Look at China's "Going Out" Policy. *CIGI Commentary*

Wang, J. (2013). China - Business Restructurings: A Case Analysis and Regulations Applicable to Business Restructuring. *ITPJ, September/October*, 317–323

Weeghel, S. (August 2013). Global Developments and Trends in International Anti-Avoidance. *Bulletin for International Taxation*, 428–435

Wei, J (17 May 2013). China Provides Favorable Beneficial Owner Guidance for Hong Kong Applicants. *Worldwide Tax Daily*, Doc 2013-11996

Wei, J. (10 January 2014). China Clarifies Preferential Export Tax Policy for Cross-Border E-Commerce. *Worldwide Tax Daily*, Doc 2014-530

Wei, J. (13 August 2013). China Clarifies Income Tax Treatment of Software Companies. *Worldwide Tax Daily*, Doc 2013-19532

Wei, J. (15 August 2013). China Simplifies Tax Procedures for Cross-Border Payments. *Worldwide Tax Daily*, Doc 2013-19730

Wei, J. (17 December 2013). Chinese Tax Authority Makes Transfer Pricing Adjustment for Domestic Transaction. *Worldwide Tax Daily*, Doc 2013-28863

Wei, J. (17 December 2013). Foreign Investor Is Subject to Transfer Pricing Adjustment on Transfer of Chinese Company. *Worldwide Tax Daily*, Doc 2013-28860

Wei, J. (18 November 2013). Foreign Investment Company Subject to Second Transfer Pricing Adjustment in China. *Worldwide Tax Daily*, Doc 2013-26494

Wei, J. (20 September 2013). China Offers Guidelines on Hong Kong Resident Status for Tax Relief. *Worldwide Tax Daily*, Doc 2013-22207

Wei, J. (24 December 2013). China Releases Guidelines for Non Resident Companies' Tax Free Reorganizations. *Worldwide Tax Daily*, Doc 2013-29520

Wei, J. (25 November 2013). Chinese-Foreign Joint Venture Pays $7.63m Chinses Transfer Pricing Adjustment. *Worldwide Tax Daily*, Doc 2013-27119

Wei, J. (25 September 2013). China Issues CNY 9.38m Tax Bill For Cayman Company's Indirect Share Transfer. *Worldwide Tax Daily*, Doc 2013-22478

Wei, J. (28 October 2013). China Denies Preferential Tax Rate for Interest Income From Back-to-Back Loans. *Worldwide Tax Daily*, Doc 2013-24857

Wei, J. (3 June 2013). New Chinese Investment Catalog Expands Scope of Beneficial Tax Rate. *Worldwide Tax Daily*, Doc 2013-13165

Wei, J. (3 September 2013). US Fund's Cayman Islands Subsidiary Pays $45.58m Tax Bill in China for Indirect Share Transfer. *Worldwide Tax Daily*, Doc 2013-20873

Wei, J. (6 January 2014). China Makes Single Largest Share Transfer Tax Assessment. *Worldwide Tax Daily*, Doc 2014-137

Wei, J. (6 May 2013). China Taxes Indirect Share Transfer in Wal-Mart Acquisition Case. *Worldwide Tax Daily*

Wei, J. (6 November 2013). China Clarifies Beneficial Owners' Status For Treaty Benefits. *Worldwide Tax Daily*, Doc 2013-24255

Wei, J. (7 August 2013). China Clarifies Enterprise Income Tax Treatment of Hybrid Investments. *Worldwide Tax Daily*, Doc 2013-19065

Wei, J. (January 2014). New China-France Tax Treaty Increases Complications. *Tax Notes International*, pages 341–347

Wei, J. (January 2014). New China-France Tax Treaty Increases Complications. *Tax Notes International*, pages 341–347

Welsh, R. (1960). Law of Taxation, Income Tax Act, 1960. *Ann. Surv. S. African L*, pages 386–401

Wescott, G. (February 2003). Measuring Governance in the Asia-Pacific Region and. *Asia-Pacific Tax Bulletin 57*, 51–57

West, C. (2016). Tax Avoidance Revisited: Exploring the Boundaries of Anti-Avoidance Rules in the EU BEPS Context Report, Tax Institute for Fiscal Research University of Cape Town South Africa. *EATLP 2016*, (pp. 1–15)

West, C. (August 2009). *PhD Thesis: The Taxation of International (non-resident) Sportspersons in South Africa*. Capetown: University of Capetown

Wheeler, J. (February 2011). The Attribution of Income in the Netherlands and the United Kingdom. *World Tax Journal*, 38–172

Wijnen, W. (October 2013). Some Thoughts on Convergence and Tax Treaty Interpretation. *Bulletin For International Taxation, 2013 (Volume 67) No. 11*, 1–9

Wilson, P. (2012). Russia and Model International Tax Treaties –Part II. *Informa UK*, www.internationaltaxreport.com, 1–12

Wilson, P. (2013). United Kingdom: New Controlled Foreign Corporation Rules; A Summary, Including Potential Impact on UK Companies with BRICS' Businesses. *International Tax Report*, Parts I, II, III and IV

Wilson, P. (June 2012). Russia and Model International Tax Treaties- Part I. *Informa, International Tax Report*

Wong, C. (1999). China-The Application of TP Rules and the Definition of Associated Enterprises. *ITPJ, November/December*, 248–252

Worstall, T. (2013). *Russians in Cyprus: It's Not About Tax It's All About The Rule of Law and Property Rights*. Forbes March 2013

Wouters, J. (February 2011). Global Tax Governance: Work in Progress. *Leuven Centre for Global Governance Studies*, Working Paper No. 59

Wunder, H. (2001). The Effect of International Tax Policy on Business Location Decisions. *24 Tax Notes International*, 1331

www.pwc.com. (15 January 2013). Indian Finance Minister Announces Decisions on Indian GAAR. *Asia Pacific Tax Newsalert*, Doc 2013-1263

Bibliography

www.pwc.com. (15 January 2013). Indian Finance Minister Announces Decisions on Indian GAAR. *Asia Pacific Tax Newsalert*, 1–3

Xavier, A. (1996). Principles for the Determination of the Income and Capital of Permanent Establishments and Their Applications to Banks, Insurance Companies and Other Financial Institutions – Brazil. *iIFA Cahiers - Vol. 81a*, 303–312

Xinhua, C. (2012). *A Guide to Doing Business in BRICS*. USA: Intercultural Publishing

Xu, Y. Old Wine in New Wineskins: The Taxation History of China. *Faculty of Law, The Chinese University of Hong Kong*, pages 1–33

Xu, Y. Tax Dispute Resolution, Judiciary Independence and Property Rights: The Case of China. *Faculty of Law, Chinese University of Hong Kong*

Yang, B. (1992). Tax Evasion and Avoidance in FDI and Countering Measures. *Journal of Xiamen University*

Yang, B. (2011). China Structuring an Overseas Investment. *Asia-Pacific Tax Bulletin, Volume 17 No 5*

Yang, H. (2009). China - A Comparative View of Transfer Pricing Documentation: New Chinese Rules and the EU Code of Conduct. *ITPJ, September/October*, 318–324

Yang, H. (2010). Tax Treaties and Tax Avoidance: Application of Anti-avoidance Provisions – China. *IFA Cahiers- Volume 95A*, 209–232

Yang, H. (2011). China Structuring an Overseas Investment – What Do We Need to Know? *Asia-Pacific Tax Bulletin, Volume 17, No. 5*, 340–355

Yang, H. (2012). China-Beneficial Ownership, Conduit Company and Treaty Shopping: Is a Capital Gains Exemption Still Available in China? *Derivatives & Financial Instruments, (Volume 14), No. 5*, 252–260

Yelery, A. (2014, No 24). *China's 'Going Out' Policy: Sub-National Economic Trajectories*. Institute of Chinese Studies

Ying, Z. (n.d.). China's Transfer Pricing System. *http://www.taxjustice.net/cms/upload/pdf/Zhang_Ying_1206_Helsinki_ppt.pdf*

Young, E. (24 June 2013). Brazil Revising 2004 Tax Treaty With Russia. *Worldwide Tax Daily*, Doc 2013-15298

Yuan, J. (August 2007). China TP under the New Law. *www.pwchk.com/webmedia/doc/633281271237582380_tp_cit_law_aug2007.pdf*, 1–9

Yuan, S. (2003). China - Changing Transfer Pricing Landscape: 'Like It or Not'. *ITPJ, July/August*, 259–262

Zakharov, A. (30 October 2013). Russian Lower House Approves Tax Code Amendments to Reveal Beneficial Owners. *Worldwide Tax Daily*, Doc 2013-25015

Zapol, D. (June 2013). Holding Company Structures for Investment into Russia in the Light of Current Developments. *International Taxation*, 752–756

Zhang, A. (June 2007). China's Tax Planning and Applicable Law under the New Corporate Income Tax. *Offshore Investment*

Zhang, M. (Vol 24, 2010). The Socialist Legal System with Chinese Characteristics: China's Discourse for the Rule of Law and a Bitter Experience. *Temple International & Comparative Law Journal, Vol. 24, p. 1, 2010*, 1

Zhang, Y. (2012). The State Administration of Taxation's Efforts Towards Anti-Avoidance. *Asia-Pacific Tax Bulletin, Volume 18, No 6*, 439–441

Zhang, Y. *China's TP System.* http://www.taxjustice.net/cms/upload/pdf/Zhang_Ying_1206_Helsinki_ppt.pdf

Zhang, Z. (2014). What Is Needed to Perfect the Chinese GAARs. *Bulletin for International Taxation, Volum 68, No 1,* 35–40

Zhu, L. (2013). *China: SAT Clarifies Meaning of Technical Services "Inseparable" from Transfer of Technology.* Deloitte Global Services Limited

Zhu, Z. (2007). *Essays On China's Tax System (PhD Thesis).* Rotterdam: Erasmus University Rotterdam

Zobalia, H. (2012). India - Structuring New Investments and Managing Existing Investments. *Asia-Pacific Tax Bulletin, (Volume 18), No. 1,* 64–70

Zobalia, H. (2013 (Volume 19), No. 3). The Anti-Avoidance Regime and the Shome Committee Recommendations. *Asia-Pacific Tax Bulletin,* 176–183

Table of Cases

Cited Cases

09AP-58460/2014, Distillery Topaz, January 2015, 86
27 February 2014 (Case No. 232/2011), 88
2015 (9) TMI 438 - ITAT PUNE, 99
A Oyj Abp, Case. No. KHO:2002:26, 20 March 2002, 141
A26-6967, September 2009, 94
A27-7455/2010, November 2011, Northern Kuzbass, 15 November 2011, No. 8654/11, 94
A40-58575/11-129-248 v. Federal Arbitration Court, 2 August 2012, 210
A40-60755/12-20-388(Eastern Value Partners Ltd), 28 November 2012, 182
A56-19578, Swedwood Tikhvin, April 2007, 94
ABC Limited v. SARS (VAT 189) [2010] ZATC 2, 6 May 2010, 69
Accolla Pillay v. Newlands Sport Bar Liquor Store 2010 (3) SA 116, 59
ADIT v. Universal International Music BV (2011-TII-22-ITAT-MUM-INTL), 176
Aditya Birla Nuvo Ltd. v. IRD, 14th July 2011
AM Moola Group Ltd v. C: SARS [2003] 65 SATC 414, 145
Amadeus Global Travel v. DCIT, ITA No. 2433 to 2145/Del/2000, 1022 to 1024/Del/2005, 30 November 2007, 209
Anglo-French Textile Co. Ltd v. Commissioner Of Income-Tax, 1953 AIR 105, Supreme Court of India, 97, 117
Anshan STB of Liaoning Province, 22 December 2015, 108
Ardex Investments Mauritius Ltd, A.A.R. No. 886 of 2010, 14 November 2011, 73, 183
Aricent Technologies (Holding) Limited v. DCIT, 21 January 2011, 73
Armstrong World Industries Mauritius Multi Consult Ltd, A.A.R. NO. 1044 OF 2011, 22 August 2012, 57
Aspect Software Inc v. IRD, ITA Nos. 1124 & 1125/Del/2014 18 May 2015, 210
Associated Wholesale Grocers, Inc. v. United States, 927 F.2d 1517, 1521 [67 AFTR 2d 91-837] (10th Cir. 1991), 66
Astellas Pharma Europe BV v. Federal Tax Service A40-155695/12, 6 February 2015, 210
Ayrshire Pullman v. CIR (1929) 14TC75, 65
Aztec Software And Technology v. ACIT, 2007, 294 ITR 32 Bang, 12 July 2007, 57

Bank Windhoek Bpk v. Rajie en 'n Ander 1994(1) SA 115 (A), 69
Bayfine UK v. Commissioners for H M Revenue and Customs, [2011] EWCA Civ 304, 65
Beijing, Xiamen, Guanghzhou, 75
Betty M. Ellis v. Commissioner of Internal Revenue, 30 September 1985, 65
Bloomberg v. Tax Inspector, Federal Arbitration Court Moscow District, No. A40-94391/10-142-134, 8 December 2010, 210
BMW India Pvt. Ltd v. IRD, ITA No. 5354/Del/2012, 16 August 2013, 214
Bosch and Another v. Commissioner for SARS (unreported Case No A94/2012, 20 November 2012), 59
Bricom Holdings Limited v. The Commissioners of Inland Revenue, IRC 1997, STC 1179, 141
Bullock v. Unit Construction Co Ltd, 1959, 38TC712., 164
C.B. Gautam v. Union Of India & Ors, 17 November 1992, 57
C.I.T. v. R.D. Aggarwal and Co, Civil Appeals Nos. 808 and 809 of 1963, 6 October 1964, 208
Cairn Energy PLC v. India http://investmentpolicyhub.unctad.org/ISDS/Details/691, 232
Canon, Sony & Others v. ADIT, 55 Taxmann.com 240 (Delhi) 2015, 16 March 2015, 214
CARF Judgment No. 1402-001.404, 9 July 2013, 55, 72
CARF Judgment, No. 1402-001.404, 55, 72
Cartier Shipping Co. Ltd. v. DDIT, 7 June 2010, ITA No. 3036/Mum/07, 56
Case 160-0, Constitutional Court, 1 April 2004, 56
Case A41-21630, Aluplast, September 2014, 94
Case AZ. II R 39/89, 29 July 1992, 54
Case I R 16/78, 26 May 1982, 54
Cecil B. Furstenberg v. Commissioner of Internal Revenue, 26 November 1984, 66
Chengdu, 14 May 2014, 118, 214
Chengdu, May 2014, 118, 214
China Mobile Vodafone, 2011, 165
Chongqing (June 2010), 74-75, 178
CIR v. Challenge Corporation Ltd [1986] STC 548 (PC), 65
CIT v. Durga Prasad More, AIR 1971 SC 2439, 56
CIT v. Fried Krupp Industries Tax Case Nos. 357 to 360 of 1976 (Reference Nos. 256 to 259 of 1976), 2 May 1980, 208
Coamo Agroindustrial Cooperativa, Extraordinary Appeal 611,586, April 2013, 127
Coca Cola India Inc. v. ACIT, Gurgaon, (2008) 116 TTJ Pune 880, 17 December 2008, 57
Commissioner for IR v. Conhage (Pty) Ltd (606/97) [1999] ZASCA 64, 68
Commissioner for the SA Revenue Service v. Mark Krok, 31 January 2014, 154
Commissioner for the South African Revenue Service v. Tradehold Ltd [2012] 3 All SA 15(SCA), 145
Commissioner of Customs and Excise v. Randles, Bros and Hudson Ltd 1941 AD 369 at 395-6, 68
Commissioner Of Income-Tax v. Hindustan Conductors Pvt. Ltd. on 13 July 1999, 81

Commissioner of IR v. Sunnyside Centre (86/95) [1996] ZASCA 102, 68
Commissioner v. Court Holding Co, 324 U.S. 331, 334 (1945), 66
Companhia Vale do Rio Doce v. Federal Union - Appeal 1,325.709 24 April 2014, 142
Comptroller of Income Tax v. AZP, 2012, Singapore, SGHC 112, 23 May 2012, 154
Comptroller of Income Tax v. BJY & Ors. - High Court of Singapore, 13th September 2013 [2013] SGHC 173, 154
Constitutional Court No. 4-0, dated 10 January 2002, 60
Constitutional Court, 2003 N9-P, 62
Constitutional Court, No. 138-O, dated 25 July 2001, 60
Crown Forest Industries Limited, 1995 2 SCR 802, 168
DCIT, Circle-7, Pune v. W.B. Engineers International Private Limited, 99
De Beers Consolidated Mines Ltd v. Howe [1906] AC 455, 164
Decision 16327.001870 / 2001-42, 15 June 2005; 101-95014, 83
Decision 9101-00287; Case No. 16327.001870 / 2001-42;Appeal No. 101-138101; Special Prosecutor, 24 August 2009, 83
Decree of the North-West District FAS on Case No. A52-4072/2012, 6 June 2014, 154
Del Commercial Properties, Inc. v. Commissioner of Internal Revenue, 8 June 2001, 66
Diageo India Private Limited v. ACIT [ITA No. 8602/Mum/2010, ITAT, 7 September 2011 (AY 2006-07)], 99
Dinurje Jewellery Pvt. Ltd, DCIT, ITAT, MA No. 419/Mum/2014, 20 February 2015, 100
Director of Income-tax, International Taxation-II, Mumbai v. Besix Kier Dabhol SA IT Appeal NO. 776 OF 2011, 30 August 2012, 82, 144
Discovery Communications India v. IRD, ITA No. 1297/2010 and ITA No. 1101/2011 24 November 2014, 214
DIT v. Copal Research Limited, Mauritius [2014] 49 Taxmann 125, 192
Dvortsovy Ryad-MS, Russian Federation Supreme Court, 25 February 2009, Decision No. 12418/08, 56,
Dynamic India Fund, 18 July 2012 A.A.R. No. 1016 of 2010, 57
E* Trade Mauritius, AAR 826 of 2009, 22 March 2010, 176
Eagle Distribuidora de Bebidas S/A v. No. 16327.000530/2005-28, Sentence No. 101-97070, 17 December 2008, 126, 130
East West Alliance Limited v. Ukraine, No. 19336/04, ECTHR (Fifth Section), Judgment (Merits and Just Satisfaction) of 23.01.2014 Strasbourg, 23 January 2014, Final, 2 June 2014, 238
Eastern Value Partners Limited, Ninth Arbitrazh Appellate Court Resolution No. 09AP-33421/2012-AK of 5 December 2012, 174
Element Trade (Monetka) No. A60-32327/2010, 63
Embraco Empresa Brasileira de Compressore, April 2013, 127
Erf 3183/1 Ladysmith (Pty) Ltd and Another v. Commissioner for Inland Revenue 1996 (3) SA 942 (A) at 953(D-E), 69
Expro Gulf Limited v. UOI (Writ Petition No. 2871/2014, 22 January 2015, 154, 190
Extraordinary Appeal (Recurso Extraordinário, RE) 601,304; Direct Actions for Unconstitutionality (Ação Direta de Inconstitucionalidade, ADI) 2390, 2386, 2397 e 2859, On 24 February 2016

Table of Cases

Federal Commercial Court of the North-West Region 18 September 2013, United-Bakers Pskov LLC/ Kellogg Group, A52-4072/2012, 121

Fisher's Executors v. CIR [1926] AC395, 65

Fosroc Chemicals India Pvt. Ltd. v. DCIT [IT(TP)A No.148/Bang/2014 - AY 2009-10] – Taxsutra.com, 102

Fuchs Lubricants (I) P. Ltd, v. Department Of Income Tax, I.T.A. No.7629 /Mum/2010, 20 November 2012, 106

Fujian (June 2010), 178

Fuzhou Tax Bureau, 2010, 194

GE India Technology Centre Private Limited v. DRP ((TS-462-HC-2011(KAR)), 114

Gerdau Açominas S/A v. National Treasury (Administrative Proceedings n. 10680.724392/2010-28), 72

Glamour Enterprises (P.) Ltd. v. Deputy Commissioner of Income-tax, Circle-6, Jaipur, 2015 (10) TMI 1387 - ITAT JAIPUR, 106

Godhra Electricity Co Ltd and Anr v. The State of Gujarat and Anr (1975) 1 SCC 199

Goldberg v. Kelly, 397 U.S. 254 (1970), 239

Gregory v. Helvering, 293 U.S. 465, 1935, 66

Guangzhou Tax Bureau, Procter and Gamble, 2002, 84

Guizhou, 2011, 193, 194, 259

Gyo-Hi, case number: 2008 (Gyo-Hi) No. 91, 29 October 2009, 141

Heilongjiang, 2013, 166, 193, 194

Higgins v. Smith, 308 U.S. 473, 477 (1940), 66

IDBI Trusteeship Services Limited v. Hubtown Limited, LSI-511-HC-Mumbai-2015, 73

Iljin Automotive (P.) Ltd. v. ACIT, 30 November 2011, 57

In Re: Star Television Entertainment Ltd., (2010) 321 ITR 1 (AAR), 60, 73

Indofood International Finance Limited v. JPMorgan Chase Bank NA, London Branch, A3/2005/2497,2 March 2006, 172

International Global Networks, ITA No. 2865/Mum/2008, 23 July 2010, 183

Interoute Communications Ltd v. Assessee on 31 March 2016, I.T.A. No. 2284/Mum/2014, 31 March 2016, 209

Intertek Testing Services v. AAR No. 751 of 2007, 7 November 2008, 183

IRC v. Duke of Westminster [1935] All ER 259 (1935), 65

ITC 569 13 SATC 447, 97

Japan-Alcohol Beverages II, WT/DS8/AB/R, 23

JC Bamford Investments, ITA No. 80/Del/2013, 4 July 2014, 177

Jiandu, 2010, 194, 195

Juggi Lal Kamlapat v. Commissioner Of Income-Tax, U.P, 1969 1 SCR 988, 183

KA40 / 9453-09-2, September 2009, 94

Keshavji Ravji & Co. v. CIT, 1990 SCR (1) 243, 1990 SCC (2) 231, 57

Khodorkovskiy and Lebedev v. Russia(applications nos. 11082/06 and 13772/05), 25 July 2013, Final 25/10/2013, 238

Kodak India Pvt. Ltd v. ACIT (ITA No. 7349Mum/2012), 101

KSPG Netherlands Holding v. Director of Income Tax International, Mumbai, 25 February 2010, 192

Kusum Products Ltd, IT Reference No. 288 of 1987, 117

Labushev v. Russia, No. 4144/06, ECTHR (first Section), Decision of 11 December 2007, 238
Laerstate v. HMRC, [2009] UKFTT 209, 164
LG Electronics India Pvt. Ltd v. IRD, ITA No. 3823/Del/2009, 17 May 2013, 214
Louisville v. Letson Louisville, C. & C.R. Co. v. Letson, 2 How. 497, 558, 11 L.Ed. 353 (1844)
Luohe, 2010, 164
M/S Nortel Networks India International Inc. DDIT, 13 June 2014, 57
M/S. Ansaldo Energia Spa v. The Income Tax Appellate Tribunal on 12 January 2009, 73
M/s.Hamon Shriram Cottrell Pvt. Ltd v. Income Tax Officer Ward 8(2), Mumbai. 400 065. PAN: AAACT2254Q, ITAT, MUMBAI, 19 April 2013, 114
Maersk Global Service Centres (India) Pvt. Ltd. v. ACIT, 29 February 2012, 57
Mammen v. DCIT (ITA No. 870/Mds/201), 21 January 2013, 154
Marcel Dassault, AAR No. 846 & 847 of 2009, 28 November 2011, 192
Marcopolo S/A v. Federal Treasury, 105-17083, 25 June 2008, 55, 104, 181
Maruti Suzuki India v. IRD, ITA No. 5237/Del/2011, 2 August 2013, 214
Mathuram Agrawal v. State of M.P., Civil Appeal No. 1990 of 1995, AIR 2000 SC 109, 67
McDowell And Co. Ltd. v. Commercial Tax Officer, 1986 AIR 649, 1985 SCR (3) 791, 17 April 1985, 67
Mitsubishi Corporation India Pvt. Ltd v. IRD, No: 5042/Del/11, 21 October 2014, 211
Mitsui and Company India Pvt. Ltd. v. ITO - WPC No. 1121/2012 & CM No. 2447/2012 - High Court of Delhi, 26th September 2012, 154
Mittal Metal v. ITO (2008) 21 SOT 186 Del, 81
Moscow Municipal Court Cassational Judgement No. 4g/2-12260/12 of 25 December 2012, 174
Motif India Infotech Pvt. Ltd. v. ACIT, 25 March 2014, 57
Mudan (July 2010), 178
Mudan, 2010; Xinjiang, 2008, 75
N A40-58575/11-129-248, 2 August 2012, 210
Nalco India Ltd v. DCIT, on 3 I.T.A No.529/Kol/2008, 3 February 2016, 216
Nantong, 2012, 75
National Industry Confederation, 2011; Direct Action of Unconstitutionality 2,588, 10 April 2013, 127
News Datacom Ltd and another v. Atkinson (Inspector of Taxes) [2006] STC (SCD) 732, 164
Nokia India Private Ltd v. Deputy Director of Income Tax, International taxation, New Delhi, ITA 3532/Del/2013, May 2015, 229, 232
Novo Nordisk India Private v. DCIT, 30 July 2015, ITAT, IT(TP)A No. 146/Bang/2015, 100, 101
Oceanic Trust Co Ltd NO, V SISM, Case No. 2011/2255556/09, 13 June 2011, 166
Oriflame Cosmetics, 9th Arbitration Court, dated 4 June 2015, Number A40-138879/14-75-404, 62, 209
Partington v. Attorney-General (1869) L.R. 4 E. & I. App. 100, 65

Table of Cases

Patrick McGrath and Ors v. Inspector of taxes JE McDermott, 7 July 1988 3 ITR 683 (1988), 65
Pegasystems Worldwide India v. ACIT, ITAT, 16 October 2015, I.T.A. No. 1936/HYD/2014, 100
People's Daily in 2013, 216
Perot Systems TSI (India) Ltd. v. DCIT (ITA Nos. 2320, 2321 and 2322/Del/2008), 100
Petrobras, 21 October 2014, 142
Prevost Car 2004-2006(IT)G and 2004-4226(IT)G, 22 April 2008, 172
Process no 5005596-52.2015.4.04.7000/PR, Federal Court of Curitiba, May 2016, 142
Qidong, 2012, 152
Qinghai, 24 September 2014, 178
R v. IRC ex parte Matrix Securities Ltd [1994] 1 WLR (HL) at p. 345C, 69, 71
Raman & Co, 1968, 67 ITR 11, 70
Ranbaxy Laboratories Ltd v. Deputy Commissioner Of Income Tax W.P.(C) 6728/2011, 24 January 2013, 114
Refinaria de Petróleo Ipiranga S/A, REsp 1.200.49214, October 2015, 88
Relier (Pty) Ltd. v. Commissioner for Inland Revenue (256/96) [1997] ZASCA 105, 69
Renta 4 SVSA. v. Russian Federation, Arbitration Institute of the Stockholm Chamber of Commerce, 20 March 2009, 231
Reznik v. Russia, ECHR 102 (2013) 4 April 2013, Case 4497/05, 238
RMM Canadian Enterprises v. MNR, 1997 DTC 302, 54
Robert M. Brittingham v. Commissioner of Internal Revenue, 23 July 1979, 54
Ruling of the of the Presidium Supreme Arbitration No. 11259/02, dated 17 December 2002, 60
Ruling of the Presidium of Supreme Arbitration Court No. 6294/01, dated 5 November 2002, 60
Ruling of the Presidium of Supreme Arbitration Court No. 7374/01, dated 18 June 2002, 60
Ruling of the Presidium of the Supreme Commercial Court No. 9408/00, dated 18 September 2001, 60
Russian Federation v. Veteran Petroleum Limited, C/09/477160 / HA ZA 15-1, 20 April 2016, 231
SA Andritz, Case No. 233,894, 6 ILTR, 604, 2004, 94
SARS v. Mark Krok, 31 January 2014 Case 1319/13, 154, 157
SARS v. NWK (27/10) [2010] ZASCA 168 (1 December 2010), 59
Sayanskhimplast LLC v. Tax Administration, A19-2735/2013, 6 February 2014, 174
Shaan Marine Services Private Limited v. IRD, 27 May 2014, 167
Shaanxi, 25 November 2011, 87
Shandong Case, June 2015, 134
Shenzen, 2011, 183, 256
Shenzhen, STB, January 2016, 215
Shenzhen, STB, 107, 116
Shiv Dutt Rai Fateh Chand v. Union of India, AIR 1984 SC 1194, 239
Smallwood Trustees Anor [2010] EWCA Civ 778, 164
Snook v. London & West Riding Investments: [1967] 2 QB at 801, 54

Table of Cases

Societe Schneider Electric, Case No. 232276, RJF 10/2002, 28 June 2002, 142
Spies v. United States, 317 U.S. 492, 498-99 (1943), 54
Sree Meenakshi Mills Ltd v. CIT (1957) 31 ITR 28, 56
SS A/S v. Skat, B-2152-10, December 2011, 172
Sun Inbev, The Moscow Arbitration Court, Court of Appeal, 10 February 2014, 101
Suzhou, 2011, 75
Suzhou, Jiangsu Province, 2012, 106
Suzuki Rus, Federal Arbitration Court, 16 September 2013, Case No. A40-111951/12-20-580
Suzuki Rus, Federal Commercial Court of the North-West District, Case A52-4072/2012, 18 September 2013, 121 (Only case number is found)
Suzuki Rus, Moscow Arbitration Court, 19 March 2013, Case No. A40-111951/2012, 101
Swarnandhra IJMII Integrated Township Development Company Pvt. Ltd. v. DCIT, in ITA no. 2072/Hyd/2011, 101
Swiss Federal Administrative Court (SFAC), 17 December 2013, 153
Switzerland - Case 2C_364 / 2012 / 2C_377 / 2012, 5 May 2015, 173
Switzerland - Case No. 6537/2010, 7 March 2012, 173
T. Rajkumar & Others v. UOI (Writ Petition Nos. 17241 / 2015), 190
T. S. Baliah v. T. S. Rengachari, 12 December 1968; 1969 AIR 701, 1969 SCR (3) 65, 56
Taizhou, March 2013, 75
Tata Industries Ltd. v. DDIT(Mum)([2011] 12 Taxmann.com 141), 176
Tata Sons Limited v. DCIT, 24 November 2010, 73
The Commissioner Of Income-Tax v. The Provident Investment Co., Ltd, 15 May 1957, 56
Tianjin, 2010, 194, 252
Timinskiy v. Russia, no. 74947/01, ECTHR (Fifth Section), Decision of 11 September 2007, 238
Tobacco Father v. COT 17 SATC 39513, 97
Tradehold Limited v. SARS, 132/11, May 2012, 145, 165, 166, 253
Tulazheldormash, Supreme Commercial Court No. 12093/11, dated 14 February 2012, 56, 63
Tza Yap Shum v. Republic of Peru (ICSID Case No. arb/07/6) award, 7 July 2011, 232
Vasco Drycleaners v. Twycross 1979 (1) SA 603 (A) at 615H in fin to 616A, 69, 76
Velcro v. Queen, 2012 TCC 57, 173
Vinco, Moscow Federal District Commercial Court No. KA-A40/8959-07, dated 10 September 2007, 67
Vodafone India Services Pvt. Ltd v. Union Of India, on 10 October 2014, WP-871-14, 100
Vodafone India Services Pvt. Ltd. v. Union of India & Ors. Writ Petition No. 1877 of 2013 decided on 29 November 2013, 122
Vodafone International Holdings B.V. v. Union of India, Case Civil Appeal No. of 2012 (arising out of S.L.P. (C) No. 26529 of 2010), 176
Vodafone International Holdings B.V. v. Union of India, Civil Appeal No. of 2012 (arising out of S.L.P. (C) No. 26529 of 2010) 20 January 2012, 176

Table of Cases

Vodafone International Holdings BV v. India, 20 January 2012, 176
Vodafone International Holdings BV v. India, 2014, 73
Vodafone, Civil Appeal No. of 2012 (arising out of S.L.P. (C) No. 26529 of 2010), 176
VodafoneChina Mobile, 2011, 194
Volvo Brasil Veículos Ltda v. Federal Revenue Service, 457.228, 18 March 2004, 177
Volvo Brasil Veículos Ltda, Case 457.228, 168, 177
Wood v. Holden [2006] EWCA Civ 26, 164
WT Ramsay Ltd v. IRC [1982] AC 300, 66
Xiamen, 20 January 2014, 118
Xiangshan, 2011, 75
Xingjiang, 2006, 74
Xinjiang (December 2008), 178, 255
Xuzhou (2010), 194
XYZ, P No. 9 of 1995, 22 December 1995, 176
Yanden Enterprises Limited, Federal Arbitration Court of the East, 6 February 2014 the Judgment No. A19-2735/2013, 174
Yangzhou (May 2010), 178, 244, 255
Yolanda Participações s/a, Recurso Especial N° 1.211.882 - RJ (2010/0159996-0), 5 April 2011, 130
Yum Restaurants (India) Pvt. Ltd, ITA No. 1097/Del/2014, 177
Zaheer Mauritius v. DIT [2014] 47 taxmann.com 247 (Delhi), 82
Zandberg v. Van Zyl 1910 AD 302, 69
Zhuizheng, March 2013, 75

Non-cited Cases

Aztec Software And Technology v. ACIT, 12 July 2007
Aztec Software And Technology v. ACIT, ITAT, 12 July 2007
Baker Hughes Singapore Pte. Ltd, v. IRD ITA No. 744/Del/13, 20 April
Bank of India v. CIT, 7 January 2015, Income Tax Appeal No. 1630 of 2012
Bharti Airtel Ltd. v. ACIT, ITA No.: 5816/Del/2012, 11 March 2014
Canadian Immigration Service Centre, May 2004, (People's Daily: National Tax http://www.xm-l-tax.gov.cn/content/3572.shtml
CARF, Judgment n. 103 07.260. Feature No. 89 ° 806
Chonqqing, 2008
CIT v. EKL APPLIANCES LTD, I.T.A. Nos.1068/2011 & I.T.A. Nos.1070/2011, 29 March 2012
CIT v. Vishakhapatnam Port Trust, 1983 144 ITR 146 AP
Companhia vale do rio doce recurso especial n° 1.325.709 - RJ (2012/0110520-7)
Company undisclosed, KA-A40/13648-10, 18 November 2010
Company, name undisclosed v. IRD, 13276, 15 May 2015
Copesul – CIA / Petroquímica do Sul (the taxpayer)
Craven v. White, [1989] AC 398
Dalian Kang, August 2002, http://www.xm-l-tax.gov.cn/content/3572.shtml

Decree of the North-West District FAS on Case No. A21-2110/2005-C1, 9 January 2007
DIT v. Morgan Stanley & Co. (2007) 292 ITR 416 (SC)
Dynamic India Fund, AAR No. 1016 of 2010, 18 July 2012
E Funds Corporation TS-63-HC-2014 (DEL)
Federal Arbitrage Court (North West District) ruling (No. A66-5524/2004, 6 October 2005)
Federal Union (National Treasury) (the tax authorities), RE 1.161.467 – RS, 17 May 2012
First Blue Home Finance Ltd v. ACIT [ITA No. 4650/Del/2011]
First Security Bank of Utah et al. v. Commissioner of Internal Revenue, 21 March 1972
Guiyang, 2011
Higher Arbitration Court, 1 March 2008
ICICI Bank Ltd v. ITA Nos. 341, 342 of 2012, 21 August 2014
India and Anr v. Azadi Bachao Andolan and Anr, 7 October 2003
India v. Azadi Bachao Andolan, 7 October 2003
Information Letter No. 71-2003 Supreme Arbitration Court in 2013
Ingemar Johannson US (1964) 336 F 2d 809
Intaxicate India Pvt. Ltd Bangalore applicant, AAR no. 100, 2015
Inter-Science Research and Development Services (Pry.) Ltd v. Republica Popular de Mocambique 1980 (2) SA 111 (T), at 124
ITO v. Right Florists Pvt Ltd, No. 1336/Kol/2011, 12 April 2013
Joint Anti-Fascist Refugee Committee v. McGrath, 341 U.S. 123, 171-72 (1951)
JSC AvtoVAZ, 990/05, June 2005
Judgement No. A40-1164/11-99-7, 28 October 2011 Ninth Arbitrazh Appellate Court, OOO Naryanmarneftegaz By Judgement No. A40-1164/11-99-7 of 27 February 2012
KA-A40/7211-10, Gidromashservice July 2010
Kehin Panalfa Ltd. v. ACIT, 6 May 2014
Khodorkovskiy v. Russia, ECHR 023 (2011) 31 May 2011
KSPG Netherlands, AAR/818/2009 2010
Lebedev v. Russia, Chamber Judgement, 25 October 2007 (application no. 4493/04)
Maruti Suzuki Ltd [TS-212-ITAT-2013(DEL)-TP]
Mashinostroyenie i Gidravlika OOO, Moscow Arbitration Court, Case No. A40-135737/14, 5 June 2015
Mauritius (XYZ India), In re (2012) 343 ITR 455 / 206 Taxman 631 (AAR) Ardex Investments Mauritius Ltd. v. N/A, 14 November 2011
Micro Ink Limited v. ACIT; ITAT, I.T.A. No. 2873/Ahd/10, 27 November 2015
Min Xavier d'Alburquerque, 1 June 1977, 143
Motorola Solutions India Pvt. v. assesse, ITAT, ITA No. 5637/Del/2011, 14 August 2014
Mr Abdul Razak A Meman, AAR No. 637 of 2004, 9 May 2005
N A40-1164/11-99-7, Naryanmarneftegas, February 2012
Navnitlal C. Javeri v. K. K. Sen, 1965 AIR 1375
Nestlé Russia, 26 June 2015, Court of Appeal Ruling No. 09AP-22271/2015 AK, Ninth Arbitration Appeal Court

Table of Cases

No. A40-65284/11-91-279, Likero-Vodochniy Zavod Topaz, February 2013
Oriflame v. FTS, 14 January 2016, Case No. 305-KG15-11546
Peoples' Union for Civil Rights v. Union of India, AIR 1997 SC 568
Plenum of the Supreme Arbitration Court, Dated 12 October 2006, Resolution No. 53
Presidium of Supreme Arbitration Court, dated 6 July 2010, N 17152/09
Presidium of the Supreme Arbitration Court, Newsletter, 17 March 2003, N71
Ram Jethmalani & Ors v. Union of India & Ors. (Writ Petition (Civil) No. 176 of 2009)
RE 80.004; Brazil, Supremo Tribunal Federal, Recurso Extraordinário 80.004/SE. Relator
Resolution of the Moscow Arbitrazh Court on Case No. A40-4757/14 75-1, 15 April 2014
Ruling No. A21-296/02-C, Federal Arbitration Court North Western District, 12 September 2002
SERCO BPO Private Limited, [2015] 60 taxmann.com 433 (Punj. & Har.)
Sesa Goa Ltd and Sterlite Industries (India) Ltd, 19 January 2015, http://www.moneycontrol.com/news/business/supreme-court-to-hear-govt-plea-against-sesa-sterlite-deal_1278204.html
Shantou, 2011
Shenzhen Pavilion Hotel Limited, July 2004, http://www.xm-l-tax.gov.cn/content/3572.shtml
Shri Mohan Manoj Dhupelia, Shri Ambrish Manoj Dhupelia and Ms. Bhavya Manoj Dhupelia v. Deputy Commissioner of Income Tax (ITA No. 3544/MUM/2011, ITA No. 3545/MUM/2011 and ITA No. 3546/MUM/2011), 31 October, 2014
Sibschwank, Federal Arbitration Court of the West Siberian district No. A70-3295/2013 of 19 February 2014
Sony Ericsson Mobile Communications India Pvt. Ltd v. CIT (ITA No. 16 of 2014), 16 March 2015
South Atlantic Islands Development Corporation Ltd v. Buchan 1971 (I) SA 234 (C), at 238
Tata Autocomp Systems Ltd. Mumbai v. Assessee, ITAT, ITA NO. 7354/MUM/11(A.Y. 2007-08)16 April 2012
Union of India and others v. Azadi Bachao Andolan and others, 263 ITR 706
United Bakers Pskov LLC, Decision of the Pskov Arbitration Court on Case No. A52-4072/2012 of 16 December 2013
Yukos Universal Limited (Isle of Man) v. The Russian Federation (PCA Case No. AA 227)

Index

A

Affirmative savings, 96
Aid agencies
  regional funding institutions, 20–21
  VAT system, 20
  World Bank, 19–20
Anti-abuse rules, 199–200
  domestic actions
    CFC rules, 201–202
    harmful tax practices, 203–205
    hybrid mismatches, 200–201
    interest deductibility, 202–203
  information gathering actions
    CbyC reporting, 220–221
    disclosure of aggressive tax planning, 219–220
  international actions
    digital economy, 205–206
    DTC abuse, 206–208
    PEs, 208–210
  MAP and mandatory and binding dispute resolution, 221–222
  tax value creation actions, 210–211
    assembled workforces, 212
    intangibles, 212–219
    location savings and other local market features, 211
    MNE group synergies, 212
Anti-avoidance rule, 95, 145
APA programme, 113–116
Arbitration
  dispute resolution, 227–228
    Brazil, 228–229
    China, 230
    India, 229–230
    OECD Model Tax Convention's Article 25(5), 228
    Russia, 230
    SA, 230
  ICSID, 232–233
  supplementary dispute resolution, 273–274
Audit selection
  transfer pricing (TP)
    Brazil, 116
    China, 118–119
    India, 117–118
    Russia, 116–117
    SARS' approach, 119
Automatic information exchange, 151
Avoidance, 64–66, 77
  CFC rules (*See* Controlled foreign company (CFC) rules)
  consequences, 77
  coordination, 77
  loopholes and intent
    Brazil, 69
    colourable device *vs.*, 70–71
    India, 70
    Russia, 69–70
    SA, 71
  significance, 76
  substance over form (*See* Substance over form doctrine)
  tax liability reduction
    Brazil, 66
    China, 67–68

Index

India, 67
Russia, 67
SA's approach to avoidance, 68–69
thin capitalization (*See* Thin capitalization)
TP (*See* Transfer pricing (TP))
Azardi principle, 175

B

Base erosion and profit shifting (BEPS)
　BEPS Final 2015 Reports (*See* BEPS Final 2015 Reports)
　recommendation
　　Action Plans, 6–7
　　contract splitting, 265–266
　　indirect asset transfers, 260–261
　　limitation of benefits, 255–257
　　main purpose tests, 258
　　savings clauses, 263–264
　　supplementary dispute resolution, 271–273
Beneficial ownership, 171–172
　BRICS: DTCs and, 179–180
　contractual obligations
　　Brazil, 173–174
　　China, 174–175
　　Russia, 174
　　SARS, 175
　definition, 172
　Description, 172–173
　DTC anti-abuse, 254–255
　possession, use, risk and control
　　Brazil: DTC benefits, 176–177
　　China, 177–178
　　SA, 178–179
BEPS. *See* Base erosion and profit shifting (BEPS)
BEPS Action Plans, 6–7
BEPS Final 2015 Reports
　anti-abuse rules (*See* Anti-abuse rules)
　base erosion and profit shifting, 197–198
　MI (*See* Multilateral instrument (MI))

SAT Beijing Conference, 198
value creation actions (*See* Tax value creation actions)
Bi-lateral investment treaties (BITs)
　arbitration, 234
　core international tax policy and law, 21–22
BITs. *See* Bi-lateral investment treaties (BITs)
Black Money Act, 63, 139, 239
BPA override, 141–142
　BRICS and, 142–145
　CFC rules, 146
　treaties and interpretation, 142
Brazil, Russia, India, China And South Africa (BRICS), 2–3
　avoidance (*See* Avoidance)
　beneficial ownership and, 179–180
　BPA override and, 142–145
　contract splitting and, 265
　DTCs and
　　indirect asset transfers, 260
　　residence and POEM, 167–171
　　savings clauses, 264
　evasion (*See* Evasion)
　FDI (*See* Foreign Direct Investment (FDI))
　illicit trade flows
　　financial outbound flows, 8
　　GFI Report, 7
　　trade mispricing analysis, 8–9
　　UNCTAD, 7–8
　indirect asset transfers, 195–196, 260
　information exchange
　　consequences of exchanging, 161–162
　　coordination and, 161
　instrument and, 267–268
　liberalization, 2–3
　LOB and, 181–184
　MI and
　　DTC abuse, 223
　　MAP binding, 223–224
　　opt out, 224

346

OECD Model DTC, 25–26
  DTC network - pre and post liberalization, 36–37
  reservations and positions on, 26–36
Peer reviews and
  AEOI, 159–160
  Global Forum, 158–159
political cooperation
  Dehli Declaration (2012), 5
  Fortaleza Declaration (2014), 5–6
tax authority (*See* Tax authority)
tax cooperation
  BEPS Action Plans, 6–7
  Ufa Declaration, 6
thin capitalization (*See* Thin capitalization)
TP (*See* Transfer pricing (TP))
treaty shopping and, 256–257
Burden of proof
  transfer pricing (TP), 119

C

CFC rules. *See* Controlled foreign company (CFC) rules
CLT. *See* Comprehensive liability test (CLT)
Comminque, 6, 189, 244, 283–285
Common Reporting Standard, 6–7, 150, 278, 282, 284
Compensatory adjustments
  primary, 120–122
  secondary, 122
Comprehensive liability test (CLT), 167–169
Contract splitting, 264
  BEPS recommendation, 265–266
  BRICS, 265
Controlled foreign company (CFC) rules, 124
  anti-avoidance rule, 145
  attributable income, 202
  BPA override, 141–142
  BRICS and, 142–145
  treaties and interpretation, 142
  BRICS cooperation, 147
  control relationship, 128–129
  DTCs and BPA override, 146
  evolution of, 126–128
  exchange controls and OFDI, 124–126
  exemptions
    blacklist countries, 135–138
    comparable tax rate, 133–134
    OECD's policy, 133
    stalling targeted OFDI, 134–135
    threshold, 134
  GAAR, 146
  notification process, 138–139
    exchange controls, 139
    taxation process, 139–140
  potentially attributed income, 129–131
  recommendations, 201–202
  significance, 147
  substance, 131–133
  tax credits, 140–141
Core international tax policy and law
  aid agencies
    regional funding institutions, 20–21
    VAT system, 20
    World Bank, 19–20
  investment treaties
    BITs, 21–22
    TIPs, 22–23
  MNEs (*See* Multi-national enterprises (MNEs))
  OECD
    Model DTC, 26–36
    policy and prisoners' dilemma, 37–46
    policy influencers, significance of, 48–49
  WTO, 23–24
Cost contribution agreements (CCAs)
TP
Country by country (CbyC) reporting
  DTC anti-abuse, 249–250

information gathering actions, 220–221
Crimes Against the Tax, Economic and Consumer Relations Systems Act, 54–55
Criminal conduct
    Evasion, 64
Cyber economy, 205

D

Deemed dividend, 92–93
Dehli Declaration (2012), 5
Development, enhancement, maintenance, protection and exploitation (DEMPE), 213–214
Digital economy, 205–206
Dispute resolution
    Arbitration, 227–228
        Brazil, 228–229
        China, 230
        India, 229–230
        OECD Model Tax Convention's Article 25(5), 228
        Russia, 230
        SA, 230
    human rights
        defence, 238–239
        International Covenant, 236–238
        OECD, 236
    investment treaties
        BITs, 230–232
        ICSID arbitration, 232–233
    supplementary (See Supplementary dispute resolution)
    WTO, 234–236
Dispute settlement understanding (DSU), 234–236
Doctrine of 'unjustified tax benefit', 62
Documentation
    TP, 111–113
Double taxation, 122–123
Double Taxation Convention (DTC)
    abuse, 206

LOB, 207
MI, 223
MPT, 207–208
affirmative savings, 96
anti-abuse (See DTC anti-abuse)
Article 26: information exchange
    OECD Model Convention, 153–154
    Russian Model, 153
BRICS and
    indirect asset transfers, 260
    savings clauses, 264
BRICS: DTC residence and POEM, 169–171
business purpose, and, 262–263
CFC rules, 146
indirect transfers, 194–195
MPT185, 187–188
override
    Article 3(2), 93
    ND Article, 94–95
    public international law, 93
residence, 167–169
savings provisions, and
    BEPS recommendation, 263–264
    BRICS and DTCs savings clauses, 264
Draft instrument, 267
DTC. See Double Taxation Convention (DTC)
DTC anti-abuse
    application
        countering abuse and investment decisions, 244–245
        uncertainty, 243–244
    domestic rules
        beneficial ownership, 254–255
        hybrid debt, 251–252
        residence, 252–254
        thin capitalization, 250–251
        transfer pricing (TP), 245
    international rules
        contract splitting, 264–266
        DTC and savings provisions, 263–264

DTCs and business purpose, 262–263
indirect asset transfers, 259–261
limitation of benefits, 255–257
main purpose tests, 257–258
multilateral instrument, 266–268
third country PEs, 261–262
structures, 243

E

Evasion, 77–78
income, concealing
Brazil, 54–55
criminal conduct, 64
existing liability, purposely not paying, 59–60
India, 56–58
Russia, 56
SA, 58–59
wilful or intentional fraudulent conduct, 61–64
transfer pricing, 110
Exchanging statistics, 151–153
Exemptions
CFC rules
blacklist countries, 135–138
comparable tax rate, 133–134
OECD's policy, 133
stalling targeted OFDI, 134–135
threshold, 134
thin capitalization, 91–92

F

FATCA. *See* Foreign Account Tax Compliance Act (FATCA)
FDI. *See* Foreign Direct Investment (FDI)
Finance Act, 192, 206, 259
Financial account information, 157–158
AEOI
legal basis for exchange, 159
procedures facilitating exchange, 159–160

BRICS and Peer reviews, 158
AEOI, 159–160
Global Forum, 158–159
Global Forum, 158–159
Foreign Account Tax Compliance Act (FATCA), 156–157
Foreign Direct Investment (FDI)
BRICS and DTC anti-abuse (*See* DTC anti-abuse)
DTC anti-abuse (*See* DTC anti-abuse)
dispute resolution, 269–274
inbound and outbound, 4
information exchange, 150
nonstock investor countries
main inbound, 4–5
main outbound, 5–6
OFDI, 3
Form 49D, 192
Fortaleza Declaration (2014), 5–6

G

GAAR. *See* General Anti-Avoidance (Abuse) Rule (GAAR)
General Anti-Avoidance (Abuse) Rule (GAAR), 75
capitalization and, 95–96
CFC rules and, 146
indirect asset transfers, 193
GFI Report, 7
Global Forum, 151, 158–159
Government lobbying, 48

H

Harmful tax practices, 203–205
Human rights
International Covenant, 236–238
OECD, 236
supplementary dispute resolution, 274
Hybrid debt
DTC anti-abuse, 251–252
Hypotheses, 14–15, 277

Index

I

Illicit trade flows
  financial outbound flows, 8
  GFI Report, 7
  trade mispricing analysis, 8–9
  UNCTAD, 7–8
Indirect asset transfers, 190–191
  BRICS and coordination, 195–196
  BRICS and DTCs, 260
  domestic rule
    China's GAAR, 193
    commercially acceptable
      transactions, 193–194
    Form 49D, 192
    immoveable property, 191
    moveable property, 191–192
  domestic rules, 259–260
  DTCs, 194–195
  Significance, 196
Industry and trade groups, 46–47
Information exchange
  BRICS
    consequences of exchanging, 161–162
    coordination and, 161
  DTCs-Article 26
    OECD Model Convention, 153–154
    Russian Model, 153
  FDI, 150
  financial account information (*See* Financial account information)
  inbound and outbound exchange, 152–153
  MNEs, 150
  multilateral agreements
    FATCA, 156–157
    MAC, 155–156
    MCAA, 156
    prior information exchange, 157
  multilateral and mutual assistance agreements, 150–151
  OECD and Revenue Rule, 150
  TIEAs, 155

Information gathering actions
  CbyC reporting, 220–221
  disclosure of aggressive tax planning, 219–220
Intangibles
  CCA, 215
  DEMPE, 213–214
  identification, 212–213
  intra-group services, 216–217
    benefits test, 217
    centralized services, 217–219
    shareholder activities and duplication, 217
Interest deductibility, 202–203
International centre for settlement of investment disputes (ICSID)
  arbitration model, 232–234
International Covenant, 236–238
International tax law, 278–282
Investment treaties
  BITs, 21–22
  TIPs, 22–23
IRD approach, 82

L

Leaders' Summit Statement, 237
Lender's residence
  thin capitalization, 89–90
Lima Declaration, 237
Limitation of benefits (LOB)
  BRICS and, 181–184
  DTC
    benefits claimed by conduits, 180–181
    Brazil, 186
    China, 186–187
    India, 186
    MPTs, 187–188
    Russia, 186
    SA, 187
  DTC abuse, 207
  MPT and, 187–188
    coordination, 189

significance, 189
Lock in, 39, 48, 279
LOB. See Limitation of benefits (LOB)

M

Main purpose test (MPT), 185, 187–188
   BEPS recommendation, 258
   BRICS and MPTs, 257–258
   DTC abuse, 207–208
Manpower, 9–11
MAP
   mandatory and binding dispute resolution, 221–222
   MI, 223–224
   supplementary dispute resolution
   BRICS dispute resolution and, 269–270
   BRICS, MAP and sovereignty, 271
   instrument and sovereignty, 270–271
MCAA. See Multilateral competent authority agreement (MCAA)
MI. See Multilateral instrument (MI)
MNEs. See Multi-national enterprises (MNEs)
MPT. See Main purpose test (MPT)
Multi-national enterprises (MNEs)
   government lobbying, 48
   group synergies, 212
   industry and trade groups, 46–47
   information exchange, 150
Multilateral and mutual assistance agreements, 150–151
Multilateral competent authority agreement (MCAA), 156
Multilateral Convention on Mutual Administrative Assistance in Tax matters, Amended by 2010 Protocol (MAC), 155–156
Multilateral instrument (MI)
   BRICS and, 223–224
   DTC abuse, 223–224
   MAP binding, 223–224

   opt out, 224
   changes and sovereignty, 266
   draft instrument, 267

N

Non-cooperative countries
   BRICS and coordination, 195–196
   Significance, 196
Non-discrimination (ND), 93–95, 250–251
Notification process
   in CFC rules, 138–139
      exchange controls, 139
      taxation process, 139–140
   in TP rules, 137, 245

O

OECD. See Organisation for Economic Cooperation and Development (OECD)
OECD Model Convention, 120
   Article 13(4), 194–195
   information exchange, 153–154
OECD Model DTC and BRICS
   DTC network – pre and post liberalization, 36–37
   reservations and positions on, 26–36
OFDI, 124–126
Organisation for Economic Cooperation and Development (OECD), 150
   human rights, 236
   information exchange, 150
   Model Convention (See OECD Model Convention)
   Model DTC (See OECD Model DTC)
   POEM defined, 165
   policy and prisoners' dilemma, 37–46
   developed and developing countries, BRICS DTC with, 39–44
   quasi developed countries, BRICS DTC with, 45–46

Index

tax incentives intended to attract FDI, 38
Ownership, beneficial. *See* Beneficial ownership

P

Permanent establishment (PE)
   activities excluded, 210
   commissionaire agreements: business presence, 208–209
   dependent agency, 209–210
Place of effective management (POEM)
   definition
      OECD, by, 165
      UN, by, 165–166
   DTCs
      BRICS: DTC residence, 169–171
      effectiveness in denying DTC benefits, 171
      residence and, 167–171
   economic activities, 167
   highest decision making, 166
   incorporation place and, 252–253
   OECD's definition, 165
   UN definition, 165–166
POEM. *See* Place of effective management (POEM)
Political cooperation
   Dehli Declaration (2012), 5
   Fortaleza Declaration (2014), 5–6
Prisoners' dilemma, 37–46

R

Regional funding institutions, 20–21
Residence
   BRICS: DTC residence, 169–171
   DTC, 167–171
   DTC anti-abuse
      decision makers' location v. economic activities location, 253–254
      incorporation place and POEM, 252–253
      effectiveness in denying DTC benefits, 171
Revenue Rule, 150

S

SAARs. *See* South Asian Association for Regional Cooperation (SAARs)
Safe harbours
   DTC anti-abuse, 248
   thin capitalization, 90–91
   transfer pricing (TP), 108–111
South Asian Association for Regional Cooperation (SAARs)
   CFC rules (*See* Controlled foreign company (CFC) rules)
   thin capitalization (*See* Thin capitalization)
   TP (*See* Transfer pricing (TP))
Sovereignty, 266, 270–271
State Administration of Taxation (SAT)
   Beijing Conference, 198
Substance over form doctrine
   Brazil's legality principle, 71–72
   China, 74–75
   India, 73–74
   Russia, 72
   SA, 75–76
Supplementary dispute resolution
   arbitration rules, 273–274
   BEPS recommendation, 271–273
   human rights, 274
   MAP
      BRICS dispute resolution and, 269–270
      BRICS, MAP and sovereignty, 271
      instrument and sovereignty, 270–271

T

Tax authority, 9
   aggregate manpower, 10
   audit and investigation manpower-absolute, 10

manpower-percentages, 10
technical assistance, 12–13
TP manpower, 11
Tax credits, 140–141
Tax information exchange agreement
    (TIEAs), 36, 155, 156, 161, 280
Tax liability
    purposely not paying existing, 59–60
Tax planning (TP)
    disclosure of aggressive TP, 219–220
Tax value creation actions, 210–211
    assembled workforces, 212
    intangibles, 212–219
    location savings and other local
        market features, 211
    MNE group synergies, 212
Taxes
    authority capacity, 277–278
    coordination and cooperation, 278
Thin capitalization
    anti-avoidance rule, 95
    associates
        Brazil, 85
        China, 87
        Russia, 86
        SA, 87–88
    BRICS and coordination, 96
    Description, 79–80
    DTC anti-abuse, 250
        arm's length lenders resident in tax
            privileged countries, 251
        ND article override, 250–251
    DTCs
        affirmative savings, 6
        override, 93–95
    excess interest: deemed dividend,
        92–93
    exchange controls, 80–81
    exemptions, 91–92
    GAAR and, 95–96
    hybrids and
        Brazil, 88
        China and SA, 88–89
    India and, 81–82
    lender's residence, 89–90

ratio or arm's length, 82–85
safe harbours, 90–91
significance, 96–97
treaty override, 93–95
Third Country PEs
    BEPS recommendation, 261–262
    domestic rules, 261
TIPs. See Treaties with investment
    provisions (TIPs)
TP. See Transfer pricing (TP)
Trade, 7–9, 46–47, 176
Transfer pricing (TP), 97–98
    APA programme, 113–116
    associates, 99
    audit selection
        Brazil, 116
        China, 118–119
        India, 117–118
        Russia, 116–117
        SARS' approach, 119
    BRICS cooperation, 123
    burden of proof, 119
    CCAs, 102
    compensatory adjustments
        primary, 120–122
        secondary, 122
    documentation, 111–113
    double taxation, 122–123
    DTC anti-abuse, 245
        APA programme, 246–247
        CbyC reporting, 249–250
        safe harbours, 248
    excessive leverage, 103
    methods, 103–108
    safe harbours, 108–109
        Brazil, 109
        China, 111
        India, 109–110
        Russia, 109
        SA, 111
    significance of, 123–124
    transactions, 100–102
    UN Transfer Pricing Manual, 119–120
Treaties with investment provisions
    (TIPs), 49, 279

core international tax policy and law, 22–23
Treaty benefits, countering
  LOB (*See* Limitation of benefits (LOB))
  POEM (*See* Place of effective management (POEM))
  resident, 163–165
Treaty shopping, 175, 181–183, 256–257

U

Ufa Declaration, 6, 11
UN BEPS Questionnaire, 198, 224
UN Human Rights Council, 237
UN Transfer Pricing Manual, 119–120
United Nations
  POEM defined, 165
United Nations Council on Trade and Development (UNCTAD), 7–8, 230, 273
Unjustified tax benefit doctrine, 62, 67, 69, 70, 77, 88, 95, 145, 146, 195, 258, 263

V

VAT system
  core international tax policy and law, 20
  SA, 206
  VCLT, 142, 144, 262, 268

W

Wilful or intentional fraudulent conduct
  ATO, 61
  China, 64
  good faith, 62
  HMRC, 61
  India, 63–64
  SARS, 64
  unjustified tax benefit doctrine, 62
Withholding Tax (WHT)
  India, 179–180
  interest and royalties, 179
Working Group on Double Taxation', 20
World Bank, 128
  core international tax policy and law, 19–20
World Trade Organisation (WTO), 234–236, 282, 284
  core international tax policy and law, 23–24

SERIES ON INTERNATIONAL TAXATION

1. Alberto Xavier, *The Taxation of Foreign Investment in Brazil*, 1980 (ISBN 90-200-0582-0).
2. Hugh J. Ault & Albert J. Rädler, *The German Corporation Tax Law with 1980 Amendments*, 1981 (ISBN 90-200-0642-8).
3. Paul R. McDaniel & Hugh J. Ault, *Introduction to United States International Taxation*, 1981 (ISBN 90-6544-004-6).
4. Albert J. Rädler, *German Transfer Pricing/Prix de Transfer en Allemagne*, 1984 (ISBN 90-6544-143-3).
5. Paul R. McDaniel & Stanley S. Surrey, *International Aspects of Tax Expenditures: A Comparative Study*, 1985 (ISBN 90-654-4163-8).
6. Kees van Raad, *Nondiscrimination in International Tax Law*, 1986 (ISBN 90-6544-266-9).
7. Sijbren Cnossen (ed.), *Tax Coordination in the European Community*, 1987 (ISBN 90-6544-272-3).
8. Ben Terra, *Sales Taxation. The Case of Value Added Tax in the European Community*, 1989 (ISBN 90-6544-381-9).
9. Rutsel S.J. Martha, *The Jurisdiction to Tax in International Law: Theory and Practice of Legislative Fiscal Jurisdiction*, 1989 (ISBN 90-654-4416-5).
10. Paul R. McDaniel & Hugh J. Ault, *Introduction to United States International Taxation* (3rd revised edition), 1989 (ISBN 90-6544-423-8).
11. Manuel Pires, *International Juridicial Double Taxation of Income*, 1989 (ISBN 90-6544-426-2).
12. A.H.M. Daniels, *Issues in International Partnership Taxation*, 1991 (ISBN 90-654-4577-3).
13. Arvid A. Skaar, *Permanent Establishment: Erosion of a Tax Treaty Principle*, 1992 (ISBN 90-6544-594-3).
14. Cyrille David & Geerten M.M. Michielse (eds), *Tax Treatment of Financial Instruments*, 1996 (ISBN 90-654-4666-4).
15. Herbert H. Alpert & Kees van Raad (eds), *Essays on International Taxation*, 1993 (ISBN 90-654-4781-4).
16. Wolfgang Gassner, Michael Lang & Eduard Lechner (eds), *Tax Treaties and EC Law*, 1997 (ISBN 90-411-0680-4).
17. Glória Teixeira, *Taxing Corporate Profits in the EU*, 1997 (ISBN 90-411-0703-7).
18. Michael Lang et al. (eds), *Multilateral Tax Treaties*, 1998 (ISBN 90-411-0704-5).
19. Stef van Weeghel, *The Improper Use of Tax Treaties*, 1998 (ISBN 90-411-0737-1).
20. Klaus Vogel (ed.), *Interpretation of Tax Law and Treaties and Transfer Pricing in Japan and Germany*, 1998 (ISBN 90-411-9655-2).
21. Bertil Wiman (ed.), *International Studies in Taxation: Law and Economics; Liber Amicorum Leif Mutén*, 1999 (ISBN 90-411-9692-7).
22. Alfonso J. Martín Jiménez, *Towards Corporate Tax Harmonization in the European Community*, 1999 (ISBN 90-411-9690-0).

23. Ramon J. Jeffery, *The Impact of State Sovereignty on Global Trade and International Taxation*, 1999 (ISBN 90-411-9703-6).
24. A.J. Easson, *Taxation of Foreign Direct Investment*, 1999 (ISBN 90-411-9741-9).
25. Marjaana Helminen, *The Dividend Concept in International Tax Law: Dividend Payments Between Corporate Entities*, 1999 (ISBN 90-411-9765-6).
26. Paul Kirchhof, Moris Lehner, Kees van Raad, Arndt Raupach & Michael-Rodi (eds), *International and Comparative Taxation: Essays in Honour of Klaus Vogel*, 2002 (ISBN 90-411-9841-5).
27. Krister Andersson, Peter Melz & Christer Silfverberg (eds), *Liber Amicorum Sven-Olof Lodin*, 2001 (ISBN 90-411-9850-4).
28. Juan Martín Jovanovich, *Customs Valuation and Transfer Pricing: Is It Possible to Harmonize Customs and Tax Rules?*, Second Edition, 2018 (ISBN 978-90-411-6134-5).
29. Stefano Simontacchi, *Taxation of Capital Gains under the OECD Model Convention: With Special Regard to Immovable Property*, 2007 (ISBN 978-90-411-2549-1).
30. Michael Lang, Josef Schuch, & Claus Staringer (eds), *Tax Treaty Law and EC Law*, 2007 (ISBN 978-90-411-2629-0).
31. Duncan Bentley, *Taxpayers' Rights: Theory Origin and Implementation*, 2007 (ISBN 978-90-411-2650-4).
32. Sergio André Rocha, *Interpretation of Double Taxation Conventions: General Theory and Brazilian Perspective*, 2008 (ISBN 978-90-411-2822-5).
33. Robert F. van Brederode, *Systems of General Sales Taxation: Theory, Policy and Practice*, 2009 (ISBN 978-90-411-2832-4).
34. John G. Head & Richard Krever (eds), *Tax Reform in the 21st Century: A Volume in Memory of Richard Musgrave*, 2009 (ISBN 978-90-411-2829-4).
35. Jens Wittendorff, *Transfer Pricing and the Arm's Length Principle in International Tax Law*, 2010 (ISBN 978-90-411-3270-3).
36. Marjaana Helminen, *The International Tax Law Concept of Dividend*, Second Edition, 2017 (ISBN 978-90-411-8394-1).
37. Robert F. van Brederode (ed.), *Immovable Property under VAT: A Comparative Global Analysis*, 2011 (ISBN 978-90-411-3126-3).
38. Dennis Weber & Stef van Weeghel, *The 2010 OECD Updates: Model Tax Convention & Transfer Pricing Guidelines - A Critical Review*, 2011 (ISBN 978-90-411-3812-5).
39. Yariv Brauner & Martin James McMahon, Jr. (eds), *The Proper Tax Base: Structural Fairness from an International and Comparative Perspective—Essays in Honour of Paul McDaniel*, 2012 (ISBN 978-90-411-3286-4).
40. Robert F. van Brederode (ed.), *Science, Technology and Taxation*, 2012 (ISBN 978-90-411-3125-6).
41. Oskar Henkow, *The VAT/GST Treatment of Public Bodies*, 2013 (ISBN 978-90-411-4663-2).
42. Jean Schaffner, *How Fixed Is a Permanent Establishment?*, 2013 (ISBN 978-90-411-4662-5).

43. Miguel Correia, *Taxation of Corporate Groups*, 2013 (ISBN 978-90-411-4841-4).
44. Veronika Daurer, *Tax Treaties and Developing Countries*, 2014 (ISBN 978-90-411-4982-4).
45. Claire Micheau, *State Aid, Subsidy and Tax Incentives under EU and WTO Law*, 2014 (ISBN 978-90-411-4555-0).
46. Robert F. van Brederode & Richard Krever (eds), *Legal Interpretation of Tax Law*, Second Edition, 2017 (ISBN 978-90-411-8473-3).
47. Radhakishan Rawal, *Taxation of Cross-border Services*, 2014 (ISBN 978-90-411-4947-3).
48. João Dácio Rolim, *Proportionality and Fair Taxation*, 2014 (ISBN 978-90-411-5838-3).
49. Paulo Rosenblatt, *General Anti-avoidance Rules for Major Developing Countries*, 2015 (ISBN 978-90-411-5839-0).
50. Gaspar Lopes Dias V.S., *Tax Arbitrage through Cross-Border Financial Engineering*, 2015 (ISBN 978-90-411-5875-8).
51. Geerten M.M. Michielse & Victor Thuronyi (eds), *Tax Design Issues Worldwide*, 2015 (ISBN 978-90-411-5610-5).
52. Oktavia Weidmann, *Taxation of Derivatives*, 2015 (ISBN 978-90-411-5977-9).
53. Chris Evans, Richard Krever & Peter Mellor (eds), *Tax Simplification*, 2015 (ISBN 978-90-411-5976-2).
54. Reuven Avi-Yonah & Joel Slemrod (eds), *Taxation and Migration*, 2015 (ISBN 978-90-411-6136-9).
55. Alexander Bosman, *Other Income under Tax Treaties: An Analysis of Article 21 of the OECD Model Convention*, 2015 (ISBN 978-90-411-6610-4).
56. John Abrahamson, *International Taxation of Manufacturing and Distribution*, 2016 (ISBN 978-90-411-6664-7).
57. Frederik Boulogne, *Shortcomings in the EU Merger Directive*, 2016 (ISBN 978-90-411-6713-2).
58. Angelika Meindl-Ringler, *Beneficial Ownership in International Tax Law*, 2016 (ISBN 978-90-411-6833-7).
59. Andreas Waltrich, *Cross-Border Taxation of Permanent Establishments: An International Comparison*, 2016 (ISBN 978-90-411-6832-0).
60. Sergio André Rocha & Allison Christians (eds), *Tax Sovereignty in the BEPS Era*, 2017 (ISBN 978-90-411-6707-1).
61. Peter Antony Wilson, *BRICS and International Tax Law*, 2018 (ISBN 978-90-411-9435-0).